REVISION CHECKLISTS	PEER EDITING CHECKLISTS	WRITING WITH A COMPUTER
Writing from Recall, **22**	Writing from Recall, **22**	Recalling, **19**
Writing from Observation, **49**	Writing from Observation, **48**	Observing, **48**
Writing from Reading, **81**	Writing from Reading, **82**	Reading, **78**
Writing from Conversation, **110**	Writing from Conversation, **111**	Conversing, **109**
Writing from Imagination, **138**	Writing from Imagination, **137**	Imagining, **134**
Analyzing a Subject, **194** Analyzing a Process, **195**	Analyzing a Subject, **193** Analyzing a Process, **194**	Analyzing, **193**
Taking a Stand, **236**	Taking a Stand, **235**	Taking a Stand, **234**
Proposing a Solution, **264**	Proposing a Solution, **262**	Proposing a Solution, **260**
Evaluating, **297**	Evaluating, **297**	Evaluating, **294**
Asking Why, **324** Determining Effects, **325**	Seeking Causes, **325** Determining Effects, **326**	Seeking Causes and Effects, **322**
Looking Over Everything, **373**	Writing from Library Research, **372**	Shaping a Draft, **364** Rewriting, **375**
Looking Over Your Results, **435**	Writing from Research in the Field, **436**	Generating Ideas, **425** Shaping a Draft, **432**
Reaching Your Goal, **524** Testing Structure, **524** Considering Your Audience, **525** Cutting and Whittling, **537**		
		Serving as a Reader, **543**

S0-AFN-967

THE
BEDFORD GUIDE
FOR COLLEGE WRITERS

with Readings and Handbook

SECOND EDITION

THE
BEDFORD GUIDE
FOR COLLEGE WRITERS

with Readings and Handbook

X. J. KENNEDY and DOROTHY M. KENNEDY

BEDFORD BOOKS of ST. MARTIN'S PRESS · BOSTON

For Bedford Books
Publisher: Charles H. Christensen
Associate Publisher: Joan E. Feinberg
Managing Editor: Elizabeth M. Schaaf
Developmental Editor: Stephen A. Scipione
Copyeditor: Barbara G. Flanagan
Text Design: Claire Seng-Niemoeller
Cover Design: Hannus Design Associates

Library of Congress Catalog Card Number: 88–63034

Manufactured in the United States of America

4   3   2

f   e   d

For information, write: St. Martin's Press, Inc.
175 Fifth Avenue, New York, NY 10010
Editorial Offices: Bedford Books *of* St. Martin's Press
29 Winchester Street, Boston, MA 02116

ISBN: 0–312–03545–4

Acknowledgments

Edward Abbey. "Disorder and Early Sorrow." From *The Journey Home* by Edward Abbey.
Copyright © 1977 by Edward Abbey. Reprinted by permission of the publisher, E. P. Dutton, a
division of Penguin Books USA Inc.

Deborah C. Andrews. From "Words about Words." Adapted with permission from *Chemical
& Engineering News,* March 13, 1989, *67*(11), pp. 45–46. Copyright 1989 American Chemical
Society.

Ed Anger. From "Junk Food Made Our Country Great." Reprinted by permission from *Weekly
World News,* January 1, 1985.

Russell Baker. "The Art of Eating Spaghetti." From *Growing Up* by Russell Baker, published
by Congdon & Weed, Inc. Copyright © 1982 by Russell Baker. Reprinted by permission of Contemporary Books, Inc.

*Acknowledgments and copyrights are continued at the back of the book on pages
783–785, which constitute an extension of the copyright page.*

Preface:

To the Instructor

This book in your hands is three full books in one. In one compact package, it offers a rhetoric (greatly revised from its first edition), a reader (with forty-eight selections), and a handbook (of about 200 pages)—all the textbooks most instructors, and their students, will need for a complete writing course. (For the instructor who prefers a shorter edition without handbook, one now exists: *The Bedford Guide for College Writers with Readings.*)

Warm response to the first edition heartened us to try to hone this book into a still more efficient instrument. In its new edition we have striven, above all, to thrust the student immediately into the act of writing. To this end we have tightened our discussion of the writing process, substituting on-the-job learning for preliminary advice. In the first edition, three chapters of sage counsel stood between the student and the act of writing. Now the student writes a paper in Chapter 1.

The Bedford Guide for College Writers seeks to bring into the classroom many recent findings of composition research. Writing, we insist, is not the laborious construction of something one *has* to say but doesn't especially want to; it is the lively and often surprising art of thinking while working with language. No one ever learned to swim by reading a book about swimming; similarly, if the student is to learn to write well, a pinch of practice is worth a pound of theory. This view is hardly original; yet perhaps the book can claim some originality in how this view is set forth. We can no longer count the ways we tried to organize the book before discovering the present way—discovered it, that is, with the help of those many discerning teachers who criticized our manuscripts and our first edition.

How the Rhetoric Book Is Built

Although the table of contents ought to speak for itself, let us quickly sum up what each of the book's four parts tries to do.

In Part One, "A Writer's Resources," the student writes by actively seeking ideas and material: by recalling, observing, reading, conversing, and imagining. The assumption is that every writer starts out with these resources, endlessly fruitful and readily available.

In Part Two, "Thinking Critically," the student fulfills five writing assignments with clear purposes: analyzing, taking a stand, proposing a solution, evaluating, and seeking causes and effects. The assumption is that these basic skills are essential to many kinds of critical and persuasive writing (including the analysis and evaluation of literature—see Chapters 6 and 9).

In Part Three, "Investigating," the student is encouraged to write from research, both in the library and in the field. Most textbooks warn that research writing is completely different from other writing tasks. But we suggest that when your students write a research paper, they make no such violent break with all they know. Chapter 12 provides a detailed introduction to the reference facilities of a typical college library. Guidelines for MLA and APA styles of documentation are placed in a separate, final chapter (Chapter 14) for ready reference.

Part Four, "Strategies: A Reference Manual," is a toolchest of techniques for generating ideas, drafting, and rewriting, in class or out, with or without a computer. These techniques are intended to serve both the instructor who wishes some specific treatment of recent concerns, such as nonlinear outlining and collaborative learning, and the instructor who wants to teach traditional outlining and the writing of thesis sentences. A final section provides instructions on manuscript style (if you don't specify otherwise) and on how to format a paper when writing with a computer.

How the Assignment Chapters Are Built

In each of the first ten assignment chapters (Parts One and Two) you will find, in sequence, the following:

1. Two short readings, one by a professional writer, one by a student writer. After each selection, our questions are designed not merely to point to what the writers are saying but to show how the writers go about writing and to provoke original thought.

2. A writing assignment general enough to let students define it for themselves and so become involved in it.

3. Detailed guidance in generating ideas, shaping a draft, and rewriting. We do not pretend that writing always proceeds by lockstep through all three stages. Sometimes we show how the stages can overlap, how a writer may backtrack—may stop revising, say, to generate new ideas—or leap ahead from one stage to another.

4. "Other Assignments," in case you prefer one of these to the main assignment or wish students to do some further writing.

5. "Applying What You Learn," a short discussion of the practical applications, in college and beyond, of the kind of writing dealt with in the chapter.

6. Two additional readings that apply the same kind of writing knowledge. If, after they write, students do more reading, they may read with a keener awareness of how a professional writer works. To be sure, you can have students read these essays *before* they write, if you so desire.

Every assignment chapter also includes checklists for discovering ideas, for revising, and for peer editing and screened boxes with activities for word processing and group learning. A guide to these lists and boxes appears on the front endpapers.

The Readings

The forty-eight readings display good writing by thirty-five professional and thirteen student writers. We have tried to select professional essays that relate to whole chapters and to feature some writers whose disciplines span the curriculum from astrophysics to zoology, including psychology, medicine, law, journalism, education, philosophy, music, film criticism, environmental studies, astronomy, history, and economics. The student essays, we think, are very good indeed, but not discouragingly dazzling.

How the Handbook Is Built

The handbook is meant to be full and adequate. No mere token section, not a handbook in name only, it is designed to serve students just as efficiently as a high-priced, separate handbook might. If you care to test this claim, glance at its table of contents and satisfy yourself that all topics typically covered in a separate handbook are indeed there. You will also find discussions of grammar, jargon, nonsexist usage, and other matters some handbooks skip or deal with cursorily. The handbook's coding system should make it easy for you to refer students to the very parts they need. By binding it together with the rhetoric-reader, the publishers hope to make it more convenient, too, for your students to consult on their own.

Boxed charts invite the student to find answers to their problems quickly. These set forth at a glance many matters of grammar and a few techniques for editing and revising. The handbook also contains more than 650 exercises for in-class or out-of-class practice. (Solutions to problems raised in some of these exercises will be found at the back of the book.) Because the handbook is part of the book, we trust, your students will always have help at their fingertips.

Writing with a Computer

Now that word processing has come to rival typewriting in popular acceptance, we have paid still more attention to the process of writing with a computer. Screened boxes in every assignment-centered chapter (Chapters 1–11 and 13) supply labor-saving tips that relate directly to each writing assignment. These are in addition to the extended discussion in Chapter 19, "Strategies for Writing with a Computer," which is addressed to the student who already knows how to use a computer but who has not yet written college papers.

Peer Editing and Group Learning

Because so many instructors now ask their students to read and comment on one another's papers—sometimes in organized groups, sometimes informally—we have strengthened the book's concern with peer editing. Exactly how does the student go about criticizing another student's paper? If you ask students to edit one another's work, refer them to the peer editing checklist in each assignment chapter. Refer them also to Chapter 18, "Strategies for Working with Fellow Writers." It contains many pointers and some illustrations: a single paragraph (and its revision after peer editing) and a whole peer-edited paper.

Peer editing, to be sure, is only one activity for collaborative learning; so in each of the assignment chapters, a box labeled "For Group Learning" crops up after every list of "Other Assignments." Some of these suggestions invite collective brainstorming and other group techniques; others call on the group to assist students in writing as individuals.

Ancillaries

An instructor's manual, *Teaching with the Bedford Guide for College Writers,* prepared by Shirley Morahan of Northeast Missouri State University, is available in two volumes. The first volume, *Practical Suggestions,* includes syllabuses, a guide (in tabular form) to the readings, a chapter on helping students make the leap to critical thinking, and a chapter on publishing student writing on campus. The second volume, *Background Readings,* is an anthology of articles taken mainly from journals of composition; these readings are connected to *The Bedford Guide* and the classroom by introductions and exercises. We hope that both the manual and the supplementary readings will prove useful to new and seasoned instructors alike.

A pop-up reference system that can be used with most word processing programs, the Hotline for *The Bedford Guide* is an on-line handbook that gives students quick, easy access to information on grammar, punctuation, mechanics, usage, and documentation models while they are writing. The Hotline is available free (in either IBM or MacIntosh version) to instructors who adopt *The Bedford Guide for College Writers.* It will be sent, upon request, to adopters who may then freely copy the disk and give it to their students.

Thanks

We continue to be grateful to the many people who gave us the benefit of their advice throughout the planning and writing of the first edition of *The*

Bedford Guide, especially to mentors Mike Rose, John J. Ruszkiewicz, and Robert A. Schwegler and also to Jane Aaron, Patricia Bizzell, Robert DiYanni, Diana Hacker, Clayton Hudnall, Richard L. Larson, Sonia Maasik, Donald McQuade, Thomas P. Miller, Shirley A. Morahan, James C. Raymond, Robert Rudolph, Nancy Sommers, and Jo Tarvers.

To Shirley A. Morahan, director of composition at Northeast Missouri State University, we owe a further, deeper debt as the author of both the first and second editions of the instructor's manual and as the editor of that manual's new companion volume. We thank her, too, for allowing us to lift from her first manual the peer editing checklists that now appear in each of our writing assignment chapters. We wanted students as well as instructors to have direct access to them.

We still feel deeply indebted to Rise B. Axelrod and Charles R. Cooper, from whose ground-breaking textbook, *The St. Martin's Guide to Writing,* we learned a whole new way of looking at the teaching of writing.

Since *The Bedford Guide* first appeared in print, our debts have multiplied. We are grateful to Em Claire Knowles of the Simmons College Graduate School of Library and Information Science, who criticized, updated, and corrected our chapter on library resources. For reviewing the first edition and supplying suggestions for the second, we thank Richard Batteiger, Oklahoma State University; John Clifford, University of North Carolina at Wilmington; Anne Doyle, University of Washington; Jennifer Ginn, North Carolina State University; Carol Peterson Haviland, California State University, San Bernardino; Nancy Joseph, York College; Marilyn Larson, Snow College; Thomas Martinez, Villanova University; Elizabeth Metzger, University of Southern Florida; Betty Pytlik, Ohio University; Sally Reagan, University of Missouri, St. Louis; Michael Robertson, Lafayette College; Shirley Rose, Eastern Michigan University; John Ruszkiewicz, University of Texas at Austin; and Robert Schwegler, University of Rhode Island.

A number of instructors at Northeast Missouri State University not only reviewed the "Applying What You Learn" sections of our writing chapters and suggested more valuable additions to them than we had room for, but led us to some of the new essays included in this edition. For their thoughtful and pertinent contributions we thank Russell G. Baughman, associate professor of chemistry; Mina Carson, assistant professor of history (now at Oregon State University); Paula S. Cochran, assistant professor of communication disorders; Elizabeth Jean Hogeland, associate professor of child and family development; Dr. Peter Saltzstein of the Academic Planning Services and the Department of Philosophy; and C. Cartwright Young of the Department of Political Science.

Instructors invited by the publisher to write comments and rate the effectiveness of our book were R. A. Beckham, Germanna Community College; Marianne Brokaw, Michigan Technological University; Audrey L. Brubaker, York College of Pennsylvania; Shirley Buettner, Kearney State College; Michael S. Cain, Catonsville Community College; Hilbert H. Campbell, Virginia Polytechnic Institute and State University; Anne Dayton, Slippery Rock University; Susan Galliano, Michigan Technological University; E. L. Graswell, Mount Olive College; Joe Hall, Oklahoma Baptist University; Mark Halpern, Central Washington University; Nan Hayes, Salisbury State University; Marlene R. Lerner, Johnson Community College; Mary P. Lyons, Bryant College; Michael McCullu, Bloomsburg University; James Oldham, Rensselaer Polytechnic Institute; Douglas A. Pearson, Jr., University of Wisconsin, Eau Claire; Mary Pelkey, Bryant College; Paul W. Rogalus, Purdue University; Elizabeth Rosner, Contra Costa College; Ruth Ann Rueln, Michigan Technological University; Walter Sanders, Mansfield University; Ruth Stratton, Broome Community College; Gail White, Northern Illinois University; Marydale Wiley, Kishwaukee College; Janice M. Wolff, Northern Illinois University.

Not least, we are grateful to publisher Charles H. Christensen and associate publisher Joan E. Feinberg, both of whom provided unstinting encouragement and inspiration, criticized plans and manuscript, and kept the faith. Editor Steve Scipione read and reread our manuscript many times, all the while suggesting improvements and refinements, painstakingly nudging us toward a better book. Elizabeth M. Schaaf once again saw the book into print and solved its problems of art and photography. Barbara Flanagan did an inspired job of copyediting. Paula Spencer prepared the index. Mary Lou Wilshaw, Carolyn Woznick, Riikka Melartin, Lynn Goldstein, Linda Faulkenstein, and Karen S. Henry deserve thanks for their many contributions, small and large. As an undergraduate student, Jane Betz contributed her essay on Kate Chopin; for this edition, she turned her editorial talents to the book's manual. Claire Seng-Niemoeller gave this edition a fresh design. Working on the book, we realized anew that to write a textbook is to take part in a collaborative writing project different only in scope from those assigned to the students for whom we write.

Joan Feinberg gave her special attention this time around to the Handbook, patiently guiding, goading, and inspiring it into shape. Carol Verburg's contribution to the Handbook was immense. Toiling for months to give finished shape to our original version, she made generous additions of her own. It was Carol Verburg who gave the whole handbook consistency—and constant intelligence. Riikka Melartin worked ably on its charts and edited our draft of the glossary on usage.

To Dorothy Kennedy's former students at Ohio University and the University of Michigan; to XJK's at Michigan, the University of California, Irvine, the University of North Carolina, Greensboro, and Tufts University—thanks for letting us learn from your writing. Last, we are grateful to the three college graduates, one college student, and one high school student in our immediate family for their extensive help and advice: Kathleen, David, Matthew, Daniel, and Joshua. Thanks to them, living students could never be far from our minds.

Brief Contents

Preface: To the Instructor   v

Introduction: To the Student   1

PART ONE
A WRITER'S RESOURCES   7

1. Writing from Recall   9

2. Writing from Observation   35

3. Writing from Reading   64

4. Writing from Conversation   95

5. Writing from Imagination   121

   Further Writing Assignments: Combining Resources   149

   Essays Combining Resources   154

PART TWO
THINKING CRITICALLY   179

6. Analyzing   181

7. Taking a Stand   220

8. Proposing a Solution   250

9. Evaluating   279

10. Seeking Causes and Effects   310

PART THREE

INVESTIGATING   341

11. Writing from Library Research   343

12. Knowing Your Library: A Directory of Sources   397

13. Writing from Research in the Field   418

14. Documenting Sources; Using a Style Book   450

PART FOUR

STRATEGIES: A REFERENCE MANUAL   469

15. Strategies for Generating Ideas   471

16. Strategies for Shaping a Draft   483

17. Strategies for Rewriting   523

18. Strategies for Working with Fellow Writers: Collaborative Learning   538

19. Strategies for Writing with a Computer   554

20. Strategies for Writing in Class   562

    A Note on Manuscript Style and Computer Formatting   577

PART FIVE

HANDBOOK   583

21. Basic Grammar   589

22. Grammatical Sentences   615

23. Effective Sentences   662

24. Punctuation   685

25. Mechanics   722

26. Word Choice   750

    A Glossary of Troublemakers   769

Answers for Lettered Exercises   787

Index   795

Correction Symbols   824

Contents

Preface: To the Instructor   v

Introduction: To the Student   1

PART ONE

A WRITER'S RESOURCES   7

1. Writing from Recall   9

LEARNING FROM OTHER WRITERS   9

- Russell Baker, THE ART OF EATING SPAGHETTI   10
- Robert G. Schreiner, WHAT IS A HUNTER? (Student Essay)   12

LEARNING BY WRITING   16

The Assignment: A Personal Experience   16
Generating Ideas   17
Shaping a Draft   20
Rewriting   21
Other Assignments   23

APPLYING WHAT YOU LEARN: SOME USES OF WRITING FROM RECALL   24

An Environmentalist Recalls   26
- Edward Abbey, DISORDER AND EARLY SORROW   26
A Journalist Recalls   31
- Brent Staples, BLACK MEN AND PUBLIC SPACE   31

2. Writing from Observation 35

LEARNING FROM OTHER WRITERS   36

* Sandy Messina, FOOTPRINTS: THE MARK OF OUR PASSING (Student Essay)   36
* Joan Didion, MARRYING ABSURD   39

LEARNING BY WRITING   41

The Assignment: Reporting on Group Behavior   41

Generating Ideas   42

Shaping a Draft   45

Rewriting   47

Other Assignments   49

APPLYING WHAT YOU LEARN: SOME USES OF WRITING FROM OBSERVATION   51

A Zoologist Observes   54

* Alexander Petrunkevitch, THE SPIDER AND THE WASP   55

A Social Commentator Observes   59

* Charlie Haas, TINSEL TEENS   59

3. Writing from Reading   64

LEARNING FROM OTHER WRITERS   65

* David Quammen, A REPUBLIC OF COCKROACHES: WHEN THE ULTIMATE EXTERMINATOR MEETS THE ULTIMATE PEST   65
* Rose Anne Federici, CONFLICTING MESSAGES: A LOOK AT A GENERATION TORN TWO WAYS (Student Essay)   70

LEARNING BY WRITING   73

The Assignment: Reading for Insight   73

Generating Ideas   74

Shaping a Draft   77

Rewriting   80

Other Assignments   83

APPLYING WHAT YOU LEARN: SOME USES OF WRITING FROM READING   84

A Paleontologist Writes from Reading   86

* Stephen Jay Gould, WOMEN'S BRAINS   86

A Novelist Writes from Reading   91

* E. L. Doctorow, A CITIZEN READS THE CONSTITUTION   92

4. Writing from Conversation   95

LEARNING FROM OTHER WRITERS   95

* Michael R. Tein, FLOWERS FOR CHAPEL STREET (Student Essay)   96
* William Least Heat Moon, A VIEW OF PREJUDICE   99

LEARNING BY WRITING   104

The Assignment: Interviewing   104

Generating Ideas   104

Shaping a Draft   108

Rewriting *110*
Other Assignments *113*
APPLYING WHAT YOU LEARN: SOME USES OF WRITING
FROM CONVERSATION 113
An Essayist Writes from Conversation *115*
• Annie Dillard, ENCOUNTERS WITH CHINESE READERS 115
An Educator Writes from Conversation *118*
• David Elkind, SUPERKIDS AND SUPER PROBLEMS 118

5. Writing from Imagination **121**
LEARNING FROM OTHER WRITERS 122
• James C. Rettie, "BUT A WATCH IN THE NIGHT": A SCIENTIFIC FABLE 122
• Jennifer Bowe, IF I COULD FOUND A COLLEGE (Student Essay) 127
LEARNING BY WRITING 131
The Assignment: What if . . . ? *131*
Generating Ideas *133*
Shaping a Draft *135*
Rewriting *136*
Other Assignments *138*
APPLYING WHAT YOU LEARN: SOME USES OF WRITING
FROM IMAGINATION 141
A Humorist Imagines *143*
• James Thurber, IF GRANT HAD BEEN DRINKING AT APPOMATTOX 143
An Astrophysicist Imagines *146*
• Alan P. Lightman, TIME TRAVEL AND PAPA JOE'S PIPE 146

Further Writing Assignments: Combining Resources **149**

Essays Combining Resources **154**
• Ralph Ellison, WHAT AMERICA WOULD BE LIKE WITHOUT BLACKS 154
• Phyllis Rose, TOOLS OF TORTURE 159
• Marie Winn, THE PLUG-IN DRUG 163
• Perri Klass, A TEXTBOOK PREGNANCY 171

PART TWO
THINKING CRITICALLY 179

6. Analyzing **181**
LEARNING FROM OTHER WRITERS 182
• Richard Polomsky, COLLECTING THE PAST (Student Essay) 182
• Paul Bodanis, WHAT'S IN YOUR TOOTHPASTE? 185
LEARNING BY WRITING 187
The Assignment: Analyzing *187*
Generating Ideas *188*

Shaping a Draft   *190*
Rewriting   *192*
Other Assignments   *195*

APPLYING WHAT YOU LEARN: SOME USES OF ANALYSIS   197
An Investigative Reporter Analyzes   *200*
• Jessica Mitford, BEHIND THE FORMALDEHYDE CURTAIN   200
A Composer Analyzes   *207*
• Aaron Copland, HOW WE LISTEN   207

A NOTE ON ANALYZING LITERATURE   212
• Kate Chopin, THE STORY OF AN HOUR   214
• Jane Betz, A DEFENSE OF THE ENDING OF "THE STORY OF AN HOUR"
(Student Essay)   217

7. Taking a Stand   220

LEARNING FROM OTHER WRITERS   221
• Suzanne Britt, THE FIRST PERSON   221
• Susan Fendel, AIDS: THE RETURN OF THE SCARLET LETTER
(Student Essay)   223

LEARNING BY WRITING   227
The Assignment: Taking a Stand   *227*
Generating Ideas   *228*
Shaping a Draft   *233*
Rewriting   *235*
Other Assignments   *236*

APPLYING WHAT YOU LEARN: SOME USES OF TAKING A STAND   238
A Philosopher Takes a Stand   *239*
• Bertrand Russell, DO WE SURVIVE DEATH?   239
An Economist Takes a Stand   *243*
• Milton Friedman, THE SOCIAL RESPONSIBILITY OF BUSINESS IS TO
INCREASE ITS PROFITS   243

8. Proposing a Solution   250

LEARNING FROM OTHER WRITERS   251
• Caryl Rivers, WHAT SHOULD BE DONE ABOUT ROCK LYRICS?   251
• Jeffrey Ting, THE DRINKING AGE: HOW WE SHOULD DETERMINE IT
(Student Essay)   254

LEARNING BY WRITING   257
The Assignment: Arguing for an Action   *257*
Generating Ideas   *258*
Shaping a Draft   *260*
Rewriting   *262*
Other Assignments   *265*

APPLYING WHAT YOU LEARN: SOME USES OF PROPOSALS   266
Two Psychologists Make a Proposal   *268*
• Edward Teyber and Charles D. Hoffman, MISSING FATHERS   269

A Physician Makes a Proposal   272
- Lewis Thomas, THE ART OF TEACHING SCIENCE   272

9. Evaluating   279

LEARNING FROM OTHER WRITERS   279
- Mark Twain, FENIMORE COOPER'S LITERARY OFFENSES   280
- Matthew A. Munich, I WANT MY MTV (Student Essay)   289

LEARNING BY WRITING   292
The Assignment: Writing an Evaluation   292
Generating Ideas   293
Shaping a Draft   295
Rewriting   296
Other Assignments   298

APPLYING WHAT YOU LEARN: SOME USES OF EVALUATING   299
A Film Critic Evaluates   301
- Pauline Kael, ROCKY   301
A Lawyer Evaluates   304
- Alan M. Dershowitz, SHOUTING "FIRE!"   304

10. Seeking Causes and Effects   310

LEARNING FROM OTHER WRITERS   311
- Katie Kennedy, WHY WE BURNED A WILDERNESS (Student Essay)   311
- Jonathan Kozol, ARE THE HOMELESS CRAZY?   315

LEARNING BY WRITING   318
The Assignment: Understanding a Change   318
Generating Ideas   319
Shaping a Draft   322
Rewriting   323
Other Assignments   326

APPLYING WHAT YOU LEARN: SOME USES OF SEEKING CAUSES
AND EFFECTS   329
A Historian Seeks Causes   331
- Joan Jacobs Brumberg, THE ORIGINS OF ANOREXIA NERVOSA   331
An Astronomer Determines Effects   334
- Carl Sagan, THE NUCLEAR WINTER   334

PART THREE

INVESTIGATING   341

11. Writing from Library Research   343

LEARNING FROM ANOTHER WRITER: ONE STUDENT'S EXPERIENCE   344

LEARNING BY WRITING   346
The Assignment: Writing from Library Research   346

Generating Ideas   348
  Choosing Your Territory   348
  Taking an Overview   349
  Stating Your Question   350
  Making a Preliminary Search   352
  Making a Working Bibliography   352
  Evaluating Your Sources   354
  Setting Out: Note Taking   357
  Writing from Sources: Quoting, Nutshelling, Paraphrasing   358
Shaping a Draft   362
  Evaluating Your Material   362
  Organizing Your Ideas   363
  From Notes to Outline to Draft   363
  Using Sources (Not Letting Sources Use You)   365
  Nutshell and Paraphrase Again: Using Long Passages   365
  Avoiding Plagiarism   369
  Ending (also Beginning)   371
Rewriting   372
  Preparing Your Manuscript   373
A COMPLETED LIBRARY RESEARCH PAPER   375
  • Lisa Chickos, EDUCATIONAL LEADERSHIP: A MAN'S WORLD
    (Student Research Paper)   376
  Other Assignments   392
APPLYING WHAT YOU LEARN: SOME USES OF LIBRARY RESEARCH   393

12. Knowing Your Library: A Directory of Sources   397
CONSULTING THE LIBRARY CATALOG   398
  Library of Congress Subject Headings   399
  Finding a Book   399
UNDERSTANDING SYSTEMS OF CLASSIFICATION   402
USING THE PERIODICALS ROOM   403
SURVEYING THE REFERENCE SECTION   403
  Encyclopedias   404
  Specialized Encyclopedias   404
  Dictionaries   405
  Bibliographies   407
  Indexes to Periodicals   407
  News Indexes   410
  Abstracts   411
  Biographical Sources   411
  Yearbooks and Almanacs   412
  Gazetteers and Atlases   412
EXPLORING OTHER SOURCES   413
  Microfilm and Microfiche   413

Databases 414
Government Documents 415
Brochures, Handouts, and Annual Reports 416

13. Writing from Research in the Field 418

Learning from Another Writer: One Student's Experience 419
Learning by Writing 420
The Assignment: Researching a Subculture 420
Generating Ideas 421
Reading for Background 422
Directing an Interview 422
Preparing a Questionnaire 424
Making a Field Trip 428
Inquiring by Telephone 429
Letter Writing 429
Using Television and Radio Programs, Films, and Recordings 430
Using a Camera or a Videocamera 430
Attending Lectures and Conferences 430
Shaping a Draft 431
Organizing Your Ideas 432
Interpreting Your Evidence 433
Using Sources (Not Letting Sources Use You) 434
Rewriting 435
Preparing Your Manuscript 436
A Completed Field Research Paper 437
• Jamie Merisotis, HOW A BONDSMAN DECIDES TO POST BAIL
(Student Research Paper) 438
Other Assignments 445
Applying What You Learn: Some Uses of Field Research 446

14. Documenting Sources; Using a Style Book 450

Citing: MLA Style 451
Listing: MLA Style 457
Citing: APA Style 461
Listing: APA Style 464

PART FOUR
STRATEGIES: A REFERENCE MANUAL   469

15. Strategies for Generating Ideas 471

Brainstorming 471
Freewriting 474
Keeping a Journal 476

ASKING A REPORTER'S QUESTIONS   478
SEEKING MOTIVES   480

16. Strategies for Shaping a Draft   483
STARTING TO WRITE   483
RESTARTING   490
STATING A THESIS   491
GROUPING YOUR IDEAS   495
OUTLINING   498
Informal Outlines   499
Formal Outlines   501
PARAGRAPHING   503
Using Topic Sentences   504
Giving Examples   506
Other Ways of Developing a Paragraph   509
Analyzing   509
Analyzing a Process   509
Comparing and Contrasting   510
Seeking Causes and Effects   511
Defining   512
Classifying   512
Using Transitions   513
Writing an Opening   516
Writing a Conclusion   518
TELLING A STORY   521

17. Strategies for Rewriting   523
REVISING DEEPLY   523
LOOKING FOR LOGICAL FALLACIES   525
STRESSING WHAT COUNTS   528
CUTTING AND WHITTLING   531

18. Strategies for Working with Fellow Writers: Collaborative Learning   538
PEER EDITING   539
SERVING AS A READER   540
LEARNING AS A WRITER   544
PEER EDITORS IN ACTION   545

19. Strategies for Writing with a Computer   554
WHAT WORD PROCESSING CAN DO   555
WHAT IT'S LIKE TO WRITE WITH A WORD PROCESSOR   555

WHAT IT TAKES 557
SPECIAL HELP FOR WRITERS 558
A FEW PRACTICAL TIPS 559
THE LIMITS OF TECHNOLOGY 560

20. Strategies for Writing in Class 562

ESSAY EXAMINATIONS 563
Learning from Another Writer 564
Generating Ideas 565
Typical Exam Questions 566
Shaping a Draft (or the Only Version) 571
Rewriting 573
SHORT-ANSWER EXAMINATIONS 575
IN-CLASS ESSAYS 575

A Note on Manuscript Style and Computer Formatting 577

PART FIVE

HANDBOOK 583

INTRODUCTION: GRAMMAR, OR THE WAY WORDS WORK 585

21. Basic Grammar 589

1. PARTS OF SPEECH 589
2. PARTS OF SENTENCES AND SENTENCE PATTERNS 598
3. PHRASES AND CLAUSES 604
4. TYPES OF SENTENCES 611

22. Grammatical Sentences 615

5. VERBS 615
6. SUBJECT-VERB AGREEMENT 630
7. PRONOUN-ANTECEDENT AGREEMENT 635
8. PRONOUN REFERENCE 638
9. PRONOUN CASE 641
10. SENTENCE FRAGMENTS 646
11. COMMA SPLICES AND FUSED SENTENCES 652
12. ADJECTIVES AND ADVERBS 657

23. Effective Sentences 662

13. MISPLACED AND DANGLING MODIFIERS 662
14. INCOMPLETE SENTENCES 665

15. MIXED CONSTRUCTIONS AND FAULTY PREDICATION   670
16. PARALLEL STRUCTURE   673
17. COORDINATION AND SUBORDINATION   677

24. Punctuation   685
18. END PUNCTUATION   685
19. THE COMMA   688
20. THE SEMICOLON   699
21. THE COLON   702
22. THE APOSTROPHE   705
23. QUOTATION MARKS   709
24. THE DASH AND THE SLASH/VIRGULE   713
25. PARENTHESES, BRACKETS, AND THE ELLIPSIS MARK   716

25. Mechanics   722
26. ABBREVIATIONS   722
27. CAPITAL LETTERS   726
28. NUMBERS   730
29. ITALICS   733
30. THE HYPHEN   736
31. SPELLING   740

26. Word Choice   750
32. APPROPRIATENESS   750
33. AVOIDING SEXISM   757
34. EXACT WORDS   760
35. WORDINESS   765

A Glossary of Troublemakers   769

Answers for Lettered Exercises   787
Index   795
Correction Symbols   824

THE
BEDFORD GUIDE
FOR COLLEGE WRITERS
with Readings and Handbook

Introduction:

To the Student

Unlike parachute jumping, writing for a college course is something you go ahead and try without first learning all there is to it. In truth, nothing anyone can tell you about writing can help you so much as learning on the job. That is why in this book we will put you in various writing situations and say, "Go to it."

By this time, we realize that you are already a writer with long experience. In earlier school years, you probably wrote book reports and essays and term papers, perhaps kept a journal. You've taken notes, written letters and post-cards to family and friends, made lists, maybe kept a diary, even tried your hand at writing stories and poetry. All this experience is about to pay off for you.

In college, you face writing tasks that will naturally look more challenging than most you have faced before. To write a psychology or economics paper, you'll find that your mind has to stretch wider than it did in writing that high school paper on flying squirrels or George Washington. From now on, you will find yourself working in broader disciplines, writing reports, gathering information from many sources, and, above all, thinking critically—not just reading books and stacking up facts, but analyzing what you learn, deciding what it means, arguing, proposing solutions to problems, and weighing the value of things. College instructors will expect you to question what they say, form your own judgments, and put them to use.

THE PROCESS OF WRITING

As you probably know, writing can seem at times a drudgery worse than scrubbing kettles; at other moments, a sport full of thrills—like whizzing downhill on skis, not knowing what you'll meet around a bend.

Surprising and unpredictable though the writing process may be, we can understand what happens in it. Nearly all writers do similar things:

> They generate ideas.
> They shape drafts.
> They rewrite.

These activities aren't lockstep stages: they don't always proceed in a straight line, like dog after cat after rat. You can skip around, taking up parts of the job in whatever order you like. While gathering material, you may feel an urge to play with a sentence until it clicks. In writing a draft, you may decide to go back and look for more material. You may find yourself dashing off, crossing out, leaping ahead, backtracking, correcting, adjusting, questioning, trying a fresh approach, failing, trying another approach, failing, trying still another approach, making a breakthrough, scrubbing, polishing—then in the end, looking up the spellings of any tricky words.

Briefly, let's run through a writer's three basic activities.

Generating Ideas

Discovering what to write about   Finding a topic you honestly want to pursue is half the task: find it, and words will flow. Often it lies near home. By observing the peacocks in her farmyard, Georgia writer Flannery O'Connor fired off an essay heard round the world. In college, of course, an instructor may hand you a writing assignment that seems to hold no personal interest for you. In that case, you face the challenge of making it your own. Take notes while you think. Jot down any likely possibilities.

Discovering material   How do you set forth your ideas and, with your reader in mind, make them clear and convincing? You'll need information to back up your ideas—facts and figures, reports and opinions, examples and illustrations. Luckily, you have endless resources at your fingertips. You can recall your own knowledge and experience, you can go out and observe, you can read, you can converse with others, you can even do some imagining. (These five great resources will be explored in Chapters 1–5.) All the while you look for material, you can be writing. You can be thinking on paper: making notes, summarizing what other writers have said, setting down your own rough ideas, leaving reminders for yourself:

When dealing with Gen. Franco, dictator of Spain, don't forget his friendship with Hitler.

Shaping a Draft

Having discovered a burning idea to write about (or at least a smoldering one) and material to back it up with, you sort out what matters most. If right away it appears that your paper has one main point to make, you're lucky. You might try to state that point in writing. You might arrange your ideas and material in what seems a clear and sensible order that will make that one point clear. But if no one main point has emerged, never mind: you may find one while you draft—that is, while you write an early version of your paper.

Usually this first version will be rough and preliminary. Drafting takes time: a paper may take two or more drafts, especially if your subject is complicated. You may have to throw out your first attempt and start over because a stronger idea has hit you. Sometimes you can expect to keep discovering ideas while you draft. By all means, welcome them.

Most writers find that it pays to let a draft run long. Later, it will be easier to cut a draft than to expand on it.

Rewriting

When you complete a draft, you might well think that your work is done. But for most professional writers, the time of revising is the time when work begins in earnest. In an apt comparison, Chinese-American writer Maxine Hong Kingston likens writing to gardening in Hawaii: a little time spent in planting, much more time spent in "cutting and pruning and hacking back." Playwright Neil Simon puts it another way: "In baseball, you get only three swings and you're out. In rewriting, you get almost as many swings as you want and you know that, sooner or later, you'll hit the ball."

Revision—the word means "seeing again"—is more than a matter of just revising words: you sometimes revise what you know. Such changes may take place at any time while you're writing, at any moment when you stop writing to reread. You can then change your plans, decide to put in or leave out, shift things around, connect things differently. If you can put aside your draft for a few hours or a day, you can reread it with fresh eyes and with a sharp pencil.

When you revise, as humorist Leo Rosten has said, "you have to put yourself in the position of the negative reader, the resistant reader, the reader who doesn't surrender easily, the reader who is alien to you as a type, even the reader who doesn't like what you are writing." Still, you should probably sit in the seat of the scornful only when your paper is well along. When your ideas first start to flow, you want to welcome them—lure them forth, not tear them apart—or they might go back into hiding.

Editing   As you work along, or near the finish of your labors (whichever you find more comfortable), you *edit* what you have written: you correct any flaws that may stand in the way of your reader's enjoyment and understanding. In editing, you usually accomplish these repairs:

> Get rid of surplus wordage.
>
> Improve your choice of words.
>
> Replace any misusages with usages that are generally acceptable.
>
> Correct your grammar: make subjects agree with verbs, pronouns with what they stand for.
>
> Rearrange words into a stronger, clearer order.

Proofreading   A final activity, proofreading is giving your paper one last look, with a dictionary at your elbow to check any doubtful spellings, and fixing any typing mistakes.

AUDIENCE AND PURPOSE

At any moment in the writing process, two questions are worth asking: "Whom do I write for?" and "Why?"

Writing for a reader   In fulfilling some relatively easy assignments—say, recalling an experience or reporting a conversation—you won't need to keep asking nervously, "Who's reading me?" You'll know. In a college writing course like this, you'll always have three or more readers: (1) yourself, (2) your instructor, and (3) your fellow students. If, as you write a paper in a college course, you believe it is going well, the chances are that your readers will think so too. But in tackling certain other assignments, you'll write more effectively if you consider your audience. Say you wish to persuade your readers to take a certain action—to ban (or approve) a law regulating the hiring of women or the sale of pornography. At some point, you might ask, What do my readers probably believe? Where is my argument likely to offend them? What objections are they likely to raise? What do they need to be told, what do they know already?

As your own first reader, you'll always want to step back from a draft and reread it *as though you weren't the writer but were someone else*, detached and objective, and not too easy to please. You will also want to comb your writing for errors before you turn it in. That is merely to follow the Golden Rule and do unto your reader as you trust other writers to do unto you.

Writing for a reason   Usually, a college writing assignment has a clear-cut purpose. Every assignment in this book asks you to write for a definite reason. In Chapter 1, you'll be asked to recall a memorable experience, and in Chapter 2, to observe people. In Part Two, purposes will become especially important. You'll write papers to analyze — to understand something by breaking it into its components — to evaluate, to see causes or effects, to set forth an opinion, to propose a solution. Aware that you write for a reason, you can concentrate on your task. From the start you can ask, What do I want to do? And, in revising, Did I do what I meant to do? As you'll find, these are very practical questions. They'll help you cut out anything irrelevant that wanders into your writing, anything that hinders your paper from getting where you want it to go.

The reason you write, and the reader you write for, will always deserve a little consideration — and in the case of certain assignments, a great deal. Throughout this book, from time to time we'll remind you of them.

WHAT MATTERS MOST

In college writing, some qualities count more than mere neatness and correctness: mastering knowledge, discovering your own ideas. The most important part of writing is getting something down on paper. Why worry if your first draft isn't neat? Drafts are only sketches, made to be torn apart. Cross out words, draw arrows, move sentences and paragraphs. Scissor your draft to bits, then Scotch-tape the pieces together in a stronger order. If your first draft looks like a rug that a bulldog has been chewing, never mind — all a reader will see is your final version.

Don't be afraid, by the way, that your readers will expect your writing to be dazzling. No writer is brilliant at all times. That's why writers have wastebaskets.

To keep thinking while you write, not merely beforehand, can yield surprising results. As your fingers type or drive a pencil, your head keeps working right along. Often, an idea will leap up and startle you. As the English writer E. M. Forster put it, "How do I know what I think until I see what I say?" Asked how she customarily wrote a poem, Anne Sexton said, "I will fool around on the typewriter. It might take me ten pages of nothing, of terrible writing, and then I'll get a line, and I'll think, 'That's what I mean.' " Though you don't need to include all the further thoughts that come to you, be willing to consider them.

USING THIS BOOK

In *The Bedford Guide for College Writers,* we too have a purpose. It is to help you write better, deeper-reaching, and more interesting papers than you have ever written before, and to do so by actually writing.

How this book is built   Right away, Part One encourages you to write, drawing on five basic resources for your ideas and material: recalling, observing, reading, conversing, and imagining. Part Two asks you to write papers that emphasize reading and thinking critically. Part Three guides you in writing research papers.

Extra help on hand   Like a kit of tools and a spare tire carried in the trunk, in the back of this book are two carefully packed reference manuals useful in day-to-day emergencies. Part Four, "Strategies," arrays advice on a number of ways to generate ideas, draft, and rewrite. Browse through them at your leisure to find out what is there. If you write with a word processor, take a look at "Strategies for Writing with a Computer" (Ch. 19). (By the way, you'll notice word processing tips embedded throughout the book: in boxes labeled "Writing with a Computer.") Whether you work with pen, typewriter, or word processor, you may want a little advice on how to prepare your manuscript. Right after the strategies section, on page 577, you'll find some guidelines you can follow if your instructor doesn't specify otherwise. Part Five, "Handbook," is a practical guide to rules and usage, covering matters such as grammar, spelling, punctuation, and choice of words. These are matters to care about in giving your paper a thorough proofreading.

As you know, your fellow students also can help you—sometimes more than a textbook or an instructor can. This book sets up opportunities for you to learn from them and to help them learn from you. If your instructor asks you to exchange your work with other students, to give and receive reactions, you'll face a challenge: just how do you go about criticizing another's writing? You'll find suggestions in Chapter 18 and also in the "Peer Editing Checklist" in every writing assignment chapter. In each of these chapters, besides, a feature called "For Group Learning" will give useful hints for ways that you and other students can help one another discover ideas as you write and rewrite your papers.

Taking it to the hoop   Like a hard game of basketball, writing a college paper is strenuous. Without getting in your way, we want to lend you all possible support. So, no doubt, does your instructor, someone closer to you than any textbook writers. Still, like even the best coaches, instructors and textbook writers can improve your game only so far. Advice on how to write won't make you a better writer. You'll learn more and have more fun when you take a few sentences to the hoop and make points yourself.

PART ONE

A WRITER'S RESOURCES

Every college writer wrestles with the question "What should I write about?" and then, after finding a topic, with the question "What should I say?" Fortunately, to answer those questions, you have five tremendous resources. With their aid, you'll never find yourself long at a loss for words.

None of these resources will be new to you. Already, you are adept at *recalling* what you know and at *observing* the world around you. You're accustomed to *reading* and *conversing* with people. And you've had experience with the richest resource of all: *imagining*.

At the start of each chapter, we offer illustrations of good writing by two writers—a college student and a professional—who draw on the same resource. Then we suggest a writing assignment: a large one that leaves you room to discover a specific topic you care about.

Immediately following the assignment you'll find suggestions to guide you in writing it. We pose questions that, if you like, you can ask yourself. Some of these questions will remind you of your audience and your purpose. Sometimes we report the experience of other students. We offer you rough guidance throughout the whole shifting, tentative, surprise-filled process of writing. But if, instead of reading our suggestions, you'd rather go ahead and write, please do. Our only aim in offering suggestions is to provide you with a trusty support system, for whenever you feel the need for it.

After you write your paper, you might care to read "Applying What You Learn." It will show you typical uses for the same kind of writing in your other college courses and in your career.

CHAPTER 1

Writing from Recall

Write from recall and you write from memory, the richest resource a writer has, and the handiest. This is clearly the case in an English course when you are asked to write of a personal experience, a favorite place, a memorable person. But even when an instructor hands you a subject that at first glance seems to have nothing to do with you, your memory is the first place to look. Suppose you have to write a psychology paper about how advertisers play on our fears. Begin with what you remember. What ads have sent chills down your back? (We recall a tire ad that showed the luckless buyer of an inferior product stuck with a blowout on a remote road on a stormy night, while the Frankenstein monster bore down on him.)

You may also need to observe, read, talk with someone, and imagine. All by itself, memory may not give you enough to write about. But whenever you need to start writing, you will rarely go wrong if you start by jotting down something remembered.

LEARNING FROM OTHER WRITERS

In this chapter you will be invited to write a whole paper from recall. First, let's illustrate what we mean. Here are two samples of good writing—one by a professional writer, one by a college student. We begin with an excerpt from columnist Russell Baker's autobiography *Growing Up*, because autobiographical writing so clearly demonstrates the uses of memory. Baker recalls what it was like to be sixteen in urban Baltimore, wondering what to do with his life.

THE ART OF EATING SPAGHETTI
Russell Baker

The only thing that truly interested me was writing, and I knew that 1
sixteen-year-olds did not come out of high school and become writers. I
thought of writing as something to be done only by the rich. It was so
obviously not real work, not a job at which you could earn a living. Still, I
had begun to think of myself as a writer. It was the only thing for which I
seemed to have the smallest talent, and, silly though it sounded when I
told people I'd like to be a writer, it gave me a way of thinking about myself
which satisfied my need to have an identity.

The notion of becoming a writer had flickered off and on in my head 2
since the Belleville days, but it wasn't until my third year in high school
that the possibility took hold. Until then I'd been bored by everything associated with English courses. I found English grammar dull and baffling.
I hated the assignments to turn out "compositions," and went at them like
heavy labor, turning out leaden, lackluster paragraphs that were agonies
for teachers to read and for me to write. The classics thrust on me to read
seemed as deadening as chloroform.

When our class was assigned to Mr. Fleagle for third-year English I 3
anticipated another grim year in that dreariest of subjects. Mr. Fleagle was
notorious among City students for dullness and inability to inspire. He was
said to be stuffy, dull, and hopelessly out of date. To me he looked to be
sixty or seventy and prim to a fault. He wore primly severe eyeglasses, his
wavy hair was primly cut and primly combed. He wore prim vested suits with
neckties blocked primly against the collar buttons of his primly starched
white shirts. He had a primly pointed jaw, a primly straight nose, and a
prim manner of speaking that was so correct, so gentlemanly, that he
seemed a comic antique.

I anticipated a listless, unfruitful year with Mr. Fleagle and for a long 4
time was not disappointed. We read *Macbeth*. Mr. Fleagle loved *Macbeth*
and wanted us to love it too, but he lacked the gift of infecting others with
his own passion. He tried to convey the murderous ferocity of Lady Macbeth
one day by reading aloud the passage that concludes

> . . . I have given suck, and know
> How tender 'tis to love the babe that milks me.
> I would, while it was smiling in my face,
> Have plucked my nipple from his boneless gums. . . .

The idea of prim Mr. Fleagle plucking his nipple from boneless gums was
too much for the class. We burst into gasps of irrepressible snickering. Mr.
Fleagle stopped.

"There is nothing funny, boys, about giving suck to a babe. It is the— 5
the very essence of motherhood, don't you see."

He constantly sprinkled his sentences with "don't you see." It wasn't a 6
question but an exclamation of mild surprise at our ignorance. "Your pronoun needs an antecedent, don't you see," he would say, very primly. "The
purpose of the Porter's scene, boys, is to provide comic relief from the
horror, don't you see."

Late in the year we tackled the informal essay. "The essay, don't you 7
see, is the. . . ." My mind went numb. Of all forms of writing, none seemed
so boring as the essay. Naturally we would have to write informal essays.
Mr. Fleagle distributed a homework sheet offering us a choice of topics.
None was quite so simpleminded as "What I Did on My Summer Vacation,"
but most seemed to be almost as dull. I took the list home and dawdled
until the night before the essay was due. Sprawled on the sofa, I finally
faced up to the grim task, took the list out of my notebook, and scanned
it. The topic on which my eye stopped was "The Art of Eating Spaghetti."

This title produced an extraordinary sequence of mental images. Surg- 8
ing up out of the depths of memory came a vivid recollection of a night in
Belleville when all of us were seated around the supper table—Uncle Allen,
my mother, Uncle Charlie, Doris, Uncle Hal—and Aunt Pat served spaghetti
for supper. Spaghetti was an exotic treat in those days. Neither Doris nor
I had ever eaten spaghetti, and none of the adults had enough experience
to be good at it. All the good humor of Uncle Allen's house reawoke in my
mind as I recalled the laughing arguments we had that night about the
socially respectable method for moving spaghetti from plate to mouth.

Suddenly I wanted to write about that, about the warmth and good 9
feeling of it, but I wanted to put it down simply for my own joy, not for Mr.
Fleagle. It was a moment I wanted to recapture and hold for myself. I wanted
to relive the pleasure of an evening at New Street. To write it as I wanted,
however, would violate all the rules of formal composition I'd learned in
school, and Mr. Fleagle would surely give it a failing grade. Never mind. I
would write something else for Mr. Fleagle after I had written this thing for
myself.

When I finished it the night was half gone and there was no time left 10
to compose a proper, respectable essay for Mr. Fleagle. There was no
choice next morning but to turn in my private reminiscence of Belleville.
Two days passed before Mr. Fleagle returned the graded papers, and he
returned everyone's but mine. I was bracing myself for a command to report
to Mr. Fleagle immediately after school for discipline when I saw him lift
my paper from his desk and rap for the class's attention.

"Now, boys," he said, "I want to read you an essay. This is titled 'The 11
Art of Eating Spaghetti.' "

And he started to read. My words! He was reading *my words* out loud 12
to the entire class. What's more, the entire class was listening. Listening
attentively. Then somebody laughed, then the entire class was laughing,
and not in contempt and ridicule, but with openhearted enjoyment. Even
Mr. Fleagle stopped two or three times to repress a small prim smile.

I did my best to avoid showing pleasure, but what I was feeling was   13
pure ecstasy at this startling demonstration that my words had the power
to make people laugh. In the eleventh grade, at the eleventh hour as it
were, I had discovered a calling. It was the happiest moment of my entire
school career. When Mr. Fleagle finished he put the final seal on my happiness by saying, "Now that, boys, is an essay, don't you see. It's—don't
you see—it's of the very essence of the essay, don't you see. Congratulations, Mr. Baker."

For the first time, light shone on a possibility. It wasn't a very heartening   14
possibility, to be sure. Writing couldn't lead to a job after high school, and
it was hardly honest work, but Mr. Fleagle had opened a door for me. After
that I ranked Mr. Fleagle among the finest teachers in the school.

Questions to Start You Thinking

1. In your own words, state what Baker believes he learned in the eleventh grade
   about the art of writing. What incidents or statements help identify this lesson for
   readers of the essay? Tell what lesson, if any, you learned from the essay.

2. What is the effect, in paragraph 3, of Baker's many repetitions of the words *prim*
   and *primly*? What other devices does Baker use to make vivid his characterization
   of Mr. Fleagle? Why do you think the author uses so much space to portray his
   teacher?

3. What does the quotation from *Macbeth* add to Baker's account? Had the quotation
   been omitted, what would have been lost?

The next essay was written by a student, Robert Schreiner. He was asked
to recall a significant event from his childhood. As you read Schreiner's recollection, notice those vivid details that help bring the incident alive.

Student Essay

WHAT IS A HUNTER?
Robert G. Schreiner

What is a hunter? This is a simple question with a   1
relatively straightforward answer. A hunter is, according to
Webster's New Collegiate Dictionary, a person that hunts game
(game being various types of animals hunted or pursued for
various reasons). However, a question that is just as simple
but without such a straightforward answer is What characteristics make up a hunter? As a child, I had always considered

the most important aspect of the hunter's person to be his
ability to use a rifle, bow, or whatever weapon was appropriate to the type of hunting being done. Having many relatives
in rural areas of Virginia and Kansas, I had been exposed to
rifles a great deal. I had done extensive target shooting
and considered myself to be quite proficient in the use of
firearms. I had never been hunting, but I had always thought
that since I could fire a rifle accurately I would make a
good hunter.

One Christmas holiday, while we were visiting our grand-   2
parents in Kansas, my grandfather asked me if I wanted to go
jackrabbit hunting with him. I eagerly accepted, anxious to
show off my prowess with a rifle. A younger cousin of mine
also wanted to come, so we all went out into the garage,
loaded two .22 caliber rifles and a 20-gauge shotgun, hopped
into the pickup truck, and drove out of town. It had snowed
the night before and to either side of the narrow road swept
six-foot-deep powdery drifts. The wind twirled the fine
crystalline snow into whirling vortexes that bounced along
the icy road and sprayed snow into the open windows of the
pickup. As we drove, my grandfather gave us some pointers
about both spotting and shooting jackrabbits. He told us
that when it snows, jackrabbits like to dig out a hollow in
the top of a snowdrift, usually near a fencepost, and lie
there soaking up the sunshine. He told us that even though
jackrabbits are a grayish brown, this coloration is excellent
camouflage in the snow, for the curled-up rabbits resemble
rocks. He then pointed out a few rabbits in such positions
as we drove along, showing us how to distinguish them from
exposed rocks and dirt. He then explained that the only way
to be sure that we killed the rabbit was to shoot for the
head and, in particular, the eye, for this was on a direct
line with the rabbit's brain. Since we were using solid
point bullets, which deform into a ball upon impact, a hit
anywhere but the head would most likely only wound the
rabbit.

My grandfather then slowed down the pickup and told us   3
to look out for the rabbits hidden in the snowdrifts. We
eventually spotted one about thirty feet from the road in a
snow-filled gully. My cousin wished to shoot the first one,
so he hopped out of the truck, balanced the .22 on the hood,
and fired. A spray of snow erupted about a foot to the left
of the rabbit's hollow. My cousin fired again, and again,
and again, the shots pockmarking the slope of the drift. He
fired once more and the rabbit bounced out of its hollow, its
head rocking from side to side. He was hit. My cousin
eagerly gamboled into the snow to claim his quarry. He
brought it back holding it by the hind legs, proudly displaying it as would a warrior the severed head of his enemy. The
bullet had entered the rabbit's right shoulder and exited
through the neck. In both places a thin trickle of crimson
marred the gray sheen of the rabbit's pelt. It quivered
slightly and its rib cage pulsed with its labored breathing.
My cousin was about to toss it into the back of the pickup
when my grandfather pointed out that it would be cruel to allow the rabbit to bleed slowly to death and instructed my
cousin to bang its head against the side of the pickup to
kill it. My cousin then proceeded to bang the rabbit's head
against the yellow metal. Thump, thump, thump, thump; after
a minute or so my cousin loudly proclaimed that it was dead
and hopped back into the truck.

The whole episode sickened me to some degree, and at the   4
time I did not know why. We continued to hunt throughout the
afternoon, and feigning boredom, I allowed my cousin and
grandfather to shoot all of the rabbits. Often, the shots
didn't kill the rabbits outright so they had to be killed
against the pickup. The thump, thump, thump of the rabbits'
skulls against the metal began to irritate me, and I was
strangely glad when we turned around and headed back toward
home. We were a few miles from the city limits when my
grandfather slowed the truck to a stop, then backed up a few
yards. My grandfather said he spotted two huge "jacks" sit-

ting in the sun in a field just off the road. He pointed
them out and handed me the .22, saying that if I didn't shoot
something the whole afternoon would have been a wasted trip
for me. I hesitated, then reluctantly accepted the rifle.
I stepped out onto the road, my feet crunching on the ice.
The two rabbits were about seventy feet away, both sitting
upright in the sun. I cocked and leveled the rifle, my elbow
held almost horizontal in the military fashion I had learned
to employ. I brought the sights to bear upon the right eye
of the first rabbit, compensated for distance, and fired.
There was a harsh snap like the crack of a whip, and a small
jolt to my shoulder. The first rabbit was gone, presumably
knocked over the side of the snowdrift. The second rabbit
hadn't moved a muscle; it just sat there staring with that
black eye. I cocked the rifle once more and sighted a second
time, the bead of the rifle just barely above the glassy
black orb that regarded me so passively. I squeezed the
trigger. Again the crack, again the jolt, and again the
rabbit disappeared over the top of the drift. I handed the
rifle to my cousin and began making my way toward the rabbits. I sank into powdery snow up to my waist as I clambered
to the top of the drift and looked over.

On the other side of the drift was a sight that I doubt   5
I will ever forget. There was a shallow, snow-covered ditch
on the leeward side of the drift and it was into this ditch
that the rabbits had fallen, at least what was left of the
rabbits. The entire ditch, in an area about ten feet wide,
was spattered with splashes of crimson blood, pink gobbets of
brain, and splintered fragments of bone. The twisted corpses
of the rabbits lay in the bottom of the ditch in small pools
of streaming blood. Of both the rabbits, only the bodies
remained, the heads being completely gone. Stumps of verte-
brae protruded obscenely from the mangled bodies, and one
rabbit's hind legs twitched spasmodically. I realized that
my cousin must have made a mistake and loaded the rifle with
hollowpoint explosive bullets instead of solid ones.

I shouted back to the pickup, explaining the situation,   6
and asked if I should bring them back anyway. My grandfather
shouted back, "No, don't worry about it, just leave them
there. I'm gonna toss these jacks by the side of the road
anyway; jackrabbits aren't any good for eatin'."

Looking at the dead, twitching bodies I thought only of   7
the incredible waste of life that the afternoon had been, and
I realized that there was much more to being a hunter than
knowing how to use a rifle. I turned and walked back to the
pickup, riding the rest of the way home in silence.

Questions to Start You Thinking

1. Where in the essay do you first begin to suspect the nature of the writer's feelings toward hunting? What in the essay or in your experience led you to this perception? Are other readers likely to have had a similar response? Why or why not?

2. What details in Schreiner's essay contribute to your understanding of his grandfather? From what the writer says about him, how would you characterize him?

3. How did the writer's understanding of himself change as a result of his hunting lesson? Would the change in outlook presented in the essay be any less evident if the first paragraph were omitted? How else might the essay be strengthened or weakened by cutting out the opening paragraph?

LEARNING BY WRITING

The Assignment: A Personal Experience

Write about a personal experience that took place at one moment in your life and that changed how you acted, thought, or felt from that moment on. Your purpose is not merely to tell an interesting story but to show your readers the importance that experience had for you. Your audience is your instructor and your fellow students.

We suggest you pick an event that happened outside your head. An encounter with a person who for some reason greatly influenced you, or with a challenge or obstacle, will be far easier to look back on (and to make vivid for your reader) than a subjective, interior experience like a religious conversion or falling in love.

Some memorable student papers we have read have recalled experiences like those that follow—some heavy, some light:

A woman recalled beginning dance lessons with an older teacher who at first seemed harsh but who turned out to be a true friend.

A woman recalled her childhood fear that her mother, injured in a car crash, would no longer be able to take care of her. (The fear proved groundless.)

A woman recalled how, as a small girl, she sneaked into a nun's room, out of curiosity stole some rosary beads, and discovered that crime does not pay.

A man recalled meeting a Native American who taught him a wider view of the natural world.

To help you fulfill this assignment, let's consider: What does writing from personal experience call for?

Generating Ideas

You may find that the minute you are asked to write about a significant experience in your life, the very incident will flash to mind. If that is the case, start writing. Most writers, though, will need a little time to shake down their memories. If you are such a writer, the following suggestions may help.

Probably what will come to you first will be recent memories, but give long-ago memories time to surface, too. Novelist Willa Cather once said, "Most of the basic material a writer works with is acquired before the age of fifteen." As we might infer from her many stories of growing up on the plains of Nebraska, she was well aware of the value of searching early memories.

Be ready for any recollections that well up unexpectedly. Often, when you are busy doing something else—observing the scene around you, talking with someone, reading about someone else's experience—the activity can trigger a recollection from the past. When a promising one surfaces, write it down. It may be the start of your paper. Perhaps, like Russell Baker, you found success only when you ignored what you thought you were supposed to do in favor of what you really wanted to do. Perhaps, like Robert Schreiner, you learned from a painful experience. If nothing much surfaces, you might want to prod your memory with the following questions.

DISCOVERY CHECKLIST: SEARCHING YOUR MEMORY

- Did you ever break a rule or rebel against authority in some memorable way? Did you learn anything from your actions? If so, what?
- What were the causes and the results of the worst fight you ever had?
- Did you ever succumb to peer pressure? Were the results of going along with the crowd good or bad? What did you learn from the experience?
- Did you ever regard a person in a certain way and then find you had to change your opinion of him or her?
- Did you ever have to choose between two equally attractive or equally dismal alternatives? What made the choice hard for you? What factors led you to decide as you did? Were you ultimately happy or unhappy with your choice?

- Did you ever make a serious error in judgment that led to disaster—or maybe to unexpected good fortune?

- Did you ever, as Robert Schreiner did, have a long-held belief or assumption challenged and toppled? Did you experience having one of your prejudices shattered?

- Was there ever a moment in your life when you decided to reform, to adopt a whole new outlook? In retrospect, would you characterize your attempt as successful, unsuccessful, laughable, painful, or what?

- Was there ever a moment in your life when you found, as Russell Baker did, that something you did just took off and seemed to do itself, and the result pleased you mightily, and perhaps pleased others, and you felt you had really learned something?

Try freewriting. You might still think, "My life hasn't had any moments important enough to write about." If you still have difficulty recalling a meaningful experience, perhaps some other means of discovery might serve you. Spend ten or fifteen minutes *freewriting*—simply writing as fast as you can whatever comes into your head, regardless of whether it seems to have anything to do with the subject at hand. If you think you have nothing to say, write "I have nothing to say" over and over, until ideas come. They will come. Don't worry at all about spelling, punctuation, coherence, or anything else. Most of what you set down that way may have to be thrown out, but you may be surprised, when you read over what you have written, to find in it the germ of a good paper. (For more about freewriting, see p. 474 in Chapter 15.)

Try brainstorming. Alone or as part of a classroom exercise, brainstorming is another good way to jog your memory. When you brainstorm, you try to come up with as many ideas as you can, without any thought for their practical applications. Start with a suggestive word or phrase—*fight, painful lesson, peer pressure*—and list under that word or phrase as many ideas as occur to you through free association. Put them down at random, in the order in which they come to you. Later you can see if anything on your list suggests a fruitful direction. (For more about brainstorming, see p. 471 in Chapter 15.)

Try reading. Browse in the autobiography of some famous person. (Helen Keller, Maya Angelou, and Alec Guinness are only a few authors of memorable autobiographies.) See the brief story told by Mahatma Gandhi in his autobiography (quoted on p. 521) and what he learned from it. As you will find from reading, not every decisive experience is earthshaking—Gandhi learned a profound lesson from giving himself a bad haircut.

Try a reporter's questions. Once you recall an experience you want to write about, ask yourself whether you feel the same about the event now as you did when it took place—or has the passage of time changed your view?

Ask the *reporter's questions,* the "five *W*'s and an *H*," that journalists find useful in their work:

Who was there?
What happened?
When did it happen?
Where did the event take place?
Why?
How did the event or events happen?

Any one of these questions can lead to further questions—and, so, to further discovery. Take, for instance, "Who was there?" If there were people besides you involved in the incident, you might also ask: What did they look like? What information about them would a reader have to know to appreciate fully the point of your story? (Remember Mr. Fleagle in Baker's reminiscence.) What did the people do? What did they say? Can you remember, or approximate, what they said? If so, might their words supply a lively quotation for your paper? Or take the question "What happened?" Think about that, and you might also ask: What were your inmost thoughts as the event took place? At what moment did you become aware that the event was no ordinary,

---

WRITING WITH A COMPUTER: RECALLING

If you write with a personal computer, you'll enjoy applying it to this assignment. You can set down your recollections rapidly, without pausing even to slam back a typewriter carriage. You might begin by making, as fast as you can, a simple on-screen list of the events you wish to record. This done, go back and flesh out the skeleton. Add any exact details that might make the experience real to your reader. Have you recalled a person? If so, add a sentence or two that will make him or her come alive ("a gray-haired gentleman who wore old white shirts with frayed collars, fond of consulting his gold pocket watch"). Did a certain locale shape your experience? (A washed-out, abandoned road is central to Edward Abbey's memoir "Disorder and Early Sorrow," p. 26.) What made that place such an unforgettable part of your experience? Keep recalling, dropping in memorable details. Before your eyes, your bare list will start becoming a meaty draft.

But if your list remains bare and you need more material, file your draft and create a fresh document. Apply to your experience the five *W*'s and an *H*. Ask yourself a reporter's questions and jot down your replies. With the power of word processing to lift the contents of one document to another, you can transfer to your draft all or any of the material you generate and work it in wherever it best fits.

everyday experience? Or weren't you aware of that until later—perhaps only now that you are writing about it? (For more advice about putting these questions to work for you, see "Asking a Reporter's Questions" on p. 478.)

Once you have a promising incident in mind, feel sure you can be honest in presenting it. If you find it too embarrassing to tell the whole truth, you might be better off choosing some other recollection.

Talk with others. As we find out in a psychology course, the memory drops as well as retains. So it may be that you will want to check your recollections against those of anyone else who shared the experience. If possible, talk to a friend or family member. See that person, or phone him or her. Did you keep a diary at the time? If so, you might glance into it and refresh your memory. Was the experience public enough (such as a riot or a blizzard) to have been recorded in a newspaper or a news magazine? If so, perhaps you can read up on it in a library. These are *possible* sources of material.

Shaping a Draft

Now, how will you tell your story? If the one experience you want to write about is burning in your mind, it may be that you can start right in and write a draft, without advance planning, instead planning and writing simultaneously, shaping your story as you go along. Such a method might work for a personal memoir like this. But whether or not you plan and draft at the same time, you'll find it reassuring to have at your elbow any jottings you made as you searched your memory.

Establish a chronology. The simplest way to recount an experience is chronologically: relating events in the order in which they occurred. In doing so, you take the King's advice to the White Rabbit in *Alice's Adventures in Wonderland:* "Begin at the beginning, and go on till you come to the end: then stop." It is possible, of course, to begin in the middle of a story, at an exciting or interesting moment, and then by a flashback to tell your readers what else they need to know. This method sometimes makes for an arresting opening. But a good rule of thumb, in relating an experience, is to set down events chronologically—unless you see a good reason to set them down in some other way.

Show what happened. How can you best make your recollections come alive for your readers? Look again at Russell Baker's account of Mr. Fleagle teaching *Macbeth* and at the way Robert Schreiner depicts his cousin putting the wounded rabbits out of their misery. Both writers have done what good novelists and story writers do: they have not merely told us what happened, they have *shown* us, by creating scenes that we can see in our mind's eye. As you tell your story, you might include at least two or three scenes of your own. Show your readers exactly what happened, what was said, who said it.

How did the other people react? Were there any sounds that contributed to the scene? Smells or tastes or textures that you want to record? (For more information about recounting an incident effectively, see "Telling a Story" on p. 521.)

Good fiction writers, and writers of true stories as well, know how to keep readers (or listeners) wondering, "What happened next?" They dole out essential information a little bit at a time so that readers have to keep reading or listening until the end to find out what they want to know. Both Baker and Schreiner save the meaning of the experience they share with us for the end of their accounts. You can decide as you write whether you think that's the best place to discuss what your experience means to you.

Often, an account of a personal experience needs no introduction: it starts with something happening and then the writer fills in whatever background a reader needs to know. Richard Rodriguez, for instance, begins *Hunger of Memory*, a memoir of his bilingual childhood, with an arresting sentence:

> I remember, to start with, that day in Sacramento, in a California now nearly thirty years past—when I first entered a classroom, able to understand about fifty stray English words.

With such a limited vocabulary, we wonder, how will the child get along? The opening hooks our attention. In the rest of his essay, Rodriguez fills us in on his family history, on the gulf he came to perceive between the public language (English) and the language of his home.

Rewriting

After you have written an early draft and have put it aside for a day or two (or, if time is tight, for a few hours), read it over as if seeing it for the first time.

When you revise, ask: What was so memorable about this experience? Do you get that across? Have you made it come alive, by recalling it in sufficient concrete detail? Notice again Robert Schreiner's attention in his second paragraph to the world outside his own skin: his close recall of the snow, of the pointers his grandfather offered about the habits of jackrabbits and the way to shoot them. If you're recalling a fire, make your reader smell the smoke. As you revise, you may well find more and more vivid details rising to the light.

Remember your purpose. Keep in mind that you want to show how the experience was a crucial one in your life. So when you look back over your draft, make sure that this importance stands out. Ask again the question you probably asked yourself when you began: How did this experience alter your life? Have you got something in there about how life (or your view of it) has been different ever since? Pay a little extra attention to this major point. Be sure that the difference you point to is genuine and specific. Don't ramble on insincerely about "significances" that don't reflect the incident's real impact on you.

Here are some other questions for you to ask as you go over your paper.

REVISION CHECKLIST: WRITING FROM RECALL

- Have you fulfilled your purpose and demonstrated that this experience changed your life?
- Is there a place in the draft that would make a better beginning?
- Do you portray any people? If so, have you told your readers enough about them to indicate their importance to you?
- If there is dialogue, does it have the ring of real speech? Read it aloud. Try it on a friend.
- If the events are not recorded in chronological order, is it easy to follow the organization you have chosen?
- Do you stick to the point? Does the draft contain extraneous thoughts, ideas, or events that ought to be struck out? (Draw a single line through any such wandering prose.)
- Consider your audience. If you were in your readers' shoes, would you want to keep reading? Have you paid enough attention to what is most dramatic, instructive, or revealing?

You may also find it helpful at this point to call upon a fellow student to read and criticize your draft. Ask your peer editor to answer the following questions as carefully as possible.

PEER EDITING CHECKLIST: WRITING FROM RECALL

- What did you, the peer editor, see as you read the essay?
- Tell the writer what you understand to be the importance of what he or she recalled.
- Tell the writer what emotions you saw (and perhaps felt) while reading the essay.
- Underline on the manuscript any sense images that seem particularly effective.
- List questions you might still have about the event the writer has recalled.

In the light of the answers to the questions you have asked yourself and your peer editor, rewrite. Keep at it until you know you've related your experience and recorded its impact as well as you know how. This may take more than one new draft. It may take several.

Then go over your paper one last time. Even the names of people and places you know well may need to be checked. Writing a paper about a remembered trip to New York, a high school student once consistently referred to "the Umpire State Building." Any encyclopedia could have put that writer straight. But don't agonize over the likelihood that you might make a spectacular boner. All writers do.

When you have made all the changes you need to make, retype or recopy or print out your paper—and hand it in.

Other Assignments

1. Choose a person outside your immediate family who had a marked effect on your life, either good or bad, and jot down ten details about that person that might help a reader understand what he or she was like. In searching your memory for details, consider the person's physical appearance, way of talking, and habits as well as any memorable incidents. When your list is finished, look back to "The Art of Eating Spaghetti" to identify the kinds of detail Baker used in his portrait of Mr. Fleagle, paying particular attention to the kinds of detail you might have included in your list but didn't. Then write a paper in which you portray that person and explore the nature of his or her impact on you.

2. Write a paper in which you remember a place you were once fond of—your grandmother's kitchen, a tree house, a library, a locker room, a clubhouse, a vacation retreat, a place where your gang got together. Try to emphasize why this place was memorable. What made it different from every other place? Why was it important to you? Do you even now think back on it? What do you feel when you remember it? (No sentimental gush, now. But don't be afraid to set down honest feeling.)

3. Write a paper in which, from memory, you inform your readers about some traditional ceremony, ritual, or observation familiar to you. Such a tradition can pertain to a holiday, a rite of passage (confirmation, bar or bas mitzvah, fraternity or sorority initiation), a sporting event, a special day on your college calendar. It might be a family custom. Explain the tradition, making use of whatever information you recall. How did the observation or custom originate? Who takes part? How has the tradition changed through the years? What does it add to the lives of those who observe it?

FOR GROUP LEARNING

To gain dry-run practice in peer editing before trying your skills on a paper by a student you know, select from this book's table of contents any student-written paper and write a detailed response to it. Do this in the form of a short letter or note to the writer. If others in your class work on the same paper, get together and compare comments. What did you notice in the paper? What did you miss that others noticed? If you have any doubts that it is worth your good time to compare your responses with other people's, this activity will convince you that several people can notice far more than one individual can.

APPLYING WHAT YOU LEARN:
SOME USES OF WRITING FROM RECALL

Autobiographers and writers of informal essays rely extensively on recall. All of us depend on recall in much of our informal, everyday writing—when we pen a letter to friends or family members, when we write out directions for someone who doesn't know where we live, when we make a diary entry, when we fill out an accident report or an application form.

Students of creative writing often find themselves reaching into their memories for experiences to write about. Recall is also an important resource for the kind of paper in which you, the expert, are asked to explain how to do something—train a puppy, drive a car, build a coffee table, make a speech, hunt for edible mushrooms. But recall also plays a role in the writing you are asked to do for classes other than English. In most papers written for a college course, you are expected to investigate, to explain an idea, or to argue. Clearly it's not enough merely to recount a personal experience, but personal experience does have a place in academic writing as support for exposition and argument. Rebecca Shriver, a student who had spent a year living and working in St. Thomas, added life and verisimilitude to her research paper analyzing cultural differences between the Virgin Islands and the United States by including not only material gathered from books and periodicals but also this telling recollection:

> Among the first things an American in the Virgin Islands will notice are the driving and the drivers. St. Thomas retains the custom, a carryover from Danish rule, of driving on the left-hand side of the road. Drivers are extremely aggressive, vocal, and heedless of others. West Indians, especially the cab drivers, virtually own the road. They stop for minutes at a time at the bottom of steep hills to chat with friends or to pick up hordes of workers. The streets resound with honks and screams as drivers yell obscenities at each other. Hitchhikers, too, are aggressive. It is nothing to notice a West Indian jumping into the back of one's truck, or schoolchildren who will tap on one's window, soliciting a ride.
>
> The mind-set of left-hand driving surfaces in an unusual way: walking habits. Since St. Thomians are so used to driving on the left, they also walk on the left, and an American who is unused to this will find himself bumping into a lot of West Indians on the sidewalk.

The writer used this recollection to make an important point: that recognizing and understanding cultural differences provide the keys to understanding. In an article called "Sex and Size," paleontologist Stephen Jay Gould makes effective use of recollection to ease his readers into a seven-page essay on a challenging subject. (Linnaeus [1707–1778], a Swedish botanist, originated the system of classifying organisms in established categories.)

As an eight-year-old collector of shells at Rockaway Beach, I took a functional but non-Linnaean approach to taxonomy, dividing my booty into "regular," "unusual," and "extraordinary." My favorite was the common slipper limpet, although it resided in the realm of the regular by virtue of its ubiquity. I loved its range of shapes and colors, and the pocket underneath that served as a protective home for the animal. My appeal turned to fascination a few years later, when I both entered puberty and studied some Linnaean taxonomy at the same time. I learned its proper name, *Crepidula fornicata*—a sure spur to curiosity. Since Linnaeus himself had christened this particular species, I marveled at the unbridled libido of taxonomy's father.

When I learned about the habits of *C. fornicata,* I felt confident that I had found the key to its curious name. For the slipper limpet forms stacks, smaller piled atop larger, often reaching a dozen shells or more. The smaller animals on top are invariably male, the larger supporters underneath always female. And lest you suspect that the topmost males might be restricted to a life of obligate homosexuality by virtue of their separation from the first large female, fear not. The male's penis is longer by far than its entire body and can easily slip around a few males to reach the females. *Crepidula fornicata* indeed: a sexy congeries.

Then, to complete the disappointing story, I discovered that the name had nothing to do with sex. Linnaeus had described the species from single specimens in museum drawers; he knew nothing of their peculiar stacking behavior. *Fornix* means "arch" in Latin, and Linnaeus chose his name to recognize the shell's smoothly domed shape.

Disappointment finally yielded to renewed interest a few years later when I learned the details of *Crepidula*'s sexuality and found the story more intriguing than ever, even if the name had been a come-on. *Crepidula* is a natural sex changer, a sequential hermaphrodite in our jargon. Small juveniles mature first as males and later change to female as they grow larger. Intermediate animals in the middle of a *Crepidula* stack are usually in the process of changing from male to female.

Usually you have to research your subject in some depth before you can write an acceptable paper about it. You need to rely on resources other than memory. Yet even as you approach an academic writing assignment, a research paper, or an argument on a topic, you can *begin* by writing down your own relevant experiences. Whether or not you use them in your finished paper, they can help direct your research. Often you *will* use them, as Shriver and Gould did, in conjunction with more academic sources. A student who has worked in a day-care center can add vigor and authority to a sociology paper on day care in the United States today by including a few pertinent illustrations based on that experience. Or if you are the person writing the paper and you lack personal experience with day care, you can illustrate a point or two with lively anecdotes remembered from your reading or from having talked with someone with firsthand experience. In a paper for a course in corporate ethics, your next-door neighbor's gleeful account of a hostile takeover, divulged at the last block party you attended, might hammer home the point you're making more effectively than any statistic. An economics paper about the recent growth of the fast-food industry could benefit immeasurably from an incident remembered from your harried days behind the counter at a McDonald's. If you grew up in an urban ghetto, your recollections might lend enormous impact to a paper arguing for or against a particular city planning proposal.

Virtually every paper, no matter what it sets out to accomplish, stands to benefit from pat, vivid examples and illustrations. When you include such examples and illustrations in your writing, your memories can prove as valuable as hidden treasure.

An Environmentalist Recalls

Edward Abbey was a distinguished environmentalist and professor at the University of Arizona. His many books expressing his concern for future generations gained him a devoted following. That he was able to laugh at himself, the following recollection amply demonstrates, but it also displays firsthand knowledge of a little-traveled corner of the West.

DISORDER AND EARLY SORROW°
Edward Abbey

The first time I investigated Big Bend National Park was a long time   1
ago, way back in '52 during my student days at the University of New Mexico. My fiancée and I drove there from Albuquerque in her brand-new Ford convertible, a gift from her father. We were planning a sort of premature, premarital honeymoon, a week in the wilderness to cement, as it were, our permanent relationship. Things began well. With all the other tourists (few enough in those days), we followed the paved road down from Marathon and into the park at Persimmon Gap, paused at the entrance station for instruction and guidance, as per regulations, and drove up into the Chisos Mountains that form the heart of this rough, rude, arid national park. We camped for a few days in the Chisos Basin, hiking the trails to Lost Mine, to the Window, to Emory Peak and Casa Grande. Some of the things I saw from those high points, looking south, attracted me. Down in those blue, magenta, and purplish desert wastes are odd configurations of rock with names like Mule Ear Peaks and Cow Heaven Anticline. I was interested; my fiancée was satisfied with long-distance photographs.

Disorder and Early Sorrow: This title is borrowed from a more serious story by German writer Thomas Mann, about a child who falls in love too early in life and meets disappointment.

When I inquired of a ranger how to get down there, he told me we'd 2
have to backpack it; there was, he said, "no road." I showed him my 1948
Texaco map; according to the map there was a road—unpaved, ungraded,
primitive to be sure, but a road all the same—leading from the hamlet of
Castolon near the southwest corner of the park to Rio Grande Village at the
east-central edge of the park. Fifty miles of desert road.

"That road is closed," the ranger told me. 3

"Closed?" 4

"Not fit for travel," he explained. "Permanently washed out. Not pa- 5
trolled. Not safe. Absolutely not recommended."

My sweetheart listened carefully. 6

I thanked him and departed, knowing at once where I wanted to go. 7
Had to go. Since we were not equipped for backpacking, it would have to
be on wheels. My fiancée expressed doubts; I reassured her. We drove
down the old road along Alamo Creek—the only road at that time—to the
mouth of Santa Elena Canyon. We contemplated the mouth of Santa Elena
Canyon for a day, then headed east to Castolon, where we stocked up on
water and food. I made no further inquiries about the desert road; I did not
wish to expose myself to any arguments.

A short distance beyond Castolon we came to a fork in the road. The 8
left-hand fork was marked by a crude, hand-painted wooden sign that said:

Staked in the middle of the right-hand fork was a somewhat more official-
looking board that said:

The left-hand fork led northeasterly, up a rocky ravine into a jumble of 9
desert hills. The other fork led southeasterly, following the course of the
Rio Grande into the wastelands of southern Big Bend. One would have liked
to meet Mr. Hartung but his road was not our road.

I pulled up the No Road sign, drove through, stopped, replaced the   10
sign. Our tire tracks in the dust showed clearly on each side of the warning
sign, as if some bodiless, incorporeal ghost of a car had passed through.
That should confuse the park rangers, I thought, if they ever came this way.
My fiancée meanwhile was objecting to the whole procedure; she felt it
was time to turn back. Gently but firmly I overruled her. We advanced,
cautiously but steadily, over the rocks and through the sand, bound for Rio
Grande Village—an easy fifty-mile drive somewhere beyond those mountains and buttes, mesas and ridges and anticlines on the east.

All went well for half a mile. Then we came to the first of a hundred   11
gulches that lie transverse to the road, formed by the rare flash floods that
drain from the hills to the river. The gulch was deep, narrow, and dry but
filled with sand and cobbles. The drop-off from bank to streambed was two
feet high. Time to build road. I got out the shovel, beveled off the edge of
the cut bank on either side, removed a few of the larger rocks, logs, and
other obstacles. Revving the Ford's hearty V-8 engine, I put her in low and
charged down, across the rocks, and up the other side. A good little car,
and it made a game effort, hanging to the lip of the far embankment while
the rear wheels spun furiously in the sand and gravel. Not quite sufficient
traction; we failed to make it. I backed down into the bottom of the gulch,
opened the trunk, took out the luggage and filled the trunk with rocks. That
helped. Gunning the engine, we made a second lunge for the top and this
time succeeded, though not without cost. I could smell already the odor of
burning clutch plate.

Onward, though my fiancée continued to demur. We plunged into and   12
up out of another dozen ravines, some of them deeper and rougher than
the first, sometimes requiring repeated charges before we could climb out.
Although the car had less than 5000 miles to its career, some parts began
to give under the strain. The right-hand door, for example, would no longer
latch. Evidently the frame or body had been forced a trifle askew, springing
the door. I wired it shut with a coat hanger. My sweetheart, in a grim mood
by this time, suggested again that we turn around. I pointed out that the
road ahead could hardly be as bad as what we had come through already
and that the only sensible course lay in a resolute advance. She was doubtful; I was wrong, but forceful. I added water to the boiling radiator, diluting
the manufacturer's coolant, and drove on.

There seemed no choice. After all, I reasoned, we had already disre-   13
garded a park ranger's instructions and a clear warning sign. Our path was
littered not only with bolts, nuts, cotter pins, and shreds of rubber but with
broken law as well. Furthermore, I had to see what lay beyond the next
ridge.

In the afternoon we bogged down halfway through a stretch of sand. I   14
spent two hours shoveling sand, cutting brush and laying it on the roadway,
and repeatedly jacking up the rear of the car as it advanced, sank, stopped.
I could have partially deflated the tires and got through more easily but we
had no tire pump, and ahead lay many miles of stony trail.

By sundown of the first day we had accomplished twenty miles. The car 15
still ran but lacked some of its youthful élan. The bright enamel finish was
scarred and scoriated, dulled by a film of dust. We made camp and ate our
meal in silence. Coyotes howled like banshees from the foothills of Back-
bone Ridge, gaunt Mexican cattle bellowed down in the river bottom, and
across the western sky hung the lurid, smoldering fires of sunset, a spectacle grim and ghastly as the announcement of the end of the world. A
scorpion scuttled out of the shadows past our mesquite fire, hunting its
evening meal. I made our bed in a dusty clearing in the cactus, but my
beloved refused to sleep with me, preferring, she said, to curl up in the
back seat of her car. The omens multiplied and all were dark. I slept alone
under the shooting stars of Texas, dreaming of rocks and shovels.

Dawn, and a dusty desert wind, and one hoot owl hooting back in the 16
bush. I crawled out of my sack and shook my boots out (in case of arach-
nids), made breakfast and prepared for another struggle through the heat,
the cactus, the rock, and, hardest of all, the unspeaking enmity of my
betrothed.

The second day was different from the first. Worse. The washouts 17
rougher than before, the ravines deeper, the sandy washes broader, the
stones sharper, the brush thornier. In the morning we had our first flat. No
repair kit, of course; no pump, no tire irons. I bolted on the spare tire,
which meant that for the next thirty miles we would have no spare. Onward.
We thrashed in and out of more gullies and gulches, burning up the pressure plate, overheating the engine, bending things. Now the other door,
the one on the driver's side, had to be secured with coat-hanger wire.
Sprung doors were always a problem with those old Ford convertibles.

We clattered on. Detouring an unnecessarily bad place on the road, I 18
veered through the cactus and slammed into a concealed rock. Bent the
tie-rod. Taking out the lug wrench, I hammered the tie-rod as straight as I
could. We drove on with the front wheels toed in at a cockeyed angle. Hard
to steer and not good for the tires, which were compelled, now one, now
the other, or both at once, to slide as well as roll, forward. They might or
might not endure for the twenty miles or so that, according to my Texaco
road map and the record of the odometer, we still had to cover.

As in any medical disorder, one malady aggravates another. Because 19
of the friction in the front end I found it harder to negotiate the car across
the washes and up out of ravines. It was no longer sufficient merely to gear
down into low, pop the clutch, and *charge!* up the far side. I had to charge
down as well as *up*. The clutch still functioned, but it was going. I prayed
for the clutch, but it was the oil pan I worried about. My fiancée, clutching
at the dashboard with both hands, jaw set and eyes shut, said nothing. I
thought of iron seizures, bleeding crankcases, a cracked block.

Nevertheless: forward. Determination is what counts. 20

Cactus, sand pits, shock-busting chuckholes, axle-breaking washouts, 21
rocks. And more rocks. Embedded like teeth in the roadway, points upward,
they presented a constant nagging threat to my peace of mind. No matter

how slowly I drove forward, lurching over the ruts at one mile an hour, there was no way I could avoid them all. I missed a few, but one of them got us, five miles short of the goal, late in the afternoon of the second day. A sharp report rang out, like a gunshot, followed by the squeal of hot air, the sigh of an expiring tire, and I knew we were in difficulty.

I stopped to inspect the damage, for form's sake, but there was really 22 nothing I could do. Nothing practical, that is, except maybe pull the wheel and roll it on to Rio Grande Village by hand where, possibly, I could have it fitted with a new tire, and roll it back here to the stricken Ford. I suggested this procedure to my one and only. She objected to being left alone in this scorching wilderness full of animals and Mexicans while I disappeared to the east. Did she wish to walk with me? No, she didn't want to do that either.

That helped make up my mind. I got back in the car, started the engine 23 and drove on, flat tire thumping on the roadway, radiator steaming, clutch smoking, oil burning, front wheels squealing, the frame and all moving parts a shuddering mass of mechanical indignation. The car clanked forward on an oblique axis, crabwise, humping up and down on the eccentric camber of the flat. Scraps of hot, smoking rubber from the shredded tire marked our progress. Late in the evening, on scalloped wheel rim and broken heart, we rumbled painfully into Rio Grande Village, pop. 22 counting dogs.

My fiancée took the first bus out of town. She had most of our money. 24 I was left behind to hitchhike through west Texas with two dollars and forty-seven cents in my pocket. The car, as I later heard, was salvaged by my sweetheart and her friends, but never recovered its original *esprit de Ford.* Nor did I ever see my fiancée again. Our permanent relationship had been wrecked, permanently. Not that I could blame her one bit. She was fully justified. Who could question that statement? All the same it hurt; the pain lingered for weeks. Small consolation to me was the homely wisdom of the philosopher, to wit:

> A woman is only a woman
> But a good Ford is a car.°

A woman . . . a car: Abbey echoes Rudyard Kipling's poem "The Betrothed," in which another man also loses his fiancée. When she makes him choose between her and cigars, he decides that "a woman is only a woman, but a good Cigar is a Smoke."

Questions to Start You Thinking

1. In his opening paragraph, how does Abbey arouse his readers' anticipation? By reading on, what do we expect to find out?

2. At what moment did you first suspect that Abbey, in his determination to travel the closed road, might be asking for trouble? At what point were you practically sure that he was making a terrible mistake?

3. Right after he recalls the NO ROAD sign, Abbey tells us, "Our tire tracks in the dust showed clearly on each side of the warning sign, as if some bodiless, incorporeal ghost of a car had passed through." What makes that sentence so effective?

4. In the last half of Abbey's memoir, as the unlucky Ford lurches onward, what vivid details strike you? What facts of the car's mechanical woes stand out? In what passages is the roughness of the terrain made unmistakably clear?

5. Although Abbey's fiancée is a central character, one whose presence is often felt, the writer never quotes her words directly or describes her in vivid detail. Do you find it a fault that he leaves her portrait so vague? What does this vagueness reveal about the narrator and his single-minded determination?

A Journalist Recalls

Brent Staples is an assistant metropolitan editor of the *New York Times.* Before joining the *Times* in 1985, he worked for several magazines and newspapers in Chicago, including the *Chicago Sun-Times.* In this essay from the December 1986 issue of *Harper's,* he shares his reflections about an urban problem that most of us have probably never thought about before.

BLACK MEN AND PUBLIC SPACE
Brent Staples

My first victim was a woman—white, well dressed, probably in her late 1 twenties. I came upon her late one evening on a deserted street in Hyde Park, a relatively affluent neighborhood in an otherwise mean, impoverished section of Chicago. As I swung onto the avenue behind her, there seemed to be a discreet, uninflammatory distance between us. Not so. She cast back a worried glance. To her, the youngish black man—a broad six feet two inches with a beard and billowing hair, both hands shoved into the pockets of a bulky military jacket—seemed menacingly close. After a few more quick glimpses, she picked up her pace and was soon running in earnest. Within seconds, she disappeared into a cross street.

That was more than a decade ago. I was twenty-two years old, a grad- 2 uate student newly arrived at the University of Chicago. It was in the echo of that terrified woman's footfalls that I first began to know the unwieldy inheritance I'd come into—the ability to alter public space in ugly ways. It was clear that she thought herself the quarry of a mugger, a rapist, or worse. Suffering a bout of insomnia, however, I was stalking sleep, not defenseless wayfarers. As a softy who is scarcely able to take a knife to a raw chicken—let alone hold one to a person's throat—I was surprised, embarrassed, and dismayed all at once. Her flight made me feel like an accomplice in tyranny. It also made it clear that I was indistinguishable from the muggers who occasionally seeped into the area from the surrounding ghetto. That first encounter, and those that followed, signified that a vast, unnerving gulf lay between nighttime pedestrians—particularly women—and me. And I soon gathered that being perceived as dangerous is a hazard in itself. I only needed to turn a corner into a dicey situation, or crowd some frightened, armed person in a foyer somewhere, or make an errant move after being pulled over by a policeman. Where fear and weapons meet—and they often do in urban America—there is always the possibility of death.

In that first year, my first away from my hometown, I was to become 3
thoroughly familiar with the language of fear. At dark, shadowy intersections, I could cross in front of a car stopped at a traffic light and elicit the *thunk, thunk, thunk, thunk* of the driver—black, white, male, or female—hammering down the door locks. On less traveled streets after dark, I grew accustomed to but never comfortable with people crossing to the other side of the street rather than pass me. Then there were the standard unpleasantries with policemen, doormen, bouncers, cabdrivers, and others whose business it is to screen out troublesome individuals *before* there is any nastiness.

I moved to New York nearly two years ago and I have remained an avid 4
night walker. In central Manhattan, the near-constant crowd cover minimizes tense one-on-one street encounters. Elsewhere—in SoHo, for example, where sidewalks are narrow and tightly spaced buildings shut out the sky—things can get very taut indeed.

After dark, on the warrenlike streets of Brooklyn where I live, I often 5
see women who fear the worst from me. They seem to have set their faces on neutral, and with their purse straps strung across their chests bandolier-style, they forge ahead as though bracing themselves against being tackled. I understand, of course, that the danger they perceive is not a hallucination. Women are particularly vulnerable to street violence, and young black males are drastically overrepresented among the perpetrators of that violence. Yet these truths are no solace against the kind of alienation that comes of being ever the suspect, a fearsome entity with whom pedestrians avoid making eye contact.

It is not altogether clear to me how I reached the ripe old age of twenty- 6
two without being conscious of the lethality nighttime pedestrians attributed to me. Perhaps it was because in Chester, Pennsylvania, the small, angry industrial town where I came of age in the 1960s, I was scarcely noticeable against a backdrop of gang warfare, street knifings, and murders. I grew up one of the good boys, had perhaps a half-dozen fistfights. In retrospect, my shyness of combat has clear sources.

As a boy, I saw countless tough guys locked away; I have since buried 7
several, too. They were babies, really—a teenage cousin, a brother of twenty-two, a childhood friend in his mid-twenties—all gone down in episodes of bravado played out in the streets. I came to doubt the virtues of intimidation early on. I chose, perhaps unconsciously, to remain a shadow—timid, but a survivor.

The fearsomeness mistakenly attributed to me in public places often 8 has a perilous flavor. The most frightening of these confusions occurred in the late 1970s and early 1980s, when I worked as a journalist in Chicago. One day, rushing into the office of a magazine I was writing for with a deadline story in hand, I was mistaken for a burglar. The office manager called security and, with an ad hoc posse, pursued me through the labyrinthine halls, nearly to my editor's door. I had no way of proving who I was. I could only move briskly toward the company of someone who knew me.

Another time I was on assignment for a local paper and killing time 9 before an interview. I entered a jewelry store on the city's affluent Near North Side. The proprietor excused herself and returned with an enormous red Doberman pinscher straining at the end of a leash. She stood, the dog extended toward me, silent to my questions, her eyes bulging nearly out of her head. I took a cursory look around, nodded, and bade her good night.

Relatively speaking, however, I never fared as badly as another black 10 male journalist. He went to nearby Waukegan, Illinois, a couple of summers ago to work on a story about a murderer who was born there. Mistaking the reporter for the killer, police officers hauled him from his car at gunpoint and but for his press credentials would probably have tried to book him. Such episodes are not uncommon. Black men trade tales like this all the time.

Over the years, I learned to smother the rage I felt at so often being 11 taken for a criminal. Not to do so would surely have led to madness. I now take precautions to make myself less threatening. I move about with care, particularly late in the evening. I give a wide berth to nervous people on subway platforms during the wee hours, particularly when I have exchanged business clothes for jeans. If I happen to be entering a building behind some people who appear skittish, I may walk by, letting them clear the lobby before I return, so as not to seem to be following them. I have been calm and extremely congenial on those rare occasions when I've been pulled over by the police.

And on late-evening constitutionals I employ what has proved to be an 12 excellent tension-reducing measure: I whistle melodies from Beethoven and Vivaldi and the more popular classical composers. Even steely New Yorkers hunching toward nighttime destinations seem to relax, and occasionally they even join in the tune. Virtually everybody seems to sense that a mugger wouldn't be warbling bright, sunny selections from Vivaldi's *Four Seasons*. It is my equivalent of the cowbell that hikers wear when they know they are in bear country.

Questions to Start You Thinking

1. What does the first paragraph of "Black Men and Public Space" lead you to expect? What is valuable in the author's strategy of beginning his essay with a recalled experience?

2. "Black Men and Public Space" is more than a memoir. What is Staples's apparent purpose in writing this essay? Sum it up in your own words.

3. Can *anyone* alter public space if he or she chooses? If so, by what means? Have you had any experience of your own that seems comparable? Get it down on paper in a paragraph or two, and plan to read your recollection in class.

4. What clues in Staples's essay reveal how the author feels about the phenomenon he has noticed—the way people react toward him?

CHAPTER 2

Writing from Observation

Most writers, we said in the last chapter, begin to write by recalling what they know. But sometimes when they sit down to write they look around the storehouse of the brain only to find empty shelves. In that case, a writer has another resource: observation.

Not enough to write about? Open your eyes—and your other senses. Take in not only what you can see but also what you can hear, smell, touch, and taste. Then, when you write, report your experiences in concrete detail. Of course, you can't record everything your senses bring you. Keeping in mind your purpose in writing and your audience will help you to select those details important to the job at hand and to pay them the most attention. Writing an account of a football game for your college newspaper, trying to make it come alive for a reader who wasn't there, you might briefly mention the weather (overcast and cold) and the buttery smell of popcorn in the air. But, hewing to your purpose to tell which team won and why, you might stress other details: the condition of the playing field (deep mud), the most spectacular plays, and which players scored.

Some writing consists almost entirely of observation: a news story by a reporter who has witnessed a fire, a clinical report by a doctor or nurse detailing a patient's condition, an account of a laboratory experiment. Travel writing, in which a traveler reports a visit to a distant place, consists largely of observation; so does descriptive writing that sets down a writer's observations of a person, place, or thing. (Such description occurs in both fiction and nonfiction.) In such kinds of writing, observation serves a definite purpose. But indeed, we can hardly think of a kind of writing that doesn't call for a writer to observe and report those observations.

LEARNING FROM OTHER WRITERS

Let's read two essays by writers who write from observation: a college student and a professional. Both essays arise from the western American desert, but there the resemblance ends. First is the student paper, written by Sandy Messina, who was invited to submit the same paper to both a course in freshman composition and another course—in her case, environmental biology.

Student Essay

FOOTPRINTS: THE MARK OF OUR PASSING
Sandy Messina

No footprints. No tracks. No marks. The Navajo leave 1 no footprints because their shoes have no heels to dig into the earth's womb. They have a philosophy--walk gently on mother earth; she is pregnant with life. In the spring, when the earth is ready to deliver, they wear no shoes at all.

As I walk across the desert, I look at my shoes etch the 2 sand dune. There they are following me: the telltale prints left on the brown earth. Each footprint has a story to tell, a story of change, a story of death. Many lives are marked by our passing. Our steps can bring death to the life of a flower, the life of a forest, the life of a friendship. Some of our passages can bring death to the life of a nation.

I see my prints dug deeply into the spawning grounds of 3 the desert lavender, the evening primrose, the desert sunflower, and the little golden gilia. Life destroyed. Birth aborted. There under each mark of my passing is death. The fetuses--seeds of desert color, spring glory, trapped just below the surface waiting parturition--crushed into lifelessness. Man walks heavily on the earth.

He tramples across America, leaving giant footprints 4
everywhere he goes. He fills swamps, furrows hillsides,
forms roads, fells trees, fashions cities. Man leaves the
prints of his lifelong quest to subdue the earth, to conquer
the wilderness. He pushes and pulls and kneads the earth
into a loaf to satisfy his own appetites. He constantly tugs
at the earth, trying to regulate it. Yet, man was not told
to regulate, restrict, restrain the Garden of Eden but to
care for it and allow it to replenish itself.

I look at my own footprints in the sand and see nearby 5
other, gentler tracks. Here on the sandy hummock I see
prints, soft and slithery. The snake goes softly on the
earth. His willowy form causes no tyranny. He has no need
to prove his prowess: he graciously gives warning and strikes
only in self-defense. He doesn't mar the surface of the
earth by his entrance, for his home is found in the burrows
of the other animals.

The spidery prints of the roadrunner, as he escapes with 6
a lizard dangling from his beak, show that he goes mercifully
on the earth. He does not use his power of flight to feed
off wide distances but instead employs his feathers to insu-
late his body from high temperatures. He takes sustenance
from the earth but does not hoard or store it.

The wood rat scrambles over the hillock to burrow be- 7
neath the Joshua tree. His clawed plantigrade feet make
sensitive little marks. He is caring of the earth. He
doesn't destroy forage but browses for food and eats cactus,
food no other animal will eat. His home is a refuge of underground runways. It even provides protection for his enemy
the snake, as well as for himself, from the heat of the day.
He never feels the compulsion to be his own person or have
his own space but lives in harmony with many other animals,
under the Joshua tree.

The Joshua tree, that prickly paragon that invades the 8
desolation of desert, welcomes to its house all who would
dwell there. Many lives depend on this odd-looking creature,

the Joshua tree. It is intimately associated with the moth, the lizard, the wood rat, the snake, the termite, the woodpecker, the boring weevil, the oriole. This spiky fellow is hospitable, tolerant, and kind on the earth. He provides a small world for other creatures: a world of pavilion, provision, protection from the harsh desert.

Unlike the Navajo's, my prints are still there in the   9
sand, but not the ruthless furrows I once perceived. My musings over nature have made my touch upon the earth lighter, softer, gentler.

Man too can walk gently on the earth. He must reflect   10
on his passing. Is the earth changed, bent and twisted, because he has traveled there, or has he considered nature as a symphony he can walk with, in euphony? He need not walk heavily on the earth, allowing the heat of adversity and the winds of circumstance to destroy him. He can walk gently on the earth, allowing life to grow undisturbed in seeming desert places until it springs forth.

Questions to Start You Thinking

1. Why doesn't the writer plunge right in and immediately start to observe? Of what use to her essay is her first paragraph?

2. In paragraph 2, how is the writer's way of walking across the earth seen as different from the Navajo way? Paragraph 3 isn't observation, but what does the writer accomplish in it? With paragraphs 4, 5, and 6, the writer returns to observing—for what purpose?

3. In the end, how has the process of observing her own footprints changed the writer's behavior? How would she change the behavior of the rest of us?

4. What specialized words suggest that this essay was written for a readership familiar with biology (her instructor and her fellow students)? Would you blast this essay for using too much *jargon,* or technical terminology?

5. How readily does Messina communicate her ideas to a general reader?

Now here is another, much different piece of writing from observation: an article that sets out to depict the marriage industry in Las Vegas. Joan Didion wrote it in 1967 for a wide, unspecialized audience—the readers of the *Saturday Evening Post,* a magazine of general circulation.

MARRYING ABSURD
Joan Didion

To be married in Las Vegas, Clark County, Nevada, a bride must swear 1
that she is eighteen or has parental permission and a bridegroom that he
is twenty-one or has parental permission. Someone must put up five dollars
for the license. (On Sundays and holidays, fifteen dollars. The Clark County
Courthouse issues marriage licenses at any time of the day or night except
between noon and one in the afternoon, between eight and nine in the
evening, and between four and five in the morning.) Nothing else is required. The State of Nevada, alone among these United States, demands
neither a premarital blood test nor a waiting period before or after the
issuance of a marriage license. Driving in across the Mojave from Los
Angeles, one sees the signs way out on the desert, looming up from that
moonscape of rattlesnakes and mesquite, even before the Las Vegas lights
appear like a mirage on the horizon: "GETTING MARRIED? Free License Information First Strip Exit." Perhaps the Las Vegas wedding industry achieved
its peak operational efficiency between 9:00 P.M. and midnight of August
26, 1965, an otherwise unremarkable Thursday which happened to be, by
presidential order, the last day on which anyone could improve his draft
status merely by getting married. One hundred and seventy-one couples
were pronounced man and wife in the name of Clark County and the State
of Nevada that night, sixty-seven of them by a single justice of the peace,
Mr. James A. Brennan. Mr. Brennan did one wedding at the Dunes and the
other sixty-six in his office, and charged each couple eight dollars. One
bride lent her veil to six others. "I got it down from five to three minutes,"
Mr. Brennan said later of his feat. "I could've married them *en masse*, but
they're people, not cattle. People expect more when they get married."

What people who get married in Las Vegas actually do expect—what, 2
in the largest sense, their "expectations" are—strikes one as a curious and
self-contradictory business. Las Vegas is the most extreme and allegorical
of American settlements, bizarre and beautiful in its venality and in its
devotion to immediate gratification, a place the tone of which is set by
mobsters and call girls and ladies' room attendants with amyl nitrite pop-
pers in their uniform pockets. Almost everyone notes that there is no "time"
in Las Vegas, no night and no day and no past and no future (no Las Vegas
casino, however, has taken the obliteration of the ordinary time sense quite
so far as Harold's Club in Reno, which for a while issued, at odd intervals
in the day and night, mimeographed "bulletins" carrying news from the
world outside); neither is there any logical sense of where one is. One is
standing on a highway in the middle of a vast hostile desert looking at an
eight-foot sign which blinks "STARDUST" or "CAESAR'S PALACE." Yes, but what
does that explain? This geographical implausibility reinforces the sense
that what happens there has no connection with "real" life; Nevada cities

like Reno and Carson are ranch towns, Western towns, places behind which there is some historical imperative. But Las Vegas seems to exist only in the eye of the beholder. All of which makes it an extraordinarily stimulating and interesting place, but an odd one in which to want to wear a candlelight satin Priscilla of Boston wedding dress with Chantilly lace insets, tapered sleeves and a detachable modified train.

And yet the Las Vegas wedding business seems to appeal to precisely 3 that impulse. "Sincere and Dignified Since 1954," one wedding chapel advertises. There are nineteen such wedding chapels in Las Vegas, intensely competitive, each offering better, faster, and, by implication, more sincere services than the next: Our Photos Best Anywhere, Your Wedding on a Phonograph Record, Candlelight with Your Ceremony, Honeymoon Accommodations, Free Transportation from Your Motel to Courthouse to Chapel and Return to Motel, Religious or Civil Ceremonies, Dressing Rooms, Flowers, Rings, Announcements, Witnesses Available, and Ample Parking. All of these services, like most others in Las Vegas (sauna baths, payroll-check cashing, chinchilla coats for sale or rent) are offered twenty-four hours a day, seven days a week, presumably on the premise that marriage, like craps, is a game to be played when the table seems hot.

But what strikes one most about the Strip chapels, with their wishing 4 wells and stained-glass paper windows and their artificial bouvardia, is that so much of their business is by no means a matter of simple convenience, of late-night liaisons between show girls and baby Crosbys. Of course there is some of that. (One night about eleven o'clock in Las Vegas I watched a bride in an orange minidress and masses of flame-colored hair stumble from a Strip chapel on the arm of her bridegroom, who looked the part of the expendable nephew in movies like *Miami Syndicate*. "I gotta get the kids," the bride whimpered. "I gotta pick up the sitter, I gotta get to the midnight show." "What you gotta get," the bridegroom said, opening the door of a Cadillac Coupe de Ville and watching her crumple on the seat, "is sober.") But Las Vegas seems to offer something other than "convenience"; it is merchandising "niceness," the facsimile of proper ritual, to children who do not know how else to find it, how to make the arrangements, how to do it "right." All day and evening long on the Strip, one sees actual wedding parties, waiting under the harsh lights at a crosswalk, standing uneasily in the parking lot of the Frontier while the photographer hired by The Little Church of the West ("Wedding Place of the Stars") certifies the occasion, takes the picture: the bride in a veil and white satin pumps, the bridegroom usually in a white dinner jacket, and even an attendant or two, a sister or a best friend in hot-pink *peau de soie*, a flirtation veil, a carnation nosegay. "When I Fall in Love It Will be Forever," the organist plays, and then a few bars of Lohengrin. The mother cries; the stepfather, awkward in his role, invites the chapel hostess to join them for a drink at the Sands. The hostess declines with a professional smile; she has already transferred her interest to the group waiting outside. One bride out, another in, and again the sign goes up on the chapel door: "One moment please—Wedding."

I sat next to one such wedding party in a Strip restaurant the last time 5 I was in Las Vegas. The marriage had just taken place; the bride still wore her dress, the mother her corsage. A bored waiter poured out a few swallows of pink champagne ("on the house") for everyone but the bride, who was too young to be served. "You'll need something with more kick than that," the bride's father said with heavy jocularity to his new son-in-law; the ritual jokes about the wedding night had a certain Panglossian character, since the bride was clearly several months pregnant. Another round of pink champagne, this time not on the house, and the bride began to cry. "It was just as nice," she sobbed, "as I hoped and dreamed it would be."

Questions to Start You Thinking

1. Where does Didion begin to observe? How much of this essay consists of observation?

2. "But Las Vegas seems to offer something other than 'convenience'; it is merchandising 'niceness' . . . to children who do not know how else to find it, how to make the arrangements" (paragraph 4). Which of Didion's observations seem to bear out this insight?

3. Reflect on the scene in the concluding paragraph: the wedding party in the restaurant. Imagine a little of this couple's story *before* the moment Didion observes. Imagine a little of it as it might unfold, say, a year later. Then reflect again on that original scene. What do Didion's observations of it reveal about what might have gone before and what might be to come?

4. Would you call Didion's attitude toward Las Vegas and its marriage chapels sneering and contemptuous? Is she wholly negative? How would you characterize her view of the city and its wedding industry? Sum up the apparent purpose of her essay.

LEARNING BY WRITING

The Assignment: Reporting on Group Behavior

Station yourself in a nearby place where you can mingle with a group of people gathered for some reason or occasion. Observe the group's behavior and in a short paper report on it. Then offer some insight. What is your main impression of the group?

This assignment is meant to start you observing closely, so we suggest you don't write from long-ago memory. Go somewhere nearby, today or as soon as possible, and open your senses. Write for your fellow students. Jot down what you can immediately see and sense. You may wish to take notes right there on the scene or minutes after you make your observations. After you have set forth your observations in detail, try to use them to form some general impression of the group or come to some realization about it.

Notice how the people in the group affect one another, how they respond. Which individuals stand out and seem to call for an especially close look? What details (of their dress, actions, speech, body language) make you want to remember them? Four student writers made these observations:

> One student recently did an outstanding job of observing a group of people nervously awaiting a road test for their driver's licenses. (She also observed them when they crossed the finish line, in most cases triumphantly.)
>
> Another observed a bar mitzvah celebration that reunited a family for the first time in many years.
>
> Still another, who works nights in the emergency room of a hospital, observed the behavior of the community of people that abruptly forms on the arrival of an accident victim (including doctors, nurses, orderlies, the patient's friends or relatives, and the patient himself or herself).
>
> A fourth student observed a knot of people that formed on a street corner to inspect a luna moth perched on a telephone pole (including a man who viewed it with alarm, a wondering toddler, and an amateur entomologist).

Expect to take at least two typewritten or three handwritten pages to cover your subject.

Generating Ideas

Setting down observations might seem a cut-and-dried task, not a matter of discovering anything. But to Joan Didion it is true discovery. "I write," she says, "entirely to find out what I'm thinking, what I'm looking at, what I see and what it means."

Do some brainstorming. First, you need to find a subject to observe. What groups of people come together for a reason? Get out your pencil and start brainstorming—listing rapidly and at random any ideas that come to mind (a technique often useful in getting started; for more advice about it, see p. 471). Here are a few questions to help you start your list.

DISCOVERY CHECKLIST: OBSERVING

- What people get together to take in some event or performance? (Spectators at a game, an audience at a play or concert—you go on.)
- What people get together to participate in some activity? (Worshipers at a religious service, students in a discussion class. . . .)
- What people assemble to receive advice or instruction? (A team receiving a briefing from a coach, actors, musicians, dancers at a rehearsal. . . .)

- What people form crowds while they are obtaining something or receiving service? (Shoppers, students in a dining hall or student union, patients in a waiting room. . . .)
- What people get together for recreation? (People at a party, at a video arcade. . . .)

Get out and look. After you make your list, go over it and put a check mark next to any possible subject that appeals to you. If no subject strikes you as compelling, go plunge into the world beyond your sleeping quarters and see what you will see. Your location might be a city street or a hillside in the country, a college building or a campus lawn, a furiously busy scene—an air terminal, a fast-food restaurant at lunch hour, or a student hangout—or one in which only two or three people are idling—sunbathers, dog walkers, or Frisbee throwers. You may soon find you have picked a likely group to observe, or you may instead find that you're getting nowhere and want to move on to another location. Move around in a group, if possible. Stand off in a corner for a while, then mix in with the throng. Get different angles of view.

Sandy Messina's essay "Footprints" began as a journal entry. In her biology course, Sandy was asked to keep a *specialized* journal in which to record her thoughts and observations on environmental biology. When she looked back over her observations of a desert walk, a subject stood out—one wide enough for a paper that she could submit to her English course as well. As you can see from her final version, to keep such a journal or notebook, occasionally jotting down thoughts and observations, creates a trove of material ready and waiting for use in more formal writing. (For further thoughts on journal keeping, see p. 476.)

Record your observations. The notes you take on your subject—or tentative subject—can be taken in any old order or methodically. One experienced teacher of writing, Myra Cohn Livingston, urges her students to draw up an "observation sheet" to organize their note taking. To use it, fold a sheet of paper in half lengthwise. On the left make a column (which might be called Objective) and list exactly what you saw, in an impartial way, like a zoologist looking at a new species of moth. Then on the right make a column (called Subjective), and list your thoughts and feelings about what you observed. For instance, an observation sheet inspired by a trip to observe people at a beach might begin this way:

OBJECTIVE	SUBJECTIVE
Two kids toss a red beach ball while a spotted dog chases back and forth trying to intercept it.	Reminds me of when I was five and my beach ball rolled under a parked car. Got stuck crawling in to

	rescue it, cried, had to be calmed down, dragged free. Never much liked beach ball after that.
College couples on dates, smearing each other with suntan lotion.	Good way to get to know each other!
Middle-aged man eating a foot-long hot dog. Mustard drips on his paunch. "Hell! I just lost two percent!"	Guy looks like a business executive: three-piece-suit type, I bet. But today he's a slob. Who cares? The beach brings out the slob in everybody.

As your own list grows, it may spill over onto a fresh sheet. Write on one side of your paper only: later, you can more easily organize your notes if you can spread them out and look at them all in one glance. Even in this sample beginning of an observation sheet, some sense is starting to take shape. At least, the second and third notes both suggest that the beach is where people come to let their hair down. That insight might turn out to be the main impression that the paper conveys. For this writing assignment, an observation sheet seems an especially useful device. The notes in column one will trigger more notes in column two. Observations, you will find, start thoughts and feelings moving.

The quality of your finished paper will probably depend not on how much you rewrite but on the truthfulness of your observations. If possible, while you write keep looking at your subject. Sandy Messina is a good, exact observer of nature: the details of the snake's "soft and slithery" print in the sand, the wood rat's "clawed plantigrade feet" (a technical word: *plantigrade* means walking with both sole and heel touching the ground).

Include images. Have you captured not just sights, but any sounds, touches, odors? A memorable *image,* or evocation of a sense experience, can do wonders for a paper. In his memoir *Northern Farm,* naturalist Henry Beston observes a remarkable sound: "the voice of ice," the midwinter sound of a whole frozen pond settling and expanding in its bed:

> Sometimes there was a sort of hollow oboe sound, and sometimes a groan with a delicate undertone of thunder. . . . Just as I turned to go, there came from below one curious and sinister crack which ran off into a sound like the whine of a giant whip of steel lashed through the moonlit air.

Apparently Beston's purpose in this passage is to report the nature of ice from his observations of it, and yet he writes accurate language that arrests us by the power of its suggestions.

When British journalist and fiction writer G. K. Chesterton wrote of ocean waves, he was tempted at first to speak of the "rushing swiftness of a wave" — a usual phrase. But instead, as he tells us in his essay, "The Two Noises," he dusted off his glasses and observed a real wave toppling.

> The horrible thing about a wave is its hideous slowness. It lifts its load of water laboriously. . . . In front of me that night the waves were not like water: they were like falling city walls. The breaker rose first as if it did not wish to attack the earth; it wishes only to attack the stars. For a time it stood up in the air as naturally as a tower; then it went a little wrong in its outline, like a tower that might some day fall.

Shaping a Draft

Having been writing, however roughly, all the while you've been observing, you will now have some rough stuff to organize. If you have made an observation sheet, you can mark it up: you can circle whatever looks useful. Maybe you can plan best while rewriting your preliminary notes into a draft. Then you'll be throwing out details that don't matter, leaving those that do.

How do you map out a series of observations? One simple way—and you could map this out in a simple scratch outline—would be to proceed spatially. In observing a landscape, you might move from left to right, from top to bottom, from near to far, from center to periphery. One of these methods might be as good as any other. However, your choice may well depend on your purpose in writing.

You might see (or feel) a reason to *move from the most prominent feature to the less prominent.* If you are writing about a sketch artist at work, say, the most prominent and interesting feature to start with might be the artist's busy, confident hands. If you are describing a basketball game, you might start with the action under a basket.

Or you might *move from specific details to a general statement of an overall impression.* In describing Fisherman's Wharf in San Francisco, you might start with sellers of shrimp cups and souvenir fishnets, tour boats loading passengers, and the smell of frying fish and go on to say, "In all this commotion and commerce, a visitor senses the constant activity of the sea."

Or you could *move from common, everyday features to the unusual features you want to stress.* After starting with the smell of frying fish and the cries of gulls, you might go on: "Yet this ordinary scene attracts visitors from afar: the Japanese sightseer, perhaps a fan of American prison films, making a pilgrimage by tour boat to Alcatraz."

How closely can you observe? Of these two copies of woodcuts by the sixteenth-century German artist known only by his signature, The Master I. B. with the Bird, one is the original, the other a forgery. Art critic William M. Ivins, Jr., remarked: "In this original the lines have

Consider your purpose. Perhaps your most important planning will take place as you answer the question What main insight or impression do I want to get across? To ask yourself this question may help you decide which impressions to include and which to omit. Joan Didion's "Marrying Absurd" leaves us with a definite impression that the Las Vegas marriage chapel scene is full of absurd incongruities. (If Didion had any further thoughts on the natural beauties of Las Vegas, she sliced them from her final version.)

intention and meaning. In the copy . . . the lines have lost their intention. They have all the characteristics of careless and unintelligent but laborious tracing." Which is which? The solution is on page 63.

Rewriting

Your rewriting, editing, and proofreading will all prove easier if you have taken accurate notes on your observations. Clearly, that is what Joan Didion did in Las Vegas: she must have copied down (or photographed) highway signs and other advertisements for marriage chapels. The ads she quotes sound authentic.

WRITING WITH A COMPUTER: OBSERVING

If you do find it necessary to make a second, follow-up trip back to the scene, word processing will help you to amplify your draft easily. You can simply drop in further details wherever they will make your paper more vivid and lifelike.

Making your observations crackle with life, by the way, isn't just a matter of trying to intensify things with adverbs such as *very*. William Allen White, famous author and Kansas newspaper editor, hated such modifiers, which he believed are usually like fifth wheels. He once instructed his reporters to change every *very* they wrote to a *damn*, then cross out all the *damn*s; they would then have stronger prose. Thanks to the miracle of word processing, you can—just for fun—readily William-Allen-White your own writing. Instruct your computer to conduct a global search-and-replace, changing every *very* to a *damn* throughout your paper. Print out the results and read it over. Then tell your computer to search out every *damn* and replace it with a space.

But what if, when you look over your draft, you find that in observing you skimped and now you don't have enough notes? If you have any doubts about your notes, go back to the scene and check them. Professional journalists often make such follow-ups.

Once you have made sure that you've accurately recorded your observations, you may find it useful to seek a fellow student's reactions to your draft. If so, ask your peer editor to answer the following questions (in writing if possible).

PEER EDITING CHECKLIST: WRITING FROM OBSERVATION

- Give your overall reaction to the entire paper.
- Describe the main insight or impression you carry away from this piece of writing.
- How well has the writer used the evidence from his or her senses? Highlight with a marker details or description in the essay that you think use that evidence effectively.
- Which sense does the writer use particularly well in writing from observation? Does he or she neglect any sense that could be used?
- Are there any places in the writing where you think the writer could or should use more details? Put stars on the manuscript where you would want more detail.
- Look at the way the writer has organized his or her observations. How well does the organization work? Do you recommend any changes?
- What three things do you like best about this piece of writing?

- On the manuscript, circle any spelling, punctuation, grammar, or word choice that made your reading of this essay more difficult than it should have been.

Not all writers rewrite in the same way. Some start tinkering early, perfecting little bits here and there. Even back in her original version of "Footprints," a few sheets of rough notes, Sandy Messina started making small improvements. In her first draft, she had written:

> Each of us must learn to walk gently on the earth. We must quit pushing and pulling and kneading it into a loaf to be our own bread.

Right away, she realized that by calling the earth "a loaf" she had already likened it to bread. So she crossed out "be our own bread" and substituted "suit our own appetites." She also crossed out verbs one at a time, as they occurred, until a strong verb came along.

> We ~~moved marched~~ trooped across America, leaving our giant footprints.

As a final test, to see what parts of your draft still need work when you rewrite, you might ask yourself these questions.

REVISION CHECKLIST: WRITING FROM OBSERVATION

- Have you gathered enough observations to make your subject understandable? Think of your audience: What can you assume your readers already know? What don't they need to be told?
- Do any of your observations need to be checked for accuracy?
- Have you observed with *all* your senses? (Smell isn't always useful, but it might be.)
- Have you accomplished your purpose: to convey clearly your overall impression of your subject and to share some telling insight about it?

Other Assignments

1. To develop your own powers of observation, follow Sandy Messina's example. Go for a walk, recording your observations in two or three detailed paragraphs. Let your walk take you either through an unfamiliar scene or through a familiar scene perhaps worth a closer look than you normally give it (such as a supermarket, a city street, or an open field). Avoid a subject so familiar that it would be difficult

for you to see it from a fresh perspective (such as a dormitory corridor or a parking lot). Sum up your impression of the place, including any opinion you form by your close observations.

2. Just for fun, here is a short, spontaneous writing exercise that might serve as a warmup for a long assignment. Lin Haire-Sargeant of Tufts University, whose students enjoyed the exercise, calls it "You Are the Detective." She asked her students to begin the assignment immediately after the class in which it was given and to turn it in by 4:05 P.M.

> Go to a nearby public place—burger joint, library, copy center, art gallery—and select a person who catches your eye, who somehow intrigues you. Try to choose someone who looks as if she or he will stay put for a while. Settle yourself where you can observe your subject unobtrusively. Take notes, if you can do so without being observed yourself.
>
> Now, carefully and tactfully (we don't want any fistfights or lawsuits) notice everything you can about this person. The obvious place to start would be with physical characteristics, but focus on other things too. How does the person talk? Move? What does body language tell you?
>
> Write a paragraph describing the person. Pretend that the person is going to hold up a bank ten minutes from now, and the police will expect you to supply a full and accurate description of him or her.

3. Observe some bird, animal, or object and record your observations in a paragraph as long as necessary.

4. Joan Didion writes from the perspective of a tourist, an outsider alert to details that reveal the distinctive character of places and people. If in the past year you, as an outsider, have visited some place, jot down from memory any details you noticed that you haven't been able to forget. Or spend a few minutes as a tourist right now. Go to a busy spot on or off campus and, in a few paragraphs, record your observations of anything you find amusing, surprising, puzzling, or intriguing.

Ask your instructor whether, for this assignment, you might write not a finished essay but a single draft. The idea would be to display your observations in the rough. If you and your instructor think it shows promise, it might be the basis for a later, more polished paper.

FOR GROUP LEARNING
Instead of soliciting written comments about your work, try reading aloud to your group the draft you have written for an assignment in this chapter. Prepare your reading beforehand and try to deliver it with some life and feeling. Ask others to stop you at any point when something isn't clear. Have pencil in hand to circle any such problem. After you've finished reading aloud, ask for reactions. If these are slow in coming, ask your listeners any of the questions in the peer editing checklist on page 48. Have your group's secretary record the most vital suggestions and reactions that your draft provokes. Expect to serve as a listening critic for other writers in your group, to help them in return.

5. From among the photographs on pages 52–53, select one to observe. In a paragraph or two, capture in words its most memorable features. Does the photograph have any center that draws your attention? What main impression or insight does the picture convey to you? See if you can put a sense of the picture into the mind of a reader who hasn't seen it at all.

APPLYING WHAT YOU LEARN: SOME USES OF WRITING FROM OBSERVATION

Many college courses designed to prepare students for a professional career involve field trips. In such courses, you are often expected to observe closely and later to write up your observations in a report. A sociology class (or maybe a class in prelaw) might visit a city police court on a Saturday morning to hear the judge trying the spouse beaters, drug pushers, streetwalkers, and peeping Toms hauled in on Friday night. A journalism class might visit the composing room of a large daily newspaper to see how a front page is made up. History students writing about local or recent events can add color by sharing their firsthand impressions of a nearby historic site. A class in early childhood education might visit a day-care center for intensive observation of one child, perhaps culminating in a written account of that child's behavior. For a language development course, observers might be asked to report on the way in which a particular child communicates: Does the child's speech exhibit immaturity? How does the child cope when someone misunderstands him or her?

Professionals in the helping professions often write case studies, sometimes for publication, sometimes not. Here, in *A Career in Speech Pathology* (1979), C. Van Riper illustrates the technique. He describes his initial observations of three severely deprived rural children in need of treatment.

> As I watched through the screen I saw the three children huddled in a corner like kittens in a cold barn, silent and not moving for almost five minutes. Then the oldest one separated from the tangle and tiptoed all around the edge of the room, listening and watching. Then he motioned the other two to come with him to the door which he found was locked. Then he spied a little blue truck which had been placed under the table (with a ball and other toys), made a dive for it, and suddenly the room was full of wild animals, fighting, snarling, making animal noises of every kind, barking, mewing, shrieking. I knocked on the door and they fled again to huddle in the corner, human again but silently frozen with terror. I sat down in a chair and played with the truck and talked to myself about what I was doing, occasionally giving them a slow smile. I held out a piece of candy but none of them would reach for it. It was an eerie first session.

Much writing in scientific and technical courses involves observation. In a report for a chemistry or biology course, you might be asked to report your

observations of a laboratory experiment ("When the hair was introduced into the condensing dish, bacteria collected in its follicles . . ."); in zoology, to observe and report on the behavior of animals. Here is a good illustration of scientific reporting from *Gorillas in the Mist,* written by Dian Fossey, a zoologist who for many years studied mountain gorillas in Rwanda, Africa. She records what a typical gorilla looks like at birth, based on her observations of scores of infant gorillas.

> The body skin color of a newly born gorilla is usually pinkish gray and may have pink concentrations of color on the ears, palms, or soles. The infant's body hair varies in color from medium brown to black and is sparsely distributed except on the dorsal surfaces of the body. The head hair is often jet black, short, and slick, and the face wizened, with a pronounced protrusion of the nasal region, giving a pig-snouted appearance. Like the nose, the ears are prominent, but the eyes are usually squinted or closed the first day following birth. The limbs are thin and spidery, and the digits typically remain tightly flexed when the baby's hands are not grasping the mother's abdominal hair. The extremities may exhibit a spastic type of involuntary thrusting movement, especially when searching for a nipple. Most of the time, however, a gorilla infant appears asleep.

In a college course in technical writing, and in many occupations, you are expected to write observations of objects, mechanisms, places of work, terrains, and other things. Richard J. Councill, chief geologist for the Seaboard System Railroad, turned in a report on two possible building sites in New Hanover County, North Carolina, for the use of a client of the railroad, a company deciding where to build a plant. Because the decision to build rested on whether adequate supplies of groundwater would be available, Councill wrote (in part):

> Both sites are characterized by rolling, sparsely wooded fossil sand dunes attaining a maximum elevation of 25–30 feet and lowlands ranging from near 0 feet to 10 feet. Depending upon elevation, the total thickness of the dunes is 45 to 60 feet. The surface and subsurface materials are essentially homogenous and consist of interbedded strata of fine to medium quartz sand, fine to coarse sand containing thin clayey sand and clay seams. Beneath these geologically young materials are intercalated beds of fine to very coarse quartz sand, glauconite, thin discontinuous broken shell beds, and clay-silt beds of the Pee Dee formation.

In this kind of writing, no doubt immensely valuable to decision making, the writer sets forth observations mingled with judgments and recommendations.

A Zoologist Observes

Alexander Petrunkevitch (1875–1964) was one of the world's foremost zoologists and, from 1910 to his retirement in 1944, a popular member of the faculty at Yale. He spent years observing the behavior of spiders and wasps. The essay that follows sets forth findings that resulted from his personal observations.

THE SPIDER AND THE WASP
Alexander Petrunkevitch

To hold its own in the struggle for existence, every species of animal 1 must have a regular source of food, and if it happens to live on other animals, its survival may be very delicately balanced. The hunter cannot exist without the hunted; if the latter should perish from the earth, the former would, too. When the hunted also prey on some of the hunters, the matter may become complicated.

This is nowhere better illustrated than in the insect world. Think of the 2 complexity of a situation such as the following: There is a certain wasp, *Pimpla inquisitor*, whose larvae feed on the larvae of the tussock moth. *Pimpla* larvae in turn serve as food for the larvae of a second wasp, and the latter in their turn nourish still a third wasp. What subtle balance between fertility and mortality must exist in the case of each of these four species to prevent the extinction of all of them! An excess of mortality over fertility in a single member of the group would ultimately wipe out all four.

This is not a unique case. The two great orders of insects, Hymenoptera 3 and Diptera, are full of such examples of interrelationship. And the spiders (which are not insects but members of a separate order of arthropods) also are killers and victims of insects.

The picture is complicated by the fact that those species which are 4 carnivorous in the larval stage have to be provided with animal food by a vegetarian mother. The survival of the young depends on the mother's correct choice of a food which she does not eat herself.

In the feeding and safeguarding of their progeny the insects and spiders 5 exhibit some interesting analogies to reasoning and some crass examples of blind instinct. The case I propose to describe here is that of the tarantula spiders and their archenemy, the digger wasps of the genus *Pepsis*. It is a classic example of what looks like intelligence pitted against instinct—a strange situation in which the victim, though fully able to defend itself, submits unwittingly to its destruction.

Most tarantulas live in the tropics, but several species occur in the 6 temperate zone and a few are common in the southern U.S. Some varieties are large and have powerful fangs with which they can inflict a deep wound. These formidable-looking spiders do not, however, attack man; you can hold one in your hand, if you are gentle, without being bitten. Their bite is dangerous only to insects and small mammals such as mice; for a man it is no worse than a hornet's sting.

Tarantulas customarily live in deep cylindrical burrows, from which they 7 emerge at dusk and into which they retire at dawn. Mature males wander about after dark in search of females and occasionally stray into houses. After mating, the male dies in a few weeks, but a female lives much longer and can mate several years in succession. In a Paris museum is a tropical specimen which is said to have been living in captivity for twenty-five years.

A fertilized female tarantula lays from 200 to 400 eggs at a time; thus 8 it is possible for a single tarantula to produce several thousand young. She takes no care of them beyond weaving a cocoon of silk to enclose the eggs. After they hatch, the young walk away, find convenient places in which to dig their burrows and spend the rest of their lives in solitude. Tarantulas feed mostly on insects and millipedes. Once their appetite is appeased, they digest the food for several days before eating again. Their sight is poor, being limited to sensing a change in the intensity of light and to the perception of moving objects. They apparently have little or no sense of hearing, for a hungry tarantula will pay no attention to a loudly chirping cricket placed in its cage unless the insect happens to touch one of its legs.

But all spiders, and especially hairy ones, have an extremely delicate 9 sense of touch. Laboratory experiments prove that tarantulas can distinguish three types of touch: pressure against the body wall, stroking of the body hair, and riffling of certain very fine hairs on the legs called trichobothria. Pressure against the body, by a finger or the end of a pencil, causes the tarantula to move off slowly for a short distance. The touch excites no defensive response unless the approach is from above, where the spider can see the motion, in which case it rises on its hind legs, lifts its front legs, opens its fangs and holds this threatening posture as long as the object continues to move. When the motion stops, the spider drops back to the ground, remains quiet for a few seconds, and then moves slowly away.

The entire body of a tarantula, especially its legs, is thickly clothed 10 with hair. Some of it is short and woolly, some long and stiff. Touching this body hair produces one of two distinct reactions. When the spider is hungry, it responds with an immediate and swift attack. At the touch of a cricket's antennae the tarantula seizes the insect so swiftly that a motion picture taken at the rate of sixty-four frames per second shows only the result not the process of capture. But when the spider is not hungry, the stimulation of its hair merely causes it to shake the touched limb. An insect can walk under its hairy belly unharmed.

The trichobothria, very fine hairs growing from disklike membranes of 11 the legs, were once thought to be the spider's hearing organs, but we now know that they have nothing to do with sound. They are sensitive only to air movement. A light breeze makes them vibrate slowly without disturbing the common hair. When one blows gently on the trichobothria, the tarantula reacts with a quick jerk of its four front legs. If the front and hind legs are stimulated at the same time, the spider makes a sudden jump. This reaction is quite independent of the state of its appetite.

These three tactile responses—to pressure on the body wall, to moving 12 of the common hair, and to flexing of the trichobothria—are so different from one another that there is no possibility of confusing them. They serve the tarantula adequately for most of its needs and enable it to avoid most annoyances and dangers. But they fail the spider completely when it meets its deadly enemy, the digger wasp *Pepsis.*

These solitary wasps are beautiful and formidable creatures. Most spe- 13 cies are either a deep shiny blue all over, or deep blue with rusty wings. The largest have a wing span of about four inches. They live on nectar. When excited, they give off a pungent odor—a warning that they are ready to attack. The sting is much worse than that of a bee or common wasp, and the pain and swelling last longer. In the adult stage the wasp lives only a few months. The female produces but a few eggs, one at a time at intervals of two or three days. For each egg the mother must provide one adult tarantula, alive but paralyzed. The tarantula must be of the correct species to nourish the larva. The mother wasp attaches the egg to the paralyzed spider's abdomen. Upon hatching from the egg, the larva is many hundreds of times smaller than its living but helpless victim. It eats no other food and drinks no water. By the time it has finished its single gargantuan meal and become ready for wasphood, nothing remains of the tarantula but its indigestible chitinous skeleton.

The mother wasp goes tarantula-hunting when the egg in her ovary is 14 almost ready to be laid. Flying low over the ground late on a sunny afternoon, the wasp looks for its victim or for the mouth of a tarantula burrow, a round hole edged by a bit of silk. The sex of the spider makes no difference, but the mother is highly discriminating as to species. Each species of *Pepsis* requires a certain species of tarantula, and the wasp will not attack the wrong species. In a cage with a tarantula which is not its normal prey the wasp avoids the spider, and is usually killed by it in the night.

Yet when a wasp finds the correct species, it is the other way about. 15 To identify the species the wasp apparently must explore the spider with her antennae. The tarantula shows an amazing tolerance to this exploration. The wasp crawls under it and walks over it without evoking any hostile response. The molestation is so great and so persistent that the tarantula often rises on all eight legs, as if it were on stilts. It may stand this way for several minutes. Meanwhile the wasp, having satisfied itself that the victim is of the right species, moves off a few inches to dig the spider's grave. Working vigorously with legs and jaws, it excavates a hole eight to ten inches deep with a diameter slightly larger than the spider's girth. Now and again the wasp pops out of the hole to make sure that the spider is still there.

When the grave is finished, the wasp returns to the tarantula to com- 16 plete her ghastly enterprise. First she feels it all over once more with her antennae. Then her behavior becomes more aggressive. She bends her abdomen, protruding her sting, and searches for the soft membrane at the point where the spider's leg joins its body—the only spot where she can penetrate the horny skeleton. From time to time, as the exasperated spider slowly shifts ground, the wasp turns on her back and slides along with the aid of her wings, trying to get under the tarantula for a shot at the vital spot. During all this maneuvering, which can last for several minutes, the tarantula makes no move to save itself. Finally the wasp corners it against some obstruction and grasps one of its legs in her powerful jaws. Now at last the harassed spider tries a desperate but vain defense. The two contestants roll over and over on the ground. It is a terrifying sight and the outcome is always the same. The wasp finally manages to thrust her sting into the soft spot and holds it there for a few seconds while she pumps in the poison. Almost immediately the tarantula falls paralyzed on its back. Its legs stop twitching; its heart stops beating. Yet it is not dead, as is shown by the fact that if taken from the wasp it can be restored to some sensitivity by being kept in a moist chamber for several months.

After paralyzing the tarantula, the wasp cleans herself by dragging her   17
body along the ground and rubbing her feet, sucks the drop of blood oozing from the wound in the spider's abdomen, then grabs a leg of the flabby, helpless animal in her jaws and drags it down to the bottom of the grave. She stays there for many minutes, sometimes for several hours, and what she does all that time in the dark we do not know. Eventually she lays her egg and attaches it to the side of the spider's abdomen with a sticky secretion. Then she emerges, fills the grave with soil carried bit by bit in her jaws, and finally tramples the ground all around to hide any trace of the grave from prowlers. Then she flies away, leaving her descendant safely started in life.

In all this the behavior of the wasp evidently is qualitatively different   18
from that of the spider. The wasp acts like an intelligent animal. This is not to say that instinct plays no part or that she reasons as man does. But her actions are to the point; they are not automatic and can be modified to fit the situation. We do not know for certain how she identifies the tarantula—probably it is by some olfactory or chemo-tactile sense—but she does it purposefully and does not blindly tackle a wrong species.

On the other hand, the tarantula's behavior shows only confusion.   19
Evidently the wasp's pawing gives it no pleasure, for it tries to move away. That the wasp is not simulating sexual stimulation is certain, because male and female tarantulas react in the same way to its advances. That the spider is not anesthetized by some odorless secretion is easily shown by blowing lightly at the tarantula and making it jump suddenly. What, then, makes the tarantula behave as stupidly as it does?

No clear, simple answer is available. Possibly the stimulation by the   20
wasp's antennae is masked by a heavier pressure on the spider's body, so that it reacts as when prodded by a pencil. But the explanation may be much more complex. Initiative in attack is not in the nature of tarantulas; most species fight only when cornered so that escape is impossible. Their inherited patterns of behavior apparently prompt them to avoid problems rather than attack them. For example, spiders always weave their webs in three dimensions, and when a spider finds that there is insufficient space to attach certain threads in the third dimension, it leaves the place and

seeks another, instead of finishing the web in a single plane. This urge to escape seems to arise under all circumstances, in all phases of life, and to take the place of reasoning. For a spider to change the pattern of its web is as impossible as for an inexperienced man to build a bridge across a chasm obstructing his way.

In a way the instinctive urge to escape is not only easier but more 21 efficient than reasoning. The tarantula does exactly what is most efficient in all cases except in an encounter with a ruthless and determined attacker dependent for the existence of her own species on killing as many tarantulas as she can lay eggs. Perhaps in this case the spider follows its usual pattern of trying to escape, instead of seizing and killing the wasp, because it is not aware of its danger. In any case, the survival of the tarantula species as a whole is protected by the fact that the spider is much more fertile than the wasp.

Questions to Start You Thinking

1. In their encounters, what is the difference between the behavior of the tarantula and that of the digger wasp? What is the effect of this difference?

2. What reasons does Petrunkevitch set forth for the tarantula's "stupid" behavior (paragraphs 20–21)? On what evidence does the author base his remark?

3. Explain the "balance between fertility and mortality" that is maintained between the tarantula and the digger wasp. Of what importance is this balance?

4. How would you characterize the audience of the *Scientific American,* whom this essay first addressed? (*Suggestion:* For clues, look at a copy of the magazine in the periodicals room of your library.) How extensive a knowledge of science does Petrunkevitch seem to expect his readers to share?

A Social Commentator Observes

Addressing a definite audience—in this case, relatively well educated, well heeled males who read *Esquire*—freelance sociologist Charlie Haas writes of crowd behavior with a perceptive eye. In this sprightly essay, he takes a close and penetrating look at Westwood Village, a neighborhood near the UCLA campus in Los Angeles from which national trends in clothes, food, music, and behavior emerge.

TINSEL TEENS
Charlie Haas

Some of us, years after graduating from college, still love college 1 towns. We hit these little European pockets of America and feel right at home, happy to see an entire local economy running on strong coffee, imported cigarettes, and used books. The Vivaldi and chess in the bus-your-own coffeehouses, the day packs and bicycles aren't clichés to us, they're fraternal high signs. Some of us like these places so much that we graduate and never move away; others collect new college towns all our lives, always looking for these funky holdouts against a landscape that lights up, beeps, and buzzes.

Westwood Village is *nothing* like that. Westwood Village, which adjoins 2 UCLA but looks like MTV, is a kids' chic business district so marvelously slick that you can enter it at twilight and glide all evening along the goofily curved and angled streets, feeling no friction and seeing, in a few blocks, the diet of hipness that will be fed to kids in slower regions for the next five years, after clearance from Westwood's spotless test boutiques.

If the currencies of past youth scenes were cultural ideas and political 3 positions, the currency of Westwood is currency, and plenty of it: this is the Greenwich Village of moneyed leisure, the Left Bank of beautiful-brute hype. You can rummage in college towns for wisdom, but you go to West-wood for cleverness—clever clothes on clever bodies, droll food at arch tables. Westwood is your college town as remade by Hollywood. On week-end nights it is hardly a college town at all. On those nights Westwood is teen heaven.

Westwood doesn't attract teenagers with bitchin' surf, straight drag 4 strips, hot dance floors, or anything so prosaically teen. If you ask a fifteen-year-old girl in state-of-the-art *haute*-tramp exposed-midriff fashion and a two-hour eye-makeup job what she likes about Westwood and close your eyes as she answers, you can imagine that you're hearing an upper-middle-class, upper-middle-aged lady describe a favored destination in Europe: "Yes, well, there are a lot of nice *shops*, you know, the *gift* shops and so on, and there are, *ah*, some nice *restaurants*, and of course it's nice to, oh, go to a restaurant and then, say, a movie. . . ."

On a Saturday afternoon the kids start drifting in from all over the city 5 to kick things off with some serious clothes shopping. Boys who can name you every designer in their outfit, from Generra all-cotton jacket down, are heard to swear undying love for the shoes at Leather Bound. The Limited Express, with technopop on the PA, offers Day-Glo sweat-fleece cardigans and other punch-line looks; a few doors down, at the other Limited store, the emphasis is on foreign designs—Forenza, Kenzo. But what is key for the Westwood girl of the moment—even more key than Esprit—is Guess?, a line of sportswear heavy on soft-shaped whites, pastels, and denims. "They'll buy anything Guess?—the *label* sells," says a seventeen-year-old salesgirl at MGA. "They spend a lot of money, but then, *clothes* are a lot of money now." The biggest hit garment with the girls is a hugely oversize white jacket with overlapping seams, a jacket so shapeless and enveloping that its wearers look like sculptures waiting to be unveiled at adulthood.

In the meantime, there is Westwood, high school polite society. The 6 Village is easily walked across, but a pedicab service has sprung up, with all the "drivers" in black bow ties and some in formal dress. For those over twenty-one there are bars with alcohol, and they too are models of decorum: upstairs at T. J. Honeycutt's, clean-cut young people dance under a mirror ball to recorded pop you can talk over. At Baxter's downstairs bar, where the cocktail waitresses wear tiny sport shorts and satin team jackets, amiable chatter drowns out the rock videos on the multiple monitors, and a banner says WEDNESDAY NIGHT IS DYNASTY NIGHT—CHAMPAGNE 25¢, 9 P.M. There are video games in Westwood, but they are massed in one arcade, just as junk-jewelry vendors are confined to one courtyard, instead of lining several sleazy blocks as they do near UC Berkeley. If down these clean streets a man must go, he can do so for hours without being asked for spare change. There is a sprinkling of kids in the spirit-of-1976 punk look; an ambling few of them say that their idea of a hot time in Westwood, like anyone else's, is dinner and a movie—though, as hard-core anarchists, they make a point of copping meals and admissions from friends with jobs on the inside.

In the restaurants, fifteen-year-old diners place polite orders with six- 7 teen-year-old waitresses, but a full-course meal is not the only option: in Westwood, not even the junk food is junk. There are bulging falafels at Me & Me; Louisiana hot links at The Wurst; a clean, well-lit building housing an international arcade of GYRO SOUVLAKI TANDOORI CURRY KEBAB. There is Fatburger, "the last great hamburger stand," where the king chili-cheese-egg burger is so wetly unmanageable that watching someone eat one is an invasion of privacy. You can buy Bordeaux-chocolate-flavored popcorn in a gourmet popcorn store, order Heath Bar chips chopped into your raspberry custard ice cream with rum-soaked raisins poured on top at an ice cream place, eat New York-style pizza in a storefront decorated as a New York subway station. When a new method is discovered for achieving treats, the technology is rushed instantly to Westwood, the Silicon Valley of silly delight.

When a new movie is released, same deal: to go to a picture here is 8 to go to a *show*, to glide under the neon-crammed marquee of a heroic old theater, up to a cashier's cage where computers monitor ticket sales, past the studio's proudest die-cut star-photo stand-ups, across the lush under-growth pictured on the old-fashioned lobby carpet, to projection and sound of a quality that has become rare.

But as sound-stage spectacles, movies in Westwood have to compete 9 with the stores. In the Nike sports-fashion store on Westwood Boulevard a giant fire-red 3-D plastic Nike swoosh logo hangs from the ceiling, its point sticking through the plate-glass window and out over the street, with faked burn damage in the masonry overhead. *Aahs!*, a store that sells the same Jetson-family T-shirts, naughty greeting cards, and candy-colored planning diaries as half a dozen other Westwood stores yet achieves distinction through sheer size, limits the number of customers, so kids line up on the sidewalk, patient victims of Saturday Night Browsing Fever. In one T-shirt store the salesgirl says that a shirt with a plain pink pig on it is her biggest seller ("I think because people consider themselves pigs"); at another, Lacoste-type knit shirts with pairs of screwing alligators are moving fast. At a third, the I FUCK ON THE FIRST DATE T-shirt is big, as are some devoted to Westwood's true compulsion: WHEN THE GOING GETS TOUGH, THE TOUGH GO SHOPPING, and I CAN'T BE OVERDRAWN, I STILL HAVE SOME CHECKS. But all of these, sweetly, are outsold by FEED THE WORLD and WAR IS STUPID.

By 10:00 P.M. the sidewalks are packed with kids from all over the city, 10 and the streets are filled with slow-cruising cars, kids striking up acquaintances in shouts, visiting one another in gridlocked Z's and Baja trucks. Even in Westwood, a fifteen-year-old's sophistication runs only so deep, and some of the kids are like farmers come to town: "Look at *that!* Look at *her!* Hey!" They are boisterous, but in a mild, vacationing way—Westwood is a place where people who live four freeway exits away become resort tourists in their own city. There are a lot of couples but also a lot of same-sex pairs and packs, and no urgent mating frenzy: a pack of boys sweeps up to a pack of girls on a corner, collects phone numbers, and breezes on. The kids are genuinely happy, which makes sense: sure, they live in the shadow of the nuclear bomb, but they also stand within walking distance of *two* all-night Fatburgers.

As it gets late a mass of kids crowd onto the wedge of sidewalk in front 11 of Glendale Federal Savings and Loan (it takes real style to look cool in front of posters about interest rates). A couple of LAPD° cops keep an eye on the crowd and hand out a few traffic tickets. "Westwood is orderly," one of them says, "because we keep it orderly. We have eight officers on foot patrol here on weekend nights, two during the week. Occasionally there will be trouble—a knife fight or something—because they're coming from all over now."

His fellow officer is letting a young woman talk him into signing a piece 12 of paper that says she got thirty-two people to sing "Row, Row, Row Your Boat." "It's for Lifespring," she says. "That's a self-awareness organization, but I'm not allowed to talk about it." Meanwhile six Asian teenage girls wearing Oreo-cookie costumes "as part of our Hell Week" for a sorority march through the crowd, followed by six Asian teenage boys who exchange graphic fantasies regarding the girls. Pledge a sorority, pledge a self-awareness scheme: one-stop shopping.

The cop's words aside, the Westwood kids look more inclined to diet 13 than riot. Adults who work in Westwood almost invariably describe weekend nights there as "a zoo." This is accurate, but perhaps in more ways than the speakers intend: Westwood is a place where kid wildness is neatly restrained, where the central pleasure is to check one another out like little loaned pandas. (Youth wants to know: Is your Guess? as good as mine?) The kids in front of Glendale Federal mill around just as they do at school recess, but this is gourmet recess, the all-city walking-around finals.

LAPD: Los Angeles Police Department.

The conventional jive about L.A. is that the neighborhoods are insular, 14
that ethnic and racial groups don't mix, and that nobody walks. The Westwood kids, ignoring all that, have fashioned an integrated promenade that
makes the adult visitors envious. Westwood is slick, but it is not a mall or
an amusement park, not forged or run by a single intelligence. Instead, it's
an actual urban neighborhood, with at least some randomness; if you've
been growing up in Woodland Hills, this alone can seem a dizzying freedom.
And Westwood actually invites kids, offers them a physical place to match
their moment. Everyone is welcome—be a punk if you want, that's fine,
punks add color, but be a *designer* punk, all right? Because this is not the
Beach, not the Valley; tonight we are playing the Palace, the Carson show,
of being a kid. A little élan; we are walking in *Westwood,* and what we do
and wear here this Saturday night they will be doing and wearing six months
from now in New York, two years from now in Cleveland, ten years from
now at nostalgia-themed charity balls.

And on Sunday morning there is a ton of litter on the sidewalk in front 15
of Glendale Federal. All of it in the trash baskets.

Questions To Start You Thinking

1. Commented a UCLA student, "The guy who wrote this essay makes it seem as if
   only teenagers flock to Westwood Village. University students hang out there,
   too." Does anything in "Tinsel Teens" serve to answer this criticism?

2. Is this essay primarily about a place or about the people who frequent that place?
   Give evidence to support your answer.

3. In one or two sentences, summarize the main impression the essay gives you of
   Westwood Village and the teenagers the author observes there. Do all of Haas's
   observations contribute to a single overall impression, or are you left with more
   than one?

4. To which of the five senses does "Tinsel Teens" especially appeal? Point to two
   or three vivid examples of sense imagery.

Solution to the Problem of the Two Woodcuts

If you identified the woodcut on page 47 as the original by the Master I. B.
with the Bird, your powers of observation are excellent. If you were wrong,
don't feel alone: in his scholarly book *The Woodcuts of the Master I. B. with
the Bird* (Berlin, 1894), art historian F. Lippmann also mistook the forgery for
the original.

CHAPTER 3

Writing from Reading

"A shut book," according to a saying, "is only a block of paper." So is an open book, until a reader interacts with it. Did you ever observe someone truly involved with a book? From time to time that reader may put down the book to doubt, to ponder, or to dream; may pick it up again, jot notes, underline or star things, leaf backward for a second glance, sigh, mutter, fidget in discomfort, nod approvingly, perhaps laugh aloud, or disgustedly slam the book shut. Such a reader mixes in, interacts with the printed page, and reads with an individual style. Not all readers are so demonstrative. Some sit quietly, hardly moving a muscle, and yet they too may be interacting, deeply involved.

The act of reading is highly personal. Do all readers extract the same things from the same reading? Surely they don't. *The Divine Comedy,* said T. S. Eliot, has as many versions as that classic poem has readers. The point is not that a book can mean any old thing you want it to, but that each reader, like each visitor to a city, has different interests and so comes away with different memories. Listening to a class discussion of a textbook all have read, you may be surprised by the range of insights reported by different readers. If you missed some of those insights when you read alone, don't feel crestfallen. Just offer any insights that come to you. Other students may be equally surprised by what you saw—something they missed entirely.

Like flints that strike against one another and cause sparks, readers and writers provoke one another. Often you go to books or journals to stimulate your own ideas. Sometimes you read in search of a topic to write about. Sometimes, when you already have a topic, you seek more ideas. Sometimes, when you have enough ideas, you turn to other writers to help you explain them or to back them up with examples and evidence. Sometimes you read because you have ideas you want to test. Reading revises your ideas.

LEARNING FROM OTHER WRITERS

Let's look at two examples of writing evidently inspired by thoughtful reading: first, an essay by David Quammen, whose wide reading contributes depth and breadth to his many writings on science. Though he gathers ideas from other sources, he also—as you'll see—propels himself from what he reads into a fresh view of his own. Originally, Quammen wrote this essay for the May 1983 issue of *Outside,* a magazine for general readers to which he contributes regularly.

A REPUBLIC OF COCKROACHES: WHEN THE ULTIMATE EXTERMINATOR MEETS THE ULTIMATE PEST
David Quammen

1   In the fifth chapter of Matthew's gospel, Christ is quoted as saying that the meek shall inherit the earth, but other opinion lately suggests that, no, more likely it will go to the cockroaches.

2   A decidedly ugly and disheartening prospect: our entire dear planet—after the final close of all human business—ravaged and overrun by great multitudes of cockroaches, whole plagues of them, whole scuttering herds shoulder to shoulder like the old herds of bison, vast cockroach legions sweeping as inexorably as driver ants over the empty prairies. Unfortunately this vision is not just the worst Kafkaesque fantasy of some fevered pessimist. There is also a touch of hard science involved.

3   The cockroach, as it happens, is a popular test subject for laboratory research. It adapts well to captivity, lives relatively long, reproduces quickly, and will subsist in full vigor on Purina Dog Chow. The largest American species, up to two inches in length and known as *Periplaneta americana,* is even big enough for easy dissection. One eminent physiologist has written fondly: "The laboratory investigator who keeps up a battle to rid his rat colony of cockroaches may well consider giving up the rats and working with the cockroaches instead. From many points of view the roach is practically made to order as a laboratory subject. Here is an animal of frugal habits, tenacious of life, eager to live in the laboratory and very

modest in its space requirements." Tenacious of life indeed. Not only in kitchen cupboards, not only among the dark corners of basements, is the average cockroach a hard beast to kill. Also in the laboratory. And so also it would be, evidently, in the ashes of civilization. Among the various biological studies for which cockroaches have served as the guinea pigs—on hormone activity, parasitism, development of resistance against insecticides, and numerous other topics—have been some rather suggestive experiments concerning cockroach survival and atomic radiation.

Survival. Over the centuries, over the millennia, over the geologic   4 epochs and periods and eras, that is precisely what this animal has proved itself to be good at. The cockroach is roughly 250 million years old, which makes it the oldest of living insects, possibly even the oldest known air-breathing animal. Admittedly "250 million years" is just one of those stupefying and inexpressive paleontological numbers, so think of it this way: long before the first primitive mammal appeared on earth, before the first bird, before the first pine tree, before even the reptiles began to assert themselves, cockroaches were running wild. They were thriving in the great humid tropical forests that covered much of the Earth then, during what geologists now call the Carboniferous period (because so much of that thick swampy vegetation was eventually turned into coal). Cockroaches were by far the dominant insect of the Carboniferous, outnumbering all other species together, and among the most dominant of animals. In fact, sometimes this period is loosely referred to as the Age of Cockroaches. But unlike the earlier trilobites, unlike the later dinosaurs, cockroaches lingered on quite successfully (though less obtrusively) long after their heyday—because, unlike the trilobites and the dinosaurs, cockroaches were versatile.

They were generalists. Those primitive early cockroaches possessed a   5 simple and very practical anatomical design that remains almost unchanged in the cockroaches of today. Throughout their evolutionary history they have avoided wild morphological experiments like those of their near relatives, the mantids and walking sticks, and so many other bizarrely evolved insects. For cockroaches the byword has been: keep it simple. Consequently today, as always, they can live almost anywhere and eat almost anything.

Unlike most insects, they have mouthparts that enable them to take   6 hard foods, soft foods, and liquids. They will feed on virtually any organic substance. One study, written a century ago and still considered authoritative, lists their food preferences as "Bark, leaves, the pith of living cycads [fern palms], paper, woollen clothes, sugar, cheese, bread, blacking, oil, lemons, ink, flesh, fish, leather, the dead bodies of other Cockroaches, their own cast skins and empty egg-capsules," adding that "Cucumber, too, they will eat, though it disagrees with them horribly." So much for cucumber.

They are flattened enough to squeeze into the narrowest hiding place, either in human habitations or in the wild. They are quick on their feet, and can fly when they need to. But the real reason for their long-continued success and their excellent prospects for the future is that, beyond these few simple tools for living, they have never specialized. 7

It happens to be the very same thing that, until recently, could be said of *Homo sapiens*. 8

Now one further quote from the experts, in summary, and because it has for our purposes here a particular odd resonance. "Cockroaches," say two researchers who worked under sponsorship of the United States Army, "are tough, resilient insects with amazing endurance and the ability to recover rapidly from almost complete extermination." 9

It was Jonathan Schell's best-selling jeremiad *The Fate of the Earth*, published in 1982, that started me thinking about cockroach survival. *The Fate of the Earth* is a very strange sort of book, deeply unappealing, not very well written, windy and repetitious, yet powerful and valuable beyond measure. In fact, it may be the dreariest piece of writing that I ever wished everyone in America would read. Its subject is, of course, the abiding danger of nuclear Armageddon. Specifically, it describes in relentless scientific detail the likelihood of total human extinction following a full-scale nuclear war. In a section that Schell titles "A Republic of Insects and Grass," there is a discussion of the relative prospects for different animal species surviving to propagate again after mankind's final war. Schell takes his facts from a 1970 symposium held at Brookhaven National Laboratory, and in summarizing that government-sponsored research he says: 10

> For example, the lethal doses of gamma radiation for animals in pasture, where fallout would be descending on them directly and they would be eating fallout that had fallen on the grass, and would thus suffer from doses of beta radiation as well, would be one hundred and eighty rads [a standard unit of absorbed radiation] for cattle; two hundred and forty rads for sheep; five hundred and fifty rads for swine; three hundred and fifty rads for horses; and eight hundred rads for poultry. In a ten-thousand-megaton attack, which would create levels of radiation around the country averaging more than ten thousand rads, most of the mammals of the United States would be killed off. The lethal doses for birds are in roughly the same range as those for mammals, and birds, too, would be killed off. Fish are killed at doses of between one thousand one hundred rads and about five thousand six hundred rads, but their fate is less predictable. On the one hand, water is a shield from radiation, and would afford some protection; on the other hand, fallout might concentrate in bodies of water as it ran off from the land. (Because radiation causes no pain, animals, wandering at will through the environment, would not avoid it.) The one class of animals containing a number of species quite likely to survive, at least in the short run, is the insect class, for which in most known cases the lethal doses lie between about two thousand rads and about a hundred thousand

rads. Insects, therefore, would be destroyed selectively. Unfortunately for the rest of the environment, many of the phytophagous species [the plant-eaters] . . . have very high tolerances, and so could be expected to survive disproportionately, and then to multiply greatly in the aftermath of an attack.

Among the most ravaging of those phytophagous species referred to by Schell is an order of insects called the Orthoptera. The order Orthoptera includes locusts, like those Moses brought down on Egypt in plagues. It also includes crickets, mantids, walking sticks, and cockroaches.   11

Ten thousand rads, according to Schell's premises, is roughly the average dosage that might be received by most living things during the week immediately following Armageddon. By coincidence, 10,000 rads is also the dosage administered to certain test animals in a study conducted, some twenty-four years ago, by two researchers named Wharton and Wharton. The write-up can be found in a 1959 volume of the journal *Radiation Research*. The experiment was performed under the auspices, again, of the U.S. Army. The radiation was administered from a two-million-electron-volt Van de Graaff accelerator. The test animals were *Periplaneta americana*, those big American cockroaches.   12

Remember now, a dose of 180 rads is enough to kill a Hereford. A horse will die after taking 350 rads. The average lethal dose for humans isn't precisely known (because no one is performing quite such systematic experiments on humans, though again the Army has come closest, with those hapless GIs forced to ogle detonations at the Nevada Test Site), but somewhere around 600 rads seems to be a near guess.   13

By contrast, cockroaches in the laboratory dosed with 830 rads routinely survive to die of old age. Their *average* lethal dose seems to be up around 3200 rads. And of those that Wharton and Wharton blasted with 10,000 rads, *half* of the group were still alive two weeks later.   14

The Whartons in their *Radiation Research* paper don't say *how much* longer those hardiest cockroaches lasted. But it was long enough, evidently, for egg capsules to be delivered, and hatch, and for the cycle of cockroach survival and multiplication—unbroken throughout the past 250 million years—to continue on. Long enough to suggest that, if the worst happened, cockroaches in great and growing number would be around to dance on the grave of the human species.   15

With luck maybe it won't happen—that ultimately ugly event foreseen so vividly by Jonathan Schell. With luck, and with also a gale of informed and persistent outrage by citizenries more sensible than their leaders. But with less luck, less persistence, what I can't help but envision for our poor raw festering planet, in those days and years after the After, is, like once before, an Age of Cockroaches.   16

If Quammen had written for a specialized scientific periodical like the *Journal of Comparative Zoology*, he would have directed any curious reader to the very page he used from other sources—as we'll show you how to do in Chapter 11, "Writing from Library Research." But because he wrote for an audience of nonspecialists—readers of a general magazine—Quammen more informally acknowledged his sources whenever he quoted or borrowed ideas. When later he collected his essays into a book, he cheerfully admitted to having "cannibalized fact and reaped understanding" from other writers. He then took pains to list his sources, as many as he could remember. Here is his list for "A Republic of Cockroaches." It will give you a sense of the reading he did in writing his essay—less than the writer of a scientific research paper might do, perhaps, but a reasonable amount for anyone writing an informal essay addressed to general readers.

PARTIAL SOURCES

Cornwell, P. B. *The Cockroach.* London: Hutchinson, 1968.

Guthrie, D. M., and A. R. Tindall. *The Biology of the Cockroach.* New York: St. Martin's Press, 1968.

Miall, L. C., and Alfred Denny. *The Structure and Life-History of the Cockroach* (Periplaneta orientalis). London: L. Reeve, 1886.

Rau, Phil. "The Life History of the American Cockroach, *Periplaneta americana* Linn. (Orthop.: Blattidae)." *Entomological News* 51 (1940).

Schell, Jonathan. *The Fate of the Earth.* New York: Knopf, 1982.

Wharton, D. R. A., and Martha L. Wharton. "The Effect of Radiation on the Longevity of the Cockroach, *Periplaneta americana*, as Affected by Dose, Age, Sex, and Food Intake." *Radiation Research* 11 (1959).

Questions to Start You Thinking

1. How did you respond to this essay? What did you star, question, underline, or comment on in the margin while you read?

2. What passages in "A Republic of Cockroaches" reveal Quammen's purpose in writing? What main idea is he driving at?

3. Apparently, Quammen was inspired by a paragraph in Jonathan Schell's *The Fate of the Earth,* and he then did further reading about cockroaches. Where in his essay does he appear to go beyond Schell and his other sources to contribute something original?

4. If, like Quammen, you had found yourself goaded to write after reading the paragraph from Schell's book that is quoted in this essay, in what other direction might your thoughts possibly have taken you? Would *your* essay have gone into detail about cockroaches?

Rose Anne Federici had been assigned to read a medical book on eating disorders for her course in nursing education. As she read, looking for passages that encouraged "further thinking," one page stood out for her. Her reflections about it sent her thoughts beyond the book's immediate subject and crystallized into the following paper.

Student Essay

CONFLICTING MESSAGES: A LOOK
AT A GENERATION TORN TWO WAYS
Rose Anne Federici

this
the reader

I belong to a generation constantly torn in two direc-   1
tions. This realization came to me unexpectedly as I was
reading Eating Disorders: The Facts by Suzanne Abraham and
Derek Llewellyn-Jones (Oxford: Oxford University Press,
1984). These two medical writers ask why eating disorders
are so prevalent among young women. Many people my age become victims of anorexia, or self-starvation, while others
overeat to the point of obesity and become victims of bulimia, or abnormal craving for food.

Why does this happen? The writers offer several possible   2
explanations. One is that women in our society today are
bombarded by two conflicting messages--eat and don't eat.
Growing confused, a person may go to either extreme, becoming
a dieter who wastes away or a foodaholic. It is in the media, the writers point out, where we often find the two messages coming at us at once. In almost any women's magazine,
right after an article on a sensational new diet guaranteed
to help us lose weight comfortably with little effort or
willpower, we get a recipe for a delectable chocolate cake or
a creamy sauce. A television commercial shows us a diet
drink or a low-calorie cereal followed by another commercial
for a burger joint or pizzeria. One minute, we receive the
message that a woman's lifework is to be thin so as to be
healthy, happy, and loved by everyone. The next minute we
are told that eating not only satisfies the appetite but also
fulfills many inner wants. It is sensuous fun, which every
woman has a right to. Sometimes, Abraham and Llewellyn-Jones
add, the contradictions beamed forth from television are
reinforced by contradictory messages in the home.

> The social (and usually family) pressures are also
> contradictory: you must eat everything other people
> give you but you must not get fat.

The provision of food is seen in our culture
as a major sign of caring; and sharing food at a
meal is seen as one of the prime social contacts.
These cultural imperatives place a burden on a
mother to provide abundant quantities of food, and
on her loving daughter or son to eat that food. It
is not surprising that in the face of the psychological bombardment of two contradictory messages,
most young women diet.

The writers suggest other possible explanations for eat- 3
ing disorders, but this one started me thinking. I believe
these writers are on to something important, and not only important for health care and preventive medicine. I suddenly
realized that in our society, people are constantly being
bombarded by contradictory messages, not only about eating
but about almost everything. For example, advertisers constantly make appeals that tug us in two different directions.
A television commercial tells us to get outdoors and explore
the wilds of America. However, while we are roughing it and
getting close to nature we are supposed to be living in a
camper with a TV set, a microwave oven, and the other comforts of home. The same discount store ad in the newspaper
that invites us to get plenty of exercise with a set of
weights also tells us to take life easy with an automatic garage door opener.

Many of these conflicting messages are beamed at people 4
of college age. We are told to assert our individuality--but
to do so by wearing a name brand of makeup, or Jams, or Jordache jeans. How we can display our very own personalities
when we are wearing what everyone else wears, we are not
told. On television news and talk shows, glamorous unmarried
mothers--Farrah Fawcett and Susan Sarandon, for example--are
presented as stars worthy of our admiration. Recently, the
same channels that feature such shows have been running public service messages aimed at unmarried women and girls:
"Don't get pregnant."

Often our parents and teachers tell us one thing, and 5

television another. "Study hard and you will achieve success," I am told every time I go home. Meanwhile, on TV, I
keep seeing people who are considered successes even though
they have probably never opened a book. They simply buy a
lottery ticket and they win a million dollars, or they record
one hit song and become rich for life. Other conflicting
messages bombard me every time I go home--"Study hard in college" and "Why don't you get out and meet people and enjoy
yourself?"

In <u>Mademoiselle</u> magazine, an interview presents a woman   6
for us to admire. After starting her own business, she has
scored a huge success and now has twenty employees. At the
same time she has a husband and three children. She maintains a "gracious home" and gives dinner parties. There may
be many miracle workers like that woman, but for me the two
messages--be a successful executive, be a wonderful wife and
mother--point in different directions. I wonder if there is
not a built-in conflict in the whole idea of becoming a big
success and still being a loving person, able to spend time
with family and friends. Being both is not impossible, but
for me it would be hard to achieve.

I realize that even on a national level, conflicting   7
messages are broadcast. We throw a big birthday party for
the Statue of Liberty while doing our best to limit the number of immigrants allowed to enter the United States. We
pride ourselves that we deinstitutionalize the mentally ill,
but we do it by sending them out onto the streets while refusing to give them the skills and the support to make it on
their own. We criticize the quality of our schools but pay
our public school teachers very little. We spend money for
"Star Wars" missiles and at the same time call for world
peace. In the name of democracy, we send financial and military aid to corrupt governments in other lands. No wonder
that, although I do not suffer from anorexia or bulimia, I
have an increasing sense that I belong to a generation torn
in different directions.

Questions to Start You Thinking

1. What did Rose Anne Federici herself add to the idea that she found in the book *Eating Disorders*?

2. What other contradictory messages are you familiar with from magazine and television advertising, from films, or from the news?

3. Do you agree that all the messages Federici cites are necessarily contradictory? Can't one diet most of the time, yet on special occasions eat a sliver of chocolate cake?

LEARNING BY WRITING

The Assignment: Reading for Insight

This assignment invites you to do some reading that will enlarge your area of knowledge. It asks you to reflect on what you read, arrive at some original insight or observation that stems from what you have read, and then write a paper in which you use your reading as the point of departure for your own ideas.

For at least five days, keep a reading journal in which you react each day to one essay, magazine article, or chapter of a book that sends your thoughts in some new and interesting direction. Then look over your journal and select the most promising entry. Develop it into a paper in which you share with your readers what you learned, your insights, your further ideas. Hand in your journal along with your paper.

Among the thoughtful papers we have seen in response to this assignment are these:

A man who had recently read about the economic law of supply and demand set out to explain that law by describing the behavior of both sellers and customers at a yard sale.

A woman, having read in her sociology textbook about the changes that city neighborhoods in the United States typically undergo in the course of fifty to a hundred years, thought about the changes that had taken place in a neighborhood she knew well and decided that the textbook's generalizations applied imperfectly.

A man, after having read and thought about George Orwell's classic essay "Shooting an Elephant," agreed with the writer that whole governments can act unwisely, seemingly for no better reason than to save face. He used as his main example U.S. policy toward Vietnam in the 1960s and 1970s.

A man, inspired by Gradgrind, the tyrannical and shortsighted schoolmaster in Charles Dickens's novel *Hard Times,* humorously insisted he had encountered as much mindlessness in the elementary school he had attended as had Dickens's characters in Gradgrind's classroom.

A woman, appalled by newspaper accounts of the 1986 nuclear disaster at Chernobyl in the Soviet Union, weighed the risks inherent in nuclear power against possible benefits to humankind.

Generating Ideas

Check current periodicals. What will you read to fulfill this assignment? Why not go to the library and browse through several current magazines, such as the *Atlantic, Harper's, New Republic, Commentary, Ms.,* and others likely to contain articles to spur you to thought. Never mind *People, Sporting News,* and other periodicals written mainly to entertain. You want good, meaty articles, conducive to reflection; if they are a bit difficult to understand and need to be read twice, so much the better. Try not to start out with ideas you already have, looking only for confirmation. You'll do better if you stay open to fresh ideas that your readings may unexpectedly trigger.

Recall your reading. What have you read lately that has started you thinking and wondering? Classics like Sigmund Freud's *The Interpretation of Dreams,* Rachel Carson's *The Sea around Us,* or Henry David Thoreau's *Walden* bristle with challenging ideas. And why not draw on some reading you've been assigned for another course? It may be a chapter in a textbook, an essay in a reader used in your college English course, or a book assigned for outside reading. We suggest you mix your choices. Try one of each: a classic, a current magazine article, a chapter from a textbook, the letters of some famous person, a thought-provoking short story, a book about art or music—whatever engages your interest. That way, your journal will contain a variety of possibilities from which you can choose the topic for your paper.

Skim and sample. As you begin your search for promising material, keep in mind that you're reading with a purpose. You can't afford the luxury of reading everything word by word; skip, skim, and sample things. Should something prove thought-provoking, you can read it more closely. When reading things for possible material, try reading just the first two paragraphs and the last two paragraphs. Those will probably alert you to the main points the writer makes. When you look into books to see if they're worth reading, skim through the first chapter and the last chapter. Then, if the book looks helpful, you can spend more time with it.

Once you zero in on a likely chapter, article, or essay, read slowly and carefully, giving yourself plenty of time to think between the lines. Try to discern the writer's opinions, even if they are unstated. Don't just soak up opinions and information. Criticize. Question. Wonder. Argue back. Dare to differ with the author whose work you're reading. Most printed pages aren't holy writ; you can doubt them. Opinions you don't agree with can be valuable if they set your own thoughts in motion.

Write while you read. Read with pencil in hand and, if you're one of those people who find it helpful (not everyone does), react in writing. Write brief notes to yourself (if you're using library materials), or mark up the text (if you own the book or magazine or have made a photocopy of it). This technique will focus your attention. Underline phrases and sentences that contain essentials. Star things you think are important. Make cross-references: "Contradicts what he said on p. 17." Jot thoughts in the margin. Besides helping you participate while you read, such notes are a wonderful help in reviewing what you have read.

On the next page, you can see how Rose Anne Federici reacted when she read Suzanne Abraham and Derek Llewellyn-Jones's *Eating Disorders: The Facts*. By the way, she had a perfect right to mark up the copy: it was an assigned textbook in her nursing education course. We don't say you need to mark up every page you read so intensively. Evidently, Federici recognized that here was an especially valuable page, with an idea she would surely want to write about.

Keep a reading journal. As the assignment suggests, keep a journal of thoughts that arise in response to your reading. Each day, after reading and thinking about the day's selection, dash out a few sentences. What do you put into a journal entry? Well, first (and this is easy), put in the title and author of any material you discuss. If as you read you come across passages you especially admire, copy them into the journal. Along with summaries and direct quotations, include your own reactions. See if you can arrive at any further insight.

This is what Rose Anne Federici did in preparing to write her essay. Shortly after she found herself interacting with this passage, Federici felt elated. In the last place she might have looked for it—a textbook for her nursing course—she had discovered a really interesting criticism of the society in which we live. This suggestion cast light not only on people who gorge or starve themselves, but on advertising, political pronouncements, and family life as well. Excited, Federici jotted her thoughts in her notebook. We give them here to illustrate a typical, spontaneous entry in a reading journal, like the one that our assignment calls for.

> "Don't eat" and "Eat"—contradictory messages. I'm pretty sure we receive other c.m.'s all the time.
>
> What about the line on mental health? Yesterday in nursing class lecturer talked about how mental patients are "deinstitutionalized"—this saves cost and is supposed to be good for them. But they are turned loose on the streets without money or support. They get in trouble, commit crimes.
>
> There's the line I get handed at home—"Study hard" vs. "Why don't you get out and meet people?"
>
> Do advertisers sometimes contradict themselves? What about politicians? I want to find some more examples. How many conflicting messages are there in our society?

As you start writing your own reading journal, you might ask the questions in the Discovery Checklist.

Eating disorders – the facts

THE SOCIAL EXPLANATION

In Western culture two contrasting messages about food and eating are offered by society, and particularly by the media. The first message is *"don't eat"* that a slim woman is successful, attractive, healthy, happy, fit, and & popular. To become slim, with all that this implies, is deemed to be a *"eat"* major pursuit of many women. The second message is that eating is a pleasurable activity which meets many needs in addition to relieving hunger, and women have a right to have these needs met. In women's magazines these two contrasting messages tend to appear inextricably mixed. In nearly every issue the magazines publish 'exciting' new diets which 'guarantee weight loss with minimum discomfort or motivation', and these diets are often followed by recipes for, and superb photographs of, luscious cakes and foods with rich sauces. It is difficult to watch television without being confronted by an advertisement for a substitute diet-food alternating with a fast food advertisement, or its equivalent. The social (and usually family) pressures are also contradictory: you must eat everything other people give you but you must not get fat.

The provision of food is seen in our culture as a major sign of caring; and sharing food at a meal is seen as one of the prime social contacts. These cultural imperatives place a burden on a mother to provide abundant quantities of food, and on her loving daughter or *YES!* son to eat that food. It is not surprising that in the face of the psychological bombardment of two contradictory messages, most young women diet. Some become 'foodaholics' and develop bulimia. Others become preoccupied with food and the avoidance of weight gain, developing bulimia or anorexia nervosa. Some decide that dieting is too disturbing to their way of life and return to eating more food than they require, becoming obese. These women may also find obesity protective against acceding to current social attitudes to sexuality, which they fear. Hidden in a fat body, they give the message that they are not attractive and do not want to form a sexual relationship.

Other contradictory messages we receive?

28

DISCOVERY CHECKLIST: RECORDING YOUR READING

- How would you state what the writer takes for granted? If a writer begins, "The serious threat of acid rain was dismissed with a collective yawn in Washington again last week," then evidently he or she assumes that acid rain is a serious menace and that legislators, too, should take it seriously.
- Do you agree with what the author has said? Does it clash with any ideas you hold dear? Does it question anything you take for granted?
- Do the writer's assertions rest on evidence? What kind of evidence? Statistics? The results of surveys? Quotations from authorities? Historical facts? Photographs? Are you convinced?
- With what do you disagree? Why?
- If you doubt the writer's statements, can you test them against anything you know or can find out?
- From any facts the writer presents, what inferences can you draw? If the writer musters facts that lead to an inescapable conclusion, might any conflicting evidence be mustered? A portrait of an unfriendly country that showed all its citizens to be rapists, drunks, and drug addicts would leave much out; evidently a different view would be possible.
- Has anything you read opened your eyes to new possibilities, new ways of looking at the world?
- Has the writer failed to tell you anything you wish you knew? If so, what?

If in your journal you write the answers to at least some of these questions, you'll have valuable thoughts on hand when you start drafting your paper.

Shaping a Draft

Select an interesting entry. Faced now with your five journal entries, how do you decide which to expand into a paper? First, ask yourself which entry most interests you. Second, ask which of your reflections would most interest your possible readers—your fellow students and your instructor. As you look over your journal entries, decide which most clearly seems to say something. Which arrives at a conclusion, however tentative? That's the one to develop.

If, before you begin to draft, you feel the need for more ideas than there are in your journal entry, backtrack for a while. Look back over what you have read and do more thinking. One of the strengths of Rose Anne Federici's paper is its convincing array of examples. After she wrote her journal entry, Federici decided it looked a little skimpy. She wished she might discover other contradictory messages. "I thought of the one about deinstitutionalizing the mentally ill but refusing to help them," she recalls, "and the one about 'get good grades but get out and see people'—I'd heard that one before. I knew there must be lots of other contradictory messages, but at first it was hard to think of any."

After a solitary, fruitless attempt at brainstorming, Federici had a conversation with three other students. She told them of her assignment, shared her preliminary thoughts, and asked, "What other contradictory messages have you heard lately?" They came up with ten further examples. Some of their ideas didn't fit Federici's specifications. It seemed easy enough to think of differing messages coming from two different sources—such as health warnings like "Don't smoke" and tobacco ads that urge the opposite. It was more difficult to come up with contradictory messages from the same source: for instance, the ad that calls on readers to "rough it in the wild" in a camper that boasts a microwave oven. As Federici began to draft, looking over the notes on her brainstorming session and on her conversation, new examples occurred to her.

Borrow honestly. The first law of writing from reading is to acknowledge fully and honestly your debt to the writer from whom you derived anything, whether it be a quotation, information, or an idea. Not to do so is to lay yourself open to the charge of plagiarism. In general, identify any source of an idea or quotation right away, as soon as you mention it in your writing. You can do this informally, as David Quammen does in "A Republic of Cockroaches." It is enough in an informal paper, for example, to say, "Renowned

---

WRITING WITH A COMPUTER: READING

Try sitting at your computer with a book in your lap, so that you can read and take notes at the same time. This way, you won't have to recopy any material you transcribe. You can write *around* it.

If you have long quotations that require extended proofreading, try this. Change the ruler you are using, and display your words in a narrow column with a justified right-hand margin. If a long passage looks like this, perhaps it will be more fun to proofread:

```
Benvenuto   Cellini,   the
celebrated   sculptor   of
the  Italian  Renaissance,
designed  for  Francis I a
famous  saltcellar  of en-
amel  and  gold,  preserved
in the Vienna Art Museum.
```

In lines so short, any errors will stand out more readily. But lest you turn in a paper that looks like a newspaper, return your ruler to its usual width after you finish proofreading.

A *portable* computer, by the way, is a great aid to reading and note taking in a library.

feminist Betty Friedan states this idea convincingly in *The Feminine Mystique*,"
and then quote Friedan.

You can acknowledge your sources in any of three ways.

Quoting. When an author expresses an idea in a way so incisive, so brilliant, or so memorable that you want to reproduce his or her words exactly,
you can quote them word for word. Direct quotations add life and color and
the sound of a speaking voice. If you leave out part of a quotation, indicate
the omissions with an ellipsis—three dots (. . .). If the ellipsis occurs at the
beginning or end of a sentence, it contains *four* dots. Why leave anything out?
Usually because, if left in, it would be too boring or cumbersome or distracting
or needlessly long—perhaps because it adds some information that mattered
to the author but doesn't matter to the point you are making.

Nutshelling. Also called *summarizing,* this is a useful way to deal with a
whole paragraph or section of a work when what you're after is just the
general drift. To save time and space and to focus on the idea, you don't want
to quote word for word. Without doing violence to an idea, you put it in a
nutshell: you express its main sense in a few words—*your own words*—and
tell where you got the idea. Jonathan Schell's long paragraph on gamma
radiation, which Quammen quotes, is a summary of research conducted at
Brookhaven National Laboratory.

Paraphrasing. This skill involves restating an author's ideas. When you
put the author's thoughts into your own words, don't let the author's words
keep slipping in. The style in paraphrasing, as in nutshelling, has to be yours.
If some other writer says, "President Wilson called an emergency meeting of
his cabinet to discuss the new crisis," and you say, "The president called on
his cabinet to hold an emergency meeting to discuss the new crisis," that isn't
far enough removed from the original. It looks like plagiarism. You could put
quotation marks around the original sentence, although it seems unmemor-
able, not worth quoting word for word. Or, better, you could write: "Sum-
moning his cabinet to an emergency session, Wilson laid forth the challenge
before them." If you deal carefully with the material, you won't have to put
quotation marks around anything in your paraphrase.

In Rose Anne Federici's "Conflicting Messages," you'll find all three methods in action: quotation, nutshell, and paraphrase. In her second paragraph,
introducing the idea she had discovered in the book she read, Federici sums
it up in a nutshell:

> One [explanation for eating disorders] is that women in
> our society today are bombarded by two conflicting mes-
> sages--eat and don't eat. Growing confused, a person may
> go to either extreme, becoming a dieter who wastes away
> or a foodaholic.

Then, apparently feeling the need to explain more fully, she immediately goes
on to paraphrase the writers' entire discussion of the two messages, with their

illustrations from women's magazines and television advertising. Thus, without borrowing the writer's very language, she produces a new version true to their ideas. Better than quoting at great length, paraphrasing here serves her purposes. Freely, she arranges the writers' points in a different order, making the idea "contradictory messages" stand last in her own paragraph—and so giving it greater emphasis. She even invents specific examples where the original writers are vague: instead of their somewhat puzzling "a fast food advertisement, or its equivalent" (whatever its equivalent is!), she bravely and faithfully substitutes "commercial for a burger joint or pizzeria." Paraphrasing a British book, she thus retains its sense while making its examples recognizably American.

Her essay clearly gains, too, from an appropriate quotation. In her third paragraph, she quotes four sentences from her original—for what reason? "Because," she explains, "I wanted to keep the exact words about the mother and her loving daughter or son. Besides, I didn't know how to paraphrase 'cultural imperatives.' I could have said 'the dictates of society' or something, but that didn't sound as good. 'Cultural imperatives' was wonderful, and I wanted to leave it alone." (You can compare her nutshell and her paraphrase with the original text she read, reproduced on p. 76.)

How do you condense another writer's thoughts? Before you paraphrase or nutshell, we suggest that you do the following.

1. Read the original passage over a couple of times. You can underline key parts or note them.
2. Without looking at it, try to state its gist—the point it makes, the main sense you remember.
3. Then go back and reread the original one more time, making sure you got its gist faithfully. Revise your paraphrase as necessary.

To paraphrase, incidentally, has another use: it is one way to understand a knotty passage that has baffled you. You can try to paraphrase it in writing, or perhaps just paraphrase it mentally.

Rewriting

Perhaps, as you look over your draft, you will feel the need to read further. Would your paper be stronger if it had more facts, statistics, or other evidence? Take the trouble to do additional reading. David Quammen, inspired by Jonathan Schell's paragraph to picture Armageddon as a victory for cockroaches, apparently found that to make his vision effective, he had to read the work of several scientists knowledgeable about cockroaches. We don't ask you at this point to write a research paper. For this assignment, just have enough facts and information at your disposal to state your ideas with confidence and authority.

As you read and write at the same time, you may find your views changing. If you rearranged your ideas drastically since starting to write, cosmetic changes may not be enough—you may have to revise thoroughly. To see how much your ideas have changed since you first wrote your journal entry, you might try to state (to yourself or in writing) what insight you had then and what insight you have now.

In looking back over your paper, you might ask the following questions.

REVISION CHECKLIST: WRITING FROM READING

- Have you given emphasis to major points in the work you read? Or did you get sidetracked and deal with the writer's incidental points, skipping over what really matters?
- If you see any long stretches without a quotation, can you come up with a good, lively direct quotation to break the monotony? Look over your reading and see where it might be helpful (and interesting) to quote a writer's very words.
- Would it ever help to state the other writer's ideas in a nutshell or to paraphrase?
- Did you make clear what you took from your source or sources?

Rose Anne Federici found that the hardest part of writing her paper was making the transition from the background material she felt her readers would need (paragraphs 1 and 2 of her finished essay) to the insights that reading the book had led her to. In her first draft she went on too long about the book she had read. Then she included in her transition almost all the suggestions that had arisen in the brainstorming session with her friends. As she set about revising, she realized that most of those ideas belonged later in the paper; and one or two, she finally had to admit, were too weak to be included at all. She coped with her problem by doing a lot of reorganizing.

~~Increasingly as I read, I realized what a valuable~~ *The writers suggest* ~~book Eating Disorders was. It gave a whole lot of~~ other reasons for eating disorders, ~~too--reasons that never would have occurred to me, like fear of sexuality, wanting to remain a child, and the need to rebel against strict parents. All these were very interesting to me,~~ but *this* ~~the~~ one ~~I have quoted~~ started me thinking. I believe these writers are on to something important, and not only *important* for health care and preventive medicine. I *suddenly realized* ~~now know~~ that in our society, people are constantly being bombarded ~~in the media and elsewhere~~ by contradictory messages**,** ~~These messages are~~ not only about eating but ~~also~~ about almost everything. For example, advertisers constantly *make* appeal~~s~~ ~~to us in ways~~ that tug us in two different directions. A

So what? [marginal note with arrows]

television commercial tells us to ~~rough it~~ *get outdoors* and explore the wilds of America. However, while we are roughing it and getting close to nature we (supposed~~ly~~ are) ~~also resid-ing~~ *to be living* in a camper with a TV set, a microwave oven, and ~~all~~ the *other* comforts of home. ~~"~~ The same discount ad in the news-paper ~~inviting~~ *that invites* us to get ~~lots~~ *plenty* of exercise with *a set of* weights also tells us to take life easy with an automatic garage door opener.

Many of these conflicting messages are beamed at people of college age. We are told ~~Advertisers tell us~~ to assert our individuality--but to do so by wearing a name brand of makeup, or Jams, or Jordache jeans. How (can we) ~~"be ourselves"~~ *display our very own personalities* when we are wearing what everyone else wears, we are not told. ~~They tell us to drive Porsches even though they ought to know we can't afford them.~~ *?* The media keeps showing us super-women with high-powered jobs and gorgeous, well-run homes and beautiful, outstanding children. Are we supposed to study hard or be social successes? ~~Are we supposed to support missile growth or stop paying taxes?~~ *What?* Mental pa-tients are "deinstitutionalized," saving costs, but they can't support themselves. On television news and talk *—Farrah Fawcett and Susan Sarandan, for example—* shows, glamorous unmarried mothers are presented as stars worthy of our admiration. Recently, the same channels *running public service announcements aimed at unmarried women and girls:* that feature such shows have been ~~advertising,~~ "Don't get pregnant."

I'm using up all my examples! Develop later?

Really needed, a three-part organization for these messages: those by advertisers, those by government, and others

Once you have a preliminary draft that you like, why not ask a friend or classmate to read your paper and answer these questions? In the light of his or her suggestions, you can then make your final revisions.

PEER EDITING CHECKLIST: WRITING FROM READING

- What is your first reaction to the essay?
- Please restate or quote the major insight that the writer shares with you from his or her reading.

- Look at the organization of the essay. Is it clear enough how parts of the essay connect to other parts? Do you recommend any changes in the ordering of parts?
- List any questions you have about what the writer wrote that you think he or she could still answer in revising.
- Did you need any additional examples or explanations of ideas or illustrations anywhere in the paper? Put stars on the manuscript where the writer needs to develop the ideas more.
- How useful and how interesting to you are the quotations the writer uses? Does the writer introduce them smoothly enough?
- Is it difficult in any places to know when the writer is explaining his or her ideas and when he or she is nutshelling or paraphrasing from reading? Underline any parts of the essay when you're not sure whose ideas you are reading.
- Does the writer use any unfamiliar words that need quick definition?
- Circle on the manuscript any spelling, punctuation, grammar, or word choice that got in the way of your reading and understanding.
- Are there any revisions you think would be essential before the writer submits the paper to the instructor?

In writing from reading, you have certain minor but important responsibilities when you proofread your final draft. If you have used any direct quotations, check them against the original source. In copying a quotation into your paper, it's easy to omit something, perhaps something essential. Of course, your main concern will be to make sure you've produced a paper in which you convey to your readers some of the power and joy of thinking, not only with the prompting of another writer, but also by thinking on your own.

Other Assignments

1. Read several comments about a recent news event by columnists and commentators in magazines and newspapers. Find two writers who disagree in their analyses. Decide which view you favor and explain it in a few paragraphs. In making your decision, you may find that you need to read still more, to know as much about the event as possible.

2. Write a letter to the editor of your local newspaper in which you take exception to the recent conduct of some world leader or celebrity as reported in the paper or to some column the newspaper printed recently. By referring to what you have read, make the grounds of your complaint clear enough so that even someone who didn't read the article you're criticizing will know what you're talking about.

3. To give yourself practice in skeptically analyzing what you read, study a story in a recent tabloid newspaper such as the *National Enquirer, Weekly World News,* or the *Star* that seems to you particularly hard to believe. Where was the story

FOR GROUP LEARNING

When your instructor assigns a paper in which you are to respond to some reading selection (or selections), first meet outside class with members of your writing group before you write. Let members of your group pool their reactions to their reading. Appoint a moderator to run a discussion. Each participant is free to take notes. To start the discussion, here are some questions that might be asked:

What problems did you have with this reading? What didn't you understand? (Be frank: no one always understands everything.) Were there any words or allusions you didn't get, that someone else might explain?

What do you take to be the author's purpose?

Is there any main point this author makes?

At any point, does the author cause you to disagree or doubt?

What, if anything, did the author do especially well?

What do you wish the author might have done instead?

What did you find out from this reading that you didn't know before?

The goal of this discussion is to give you a better understanding and appreciation of the reading than you alone might derive so that you might come up with more ideas for your own paper.

said to take place? What reliable witnesses were there? How could a skeptic verify the truth of the story? What inferences can you draw about the story, the reporter, and the newspaper that printed it?

4. Compare two history books in their accounts of a celebrated event—the Declaration of Independence, the bombing of Hiroshima, or any other event you wish to read more about. One of the books should be recent, the other at least thirty years old. Describe the differences in the two versions. How do you account for them?

APPLYING WHAT YOU LEARN: SOME USES OF WRITING FROM READING

In college, writing from your reading is an activity you'll take part in almost daily. Many instructors, to encourage you to read and write continually, will ask you to keep a notebook of your reading and occasionally may ask you to turn it in for inspection. Writing about your reading, as you often do in taking tests and examinations, is intended to demonstrate your mastery of it. (For advice about writing essay examinations, see Chapter 20.)

For other college writing assignments, reading will be just one of your resources. An education course, to take an instance, might ask you to combine reading and observing: to watch a toddler for an hour a day over the course of a week, keep a detailed record of her appearance and her actions, compare those with what is average for a child of her age (information you would find by reading), and then draw some conclusions about her behavior. In the field of human development, students are constantly asked to make informed judgments on current issues (abortion, day care, and joint custody, to name a few) by learning to understand the differing views presented in the books and articles they are assigned to read. Further, they learn to be advocates for troubled children and their families not only by reading and researching legislative bills but also by writing letters against or in support of those bills.

At home or in high school you may have read general magazines like *Newsweek* and *National Geographic,* which most literate readers can take pleasure in. But later in college, many of your courses will oblige you to read periodicals of a different kind: journals written and read by trained specialists. Many specialists, from physicists to physicians, write articles for others in their field, sharing what they know. Doctors and other health professionals report new diseases or new treatments; scientists and technicians advance new theories; literary critics make fresh ventures into literary criticism; historians address other historians, enlarging on and reinterpreting knowledge of the past. As part of your training in a special discipline, you may be introduced to the *Journal of Comparative Behavior, Nature, Educational Research, American Journal of Sociology, PMLA,* or *Foreign Affairs.* You will often be asked to report on an article, reading it critically, perhaps summarizing or paraphrasing its essentials, and finally adding a thoughtful comment. Doing so, you absorb the vocabulary and habits of thought of your chosen field of work and make them your own. You see how skilled writers prove and demonstrate, evaluate, explain, select useful details, assert, affirm, deny, try to convince.

Many a learned article begins with a short review of previous research, which the writer is about to dash to pieces. In some professional journals, though, summary or paraphrase of other writing may be an end in itself. Attorney Peter L. Knox, who in addition to practicing his profession writes articles about pension tax laws for professional journals such as *Taxation for Accountants* and the *Journal of Taxation,* says that writing for him is often a matter of reading difficult writing (like rulings of the tax court and the *Internal Revenue Manual*) and condensing it in plainer prose—"expressing in an organized, somewhat literary form a set of complex rules." You can see how such an article might greatly help other tax lawyers struggling to understand a long, crucially important entry about changing a pension plan, as in this example from *Final and Temporary IRS Regulations:*

§ 1.401(b)-1 Certain retroactive changes in plan [TD 7437, filed 9-23-76].

(a) *General rule.* Under section 401(b) a stock bonus, pension, profit-sharing, annuity, or bond purchase plan which does not satisfy the requirements of section 401(a) on any day solely as a result of a disqualifying provision (as defined in paragraph (b) of this section) shall be considered to have satisfied such requirement on such date if, on or before the last day of the remedial amendment period (as determined under paragraphs (c), (d) and (e) of this section) with respect to such disqualifying provision, all provisions of the plan which are necessary to satisfy all requirements of sections 401(a), 403(a), or 405(a) are in effect and have been made effective for all purposes for the whole of such period.

The entry goes on like that for three and a half large pages of fine print divided into subsections, some with roman numerals. Bewildering as such material may be—probably no one reads IRS regulations for entertainment—thousands of a client's dollars may be riding on an attorney's ability to interpret that entry correctly. In an article explaining the passage to his fellow pension plan professionals, Knox helpfully begins, "Section 401(b) provides a way for retirement plans to be retroactively corrected" and goes on to tell how it is generally applied. Obviously, the law could not function without its interpreters, who translate its complex language into simpler directives that other people can follow. Besides, the interpreters foresee difficulties that can arise in real life when professionals try to apply the law. No mere exercise in translation, such specialized nutshelling and paraphrasing, it seems, calls for hard, even imaginative, thought.

We have been viewing books and articles as *immediately* useful sources of ideas and information. But sometimes there is a time lag: you read Melville's novel *Moby-Dick* or Thorstein Veblen's *The Theory of the Leisure Class* and, although your reading isn't immediately useful to the paper you have to write, something from it remains with you, perhaps nothing but a phrase, an example, a stray idea, a way of constructing a sentence. Perhaps months later, when you are writing another paper, it returns to the forefront of your mind. In truth, writing from reading is useful to you in ways we haven't begun to indicate. We hold this truth to be self-evident: that the better you read—the more alertly, critically, questioningly—the better you write.

A Paleontologist Writes from Reading

Distinguished for his many books and more than a hundred articles, Stephen Jay Gould writes for a large audience that includes both his fellow scientists and the general reader. The essay that follows, collected in *The Panda's Thumb* (1980), is one of several in which Gould deflates scientific attempts to prove the biological superiority of white males. His reading supplies him with powerful ammunition.

WOMEN'S BRAINS
Stephen Jay Gould

In the prelude to *Middlemarch*, George Eliot lamented the unfulfilled   1
lives of talented women:

> Some have felt that these blundering lives are due to the inconvenient indefiniteness with which the Supreme Power has fashioned the natures of women: if there were one level of feminine incompetence as strict as the ability to count three and no more, the social lot of women might be treated with scientific certitude.

Eliot goes on to discount the idea of innate limitation, but while she wrote in 1872, the leaders of European anthropometry were trying to measure "with scientific certitude" the inferiority of women. Anthropometry, or measurement of the human body, is not so fashionable a field these days, but it dominated the human sciences for much of the nineteenth century and remained popular until intelligence testing replaced skull measurement as a favored device for making invidious comparisons among races, classes, and sexes. Craniometry, or measurement of the skull, commanded the most attention and respect. Its unquestioned leader, Paul Broca (1824–80), professor of clinical surgery at the Faculty of Medicine in Paris, gathered a school of disciples and imitators around himself. Their work, so meticulous and apparently irrefutable, exerted great influence and won high esteem as a jewel of nineteenth-century science.

Broca's work seemed particularly invulnerable to refutation. Had he not measured with the most scrupulous care and accuracy? (Indeed, he had. I have the greatest respect for Broca's meticulous procedure. His numbers are sound. But science is an inferential exercise, not a catalog of facts. Numbers, by themselves, specify nothing. All depends upon what you do with them.) Broca depicted himself as an apostle of objectivity, a man who bowed before facts and cast aside superstition and sentimentality. He declared that "there is no faith, however respectable, no interest, however legitimate, which must not accommodate itself to the progress of human knowledge and bend before truth." Women, like it or not, had smaller brains than men and, therefore, could not equal them in intelligence. This fact, Broca argued, may reinforce a common prejudice in male society, but it is also a scientific truth. L. Manouvrier, a black sheep in Broca's fold, rejected the inferiority of women and wrote with feeling about the burden imposed upon them by Broca's numbers:

> Women displayed their talents and their diplomas. They also invoked philosophical authorities. But they were opposed by *numbers* unknown to Condorcet or to John Stuart Mill. These numbers fell upon poor women like a sledge hammer, and they were accompanied by commentaries and sarcasms more ferocious than the most misogynist imprecations of certain church fathers. The theologians had asked if women had a soul. Several centuries later, some scientists were ready to refuse them a human intelligence.

Broca's argument rested upon two sets of data: the larger brains of men in modern societies, and a supposed increase in male superiority through time. His most extensive data came from autopsies performed personally in four Parisian hospitals. For 292 male brains, he calculated an average weight of 1325 grams; 140 female brains averaged 1144 grams for a difference of 181 grams, or 14 percent of the male weight. Broca understood, of course, that part of this difference could be attributed to the greater height of males. Yet he made no attempt to measure the effect of size alone and actually stated that it cannot account for the entire difference because we know, a priori, that women are not as intelligent as men (a premise that the data were supposed to test, not rest upon):

> We might ask if the small size of the female brain depends exclusively upon the small size of her body. Tiedemann has proposed this explanation. But we must not forget that women are, on the average, a little less intelligent than men, a difference which we should not exaggerate but which is, nonetheless, real. We are therefore permitted to suppose that the relatively small size of the female brain depends in part upon her physical inferiority and in part upon her intellectual inferiority.

In 1873, the year after Eliot published *Middlemarch,* Broca measured the cranial capacities of prehistoric skulls from L'Homme Mort cave. Here he found a difference of only 99.5 cubic centimeters between males and females, while modern populations range from 129.5 to 220.7. Topinard, Broca's chief disciple, explained the increasing discrepancy through time as a result of differing evolutionary pressures upon dominant men and passive women:

> The man who fights for two or more in the struggle for existence, who has all the responsibility and the cares of tomorrow, who is constantly active in combating the environment and human rivals, needs more brain than the woman whom he must protect and nourish, the sedentary woman, lacking any interior occupations, whose role is to raise children, love, and be passive.

In 1879, Gustave Le Bon, chief misogynist of Broca's school, used these data to publish what must be the most vicious attack upon women in modern scientific literature (no one can top Aristotle). I do not claim his views were representative of Broca's school, but they were published in France's most respected anthropological journal. Le Bon concluded:

> In the most intelligent races, as among the Parisians, there are a large number of women whose brains are closer in size to those of gorillas than to the most developed male brains. This inferiority is so obvious that no one can contest it for a moment; only its degree is worth discussion. All psychologists who have studied the intelligence of women, as well as poets and novelists, recognize today that they represent the most inferior forms of human evolution and that they are closer to children and savages than to an adult, civilized man. They excel in fickleness, inconstancy, absence of thought and logic, and incapacity to reason. Without doubt there exist some distinguished women, very superior to the average man, but they are as exceptional as the birth of any monstrosity, as, for example, of a gorilla with two heads; consequently, we may neglect them entirely.

Nor did Le Bon shrink from the social implications of his views. He was horrified by the proposal of some American reformers to grant women higher education on the same basis as men:

> A desire to give them the same education, and, as a consequence, to propose the same goals for them, is a dangerous chimera. . . . The day when, misun-

derstanding the inferior occupations which nature has given her, women leave the home and take part in our battles; on this day a social revolution will begin, and everything that maintains the sacred ties of the family will disappear.

Sound familiar?[1]

I have reexamined Broca's data, the basis for all this derivative pronouncement, and I find his numbers sound but his interpretation ill-founded, to say the least. The data supporting his claim for increased difference through time can be easily dismissed. Broca based his contention on the samples from L'Homme Mort alone—only seven male and six female skulls in all. Never have so little data yielded such far ranging conclusions.

In 1888, Topinard published Broca's more extensive data on the Parisian hospitals. Since Broca recorded height and age as well as brain size, we may use modern statistics to remove their effect. Brain weight decreases with age, and Broca's women were, on average, considerably older than his men. Brain weight increases with height, and his average man was almost half a foot taller than his average woman. I used multiple regression, a technique that allowed me to assess simultaneously the influence of height and age upon brain size. In an analysis of the data for women, I found that, at average male height and age, a woman's brain would weigh 1212 grams. Correction for height and age reduces Broca's measured difference of 181 grams by more than a third, to 113 grams.

I don't know what to make of this remaining difference because I cannot assess other factors known to influence brain size in a major way. Cause of death has an important effect: degenerative disease often entails a substantial diminution of brain size. (This effect is separate from the decrease attributed to age alone.) Eugene Schreider, also working with Broca's data, found that men killed in accidents had brains weighing, on average, 60 grams more than men dying of infectious diseases. The best modern data I can find (from American hospitals) records a full 100-gram difference between death by degenerative arteriosclerosis and by violence or accident. Since so many of Broca's subjects were very elderly women, we may assume that lengthy degenerative disease was more common among them than among the men.

More importantly, modern students of brain size still have not agreed on a proper measure for eliminating the powerful effect of body size. Height is partly adequate, but men and women of the same height do not share the same body build. Weight is even worse than height, because most of its variation reflects nutrition rather than intrinsic size—fat versus skinny exerts little influence upon the brain. Manouvrier took up this subject in

8

9

10

11

---

[1]When I wrote this essay, I assumed that Le Bon was a marginal, if colorful, figure. I have since learned that he was a leading scientist, one of the founders of social psychology, and best known for a seminal study on crowd behavior, still cited today (*La psychologie des foules*, 1895), and for his work on unconscious motivation.—Gould's note.

the 1880s and argued that muscular mass and force should be used. He tried to measure this elusive property in various ways and found a marked difference in favor of men, even in men and women of the same height. When he corrected for what he called "sexual mass," women actually came out slightly ahead in brain size.

Thus, the corrected 113-gram difference is surely too large; the true figure is probably close to zero and may as well favor women as men. And 113 grams, by the way, is exactly the average difference between a 5 foot 4 inch and a 6 foot 4 inch male in Broca's data. We would not (especially us short folks) want to ascribe greater intelligence to tall men. In short, who knows what to do with Broca's data? They certainly don't permit any confident claim that men have bigger brains than women. 12

To appreciate the social role of Broca and his school, we must recognize that his statements about the brains of women do not reflect an isolated prejudice toward a single disadvantaged group. They must be weighed in the context of a general theory that supported contemporary social distinctions as biologically ordained. Women, blacks, and poor people suffered the same disparagement, but women bore the brunt of Broca's argument because he had easier access to data on women's brains. Women were singularly denigrated but they also stood as surrogates for other disenfranchised groups. As one of Broca's disciples wrote in 1881: "Men of the black races have a brain scarcely heavier than that of white women." This juxtaposition extended into many other realms of anthropological argument, particularly to claims that, anatomically and emotionally, both women and blacks were like white children—and that white children, by the theory of recapitulation, represented an ancestral (primitive) adult stage of human evolution. I do not regard as empty rhetoric the claim that women's battles are for all of us. 13

Maria Montessori did not confine her activities to educational reform for young children. She lectured on anthropology for several years at the University of Rome, and wrote an influential book entitled *Pedagogical Anthropology* (English edition, 1913). Montessori was no egalitarian. She supported most of Broca's work and the theory of innate criminality proposed by her compatriot Cesare Lombroso. She measured the circumference of children's heads in her schools and inferred that the best prospects had bigger brains. But she had no use for Broca's conclusions about women. She discussed Manouvrier's work at length and made much of his tentative claim that women, after proper correction of the data, had slightly larger brains than men. Women, she concluded, were intellectually superior, but men had prevailed heretofore by dint of physical force. Since technology has abolished force as an instrument of power, the era of women may soon be upon us: "In such an epoch there will really be superior human beings, there will really be men strong in morality and in sentiment. Perhaps in this way the reign of women is approaching, when the enigma of her anthropological superiority will be deciphered. Woman was always the custodian of human sentiment, morality and honor." 14

This represents one possible antidote to "scientific" claims for the con- 15
stitutional inferiority of certain groups. One may affirm the validity of biological distinctions but argue that the data have been misinterpreted by
prejudiced men with a stake in the outcome, and that disadvantaged groups
are truly superior. In recent years, Elaine Morgan has followed this strategy
in her *Descent of Woman,* a speculative reconstruction of human prehistory
from the woman's point of view—and as farcical as more famous tall tales
by and for men.

I prefer another strategy. Montessori and Morgan followed Broca's phi- 16
losophy to reach a more congenial conclusion. I would rather label the
whole enterprise of setting a biological value upon groups for what it is:
irrelevant and highly injurious. George Eliot well appreciated the special
tragedy that biological labeling imposed upon members of disadvantaged
groups. She expressed it for people like herself—women of extraordinary
talent. I would apply it more widely—not only to those whose dreams are
flouted but also to those who never realize that they may dream—but I
cannot match her prose. In conclusion, then, the rest of Eliot's prelude to
Middlemarch:

> The limits of variation are really much wider than anyone would imagine from
> the sameness of women's coiffure and the favorite love stories in prose and
> verse. Here and there a cygnet is reared uneasily among the ducklings in the
> brown pond, and never finds the living stream in fellowship with its own oary-
> footed kind. Here and there is born a Saint Theresa, foundress of nothing,
> whose loving heartbeats and sobs after an unattained goodness tremble
> off and are dispersed among hindrances instead of centering in some long-
> recognizable deed.

Questions to Start You Thinking

1. What flaws does Gould find in the reasoning of Paul Broca?
2. In paragraph 10 Gould admits his inability to "assess other factors known to influence brain size in a major way." Does this admission strengthen or weaken his case?
3. What is Gould's conclusion about biological arguments for the superiority of certain groups?
4. If there is a lesson to be learned from Gould's essay about the respect generally granted to the written word, what is it?

A Novelist Writes from Reading

A novelist whose work not only has pleased critics but also has topped best-seller lists, E. L. Doctorow has drawn real characters, settings, and situations from the American past. In his recent *Billy Bathgate* (1988), for instance, he portrays Dutch Schultz, a gangster who flourished in the 1930s. In this essay, Doctorow's keen interest in history leads him to a fresh and possibly controversial rereading of a classic American document.

A CITIZEN READS THE CONSTITUTION
E. L. Doctorow

Not including the amendments, it is approximately 5000 words long— 1
about the length of a short story. It is an enigmatically dry, unemotional
piece of work, tolling off in its monotone the structures and functions of
government, the conditions and obligations of office, the limitations of
powers, the means for redressing crimes and conducting commerce. It
makes itself the supreme law of the land. It concludes with instructions on
how it can amend itself, and undertakes to pay all the debts incurred by
the states under its indigent parent, the Articles of Confederation.

It is no more scintillating as reading than I remember it to have been 2
in Mrs. Brundage's seventh-grade civics class at Joseph H. Wade Junior
High School. It is 5000 words but reads like 50,000. It lacks high rhetoric
and shows not a trace of wit, as you might expect, having been produced
by a committee of lawyers. It uses none of the tropes of literature to create
empathetic states in the mind of the reader. It does not mean to persuade.
It abhors metaphor as nature abhors a vacuum.

One's first reaction upon reading it is to rush for relief to an earlier 3
American document, as alive with passion and the juices of outrage as the
work of any single artist:

> We hold these truths to be self-evident, that all men are created equal,
> that they are endowed by their Creator with certain unalienable Rights, that
> among these are Life, Liberty and the pursuit of Happiness. That to secure
> these rights, Governments are instituted among Men, deriving their just powers
> from the consent of the governed. That whenever any Form of Government
> becomes destructive of these ends, it is the Right of the People to alter or to
> abolish it, and to institute new Government.

Here is the substantive diction of a single human mind—Thomas Jef- 4
ferson's, as it happens—even as it speaks for all. It is engaged in the art
of literary revolution, rewriting history, overthrowing divine claims to rule
and genealogical hierarchies of human privilege as cruel frauds, defining
human rights as universal and distributing the source and power of government to the people governed. It is the radical voice of national liberation, combative prose lifting its musketry of self-evident truths and firing
away.

What reader does not wish the Constitution could have been written out 5
of something of the same spirit? Of course, we all know instinctively that
it could not, that statute-writing in the hands of lawyers has its own demands, and those are presumably precision and clarity, which call for sentences bolted at all four corners with *wherein*'s and *whereunder*'s and
thereof's and *therein*'s and notwithstanding the *foregoing*'s.

Still and all, our understanding of the Constitution must come of an 6
assessment of its character as a composition, and it would serve us to

explore further why it is the way it is. . . . It is true but not sufficient to say that the Constitution reads as it does because it was written by a committee of lawyers. Something more is going on here. Every written composition has a voice, a persona, a character of presentation, whether by design of the author or not. The voice of the Constitution is a quiet voice. It does not rally us; it does not call on self-evident truths; it does not arm itself with philosophy or political principle; it does not argue, explain, condemn, excuse or justify. It is postrevolutionary. Not claiming righteousness, it is, however, suffused with rectitude. It is this way because it seeks standing in the world, the elevation of the unlawful acts of men—unlawful first because the British government has been overthrown, and second because the confederation of the states has been subverted—to the lawful standing of nationhood. All the *herein*'s and *whereas*'s and *thereof*'s are not only legalisms; they also happen to be the diction of the British Empire, the language of the deposed. Nothing has changed that much, the Constitution says, lying; we are nothing that you won't recognize.

But there is something more. The key verb of the text is *shall,* as in   7 "All legislative powers herein granted shall be vested in a Congress of the United States which shall consist of a Senate and a House of Representatives," or "New States may be admitted by the Congress into this Union; but no new State shall be formed or erected within the jurisdiction of any other State." The Constitution does not explicitly concern itself with the grievances that brought it about. It is syntactically futuristic: it prescribes what is to come. It prophesies. Even today, living two hundred years into the prophecy, we read it and find it still ahead of us, still extending itself in time. The Constitution gives law and assumes for itself the power endlessly to give law. It ordains. In its articles and sections, one after another, it offers a ladder to heaven. It is cold, distant, remote as a voice from on high, self-authenticating.

Through most of history kings and their servitor churches did the ordaining, and always in the name of God. But here the people do it: "We the People . . . do ordain and establish this Constitution for the United States." And the word for God appears nowhere in the text. Heaven forbid! In fact, its very last stricture is that "no religious test shall ever be required as a qualification to any office or public trust under the United States."

The voice of the Constitution is the inescapably solemn self-consciousness of the people giving the law unto themselves. But since in the Judeo-Christian world of Western civilization all given law imitates God—God being the ultimate lawgiver—in affecting the transhuman voice of law, that dry monotone that disdains persuasion, the Constitution not only takes on the respectable sound of British statute, it more radically assumes the character of scripture.

The ordaining voice of the Constitution is scriptural, but in resolutely   10 keeping the authority for its dominion in the public consent, it presents itself as the sacred text of secular humanism.

I wish Mrs. Brundage had told me that back in Wade Junior High School.   11
I wish Jerry Falwell's and Jimmy Swaggart's and Pat Robertson's teach-   12
ers had taught them that back in their junior high schools.

Questions to Start You Thinking

1. What differences does Doctorow find between the prose of the Constitution and that of the Declaration of Independence? How does he account for the differences?

2. What seems to you the reason for Doctorow's emphasis on what the Constitution is *not*? Where in the essay does he shift his attention to what the Constitution *is*? What, according to the author, are the Constitution's chief strengths?

3. In paragraph 6, Doctorow accuses the Constitution of "lying." What does he mean?

4. In this essay Doctorow shares the insights he has gained from his close reading of the Constitution. Does he back them up with sufficient evidence? Which of his insights seem to you the most valuable?

CHAPTER 4

Writing from Conversation

Don't know what to write about? Go talk with someone. When you exchange facts, thoughts, and feelings with people, you both give and receive. Not only do you find out things from others that you didn't know, but by speaking your own thoughts and feelings, you shape them and define them in words.

Listen closely to an hour's discussion between a class and an anthropology professor, and you might get enough material for a whole paper. Just as likely, you might get a paper's worth of information, thoughts, and feelings from a five-minute exchange with a mechanic who relines brakes. Both are experts. But even people who aren't experts in the usual sense of the word may provide you with material.

As this chapter suggests, you can direct a conversation, ask questions to elicit what you want to find out. You do so in that special kind of conversation called *interviewing*. Newspaper reporters, as you know, interview people continually, and college writers can do so as well. An interview is a conversation with a purpose: usually to help you know the other person or to find out what the other person knows.

LEARNING FROM OTHER WRITERS

Here are two fine essays whose writers met ordinary people face to face and reported their conversations. The student essay by Michael R. Tein was written for a college English course.

Student Essay

FLOWERS FOR CHAPEL STREET
Michael R. Tein

Few people on New Haven's Chapel Street ever notice   1
Louie Weisser. He presses his round back to the cement
storefront, his hands reach deep into his pockets rattling
his change, and he surveys his flowers. He sells them from a
pushcart the way he saw done on the Lower East Side of New
York City where he was born 72 years ago. He wears the same
clothes almost every day: a burgundy knit-collar shirt, a
stained tan V-neck, baggy herringbone trousers, and cloth
lace shoes. A blue nylon hunting cap with earflaps hugs his
head. It seems to be sewn right into his sparse scalp with
the threads of hair that remain. His cropped mustache has
browned under his nostrils from the smoke of thousands of
cigarettes. Louie draws a Lucky Strike from its box and
crimps the pack's edge so the remaining smokes stay huddled
together. The cellophane crinkles as he shoves them back
into his pocket. "I started smokin' these 'cause my father
smoked 'em. I used to steal them from him when I was a kid."

Louie isn't much of a flower man. He drove a local bus   2
for 38 years ("a couple million miles, I would figure") before he started to help out his son's infant flower business.
His brother "got a B.S. and M.S. and all that" and was graduated from Yale, class of 1927. Lou thinks that he might have
prospered in business but has no regrets. Someone has to be
the working man.

Louie's years make him a remnant. He misses the five-   3
cent cup of coffee and the quarter pack of Luckys, but what
he remembers most is the prejudice. His brother's credentials could only get him a job driving his father's laundry
truck. "Are you Jewish?" job interviewers asked. "Well, we
don't hire Jews." Lou's former employer, the Connecticut

Transit bus company, spurned blacks from the payroll. "It
was strictly a white man's job. Now they got women, blacks,
they got everything now. They have quotas, they gotta.
It's a law now. It's not that they wanna do it, they're
forced to do it." He remembers going into a diner as a youth
and having the waitress refuse to serve his black friend.
"So we all walked out, in protest you know, to say 'the hell
with you.' We were kids, we almost started a riot there, you
know, my younger days." He laughs. "Ain't that stupid."

Louie cannot fathom stereotypes. "They say that all the 4
Jews have money," he remarks. "That's not true. You look
at the millionaires in this country and how many Jews do you
find? Kennedys aren't Jewish, the Rockefellers aren't Jewish.
Why do they say the Jews have money? We never hurt, robbed,
or stole from anybody."

Lou balks at any distinction between races or religions. 5
He married a Protestant and his two sons were baptized at
Trinity Church a block away on the New Haven Green. "Just
live up to those ten commandments and you've got it made," he
says. "Everybody was Jewish before the advent of Christ.
Christians came from the word 'Christ' and Christ was Jewish.
I'm modernized," Lou proclaims. "I don't even go to shul
anymore."

A few times each day, Louie ventures into the Copper 6
Kitchen for a cup of coffee and a buttered Danish. He smokes
a cigarette, spins his ashtray back and forth, and tries to
work out the day's crossword, which he never finishes. He
files it in his back pocket. He eyes his cart through the
luncheonette entrance. Maybe a customer will come, maybe
not. "You may be wise, but I'm Weisser," he shrugs his
shoulders. "I got these old jokes." Lou chuckles to himself
as he waves his cigarette at the waitress to signal for a re-
fill.

Louie peddles all day until about six o'clock. The 7
construction work clouds the street with its refuse, jackham-

mers pound the pavement, and Yale students scurry by beneath
the shadow of Vanderbilt and Bingham Halls. Lou is oblivious
to the tumult. His flowers are his Garden of Eden. With
each rose or swamp lily ("believe it or not, a swamp lily")
that he sells, his innocent, toothy, stubble-lined smile reveals that this flower is his message of love and relief to a
world which is far too complex, a world which has swept him
along, rudderless, in its current. His family sailed from
Russia to "the United States of America--the land of opportunity." The terms are still interchangeable for him. Lou was
not the smart one. He drove a bus while his brother studied
chemistry. His sons are grown. One is a teacher. The
other is now his employer in the flower business. He wor-
ships both their achievements and failures, and his eyes
bulge out and shine when he speaks of them.

Lou's eyes are his most remarkable feature. The years   8
have pushed them back into the folds of skin, and a yellow
film coats the veiny whites. Each iris glows a deep purple.
Once, his eyes might have been a hazel or blue, but they have
filtered out so much darkness from his world that the residue
seems to persist. He sees only good.

"I made friends with these people." Louie points to the   9
stores behind him. "I don't hurt anybody or block anything."
Lou sets a high premium on friends. He needs them. An old
black man shuffles along behind Lou. A crumpled hat wraps
his head. He smiles at Lou through crooked and rotting teeth
as he pushes a grocery cart containing fifteen or so discarded cans. "That's my friend Richard. He looks about my
age. He used to work in a restaurant washing dishes, now
he's on social security." Richard does not beg. He returns
New Haven's cans for the five-cent deposit, and Lou respects
him for that. He pities the young bums who ask him for dimes
to buy cheap wine. After a while he stops giving. "I don't
think that I should support that."

Lou is a terrible businessman. His heart beats with the   10
people and not with the buck. His son tells him to charge

two dollars per rose; "for you, one dollar," Louie says. But with Louie, "for you" includes almost everyone, that is to say, all of his friends.

So Lou Weisser smiles and talks to Chapel Street, and   11
Chapel Street buys his flowers. The buses roll by, stores open and close, but few are able to pass without a word to Lou. "I'm really not the important part here," he says. "I'm just the background."

Questions to Start You Thinking

1. Where in his essay does Tein rely directly on conversation with his subject? Summarize what you think the old man's words reveal about his values and his outlook on life.

2. Go back to "Flowers for Chapel Street" and reread it quickly, looking for answers to these questions about Tein's strategies as a writer: (a) Which of the resources other than conversing (recalling, reading, observing, imagining) does Tein employ? (b) Which of Louie Weisser's physical characteristics does the writer choose to emphasize?

3. In paragraph 10, Tein calls Louie "a terrible businessman." To what extent is this a negative criticism of the man?

4. In its early drafts, "Flowers for Chapel Street" had one sentence added to its conclusion: "On the contrary, Lou, more like the director." Why do you think Tein removed it? Which ending do you prefer?

William Least Heat Moon's conversation with Barbara Pierre, in St. Martinville, Louisiana, appears in the author's acclaimed *Blue Highways* (1982), aptly subtitled *A Journey into America*. The author, a "mixed-blood" who signs himself with a translation of his Sioux tribal name, wrote his book after traveling through the country on small roads, visiting and talking with unsung people wherever he encountered them.

A VIEW OF PREJUDICE
William Least Heat Moon

Because of a broken sealed-beam headlight and Zatarain's Creole Mus-   1
tard, an excellent native mustard, I met Barbara Pierre. I had just come out of Dugas' grocery with four jars of Zatarain's, and we almost collided on the sidewalk. She said, "You're not from St. Martinville, are you? You can't be."

"I'm from Missouri."   2

"What in the world are you doing here? Got a little Huck Finn in you?"   3

"Just followed the bayou. Now I'm looking for the Ford agency." 4

"Coincidences. I work there. I'll show you the way." 5

She was a secretary at the agency and took classes at the University 6
of Southwestern Louisiana in Lafayette when she could. I asked about St.
Martinville, but she had to start working before we could say much.

"Here's an idea," she said. "Come by at noon and we can have lunch 7
at my place. I live in the project on the other side of the bayou."

I picked her up at twelve. She asked about the trip, especially about 8
Selma and how things were as I saw them. "A white man griped about
changes, and a black said there weren't enough changes to gripe about."

"That's us too. What we want is slow coming—if it's coming at all. Older 9
blacks here are scared of whites and won't do much for change if it means
risk. Others don't care as long as everything gets smothered over with
politeness by whites. Young blacks see the hypocrisy—even when it's not
there. But too many of them are juked on drugs, and that's where some of
this town wants us."

"Don't any whites here try to help?" 10

"A few, but if a white starts helping too much, they get cut off or shut 11
down by the others and end up paying almost the price we do. Sure, we
got good whites—when they're not scared out of showing sympathy."

On Margaret Street, she pointed to her apartment in a small one-story 12
brick building. Standard federal housing. As we went to the door, a shadowy
face watched from behind a chintz curtain in another apartment.

"See that? Could be the start of bad news," she said. 13

"Maybe I should leave. I don't want to cause trouble for you." 14

"Too late. Besides, I live my own life here. I won't be pushed. But it'll 15
come back in some little way. Smart remark, snub. One old white lady kicks
me at the library. Swings her feet under the table because she doesn't want
my kind in there. I could break her in two, she's so frail. She'll be kicking
like a heifer if she gets wind of this."

Barbara Pierre's apartment was a tidy place but for books on the sofa. 16
"You can see I still use the library even with the nuisances. The kicking
bitch hides books I return so I get overdue notices and have to go prove I
turned the book in. I explain what's going on, but nothing changes. Simplest
thing is trouble."

"That's what I heard in Selma." 17

"I'm not alone, but sometimes it seems like a conspiracy. Especially in 18
little towns. Gossip and bigotry—that's the blood and guts."

"Was that person who just looked out the window white?" 19

"Are you crazy? Nobody on this end of Margaret Street is white. That's 20
what I mean about us blacks not working together. Half this town is black,
and we've only got one elected black official. Excuse my language, but for
all the good he does this side of the bayou, he's one useless black mofo."

"Why don't you do something? I mean you personally." 21

"I do. And when I do, I get both sides coming down on me. Including 22

Barbara Pierre in St. Martinville, Louisiana

my own family. Everywhere I go, sooner or later, I'm in the courtroom. Duplicity! That's my burning pot. I've torn up more than one court of law."

We sat down at her small table. A copy of *Catch-22* lay open. 23

"Something that happened a few years ago keeps coming back on me. 24 When I was living in Norristown, outside Philadelphia, I gained a lot of weight and went to a doctor. She gave me some diet pills but never explained they were basically speed, and I developed a minor drug problem.

I went to the hospital and the nuns said if I didn't sign certain papers they couldn't admit me. So I signed and they put me in a psychiatric ward. Took two hellish weeks to prove I didn't belong there. God, it's easy to get somebody adjudicated crazy."

"Adjudicated?" 25

"You don't know the word, or you didn't think I knew it?" 26

"It's the right word. Go on." 27

"So now, because I tried to lose thirty pounds, people do a job on my 28 personality. But if I shut up long enough, things quiet down. Still, it's the old pattern: any nigger you can't control is crazy."

As we ate our sandwiches and drank Barq's rootbeer, she asked whether 29 I had been through Natchitoches. I said I hadn't.

"They used to have a statue up there on the main street. Called the 30 'Good Darkie Statue.' It was an old black man, slouched shoulders, big possum-eating smile. Tipping his hat. Few years ago, blacks made them take it down. Whites couldn't understand. Couldn't see the duplicity in that statue—duplicity on *both* sides. God almighty! I'll promise them one thing: ain't gonna be no more gentle darkies croonin' down on the levee."

I smiled at her mammy imitation, but she shook her head. "In the sixties 31 I wanted that statue blown to bits. It's stored in Baton Rouge now at LSU, but they put it in the wrong building. Ought to be in the capitol reminding people. Preserve it so nobody forgets. Forgives, okay—but not forgets."

"Were things bad when you were a child?" 32

"Strange thing. I was born here in 'forty-one and grew up here, but I 33 don't remember prejudice. My childhood was warm and happy—especially when I was reading. Maybe I was too young to see. I don't know. I go on about the town, but I love it. I've put my time in the cities—New Orleans, Philly. Your worst Southern cracker is better than a Northern liberal, when it comes to duplicity anyway, because you know right off where the cracker crumbles. With the Northerner, you don't know until it counts, and that's when you get a job done on yourself."

"I'd rather see a person shut up about his prejudices." 34

"You haven't been deceived. Take my job. I was pleased to get it. 35 Thought it was a breakthrough for me and other blacks here. Been there three weeks, and next Wednesday is my last day."

"What happened?" 36

"Duplicity's what happened. White man in the shop developed a bad 37 back, so they moved him inside. His seniority gets my job. I see the plot—somebody in the company got pressured to get rid of me."

"Are you going to leave town?" 38

"I'm staying. That's my point. I'll take St. Martinville over what I've seen 39 of other places. I'm staying here to build a life for myself and my son. I'll get married again. Put things together." She got up and went to the window. "I don't know, maybe I'm too hard on the town. In an underhanded way, things work here—mostly because old blacks know how to get along with whites. So they're good darkies? They own their own homes. They don't live in a rat-ass ghetto. There's contentment. Roots versus disorder." She stopped abruptly and smiled. "Even German soldiers they put in the POW camp here to work the cane fields wanted to stay on."

We cleared the table and went to the front room. A wall plaque: 40

OH LORD, HELP ME THIS DAY
TO KEEP MY BIG MOUTH SHUT.

On a bookshelf by the window was the two-volume microprint edition of the *Oxford English Dictionary*, the one sold with a magnifying glass.

"I love it," she said. "Book-of-the-Month Club special. Seventeen-fifty.   41
Haven't finished paying for it though."

"Is it the only one in town?"   42

"Doubt it. We got brains here. After the aristocracy left Paris during the   43
French Revolution, a lot of them settled in St. Martinville, and we got known as *Le Petit Paris*. Can you believe this little place was a cultural center only second to New Orleans? Town started slipping when the railroad put the bayou steamers out of business, but the church is proof of what we had."

"When you finish the college courses, what then?"   44

"I'd like to teach elementary school. If I can't teach, I want to be a   45
teacher's aide. But—here's a big 'but'—if I can make a living, I'll write books for children. We need black women writing, and my courses are in journalism and French. Whatever happens, I hope they don't waste my intelligence."

She went to wash up. I pulled out one of her books: *El Señor Presidente*   46
by Guatemalan novelist Miguel Asturias. At page eighty-five she had underlined two sentences: "The chief thing is to gain time. We must be patient."

On the way back to the agency, she said, "I'll tell you something that   47
took me a long time to figure out—but I know how to end race problems."

"Is this a joke?"   48

"Might as well be. Find a way to make people get bored with hating   49
instead of helping. Simple." She laughed. "That's what it boils down to."

Questions to Start You Thinking

1. What feelings about her town and about the people in it does Barbara Pierre reveal as she talks? What reasons does she give for wanting to stay in St. Martinville?

2. Based on evidence from the essay, what proportion of his conversation with Pierre would you say the author has included? For what reasons do you think he omitted the rest?

3. To what extent does the author's conversation with Pierre provide insights into more than individual personality?

4. Imagine that you have a chance to interview Barbara Pierre. Make a list of ten questions that you would ask her, questions that either extend topics covered in William Least Heat Moon's essay or that cover areas on which you think Pierre's comments might be interesting.

LEARNING BY WRITING

The Assignment: Interviewing

Write a paper about someone you know, a paper that depends primarily on a conversation with that person. Write about any acquaintance, friend, or relative whose traits, interests, activities, background, or outlook on life you think will interest your readers. It need not be anyone remarkable. Your purpose is to show as thoroughly as you can this person's character and personality as revealed through his or her conversation—in other words, to bring your subject alive for your readers.

Among student papers we have read that grew out of a similar assignment were the following.

> A man wrote about a high school science teacher who had quit teaching for a higher-paying job in the computer industry only to return three years later to the classroom.

> A man wrote about an acquaintance who had embraced the hippie lifestyle in the 1960s by "dropping out" of mainstream society.

> A woman recorded the thoughts and feelings of a discouraged farmer she had known since childhood.

> A man wrote what he learned about one woman's aspirations when he interviewed the most ardent feminist he knew.

If you would prefer not to write about a person but rather interview someone for information *about* something, see "Other Assignments" (p. 113).

Generating Ideas

It may be that the minute you read the assignment, an image of the perfect subject will flash into your mind. If that's the case, consider yourself lucky and go at once in search of that person to set up an appointment. If, on the other hand, you draw a blank at first, you'll need to spend a little time casting about for a likely person to interview. As you begin examining the possibilities, you may find it helpful to consider one or more of the following questions.

DISCOVERY CHECKLIST: INTERVIEWING

- Of the people you know, which ones do you most enjoy talking with?
- Are you acquainted with anyone whose life has been unusually eventful, stressful, or successful? If not, don't be discouraged. Even unspectacular lives, as Tein and Least Heat Moon demonstrate, can make interesting reading.

- Among the people you know, which have passionate convictions about society, politics, sex, childrearing, or any other topic on which you'd expect them to hold forth in lively words? A likely subject may be someone actively engaged in a cause.
- Do you know anyone who has traits you particularly respect and admire — or deplore?
- Is there anyone whose background and life history you would like to know more about?
- Is there anyone in your area whose lifestyle is utterly different from your own and from that of most people you know?
- Is there anyone whose line of work you'd like to know more about?

Set up your interview. You might list the names of a few people you'd like to talk with and then find out whether your prospective source will grant you an interview. Make sure that your subject can talk with you at some length — an hour, say. That should be enough time for you to conduct a thorough interview.

You'll want to make sure, too, that this person has no objections to appearing in your paper. If you sense any reluctance on your prospective subject's part, probably your wisest course is to go in search of a new subject.

There's an advantage to scheduling the interview on your subject's own ground: his or her home or workplace. As we've seen from both Tein's and Least Heat Moon's essays, an interviewer can learn a great deal from the objects with which a person surrounds himself or herself, and an interview can gain a great deal of life.

Don't be timid about asking for an interview. When you interview a subject, you acknowledge that person as someone with valuable things to say. Most people will be flattered by your interest in them and their lives.

Prepare questions. The interview will go better if you meet your subject at the appointed time and come prepared with some questions to ask. Give these careful thought. What kinds of questions will encourage your subject to open up? Questions about the person's background, everyday tasks, favorite leisure-time activities, hopes, and aspirations are likely to bring forth answers that you'll want to record. Sometimes a question that asks your subject to do a little imagining will elicit a revealing response. (If your house were on fire, what are the first objects you'd try to save from the flames? If you were stranded on a desert island, what books would you like to have with you?) You won't find out everything there is to know about the person you're interviewing. You'll have to focus on whatever aspect of that person's life you think will best reveal his or her character. Good questions will enable you to lead the conversation where you want it to go and get it back on track when it strays too far afield. Such questions will also help you avoid awkward silences. Here are some of the questions Michael Tein had scribbled down before going to see Louie Weisser, a man with whom he seems to have had only a slight acquaintance:

Where do you live?
Does your family live in New Haven?
When is business best?
Where do you get your flowers?
Who are your customers?
Does the construction bother you?
Does the noise bother you?
Is this the best street corner?
Any trouble with robbers?
Competition?
What got you involved in the flower business?

Probably Tein didn't have to use all those questions. One good question can get some people going for hours. Some experts insist that four or five are enough to bring to any interview, but we believe it's better to err on the side of too many than too few. If, when you're actually talking with your subject, some of the questions you wrote strike you as downright silly, you can easily skip them. Some of Tein's questions would have elicited very brief answers. Others—like "What got you involved in the flower business?"—clearly inspired Louie to respond with enthusiasm.

Be open and observant. Michael Tein was willing to let the conversation stray down interesting byways. Sometimes the key question, the one that takes the interview in its most rewarding direction, is the one the interviewer didn't write down in advance, one that simply grew out of something the subject said. Tein allowed Louie to answer some questions he hadn't even asked, and he really *listened* to what Louie was saying. William Least Heat Moon, in the account of his conversation with Barbara Pierre, demonstrates both the same flexibility and the same genuine interest in his subject. Of course, if the conversation heads toward a dead end, you can always bring it back by volunteering, "But to get back to what you were saying about. . . ."

During his interview, Least Heat Moon does something else that will later add vividness to his chapter about Barbara Pierre. In her apartment he uses his eyes as well as his ears. He observes what's in the room—books on the sofa, an open copy of *Catch-22* on the table, a wall plaque, an edition of the *Oxford English Dictionary,* a Guatemalan novel in which Pierre had underlined two sentences. He asks about the details that interest him, and he works Pierre's answers into his account. When you conduct an interview, you too can notice and ask about distinctive items in the subject's environment. It may encourage your subject to reveal unexpected facets of his or her personality.

Sometimes a question won't interest your subject as much as you'd hoped it would. Sometimes the person you're interviewing may seem reluctant to answer a question, especially if you're unwittingly trespassing into private territory. Don't badger. If you have the confidence to wait silently for a bit, you might be rewarded. But if the silence persists, just go on to the next question.

Decide how to record the interview. Many interviewers advise against bringing a tape recorder to an interview on the grounds that sometimes it inhibits the person being interviewed. Too often, it makes the interviewer lazy about really concentrating on what the subject is saying. Too often, the objections go, it tempts the interviewer simply to quote the rambling conversation as it appears on the tape without shaping it into good writing. If you do bring a tape recorder to your interview, be sure that the person you're talking with has no objections to it. Arm yourself with a pad of paper and a pen or a few sharp pencils just in case the recorder malfunctions or the tape runs out before the interview ends. And don't let your mind wander. Martha Weinman Lear, a former editor with the *New York Times Magazine,* tape-records interviews but at the same time takes notes. "With the notes I hit all the high points, everything I know I want to use in the story. Then I can go back to expand on those points without having to listen to four hours of tapes, three-and-a-half hours of which might be garbage."[1]

Many interviewers approach their subjects without a tape recorder, with only paper and pen or pencil so that they can take notes unobtrusively as the interview proceeds. However, you won't be able to write down everything the person says as he or she is talking. It's more important to look your subject in the eye and keep the conversation lively than to scribble down everything he or she says. But be sure to record on the scene whatever you want to remember in exact detail: names and dates, numbers, addresses, whatever. If the person you're interviewing says anything that is so memorable that you want to record it exactly, take time to jot down the speaker's words just as he or she said them. Put quotation marks around them so that when you transcribe your notes later, you can put them, quoted, into your paper.

What about a telephone interview? It may sound like an easy way to work, but it is often less valuable than talking with the subject in person. You won't be able to duplicate by phone the lively interplay you can achieve in a successful face-to-face encounter. You'll be unable to observe the subject's possessions and environment, which so often reveal a person's personality, or see your subject's smiles, frowns, or other body language. Meet with your subject in person if at all possible.

As soon as the interview ends, rush to the nearest available desk or table and write down everything you remember but were unable to record during the conversation. Do this while the conversation is still fresh in your mind.

---

[1] Quoted in "The Art of Interviewing," text of a symposium, *The Author's Guild Bulletin* June–July 1982, p. 17.

The questions you took with you into the interview will guide your memory, as will any notes you took while your subject talked.

Shaping a Draft

If you now have plenty of material and feel you know what matters, you are ready to start writing your first draft immediately. You have a good notion of what to include, what to emphasize, what to quote directly, what to sum up. But if your notes seem a confused jumble, you may need to approach your first draft more slowly. What are you to do with the bales of material you have amassed during the interview? Inevitably, much of what you collected will be "garbage," as Martha Weinman Lear calls it. Does that mean you should have collected less? No, it means that as you plan, you have to zero in on what is most valuable and throw out the rest. How do you do this?

Evaluate your material. Start by making a list of those details you're already pretty sure you want to include. To guide you as you sift and evaluate your material, you may find it useful to ask yourself a few questions.

What part of the conversation gave you the most insight into your subject's character and circumstances?

Which of the direct quotations you wrote down reveal the most about your subject? Which are the most amusing, pithy, witty, surprising, or outrageous?

Which of the objects that you observed in the subject's environment provided you with valuable clues about your subject's interests?

What, if anything, did your subject's body language reveal? Did it give evidence of discomfort, pride, self-confidence, shyness, pomposity?

Did the tone of voice of the person you interviewed tell you anything about his or her state of mind?

Is there one theme, one emphasis that runs through the material you have written down? If so, what is it?

If you have a great deal of material and if, as often happens, your subject's conversation tended to ramble, you may want to emphasize just one or two things about him or her: a personality trait, the person's views on one particular topic, the influences that shaped the views he or she holds today. More than likely your notes will reveal some dominant impression around which to organize your portrait.

As interviews go, William Least Heat Moon's is a bit unusual in that, without in any way detracting from his subject, the author reveals much about himself as well. Michael Tein concentrates exclusively on what Lou Weisser told him. Probably it's easier to leave yourself out and concentrate on your subject. That way you have to concern yourself with only one side of the conversation.

As you write, you may find yourself unable to read your hasty handwriting, or you may discover you need some crucial bit of information that somehow escaped you when you were taking notes. In such a case, telephone the person you interviewed so that you can check out what you need to know. Have your questions ready so that you do not need to take much of your subject's time.

Bring your subject alive. At the beginning of your paper, can you introduce the person you interviewed in a way that will frame him or her immediately in your reader's mind? A quotation, a bit of physical description, a portrait of your subject at home or at work can bring the person instantly to life.

From time to time you'll want to quote your subject directly. Be as accurate as possible, and don't put into quotation marks something your subject couldn't possibly have uttered. Sometimes you may care to quote a whole sentence or more, sometimes just a phrase. Tein smoothly works a brief direct quotation into paragraph 2 of "Flowers for Chapel Street":

> His brother "got a B.S. and M.S. and all that" and
> was graduated from Yale, class of 1927.

Only the words in quotation marks are actually Louie's, and they make clear the old man's rather casual attitude toward academic achievement. In the rest of the paragraph, Tein merely sums up much of what Lou has told him. Throughout his paper he moves gracefully back and forth between direct quotation and summing up.

In *Reporting,* a collection of interviews, noted reporter Lillian Ross suggests that when you quote directly the person you have interviewed, you

---

WRITING WITH A COMPUTER: CONVERSING

One problem with turning conversation into writing is that the results may not make easy reading. There are differences between what we say and what we write. When people talk, their facial expression, voice inflections, and gestures can lend interest and emphasis to their words. But sometimes even the conversation of a lively speaker, transcribed word for word, will sound dull and long-winded.

Word processing can help you counter this problem. Set down your subject's words as fully as you can recall. If you tape-recorded them, set them down word for word. Then scroll through the results on the screen. What parts stand out? What remarks, just as they are, will be interesting and revealing and will help fulfill the purpose of your paper? Highlight these in bold or with underlining (which you can easily undo), or with another highlighting tool that your word processing program provides. Since you can delete with a couple of keystrokes, it will be easy to keep the best material and cut the rest. Or on the screen, you can readily replace any comment that seems tedious with a terse summary.

work hard to "find the quotations that get to the truth of what that person is. That does not mean that you make up quotations. Somewhere along the line, in the time you spend with your subject, you will find the quotations that are significant—that reveal the character of the person, that present as close an approximation of the truth as you can achieve." Keep writing until you believe you have come close to that truth.

Rewriting

Wait a few hours or a few days before you look again at the early draft you have written. As you pick it up to read it over, keep in mind that your purpose was to bring alive for your reader the person you interviewed. Your main task now is to make sure you have succeeded in doing that. This brief self-quiz may help you in reviewing your work.

REVISION CHECKLIST: WRITING FROM CONVERSATION

- Have you merely skimmed over what the person said to you, or have you been careful to represent the conversation in enough detail to reveal a unique individual, worth paying attention to?
- Are some statements you quoted of lesser importance, better suited to summing up or indirect quotation ("He said that he had suffered enough") than to direct quotation ("He said, 'I have suffered enough' ")? Should some of what you merely summed up be given greater prominence?
- Have you included details that show what your subject most cares about?
- Have you put in a few of your own observations, inspired perhaps by objects you noticed in the place where the interview was conducted?
- Do the person's voice, bearing, and gestures come through in your writing?
- Read the direct quotations out loud. Do they sound likely to have come out of the mouth of the person you're portraying?
- Do the things he or she says reveal personality, character, mood?
- If any of your classmates are acquainted with your subject, do you think they would be able to recognize him or her from what you have written, even if the person's name were omitted from your account? Find out.
- Does any of the material you put into your paper strike you now as drivel? If so, be merciless about getting rid of it.
- Do any additional details, left out of your early draft, now seem worth putting in after all? If so, it's not too late to find a place for them and add them. Skim over your interview notes or listen again to selected parts of your tape recording for material whose significance may not have struck you while you were deciding what to include.
- Could your paper have a stronger beginning?
- What can you strike out?

If you find it hard to criticize your own work, ask a friend to read your draft and suggest how to make the portrait more vivid, clear, and honest.

PEER EDITING CHECKLIST: WRITING FROM CONVERSATION

- Give your overall reaction to the paper.
- What seems to make the person interviewed interesting to the writer? What do you understand to be the writer's major impression of or insight into the person? "Nutshell" this.
- Do you have any questions about this person that you'd like answered in the paper but that aren't?
- Does the writer tell you anything about the person that seems unconnected to his or her major impression or insight?
- How does the person interviewed "sound" to you? Has the writer quoted anything that seems at odds with the general impression you now have of the person?
- Would you leave out any of the conversation the writer used? Underline any that you find not connected to the major impression or insight.
- Look at how the writer has arranged the materials. Would you suggest any changes in their organization?
- Does each part connect logically with other parts? Put a star anywhere that you think the writer needs to work more on transitions.
- Look particularly at the beginning of the essay. Did the writer make you want to get to know the person? If so, how? If not, what got in your way?
- Circle on the manuscript any problems with spelling, punctuation, grammar, or word choice that hindered you as you read.

Double-check your quotations. As you write your final draft, be sure that where you have omitted words from a direct quotation, you have substituted an ellipsis mark (. . .)—three dots that show where omissions have occurred—and that the sentence that contains the ellipsis makes sense. Suppose you want to quote Marta, who was interviewed by anthropologist Oscar Lewis for his landmark study of a poor Mexican family, *The Children of Sanchez* (New York: Random House, 1961). Marta said, "I had been living in the Casa Grande, but there was an argument with Delila and I moved to my aunt Guadalupe's again, this time staying until just before Trini was born." Suppose that you want to quote just part of that sentence in your paper. You might do it like this: "I had been living in the Casa Grande, but there was an argument with Delila and I moved to my aunt Guadalupe's . . . staying until just before Trini was born." The sentence is faithful enough to the original so that it doesn't distort the speaker's words, but the three dots indicate that something has been omitted.

Occasionally you may have included a quotation within a quotation, as Lewis does a little later in his interview with Marta, who says, "When Guadalupe had gone begging Prudencia to let them stay in a corner of her room, she was told, 'My house is yours, but there is no room for your son.' " When you quote your subject quoting someone else, your subject's words appear in regular quotation marks, the other person's in *single* quotation marks. If your written interview, like William Least Heat Moon's, contains dialogue, be sure to start a new paragraph each time a different person speaks.

Whenever you, the writer, want to emphasize something your subject didn't, underline the material and add "emphasis mine" in brackets:

```
"I've always believed that if you bring children into the
world, you owe them at least twenty years of your-
self" [emphasis mine].
```

As you can see from these illustrations, quoting from conversation requires special attention to punctuation, and you should check your paper carefully for mechanical errors before you hand it in.

FOR GROUP LEARNING
Take part in a collective interview. Let your whole class or just your writing group interview someone who has some special knowledge or who represents a walk of life that you want to learn more about. Of course, this means finding a person likely to have something of interest to say who wouldn't mind meeting with your whole class or group. (Public figures, like writers, who occasionally visit schools, are used to facing the questions of a whole class.)

Before your subject arrives, let your class or your writing group take time for preparatory discussion: What do you want to find out? What questions or lines of questioning do you wish to pursue? (If the outcome of the interview will be one group-written paper, then the group might appoint two members to act as reporters or recording secretaries and take notes.) We suggest that when the interviewee is present, each questioner be allowed (as far as time permits) to ask all of his or her main questions before yielding the floor to the next questioner. This way each person can pursue a line of thought all the way. Later, students may write their individual papers based on the group interview, showing what they have learned not only from their own questions but from everybody's.

An alternative plan is to collaborate on the paper. Your writing group might meet after the interview to sift what you learned. The two reporters who took notes during the interview might show (or read aloud) their notes to the group to check the accuracy of both questions and answers. To parcel out the project fairly, these reporters shouldn't be asked to write the paper, too. Designate two or three others to write what the group has learned. One might write a draft and the others polish it.

Other Assignments

1. Write a paper based on an interview with at least two members of your extended family about some incident that is part of your family lore. You may find yourself amused to notice that different people's accounts of the event don't always agree. If you can't reconcile them, combine them into one vivid account, noting that some details may be more trustworthy than others. Give credit to your sources. The paper that results might just be worth saving for posterity.

2. Interview someone who is in a line of work you think you might like to enter yourself. Find out what this person recommends you do to prepare for the job that interests you. Then write a paper detailing your subject's advice.

3. Interview a mother you know to find out what it was like for her to give birth, and write a paper in which you discuss her reactions to the event. (To ask pertinent questions, you may have to do some background reading to find out what the usual childbirth practices are in this country today, what objections have been raised about them in recent years, and what alternatives are available.) Ask what the mother might do differently if she were able to relive the experience.

4. After briefly questioning fifteen or twenty students on your campus to find out what careers they are preparing for, write a short essay summing up what you find out. Are students at your college more intent on earning money than on other pursuits? How many of them are choosing lucrative careers because they have to pay back huge college loans? Are any of them unhappy with the direction they have chosen? Provide some quotations to flesh out your survey. From the information you have gathered, would you call your classmates materialists? Idealists? Practical people?

APPLYING WHAT YOU LEARN: SOME USES OF WRITING FROM CONVERSATION

Interviewing is a familiar tool of many writers in the world beyond college. Biographers who write about someone living often conduct extensive interviews with their subjects to guarantee accuracy. Usually they interview friends, relatives, and other associates to round out their picture of a person. Likewise, news reporters and commentators often rely on interviews with "informed sources" (generally public officials, some of whom don't want to be named). Another familiar kind of interview is that in which some author, actor, or political figure airs his or her views on a variety of subjects. Such interviews are written by people who have talked with their subjects, sometimes by telephone but usually face to face.

Often in college writing you find yourself interviewing people not because you are interested in their personalities but because they can contribute valuable insights to what you are studying. Students of human development often interview people at various stages of the life cycle. They talk to men and women about the transition from student life to the working world, to mothers about the experience of giving birth, to old people about widowhood or retirement. One line of questioning, for instance, helps them find out how well these older men and women are carrying out the "life review" that therapists like Erik Erikson find so important to ending life with integrity. Sometimes, too, these students collect oral histories, either purely autobiographical ones or those that center on particular events from the past. In recent years historians themselves, acknowledging that "ordinary" people matter, both individually and collectively, have shown increasing interest in gathering and publishing oral histories and in mining those from the past. One such collection that throws vivid light on the civil rights movement is Howell Raines's *My Soul Is Rested* (New York: Putnam's, 1977). In the following excerpt the author records the words of Franklin McCain, who participated in the now famous sit-in at Woolworth's in Greensboro, N.C., on February 1, 1960.

> Once getting there . . . we did make purchases of school supplies and took the patience and time to get receipts for our purchases, and Joseph and myself went over to the counter and asked to be served coffee and doughnuts. As anticipated, the reply was, "I'm sorry, we don't serve you here." And of course we said, "We just beg to disagree with you. We've in fact already been served; you've served us already and that's just not quite true. . . . We wonder why you'd invite us in to serve us at one counter and deny service at another. If this is a private club or private concern, then we believe you ought to sell membership cards and sell only to persons who have a membership card. If we don't have a card, then we'd know pretty well that we shouldn't come in or even attempt to come in." That didn't go over too well. . . . And the only thing that an individual in her case or position could do is, of course, call the manager. [Laughs]

A memorable quotation from an expert can lend great life and conviction to a factual paper or article. To write "The Superstars of Heart Research" for *Boston* magazine, reporter Philip Zaleski gathered information by talking with surgeons and scientists and, as in the following paragraph, with an official of a national health organization.

> "If you ever want to alter people's lifestyles," says Barnie Duane of the American Heart Association, "let them watch a coronary bypass. It's the most horrendous thing I've ever seen. I watched my first one at Massachusetts General with a bunch of kids. Some of them fainted. We observed from a glass dome just four feet above the head of the surgeon, so we had a perfect view. Two teams of doctors worked simultaneously. One stood at the patient's feet, cutting a huge vein out of his leg. The other stood at his chest, ripping open the sternum with a saw—*zip!* Then they cracked open his ribs with giant clamps—*snap! snap! snap!* The surgeons lifted out a damaged artery and held it up to our view and squeezed. Cholesterol squirted out like toothpaste from a tube. It's guaranteed to change your life."

In professional scholarly research, dozens of interviews may be necessary. The five sociologists who wrote the much-acclaimed *Habits of the Heart: Individualism and Commitment in American Life* (Berkeley: University of California Press, 1985) used as their sources not only books and periodicals but also extensive interviews with both ordinary citizens and professionals in various fields. Note how this example from a chapter written by Ann Swidler enlivens its discussion with pointed, informative quotations that read like spoken words:

> Asked why she went into therapy, a woman summed up the themes that recur again and again in accounts by therapists and their clients: "I was not able to form close relationships to people, I didn't like myself, I didn't love myself, I didn't love other people." In the therapeutic ideology, such incapacities are in turn related to a failure fully to accept, fully to love, one's self.
>
> As the therapist Margaret Oldham puts it, many of the professionally trained, upper-middle-class young adults who come to her, depressed and lonely, are seeking "that big relationship in the sky—the perfect person." They want "that one person who is going to stop making them feel alone." But this search for a perfect relationship cannot succeed because it comes from a self that is not full and self-sustaining. The desire for relatedness is really a reflection of incompleteness, of one's own dependent needs.
>
> Before one can love others, one must learn to love one's self. A therapist can teach self love by offering unconditional acceptance. As a Rogersian therapist observes, "There's nobody once you leave your parents who can just say you are O.K. with us no matter what you do." He continues, "I'm willing to be a motherer." ... Another, more behavioristic therapist concurs, saying he works by "giving them just lots of positive reinforcement in their selves; continually pointing out things that are good about them, feeding them with it over and over again." Thus the initial ingredient in the development of a healthy, autonomous self may be love from the ideal, understanding surrogate parent-lover-friend—the therapist. Unlike that of lovers, and friends, however, the purpose of the therapist's love is not to create a lasting relationship of mutual commitment, but to free people of their dependence so that ultimately they can love themselves.

An Essayist Writes from Conversation

After talking with many Chinese in their own land, poet and essayist Annie Dillard, in this chapter from *Encounters with Chinese Writers* (1984), reports what she learned of the reading habits of a different culture.

ENCOUNTERS WITH CHINESE READERS
Annie Dillard

In Beijing Library—the national library—I was standing by the English   1
card catalogue with Song Hua. He is a young and very jolly interpreter,
whose gestures are extreme. When he is embarrassed, he covers his face
with both hands; when he laughs, he tends to fall over; when he makes a
mistake, he strikes himself on the skull with a fist. I liked him.

The Beijing Library has 11 million 100 thousand books, and 200 chairs.   2
We were standing among several dozen of these chairs pushed up to tables.
The chairs were all taken, this day as every day; many people were taking

notes in minuscule characters on tiny pieces of paper. Most people, in fact, seemed to have located one such tiny piece of paper to bring to the library for this purpose. There is not much paper in China. There are not many books, either, comparatively; Red Guards burned so many. And, alas, most of the people can't read most of the books; the books tend to be in classical Chinese, in old-style characters, and most people read only the modern, simplified characters not firmly established until the 1950s. On the other hand, partly as a result of the introduction of simplified characters, and partly as a result of the Communist party, literacy has soared.

From any public library, Song Hua told me, *people* may not borrow   3
books. People apply to their production units and show good reason why they wish to read a particular book. If the book is not in their production unit's library, the unit gives them written permission to try to get the book at the public library.

"What's a good reason for borrowing a book?"   4

"You need the information for your work."   5

"What if you were an engineer and wanted to borrow a book of litera-   6
ture?"

To my astonishment, Song Hua burst into laughter. He doubled over as   7
if kicked, he gasped for breath, he hugged his ribs and stamped his foot. I looked down the back of his neck. Gradually his head rose again; his face was splintered with hilarity. He gave me a sidelong "oh, you card" look, and said, as clearly as he could, "But you couldn't . . . if you were an engineer . . . get to read . . . a book of literature!" And off he rolled again into squalls of laughter.

Naturally I thought I failed to make the question clear. I still wonder   8
about this. I repeated the question in different terms. Same thing. This absurdity was clearly making Song Hua's day. He looked up at the ceiling helplessly, as if imploring a hidden cameraman to help him consider the idea of an engineer borrowing a book of literature. (Did he think I meant literary criticism?) He fell towards the floor again, straightened up by steadying himself on the card catalogue, and answered as he had before.

At Shanghai's Fudan University I talked to an anatomy professor who   9
had toured fifteen American universities. He was impressed by the modern equipment available to students, by the democratic way professors treated both staff and students, and, especially, by the *diligence* of U.S. students. Now, a year after his visit, he still couldn't get over the way students were able to learn directly and independently from books. He said—and his voice was still incredulous—that he had spoken at Johns Hopkins with a Taiwanese student who was taking a physiology course. This student had told him that for that course they were all expected to read: *two books*. The course was only twelve weeks long and met only three times a week. I nodded. The students didn't read the two books in class, but were expected to read the books outside of class, and learn *directly* from them. Students at American universities ordinarily took *four* such courses.

Ways of learning differ, of course. In a country with so many people, 10
so many meetings, and so few books, it makes sense to be able to absorb
most of your information through your ears. Stephen Greenblatt, from
Berkeley, who taught Shakespeare at Beijing University recently, reported
on the solemn intensity with which his students listened to his words, as
if memorizing them. New American "styles of learning" studies show that
many Americans, like others worldwide, learn better from hearing things
than from reading them.

The newest Chinese literature, which depicts the life of educated peo- 11
ple, has as an inadvertent running theme a dreary collective description of
how different families share desk time. Usually the child uses the desk
first, then the mother, and then, after the others go to sleep, the father.
All this emphasis on the desk indicates that people are perfectly capable
of working alone, as indeed they are. The park benches in China are full of
people silently studying books, often textbooks.

I talked with a man in his fifties who had written several novels and 12
books of short stories. "What do you read for pleasure?" He was an educated man of good will, a friendly man; the question bewildered him. "We
do not read for pleasure," he said quietly.

My question had gone astray. It was the term "for pleasure." Reading 13
for pleasure is not something a serious writer would admit to doing. A writer
reads, of course; he or she calls it "studying," and it is part of work for
China. Many writers read widely in contemporary literature, and study classical works like *The Dream of the Red Chamber*, or modern classics like
the works of Lu Xun, in depth and repeatedly, in the scholarly tradition
which obtains everywhere. In fact, classical scholarship is a safe refuge for
Chinese people who love literature for its own sake.

I asked a middle-aged writer whose literary ambitions, love of literature, 14
and breadth of education I thought I knew pretty well, "How many books,
roughly, would you say you read a year, on your own?" "One," he said,
embarrassed. "Maybe two." He was helping his son study for university
entrance exams. He had almost no free time. He and his wife, who had
been married for nineteen years, were saving to buy some furniture. Not
additional furniture—just furniture.

A Chinese student in the United States reported, gleeful and awed, to 15
his professor at the University of Indiana, "In the U.S., the only limit on
access to books is how many times you care to—well—raise your arm to
take the book from the shelf."

Questions to Start You Thinking

1. What are the chief differences Dillard finds between reading habits in China and
   those in this country? What reasons does she suggest for these differences?

2. In light of what most educators and other commentators say about students in

our country today, how do you account for the Chinese anatomy professor's awe at the "diligence" of American students (paragraph 9)?

3. Compile a list of questions you might ask a foreign student if you wanted to find out his or her impressions of the United States.

An Educator Writes from Conversation

David Elkind, a well-known professor of child studies, was among the first to decry the disturbing trend among middle-class American parents to push their children to achieve. In his book *The Hurried Child* (1981), he laid the groundwork for the view he states in this recent essay.

SUPERKIDS AND SUPER PROBLEMS
David Elkind

Not so long ago, most parents wanted their kids to be like everybody 1 else. They were often as upset if a child were precocious as they were if the child were slow. Precocity was looked upon as being bad for the child's psychological health. The assumption was "early ripe, early rot."

Now that has changed. For many parents today there is no such thing 2 as going too fast, and their major concern is that their child stay ahead of the pack. Far from presuming that precocity has bad effects psychologically, they believe that being above the norm brings many benefits. The assumption is "early ripe, early rich!"

The major consequence of this new parenting psychology is that many 3 contemporary parents are putting tremendous pressure on children to perform at ever-earlier ages. A first grade teacher told me that an irate mother screamed at her because she had given the woman's son a "Satisfactory." "How is he ever going to get into M.I.T. if you give him a 'Satisfactory!' " the mother wailed.

Many parents now enroll their child in prestigious nursery schools as 4 soon as the pregnancy is confirmed. And once the child is old enough, they coach the child for the screening interview. "When they count everything in sight," one nursery school director said, "you know they have been drilled before the interview." Parents believe that only if the child gets into this or that prestigious nursery school will he or she ever have a chance at getting into Harvard, Yale, or Stanford. For the same reason, our elementary schools are suddenly filled with youngsters in enriched and accelerated programs.

It is not just in academics that children are being pushed harder at 5 ever-earlier ages. Some parents start their preschool children in sports such as tennis and swimming in hopes that they will become Olympic athletes. A young man who attended one of my child development lectures stopped by afterward to ask me a question. He works as a tennis instructor at an exclusive resort hotel in Florida and wanted to know how to motivate his students. When I asked how old they were he told me that they ranged in age from three to five years!

The pressure to make ordinary children exceptional has become almost   6
an epidemic in sports. I had high hopes for soccer, which can be played by all makes and models of children, big, small, and in between. But in most states soccer has become as competitive and selective as baseball, football, and hockey. The star mentality prevails, and the less talented youngster simply doesn't get to participate. Play is out and competition is in.

The pressure for exceptionality is equally powerful at the secondary   7
level. High school students are pressured not only to get good grades but to get into as many advanced-placement classes as possible. Around the country private tutoring centers are sprouting up like dandelions in the spring, offering lessons in everything from beginning reading to taking college entrance exams. Other parents urge their children to start dating at an early age so that they will have good interpersonal skills and a better chance to win the most eligible mates.

Clearly, there is nothing wrong with wanting children to do their best.   8
It is not the normal, healthy desire of parents to have successful children that is the problem, but the excessive pressure some parents are putting on children.

Why this push for excellence? Since parents today are having fewer   9
children, their chances of having "a child to be proud of" are lower than when families were larger. The cost of child rearing has also increased dramatically, so a successful child also protects one's investment. But most of all, many of today's parents have carved out their own successful careers and feel very much in charge of their lives. They see no reason they should not take charge of child rearing in the same manner and with the same success. A successful child is the ultimate proof of their success.

The result is that many parents are far too intrusive. By deciding what   10
and when children should learn, they rob them of the opportunity to take the initiative, to take responsibility for their mistakes and credit for their achievements. Such practices run the risk of producing children who are dependent and lacking in self-esteem. Today's parents want superkids, but what they are often getting are super problems.

Although correlation is certainly not causation, it is hard not to connect   11
the reported increase in stress symptoms over the last decade with the pressure on today's children to be superkids. The stories I hear as I travel about the country are frightening. A girl who was involved in four different out-of-school activities (ballet, horseback riding, Brownies, and music lessons) developed severe facial tics at age eight. Irving Sigel of Educational Testing Service tells the story of a six-year-old who, while doing her homework, asked her mother, "If I don't get these right, will you kill me?" A

woman told me that her seven-year-old grandson ran away from home (and all the after-school lessons) and came to her house, where he could have milk and cookies and play with the dog. One mother asked me if I could cure her six-year-old son of his nail biting by hypnosis or by teaching him relaxation. When I suggested that a less demanding extracurricular program might help, she replied, "Oh no, we can't do that."

Such child behavior problems are symptomatic of our times. Our trouble   12
is that we always seem to go to extremes. Parents are either too permissive or too pushy. Healthy child rearing demands a middle ground. Certainly we need to make demands on our children. But they have to be tailored to the child's interests and abilities. We put our children at risk for short-term stress disorders and long-term personality problems when we ignore their individuality and impose our own priorities "for their own good."

I believe that we need to abandon the false notions that we can create   13
exceptional children by early instruction, and that such children are symbols of our competence as parents. And I believe we should be as concerned with character as with success. If we have reared a well-mannered, good, and decent person, we should take pleasure and pride in that fact. More likely than not, if we have achieved those goals, the child's success will take care of itself. Each child has a unique pattern of qualities and abilities that makes him or her special. In this sense, every single child is a superkid.

Questions to Start You Thinking

1. Where in his essay does Elkind use the resource of conversing to good effect?
2. According to the author, what factors motivate parents to push their children?
3. Elkind speaks of "the normal, healthy desire of parents to have successful children." How might such a desire be satisfied without pushing?
4. What other dubious childrearing practices seem to you worth criticizing?

CHAPTER 5

Writing from Imagination

"Imagination," said Albert Einstein, "is more important than knowledge." Coming from a theoretical physicist who widened our knowledge of the universe, the remark is striking. When we speak of "imaginative writing" we usually mean stories, poems, or plays. And yet storytellers, poets, and playwrights have no monopoly on imagination. Scientists, economists, and historians need it, too; so do authors of college reports, blue book exams, and research papers.

In one familiar sense of the word, imagining is nothing but daydreaming—imagining yourself wafted from a cold and rainy city street to a sunny beach in the tropics. Enlarging that definition a little, the *Shorter Oxford Dictionary* calls imagination "forming a mental concept of what is not actually present to the senses . . . of actions and events not yet in existence." That definition is all right as far as it goes. Still, for many writers and artists, imagination is a far larger resource. It is nothing less than a "magical power," in the view of poet and critic Samuel Taylor Coleridge, one that can reveal in familiar objects "novelty and freshness." Sometimes it brings new things into existence by combining old things that already exist. Lewis Carroll, whose Alice books seem remote from actual life, drew the stuff of his fantastic adventures from his friendship with a real child and some of his fantastic characters from real persons in England. (His portrait of the Mad Hatter resembles one Theophilus Carter, an eccentric Oxford furniture dealer.) Instead of creating out of thin air, imaginative writers often build from materials they find at hand. "The imagination," said poet Wallace Stevens, "must not detach itself from reality."

As many writers have testified, imagining is often playful: a fruitful kind of fooling around. Ursula LeGuin, writer of science fiction, calls imagination "the free play of the mind." In her essay "Why Are Americans Afraid of Dragons?" she explains:

> By "free" I mean that the action is done without an immediate object of profit—spontaneously. That does not mean, however, that there may not be a purpose behind the free play of the mind, a goal; and the goal may be a very serious object indeed. Children's imaginative play is clearly a practicing at the acts and emotions of adulthood; a child who did not play would not become mature. As for the free play of an adult mind, its result may be *War and Peace,* or the theory of relativity.

Though the result may not be Leo Tolstoy's classic novel or Einstein's theory, a college writer will find that such free play with language and ideas can be valuable and productive—and fun besides.

LEARNING FROM OTHER WRITERS

It appears that, to be a whole writer and a whole human being, each of us needs both a logical, analytical mind and what Shakespeare called "the mind's eye"—the faculty of imagining. In this chapter, we don't presume to tell you how to imagine. We only suggest how to use any imagination you have already. To begin, here are two examples of imaginative writing, the first by a professional and the second by a student of education. An economist by profession, author of many scholarly articles and reports, James C. Rettie is remembered mainly for writing a single famous work: the following essay, many times reprinted in textbooks and anthologies. In writing it, Rettie apparently drew some of his ideas from a U.S. government pamphlet, "To Hold the Soil," prepared by the Department of Agriculture. His approach to this material, we think, shows imaginative flair.

"BUT A WATCH IN THE NIGHT": A SCIENTIFIC FABLE
James C. Rettie

Out beyond our solar system there is a planet called Copernicus. It came into existence some four or five billion years before the birth of our Earth. In due course of time it became inhabited by a race of intelligent men.   1

About 750 million years ago the Copernicans had developed the motion picture machine to a point well in advance of the stage that we have reached. Most of the cameras that we now use in motion picture work are   2 geared to take twenty-four pictures per second on a continuous strip of film. When such film is run through a projector, it throws a series of images on the screen and these change with a rapidity that gives the visual impression of normal movement. If a motion is too swift for the human eye to see it in detail, it can be captured and artificially slowed down by means of the slow-motion camera. This one is geared to take many more shots per second—ninety-six or even more than that. When the slow motion film is projected at the normal speed of twenty-four pictures per second, we can see just how the jumping horse goes over a hurdle.

What about motion that is too slow to be seen by the human eye? That 3 problem has been solved by the use of the time-lapse camera. In this one, the shutter is geared to take only one shot per second, or one per minute, or even one per hour—depending upon the kind of movement that is being photographed. When the time-lapse film is projected at the normal speed of twenty-four pictures per second, it is possible to see a bean sprout growing up out of the ground. Time-lapse films are useful in the study of many types of motion too slow to be observed by the unaided human eye.

The Copernicans, it seems, had time-lapse cameras some 757 million 4 years ago and they also had superpowered telescopes that gave them a clear view of what was happening upon this Earth. They decided to make a film record of the life history of Earth and to make it on the scale of one picture per year. The photography has been in progress during the last 757 million years.

In the near future, a Copernican interstellar expedition will arrive upon 5 our Earth and bring with it a copy of the time-lapse film. Arrangements will be made for showing the entire film in one continuous run. This will begin at midnight of New Year's Eve and continue day and night without a single stop until midnight of December 31. The rate of projection will be twenty-four pictures per second. Time on the screen will thus seem to move at the rate of twenty-four years per second; 1440 years per minute; 86,400 years per hour; approximately two million years per day; and sixty-two million years per month. The normal life-span of individual man will occupy about three seconds. The full period of earth history that will be unfolded on the screen (some 757 million years) will extend from what the geologists call Pre-Cambrian times up to the present. This will, by no means, cover the full time-span of the earth's geological history, but it will embrace the period since the advent of living organisms.

During the months of January, February, and March the picture will be 6 desolate and dreary. The shape of the land masses and the oceans will bear little or no resemblance to those that we know. The violence of geological erosion will be much in evidence. Rains will pour down on the land and promptly go booming down to the seas. There will be no clear streams anywhere except where the rains fall upon hard rock. Everywhere on the steeper ground the stream channels will be filled with boulders hurled down by rushing waters. Raging torrents and dry stream beds will keep alternating in quick succession. High mountains will seem to melt like so much butter in the sun. The shifting of land into the seas, later to be thrust up as new mountains, will be going on at a grand scale.

Early in April there will be some indication of the presence of single-celled living organisms in some of the warmer and sheltered coastal waters. By the end of the month it will be noticed that some of these organisms have become multicellular. A few of them, including the Trilobites, will be encased in hard shells. 7

Toward the end of May, the first vertebrates will appear, but they will still be aquatic creatures. In June about 60 percent of the land area that we know as North America will be under water. One broad channel will occupy the space where the Rocky Mountains now stand. Great deposits of limestone will be forming under some of the shallower seas. Oil and gas deposits will be in process of formation—also under shallow seas. On land there will still be no sign of vegetation. Erosion will be rampant, tearing loose particles and chunks of rock and grinding them into sand and silt to be spewed out by the streams into bays and estuaries. 8

About the middle of July the first land plants will appear and take up the tremendous job of soil building. Slowly, very slowly, the mat of vegetation will spread, always battling for its life against the power of erosion. Almost foot by foot, the plant life will advance, lacing down with its root structures whatever pulverized rock material it can find. Leaves and stems will be giving added protection against the loss of the soil foothold. The increasing vegetation will pave the way for the land animals that will live upon it. 9

Early in August the seas will be teeming with fish. This will be what geologists call the Devonian period. Some of the races of these fish will be breathing by means of lung tissue instead of through gill tissues. Before the month is over, some of the lung fish will go ashore and take on a crude lizard-like appearance. Here are the first amphibians. 10

In early September the insects will put in their appearance. Some will look like huge dragonflies and will have a wing spread of 24 inches. Large portions of the land masses will now be covered with heavy vegetation that will include the primitive spore-propagating trees. Layer upon layer of this plant growth will build up, later to appear as the coal deposits. About the middle of this month, there will be evidence of the first seed-bearing plants and the first reptiles. Heretofore, the land animals will have been amphibians that could reproduce their kind only by depositing a soft egg mass in quiet waters. The reptiles will be shown to be freed from the aquatic bond because they can reproduce by means of a shelled egg in which the embryo and its nurturing liquids are sealed and thus protected from destructive evaporation. Before September is over, the first dinosaurs will be seen—creatures destined to dominate the animal realm for about 140 million years and then to disappear. 11

In October there will be series of mountain uplifts along what is now 12
the eastern coast of the United States. A creature with feathered limbs—
half bird and half reptile in appearance—will take itself into the air. Some
small and rather unpretentious animals will be seen to bring forth their
young in a form that is a miniature replica of the parents and to feed these
young on milk secreted by mammary glands in the female parent. The
emergence of this mammalian form of animal life will be recognized as
one of the great events in geologic time. October will also witness the high
water mark of the dinosaurs—creatures ranging in size from that of the
modern goat to monsters like Brontosaurus that weighed some 40 tons.
Most of them will be placid vegetarians, but a few will be hideous-looking
carnivores, like Allosaurus and Tyrannosaurus. Some of the herbivorous
dinosaurs will be clad in bony armor for protection against their flesh-eating
comrades.

November will bring pictures of a sea extending from the Gulf of Mexico 13
to the Arctic in space now occupied by the Rocky Mountains. A few of the
reptiles will take to the air on bat-like wings. One of these, called Ptera-
nodon, will have a wingspread of 15 feet. There will be a rapid development
of the modern flowering plants, modern trees, and modern insects. The
dinosaurs will disappear. Toward the end of the month there will be a
tremendous land disturbance in which the Rocky Mountains will rise out of
the sea to assume a dominating place in the North American landscape.

As the picture runs on into December it will show the mammals in 14
command of the animal life. Seed-bearing trees and grasses will have
covered most of the land with a heavy mantle of vegetation. Only the areas
newly thrust up from the sea will be barren. Most of the streams will be
crystal clear. The turmoil of geologic erosion will be confined to localized
areas. About December 25 will begin the cutting of the Grand Canyon of
the Colorado River. Grinding down through layer after layer of sedimentary
strata, this stream will finally expose deposits laid down in Pre-Cambrian
times. Thus in the walls of that canyon will appear geological formations
dating from recent times to the period when the Earth had no living organisms upon it.

The picture will run on through the latter days of December and even 15
up to its final day with still no sign of mankind. The spectators will become
alarmed in the fear that man has somehow been left out. But not so;
sometime about noon on December 31 (one million years ago) will appear
a stooped, massive creature of man-like proportions. This will be Pithecan-
thropus, the Java ape man. For tools and weapons he will have nothing but
crude stone and wooden clubs. His children will live a precarious existence
threatened on the one side by hostile animals and on the other by tremendous climatic changes. Ice sheets—in places 4000 feet deep—will form
in the northern parts of North America and Eurasia. Four times this glacial
ice will push southward to cover half the continents. With each advance

the plant and animal life will be swept under or pushed southward. With each recession of the ice, life will struggle to reestablish itself in the wake of the retreating glaciers. The woolly mammoth, the musk ox, and the caribou all will fight to maintain themselves near the ice line. Sometimes they will be caught and put into cold storage—skin, flesh, blood, bones, and all.

The picture will run on through supper time with still very little evidence of man's presence on the earth. It will be about 11 o'clock when Neanderthal man appears. Another half hour will go by before the appearance of Cro-Magnon man living in caves and painting crude animal pictures on the walls of his dwelling. Fifteen minutes more will bring Neolithic man, knowing how to chip stone and thus produce sharp cutting edges for spears and tools. In a few minutes more it will appear that man has domesticated the dog, the sheep and, possibly, other animals. He will then begin the use of milk. He will also learn the arts of basket weaving and the making of pottery and dugout canoes. 16

The dawn of civilization will not come until about five or six minutes before the end of the picture. The story of the Egyptians, the Babylonians, the Greeks, and the Romans will unroll during the fourth, the third, and the second minute before the end. At 58 minutes and 43 seconds past 11:00 P.M. (just 1 minute and 17 seconds before the end) will come the beginning of the Christian era. Columbus will discover the new world 20 seconds before the end. The Declaration of Independence will be signed just 7 seconds before the final curtain comes down. 17

In those few moments of geologic time will be the story of all that has happened since we became a nation. And what a story it will be! A human swarm will sweep across the face of the continent and take it away from the . . . red men. They will change it far more radically than it has ever been changed before in a comparable time. The great virgin forests will be seen going down before ax and fire. The soil, covered for eons by its protective mantle of trees and grasses, will be laid bare to the ravages of water and wind erosion. Streams that had been flowing clear will, once again, take up a load of silt and push it toward the seas. Humus and mineral salts, both vital elements of productive soil, will be seen to vanish at a terrifying rate. The railroads and highways and cities that will spring up may divert attention, but they cannot cover up the blight of man's recent activities. In great sections of Asia, it will be seen that man must utilize cow dung and every scrap of available straw or grass for fuel to cook his food. The forests that once provided wood for this purpose will be gone without a trace. The use of these agricultural wastes for fuel, in place of returning them to the land, will be leading to increasing soil impoverishment. Here and there will be seen a dust storm darkening the landscape over an area a thousand miles across. Man-creatures will be shown counting their wealth in terms of bits of printed paper representing other bits of a scarce but comparatively useless yellow metal that is kept buried in 18 strong vaults. Meanwhile, the soil, the only real wealth that can keep mankind alive on the face of this earth, is savagely being cut loose from its ancient moorings and washed into the seven seas.

We have just arrived upon this earth. How long will we stay?   19

Questions to Start You Thinking

1. The title of Rettie's essay alludes to Psalms 90:4 in the King James version of the Bible: "For a thousand years in Thy sight are but as yesterday when it is past, and as a watch in the night." Can you explain this quotation? What light does it cast on the essay?

2. Sum up the purpose of this essay as a whole.

3. Do you have any trouble accepting Rettie's notion of a movie whose screening takes a year? What commonplace, practical objections to such a movie occur to you? Is Rettie's analogy silly, or does it serve him well?

4. What is the value of the essay's subtitle, "A Scientific Fable"? What is a fable? Why can this essay be so designated?

Student Jennifer Bowe faced this challenging assignment: "Imagine your ideal college. Conceive it to fit your own wishes and deepest desires. Then describe it in writing. Perhaps this college might bring together the strong points of several real colleges—faculty, curriculum, location, facilities, or other prominent features—in a new combination. Propose a philosophy for your college, one that might lead to original methods of instruction."

To generate ideas, Bowe first took part in a two-hour brainstorming session with three of her peers. She scribbled eight pages of ideas, pondered them, and then wrote. The following paper, though lighthearted, makes interesting criticisms of conventional methods of instruction.

Student Essay

IF I COULD FOUND A COLLEGE
Jennifer Bowe

Welcome to Sundial College. Jennifer Bowe, founder.   1
(That's me, that statue on horseback in front of the administration building.)

When you visit the campus of Sundial for the first time,   2
you notice something strange. The position of the sun never
changes, for Sundial College takes its name from its design,
which is as unique as its educational philosophy. The whole
campus rests on an enormous disk that rotates with the sun,

almost imperceptibly, so that the sun always shines down on
the college from the same direction. Rather than rising in
the east and setting in the west, the sun appears to rise
straight up and set straight down again. This odd design is
not merely an advertising gimmick to make the college sound
unique; it is quite practical. Classrooms are built to receive maximum sunlight at all times, thus saving in heating
costs more than enough to pay for running the giant motor
that turns the campus. Students reading on the lawn do not
need to keep moving their blankets to stay in the sun or the
shade. Greenhouses stay sunny all day long. Night Owl
Hall, the dorm for people who like to stay up late, has its
back to the sun, so that its late sleepers will receive no
unwanted morning light. Lark Hall, for early risers, lights
up with the dawn. Out of necessity, the Astronomy Department
is located just outside the central disk, so that its instruments are in harmony with the rest of the earth. At the hub
of the campus wheel is a great sundial--fixed, keeping faithful time.

Sundial College operates on the philosophy that college   3
should prepare one to think independently. It believes that
the best kind of learning takes place outside of class. For
this reason, there are no classes. I insisted on making this
experiment when I founded the college. In classes where
students talk a lot, too much time is spent on chatter. I
have heard some great lectures, but they have been frustrating. When you try to take notes on a lecture, you just get
all the names spelled wrong. I believe you can obtain
knowledge faster and more accurately by reading a book.

Sundial students take only one course at a time, so as   4
to concentrate on it without being distracted by other
courses. Each course lasts from two to six weeks, as long as
necessary. On the first day of a course, each student visits
the professor, who hands out a reading list and some writing
assignments. The college library is open day and night and

has bunk beds for people to take naps. Access to the professors is easy. Each student has a weekly appointment with the professor (the one whose course he or she is now taking) to ask questions and receive feedback on reading and writing assignments.

In this college without classes, does the student lack   5
the stimulus of classroom-type discussion? On the contrary, group discussions among students in a course take place daily, outdoors in the sun, so that students can freely talk together without being graded on what they say. At the end of the course there is a test, not graded but marked pass or fail. If a student fails, he or she goes to the instructor, who finds out whether the student didn't do the work or didn't understand it. Those who fail get a second chance. If they fail again, they receive no credit for the course. None of the courses prepares students for careers; the courses only train their minds. I admit that careers are naturally important to some students, and an active work-study program finds paying jobs for those who want to take off and work for a semester.

The students come from every walk of life and from every   6
country. The faculty, brilliant people in their twenties and a few older scholars, come from all over the world. Enthusiasm for teaching, not famous publications, is the most important criterion in hiring them. More than half are women. All have to be approved by a student council before they are rehired. Besides these regular faculty, a group of "wandering scholars" spend their time roaming around campus engaging students in intellectual bull sessions. Some are famous scholars retired from other universities; some are just brilliant bums who can talk interestingly and stimulate students to think.

Although the campus stays fixed in its place in the sun,   7
it is always in a whirl of exciting activity. Each student sets time aside for strolling around the campus taking in

events. Foreign films, good Hollywood films, and documentaries of all kinds run day and night in a ten-screen theater. Lectures, plays, and concerts are held at all hours.
A computer room has every kind of educational software.
Rooms with VCR's contain thousands of videotapes. Everything
is designed to keep the student body thinking at all times.

The Sundial experience, of course, is not entirely an   8
intellectual one. There is a lively social life. When I
founded Sundial, I insisted on no fraternities, because frats
induce vomiting, especially at their beer parties. There
aren't any sororities either, to divide the student body into
castes. The students at Sundial are unified in spirit, and
campus parties and barbecues leave nobody out in the cold.
An essential center of society is the campus pub. Sundial's
has dark brown walls, booths with vinyl cushions, a dart
board, Sundialburgers (with a wedge of onion for the gnomon),
and several of the "wandering scholars" always hanging around
challenging students to argue with them. A friendly old
proprietor named Curly, who has been on the scene for thirty-
five years, gives out sympathy and five-dollar loans to students short of cash.

Sports are laid-back and informal. The teams are really   9
just clubs, which anyone may join. I don't believe in sensational football and basketball teams with star players,
supported on money given by the alumni. Alumni always like
to support sports teams because they can't cheer for students
in class taking tests.

To finance such a college without alumni support is not   10
easy. Luckily, in founding Sundial I had several billion
dollars to endow it with. My continued generosity keeps the
tuition fees down to about half those at a community college.
Financial aid for those who need it is available and is the
highest in the country. No scholarships need to be repaid,
no part-time work is required, and substantial travel bonuses
are given to students who have to come a long way.

In fact, Sundial is such a pleasant place that it has 11
one serious problem: how to make everyone go home for the
summer. However, its problem has a built-in solution. Once
again, the design of its revolving campus proves the wisdom
and foresight of its founder. When the school year ends, the
dorms are locked, keeping everyone outside. Then the huge
disk of Sundial College accelerates, faster and faster,
reaching a dizzying speed, until every last student takes
off.

Questions to Start You Thinking

1. In what remarks does Jennifer Bowe seem to be kidding? Which does she apparently mean us to take seriously?
2. What features of Sundial College appeal to you? Do any strike you as mistakes?
3. If you were designing your own ideal college, how would you state its philosophy?

LEARNING BY WRITING

The Assignment: "What if . . . ?"

Write an essay in answer to a question that begins "What if . . . ?"

You might imagine a past that unfolded differently: for instance, "What if the airplane had never been invented?" You might imagine a reversal of present-day fact: "What if men had to bear children?" Or you might imagine an event in the future: "What if the United States and the Soviet Union were to reach agreement on gradual and total nuclear disarmament?"

Envision in specific detail a world in which the supposition is true. Your purpose is to make the supposition seem credible and convincing to your reader.

Unless your instructor encourages you to do so, don't write a story. To be sure, you could conceivably write this paper as science fiction. In answer to the question "What if time travel were possible?" you might begin: "As I walked into Me-opolis in 2500 A.D., the mayor rushed up to me. 'A terrible plague of headaches has struck our city!' he shouted. Luckily, I still had my bottle of Tylenol from the twentieth century. . . ." But instead, write imaginative *nonfiction*.

To help you start imagining, here are some topics that students generated for this assignment. Some may reveal interesting dimensions in your possible major field of study; some are less serious.

A DIFFERENT PAST

What if the Equal Rights Amendment had become law?

What if the South had won the Civil War?

What if continental drift had never taken place and the Americas, Africa, and Eurasia were still one connected land mass?

What if *Homo sapiens* had not straightened up but still walked on all fours? (One first thought: Basketball rims would be lower.)

What if Sigmund Freud had never lived?

A DIFFERENT PRESENT

What if no one needed to sleep?

What if knees bent the other way? (How would chairs, cars, and bicycles have to be redesigned?)

What if smoking were good for you?

What if the human eye could perceive only two dimensions?

What if it were possible to travel backward in time? If you could do so, to what earlier eras would you go? (Alternative: What if you could meet any six prominent persons who ever lived? Whom would you choose?)

A POSSIBLE FUTURE

What if a woman were elected the next president of the United States?

What if the United Nations were to create and control a powerful army?

What if a space station, capable of sustaining hundreds of people, were placed in orbit?

What if the salaries of all teachers in public schools and colleges were increased by fifty percent, effective immediately?

What if legislation were passed limiting couples to two children?

We know of several thought-provoking papers that resulted when students were asked to answer a question that began "What if . . .?"

For a research paper in a course in European history, writing of the French Revolution, one student tried to imagine what it was like to be a citizen of Paris in 1789.

For a paper in economics, a man looked at government aid to disadvantaged people in urban ghettos, thinking and writing first as a liberal (his own conviction) and then—by an act of imagination—thinking and writing as a conservative.

In a research paper about space law, written in 1986, one student used both existing documents and his power to envision future conflicts and problems to propose answers to legal questions likely to be crucial in the future: Should discoverers of resources on the moon be allowed to keep them? Should probes be allowed for a scientific purpose (which might involve quarrying and removing material), or should international law protect the moon's existing surface? (And how should the law define a scientific purpose?)

A woman imagined a contemporary American child's day in a world in which television had not been invented.

Generating Ideas

In making your own list of "What if" questions, you may find it helpful to brainstorm, either by yourself or (as Jennifer Bowe did) with the aid of a group. Sometimes two or three imaginations are better than one. (For helpful tips on brainstorming, see p. 471.)

To help you in generating "What if's," here are a few questions.

DISCOVERY CHECKLIST: IMAGINING POSSIBILITIES

- What event in history has always intrigued you?
- What common assumption—something we all take for granted—might be questioned or denied? (It might be a scientific opinion, such as the influential view of the surgeon general that smoking is injurious to health.)
- What future event do you most look forward to?
- What present-day problem or deplorable condition do you wish to see remedied?

Jot down as many "What if" questions as you can think of, do some trial imagining, and then choose the topic that seems most promising. Say you pick as your topic "What if the average North American life span were to lengthen to more than a century?" You might begin by reflecting on some of the ways in which society would have to change. When ideas start to flow, then, pencil in hand, start listing them. No doubt a lengthened life span would mean that a greater proportion of the populace would be old. Ask questions: How would that fact affect doctors and nurses, hospitals, and other medical facilities? How might city planners respond to the needs of so many more old people? What would the change mean for retail merchants? For television programming? For the social security system?

Although there are no fixed rules to follow in imagining, all of us tend to imagine in familiar ways. Being acquainted with these ways may help you fulfill your assignment.

Shifting perspective In imagining, a writer sometimes thinks and perceives from another person's point of view. At one moment in imagining her ideal college, Jennifer Bowe stops and realizes that many students, unlike herself, want a college to prepare them for a career. She then alters her concept of Sundial College to include a work-study program.

Envisioning Imagining what might be, seeing in the mind's eye and in graphic detail, is the process of envisioning. A writer might imagine a utopia or ideal state, as did Thomas More in *Utopia* (1516), or an anti-utopia, as did George Orwell in his 1948 novel of a grim future, *1984.* By envisioning, you can conceive of other possible alternatives: to imagine, say, a different and better way of treating illness, of electing a president or a prime minister. The student who wrote about the French Revolution by imagining life in Paris in 1789 had to envision.

Sometimes in envisioning, you will find a meaningful order in what had seemed a chaotic jumble. Leonardo da Vinci, in his notebooks, tells how, when starting to conceive a painting, he would gaze at an old stained wall made of various stones until he began to see "landscapes adorned with mountains, rivers, rocks, trees, plains, . . . combats and figures in quick movement, and strange expressions of faces, and outlandish costumes, and an infinite number of things." Not everyone might see that much in a wall, but da Vinci's method is familiar to writers who have worked in an imaginative way—who also have looked into a confused and random array of stuff and envisioned in it a meaningful arrangement.

Synthesizing Synthesizing (generating new ideas by combining previously separate ideas) is the opposite of analyzing (breaking down into component parts). In synthesizing, a writer brings together materials, perhaps old and familiar materials, and fuses them into something new. A writer makes fresh connections. Surely Picasso achieved a synthesis when, in making a metal sculpture of a baboon and needing a skull for the animal, he clapped on the baboon's neck a child's toy car. With its windshield like a pair of eyes and its mouthlike bumper, the car didn't just look like a baboon's skull: it *became* one. German chemist Friedrich Kekulé rightly guessed the structure of the benzene molecule when, in reverie, he imagined a snake swallowing its own tail. In a flash he realized that the elusive molecule was a ring of carbon atoms, not a chain, as earlier chemists had believed. Surely to bring together the benzene molecule and a snake was a feat of imaginative synthesis.

WRITING WITH A COMPUTER: IMAGINING
Did you ever try "invisible writing"? This is a technique to make yourself less self-conscious while you write—as you'll especially need to be when you're imagining. Twist down the contrast control on your computer monitor so that you can't see any words appearing on your screen. Then write. Do you feel slightly at sea? Don't worry—keep writing. Then twist the contrast back up and behold what you have written. The advantage of this trick is that you won't be fussing over particular words (and spelling errors); you'll be able to devote your full attention to imagining.

If your computer has reverse-screen capability, instead of writing in black on a white background, try writing in white on black. This technique may hint to your unconscious: What I'm writing is unusual, special, and strange. See if, with any luck, the fresh look of what you write will trigger some fresh ideas.

Some things cannot be totally reduced to rule and line, and imagination is one of them. But we hope you will accept that imagining is a practical activity of which you are fully capable. The more words you put on paper, the more often you will find that you can discover surprising ideas, original examples, unexpected relationships. The more you write, the more you involve yourself with language, that fascinating stained wall that invites you to find fresh shapes in it.

Shaping a Draft

We trust we haven't given you the impression that all imagining takes place *before* you write. On the contrary, you'll probably find yourself generating more ideas—perhaps more imaginative and startling ideas—in the act of writing.

Though in writing a "What if" paper you are freely imagining, you'll still need to lay out your ideas in a clear and orderly fashion so that readers can take them in. Some writers prefer to outline (as we discuss on p. 498). However, you might find that in fulfilling this assignment all the outline you will need is a list of points not to forget. If in writing your "What if" paper you enjoy yourself and words flow readily, by all means let the flow carry you along. In that happy event, you may be able to plan at the same time that you write your first draft.

To help your reader envision your imagined world just as vividly as you do, your "What if" could use an engaging (and convincing) opening. James Rettie's "But a Watch in the Night" has such a beginning: in his opening paragraphs, Rettie arrests us by matter-of-factly describing a far-off planet with a civilization so advanced that intelligent beings there were able to take moving pictures of life on earth. This introductory illustration makes us almost willing to suppose, for the moment, that the planet Copernicus and its time-lapse cameras may indeed exist. In relying on equally concrete specifics (such as her detail about the perpendicular sunrise), Jennifer Bowe makes her description of Sundial's campus ring almost true. Like Rettie and Bowe, use specific details and concrete examples. You'll need to make your vision appear tangible, as if it really could exist.

The ending of Bowe's paper, too, works well. It pushes to an incredible extreme the notion of a campus built on a turntable. If we have been persuaded to accept the possibility of such a revolving campus, carried along by the writer's serious discussion of novel teaching methods, the ending takes us by surprise. Perhaps we laugh, feeling as though a rug has been yanked out from under us.

Often, imaginative writing appeals to the mind's eye. For some accessible picture-filled writing, see the sports pages of a daily newspaper. Sports writer Bugs Baer once wrote of fireball pitcher Lefty Grove: "He could throw a lambchop past a wolf." Dan Shaughnessy in the *Boston Globe* described pitcher Roger Clemens: "Watching the Mariners try to hit Clemens was like watching a stack of waste paper dive into a shredder." Such language isn't mere decoration: it points to a truth and puts vivid pictures in the reader's "mind's eye." (For more about writing with *images*—language that evokes sense experiences, not always sight—look back over pp. 44–45.)

Imagination isn't a constant flame: sometimes it flickers and wavers. If in shaping your draft you get stuck and words don't flow, you may find it helpful to shift your perspective. Try imagining the past, present, or future *as if you were somebody else.* Perhaps you will then see fresh possibilities in your topic. Also helpful may be what all writers do now and then: take a walk, relax, do something else for a while. Then return to your draft and try to look at it with a *reader's* eyes.

Rewriting

As Jennifer Bowe reread her first draft, which she had typed, she thought of additional details: the scholarly bums who wander around provoking intellectual conversation, the Sundialburger with the onion casting a shadow. She added these details in pen, later incorporating them into her final version. Do you need more detail in places to make your vision clear and convincing? Then make yourself comfortable and do some more imagining.

In beginning to write her essay on Sundial College, Jennifer Bowe reported that her hardest problem was to introduce "the basically wacky idea" of a campus built on a turntable. "I didn't know how I'd ever get anybody to believe in that campus," she said, "so I tried to describe it in detail, keeping a straight face." She had to try several times before she achieved a result that pleased her. Here is an earlier draft of that troublesome paragraph.

> *When you*   *for the first time, you*
> ~~Anyone who~~ visit*s* the Sundial campus‚notice*s* some-
> thing strange. ⌐Sundial College takes its name from its⌐
>   *which is as*
> design‚ unique as its educational philosophy⫽ ~~so~~ ╕he posi-
>   *for*
> ⌐tion of the sun never changes‚⌐ At the hub of the campus
> ⌐wheel is a great sundial--fixed, keeping faithful time.⌐
>   *rests*   *an enormous*   *rotates*
> The whole campus ~~rotates~~ on ~~a big~~ disk that ~~moves~~ with
> the sun, almost imperceptibly, so that the sun always
> shines down on the college from the same direction. This
> ⌐odd design is not merely an advertising gimmick to make
> ⎮the college sound unique; it is quite practical. Rather
> ⎮than rising in the east and setting in the west, the sun
> ⌐appears to rise straight up and set straight down again.
> *Classrooms are built to receive maximum sunlight at all times, thus saving in*
> ~~The~~ heating costs ~~saved are~~ more than enough to pay for
> running the giant motor that turns the campus. Students

Good way to end the ¶!

Reverse these two sentences.

reading on the lawn do not need to keep moving their
blankets to stay in the sun or the shade.   Greenhouses
stay sunny
~~are in the sun~~ all day long, ~~and the dorm for anyone who~~   *Night Owl Hall, the dorm for people*
who like to stay up late,
~~likes to stay up late~~ has its back to the sun, so that
                                    will   *no*
its late sleepers ~~don't~~ receive ⌃ unwanted morning light.
Lark Hall,
~~There's also a hall~~ for early risers ~~that~~ lights up ⌃ *with the*
                                                                    dawn.
~~early.~~   Although the campus stays fixed in its place in
the sun, it is always in a whirl of exciting activity.

Doesn't belong in this ¶

Jennifer Bowe could see that, to seem convincing to her readers, the paragraph needed reorganizing; and some details had to be more specific. Giving names to the dorms helped. The last sentence clearly introduced a whole new direction. Eventually it began paragraph 7. The completed essay's sentence about the astronomy department was a later addition, inspired by a peer reader's objection that Bowe's campus would play havoc with the study of astronomy.

Ask a fellow student to let you know if he or she has any doubts about what you've written. Here is a list of questions for your peer reader to answer.

PEER EDITING CHECKLIST: WRITING FROM IMAGINATION

- What is your overall reaction to the paper?
- What do you like best about the writer's "What if" thinking?
- What did you find hardest to follow or imagine or accept? Is it because of the ideas themselves or the way the writer presents them or both? List your problems with the "What if's" and explain why they are problems by questioning the writer about them.
- Could what the writer imagines possibly exist? Where should he or she add any details, examples, description, or images to make it seem more possible? Put stars on the manuscript where the writer needs to make the ideas more plausible.
- Look at the way the writer has arranged the materials. Would you make any changes in their organization?
- Can you suggest any other effects of the writer's "What if" thinking?
- Circle on the manuscript any word choice that particularly obstructs your reading and understanding of the essay.
- Put a check mark by any spelling, verb tense, grammar, or punctuation that needs attention.
- If you were handing in this paper for evaluation, what would you be certain to work further on?

A minor problem in envisioning may be to keep your verb tenses straight. As she imagined her ideal college, Jennifer Bowe found herself waffling between the future tense ("you *will notice* something strange") and the conditional ("the huge disk of Sundial College *would accelerate*"). Aware of this problem, she went through her draft and changed all tenses to the present. She had hit upon the simplest solution. In envisioning your imaginary world, why not hold it in the mind's eye as though it now exists?

The belief of poet William Butler Yeats that inspiration can come in rewriting as well as in writing may hold true when you write your "What if" paper. As you revise, you may find fresh and imaginative ideas occurring for the first time. If they occur, by all means let them in.

While you review your paper, you might consider the following points.

REVISION CHECKLIST: WRITING FROM IMAGINATION

- Is your vision consistent? Do all the parts of your vision get along with all the others? Or is some part discordant, needing to be cut out?

- Does your paper at any point need more information about the real world? If so, where might you find it: what can you read, whom can you talk with, what can you observe?

- Have you used any facts that need verifying, any words that need checking? (Jennifer Bowe recalls: "I was glad about finding the right name for the upright hand in the middle of a sundial—the *gnomon*. I didn't know what to call it until I looked up *sundial* in my dictionary and found a picture of a typical sundial, with the names of its parts.")

- What difficulties did you run into in writing your "What if"? Did you overcome them? Are any still present that bother you? If so, what can you do about them?

- Is this vision plausible? Could the world you imagine possibly exist? What physical details, vivid description, images, and illustrations can you add that will make your vision seem real?

Other Assignments

1. Like Jennifer Bowe, author of "If I Could Found a College," imagine an ideal: a person, place, or thing that to your mind would be virtually perfect. Shape this ideal to your own desires. Then put it in writing. Perhaps this ideal might combine the best features of two or three real people, places, or things. Set forth your vision in writing as if you are trying to be useful to someone attempting to achieve something excellent for a practical reason: to improve himself or herself, to build a new town or city or college from the ground up.

If, like Bowe, you envision your ideal college, you will have a decision to make early. Will you imagine a college as conceivably it could exist today (if you too had several billion dollars)? Or will you imagine a college of the future, which could be more nearly perfect (utilizing what science has not yet discovered)? If your ideal could exist only in the future, will you imagine the near future (say, 2000 A.D.) or a more remote future?

In describing your ideal person, city, or college, you may be tempted to build up to a surprise ending. It might seem a great trick to reveal at the end (surprise, surprise!) that your ideal city is really good old Topeka, the best place on earth, or that your ideal mother is really your own real-life mother after all. But it probably won't be a convincing way to write your paper. Nothing that exists is ideal. Simply to describe what exists won't take any imagining.

2. Imagine two alternative versions of your own future, say, ten years down the road: the worst possible future you could have and the best possible. Describe each in detail. This assignment may help you in making long-term plans. (If you would prefer not to limit your vision to your own future, imagine the future of your hometown or city, your region, or your country).

3. Recall the way you envisioned something before you experienced it; then describe the reality you found instead. For instance: "My Dream of College and the Reality," "The London I Expected and the London I Found," "A Eurythmics Concert I Looked Forward To and What I Got." Your expectations, of course, might be good or bad; the reality might be a disappointment or a pleasant surprise. But if possible, pick some topic about which your ideas changed drastically. Write to show your fellow students how your mental picture changed. They might be interested because their mental pictures might coincide with yours (before or after your change).

4. Draw a connection between two things you hadn't ever thought of connecting before. Start with something that interests you—running, moviegoing, sports cars—and try relating it to something remote from it. Connect it to rainstorms, travel, or children's play. See what both have in common and explain their similarity in two or three paragraphs: "The Pleasures of Running in Rain," "Moviegoing: Traveling Vicariously," "Sports Car Buffs as Grown-up Players with Toys," or whatever more appealing topic you can generate.

5. Here are a few short exercises designed to limber your imagination.

   a. By penciling a big *X*, divide a sheet of paper into quarters. In each quarter draw a person, a bird, an animal, a fanciful monster, a machine, or anything else you wish. Diversify the drawings: don't draw birds in all four squares; mix up your subject matter. A wildly assorted mixture will work well for this. The drawings, which can be comic or serious or both, don't need to be of museum quality; they are only for your own use. When you are done, contemplate your four drawings. Then write a one-page story that brings all four subjects together.

   b. Envision the place where you lived for the largest part of your life. Then visualize how it would have looked a hundred years ago or (if you like) how it will look a hundred years from now. Write a passage or paragraph rapidly, setting down any details you can see in your mind's eye.

   c. Divide a sheet of paper into two columns. Write in the left column the names of a list of objects that (for no special reason) please you, intrigue you, or make you laugh. You might make this list from both memory and immediate observation—by just looking around. Then in the right column, for each object complete a sentence that makes a metaphor. For instance, one such list might begin:

> An ant carrying something
> My poodle
> A sailboat
> Althea's elbows

Write rapidly, without trying to be brilliant. Compare each object with another object far removed from it, but in which you can find some similarity. The list might then give rise to metaphors such as these:

> An ant carrying something is a piano mover.
> My poodle is a barking marshmallow.
> A sailboat is a bird with one wing.
> Althea's elbows are a couple of unripe strawberries.

Not all your metaphors will be worth keeping; not all will make sense to anyone else. You have to expect some kernels not to pop. But if you get any metaphors you like, why not share them with the class? (Metaphors like these, incidentally, are sometimes poems in their infancy. If any metaphor turns you on, by all means keep writing—whether in prose or in verse.)

d.   Here is an exercise involving wordplay and other free play of the imagination. Choose a noun with interesting sounds or suggestions, a word or phrase you don't use daily: *luminosity, tyrannosaur, potato mashers, chromosome, platypus,* or perhaps a name such as *Amazon, Peter Ilyich Tchaikovsky.* Then rapidly write a series of statements, each beginning with that word or phrase. The statements need not follow logically or tell a story. Example:

> Peter Ilyich Tchaikovsky was always too shy to ask the prom queen for a date.

FOR GROUP LEARNING

Like Jennifer Bowe, who brainstormed with three friends before she wrote "If I Could Found a College," try a brainstorming session with your writing group to generate ideas for your own paper. When you do this as a group, appoint a recording secretary to set down ideas as fast as they can be transcribed. If possible, meet in an unused classroom or conference room with plenty of chalkboard space so that all present can see the ideas in the act of being recorded. Don't be surprised if this activity seems wild and chaotic; order can emerge from it. Limit your initial brainstorming session to ten or twelve minutes, then stop to discuss the results, circling on the chalkboard any items that draw strong reactions from the group. These may be the seeds that will grow a memorable paper. If nothing much comes out of this first session, brainstorm again. (For further advice on how to brainstorm, see p. 471.)

Peter Ilyich Tchaikovsky attempted to fly by flapping his arms but usually fell on his face.

Peter Ilyich Tchaikovsky couldn't cross the Delaware standing up in a row-boat like George Washington—the Delaware was always frozen and the rowboat leaked.

So far, without deliberate effort on the writer's part, connections are emerging: Peter Ilyich Tchaikovsky is becoming a distinctive and consistent character. That is how the imagination often operates. Our example may be absurd, but it exhibits a truth. "Language," says teacher and researcher Ann Berthoff, "enables us to make the meanings by whose means we discover further meanings."

APPLYING WHAT YOU LEARN: SOME USES OF WRITING FROM IMAGINATION

Imagination, we have suggested, is tremendously useful in much college writing, not only in a creative writing course. In scholarly writing, imagination is essential—as scholarly writers keep insisting. French philosopher of history Paul Veyne points out that a historian has to infer the motives of persons long dead. Understanding the past, Veyne argues, is often a matter of imaginatively "filling in" what cannot be completely documented. In the field of geography, according to Robert W. Durrenberger in *Geographical Research and Writing,* a student who wishes to do research needs most of all to develop imagination. "Admittedly, an individual cannot be taught how to be creative," Durrenberger concedes. "But he can observe those who are creative and be on the lookout for new and original approaches to the solutions of problems."

To show you how you can usefully apply the ways of imagining to your writing in college and beyond, let's consider them one at a time: shifting perspective, envisioning, and synthesizing.

Shifting perspective   The next time you are given an assignment in another course, try looking at the entire topic through someone else's eyes—someone unlike yourself. This way of imagining is often at work in specialized and professional writing. Philosophers and science writers challenge us, as Dr. Peter Saltzstein of Northeast Missouri State University puts it, to "step outside of received opinion or commonly held beliefs and examine those beliefs through the use of alternative perspectives." Thus John Locke, in his *Second Treatise of Government,* calls on his readers to imagine a world owned by all individuals in common, without private ownership. And science writer Garrett Hardin takes a skeptical look at some prevalent popular assumptions. In the following passage from *Naked Emperors: Essays of a Taboo-Stalker,* Hardin shifts perspectives. He imagines that an economist asks an ecologist, "Would you plant a redwood tree in your back yard?" When the ecologist says that he would, the economist charges him with being a fool—in economic terms.

The economist is right, of course. The supporting economic analysis is easily carried out. A redwood tree can hardly be planted for less than a dollar. To mature [it] takes some two thousand years, by which time the tree will be about three hundred feet high. How much is the tree worth then? An economist will insist, of course, on evaluating the forest giant as lumber. Measured at a man's height above the ground, the diameter of the tree will be about ten feet, and the shape of the shaft from there upward is approximately conical. The volume of this cone is 94,248 board feet. At a "stumpage" price of 15 cents a board foot—the approximate price a lumberer must pay for a tree unfelled, unmilled, untransported—the tree would be worth some $14,000.

That may sound like a large return on an investment of only one dollar, but we must not forget how long the investment took to mature: 2000 years. Using the exponential formula to calculate the rate of compound interest we find that the capital earned slightly less than one-half of 1 percent per year. Yes, a man would be an economic fool to put his money into a redwood seedling when so many profitable opportunities lie at hand.

Hardin, of course, is being unfair to economists, many of whom are undoubtedly capable of feeling awe before a giant redwood. But his momentary shift to the strict dollars-and-cents point of view enables him to conclude that, if we care for the future and for our descendants, we sometimes need to act without regard for economics.

Envisioning   Some challenging assignments you'll meet in a college course will set forth a problem and ask you to envision a solution. The following question, from a final examination in an economics course, asks the student to imagine a better procedure:

As we have seen, methods of stabilizing the dollar have depended on enlisting the cooperation of large banks and foreign governments, which has not always been forthcoming. Propose a better, alternative way for our own government to follow in protecting the value of its currency from severe fluctuations.

An effective answer to that question would be based on facts that the student has learned. What the exam question tries to provide is not just practice in recalling facts but also training in bringing them together and applying them.

Students in family science courses may be asked to envision ideal situations, play devil's advocate, even take a stand in opposition to their own when learning to debate issues informatively. In envisioning an ideal, as Jennifer Bowe does in her Sundial College paper, a writer sets up an imagined goal and perhaps also begins thinking about how to achieve it. In his epoch-making speech in Washington, D.C., on the 1963 centennial of Lincoln's Emancipation Proclamation, Martin Luther King, Jr., set forth his vision of an unsegregated future:

I have a dream that one day on the red hills of Georgia the sons of former slaves and the sons of former slave owners will be able to sit down together at the table of brotherhood. . . . I have a dream that my four little children will one day live in a nation where they will not be judged by the color of their skin but by the content of their character.

Synthesizing   Combining unlike things and drawing unexpected conclusions may result in a lively and revealing paper. But in explaining almost anything, an imaginative writer can make metaphors and draw connections. Sylvan Barnet, in *A Short Guide to Writing about Art* (Boston: Little, Brown, 1989), questions whether a period of art can be entirely "Gothic" in spirit. To make a highly abstract idea clear, he introduces a brief *analogy,* a metaphor that likens the unfamiliar thing to something familiar:

> Is there really an all-embracing style in a given period? One can be skeptical, and a simple analogy may be useful. A family often consists of radically different personalities: improvident husband, patient wife, one son an idler and the other a go-getter, one daughter wise in her choice of a career and the other daughter unwise. And yet all may have come from the same culture.

To be sure, imagining has practical applications beyond the writing of college papers and scholarly articles. Asked why World War I took place, Franz Kafka, one of the most influential writers of our century, gave a memorable explanation: the war was caused by a "monstrous lack of imagination." Evidently if we are to survive, we would do well to imagine both World War III and its alternatives—not only the consequences of the problems we now face, but also the solutions.

A Humorist Imagines

James Thurber kept people laughing for many years with his distinctive cartoons, stories, and reminiscences. In the following essay, from *The Middle Aged Man on the Flying Trapeze* (1950), he displays not only his famous sense of humor but also a remarkable ability to reimagine a historical event.

IF GRANT HAD BEEN DRINKING AT APPOMATTOX
James Thurber

The morning of the ninth of April, 1865, dawned beautifully. General   1
Meade was up with the first streaks of crimson in the eastern sky. General Hooker and General Burnside were up, and had breakfasted, by a quarter after eight. The day continued beautiful. It drew on toward eleven o'clock. General Ulysses S. Grant was still not up. He was asleep in his famous old navy hammock, swung high above the floor of his headquarters' bedroom. Headquarters was distressingly disarranged: papers were strewn on the floor; confidential notes from spies scurried here and there in the breeze from an open window; the dregs of an overturned bottle of wine flowed pinkly across an important military map.

Corporal Shultz, of the Sixty-fifth Ohio Voluntary Infantry, aide to General Grant, came into the outer room, looked around him, and sighed. He entered the bedroom and shook the General's hammock roughly. General Ulysses S. Grant opened one eye.   2

"Pardon, sir," said Corporal Shultz, "but this is the day of surrender. You ought to be up, sir."   3

"Don't swing me," said Grant, sharply, for his aide was making the hammock sway gently. "I feel terrible," he added, and he turned over and closed his eye again.   4

"General Lee will be here any minute now," said the Corporal firmly, swinging the hammock again.   5

"Will you cut that out?" roared Grant. "D'ya want to make me sick, or what?" Shultz clicked his heels and saluted. "What's he coming here for?" asked the General.   6

"This is the day of surrender, sir," said Shultz. Grant grunted bitterly.   7

"Three hundred and fifty generals in the Northern armies," said Grant, "and he has to come to *me* about this. What time is it?"   8

"You're the Commander-in-Chief, that's why," said Corporal Shultz. "It's eleven twenty-five, sir."   9

"Don't be crazy," said Grant. "Lincoln is the Commander-in-Chief. Nobody in the history of the world ever surrendered before lunch. Doesn't he know that an army surrenders on its stomach?" He pulled a blanket up over his head and settled himself again.   10

"The generals of the Confederacy will be here any minute now," said the Corporal. "You really ought to be up, sir."   11

Grant stretched his arms above his head and yawned.   12

"All right, all right," he said. He rose to a sitting position and stared about the room. "This place looks awful," he growled.   13

"You must have had quite a time of it last night, sir," ventured Shultz.   14

"Yeh," said General Grant, looking around for his clothes. "I was wrassling some general. Some general with a beard."   15

Shultz helped the commander of the Northern armies in the field to find his clothes.   16

"Where's my other sock?" demanded Grant. Shultz began to look around for it. The General walked uncertainly to a table and poured a drink from a bottle.   17

"I don't think it wise to drink, sir," said Shultz.   18

"Nev' mind about me," said Grant, helping himself to a second, "I can take it or let it alone. Didn' ya ever hear the story about the fella went to Lincoln to complain about me drinking too much? 'So-and-So says Grant drinks too much,' this fella said. 'So-and-So is a fool,' said Lincoln. So this fella went to What's-His-Name and told him what Lincoln said and he came roarin' to Lincoln about it. 'Did you tell So-and-So I was a fool?' he said. 'No,' said Lincoln, 'I thought he knew it.' " The General smiled, reminiscently, and had another drink. "*That's* how I stand with Lincoln," he said, proudly.   19

The soft thudding sound of horses' hooves came through the open   20
window. Shultz hurriedly walked over and looked out.

"Hoof steps," said Grant, with a curious chortle.   21

"It is General Lee and his staff," said Shultz.   22

"Show him in," said the General, taking another drink. "And see what   23
the boys in the back room will have."

Shultz walked smartly over to the door, opened it, saluted, and stood   24
aside. General Lee, dignified against the blue of the April sky, magnificent
in his dress uniform, stood for a moment framed in the doorway. He walked
in, followed by his staff. They bowed, and stood silent. General Grant stared
at them. He only had one boot on and his jacket was unbuttoned.

"I know who you are," said Grant. "You're Robert Browning, the poet."   25

"This is General Robert E. Lee," said one of his staff, coldly.   26

"Oh," said Grant, "I thought he was Robert Browning. He certainly looks   27
like Robert Browning. There was a poet for you, Lee: Browning. Did ja ever
read 'How They Brought the Good News from Ghent to Aix'? 'Up Derek, to
saddle, up Derek, away; up Dunder, up Blitzen, up Prancer, up Dancer, up
Bouncer, up Vixen, up—' "

"Shall we proceed at once to the matter in hand?" asked General Lee,   28
his eyes disdainfully taking in the disordered room.

"Some of the boys was wrassling here last night," explained Grant. "I   29
threw Sherman, or some general a whole lot like Sherman. It was pretty
dark." He handed a bottle of Scotch to the commanding officer of the
Southern armies, who stood holding it, in amazement and discomfiture.
"Get a glass, somebody," said Grant, looking straight at General Longstreet. "Didn't I meet you at Cold Harbor?" he asked. General Longstreet
did not answer.

"I should like to have this over with as soon as possible," said Lee.   30
Grant looked vaguely at Shultz, who walked up close to him, frowning.

"The surrender, sir, the surrender," said Corporal Shultz in a whisper.   31

"Oh sure, sure," said Grant. He took another drink. "All right," he said.   32
"Here we go." Slowly, sadly, he unbuckled his sword. Then he handed it to
the astonished Lee. "There you are, General," said Grant. "We dam' near
licked you. If I'd been feeling better we *would* of licked you."

Questions to Start You Thinking

1. Is Thurber's essay based on any resource besides imagination? Explain.

2. One reader of this essay remarked, "I laughed out loud with surprise when I got
   to the last line. Yet I accepted the ending. And when I looked back over the essay,
   I saw how carefully Thurber had set it up." What evidence can you find in the
   essay of this painstaking care on Thurber's part?

3. What other historical events, given a slight twist, might supply the basis of a
   humorous essay?

An Astrophysicist Imagines

Recently, Alan Lightman, who teaches astronomy and physics, has been writing remarkably clear essays on science for a general audience. In the essay that follows, where does Lightman begin imagining? For what purpose? With what results?

TIME TRAVEL AND PAPA JOE'S PIPE
Alan P. Lightman

When astronomers point their telescopes to the nearest large galaxy, Andromeda, they see it as it was two million years ago. That's about the time Australopithecus was basking in the African sun. This little bit of time travel is possible because light takes two million years to make the trip from there to here. Too bad we couldn't turn things around and observe Earth from some cozy planet in Andromeda. 1

But looking at light from distant objects isn't real time travel, the in-the-flesh participation in past and future of Mark Twain's Connecticut Yankee or H. G. Wells's Time Traveler. Ever since I've been old enough to read science fiction, I've dreamed of time traveling. The possibilities are staggering. You could take medicine back to fourteenth-century Europe and stop the spread of plague, or you could travel to the twenty-third century, where people take their annual holidays in space stations. 2

Being a scientist myself, I know that time travel is quite unlikely according to the laws of physics. For one thing, there would be causality violation. If you could travel backward in time, you could alter a chain of events with the knowledge of how they would have turned out. Cause would no longer always precede effect. For example, you could prevent your parents from ever meeting. Contemplating the consequences of that will give you a headache, and science fiction writers for decades have delighted in the paradoxes that can arise from traveling through time. 3

Physicists are, of course, horrified at the thought of causality violation. Differential equations for the way things should behave under a given set of forces and initial conditions would no longer be valid, since what happens in one instant would not necessarily determine what happens in the next. Physicists do rely on a deterministic universe in which to operate, and time travel would almost certainly put them and most other scientists permanently out of work. 4

But even within the paradigms of physics, there are some technical difficulties for time travel, over and above the annoying fact that its existence would altogether do away with science. The manner in which time flows, as we now understand it, was brilliantly elucidated by Albert Einstein in 1905. First of all, Einstein unceremoniously struck down the Aristotelian and Newtonian ideas of the absoluteness of time, showing that the 5 measured rate at which time flows can vary between observers in relative motion with respect to each other. So far this looks hopeful for time travel.

Einstein also showed, however, that the measured time order of two 6 events could not be reversed without relative motions exceeding the speed of light. In modern physics the speed of light, 186,000 miles per second, is a rather special speed; it is the propagation speed of all electromagnetic radiation in a vacuum, and appears to be nature's fundamental speed limit. From countless experiments, we have failed to find evidence of anything traveling faster than light.

There is another possible way out. In 1915 Einstein enlarged his 1905 7 theory, the Special Theory of Relativity, to include the effects of gravity; the later theory is imaginatively named the General Theory of Relativity. Both theories have remarkably survived all the experimental tests within our capability. According to the General Theory, gravity stretches and twists the geometry of space and time, distorting the temporal and spatial separation of events.

The speed of light still cannot be exceeded locally—that is, for brief 8 trips. But a long trip might sneak through a short cut in space created by gravitational warping, with the net result that a traveler could go between two points by one route in less time than light would require by another route. It's a little like driving from Las Vegas to San Francisco, with the option of a detour around Death Valley. In some cases, these circuitous routes might lead to time travel, which would indeed raise the whole question of causality violation.

The catch is that it is impossible to find any concrete solutions of 9 Einstein's equations that permit time travel and are at the same time well behaved in other respects. All such proposals either require some unattainable configuration of matter, or else have at least one nasty point in space called a "naked singularity" that lies outside the domain of validity of the theory. It is almost as if General Relativity, when pushed toward those circumstances in which all of physics is about to be done away with, digs in its heels and cries out for help.

Still, I dream of time travel. There is something very personal about 10 time. When the first mechanical clocks were invented, marking off time in crisp, regular intervals, it must have surprised people to discover that time flowed outside their own mental and physiological processes. Body time flows at its own variable rate, oblivious to the most precise hydrogen maser clocks in the laboratory.

In fact, the human body contains its own exquisite timepieces, all with 11 their separate rhythms. There are the alpha waves in the brain; another clock is the heart. And all the while tick the mysterious, ruthless clocks that regulate aging.

Nowhere is the external flow of time more evident than in the space- 12 time diagrams developed by Hermann Minkowski, soon after Einstein's early work. A Minkowski diagram is a graph in which time runs along the vertical axis and space along the horizontal axis. Each point in the graph has a time coordinate and a space coordinate, like longitude and latitude, except far more interesting. Instead of depicting only where something is, the diagram tells us when as well.

In a Minkowski diagram, the entire life history, past and future, of a 13 molecule or a man is simply summarized as an unbudging line segment. All this on a single piece of paper. There is something disturbingly similar about a Minkowski diagram and a family tree, in which several generations, from long dead relatives to you and your children, move inevitably downward on the page. I have an urgent desire to tamper with the flow.

Recently, I found my great-grandfather's favorite pipe. Papa Joe, as he 14 was called, died more than fifty years ago, long before I was born. There are few surviving photographs or other memorabilia of Papa Joe. But I do have this pipe. It is a fine old English briar, with a solid bowl and a beautiful straight grain. And it has a silver band at the base of the stem, engraved with three strange symbols. I should add that in well-chosen briar pipes the wood and tobacco form a kind of symbiotic relationship, exchanging juices and aromas with each other, and the bowl retains a slight flavor of each different tobacco smoked in the pipe.

Papa Joe's pipe had been tucked away in a drawer somewhere for years, 15 and was in good condition when I found it. I ran a pipe cleaner through it, filled it with some tobacco I had on hand, and settled down to read and smoke. After a couple of minutes, the most wonderful and foreign blend of smells began wafting from the pipe. All the various tobaccos that Papa Joe had tried at one time or another in his life, all the different occasions when he had lit his pipe, all the different places he had been that I will never know—all had been locked up in that pipe and now poured out into the room. I was vaguely aware that something had got delightfully twisted in time for a moment, skipped upward on the page. There *is* a kind of time travel to be had, if you don't insist on how it happens.

Questions to Start You Thinking

1. "Time travel is quite unlikely according to the laws of physics," Lightman admits in paragraph 3. How, then, do you account for his essay about time travel? For what apparent purpose or purposes does he write? Is Lightman's essay mere entertainment, or does it tell you anything you didn't know before? If so, what?

2. Does the author's emphasis on Papa Joe's pipe at the end of his essay seem misplaced? What does the pipe have to do with time travel?

3. Review the discussion of imagining that opens this chapter. How does Lightman's essay demonstrate imagining?

Further
Writing Assignments:
Combining Resources

Suppose that, in writing a psychology paper drawn from your reading in Sigmund Freud's *Interpretation of Dreams,* you remember a vivid dream you had wherein, say, you found yourself barefoot, climbing a mountain of ice cream. Unless your assignment told you, "Keep your own dreams out of this," why not go ahead and recall it in writing? Your five resources (recalling, observing, reading, conversing, and imagining) don't need to be kept in separate compartments. Besides, they may prove useful to you in virtually any college assignment you may write.

For practice in combining your resources, here are assignments that tap more than one of them.

Recalling and Observing

Visit and describe a place long familiar to you, a place that has undergone changes over the years. These changes may be external and visible, or they may have occurred in *you:* in the way you now see the place, as opposed to the way it once seemed to you. Make comparisons between the way the place is now and how it used to be.

Recalling and Observing

Like Joan Didion, who observes the wedding chapel scene in "Marrying Absurd" (p. 39), have you ever been in a place you thought fake, tacky, or depressingly pretentious? If so, what did you observe at the time that gave you such an impression? Write a short description, recalling what you observed.

Recalling and Reading

Recall a subject you know well—a sport, a business, a film or current television program, a city. Then find out what another writer has had to say about it. (Recent numbers of the *Readers' Guide to Periodical Literature* in your library's reference room will lead you to promising magazine articles.)

In a short paper that you'd be willing to have your fellow students read, compare the writer's view of the subject with your own knowledge drawn from recall. What does the writer tell you that you find enlightening? What do you know from your own experience that the professional writer left out?

Recalling, Observing, and Conversing

What changes have taken place in television programs for children and young people since you were a child? Discuss some of those changes with a group of your fellow students. What changes in society—in manners and attitudes—do they mirror?

Perhaps you can observe reruns of *The Brady Bunch* or *The Partridge Family* or recall *Mr. Rogers* or *Captain Kangaroo* or any other programs you used to watch. How, you might inquire, do the script writers regard women? How has the American family changed over the years? Do most families still enjoy the sit-down-together family dinner at home? Is the loving, uniformed servant like the Bradys' Alice a familiar figure in many households today? (It might be risky to assume that she was familiar back then.) Are there programs on the air today with which you might compare these beloved antiques? Twist that dial, probe, ponder. Since you were eight years old, what shifts have taken place in the national consciousness?

Reading and Conversing

Browse through a few articles in current magazines. (The magazines need not be *Time* or *Newsweek:* why not look around your library's periodicals room and meet an interesting magazine or professional journal you hadn't known before?) Keep browsing until you find an article that provokes you to strong feeling. Maybe it will anger you, disturb or frighten you, or make you wonder how any writer could be that dumb. Make a photocopy of the article.

Write your interpretation of the article. What message does it convey? What does it demonstrate?

Next, show the article to another student. Ask him or her to read it closely and discuss it with you. Compare your interpretations; see whether either of you missed anything interesting.

Finally, write a second account of what you now think the article is saying. If your original interpretation hasn't changed (or, if you like, even if it has), write an answer or retort to the writer.

Observing and Imagining

Do writing assignment 2 on page 50—observing, like a good detective, another person in a public place without that person observing you. Then add the following step.

Piece together the person's probable situation at home or on the job. Feel free to speculate. What do you think your subject does in everyday life, when you aren't around to observe?

Reading and Imagining

Read a news account of an event in a distant country. Then put yourself in the shoes of the people affected: imagine that this event has taken place in your own neighborhood. How would the event affect you and people you know?

Reading, Observing, and Imagining

Here is the opening of an article, "The Tactile Land," by naturalist Robert Finch in *Sanctuary* magazine, a publication of the Massachusetts Audubon Society. Read it and briefly react to it, trying it on your own experience. Then observe something and report it as Finch reports the mother's caress. If you were to take Finch's kind of observing to heart, how might it change your view of the world?

> Several years ago, as I sat in a maternity clinic waiting room anticipating the birth of my second child, I happened to see a young mother across the way just as she reached out, and, in a purely unconscious gesture, casually caressed the head of her little boy, just beyond his ear. Because I had performed that same unconscious parental gesture hundreds of times, I not only saw the movement of her hand but felt it—felt the curve of the child's head, the fine texture of the hair, the swirl and dip of the crown, the hollow behind the ear, the small, soft, fleshy fold of ear lobe. From unpremeditated and forgotten affection there now rose, with this sight, palpable ripples of remembered feeling, tactile memories surfacing to color, warm, and revivify this simple visual scene. It was real to me, this tracing of the child's head by the woman; it enriched not only the present moment, but gave back to me parts of my own life that had gone unrecognized at the time.
>
> That was the first time I became strongly aware of the great difference between merely observing an action or a scene and seeing it infused with the

memory of tactile and emotional sensation. Drugs and danger, we are told, can heighten or expand the senses, but it seems to me that life is vivid to us primarily insofar as we have previously insinuated ourselves into it and gives us back a part of ourselves as we behold it in others in just such numerous, characteristically small ways.

Recalling, Observing, Reading, and Conversing

What does a professional critic of architecture think of a contemporary shopping mall? Barrie B. Greenbie examines malls in his study *Spaces: Dimensions of the Human Landscape.* Read the passage critically. How well do Greenbie's observations fit any mall or malls you know?

> The term *mall,* which used to mean a large, outdoor, public place, now refers to such a place under a roof. In some ways, the good shopping centers have returned the market street to the pedestrian better than have the central business districts of towns because the cars are left outside. A few of these shopping malls are as colorful and interesting as any other bazaars. A number of studies, including one in which I participated, have shown that people go to them as much for sociability as to purchase necessities. Youth gangs, which used to hang out around the neighborhood candy store, now drag race over to the local shopping plaza and hang out there.
>
> The typical design of shopping centers calls for one or more large department stores as "anchors" (really magnets), between which are strung the smaller stores for so-called impulse shopping. Not only are they a place for strolling and people-watching, but for many community functions, such as charity fund drives, which used to be associated with central business districts. The shops generally do not have the personality of those operated by individual proprietors; most mall developers will rent space only to chains, which are viewed as being more reliable tenants than single-owner stores. The merchandise tends to be monotonously similar, with emphasis on products for youth. Most such emporiums do not offer the unique sense of place and the sensual variety of an old city center, but they are nevertheless very sociable promenades. . . . Their greatest weakness, as compared with lively pedestrian spaces downtown, is that they have no visible relationship to a larger exterior environment. That has been given over to parking. For example, the shopping mall which is the major public node of the "new town" of Columbia, Maryland, is as bleak on the outside as any warehouse, perhaps more so. Inside, however, it is an elegant commercial plaza, with pedestrian streets surrounded by lively architecture and spaces that can only be described as parks.

Discuss this passage in class or outside of class. Try to state what Greenbie apparently feels toward shopping malls and toward old city centers. In the usual designs or arrangements of places where people may shop, stroll, and congregate, what does he admire? What does he condemn?

In a paragraph or two based on your own recollections and observations, nourished too from your class discussion or conversation, write for or against Greenbie's view of a typical shopping mall of today. Don't hesitate to set forth your own likes and dislikes.

Recalling, Observing, Reading, Conversing, and Imagining

Recall an event of national or international significance that took place in your own lifetime: a disaster, an important discovery or breakthrough, a famous trial, whatever. Discuss the event with your peers to compare memories of it. Do some background reading so that you're sure you've got the facts straight, list some visible results that followed from this event, and then, in writing, imagine ways in which the world would now be different if the event had never occurred.

Essays Combining Resources

Over a long and distinguished career, black author and teacher Ralph Ellison has written essays, criticism, stories, and a novel about growing up black in America that many consider a classic: *Invisible Man* (1952). In this well-documented, imaginative essay, he wonders: What if American history had gone in a different direction?

WHAT AMERICA WOULD BE LIKE WITHOUT BLACKS
Ralph Ellison

The fantasy of an America free of blacks is at least as old as the dream 1 of creating a truly democratic society. While we are aware that there is something inescapably tragic about the cost of achieving our democratic ideals, we keep such tragic awareness segregated to the rear of our minds. We allow it to come to the fore only during moments of great national crisis.

On the other hand, there is something so embarrassingly absurd about 2 the notion of purging the nation of blacks that it seems hardly a product of thought at all. It is more like a primitive reflex, a throwback to the dim past of tribal experience, which we rationalize and try to make respectable by dressing it up in the gaudy and highly questionable trappings of what we call the "concept of race." Yet, despite its absurdity, the fantasy of a blackless America continues to turn up. It is a fantasy born not merely of racism but of petulance, of exasperation, of moral fatigue. It is like a boil bursting forth from impurities in the bloodstream of democracy.

In its benign manifestations, it can be outrageously comic—as in the picaresque adventures of Percival Brownlee who appears in William Faulkner's story "The Bear." Exasperating to his white masters because his aspirations and talents are for preaching and conducting choirs rather than for farming, Brownlee is "freed" after much resistance and ends up as the prosperous proprietor of a New Orleans brothel. In Faulkner's hands, the uncomprehending drive of Brownlee's owners to "get shut" of him is comically instructive. Indeed, the story resonates certain abiding, tragic themes of American history with which it is interwoven, and which are causing great turbulence in the social atmosphere today. I refer to the exasperation and bemusement of the white American with the black, the black American's ceaseless (and swiftly accelerating) struggle to escape the misconceptions of whites, and the continual confusing of the black American's racial background with his individual culture. Most of all, I refer to the recurring fantasy of solving one basic problem of American democracy by "getting shut" of the blacks through various wishful schemes that would banish them from the nation's bloodstream, from its social structure, and from its conscience and historical consciousness.

This fantastic vision of a lily-white America appeared as early as 1713, with the suggestion of a white "native American," thought to be from New Jersey, that all the Negroes be given their freedom and returned to Africa. In 1777, Thomas Jefferson, while serving in the Virginia legislature, began drafting a plan for the gradual emancipation and exportation of the slaves. Nor were Negroes themselves immune to the fantasy. In 1815, Paul Cuffe, a wealthy merchant, shipbuilder, and landowner from the New Bedford area, shipped and settled at his own expense thirty-eight of his fellow Negroes in Africa. It was perhaps his example that led in the following year to the creation of the American Colonization Society, which was to establish in 1821 the colony of Liberia. Great amounts of cash and a perplexing mixture of motives went into the venture. The slaveowners and many Border-state politicians wanted to use it as a scheme to rid the country not of slaves but of the militant free Negroes who were agitating against the "peculiar institution." The abolitionists, until they took a lead from free Negro leaders and began attacking the scheme, also participated as a means of righting a great historical injustice. Many blacks went along with it simply because they were sick of the black and white American mess and hoped to prosper in the quiet peace of the old ancestral home.

Such conflicting motives doomed the Colonization Society to failure, but what amazes one even more than the notion that anyone could have believed in its success is the fact that it was attempted during a period when the blacks, slave and free, made up eighteen percent of the total population. When we consider how long blacks had been in the New World and had been transforming it and being Americanized by it, the scheme appears not only fantastic, but the product of a free-floating irrationality. Indeed, a national pathology.

Nevertheless, some of the noblest of Americans were bemused. Not only Jefferson but later Abraham Lincoln was to give the scheme credence. According to historian John Hope Franklin, Negro colonization seemed as important to Lincoln as emancipation. In 1862, Franklin notes, Lincoln called a group of prominent free Negroes to the White House and urged them to support colonization, telling them, "Your race suffers greatly, many of them by living among us, while ours suffers from your presence. If this is admitted, it affords a reason why we should be separated." 6

In spite of his unquestioned greatness, Abraham Lincoln was a man of his times and limited by some of the less worthy thinking of his times. This is demonstrated both by his reliance upon the concept of race in his analysis of the American dilemma and by his involvement in a plan of purging the nation of blacks as a means of healing the badly shattered ideals of democratic federalism. Although benign, his motive was no less a product of fantasy. It envisaged an attempt to relieve an inevitable suffering that marked the growing pains of the youthful body politic by an operation which would have amounted to the severing of a healthy and indispensable member. 7

Yet, like its twin, the illusion of secession, the fantasy of a benign amputation that would rid the country of black men to the benefit of a nation's health not only persists; today, in the form of neo-Garveyism,° it fascinates black men no less than it once hypnotized whites. Both fantasies become operative whenever the nation grows weary of the struggle toward the ideal of American democratic equality. Both would use the black man as a scapegoat to achieve a national catharsis, and both would, by way of curing the patient, destroy him. 8

What is ultimately intriguing about the fantasy of "getting shut" of the Negro American is the fact that no one who entertains it seems ever to have considered what the nation would have become had Africans *not* been brought to the New World, and had their descendants not played such a complex and confounding role in the creation of American history and culture. Nor do they appear to have considered with any seriousness the effect upon the nation of having any of the schemes for exporting blacks succeed beyond settling some fifteen thousand or so in Liberia. 9

We are reminded that Daniel Patrick Moynihan, who has recently aggravated our social confusion over the racial issue while allegedly attempting to clarify it, is coauthor of a work which insists that the American melting 10

neo-Garveyism: Referring to Marcus Aurelius Garvey (1887–1940), a black Jamaican leader active in this country from 1916 to 1925. He advocated separation and emigration to Africa for American blacks.

pot didn't melt because our white ethnic groups have resisted all assimilative forces that appear to threaten their identities. The problem here is that few Americans know who and what they really are. That is why few of these groups—or at least few of the children of these groups—have been able to resist the movies, television, baseball, jazz, football, drum-majoretting, rock, comic strips, radio commercials, soap operas, book clubs, slang, or any of a thousand other expressions and carriers of our pluralistic and easily available popular culture. And it is here precisely that ethnic resistance is least effective. On this level the melting pot did indeed melt, creating such deceptive metamorphoses and blending of identities, values, and lifestyles that most American whites are culturally part Negro American without even realizing it.

If we can resist for a moment the temptation to view everything having   11
to do with Negro Americans in terms of their racially imposed status, we become aware of the fact that for all the harsh reality of the social and economic injustices visited upon them, these injustices have failed to keep Negroes clear of the cultural mainstream; Negro Americans are in fact one of its major tributaries. If we can cease approaching American social reality in terms of such false concepts as white and nonwhite, black culture and white culture, and think of these apparently unthinkable matters in the realistic manner of Western pioneers confronting the unknown prairie, perhaps we can begin to imagine what the United States would have been, or not been, had there been no blacks to give it—if I may be so bold as to say—color.

For one thing, the American nation is in a sense the product of the   12
American language, a colloquial speech that began emerging long before the British colonials and Africans were transformed into Americans. It is a language that evolved from the king's English but, basing itself upon the realities of the American land and colonial institutions—or lack of institutions—began quite early as a vernacular revolt against the signs, symbols, manners, and authority of the mother country. It is a language that began by merging the sounds of many tongues, brought together in the struggle of diverse regions. And whether it is admitted or not, much of the sound of that language is derived from the timbre of the African voice and the listening habits of the African ear. So there is a *de'z* and *do'z* of slave speech sounding beneath our most polished Harvard accents, and if there is such a thing as a Yale accent, there is a Negro wail in it—doubtlessly introduced there by Old Yalie John C. Calhoun, who probably got it from his mammy.

Whitman viewed the spoken idiom of Negro Americans as a source for   13
a native grand opera. Its flexibility, its musicality, its rhythms, freewheeling diction, and metaphors, as projected in Negro American folklore, were absorbed by the creators of our great nineteenth-century literature even when the majority of blacks were still enslaved. Mark Twain celebrated it in the prose of *Huckleberry Finn;* without the presence of blacks, the book could

not have been written. No Huck and Jim, no American novel as we know it. For not only is the black man a cocreator of the language that Mark Twain raised to the level of literary eloquence, but Jim's condition as American and Huck's commitment to freedom are at the moral center of the novel.

In other words, had there been no blacks, certain creative tensions   14 arising from the cross-purposes of whites and blacks would also not have existed. Not only would there have been no Faulkner; there would have been no Stephen Crane, who found certain basic themes of his writing in the Civil War. Thus, also, there would have been no Hemingway, who took Crane as a source and guide. Without the presence of Negro American style, our jokes, our tall tales, even our sports would be lacking in the sudden turns, the shocks, the swift changes of pace (all jazz-shaped) that serve to remind us that the world is ever unexplored, and that while a complete mastery of life is mere illusion, the real secret of the game is to make life swing. It is its ability to articulate this tragic-comic attitude toward life that explains much of the mysterious power and attractiveness of that quality of Negro American style known as "soul." An expression of American diversity within unity, of blackness with whiteness, soul announces the presence of a creative struggle against the realities of existence.

Without the presence of blacks, our political history would have been   15 otherwise. No slave economy, no Civil War; no violent destruction of the Reconstruction; no K.K.K. and no Jim Crow system. And without the disenfranchisement of black Americans and the manipulation of racial fears and prejudices, the disproportionate impact of white Southern politicians upon our domestic and foreign policies would have been impossible. Indeed, it is almost impossible to conceive of what our political system would have become without the snarl of forces—cultural, racial, religious—that make our nation what it is today.

Absent, too, would be the need for that tragic knowledge which we try   16 ceaselessly to evade: that the true subject of democracy is not simply material well-being but the extension of the democratic process in the direction of perfecting itself. And that the most obvious test and clue to that perfection is the inclusion—*not* assimilation—of the black man.

Questions to Start You Thinking

1. How many of the five resources for writers does Ellison use in his essay? Which one predominates?

2. What purpose is served by paragraphs 4–7?

3. Ellison makes a startling statement: that "most American whites are culturally part Negro American without even realizing it." What does he mean by this statement? What evidence does he give to support it?

4. What does Ellison have to say about democracy? Does his view of it differ from your own? If so, how?

Phyllis Rose, a professor of English at Wesleyan University, has written notable biographies: *Woman of Letters: A Life of Virginia Woolf* (1978) and a study of the wives of famous Englishmen, *Parallel Lives: Five Victorian Marriages* (1983). In an essay that draws on more than one resource, she brings fresh insight to a horrifying subject.

TOOLS OF TORTURE
Phyllis Rose

In a gallery off the rue Dauphine, near the *parfumerie*° where I get my   1
massage, I happened upon an exhibit of medieval torture instruments. It made me think that pain must be as great a challenge to the human imagination as pleasure. Otherwise there's no accounting for the number of torture instruments. One would be quite enough. The simple pincer, let's say, which rips out flesh. Or the head crusher, which breaks first your tooth sockets, then your skull. But in addition I saw tongs, thumb-screws, a rack, a ladder, ropes and pulleys, a grill, a garrote, a Spanish horse, a Judas cradle, an iron maiden, a cage, a gag, a strappado, a stretching table, a saw, a wheel, a twisting stork, an inquisitor's chair, a breast breaker, and a scourge. You don't need complicated machinery to cause incredible pain. If you want to saw your victim down the middle, for example, all you need is a slightly bigger than usual saw. If you hold the victim upside down so the blood stays in his head, hold his legs apart, and start sawing at the groin, you can get as far as the navel before he loses consciousness.

Even in the Middle Ages, before electricity, there were many things you   2
could do to torment a person. You could tie him up in an iron belt that held the arms and legs up to the chest and left no point of rest, so that all his muscles went into spasm within minutes and he was driven mad within hours. This was the twisting stork, a benign-looking object. You could stretch him out backward over a thin piece of wood so that his whole body weight rested on his spine, which pressed against the sharp wood. Then you could stop up his nostrils and force water into his stomach through his mouth. Then, if you wanted to finish him off, you and your helper could jump on his stomach, causing internal hemorrhage. This torture was called the rack. If you wanted to burn someone to death without hearing him scream, you could use a tongue lock, a metal rod between the jaw and collarbone that prevented him from opening his mouth. You could put a person in a chair with spikes on the seat and arms, tie him down against the spikes and beat him, so that every time he flinched from the beating he drove his own flesh deeper onto the spikes. This was the inquisitor's chair. If you wanted to make it worse, you could heat the spikes. You could

parfumerie: Parisian perfume shop and beauty parlor.

suspend a person over a pointed wooden pyramid and whenever he started to fall asleep, you could drop him onto the point. If you were Ippolito Marsili, the inventor of this torture, known as the Judas cradle, you could tell yourself you had invented something humane, a torture that worked without burning flesh or breaking bones. For the torture here was supposed to be sleep deprivation.

The secret of torture, like the secret of French cuisine, is that nothing 3
is unthinkable. The human body is like a foodstuff, to be grilled, pounded, filleted. Every opening exists to be stuffed, all flesh to be carved off the bone. You take an ordinary wheel, a heavy wooden wheel with spokes. You lay the victim on the ground with blocks of wood at strategic points under his shoulders, legs, and arms. You use the wheel to break every bone in his body. Next you tie his body onto the wheel. With all its bones broken, it will be pliable. However, the victim will not be dead. If you want to kill him, you hoist the wheel aloft on the end of a pole and leave him to starve. Who would have thought to do this with a man and a wheel? But, then, who would have thought to take the disgusting snail, force it to render its ooze, stuff it in its own shell with garlic butter, bake it, and eat it?

Not long ago I had a facial—only in part because I thought I needed 4
one. It was research into the nature and function of pleasure. In a dark booth at the back of the beauty salon, the aesthetician put me on a table and applied a series of ointments to my face, some cool, some warmed. After a while she put something into my hand, cold and metallic. "Don't be afraid, madame," she said. "It is an electrode. It will not hurt you. The other end is attached to two metal cylinders, which I roll over your face. They break down the electricity barrier on your skin and allow the moisturizers to penetrate deeply." I didn't believe this hocus-pocus. I didn't believe in the electricity barrier or in the ability of these rollers to break it down. But it all felt very good. The cold metal on my face was a pleasant change from the soft warmth of the aesthetician's fingers. Still, since Algeria° it's hard to hear the word "electrode" without fear. So when she left me for a few minutes with a moist, refreshing cheesecloth over my face, I thought, What if the goal of her expertise had been pain, not moisture? What if the electrodes had been electrodes in the Algerian sense? What if the cheesecloth mask were dipped in acid?

In Paris, where the body is so pampered, torture seems particularly 5
sinister, not because it's hard to understand but because—as the dark side of sensuality—it seems so easy. Beauty care is among the glories of Paris. *Soins esthétiques*° include makeup, facials, massages (both relaxing and

---

Algeria: During the Algerian war of 1956–62, in which this former French colony rebelled and achieved independence, French authorities were accused of torturing members of the National Liberation Front by the use of electric shock.
Soins esthétiques: Beauty treatments.

reducing), depilations (partial and complete), manicures, pedicures, and tanning, in addition to the usual run of *soins* for the hair: cutting, brushing, setting, waving, styling, blowing, coloring, and streaking. In Paris the state of your skin, hair, and nerves is taken seriously, and there is little of the puritanical thinking that tries to persuade us that beauty comes from within. Nor do the French think, as Americans do, that beauty should be offhand and low-maintenance. Spending time and money on *soins esthétiques* is appropriate and necessary, not self-indulgent. Should that loving attention to the body turn malevolent, you have torture. You have the procedure— the aesthetic, as it were—of torture, the explanation for the rich diversity of torture instruments, but you do not have the cause.

Historically torture has been a tool of legal systems, used to get information needed for a trial or, more directly, to determine guilt or innocence. In the Middle Ages confession was considered the best of all proofs, and torture was the way to produce a confession. In other words, torture didn't come into existence to give vent to human sadism. It is not always private and perverse but sometimes social and institutional, vetted by the government and, of course, the Church. (There have been few bigger fans of torture than Christianity and Islam.) Righteousness, as much as viciousness, produces torture. There aren't squads of sadists beating down the doors to the torture chambers begging for jobs. Rather, as a recent book on torture by Edward Peters says, the institution of torture creates sadists; the weight of a culture, Peters suggests, is necessary to recruit torturers. You have to convince people that they are working for a great goal in order to get them to overcome their repugnance to the task of causing physical pain to another person. Usually the great goal is the preservation of society, and the victim is presented to the torturer as being in some way out to destroy it.

From another point of view, what's horrifying is how easily you can persuade someone that he is working for the common good. Perhaps the most appalling psychological experiment of modern times, by Stanley Milgram, showed that ordinary, decent people in New Haven, Connecticut, could be brought to the point of inflicting (as they thought) severe electric shocks on other people in obedience to an authority and in pursuit of a goal, the advancement of knowledge, of which they approved.° (Milgram

Perhaps the most appalling . . . approved: Milgram, a clinical psychologist, conducted a famous and controversial experiment in 1963 at Yale University. The subjects, called "teachers," were charged with administering painful electric shocks to a "learner" whenever he made an error in repeating a list from memory. The learner, supposedly strapped in a chair, was invisible to the teacher. Over an intercom, an actor playing the learner gave realistic screams after each shock and pretended to plead for mercy. If the teacher hesitated to inflict more punishment, a psychologist in a white coat would urge him to step up the intensity of the shock. Milgram found that 65 percent of the subjects failed to break off the experiment but kept increasing the shocks up to the highest level. The experiment, he concluded, helped account for the behavior of ordinary citizens in Nazi Germany who, feeling no personal responsibility, obeyed instructions from authority. (For an account of Milgram's experiment, see Henry Gleitman, *Basic Psychology* [New York: Norton, 1983], 364–66.)

used—some would say abused—the prestige of science and the university to make his point, but his point is chilling nonetheless. We can cluck over torture, but the evidence at least suggests that with intelligent handling most of us could be brought to do it ourselves.

In the Middle Ages, Milgram's experiment would have had no point. It would have shocked no one that people were capable of cruelty in the interest of something they believed in. That was as it should be. Only recently in the history of human thought has the avoidance of cruelty moved to the forefront of ethics. "Putting cruelty first," as Judith Shklar says in *Ordinary Vices*, is comparatively new. The belief that the "pursuit of happiness" is one of man's inalienable rights, the idea that "cruel and unusual punishment" is an evil in itself, the Benthamite° notion that behavior should be guided by what will produce the greatest happiness for the greatest number—all these principles are only two centuries old. They were born with the eighteenth-century democratic revolutions. And in two hundred years they have not been universally accepted. Wherever people believe strongly in some cause, they will justify torture—not just the Nazis, but the French in Algeria.

Many people who wouldn't hurt a fly have annexed to fashion the imagery of torture—the thongs and spikes and metal studs—hence reducing it to the frivolous and transitory. Because torture has been in the mainstream and not on the margins of history, nothing could be healthier. For torture to be merely kinky would be a big advance. Exhibitions like the one I saw in Paris, which presented itself as educational, may be guilty of pandering to the tastes they deplore. Solemnity may be the wrong tone. If taking one's goals too seriously is the danger, the best discouragement of torture may be a radical hedonism that denies that any goal is worth the means, that refuses to allow the nobly abstract to seduce us from the sweetness of the concrete. Give people a good croissant and a good cup of coffee in the morning. Give them an occasional facial and a plate of escargots.° Marie Antoinette picked a bad moment° to say "Let them eat cake," but I've often thought she was on the right track.

All of which brings me back to Paris, for Paris exists in the imagination of much of the world as the capital of pleasure—of fun, food, art, folly, seduction, gallantry, and beauty. Paris is civilization's reminder to itself that nothing leads you less wrong than your awareness of your own pleasure and a genial desire to spread it around. In that sense the myth of Paris constitutes a moral touchstone, standing for the selfish frivolity that helps keep priorities straight.

Benthamite: Disciple of Jeremy Bentham, an eighteenth-century English jurist and social philosopher. A materialist, Bentham founded utilitarianism, the school of thought that holds that the rightness or wrongness of an action should be determined from its results.
escargots: Snails.
Marie Antoinette . . . a bad moment: According to a famous anecdote, Marie made her remark when an official explained why the people of Paris were angry: "Because they have no bread."

Questions to Start You Thinking

1. In the opening paragraphs of this essay, where do you find the author recalling? Imagining? Upon what other resource or resources does she draw for material?
2. In paragraph 5, Rose juxtaposes torture with French cooking; in paragraphs 4 and 5, torture with elaborate beauty treatments. What is her point? How convincing is her attempt to find in these dissimilar things a common denominator?
3. Which of these statements comes closest to Rose's apparent purpose in writing? (1) To fill us with horror at humans' inhumanity to other humans; (2) to explain why the custom of torture began; (3) to defend "selfish frivolity."
4. What audience do you find Rose addressing? Try to tell from her allusions, her choice of words.
5. The *tone* of a piece of writing is its author's attitude toward his or her material. How would you describe the tone of Rose's essay? Does it seem incongruous for a discussion of torture? What, in Rose's view, are the dangers of "taking one's goals too seriously" (paragraph 9)?

Czech-born Marie Winn's landmark book *The Plug-in Drug: Television, Children, and the Family* attracted wide attention when it appeared in 1977. The following essay, taken from that book, still seems as fresh and pointed as when it was written.

THE PLUG-IN DRUG
Marie Winn

A quarter of a century after the introduction of television into American 1 society, a period that has seen the medium become so deeply ingrained in American life that in at least one state the television set has attained the rank of a legal necessity, safe from repossession in case of debt along with clothes, cooking utensils, and the like, television viewing has become an inevitable and ordinary part of daily life. Only in the early years of television did writers and commentators have sufficient perspective to separate the activity of watching television from the actual content it offers the viewer. In those early days writers frequently discussed the effects of television on family life. However, a curious myopia afflicted those early observers: almost without exception they regarded television as a favorable, beneficial, indeed, wondrous influence upon the family.

"Television is going to be a real asset in every home where there are 2 children," predicts a writer in 1949.

"Television will take over your way of living and change your children's 3 habits, but this change can be a wonderful improvement," claims another commentator.

"No survey's needed, of course, to establish that television has brought   4
the family together in one room," writes the *New York Times* television critic
in 1949.

Each of the early articles about television is invariably accompanied by   5
a photograph or illustration showing a family cozily sitting together before
the television set, Sis on Mom's lap, Buddy perched on the arm of Dad's
chair, Dad with his arm around Mom's shoulder. Who could have guessed
that twenty or so years later Mom would be watching a drama in the kitchen,
the kids would be looking at cartoons in their room, while Dad would be
taking in the ball game in the living room?

Of course television sets were enormously expensive in those early   6
days. The idea that by 1975 more than 60 percent of American families
would own two or more sets was preposterous. The splintering of the
multiple-set family was something the early writers could not foresee. Nor
did anyone imagine the number of hours children would eventually devote
to television, the common use of television by parents as a child pacifier,
the changes television would effect upon childrearing methods, the increasing domination of family schedules by children's viewing requirements—in short, the *power* of the new medium to dominate family life.

After the first years, as children's consumption of the new medium   7
increased, together with parental concern about the possible effects of so
much television viewing, a steady refrain helped to soothe and reassure
anxious parents. "Television always enters a pattern of influences that already exist: the home, the peer group, the school, the church and culture
generally," write the authors of an early and influential study of television's
effects on children. In other words, if the child's home life is all right,
parents need not worry about the effects of all that television watching.

But television does not merely influence the child; it deeply influences   8
that "pattern of influences" that is meant to ameliorate its effects. Home
and family life have changed in important ways since the advent of television. The peer group has become television-oriented, and much of the
time children spend together is occupied by television viewing. Culture
generally has been transformed by television. Therefore it is improper to
assign to television the subsidiary role its many apologists (too often members of the television industry) insist it plays. Television is not merely one
of a number of important influences upon today's child. Through the
changes it has made in family life, television emerges as *the* important
influence in children's lives today.

THE QUALITY OF FAMILY LIFE

Television's contribution to family life has been an equivocal one. For while   9
it has, indeed, kept the members of the family from dispersing, it has not
served to bring them *together.* By its domination of the time families spend
together, it destroys the special quality that distinguishes one family from
another, a quality that depends to a great extent on what a family *does,*

what special rituals, games, recurrent jokes, familiar songs, and shared activities it accumulates.

"Like the sorcerer of old," writes Urie Bronfenbrenner,° "the television set casts its magic spell, freezing speech and action, turning the living into silent statues so long as the enchantment lasts. The primary danger of the television screen lies not so much in the behavior it produces—although there is danger there—as in the behavior it prevents: the talks, the games, the family festivities and arguments through which much of the child's learning takes place and through which his character is formed. Turning on the television set can turn off the process that transforms children into people." 10

Yet parents have accepted a television-dominated family life so completely that they cannot see how the medium is involved in whatever problems they might be having. A first grade teacher reports: 11

"I have one child in the group who's an only child. I wanted to find out more about her family life because this little girl was quite isolated from the group, didn't make friends, so I talked to her mother. Well, they don't have time to do anything in the evening, the mother said. The parents come home after picking up the child at the baby-sitter's. Then the mother fixes dinner while the child watches TV. Then they have dinner and the child goes to bed. I said to this mother, 'Well, couldn't she help you fix dinner? That would be a nice time for the two of you to talk,' and the mother said, 'Oh, but I'd hate to have her miss *Zoom*.° It's such a good program!' " 12

Even when families make efforts to control television, too often its very presence counterbalances the positive features of family life. A writer and mother of two boys aged three and seven described her family's television schedule in an article in the *New York Times*: 13

> We were in the midst of a full-scale War. Every day was a new battle and every program was a major skirmish. We agreed it was a bad scene all around and were ready to enter diplomatic negotiations. . . . In principle we have agreed on 2½ hours of TV a day, *Sesame Street, Electric Company* (with dinner gobbled up in between) and two half-hour shows between 7 and 8:30 which enables the grown-ups to eat in peace and prevents the two boys from destroying one another. Their pre-bedtime choice is dreadful, because, as Josh recently admitted, "There's nothing much on I really like." So . . . it's *What's My Line* or *To Tell the Truth*. . . . Clearly there is a need for first-rate children's shows at this time.

Consider the "family life" described here: Presumably the father comes home from work during the *Sesame Street–Electric Company* stint. The children are either watching television, gobbling their dinner, or both. While the parents eat their dinner in peaceful privacy, the children watch another hour of television. Then there is only a half-hour left before bedtime, just 14

Urie Bronfenbrenner: American psychologist.
Zoom: Popular 1970s public television program for elementary school children.

enough time for baths, getting pajamas on, brushing teeth, and so on. The children's evening is regimented with an almost military precision. They watch their favorite programs, and when there is "nothing much on I really like," they watch whatever else is on—because *watching* is the important thing. Their mother does not see anything amiss with watching programs just for the sake of watching; she only wishes there were some first-rate children's shows on at those times.

Without conjuring up memories of the Victorian era with family games, 15 and long, leisurely meals, and large families, the question arises: Isn't there a better family life available than this dismal, mechanized arrangement of children watching television for however long is allowed them, evening after evening?

Of course, families today still do *special* things together at times: go 16 camping in the summer, go to the zoo on a nice Sunday, take various trips and expeditions. But their *ordinary* daily life together is diminished—that sitting around at the dinner table, that spontaneous taking up of an activity, those little games invented by children on the spur of the moment when there is nothing else to do, the scribbling, the chatting, and even the quarreling, all the things that form the fabric of a family, that define a childhood. Instead, the children have their regular schedule of television programs and bedtime, and the parents have their peaceful dinner together.

The author of the article in the *Times* notes that "keeping a family sane 17 means mediating between the needs of both children and adults." But surely the needs of adults are being better met than the needs of the children, who are effectively shunted away and rendered untroublesome, while their parents enjoy a life as undemanding as that of any childless couple. In reality, it is those very demands that young children make upon a family that lead to growth, and it is the way parents accede to those demands that builds the relationships upon which the future of the family depends. If the family does not accumulate its backlog of shared experiences, shared *everyday* experiences that occur and recur and change and develop, then it is not likely to survive as anything other than a caretaking institution.

FAMILY RITUALS

Ritual is defined by sociologists as "that part of family life that the family 18 likes about itself, is proud of and wants formally to continue." Another text notes that "the development of a ritual by a family is an index of the common interest of its members in the family as a group."

What has happened to family rituals, those regular, dependable, re- 19 current happenings that gave members of a family a feeling of *belonging* to a home rather than living in it merely for the sake of convenience, those experiences that act as the adhesive of family unity far more than any material advantages?

Mealtime rituals, going-to-bed rituals, illness rituals, holiday rituals, 20 how many of these have survived the inroads of the television set?

A young woman who grew up near Chicago reminisces about her child- 21
hood and gives an idea of the effects of television upon family rituals:

"As a child I had millions of relatives around—my parents both come 22
from relatively large families. My father had nine brothers and sisters. And
so every holiday there was this great swoop-down of aunts, uncles, and
millions of cousins. I just remember how wonderful it used to be. These
thousands of cousins would come and everyone would play and ultimately,
after dinner, all the women would be in the front of the house, drinking
coffee and talking, all the men would be in the back of the house, drinking
and smoking, and all the kids would be all over the place, playing hide and
seek. Christmastime was particularly nice because everyone always brought
all their toys and games. Our house had a couple of rooms with go-through
closets, so there were always kids running in a great circle route. I remember it was just wonderful.

"And then all of a sudden one year I remember becoming suddenly 23
aware of how different everything had become. The kids were no longer
playing Monopoly or Clue or the other games we used to play together. It
was because we had a television set which had been turned on for a football
game. All of that socializing that had gone on previously had ended. Now
everyone was sitting in front of the television set, on a holiday, at a family
party! I remember being stunned by how awful that was. Somehow the
television had become more attractive."

As families have come to spend more and more of their time together 24
engaged in the single activity of television watching, those rituals and
pastimes that once gave family life its special quality have become more
and more uncommon. Not since prehistoric times when cave families
hunted, gathered, ate, and slept, with little time remaining to accumulate
a culture of any significance, have families been reduced to such a same-
ness.

REAL PEOPLE

It is not only the activities that a family might engage in together that are 25
diminished by the powerful presence of television in the home. The relationships of the family members to each other are also affected, in both
obvious and subtle ways. The hours that the young child spends in a one-
way relationship with television people, an involvement that allows for no
communication or interaction, surely affect his relationships with real-life
people.

Studies show the importance of eye-to-eye contact, for instance, in 26
real-life relationships, and indicate that the nature of a person's eye-con-
tact patterns, whether he looks another squarely in the eye or looks to the
side or shifts his gaze from side to side, may play a significant role in his
success or failure in human relationships. But no eye contact is possible
in the child-television relationship, although in certain children's programs
people purport to speak directly to the child and the camera fosters this
illusion by focusing directly upon the person being filmed. (Mr. Rogers is

an example, telling the child, "I like you, you're special," etc.) How might such a distortion of real-life relationships affect a child's development of trust, of openness, of an ability to relate well to other *real* people?

Bruno Bettelheim° writes: 27

> Children who have been taught, or conditioned, to listen passively most of the day to the warm verbal communications coming from the TV screen, to the deep emotional appeal of the so-called TV personality, are often unable to respond to real persons because they arouse so much less feeling than the skilled actor. Worse, they lose the ability to learn from reality because life experiences are much more complicated than the ones they see on the screen.

A teacher makes a similar observation about her personal viewing ex-   28
periences:

"I have trouble mobilizing myself and dealing with real people after   29
watching a few hours of television. It's just hard to make that transition from watching television to a real relationship. I suppose it's because there was no effort necessary while I was watching, and dealing with real people always requires a bit of effort. Imagine, then, how much harder it might be to do the same thing for a small child, particularly one who watches a lot of television every day."

But more obviously damaging to family relationships is the elimination   30
of opportunities to talk, and perhaps more important, to argue, to air griev-ances, between parents and children and brothers and sisters. Families frequently use television to avoid confronting their problems, problems that will not go away if they are ignored but will only fester and become less easily resolvable as time goes on.

A mother reports: 31

"I find myself, with three children, wanting to turn on the TV set when   32
they're fighting. I really have to struggle not to do it because I feel that's telling them this is the solution to the quarrel—but it's so tempting that I often do it."

A family therapist discusses the use of television as an avoidance   33
mechanism:

"In a family I know the father comes home from work and turns on the   34
television set. The children come and watch with him and the wife serves them their meal in front of the set. He then goes and takes a shower, or works on the car or something. She then goes and has her own dinner in front of the television set. It's a symptom of a deeper-rooted problem, sure. But it would help them all to get rid of the set. It would be far easier to work on what the symptom really means without the television. The tele-vision simply encourages a double avoidance of each other. They'd find out more quickly what was going on if they weren't able to hide behind the TV. Things wouldn't necessarily be better, of course, but they wouldn't be anesthetized."

Bruno Bettelheim: American psychiatrist, writing in *The Informed Heart* (1960).

The decreased opportunities for simple conversation between parents 35
and children in the television-centered home may help explain an observation made by an emergency room nurse at a Boston hospital. She reports
that parents just seem to sit there these days when they come in with a
sick or seriously injured child, although talking to the child would distract
and comfort him. "They don't seem to know *how* to talk to their own children
at any length," the nurse observes. Similarly, a television critic writes in
the *New York Times:* "I had just a day ago taken my son to the emergency
ward of a hospital for stitches above his left eye, and the occasion seemed
no more real to me than Maalot or 54th Street, south-central Los Angeles.
There was distance and numbness and an inability to turn off the total
institution. I didn't behave at all; I just watched."

A number of research studies substantiate the assumption that tele- 36
vision interferes with family activities and the formation of family relationships. One survey shows that 78 percent of the respondents indicated no
conversation taking place during viewing except at specified times such as
commercials. The study notes: "The television atmosphere in most households is one of quiet absorption on the part of family members who are
present. The nature of the family social life during a program could be
described as 'parallel' rather than interactive, and the set does seem to
dominate family life when it is on." Thirty-six percent of the respondents
in another study indicated that television viewing was the only family activity participated in during the week.

In a summary of research findings on television's effect on family in- 37
teractions, James Gabardino states: "The early findings suggest that television had a disruptive effect upon interaction and thus presumably human
development. . . . It is not unreasonable to ask: 'Is the fact that the average
American family during the 1950s came to include two parents, two children and a television set somehow related to the psychosocial characteristics of the young adults of the 1970s?' "

UNDERMINING THE FAMILY

In its effect on family relationships, in its facilitation of parental withdrawal 38
from an active role in the socialization of their children, and in its replacement of family rituals and special events, television has played an important role in the disintegration of the American family. But of course it has
not been the only contributing factor, perhaps not even the most important
one. The steadily rising divorce rate, the increase in the number of working
mothers, the decline of the extended family, the breakdown of neighborhoods and communities, the growing isolation of the nuclear family—all
have seriously affected the family.

As Urie Bronfenbrenner suggests, the sources of family breakdown do 39
not come from the family itself, but from the circumstances in which the
family finds itself and the way of life imposed upon it by those circumstances. "When those circumstances and the way of life they generate

undermine relationships of trust and emotional security between family members, when they make it difficult for parents to care for, educate and enjoy their children, when there is no support or recognition from the outside world for one's role as a parent and when time spent with one's family means frustration of career, personal fulfillment and peace of mind, then the development of the child is adversely affected," he writes.

But while the roots of alienation go deep into the fabric of American   40
social history, television's presence in the home fertilizes them, encourages their wild and unchecked growth. Perhaps it is true that America's commitment to the television experience masks a spiritual vacuum, an empty and barren way of life, a desert of materialism. But it is television's dominant role in the family that anesthetizes the family into accepting its unhappy state and prevents it from struggling to better its condition, to improve its relationships, and to regain some of the richness it once possessed.

Others have noted the role of mass media in perpetuating an unsatis-   41
factory status quo. Leisure-time activity, writes Irving Howe,° "must provide relief from work monotony without making the return to work too unbearable; it must provide amusement without insight and pleasure without disturbance—as distinct from art which gives pleasure through disturbance. Mass culture is thus oriented towards a central aspect of industrial society: the depersonalization of the individual." Similarly, Jacques Ellul° rejects the idea that television is a legitimate means of educating the citizen: "Education . . . takes place only incidentally. The clouding of his consciousness is paramount."

And so the American family muddles on, dimly aware that something   42
is amiss but distracted from an understanding of its plight by an endless stream of television images. As family ties grow weaker and vaguer, as children's lives become more separate from their parents', as parents' educational role in their children's lives is taken over by television and schools, family life becomes increasingly more unsatisfying for both parents and children. All that seems to be left is Love, an abstraction that family members *know* is necessary but find great difficulty giving each other because the traditional opportunities for expressing love within the family have been reduced or destroyed.

For contemporary parents, love toward each other has increasingly   43
come to mean successful sexual relations, as witnessed by the proliferation of sex manuals and sex therapists. The opportunities for manifesting other forms of love through mutual support, understanding, nurturing, even, to use an unpopular word, *serving* each other, are less and less available as mothers and fathers seek their independent destinies outside the family.

As for love of children, this love is increasingly expressed through sup-   44
plying material comforts, amusements, and educational opportunities. Par-

Irving Howe: American critic, writing in "Notes on Mass Culture" (1960).
Jacques Ellul: French sociologist, writing in *The Technological Society* (1964).

ents show their love for their children by sending them to good schools and camps, by providing them with good food and good doctors, by buying them toys, books, games, and a television set of their very own. Parents will even go further and express their love by attending PTA meetings to improve their children's schools, or by joining groups that are acting to improve the quality of their children's television programs.

But this is love at a remove, and is rarely understood by children. The more direct forms of parental love require time and patience, steady, dependable, ungrudgingly given time actually spent *with* a child, reading to him, comforting him, playing, joking, and working with him. But even if a parent were eager and willing to demonstrate that sort of direct love to his children today, the opportunities are diminished. What with school and Little League and piano lessons and, of course, the inevitable television programs, a day seems to offer just enough time for a good-night kiss. 45

Questions to Start You Thinking

1. What, as best you can infer it, is Winn's purpose in writing? Does she at any place depart from it, or does everything in the essay work to fulfill this purpose? (Don't answer without carefully looking through the essay one more time.)

2. In paragraphs 9 and 18–24, Winn makes much of those "family rituals" that she believes television has destroyed. Test the author's complaints against your own recalled experience and your own observations.

3. Notice where Winn brings in expert testimony: quotations from her reading and from conversation with a young woman (paragraphs 21–23). What does this material lend to her essay's effectiveness?

4. Winn's essay is a self-contained chapter from her book *The Plug-in Drug,* first published in 1977. Over the years since Winn wrote, do you think the situation she describes has changed, become worse, or been alleviated? From what resources do you draw evidence for your answer?

In *A Not Entirely Benign Procedure* (1987), Perri Klass gives a frank account of her experiences in medical school. But this chapter from it is much more than a simple memoir: Klass sets forth thoughtful views on the way physicians are educated. Now a pediatrician, Klass continues to be a widely published author as well.

A TEXTBOOK PREGNANCY
Perri Klass

I learned I was pregnant the afternoon of my anatomy exam. I had spent the morning taking first a written exam and then a practical, centered around fifteen thoroughly dissected cadavers, each ornamented with little paper tags indicating structures to be identified. 1

My classmates and I were not looking very good, our hair unwashed, our faces pale from too much studying and too little sleep. Two more exams and our first year of medical school would be over. We all knew exactly what we had to do next: go home and study for tomorrow's exam. I could picture my genetics notes lying on my desk, liberally highlighted with pink marker. But before I went home I had a pregnancy test done. 2

My period was exactly one day late, hardly worth noticing—but the month before, for the first time in my life, I had been trying to get pregnant. Four hours later I called for the test results. 3

"It's positive," the woman at the lab told me. 4

With all the confidence of a first-year medical student, I asked, "Positive, what does that mean?" 5

"It means you're pregnant," she told me. "Congratulations." 6

Somewhat later that afternoon I settled down to make final review notes for my genetics exam. *Down's syndrome*, I copied carefully onto a clean piece of paper, *most common autosomal disorder, 1 per 700 live births.* I began to feel a little queasy. Over the next twenty-four hours, I was supposed to learn the biological basis, symptoms, diagnosis, and treatment of a long list of genetic disorders. Almost every one was something that could conceivably already be wrong with the embryo growing inside me. I couldn't even think about it; I had to put my notes aside and pass the exam on what I remembered from the lectures. 7

Over the past months, as I have gone through my pregnancy, and also through my second year of medical school, I have become more and more aware of these two aspects of my life influencing each other, and even sometimes seeming to oppose each other. As a medical student, I was spending my time studying everything that can go wrong with the human body. As a pregnant woman, I was suddenly passionately interested in healthy physiological processes, in my own normal pregnancy and the growth of my baby. And yet pregnancy put me under the care of the medical profession—my own future profession—and I found myself rebelling as a mother and a patient against the attitudes that were being taught to me, particularly the attitude that pregnancy is a perilous, if not pathological, condition. The pregnancy and the decisions I had to make about my own health care changed my feelings about medicine and about the worldview of emergency and intervention which is communicated in medical training. My pregnancy became for me a rebellion against this worldview, a chance to do something healthy and normal with my body, something that would be a joyous event, an important event, a complex event, but not necessarily a medical event. 8

Medical school lasts four years, followed by internship and residency—three years for medicine, five to seven for surgery. And then maybe a two-year fellowship. 9

"The fellowship years can be a good time to have a baby," advised one physician. She was just finishing a fellowship in primary care. "Not intern- 10 ship or residency, God knows—that's when everyone's marriage breaks up since you're working eighty hours a week and you're so miserable all the time."

I am twenty-six. After college, I didn't go straight to medical school, but spent two years doing graduate work in biology and one living abroad. I'll probably have reached the fellowship stage by around thirty-three. It seemed like a long time to wait.

The more I thought about it, the more it seemed to me that there was no time in the next seven or so years when it would be as feasible to have a baby as it is now. As a medical student, I have a flexibility that I will not really have further on, a freedom to take a couple of months off or even a year if I decide I need it, and without unduly disrupting the progress of my career. Larry, who is also twenty-six, has just finished his doctoral dissertation on Polish-Vatican relations in the late eighteenth century, and is teaching at Harvard. He also has a great deal of flexibility. Both our lives frequently feel a little frantic, but we don't find ourselves looking ahead to a less complex, less frantic future.

I decided not to take a leave of absence this year. Instead, Larry and I have started on the juggling games which will no doubt be a major feature of the years ahead; I took extra courses last year so I could manage a comparatively light schedule this spring and stay with the baby two days a week while Larry worked at home for the other three. Perfect timing is of course of the essence; happily, we'd already managed to conceive the baby so it would be born between the time I took my exams in December and the time I started work at the hospital in March.

There was one other factor in my decision to have a baby now. All through my first year of medical school, in embryology, in genetics, even in public health, lecturers kept emphasizing that the ideal time to have a baby is around the age of twenty-four. Safest for the mother. Safest for the baby. "Do you think they're trying to tell us something?" grumbled one of my classmates after a particularly pointed lecture. "Like why are we wasting these precious childbearing years in school? It almost makes you feel guilty about waiting to have children."

Ironically, I know no one else my age who is having a baby. The women in my childbirth class were all in their mid-thirties. "Having a baby is a very nineteen-eighties thing to do," said a friend who is a twenty-seven-year-old corporate lawyer in New York. "The only thing is, you and Larry are much too young." In medical school one day last month, a lecturer mentioned the problem of teenage pregnancy, and I imagined that my classmates were turning to look at me.

In theory, medical education teaches first about normal anatomy, normal physiology, and then builds upon this foundation by teaching the processes of pathology and disease. In practice, everyone—student and teacher alike—is eager to get to the material with "clinical relevance" and the whole thrust of the teaching is toward using examples of disease to illustrate normal body functions by showing what happens when such functions break down. This is the way much of medical knowledge is garnered, after all—we understand sugar metabolism partially because of studies on diabetics, who can't metabolize sugar normally. "An experiment of nature" is the phrase often used.

Although we had learned a great deal about disease, we had not, in 17 our first year of medical school, learned much about the nitty-gritty of medical practice. As I began to wonder more about what was happening inside me and about what childbirth would be like, I tried to read my embryology textbook, but again the pictures of the various abnormal fetuses upset me. So I read a couple of books that were written for pregnant women, not medical students, including *Immaculate Deception* by Suzanne Arms, a passionate attack on the American way of childbirth which argues that many routine hospital practices are psychologically damaging and medically hazardous. In particular, Arms protested the "traditional birth," the euphemism used in opposition to "natural birth." Traditional often means giving birth while lying down, a position demonstrated to be less effective and more dangerous than many others, but convenient for the doctor. An intravenous line is often attached to the arm and an electronic fetal heart monitor strapped to the belly. Traditional almost always means a routine episiotomy, a surgical incision in the perineum to allow the baby's head to emerge without tearing the mother.

In our reproductive medicine course this fall, the issue of home birth 18 came up exactly once, in a "case" for discussion. "BB is a 25-year-old married graduate student . . . ," the case began. BB had a completely normal pregnancy. She showed no unusual symptoms and had no relevant past medical problems. When the pregnancy reached full term, the summary concluded, "no factors have been identified to suggest increased risk." Then, the first question: "Do you think she should choose to deliver at home?"

The doctor leading our discussion section read the question aloud and 19 waited. "No," chorused the class.

"Why not?" asked the doctor. 20

"Well, there's always the chance of a complication," said one of the 21 students.

Sure enough, after answering the first set of questions, we went on 22 with BB's case, and it turned out that she went two and a half weeks past her due date, began to show signs of fetal distress, and was ultimately delivered by cesarean after the failure of induced labor. It was clear what the lesson was that BB was supposed to teach us. It was hard to read the case without getting the impression that all of these problems were some kind of divine retribution for even considering a home birth.

In fact, Larry and I eventually decided on a hospital birth with a doctor 23 whose orientation was clearly against intervention except where absolutely necessary; he did not feel that procedures that can help in the event of complications should be applied across the board. It pleased me that he volunteered the cesarean and episiotomy figures for his practice, and also that he regarded the issue of what kind of birth we wanted as an appropriate subject for discussion at our very first meeting. ("A low-tech birth?" he said, sounding amused. "You're at Harvard Medical School and you want a low-tech birth?") He seemed to accept that there were consumer issues involved in choosing a doctor—that expectant parents are entitled to an explanation of the doctor's approach early in the pregnancy, when changing doctors is still a reasonable possibility.

At the beginning of my eighth month, we went to the first meeting of a 24 prepared-childbirth class sponsored by the hospital we had decided to use. I had great hopes of this class; I was tired of feeling like the only pregnant person in the world. My medical school classmates had continued to be extremely kind and considerate, but as I moved around the medical school I was beginning to feel like a lone hippopotamus in a gaggle of geese. I wanted some other people with whom Larry and I could go over the questions we discussed endlessly with each other: How do we know when it's time to leave for the hospital? What is labor going to *feel* like? What can we do to make it go more easily?

The prepared-childbirth class met in the hospital. At the first meeting, 25 it became clear that its major purpose was to prepare people to be good patients. The teacher was exposing us to various procedures so we would cooperate properly when they were performed on us. Asked whether a given procedure was absolutely necessary, the teacher said that was up to the doctor.

I found a childbirth class that met at a local day-care center; we sat 26 on cushions on the floor, surrounded by toys and children's artwork. Many members of the class were fairly hostile toward the medical profession; once again I was greeted with remarks like "A medical student and you think you want a natural birth? Don't you get thrown out of school for that?" This class was, if anything, designed to teach people how to be "bad patients." The teacher explained the pros and cons of the various interventions, and we discussed under what circumstances we might or might not accept them.

The childbirth classes not only prepared me well for labor but also 27 provided that sense of community I wanted. Yet they also left me feeling pulled between two poles, especially if I went to medical school during the day to discuss deliveries going wrong in one catastrophic way after another ("C-section, C-section!" my discussion section once chanted when the teacher asked what we would do next) and then later to childbirth class in the evening to discuss ways to circumvent unwanted medical procedures. As a student of the medical profession, I know I am being trained to rely heavily on technology, to assume that the risk of acting is almost always preferable to the risk of not acting. I consciously had to fight these attitudes when I thought about giving birth.

In our reproductive medicine course, the emphasis was on the abnor- 28
mal, the pathological. We learned almost nothing about normal pregnancy;
the only thing said about nutrition, for example, was said in passing—that
nobody knows how much weight a pregnant woman should gain, but "about
twenty-four pounds" is considered good. In contrast, I and the other women
in my childbirth class were very concerned with what we ate; we were always
exchanging suggestions on how to get through those interminable four
glasses of milk a day. We learned nothing in medical school about exercise,
though exercise books and classes aimed at pregnant women continue to
proliferate—will we, as doctors, be able to give valid advice about diet and
exercise during pregnancy? We learned nothing about any of the problems
encountered in a normal pregnancy; the only thing said about morning
sickness was that it could be controlled with a drug—a drug which, as it
happens, many pregnant women are reluctant to take because some studies have linked it to birth defects. We learned nothing about the emotional
aspects of pregnancy, nothing about helping women prepare for labor and
delivery. In other words, none of my medical school classmates, after the
course, would have been capable of answering even the most basic questions about pregnancy asked by the people in my childbirth class. The
important issues for future doctors simply did not overlap with the important
issues for future parents.

I sat with my classmates in our reproductive medicine course in Am- 29
phitheater E at Harvard Medical School and listened to the lecture on the
disorders of pregnancy. The professor discussed ectopic pregnancy, tox-
emia, spontaneous abortion, and major birth defects. I was eight months
pregnant. I sat there rubbing my belly, telling my baby, don't worry, you're
okay, you're healthy. I sat there wishing that this course would tell us more
about normal pregnancy, that after memorizing all the possible disasters,
we would be allowed to conclude that pregnancy itself is not a state of
disease. But I think most of us, including me, came away from the course
with a sense that in fact pregnancy is a deeply dangerous medical condition, that one walks a fine line, avoiding one serious problem after another,
to reach the statistically unlikely outcome of a healthy baby and a healthy
mother.

I mentioned this to my doctor, explaining that I was tormented by fears 30
of every possible abnormality. "Yes," he said, "normal birth is not honored
enough in the curriculum. Most of us doctors are going around looking
for pathology and feeling good about ourselves when we find it because
that's what we were trained to do. We aren't trained to find joy in a normal
pregnancy."

I tried to find joy in my own pregnancy. I am sure that the terrors that 31
sometimes visited me in the middle of the night were no more intense than
those that visit most expectant mothers: Will the labor go well? Will the
baby be okay? I probably had more specific fears than many, as I lay awake
wondering about atrial septal heart defects or placenta previa and hem-

orrhage. And perhaps I did worry more than I might once have done, because my faith in the normal had been weakened. I too, in my dark moments, had begun to see healthy development as less than probable, as the highly unlikely avoidance of a million abnormalities. I knew that many of my classmates were worrying with me; I cannot count the number of times I was asked whether I had had an amniocentesis. When I pointed out that we had been taught that amniocentesis is not generally recommended for women under the age of thirty-five, my classmates tended to look worried and mutter something about being *sure.*

The climax came when a young man in my class asked me, "Have you had all those genetic tests? Like for sickle-cell anemia?" 32

I looked at him. He is white. I am white. "I'm not in the risk group for sickle-cell," I said gently. 33

"Yeah, I know," he said, "but if there's even a one-in-a-zillion chance—" 34

I see all of us, including myself, absorbing the idea that when it comes to tests, technology, interventions, more is better. There was no talk in the reproductive medicine course about the negative aspects of intervention, and the one time a student asked in class about the "appropriateness" of fetal monitoring, the question was cut off with a remark that there was no time to discuss issues of "appropriateness." There was also no time really to discuss techniques for attending women in labor—except as they related to labor emergencies. 35

I see us absorbing the attitude, here as in other courses, that the kinds of decisions that have to be made are absolutely out of the reach of non-physicians. The risks of devastating catastrophe are so constant—how can we let patients take chances like this with their lives? Those dangers which can actually be controlled by the patients, the pregnant women—cigarettes, alcohol—are deemphasized. Instead, we are taught to think in terms of medical emergencies. And gradually pregnancy itself begins to sound like a medical emergency in which the pregnant woman, referred to as "the patient," must be carefully guided to a safe delivery, almost in spite of herself. And as we spend more and more time absorbing the vocabulary of medicine, it becomes harder to think about communicating our knowledge to those who lack that vocabulary. 36

There have been very positive aspects of having the baby while in medical school. For one thing, the anatomy and physiology and embryology I have learned deepened my awe of the miracle going on inside me. When I looked ahead to the birth, I thought of what we learned about the incredible changeover that takes place during the first minutes of life, about the details of the switch to breathing air, the changes in circulation. I feel that because of what I have learned I appreciated the pregnancy in a way I never could have before, and I am grateful for that appreciation. 37

Another wonderful thing about having my baby while in medical school was the support and attention from my classmates. Perhaps because having a baby seems a long way off to many of them, there has been some 38 tendency to regard mine as a "class baby." People asked me all the time to promise that I would bring it to lecture; the person who shows the slides offered to dim the lights for a soothing atmosphere if I wanted to nurse in class. My classmates held a baby shower for Larry and me, and presented us with a fabulous assortment of baby items. At the end of the shower, I lay back on the couch with five medical students feeling my abdomen, finding the baby's bottom, the baby's foot.

Our son, Benjamin Orlando, was born on January 28, 1984. Naturally, I would like to be able to say that all our planning and preparing was rewarded with a perfectly smooth, easy labor and delivery, but of course biology doesn't work that way. The experience did provide me with a rather ironic new wrinkle on the whole idea of interventions. Most of the labor was quite ordinary. "You're demonstrating a perfect Friedman labor curve," the doctor said to me at one point, "you must have been studying!" At the end, however, I had great difficulty pushing the baby out. After the pushing stage had gone on for quite a while, I was absolutely exhausted, though the baby was fine; there were no signs of fetal distress and the head was descending steadily. Still, the pushing had gone on much longer than is usual, and I was aware that there were now two doctors and a number of nurses in the birthing room. Suddenly I heard one of the doctors say something about forceps. At that moment, I found a last extra ounce of strength and pushed my baby out. As I lay back with my son wriggling on my stomach, the birthing room suddenly transformed into the most beautiful place on earth, I heard one of the nurses say to another, "You see this all the time with these birthing-room natural-childbirth mothers—you just mention forceps and they get those babies born." 39

Questions to Start You Thinking

1. On which of the five resources for writers does Klass draw in writing her essay?
2. Sum up the dilemma in which the author found herself as a pregnant medical student.
3. What is Klass's purpose in this essay? For what audience does she write?

PART TWO

THINKING
CRITICALLY

*C*ritic, from the Greek word *kritikos*, means "one who can judge and discern." If college leaves you better able to judge and discern—able to tell what is more important or less important, able to make distinctions and recognize differences, able to grasp involved concepts and get to the bottom of things—then it will have given you your money's worth.

This part of the book will show you five typical college writing tasks in which you think critically and fulfill a purpose: analyzing, taking a stand, proposing a solution, evaluating, and seeking causes and effects. Not that all of them will be news to you. You wrote evaluations back in grade school if you ever produced book reports that ended with statements like "I would recommend this book highly to anyone interested in polar bears." To be sure, a paper you write in college will go more deeply into the subject and will set forth your reasons for the recommendation. You will be writing for a more demanding audience who may not be as easily persuaded as a high school class or teacher. Still, if you find anything old and familiar in the following five chapters, don't be surprised.

CHAPTER 6

Analyzing

Many times in college you will be asked to understand some matter that seems complicated: an earthquake, the metabolism of a cell, the Federal Reserve Bank, the Protestant Reformation. Viewed as a whole, such a subject may look intimidating. But often you can simplify your task by *analyzing* your subject: by dividing it into its parts and then dealing with it one part at a time.

Analysis is already familiar to you. If you took high school chemistry, you probably analyzed water: you separated it into hydrogen and oxygen, its two elements. You've heard many a television commentator analyze the news. Did a riot break out in Bombay? Trying to help us understand what happened, the commentator tells us what made up the event: who the protesters were, whom they protested to, what they were protesting. Analyzing a news event may produce results less certain and clear-cut than analyzing a chemical compound, but the principle is similar: to take something apart and find out what makes it up, for the purpose of understanding it better. In a college writing assignment you might analyze anything from a contemporary subculture (What social groups make up the homeless population of Los Angeles?) to an ecosystem (What animals, plants, and minerals coexist in a rain forest?).

Not only can you analyze a subject that just sits there, you can analyze an action as well. You can write a *process analysis,* a step-by-step explanation of one of two processes:

How something happens: how an unborn infant develops, how a glacier forms, how the music industry builds a song into a top-40 hit. This is an *informative* process analysis, one that shows how something takes place by dividing it into its successive stages.

How to do something: how to ski, how to conduct yourself during a job interview, how to perform the Heimlich maneuver, how to build a hang glider. This is a *directive* process analysis, one that gives the reader step-by-step instructions in how to do something.

Whether you analyze a process or analyze some other subject, you'll be thinking in a basically similar way. You'll be dividing something into its components, the more readily to make sense of it.

LEARNING FROM OTHER WRITERS

Richard Polomsky, a student who knows a great deal about fossil collecting, wrote the following process analysis to share his knowledge with his English class. In it he gives step-by-step directions for fossil hunting and preservation.

Student Essay

COLLECTING THE PAST
Richard Polomsky

There are a wide variety of locations where one could search for fossilized remains of plant and animal life. One spot in particular, near Chicago, has yielded some of the world's most interesting varieties of fossilized remains, and I will describe how to locate, reveal, clean, and care for them. 1

About forty miles southwest of Chicago lies an area that has been associated with geological interest for over a hundred years, the Braidwood-Coal City-Mazon Creek group of towns. Around 1865, coal was mined extensively in quarries situated in and around these towns. The coal did not last, however, and all that is left now are large gaping quarries filled with water, not coal. 2

On the edges of some of the quarries, large mounds of shale protrude from the ground with their layers of strata pointing perpendicular to the ground's surface. Within the layers of shale, ironstone nodules can be found, which look 3 much like small to large hamburger patties that taper to the edge. The fossilized remains contained within often are representative of the life that existed during the Pennsylvanian period, about 280 to 325 million years ago. If you want to collect the nodules, it's best to wait until after a strong thunderstorm passes through the area. Then the nodules are washed out of the surrounding shale and roll down the sides of the mounds, so that you may come by later to simply collect them, as though on an Easter egg hunt.

No special equipment is necessary to collect the nod- 4
ules, except for a heavy canvas sack to hold them and a hard hat to protect your head from any late arriving nodules. If you want to begin preparing the nodules in the field, you should be sure to bring a good-sized hammer (a 42-ounce one should be fine), eye protection goggles, and a brush with which to clean the fossils.

If you just collect them and bring them back to your 5
"lab," you will still need the same equipment, but you shouldn't attempt to work in the field without these tools.

Once back in the lab, set up a large piece of rock, to 6
be used as an anvil. Put on the safety goggles and pick up a nodule. Place it on the anvil so that the thinner edge is perpendicular to the anvil's surface. Next pick up the hammer and strike the nodule on the top edge. At first, don't use too much pressure applying the blows. If there is a delicately preserved fossil within the nodule, it would be a shame to crush it. If the first blows don't open it, gradually increase the pressure until the nodule splits to reveal the fossil, or absence of a fossil, as is sometimes the case.

From personal experience, I have discovered that you 7
must be relentless in your search for fossils and collect several piles of rubble before you split the first fossil that reveals the approximately three-hundred-million-year-old impression of a tree fern, spider, jellyfish, shrimp, amphibian, or any of the other hundreds of species that once occupied the area when it was a steamy swamp at the edge of a

saltwater sea. If you are fortunate enough to find a fossil, brush it lightly to remove any extraneous dirt from the specimen. You may then wish to glue both the positive and negative halves of the specimen side by side on a piece of corrugated cardboard with rubber cement. If collecting fossils is to become a serious endeavor for you, then you will probably want to build a cabinet with a series of drawers stacked one on top of the other. They should only be a couple of inches thick so that more drawers can fit into the cabinet. If you do not wish to glue the two halves of the fossil to a card, place them back together tightly and wrap them with several layers of soft paper. Then neatly stack them in the cabinet until you can get back to study and classify them. If you aren't motivated to build a cabinet, a shoebox would suffice for storage.

The act of collecting the nodules is extremely enjoyable 8 if performed on a nice day. It involves a healthy walk in the outdoors, generally for quite a few hours. You learn a little about patience as you sift through pile after pile of nodules only to have them yield a tiny handful of interesting specimens.

The greatest reward from collecting and studying the 9 fossils is that if you should happen to make a find that can be verified as being a previously undiscovered species by officials of the Field Museum of Natural History in Chicago, more than likely the new species would be named after you. This would be quite a feat for an amateur. Imagine being remembered through history as the discoverer of a new species of plant or animal that remained unknown for nearly three hundred million years, until you exposed it for the first time.

Questions to Start You Thinking

1. What details in Polomsky's essay convince you that he knows what he's talking about? What details reveal his love and enthusiasm for fossil hunting?
2. How clear are Polomsky's directions? If you had the opportunity to follow them,

would you know what to do? Are there any places in the essay where the writer might be clearer, where you could use further advice?

3. What other uses of leisure time might lend themselves to a written process analysis? Are you (or is anyone you know, whom you might talk with) a part-time expert in a special field of knowledge?

Mathematician Paul Bodanis, in *The Secret House,* revels in what a microscope reveals. Analyzing items ordinarily found in an American household, Bodanis lets his readers in on surprising trade secrets. The essay that follows is taken from Bodanis's lively and eye-opening book.

WHAT'S IN YOUR TOOTHPASTE?
Paul Bodanis

Into the bathroom goes our male resident, and after the most pressing 1
need is satisfied it's time to brush the teeth. The tube of toothpaste is squeezed, its pinched metal seams are splayed, pressure waves are generated inside, and the paste begins to flow. But what's in this toothpaste, so carefully being extruded out?

Water mostly, 30 to 45 percent in most brands: ordinary, everyday 2
simple tap water. It's there because people like to have a big gob of toothpaste to spread on the brush, and water is the cheapest stuff there is when it comes to making big gobs. Dripping a bit from the tap onto your brush would cost virtually nothing; whipped in with the rest of the toothpaste the manufacturers can sell it at a neat and accountant-pleasing $2 per pound equivalent. Toothpaste manufacture is a very lucrative occupation.

Second to water in quantity is chalk: exactly the same material that 3
schoolteachers use to write on blackboards. It is collected from the crushed remains of long-dead ocean creatures. In the Cretaceous seas chalk particles served as part of the wickedly sharp outer skeleton that these creatures had to wrap around themselves to keep from getting chomped by all the slightly larger other ocean creatures they met. Their massed graves are our present chalk deposits.

The individual chalk particles—the size of the smallest mud particles 4
in your garden—have kept their toughness over the aeons, and now on the toothbrush they'll need it. The enamel outer coating of the tooth they'll have to face is the hardest substance in the body—tougher than skull, or bone, or nail. Only the chalk particles in toothpaste can successfully grind into the teeth during brushing, ripping off the surface layers like an abrading wheel grinding down a boulder in a quarry.

The craters, slashes, and channels that the chalk tears into the teeth 5
will also remove a certain amount of build-up yellow in the carnage, and it is for that polishing function that it's there. A certain amount of unduly

enlarged extra-abrasive chalk fragments tear such cavernous pits into the teeth that future decay bacteria will be able to bunker down there and thrive; the quality control people find it almost impossible to screen out these errant super-chalk pieces, and government regulations allow them to stay in.

In case even the gouging doesn't get all the yellow off, another substance is worked into the toothpaste cream. This is titanium dioxide. It comes in tiny spheres, and it's the stuff bobbing around in white wall paint to make it come out white. Splashed around onto your teeth during the brushing it coats much of the yellow that remains. Being water soluble it leaks off in the next few hours and is swallowed, but at least for the quick glance up in the mirror after finishing it will make the user think his teeth are truly white. Some manufacturers add optical whitening dyes—the stuff more commonly found in washing machine bleach—to make extra sure that that glance in the mirror shows reassuring white. 6

These ingredients alone would not make a very attractive concoction. They would stick in the tube like a sloppy white plastic lump, hard to squeeze out as well as revolting to the touch. Few consumers would savor rubbing in a mixture of water, ground-up blackboard chalk, and the whitener from latex paint first thing in the morning. To get around that finicky distaste the manufacturers have mixed in a host of other goodies. 7

To keep the glop from drying out, a mixture including glycerine glycol— related to the most common car antifreeze ingredient—is whipped in with the chalk and water, and to give *that* concoction a bit of substance (all we really have so far is wet colored chalk) a large helping is added of gummy molecules from the seaweed *Chondrus Crispus.* This seaweed ooze spreads in among the chalk, paint, and antifreeze, then stretches itself in all directions to hold the whole mass together. A bit of paraffin oil (the fuel that flickers in camping lamps) is pumped in with it to help the moss ooze keep the whole substance smooth. 8

With the glycol, ooze, and paraffin we're almost there. Only two major chemicals are left to make the refreshing, cleansing substance we know as toothpaste. The ingredients so far are fine for cleaning, but they wouldn't make much of the satisfying foam we have come to expect in the morning brushing. 9

To remedy that every toothpaste on the market has a big dollop of detergent added too. You've seen the suds detergent will make in a washing machine. The same substance added here will duplicate that inside the mouth. It's not particularly necessary, but it sells. 10

The only problem is that by itself this ingredient tastes, well, too like detergent. It's horribly bitter and harsh. The chalk put in toothpaste is pretty foul-tasting too for that matter. It's to get around that gustatory discomfort that the manufacturers put in the ingredient they tout perhaps the most of all. This is the flavoring, and it has to be strong. Double rectified peppermint oil is used—a flavorer so powerful that chemists know better than to sniff 11 it in the raw state in the laboratory. Menthol crystals and saccharin or other sugar simulators are added to complete the camouflage operation.

Is that it? Chalk, water, paint, seaweed, antifreeze, paraffin oil, deter- 12 gent, and peppermint? Not quite. A mix like that would be irresistible to the hundreds of thousands of individual bacteria lying on the surface of even an immaculately cleaned bathroom sink. They would get in, float in the water bubbles, ingest the ooze and paraffin, maybe even spray out enzymes to break down the chalk. The result would be an uninviting mess. The way manufacturers avoid that final obstacle is by putting something in to kill the bacteria. Something good and strong is needed, something that will zap any accidentally intrudant bacteria into oblivion. And that something is formaldehyde—the disinfectant used in anatomy labs.

So it's chalk, water, paint, seaweed, antifreeze, paraffin oil, detergent, 13 peppermint, formaldehyde, and fluoride (which can go some way towards preserving children's teeth)—that's the usual mixture raised to the mouth on the toothbrush for a fresh morning's clean. If it sounds too unfortunate, take heart. Studies show that thorough brushing with just plain water will often do as good a job.

Questions to Start You Thinking

1. What is the tone of Bodanis's essay? What does the essay gain from the author's use of this tone?
2. What is the author's main point?
3. Does your toothpaste tube list ingredients?
4. What is the author's apparent purpose? Does he address any particular audience?

LEARNING BY WRITING

The Assignment: Analyzing

Write an essay analyzing a subject *or* a process that you know well (or want to find out about). The purpose of your analysis will be to make the process or subject clear to an audience of your fellow students.

Here are instances of college writers who successfully responded to this type of assignment:

WRITERS WHO ANALYZED A SUBJECT

One student sliced the British Isles into geologic regions and assessed the mineral wealth in each.

A woman who plans a career as a consultant in time and motion study divided a typical day in the life of a college student into the segments that compose it (class time, study time, feeding time, grooming time, recreation time, social time, waste time) and suggested ways to make more efficient use of the student's time.

A student of psychology divided the human brain into its parts and described the function of each.

A speech student analyzed a piece of educational software for its assumptions about learning.

WRITERS WHO ANALYZED A PROCESS

A man who had dropped out of an airline's training program for flight attendants told the stages of training that an applicant goes through before receiving wings.

A woman who had worked in a clinic guided her readers through the steps by which a doctor examines a heart patient and conducts diagnostic tests.

A man wrote a step-by-step account of how a lobbyist seeks to influence a legislator.

A woman who had taken part in a summer seminar in wildlife management described, step by step, the process of banding birds to trace their patterns of migration.

A woman told how to make an excellent grilled cheese sandwich in a dorm room by using an electric iron.

Generating Ideas

Your first task is to pick a topic you care about. The paper topics just listed may help start your own ideas flowing. Do some idle, relaxed thinking, with pencil and paper at hand. Or do some fast scribbling (see "Freewriting," p. 474). Try to come up with something complicated that you understand and would really like to analyze or something you would like to understand more clearly yourself.

Suggestions for analyzing a subject   Right away, decide on the principle you will follow in your analysis. Just as you can slice a carrot in many ways, you can find many ways to analyze a subject. You might divide your home state into geographic regions, or you might divide it on the basis of different patterns of speech heard in each area. Before you begin, decide your reason for analyzing. What do you hope to demonstrate? If, for instance, you plan to write an analysis of New York City for the purpose of showing its ethnic composition, you might work through the city, dividing it into neighborhoods—Harlem, Spanish Harlem, Yorkville, Chinatown, Little Italy.

Ask yourself the following questions before you write.

DISCOVERY CHECKLIST: FOCUSING ON YOUR TASK

- Have you found a subject that interests you and that seems worthwhile to analyze?
- Is your basis—the principle you will follow in your analysis—clear to you, so that you can make it clear to your audience?

- In thinking about your essay, have you left out any obvious parts that a reader might expect to find? Some readers might object to an analysis dividing pop music into rap, rock, and jazz fusion on the grounds that it has a few holes.

- Exactly what will you be trying to achieve in your essay? Make sure before you begin that your analysis has a purpose: that it will demonstrate something or tell your readers something they didn't know before.

Suggestions for analyzing a process   What process will you analyze? It may be that at work, in the library, in a laboratory, or in a classroom, you have experienced, read about, or observed something done or something happening. If that is the case, you're an expert right now; you're well equipped to write. But if a workable idea doesn't spring to mind, drum up ideas by asking yourself a few questions.

DISCOVERY CHECKLIST: ANALYZING A PROCESS

- What processes are you already familiar with?
- What ones might you go out and observe?
- What ones have you read about or would like to read about?
- From among your friends (perhaps including your instructors), whose expertise can you tap?
- What processes can you imagine happening, say, in the future?
- What processes have you learned about in classes other than English? Has anyone in your family or among your friends ever asked you to explain one of them?
- Is there a process you've wondered about but have never had the time to investigate thoroughly? Can you do so now?

Brainstorm. For a start, do a little brainstorming. Jot down a list of titles that you think you could develop into papers worth reading. For an *informative* process analysis (explaining how something happens), these might be "How a Hospital Emergency Room Responds to an Accident Case," "How a Large Telescope Functions," "How Glaciers Are Formed," "How an Artist Draws a Portrait," "What Would Have Happened If Halley's Comet Had Struck the Earth." (We'll get to the directive or "how to" kind of paper in a moment. For more suggestions on brainstorming, or rapidly listing ideas, see p. 471.)

What you include on such a list will depend, of course, on what you know or can find out. At this point, though, you don't have to know every detail. It's always possible, at any stage, to fill in the gaps in your knowledge by reading, talking with experts, or (if possible) observing the process. What you need to do at first is just to choose a couple of paths for your thoughts to follow and eventually narrow your choices to one.

If your expertise involves a skill that you can teach your readers, you can write instead a *directive* process analysis. Do you know how to identify crystals with a microscope, navigate a sailboat, create graphs with a computer, teach someone how to drive, film a documentary, recognize the composer of a piece of chamber music, identify constellations? You'll find readers eager to learn those skills and many more. What process do you know most about? A list of possible topics might include "How to Renovate an Old House," "How to Choose Spreadsheet Software for a Small Business," "How to Record a Rock Group," "How to Train for Distance Running," "How to Silkscreen a Poster," "How to Recognize a Fourteenth-Century Italian Painting," "How to Repossess a Car."

Remember your reader. When you decide on a topic, keep asking questions about it. Is there background information your reader will need to understand the process? List any such information. (Look back at Polomsky's "Collecting the Past" and notice how much general information he includes right at the start.)

If you're writing a "how to" essay, do you know any trade secrets that will make what you're teaching easier for your reader to master? Jot them down.

What preliminary steps, if any, will the reader need to take to follow your directions? ("Sharpen a pair of shears. . . .") What materials are called for? List them: "a fifty-foot roll of sailcloth; a yardstick or measuring tape; one twelve-foot pine trunk at least twenty-four inches thick, trimmed of branches. . . ." Any ideas or information, however small, that you can put on paper now, you will soon be thankful for.

Shaping a Draft

In analyzing either a subject or a process, it is crucial to organize your material in some logical, easy-to-follow order. Some kind of outline—whether extremely detailed or rough—will save you time and avoid confusion.

Drafting a subject analysis   The outline for a written analysis might be a pielike circle with the slices labeled. If you make the slices larger or smaller according to their relative importance, the sketch might give you some notion of how much time to spend explaining each part. The pie outline for a paper analyzing the parts of a radio station's twenty-four-hour broadcast day might look like the illustration on page 191. If you need to subdivide any parts into smaller ones, clearly indicate the subdivisions in your writing so that your readers won't get lost.

Another way to plan your paper is to arrange your divisions from smallest to largest—or any other order that makes sense to you. Some writers like to start either a subject analysis or a process analysis by telling their readers

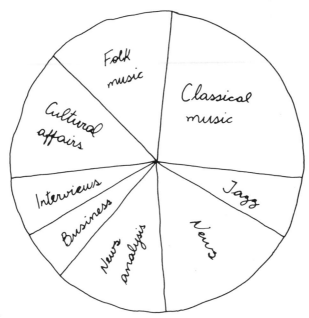

Pie outline of a radio station's broadcast day.

the divisions they are going to slice their subject into ("A typical political party has these components . . ."). Julius Caesar opens his *Commentaries on the Gallic War* with a famous division: "All Gaul is divided into three parts." That is one clear-cut way to go. Still, it takes some of the fun out of an essay, and some writers prefer to keep the reader guessing: What division is coming next?

As you write, the following suggestion may help you keep your material clearly in mind: if you haven't already done so, you might invent a name or label for each slice you mention to distinguish it from all the others. This device will also help your readers to keep the divisions straight.

Drafting a process analysis   If you have done enough thinking about your process analysis as you generated ideas, you'll have greatly lightened your next task: to map out the steps or stages in the process you are going to explain. You'll find a list of steps useful even if you're going to write just one paragraph.

Plot your paper. Let's say you are writing an *informative* process analysis. Into what stages will you divide the process? Make a list. In what order do these stages generally occur?

If you're writing a *directive* or "how to" analysis, what steps will your readers have to master to succeed in learning the skill? In what order do they need to perform those steps?

For either kind of process analysis, zero in on any parts that threaten to be complicated. Which stages or steps will take the most explaining? Underline or star these. This device will remind you, when you write your draft, to slow down and cover that stage or step with special care.

If you can, arrange all the stages or steps in chronological order. This will be easy if you're writing a "how to" essay, perhaps harder if you're writing an informative paper about an event in which everything seems to happen at once, say, how a tornado strikes. If you cannot explain your subject step by step, try explaining it part by part—the tornado's action observed at its center, its action observed at its edge—until you have covered everything necessary to make the process understandable.

Review your list once more, making sure you've included every small stage or step necessary.

Now your trusty list of steps or stages can serve as an outline. As you write your draft, concentrate on including every possible step in the process you're analyzing, even if it seems obvious. It's better at this point to put in too much detail than to put in too little. Later you can cross out what seems superfluous. Always keep in mind that what you're saying is probably news to your readers.

Use time markers. In drafting your paper, help your readers follow the steps in your analysis by putting in *time markers*: words and phrases like *then, next, soon, after, while, first, a year, later, in two hours, by the following day, during the second week, as yet, at the same time, at present.* By making clear exactly when some action occurs relative to other actions, time markers serve as signposts to keep your readers from getting lost in a forest of details. Look back at Richard Polomsky's essay about fossil hunting and notice how he uses time markers to keep his readers on the track: *Then* and *later* in paragraph 3, *Once back in the lab, Next,* and *At first* in paragraph 6, *then* (three times) in paragraph 7. Unobtrusively the time markers define each new stage of the process.

You needn't overload your writing with time markers. Use just enough so that the steps in the process will be clear. Not every sentence needs a time marker, and you'll want to avoid repeating the same ones too often ("After the seventh day . . . ," "After the eighth day . . ."). Vary them, use them with care, and they will keep your readers with you every step of the way through even the most tangled time sequences.

Rewriting

A paper that analyzes a subject or a process often turns out to be among the best essays that college students write. The secret is to care about what you say and to organize your essay so that it won't look (and read) like a lifeless stack of blocks. As you revise, you'll find it useful to concentrate on making sure that your essay is meaty enough. If you find places that are thin, flesh them out with details and examples that will bring your analysis alive.

WRITING WITH A COMPUTER: ANALYZING

When you use *time markers*, discussed on the opposite page, your computer can help you tell whether your paper needs more of them.

Go through your draft and highlight any time markers in **boldface**, CAPITALS, or whatever form of highlighting your program supplies. This will make them stand out. How frequently do you remember to use them? If you find no time markers at all, you could use some; if you find fewer than one or two in a hundred words, then you could probably use more. Word processing will let you drop these valuable transitions right into place. Remove all the highlighting, of course, before printing out your finished paper.

Rewriting a subject analysis How can you make sure that your reader will be able to follow your thinking as you analyze? You can make your essay as readable as possible by using transitions, those valuable words and phrases that introduce and connect ideas. (See "Using Transitions," p. 513.)

If, on rereading your paper you find any sentence that now strikes you as awkward or murky, just cross it out. Perhaps it needs a second try, or perhaps you can do without it altogether.

Once you have a legible draft, why not call on the services of a trustworthy peer editor? Ask him or her to answer the following questions.

PEER EDITING CHECKLIST: ANALYZING A SUBJECT

- Describe your first reaction to the paper.
- What seems to be the writer's purpose in writing this essay?
- Restate the writer's division into parts by drawing a pie and labeling each slice. Are any of the slices disproportionate? Is it clear why the writer makes one slice larger or smaller?
- If the writer subdivided, has she or he clearly situated the subdivisions within the larger division? Tell the writer where he or she needs to be clearer.
- Circle on the manuscript any places where spelling, grammar, word choice, or punctuation looks problematic to you.

Once you have your peer editor's assessment in hand, go over your paper carefully, making every effort to incorporate his or her suggestions. Depending on how accurately or inaccurately your reader has seen your purpose, you'll want to accept more suggestions—or fewer. Then, as you prepare to write your final draft, ask *yourself* the following questions. Until you can answer them all to your complete satisfaction, you probably still have more work to do on your analysis.

REVISION CHECKLIST: ANALYZING A SUBJECT

- Have you explained each part completely enough that a reader will understand it?
- Have you shown how each part functions, how it relates to the whole?
- Have you made clear your basis for dividing—the principle on which you slice?
- Do you give your audience a sense of having beheld the subject as a whole? Perhaps your concluding paragraph affords you a chance to bring all the separate parts back together and affirm what your dividing has explained.
- In your conclusion, do you show your readers that all this work has taught them something?

Rewriting a process analysis   Reread your draft in a picky, hard-to-please way. Put yourself in the place of a dim-bulb reader who can't follow any process without the writer leading him or her by the hand. This will help you notice any places where you (as a reader) need more help. Because your purpose is to provide your readers with information or a new skill that they will find truly valuable, this might be a good time to see whether another person can understand the process you're analyzing as well as you can. Enlist the services of a friend, a peer editor. Ask her or him to answer the following questions.

PEER EDITING CHECKLIST: ANALYZING A PROCESS

- Describe your first response to the essay.
- Do you think you understand this process well enough to explain it to someone else? If not, what questions do you have about the process?
- Even if the writer is analyzing a process that you didn't think you had any interest in, has she or he captured your interest? Underline any passages where the writer has failed to do so.
- Does the writer need to clarify any directions? Do you need any additional information? Put stars on the manuscript where you need more direction or help.
- Has the writer arranged the stages of the process in the clearest and most logical way that you can imagine? List any changes you would recommend.
- Do you have any trouble with the writer's word choice?
- Circle on the essay any problems with use of personal pronouns, tense, spelling, or punctuation that made this paper hard to read or follow.

Check your paper for inconsistencies of person. Process analysis tempts writers to switch from *I* to *one* to *you* without reason. If you used *one* at the start of your paper, make sure you've used it throughout.

Too heavy use of the passive voice ("It is known that . . .") is another pit that process analysis can fall into. Look for such constructions, and when you find any, change them to the active voice ("We all know that . . ."). An occasional passive is inevitable, but too many rob your writing of life. The exception to this advice occurs in scientific writing, where an objective tone is required and is generally achieved with the use of the passive voice.

Look too for language that might give your reader difficulty. Circle any specialized or technical words. Do they need defining?

Here are a few more questions to ask yourself while you read as a hard-to-please reader.

REVISION CHECKLIST: ANALYZING A PROCESS

- Is the nature of the process clear: what it will lead to, what it will accomplish?
- Have you put your steps or stages in the most logical possible order?
- If your process includes a number of smaller steps or stages, have you left any out?
- Wherever you have circled a technical word or specialized language, can you put your idea in any simpler terms?
- Have you included enough time markers so that your readers can easily follow the steps in the process you have analyzed?
- If you're writing a directive paper, is there any moment in the process when things are likely to go wrong? Can you alert your reader to possible problems and give advice for solving them?
- Does your own interest in the knowledge you're sharing with your readers shine through? If not, what can you do to make that interest evident?

Other Assignments

1. In a paragraph, analyze one of the following subjects by dividing it into its basic parts or elements.

> A symphony orchestra
> A colony of insects, a flock of birds, a school of fish
> The human heart
> The United Nations organization
> A computer or other technological device
> A basketball, football, or hockey team
> A painting or statue
> A radio telescope
> A hospital or other institution
> An essay, short story, novel, or play

A scientific theory
An era in history
A child's first year
A famous and influential idea

2. Write an informative paragraph or two, explaining how any of the following takes place (or took place).

How a rumor starts
How a bird learns to fly
How a jury is selected
How the Grand Canyon was formed
How a cow dog does its job
How the ozone layer has been damaged by chemical agents
How someone becomes a Democrat or a Republican
How a closed-end equity mutual fund operates
How a psychiatrist diagnoses an illness
How acid rain is formed
How an expert detects an art forgery

For practice in writing a brief directive process analysis, explain in a page or two how to do one of the following.

Judge the effectiveness of an advertisement
Choose an academic major
Win an election
Write a news story
Overcome an addiction
Harness solar energy to perform a useful task
Administer the Heimlich maneuver to someone choking on food
Register a patent
Take a market sampling
Lodge a complaint with authorities
Prevent a certain sports injury
Dissect a frog

3. From any textbook you are currently using in another course, choose a chapter in which a process is analyzed. Psychology, geology, chemistry, physics, biology, botany, zoology, engineering, computer programming, business, nursing, and education courses are likely candidates to supply processes.

FOR GROUP LEARNING
We've all bought items we have to assemble ourselves: bicycles, stereos, can openers. Some come with instructions so confusing that even an engineer might be hard pressed to follow them. See if you can find such a set of instructions, whatever its quality. Read it aloud to your class or writing group. What makes it clear—or dense? Together, try to rewrite any puzzling instructions so that anyone may easily follow them.

In a short paper of two or three paragraphs, including just the high points, explain the process. Your audience will be a fellow student who has not read the textbook or taken the course.

This assignment is a matter of paraphrasing or "nutshelling" another writer's ideas and observations in your own words—a skill useful in many professional situations that involve writing from reading. (In a corporation, a senior executive might say, "Here, read all this stuff and write me a short report on what's in it.")

APPLYING WHAT YOU LEARN: SOME USES OF ANALYSIS

As you have no doubt seen already, many different college courses will give you an opportunity to analyze a subject. In explaining for a political science course how the power structure in Iran works, you might divide the government into its branches, explain each, and then factor in the influence of religion. In a nutrition class, you might submit an essay outlining the components of a healthy diet. In a paper for a course on art history, you might single out each element of a Rembrandt painting: perhaps its human figures, their clothing, the background, the light.

You won't always write papers entirely devoted to analyzing. But you may often find analysis useful in writing *part* of an explanatory paper: a paragraph or a section. In the middle of his essay "Things Unflattened by Science," Lewis Thomas pauses to divide biology into three parts.

> We can imagine three worlds of biology, corresponding roughly to the three worlds of physics: the very small world now being explored by the molecular geneticists and virologists, not yet as strange a place as quantum mechanics but well on its way to strangeness; an everyday, middle-sized world where things are as they are; and a world of the very large, which is the whole affair, the lovely conjoined biosphere, the vast embryo, the closed ecosystem in which we live as working parts, the place for which Lovelock and Margulis invented the term "Gaia" because of its extraordinary capacity to regulate itself. This world seems to me an even stranger one than the world of very small things in biology: it looks like the biggest organism I've ever heard of, and at the same time the most delicate and fragile, exactly the delicate and fragile creature it appeared to be in those first photographs taken from the surface of the moon.

Analysis helps readers understand something complex: they can more readily take in the subject in a series of bites than in one gulp. For this reason, college textbooks do a lot of analyzing: an economics book divides a labor union into its component parts, an anatomy text divides the hand into the bones, muscles, and ligaments that make it up. In *Cultural Anthropology: A Perspective on the Human Condition* (1987), authors Emily A. Schultz and Robert H. Lavenda briefly but effectively demonstrate by analysis how a metaphor like "The Lord is my shepherd" makes a difficult concept ("The Lord") easy to understand.

The first part of a metaphor, the **metaphorical subject,** indicates the domain of experience that needs to be clarified (e.g., "the Lord"). The second part of a metaphor, the **metaphorical predicate,** suggests a domain of experience which is familiar (e.g., sheep-herding) and which may help us understand what "the Lord" is all about.

You will also find yourself from time to time being called upon to set forth an informative process analysis, tracing the steps by which something takes place: the formation of a star, a mountain, or a human embryo; the fall of Rome, the awarding of child custody in a divorce case, or the election of a president. Lab reports are good examples of such process analyses. For a marine biology course at his university, student Edward R. Parton did an experiment involving sea urchins, which he then described in a very fine lab report. He began the "Materials and Methods" section of his report with this paragraph, which reveals how to tell a male sea urchin from a female. (Evidently this is not a problem for sea urchins, but it is one for biologists.)

Because sea urchins (Strongylocentralus purpuratus) do not have any distinguishing characteristics that identify their sex, several sea urchins were tested so that spermatozoa and eggs could be obtained. A sample of 4 or 5 sea urchins were injected with 2.0 ml of 0.5 M potassium chloride (0.5 MKCl) by a hypodermic syringe into the soft, fleshy area on each of the sea urchins' oral side. The injected sea urchins were set aside for 5 minutes with their oral sides facing up. The injected 0.5 MKCl made the gonad muscles of each sea urchin contract, thus releasing gametes to the external environment in a mucus-like fluid. If the fluid excreted was yellow, it signified the eggs of a female sea urchin. A male sea urchin excreted blue seminal fluid. But if the identification procedures didn't uncover both a male and female sea urchin from the sample of 4 or 5 sea urchins, additional sea urchins were injected with 2.0 ml of 0.5 MKCl each, following the same identification procedures until at least one male and one female were obtained.

Sometimes, though, process analysis will make up just *part* of what you are asked to write. You'll introduce it wherever in your essay, article, or report you need to explain how something comes about. Here, to take an example from a professional writer, is an informative process analysis—a passage from *The Perceptual World of the Child* by T. G. R. Bower. The author finds it necessary to stop partway through the chapter he calls "Some Complex Effects of Simple Growth" to explain in brief the workings of the human eye.

> Finally we come to the most complex sensory system, the eye and its associated neural structures. The eye is an extremely intricate and complex organ. Light enters the eye through the cornea, passes through the anterior chamber and thence through the pupil to the lens. The lens is a soft transparent tissue that can stretch out and get thinner or shorten and thicken, thus focusing the rays of light and enabling images of objects at different distances to be seen clearly. The lens focuses the light on the retina, which is the thin membrane covering the posterior surface of the eyeball. The nerve cells in the retina itself are sensitive to spots of light. Each nerve cell at the next level of analysis in the brain receives inputs from a number of these retinal nerve cells and responds best to lines or long edges in particular orientations. Numbers of these nerve cells feed into the next level, where nerve cells are sensitive to movement of lines in particular orientations in particular directions. There are other levels that seem sensitive to size, and still others that respond to specific differences in the signals from the two eyes.

Directive or "how to" writing is also demanded of college students. In an education class, you might be asked to describe how to write a lesson plan; in geometry class, how to introduce a new concept; in a psychology class, how to identify family types (open, closed, random, synchronous). In a course on communication disorders, you might be assigned papers on subjects as varied as how to approach a reluctant child in a therapy session, how to give a hearing test, and how to teach someone a new word.

Models of directive or "how to" writing are often found in textbooks such as *Surveying,* by Francis H. Moffitt and Harry Bouchard. The following passage instructs students in using a surveyor's telescope.

> When sighting through the telescope of a surveying instrument, whether it's a level, a transit, a theodolite, or an alidade, the observer must first focus the eyepiece system to *his individual eye.* This is most easily done by holding an opened field book about six inches in front of the objective lens and on a slant in order to obscure the view ahead of the telescope and to allow light to enter the objective lens. . . . The *eyepiece* is now twisted in or out until the cross hairs are sharp and distinct. Now, with the eyepiece system focused, the telescope is pointed at the object to be sighted, with the observer looking along the top of the telescope barrel (some telescopes are provided with peep sights with which to make this initial alignment). The rotational motion is then clamped. The object to be sighted should now be in the field of view. The tangent screw is then used to bring the line of sight directly on the point.

As you enter the world of work, you will probably find yourself called upon any number of times to analyze a process—in lab reports, technical writing of all sorts, business reports and memos, case studies, nursing records, treatment histories, and a host of other kinds of writing, depending on your career. You'll find it immensely useful to know how to explain a process from its beginning to its end.

An Investigative Reporter Analyzes

Jessica Mitford, born in England, has become one of the most widely acclaimed reporters in the United States. Because she unflinchingly exposes what she regards as corruption, abuse, and absurdity, *Time* once called her "Queen of the Muckrakers." The following essay is drawn from her most famous (or notorious) book, *The American Way of Death* (1963).

BEHIND THE FORMALDEHYDE CURTAIN
Jessica Mitford

The drama begins to unfold with the arrival of the corpse at the mortuary. 1

Alas, poor Yorick!° How surprised he would be to see how his counter- 2
part of today is whisked off to a funeral parlor and is in short order sprayed, sliced, pierced, pickled, trussed, trimmed, creamed, waxed, painted, rouged, and neatly dressed—transformed from a common corpse into a Beautiful Memory Picture. This process is known in the trade as embalming and restorative art, and is so universally employed in the United States and Canada that the funeral director does it routinely, without consulting corpse or kin. He regards as eccentric those few who are hardy enough to suggest that it might be dispensed with. Yet no law requires embalming, no religious doctrine commends it, nor is it dictated by considerations of health, sanitation, or even of personal daintiness. In no part of the world but in Northern America is it widely used. The purpose of embalming is to make the corpse presentable for viewing in a suitably costly container; and here too the funeral director routinely, without first consulting the family, prepares the body for public display.

Is all this legal? The processes to which a dead body may be subjected 3
are after all to some extent circumscribed by law. In most states, for instance, the signature of next of kin must be obtained before an autopsy may be performed, before the deceased may be cremated, before the body may be turned over to a medical school for research purposes; or such provision must be made in the decedent's will. In the case of embalming, no such permission is required nor is it ever sought. A textbook, *The Prin-*

Alas, poor Yorick! Mitford echoes Shakespeare: Hamlet's line as he examines the skull of his old friend, the court jester who was buried without a coffin in a common grave (*Hamlet* V, i, 184).

ciples and Practices of Embalming, comments on this: "There is some question regarding the legality of much that is done within the preparation room." The author points out that it would be most unusual for a responsible member of a bereaved family to instruct the mortician, in so many words, to "*embalm*" the body of a deceased relative. The very term "embalming" is so seldom used that the mortician must rely upon custom in the matter. The author concludes that unless the family specifies otherwise, the act of entrusting the body to the care of a funeral establishment carries with it an implied permission to go ahead and embalm.

Embalming is indeed a most extraordinary procedure, and one must 4 wonder at the docility of Americans who each year pay hundreds of millions of dollars for its perpetuation, blissfully ignorant of what it is all about, what is done, how it is done. Not one in ten thousand has any idea of what actually takes place. Books on the subject are extremely hard to come by. They are not to be found in most libraries or bookshops.

In an era when huge television audiences watch surgical operations in 5 the comfort of their living rooms, when, thanks to the animated cartoon, the geography of the digestive system has become familiar territory even to the nursery school set, in a land where the satisfaction of curiosity about almost all matters is a national pastime, the secrecy surrounding embalming can, surely, hardly be attributed to the inherent gruesomeness of the subject. Custom in this regard has within this century suffered a complete reversal. In the early days of American embalming, when it was performed in the home of the deceased, it was almost mandatory for some relative to stay by the embalmer's side and witness the procedure. Today, family members who might wish to be in attendance would certainly be dissuaded by the funeral director. All others, except apprentices, are excluded by law from the preparation room.

A close look at what does actually take place may explain in large 6 measure the undertaker's intractable reticence concerning a procedure that has become his major *raison d'être*. Is it possible he fears that public information about embalming might lead patrons to wonder if they really want this service? If the funeral men are loath to discuss the subject outside the trade, the reader may, understandably, be equally loath to go on reading at this point. For those who have the stomach for it, let us part the formaldehyde curtain. . . .

The body is first laid out in the undertaker's morgue—or rather, Mr. 7 Jones is reposing in the preparation room—to be readied to bid the world farewell.

The preparation room in any of the better funeral establishments has 8 the tiled and sterile look of a surgery, and indeed the embalmer-restorative artist who does his chores there is beginning to adopt the term "derma-surgeon" (appropriately corrupted by some mortician-writers as "demi-surgeon") to describe his calling. His equipment, consisting of scalpels, scissors, augers, forceps, clamps, needles, pumps, tubes, bowls, and basins, is crudely imitative of the surgeon's, as is his technique, acquired in a nine- or twelve-month post-high-school course in an embalming school. He is supplied by an advanced chemical industry with a bewildering array of fluids, sprays, pastes, oils, powders, creams, to fix or soften tissue, shrink or distend it as needed, dry it here, restore the moisture there. There are cosmetics, waxes, and paints to fill and cover features, even plaster of Paris to replace entire limbs. There are ingenious aids to prop and stabilize the cadaver: a Vari-Pose Head Rest, the Edwards Arm and Hand Positioner, the Repose Block (to support the shoulders during the embalming), and the Throop Foot Positioner, which resembles an old-fashioned stocks.

Mr. John H. Eckels, president of the Eckels College of Mortuary Science, thus describes the first part of the embalming procedure: "In the hands of a skilled practitioner, this work may be done in a comparatively short time and without mutilating the body other than by slight incision—so slight that it scarcely would cause serious inconvenience if made upon a living person. It is necessary to remove the blood, and doing this not only helps in the disinfecting, but removes the principal cause of disfigurements due to discoloration." 9

Another textbook discusses the all-important time element: "The earlier this is done, the better, for every hour that elapses between death and embalming will add to the problems and complications encountered. . . ." Just how soon should one get going on the embalming? The author tells us, "On the basis of such scanty information made available to this profession through its rudimentary and haphazard system of technical research, we must conclude that the best results are to be obtained if the subject is embalmed before life is completely extinct—that is, before cellular death has occurred. In the average case, this would mean within an hour after somatic death." For those who feel that there is something a little rudimentary, not to say haphazard, about this advice, a comforting thought is offered by another writer. Speaking of fears entertained in early days of premature burial, he points out, "One of the effects of embalming by chemical injection, however, has been to dispel fears of live burial." How true; once the blood is removed, chances of live burial are indeed remote. 10

To return to Mr. Jones, the blood is drained out through the veins and replaced by embalming fluid pumped in through the arteries. As noted in *The Principles and Practices of Embalming*, "every operator has a favorite injection and drainage point—a fact which becomes a handicap only if he fails or refuses to forsake his favorites when conditions demand it." Typical favorites are the carotid artery, femoral artery, jugular vein, subclavian vein. There are various choices of embalming fluid. If Flextone is used, it will produce a "mild, flexible rigidity. The skin retains a velvety softness, the tissues are rubbery and pliable. Ideal for women and children." It may be blended with B. and G. Products Company's Lyf-Lyk tint, which is guaranteed to reproduce "nature's own skin texture . . . the velvety appearance of living tissue." Suntone comes in three separate tints: Suntan; Special Cosmetic 11

Tint, a pink shade "especially indicated for female subjects"; and Regular Cosmetic Tint, moderately pink.

About three to six gallons of a dyed and perfumed solution of formal- 12 dehyde, glycerin, borax, phenol, alcohol, and water is soon circulating through Mr. Jones, whose mouth has been sewn together with a "needle directed upward between the upper lip and gum and brought out through the left nostril," with the corners raised slightly "for a more pleasant expression." If he should be bucktoothed, his teeth are cleaned with Bon Ami and coated with colorless nail polish. His eyes, meanwhile, are closed with flesh-tinted eye caps and eye cement.

The next step is to have at Mr. Jones with a thing called a trocar. This 13 is a long, hollow needle attached to a tube. It is jabbed into the abdomen, poked around the entrails and chest cavity, the contents of which are pumped out and replaced with "cavity fluid." This done, and the hole in the abdomen sewn up, Mr. Jones's face is heavily creamed (to protect the skin from burns which may be caused by leakage of the chemicals), and he is covered with a sheet and left unmolested for a while. But not for long— there is more, much more, in store for him. He has been embalmed, but not yet restored, and the best time to start the restorative work is eight to ten hours after embalming, when the tissues have become firm and dry.

The object of all this attention to the corpse, it must be remembered, 14 is to make it presentable for viewing in an attitude of healthy repose. "Our customs require the presentation of our dead in the semblance of normality . . . unmarred by the ravages of illness, disease, or mutilation," says Mr. J. Sheridan Mayer in his *Restorative Art*. This is rather a large order since few people die in the full bloom of health, unravaged by illness and unmarked by some disfigurement. The funeral industry is equal to the challenge: "In some cases the gruesome appearance of a mutilated or disease-ridden subject may be quite discouraging. The task of restoration may seem impossible and shake the confidence of the embalmer. This is the time for intestinal fortitude and determination. Once the formative work is begun and affected tissues are cleaned or removed, all doubts of success vanish. It is surprising and gratifying to discover the results which may be obtained."

The embalmer, having allowed an appropriate interval to elapse, re- 15 turns to the attack, but now he brings into play the skill and equipment of sculptor and cosmetician. Is a hand missing? Casting one in plaster of Paris is a simple matter. "For replacement purposes, only a cast of the back of the hand is necessary; this is within the ability of the average operator and is quite adequate." If a lip or two, a nose or an ear should be missing, the embalmer has at hand a variety of restorative waxes with which to model replacements. Pores and skin texture are simulated by stippling with a little brush, and over this cosmetics are laid on. Head off? Decapitation cases are rather routinely handled. Ragged edges are trimmed, and head joined to torso with a series of splints, wires, and sutures. It is a good idea to have a little something at the neck—a scarf or a high collar—when time for viewing comes. Swollen mouth? Cut out tissue as needed from inside the lips. If too much is removed, the surface contour can easily be restored by padding with cotton. Swollen necks and cheeks are reduced by removing tissue through vertical incisions made down each side of the neck. "When the deceased is casketed, the pillow will hide the suture incisions . . . as an extra precaution against leakage, the suture may be painted with liquid sealer."

The opposite condition is more likely to present itself—that of emacia-   16
tion. His hypodermic syringe now loaded with massage cream, the embalmer seeks out and fills the hollowed and sunken areas by injection. In this procedure the backs of the hands and fingers and the under-chin area should not be neglected.

Positioning the lips is a problem that recurrently challenges the inge-   17
nuity of the embalmer. Closed too tightly, they tend to give a stern, even disapproving expression. Ideally, embalmers feel, the lips should give the impression of being ever so slightly parted, the upper lip protruding slightly for a more youthful appearance. This takes some engineering, however, as the lips tend to drift apart. Lip drift can sometimes be remedied by pushing one or two straight pins through the inner margin of the lower lip and then inserting them between the two front upper teeth. If Mr. Jones happens to have no teeth, the pins can just as easily be anchored in his Armstrong Face Former and Denture Replacer. Another method to maintain lip closure is to dislocate the lower jaw, which is then held in its new position by a wire run through holes which have been drilled through the upper and lower jaws at the midline. As the French are fond of saying, *il faut souffrir pour être belle.*°

If Mr. Jones has died of jaundice, the embalming fluid will very likely   18
turn him green. Does this deter the embalmer? Not if he has intestinal fortitude. Masking pastes and cosmetics are heavily laid on, burial garments and casket interiors are color-correlated with particular care, and Jones is displayed beneath rose-colored lights. Friends will say "How *well* he looks." Death by carbon monoxide, on the other hand, can be rather a good thing from the embalmer's viewpoint: "One advantage is the fact that this type of discoloration is an exaggerated form of a natural pink coloration." This is nice because the healthy glow is already present and needs but little attention.

The patching and filling completed, Mr. Jones is now shaved, washed,   19
and dressed. Cream-based cosmetic, available in pink, flesh, suntan, brunette, and blond, is applied to his hands and face, his hair is shampooed and combed (and, in the case of Mrs. Jones, set), his hands manicured. For the horny-handed son of toil special care must be taken; cream should be applied to remove ingrained grime, and the nails cleaned. "If he were

---

il faut . . . belle: You have to suffer to be beautiful.

not in the habit of having them manicured in life, trimming and shaping is advised for better appearance—never questioned by kin."

Jones is now ready for casketing (this is the present participle of the 20 verb "to casket"). In this operation his right shoulder should be depressed slightly "to turn the body a bit to the right and soften the appearance of lying flat on the back." Positioning the hands is a matter of importance, and special rubber positioning blocks may be used. The hands should be cupped slightly for a more lifelike, relaxed appearance. Proper placement of the body requires a delicate sense of balance. It should lie as high as possible in the casket, yet not so high that the lid, when lowered, will hit the nose. On the other hand, we are cautioned, placing the body too low "creates the impression that the body is in a box."

Jones is next wheeled into the appointed slumber room where a few 21 last touches may be added—his favorite pipe placed in his hand or, if he was a great reader, a book propped into position. (In the case of little Master Jones a Teddy bear may be clutched.) Here he will hold open house for a few days, visiting hours 10 A.M. to 9 P.M.

All now being in readiness, the funeral director calls a staff conference 22 to make sure that each assistant knows his precise duties. Mr. Wilber Kriege writes: "This makes your staff feel that they are a part of the team, with a definite assignment that must be properly carried out if the whole plan is to succeed. You never heard of a football coach who failed to talk to his entire team before they go on the field. They have drilled on the plays they are to execute for hours and days, and yet the successful coach knows the importance of making even the bench-warming third-string substitute feel that he is important if the game is to be won." The winning of *this* game is predicated upon glass-smooth handling of the logistics. The funeral director has notified the pallbearers whose names were furnished by the family, has arranged for the presence of clergyman, organist, and soloist, has provided transportation for everybody, has organized and listed the flowers sent by friends. In *Psychology of Funeral Service* Mr. Edward A. Martin points out: "He may not always do as much as the family thinks he is doing, but it is his helpful guidance that they appreciate in knowing they are proceeding as they should. . . . The important thing is how well his services can be used to make the family believe they are giving unlimited expression to their own sentiment."

The religious service may be held in a church or in the chapel of the 23 funeral home; the funeral director vastly prefers the latter arrangement, for not only is it more convenient for him but it affords him the opportunity to show off his beautiful facilities to the gathered mourners. After the clergyman has had his say, the mourners queue up to file past the casket for a last look at the deceased. The family is *never* asked whether they want an open-casket ceremony; in the absence of their instruction to the contrary, this is taken for granted. Consequently well over 90 percent of all American funerals feature the open casket—a custom unknown in other parts of the world. Foreigners are astonished by it. An English woman living in San Francisco described her reaction in a letter to the writer:

> I myself have attended only one funeral here—that of an elderly fellow worker of mine. After the service I could not understand why everyone was walking towards the coffin (sorry, I mean casket), but thought I had better follow the crowd. It shook me rigid to get there and find the casket open and poor old Oscar lying there in his brown tweed suit, wearing a suntan makeup and just the wrong shade of lipstick. If I had not been extremely fond of the old boy, I have a horrible feeling that I might have giggled. Then and there I decided that I could never face another American funeral—even dead.

The casket (which has been resting throughout the service on a Classic Beauty Ultra Metal Casket Bier) is now transferred by a hydraulically operated device called Porto-Lift to a balloon-tired, Glide Easy casket carriage which will wheel it to yet another conveyance, the Cadillac Funeral Coach. This may be lavender, cream, light green—anything but black. Interiors, of course, are color-correlated, "for the man who cannot stop short of perfection."   24

At graveside, the casket is lowered into the earth. This office, once the prerogative of friends of the deceased, is now performed by a patented mechanical lowering device. A "Lifetime Green" artificial grass mat is at the ready to conceal the sere earth, and overhead, to conceal the sky, is a portable Steril Chapel Tent ("resists the intense heat and humidity of summer and the terrific storms of winter . . . available in Silver Grey, Rose or Evergreen"). Now is the time for the ritual scattering of earth over the coffin, as the solemn words "earth to earth, ashes to ashes, dust to dust" are pronounced by the officiating cleric. This can today be accomplished "with a mere flick of the wrist with the Gordon Leak-Proof Earth Dispenser. No grasping of a handful of dirt, no soiled fingers. Simple, dignified, beautiful, reverent! The modern way!" The Gordon Earth Dispenser (at $5) is of nickel-plated brass construction. It is not only "attractive to the eye and long wearing"; it is also "one of the 'tools' for building better public relations" if presented as "an appropriate non-commercial gift" to the clergyman. It is shaped something like a saltshaker.   25

Untouched by human hand, the coffin and the earth are now united.   26

It is in the function of directing the participants through this maze of gadgetry that the funeral director has assigned to himself his relatively new role of "grief therapist." He has relieved the family of every detail, he has revamped the corpse to look like a living doll, he has arranged for it to nap for a few days in a slumber room, he has put on a well-oiled performance in which the concept of *death* has played no part whatsoever—unless it was inconsiderately mentioned by the clergyman who conducted the religious service. He has done everything in his power to make the funeral a real pleasure for everybody concerned. He and his team have given their all to score an upset victory over death.   27

Questions to Start You Thinking

1. Do you think Mitford goes into too much unpleasant detail about her topic? To what extent does it serve her purpose?

2. Into what stages has the author divided the embalming process? Where does she make good use of time markers?

3. How would an essay analyzing the process of embalming have to differ from Mitford's if it were written for an audience of professional morticians?

4. What is Mitford's attitude toward her material? Point to passages that make this attitude clear.

5. Write a few paragraphs analyzing your emotional reactions to Mitford's essay.

A Composer Analyzes

In the following essay, eminent American composer Aaron Copland writes with a purpose: to analyze how we listen to music. As he makes clear, listening isn't a step-by-step activity, and so he does not try to treat it in chronological order as he might do in a process analysis. Rather, his essay divides the way we listen into three elements or planes. All three exist simultaneously.

HOW WE LISTEN
Aaron Copland

We all listen to music according to our separate capacities. But, for 1 the sake of analysis, the whole listening process may become clearer if we break it up into its component parts, so to speak. In a certain sense we all listen to music on three separate planes. For lack of a better terminology, one might name these: (1) the sensuous plane, (2) the expressive plane, (3) the sheerly musical plane. The only advantage to be gained from me-chanically splitting up the listening process into these hypothetical planes is the clearer view to be had of the way in which we listen.

The simplest way of listening to music is to listen for the sheer pleasure 2 of the musical sound itself. That is the sensuous plane. It is the plane on which we hear music without thinking, without considering it in any way. One turns on the radio while doing something else and absent-mindedly bathes in the sound. A kind of brainless but attractive state of mind is engendered by the mere sound appeal of the music.

You may be sitting in a room reading this book. Imagine one note struck 3 on the piano. Immediately that one note is enough to change the atmos-phere of the room—proving that the sound element in music is a powerful and mysterious agent, which it would be foolish to deride or belittle.

The surprising thing is that many people who consider themselves qual- 4 ified music lovers abuse that plane in listening. They go to concerts in order to lose themselves. They use music as a consolation or an escape. They enter an ideal world where one doesn't have to think of the realities of everyday life. Of course they aren't thinking about the music either. Music allows them to leave it, and they go off to a place to dream, dreaming because of and apropos of the music yet never quite listening to it.

Yes, the sound appeal of music is a potent and primitive force, but you 5 must not allow it to usurp a disproportionate share of your interest. The sensuous plane is an important one in music, a very important one, but it does not constitute the whole story.

There is no need to digress further on the sensuous plane. Its appeal 6 to every normal human being is self-evident. There is, however, such a thing as becoming more sensitive to the different kinds of sound stuff as used by various composers. For all composers do not use that sound stuff in the same way. Don't get the idea that the value of music is commensurate with its sensuous appeal or that the loveliest sounding music is made by the greatest composer. If that were so, Ravel would be a greater creator than Beethoven. The point is that the sound element varies with each composer, that his usage of sound forms an integral part of his style and must be taken into account when listening. The reader can see, therefore, that a more conscious approach is valuable even on this primary plane of music listening.

The second plane on which music exists is what I have called the ex- 7 pressive one. Here, immediately, we tread on controversial ground. Composers have a way of shying away from any discussion of music's expressive side. Did not Stravinsky himself proclaim that his music was an "object," a "thing," with a life of its own, and with no other meaning than its own purely musical existence? This intransigent attitude of Stravinsky's may be due to the fact that so many people have tried to read different meanings into so many pieces. Heaven knows it is difficult enough to say precisely what it is that a piece of music means, to say it definitely, to say it finally so that everyone is satisfied with your explanation. But that should not lead one to the other extreme of denying to music the right to be "expressive."

My own belief is that all music has an expressive power, some more 8 and some less, but that all music has a certain meaning behind the notes and that that meaning behind the notes constitutes, after all, what the piece is saying, what the piece is about. This whole problem can be stated quite simply by asking, "Is there a meaning to music?" My answer to that would be "Yes." And "Can you state in so many words what the meaning is?" My answer to that would be "No." Therein lies the difficulty.

Simple-minded souls will never be satisfied with the answer to the 9 second of these questions. They always want music to have a meaning, and the more concrete it is the better they like it. The more the music reminds them of a train, a storm, a funeral, or any other familiar conception the more expressive it appears to be to them. This popular idea of music's

meaning—stimulated and abetted by the usual run of musical commentator—should be discouraged wherever and whenever it is met. One timid
lady once confessed to me that she suspected something seriously lacking
in her appreciation of music because of her inability to connect it with
anything definite. That is getting the whole thing backward, of course.

Still, the question remains, How close should the intelligent music lover   10
wish to come to pinning a definite meaning to any particular work? No closer
than a general concept, I should say. Music expresses, at different moments, serenity or exuberance, regret or triumph, fury or delight. It expresses each of these moods, and many others, in a numberless variety of
subtle shadings and differences. It may even express a state of meaning
for which there exists no adequate word in any language. In that case,
musicians often like to say that it has only a purely musical meaning. They
sometimes go farther and say that *all* music has only a purely musical
meaning. What they really mean is that no appropriate word can be found
to express the music's meaning and that, even if it could, they do not feel
the need of finding it.

But whatever the professional musician may hold, most musical novices   11
still search for specific words with which to pin down their musical reactions. That is why they always find Tchaikovsky easier to "understand" than
Beethoven. In the first place, it is easier to pin a meaning-word on a Tchaikovsky piece than on a Beethoven one. Much easier. Moreover, with the
Russian composer, every time you come back to a piece of his it almost
always says the same thing to you, whereas with Beethoven it is often quite
difficult to put your finger right on what he is saying. And any musician will
tell you that that is why Beethoven is the greatest composer. Because music
which always says the same thing to you will necessarily soon become dull
music, but music whose meaning is slightly different with each hearing has
a greater chance of remaining alive.

Listen, if you can, to the forty-eight fugue themes of Bach's *Well Tem-*   12
pered Clavier. Listen to each theme, one after another. You will soon realize
that each theme mirrors a different world of feeling. You will also soon
realize that the more beautiful a theme seems to you the harder it is to
find any word that will describe it to your complete satisfaction. Yes, you
will certainly know whether it is a gay theme or a sad one. You will be able,
in other words, in your own mind, to draw a frame of emotional feeling
around your theme. Now study the sad one a little closer. Try to pin down
the exact quality of its sadness. Is it pessimistically sad or resignedly sad;
is it fatefully sad or smilingly sad?

Let us suppose that you are fortunate and can describe to your own   13
satisfaction in so many words the exact meaning of your chosen theme.
There is still no guarantee that anyone else will be satisfied. Nor need they
be. The important thing is that each one feel for himself the specific expressive quality of a theme or, similarly, an entire piece of music. And if it

is a great work of art, don't expect it to mean exactly the same thing to you each time you return to it.

Themes or pieces need not express only one emotion, of course. Take 14 such a theme as the first main one of the *Ninth Symphony*,° for example. It is clearly made up of different elements. It does not say only one thing. Yet anyone hearing it immediately gets a feeling of strength, a feeling of power. It isn't a power that comes simply because the theme is played loudly. It is a power inherent in the theme itself. The extraordinary strength and vigor of the theme results in the listener's receiving an impression that a forceful statement has been made. But one should never try to boil it down to "the fateful hammer of life," etc. That is where the trouble begins. The musician, in his exasperation, says it means nothing but the notes themselves, whereas the nonprofessional is only too anxious to hang on to any explanation that gives him the illusion of getting closer to the music's meaning.

Now, perhaps, the reader will know better what I mean when I say that 15 music does have an expressive meaning but that we cannot say in so many words what that meaning is.

The third plane on which music exists is the sheerly musical plane. 16 Besides the pleasurable sound of music and the expressive feeling that it gives off, music does exist in terms of the notes themselves and of their manipulation. Most listeners are not sufficiently conscious of this third plane. . . .

Professional musicians, on the other hand, are, if anything, too con- 17 scious of the mere notes themselves. They often fall into the error of becoming so engrossed with their arpeggios° and staccatos° that they forget the deeper aspects of the music they are performing. But from the layman's standpoint, it is not so much a matter of getting over bad habits on the sheerly musical plane as of increasing one's awareness of what is going on, insofar as the notes are concerned.

When the man in the street listens to the "notes themselves" with any 18 degree of concentration, he is most likely to make some mention of the melody. Either he hears a pretty melody or he does not, and he generally lets it go at that. Rhythm is likely to gain his attention next, particularly if it seems exciting. But harmony and tone color are generally taken for granted, if they are thought of consciously at all. As for music's having a definite form of some kind, that idea seems never to have occurred to him.

It is very important for all of us to become more alive to music on its 19 sheerly musical plane. After all, an actual musical material is being used. The intelligent listener must be prepared to increase his awareness of the

---

Ninth Symphony: Final symphony of Ludwig van Beethoven (1770–1827).
arpeggios: The playing of the tones of a chord in succession instead of together.
staccatos: Groups of disconnected notes played rapidly.

musical material and what happens to it. He must hear the melodies, the rhythms, the harmonies, the tone colors in a more conscious fashion. But above all he must, in order to follow the line of the composer's thought, know something of the principles of musical form. Listening to all of these elements is listening on the sheerly musical plane.

Let me repeat that I have split up mechanically the three separate [20] planes on which we listen merely for the sake of greater clarity. Actually, we never listen on one or the other of these planes. What we do is to correlate them—listening in all three ways at the same time. It takes no mental effort, for we do it instinctively.

Perhaps an analogy with what happens to us when we visit the theater [21] will make this instinctive correlation clearer. In the theater, you are aware of the actors and actresses, costumes and sets, sounds and movements. All these give one the sense that the theater is a pleasant place to be in. They constitute the sensuous plane in our theatrical reactions.

The expressive plane in the theater would be derived from the feeling [22] that you get from what is happening on the stage. You are moved to pity, excitement, or gaiety. It is this general feeling, generated aside from the particular words being spoken, a certain emotional something which exists on the stage, that is analogous to the expressive quality in music.

The plot and plot development is equivalent to our sheerly musical [23] plane. The playwright creates and develops a character in just the same way that a composer creates and develops a theme. According to the degree of your awareness of the way in which the artist in either field handles his material will you become a more intelligent listener.

It is easy enough to see that the theatergoer never is conscious of any [24] of these elements separately. He is aware of them all at the same time. The same is true of music listening. We simultaneously and without thinking listen on all three planes.

In a sense, the ideal listener is both inside and outside the music at [25] the same moment, judging it and enjoying it, wishing it would go one way and watching it go another—almost like the composer at the moment he composes it; because in order to write his music, the composer must also be inside and outside his music, carried away by it and yet coldly critical of it. A subjective and objective attitude is implied in both creating and listening to music.

What the reader should strive for, then, is a more *active* kind of listen- [26] ing. Whether you listen to Mozart or Duke Ellington,° you can deepen your understanding of music only by being a more conscious and aware listener—not someone who is just listening, but someone who is listening *for* something.

Duke Ellington: Edward Kennedy Ellington (1899–1974), American pianist, bandleader, and composer, whose innovative music profoundly influenced the history of jazz.

Questions to Start You Thinking

1. What reason does the author give for dividing the way we listen into three separate components, or planes? What does the essay gain from his having done so?

2. In paragraphs 21–24, the author makes an analogy to help explain what he's talking about. Can you think of other analogies that would make Copland's divisions clear?

3. What, if anything, has Copland taught you about being an intelligent listener? Does he say anything that you disagree with, that doesn't coincide with your experience?

4. What other large concepts might be most easily analyzed?

A NOTE ON ANALYZING LITERATURE

You just might, in your college career, take one or more literature courses. Literary study has long been recognized as an essential in most college curricula, for to read a masterpiece (*Hamlet,* say, or *The Awakening*) offers rewards beyond those measurable in dollars and cents. Still, any time spent with Shakespeare's great play or Kate Chopin's classic American novel may not hurt you, after all, in the job market. Because the study of literature calls for critical thinking, lately even some personnel managers of large corporations have been unfurling the welcome mats for English and foreign language majors.

More often than not, a writing assignment in a literature course will ask you for some kind of analysis. You'll be expected to read closely a story, poem, or play, see it as divisible into its elements, and write about at least one of them. What might these elements be? Let's list a few. Read this list and you'll get a handy glossary of terms to use in discussing literature.

Characters are imagined people in a story, poem, or play.

Form, in poetry, is a structure of sound and rhythm. The kind of poetry called *formal verse* usually has rhyme, meter, and stanzas, but actually, every poem has a form, even *free verse,* poetry that doesn't contain rhyme, meter, and stanzas. Form is whatever shape you see on the page, whatever structure you hear when the poem is read aloud.

Images, in poetry, are words or groups of words that refer to any sense experience: seeing (a window "diamonded with panes"), hearing ("snarling trumpets"), smelling ("incense sweet"), tasting (someone "can burst Joy's grape against his palate fine"), touching ("damp and slippery footing"), feeling heat or cold (a hare "limped trembling through the frozen grass"), or feeling pain or thirst ("a burning forehead and a parching tongue")—to take examples from John Keats.

Irony results from our sense of some discrepancy. A simple kind of irony, *sarcasm,* occurs when you say a thing but mean the opposite: "I just love scrubbing the floor." In literature, an *ironic situation* sets up a wry contrast or incongruity. In Edgar Allan Poe's story "The Cask of Amontillado," a grim murder takes place during a Mardi Gras celebration.

Point of view is the angle from which a story is told. Who is the *narrator,* who tells the story? It might be the author, it might be some character in the story. If a character, what part does he or she play, and what limits does the author place on that character's knowledge? Answer those questions and you define the story's point of view. The two most usual points of view are those of a first-person narrator ("I") and a third-person narrator, not a participating character but the voice of the author or some other outsider. A story has an *ironic point of view* when we sense a difference between the author and the character telling the story. Part of William Faulkner's *The Sound and the Fury* is told through the eyes of an idiot, but Faulkner himself was one smart man.

Plot in a story or play is the arrangement of events. It places the *protagonist,* or main character, in a *dramatic situation*—in conflict with some other person or force. A *crisis* is the turning point in the action: receiving a death threat, the protagonist buys a gun. Events reach a *climax* when the outcome is to be decided. (Protagonist and enemy face each other, ready to draw.) The outcome itself is called the *resolution* or *conclusion.* Many contemporary stories and plays let events unfold without any apparent plot.

Setting, in a story or play, is the time and place where events transpire. The season or the weather may be part of the setting.

A *symbol* is a visible object or action that hints at many meanings besides itself. It doesn't "stand for" anything, it just hints. In Faulkner's "The Bear," a huge old beast with one trap-injured foot suggests a vanishing wilderness, a challenge that a boy must face to become a man, and more. In that story, as in many, figure out what the symbol suggests and you can state the *theme.*

Theme is the main idea or insight a work contains. You can often sum it up in a sentence. In Aesop's fable of the fox and the grapes, the theme is stated at the end: "Moral: It is easy to scorn what cannot be attained." In a longer work, the theme may not be obvious, and there may be different ways of stating it.

Before writing your analysis of a story, poem, or play, read the text at least three times, each time for a different purpose:

Read for the big picture. Read for an overall idea of what the work contains. Then—

Read for pleasure. Finally—

Read purposefully. Read with an eye for what you seek in the work: characters, themes, form, or whatever. Read with pencil in hand. Make notes—in the margins if the copy is yours and on paper or index cards if it isn't. Is there an especially hard part? Try writing a paraphrase. (See p. 360.) If you're analyzing a difficult poem, reading it aloud to yourself may help it make sense to you.

As you write your analysis, don't worry about impressing your reader with your brilliance. Though you need a critical vocabulary, use only terms that are part of you. The writer who writes, "The myth imagery in this story is highly symbolic in theme" is about as clear as corned beef hash. Assume, by the way, that your reader, too, has read the work you're analyzing. This assumption will save you a lot of wordy summarizing ("On the next page the bear comes out of the woods and the boy Jody is awed"). We suggest you regard your reader as a friend in whose company you are studying something already familiar to both of you.

In analyzing a literary work, you'll probably find yourself making up your mind about it. Say you're analyzing a story for its characters. You might find yourself asking, Are they convincing human beings, or are they wooden dolls? Do they behave consistently, with some believable *motivation*—some reason to act or react the way they do? Analysis easily leads to evaluating—making a judgment. Often in writing about literature you'll find yourself analyzing and evaluating at the same time.

Evaluating, or judging, is discussed thoroughly in Chapter 9, but to give a preview of how the skills of analysis and evaluation can be combined and brought to bear on literature, here is one of the most widely reprinted works of an acclaimed American storyteller, Kate Chopin (1851–1904), followed by a student's analysis of the story. Chopin's work has lately been enjoying a revival of interest, after long neglect. *The Awakening* (1899), a novel about a woman who seeks sexual and professional independence, caused shock and anger in its day, and its author was able to find few magazines willing to print her work after the book was published. Even in our day, "The Story of an Hour" has had its detractors, and in reply to them English major Jane Betz has written a sensitive defense of it.

THE STORY OF AN HOUR
Kate Chopin

Knowing that Mrs. Mallard was afflicted with a heart trouble, great care   1
was taken to break to her as gently as possible the news of her husband's death.

It was her sister Josephine who told her, in broken sentences, veiled   2
hints that revealed in half concealing. Her husband's friend Richards was there, too, near her. It was he who had been in the newspaper office when intelligence of the railroad disaster was received, with Brently Mallard's name leading the list of "killed." He had only taken the time to assure himself of its truth by a second telegram, and had hastened to forestall any less careful, less tender friend in bearing the sad message.

She did not hear the story as many women have heard the same, with   3
a paralyzed inability to accept its significance. She wept at once, with sudden, wild abandonment, in her sister's arms. When the storm of grief had spent itself she went away to her room alone. She would have no one follow her.

There stood, facing the open window, a comfortable, roomy armchair. 4
Into this she sank, pressed down by a physical exhaustion that haunted her
body and seemed to reach into her soul.

She could see in the open square before her house the tops of trees 5
that were all aquiver with the new spring life. The delicious breath of rain
was in the air. In the street below a peddler was crying his wares. The notes
of a distant song which some one was singing reached her faintly, and
countless sparrows were twittering in the eaves.

There were patches of blue sky showing here and there through the 6
clouds that had met and piled one above the other in the west facing her
window.

She sat with her head thrown back upon the cushion of the chair, quite 7
motionless, except when a sob came up into her throat and shook her, as
a child who has cried itself to sleep continues to sob in its dreams.

She was young, with a fair, calm face, whose lines bespoke repression 8
and even a certain strength. But now there was a dull stare in her eyes,
whose gaze was fixed away off yonder on one of those patches of blue sky.
It was not a glance of reflection, but rather indicated a suspension of
intelligent thought.

There was something coming to her and she was waiting for it, fearfully. 9
What was it? She did not know; it was too subtle and elusive to name. But
she felt it, creeping out of the sky, reaching toward her through the sounds,
the scents, the color that filled the air.

Now her bosom rose and fell tumultuously. She was beginning to rec- 10
ognize this thing that was approaching to possess her, and she was striving
to beat it back with her will—as powerless as her two white slender hands
would have been.

When she abandoned herself a little whispered word escaped her 11
slightly parted lips. She said it over and over under her breath: "Free, free,
free!" The vacant stare and the look of terror that had followed it went from
her eyes. They stayed keen and bright. Her pulses beat fast, and the cours-
ing blood warmed and relaxed every inch of her body.

She did not stop to ask if it were not a monstrous joy that held her. A 12
clear and exalted perception enabled her to dismiss the suggestion as
trivial.

She knew that she would weep again when she saw the kind, tender 13
hands folded in death; the face that had never looked save with love upon
her, fixed and gray and dead. But she saw beyond that bitter moment a
long procession of years to come that would belong to her absolutely. And
she opened and spread her arms out to them in welcome.

There would be no one to live for during those coming years; she would 14
live for herself. There would be no powerful will bending her in that blind
persistence with which men and women believe they have a right to impose
a private will upon a fellow creature. A kind intention or a cruel intention

made the act seem no less a crime as she looked upon it in that brief moment of illumination.

And yet she had loved him—sometimes. Often she had not. What did it matter! What could love, the unsolved mystery, count for in face of this possession of self-assertion which she suddenly recognized as the strongest impulse of her being. 15

"Free! Body and soul free!" she kept whispering. 16

Josephine was kneeling before the closed door with her lips to the keyhole, imploring for admission. "Louise, open the door! I beg; open the door—you will make yourself ill. What are you doing, Louise? For heaven's sake open the door." 17

"Go away. I am not making myself ill." No; she was drinking in a very elixir of life through that open window. 18

Her fancy was running riot along those days ahead of her. Spring days, and summer days, and all sorts of days that would be her own. She breathed a quick prayer that life might be long. It was only yesterday she had thought with a shudder that life might be long. 19

She arose at length and opened the door to her sister's importunities. There was a feverish triumph in her eyes, and she carried herself unwittingly like a goddess of Victory. She clasped her sister's waist, and together they descended the stairs. Richards stood waiting for them at the bottom. 20

Some one was opening the front door with a latchkey. It was Brently Mallard who entered, a little travel-stained, composedly carrying his grip-sack and umbrella. He had been far from the scene of the accident, and did not even know there had been one. He stood amazed at Josephine's piercing cry; at Richards' quick motion to screen him from the view of his wife. 21

But Richards was too late. 22

When the doctors came they said she had died of heart disease—of joy that kills. 23

Questions to Start You Thinking

1. How heartfelt is the "storm of grief" that sweeps over Mrs. Mallard when first she hears the report of her husband's death? Why then, only minutes later, does she whisper "Free, free, free!"? Do you find this account of a woman's emotions true to life or hard to believe? Discuss.

2. An opinion: "There's a simple reason why Mrs. Mallard dies. As we are told in the opening sentence, she has heart trouble and can't stand the slightest shock." What other reason for Mrs. Mallard's collapse does this explanation fail to take into account?

3. What does Kate Chopin tell us about love and marriage? How would you sum up her theme (the main idea or insight the story reveals)? Write it out in a sentence to read in class.

4. Would you call this a "trick ending" story, one containing an artificial surprise that the writer whips out at the end like a rabbit out of a hat? Or would you defend the ending as logical, natural, convincing, prepared for? (After you have thought about this, read on and see how Jane Betz explains the ending and why she praises it.)

Student Essay

A DEFENSE OF THE ENDING
OF "THE STORY OF AN HOUR"
Jane Betz

Some readers complain that the ending to Kate Chopin's   1
"The Story of an Hour" is a cheap trick, an unwanted surprise
that comes like a killer through an old woman's bedroom window in a low-grade horror movie. Probably such readers are
confused by Mrs. Mallard's behavior throughout the story, for
they must not see how the author prepares her readers for the
ending. Mrs. Mallard spends her last hour getting acquainted
with death: she meets it, visits with it, understands it, and
finally--logically--she knows it. In the course of an hour
Louise Mallard is gracefully initiated into the world outside
her window. Chopin gives us the most clearly inevitable
conclusion possible and still manages to surprise us with it.
The "trick" to the story does not lie in the ending but in
the author's talent for giving "veiled hints that reveal in
half-concealing." She reveals enough hints not only to justify the ending but to necessitate it, and she holds enough
back to keep the reader from knowing what's coming.

Louise Mallard does not react to her husband's death the   2
way another wife would. Instead of rejecting the news, ignoring it, or slowly taking it in with a muddled and dull acceptance, Mrs. Mallard recognizes its significance at once.
She regards the news with sadness and terror, knowing what
she sees.

After her "storm of grief" Mrs. Mallard looks at the   3
world as she never has before. She goes upstairs and surveys
the view from her western window through blank, fixed eyes.

Exhaustion presses her into her armchair and she throws her
head back and sobs like "a child who has cried itself to
sleep." She colors the view from her window with mixed feelings of youth and age: simultaneously she is seeing its
beauty for the first time and saying good-bye to its comfortable familiarity for the last. The easy chair, the western
window, the sleep of a child, and the suspension of intelligent thought call to her like the sirens.

Mrs. Mallard resists seeing paradise in that view: even   4
through her exhaustion and her fuzzy inability to think she
resists it instinctively. She tries to close her eyes to the
blue sky, her ears to the sparrows, and her mind to the
thought of how much she would like to melt into that picture.

She holds on to the life she knows with white knuckles,   5
but her two slender white hands are powerless. The most sa-
lient and appealing offer of the world outside her window
fights its way through to her and releases her grip; the sirens will have her understand that they're offering her freedom. As soon as she sees the possibility of freedom Mrs.
Mallard frees herself from the petty distinctions that were
weighing her down. Important and unimportant are sorted out.
It does not matter to her if her joy is "monstrous" or not:
it is joy. It makes no difference whether someone else's
will to control her life was kind or cruel: it was unjusti-
fied. There's no point in asking if she always loved her
husband or if she didn't sometimes; he's gone now. Mrs.
Mallard concentrates upon the word free, which only has meaning as an absolute.

But absolutes do not exist on earth, and Mrs. Mallard is   6
yearning for a freedom that she cannot attain. In our lives
the word freedom is always qualified, and the pressure to ca-
ter to the desires of others comes down hard on even the
"most free." The vision for the future that has grabbed Mrs.
Mallard with such a firm grip can lead her nowhere but to
death.

Unaware that she faces the choice between life and   7
death, Mrs. Mallard descends the stairs "like a goddess of
Victory," already more immortal than earthly.   Armed with her
vision of perfection and prepared to fuse that vision onto
her everyday world, she goes down to meet the others.   At the
bottom of the stairs Louise Mallard confronts the crowded
world where our dreams are constantly compromised by our
realities, and she does not care to stay.

Questions to Start You Thinking

1. How convincing do you find Jane Betz's point about Mrs. Mallard's moving closer to the absolute, or eternity, as the story proceeds? To what evidence in the story does Betz point?
2. Whether or not you agree with Betz's analysis and evaluation, what did this student critic help you notice in the story or realize about it?

CHAPTER 7

Taking a Stand

In college, both in class and outside of class, you'll hear controversial issues discussed: zero population growth, affirmative action, AIDS testing, gun control. In some fields of study, experts don't always agree, and issues go on and on being controversies for years. Ethical questions arise in the study of business, medical care, genetic engineering. That is why, in your college writing, you will soon find yourself taking up pen (or typewriter or word processor) in a cause. To take your stand on an issue will help you understand the controversy and clarify what you believe.

Writing of this kind has a twofold purpose: to state an opinion and to win the reader's respect for it. The reader's own mind might alter from reading what you say; then again, it might not. But at least, if you fulfill your purpose, your reader will see good reasons for your thinking the way you do.

In taking a stand, you do three things:

You state what you believe.

You enlist your reader's trust. You do this by demonstrating that you know what you're talking about.

You consider what your reader probably thinks and feels. As writers, in the words of writing specialist Maxine Hairston, "we have to care more about communicating with [readers] than about showing them the error of their ways."

LEARNING FROM OTHER WRITERS

Like Russell Baker, whose "The Art of Eating Spaghetti" is reprinted in Chapter 1, Suzanne Britt is a southern-born writer of lively informal essays that set forth serious views. In this example, she voices an opinion that every college writer might consider. Notice where Britt states her claim: not only at the conclusion of her essay, but in her opening paragraph.

THE FIRST PERSON
Suzanne Britt

1   I have it on the good authority of a college freshman that English teachers are still forbidding students the use of the first-person point of view. These teachers do so on the moral, not literary or grammatical, grounds that the middle letter in sin is "I." Well, I object. The admonition against "I" is absurd and will, I hope, come to an end in the waning decades of the twentieth century.

2   English teachers are foolish to deprive students of the only point of view they have available to them: their own. In fact, people might have trouble writing well because, from an early age, they have received these binding, unexamined maxims, the rules that stifle or kill. Why should the "I" be so cruelly chastised by the puritanical, selfless set? After all, each person is the central figure in the drama of his own life, the point at which all that he is or becomes begins.

3   Our guilt about "I" arises from Christian pronouncements about the sin of pride, Freudian theories about the tyranny of the ego, and best-selling books about the dangers of narcissism, such as the one by Christopher Lasch.° We are all afraid that a clear, strong "I" might be neurotic or downright wicked.

4   Ironically, at the same time Lasch was lambasting us for our self-absorption, we were beginning to assert the "I." Ours is the century in which we have tried to find ourselves, to recover our identities, to become well-defined, individualistic nonconformists. We have been pleased to be different, to be ourselves, to unmask. Proponents of transactional analysis encouraged us to send I-messages, not You-messages. Psychologists picked up the TA refrain, pushing diffuse, fragmented people to face themselves; to depend on the "I" they had so long denied; to refer to, use, and trust the "I."

---

one by Christopher Lasch: The Culture of Narcissism (New York: Norton, 1979).

So we have been torn. While the moralists were telling us the "I" was the center of pride, the psychologists were telling us that a strong, healthy identity, a clear-cut "I," could make us feel and function better than a whole lifetime of tiresome selflessness.

I-messages were hardest for women. Women were raised to give in to you. Some women, even in their early thirties, didn't have an "I." I was one. My messages were all for you. Where do you want to go, dear? What do you want to do? What career plans do you have? What do you believe? How do you feel? What do you want for supper? When do you want to eat it? These questions determined my personality, behavior, ethics. I began to suspect that too many puritans had gotten hold of me, whereas the TA people had grabbed all the fellows. Women who had a strong "I" were arrogant and stuck up. Men who had a strong "I" were forthright, bold, brave, confident, and determined.

When my English teacher forbade me to set foot in "I" country, I was too well indoctrinated to pose some obvious questions and challenges. The fact is, the strong, first-person "I" voice has been prevalent in every age, genre, and circumstance of great literature and history: the "I" in St. Paul's letters, in *Pilgrim's Progress*, in *Moby-Dick*, in Walt Whitman's *Song of Myself*, in Augustine's *Confessions*, in Sherwood Anderson's short stories, in Sylvia Plath's poems, in Lamb's essays, in Thoreau's *Walden*. The harder task is to find a piece of great literature that doesn't use the first-person point of view.

I think too, with some glee, of all the robust, oft-quoted I-messages sent by great men and women in all ages: Julius Caesar's "I came, I saw, I conquered"; Descartes's "I think, therefore I am"; Tennyson's "I am the heir of all ages"; MacArthur's "I shall return"; Queen Victoria's "We are not amused"; Edna Millay's "I am not resigned."

The strong "I" voice is heard less and less in this age of the committee decision, the corporate response, the governmental process. We hide behind the bland, safe, irresponsible wordiness of the passive voice. It is felt that bombs should be dropped, heads should be rolled, funds should be withdrawn, positions should be terminated. The subject, the doer, the "I" is gone. Truman may have been the last president to use the "I" responsibly. The only I-messages I can recall from recent presidents were either denials of responsibility or lies: Nixon's "I am not a crook"; Carter's "I will never lie to you."

I like "I" and have decided to use it. "I" is the place where every story begins, every energy flows, every character emerges, every self achieves definition. "I" is autonomous. Maybe the people of this century are waiting for someone brave enough to speak, write, and act in the first person and to take responsibility for those words and actions. If "I" is the center of sin, as some English teachers claim, then some of our greatest spiritual leaders were sinful. Example: I am the way, the truth, and the life.

Questions to Start You Thinking

1. What impression of Suzanne Britt do you get from reading her essay? Would you call her an objective, detached, unemotional writer, or what? In your answer, draw evidence from her choice of words.

2. How does Britt show her awareness of people with different views, those reluctant to use the first person?

3. Have any of your teachers encouraged or discouraged you to write in the first person? What is your opinion of first-person writing now that you have read Britt's essay?

4. Where in her essay does Britt go beyond the realm of writing for her examples? Why do you suppose she does?

5. What counterarguments to Britt's claim can you raise? Can you think of any writing situations in which this writer's insistence on the first-person *I* might be bad advice?

Susan Fendel, inspired by an anatomy and physiology lecture, wrote the following student essay on AIDS for her English composition class. As she pondered the disease and its consequences, she felt that she wanted to change the minds of her audience, her fellow students. She wished to "get under everyone's skin," to take a stand against the emotional isolation AIDS victims so often suffer, against injustices they receive at the hands of a frightened public.

Student Essay

AIDS: THE RETURN OF THE SCARLET LETTER
Susan Fendel

The word AIDS has become a part of our present lingo, 1
abbreviating acquired immune deficiency syndrome into a more
palatable term for the mysterious virus. In the media and in
casual conversation, the topic of AIDS quickly approaches
epidemic proportions, as does the disease itself. Currently,
AIDS ranks as the new disease of our times. The many serious
and frustrating problems of stopping this virus, the fear
that accompanies the explosion of AIDS in our country, and
the consequent isolation caused by the stigmas placed on
those afflicted with the disease are just a few of the issues
that arise with this controversial topic.

Acquired immune deficiency syndrome is a name that con-   2
veniently describes the virus--more correctly called human T-
lymphotropic type III--which forces the body's immunity to
become deficient, rendering the human body useless in protection against infection.

Kaposi's sarcoma, for example, which is a form of skin   3
cancer unknown to North America before the onset of AIDS, develops into a fatal disease in itself in the AIDS-affected
immune system. The cancer spreads from the endothelium cells
of blood vessels into the dermis (skin) and throughout the
body, making what should be a treatable form of cancer into a
deadly disease.

Researchers have been frustrated for years by the puzzle   4
of how to kill a virus without killing the human cell it attaches itself to--called the host cell. AIDS introduces a
new kink to this enigma because it is a virus that manifests
itself in the immune system (more specifically, the T cell),
disabling the body's ability to produce defenses (called an-
tibodies) against invading infection and disease. Therefore,
as in the previous example, other diseases like cancer act as
predators, attacking organs already weakened. This results
in a multidiseased body, complicated by the ever-present AIDS
virus within the cells, which reduces the chances of recovery
from the secondary diseases.

As scientists struggle to solve this puzzle, the public   5
reaction to this virus splashes upon our sexually revolution-
ized society like a bucket of cold water. "Sexual partners
need to be carefully chosen" is the new national message.
The conservatives nod their heads wisely, considering this
disease to be a punishment wrought by God--like the plague--
to admonish the promiscuous of our culture. This belief was
even more prevalent when just a few years ago AIDS afflicted
the homosexual and drug addict groups almost exclusively.
The general population approached the subject of AIDS with a
shrug and a negligent comment about getting and deserving.

But AIDS finally struck a common nerve. It has become a   6

frightening disease because of its expansion into the "innocent" groups category. Presently, children, hemophiliacs,
and heterosexuals are falling victim. The percentage of the
heterosexual group infected with the disease is increasing
rapidly. Out of 30,000 people affected, 3.8 percent of those
fall into the heterosexual group and close to 7 percent in
the other "low-risk" groups combined. This figure is expected to double by 1990.

Because of this disease's new lack of discrimination, 7
what was once considered a health problem for a few minorities has become a hazard for almost everyone. The security
once felt about not contracting AIDS has ended and has been
replaced with increasing anxiety. Also disconcerting is that
scientists have no idea of how to overcome this disease,
which is, in fact, reported to be 100 percent fatal.

Ultimately, the emotional isolation in which AIDS vic- 8
tims are instantly placed is perhaps the most tragic element
of the AIDS phenomenon. This disease tortures not only the
body but also the ego, the psyche, and the lifestyle of those
it afflicts. The distancing by others, which creates this
isolation, is a cruel and unacceptable reaction. Our culture
has been educated in the ways this disease is transmitted.
It is general knowledge that AIDS cannot be contracted
through casual contact; yet the ostracism continues.

In 1986, a child in Denver was not allowed to attend his 9
public school because he had contracted AIDS through a
"tainted" blood transfusion. The courts overruled the
school's decision, saying that he had a right to attend because he offered no danger to the other students. Parents
responded by pulling their own children from the school,
still terrified by the unknown factors of the disease. The
psychological damage to this young child, already dealing
with a painful disease, seems unnecessarily cruel.

Stigmas often spring from fear within individuals. To 10
isolate that which threatens us, to turn away regardless of
the facts or truths we have learned, remains, though perhaps

not admirable, a part of human nature. Within us still lies the instinctive resistance to jeopardizing our own safety from the deadly disease as we continue to set apart those afflicted with AIDS from those who are not. This unwillingness to (literally) extend a hand will hopefully dissipate along with the extinction of the lingering suspicion of contagion.

Society has always shunned what it fears, ostracizing people at a time when they most need support. But in the case of AIDS, families often react so negatively to the diagnosis that the person suffering is cast out, losing contact with loved ones. With other diseases (even cancer has carried less of a stigma in the last few years), the family support system is an important part in the patient's reconciliation with the disease and pending death. Sadly, the AIDS victim stands alone, labeled because of some presumed indiscretion.   11

The prejudice toward the people in high-risk categories --the homosexuals and addicts--continues to make the public unyielding in its harsh discrimination against anyone afflicted with AIDS.   12

But attention is finally focusing on the size of the AIDS problem. Support groups have been organized in almost all of the major cities, and research efforts to isolate the AIDS virus have been given important funding. Slowly, the awareness of the facts of this disease is growing. Perhaps the stigma of having AIDS will eventually lose its strength.   13

Public opinion is starting to come to terms with the disease and treat it as a deadly health problem rather than with embarrassment and disregard. It will take time before AIDS is not thought of as another venereal disease that points a finger at the promiscuous of our nation.   14

AIDS is frightening. Yet all of the current information emphasizes that the risk of contracting AIDS does not increase by being kind. So there is no need to place upon these people that scarlet letter A, ostracizing people at a time when they need comfort and acceptance. We have come too   15 far as a culture to turn away from scientific data and to rely solely on our moral judgments to make responsible decisions.

In our civilized society, the key to understanding is accepting diversity and adversity; being able to distinguish the difference between real and exaggerated threats; and realizing that judgment does not cleanse us from that which we judge but instead burdens us with attitudes and fear that are contagious.   16

Questions to Start You Thinking

1. What do Fendel's first four paragraphs contribute to her essay? Would the paper be as convincing if she had omitted them?

2. At what places in her essay does Fendel's stand emerge most clearly?

3. Make a list of public attitudes about which you might take a stand. How many examples and illustrations can you assemble in support of your stand? How many points can you think of that oppose your beliefs? Develop your notes into an essay.

LEARNING BY WRITING

The Assignment: Taking a Stand

Find a controversy that arouses your interest. It might be an issue currently in the news or it might be a long-lasting one such as "In our public schools, does the fundamentalist explanation for the origin of species deserve equal time with Darwin's?" or "Are fraternities on campus a good thing or a baleful one?" Your purpose in this paper isn't to try to *solve* a large social or moral problem, but just to make clear where you stand and why. First state your view and then your reasons for holding it. Your audience, you can assume, are people who may be familiar with the controversy but who have not yet taken sides.

Recently we have read good papers that take a stand, written by students at several colleges. Here are brief summaries of a few of them.

> A woman who earns her own way through college countered the received opinion that working full- or part-time during the school year provides a college student with valuable knowledge. Citing her own painful experience in having to drop out of college twice, she maintained that a student who can devote full time to her studies is far better off.

A woman attacked her history textbook's account of the burning of Joan of Arc on the grounds that the author had characterized Joan as "an ignorant farm girl subject to religious hysteria."

A married couple, with the encouragement of their sociology instructor, collaborated on a paper in favor of early marriage.

A woman wrote a letter to her congressional representative calling a bill that would remove a parcel of recreational land from the administration of the Bureau of Land Management "a misguided proposal" that would encourage new development by builders heedless of the environment.

A man, citing history and Christian doctrine, gave his reasons for preferring to keep prayer out of public school classrooms.

A man, decrying the "emotional publicity" that follows shooting incidents, took a stand against gun control. He challenged arguments and statistics put forth by advocates of stricter gun control laws and defended the right of citizens to carry weapons.

A woman in an education course disputed the claim of E. D. Hirsch, Jr., in his book *Cultural Literacy,* that we must give schoolchildren a grounding in facts common to our culture, including history, literature, mythology, science, geography, and sports. As a Hispanic, she maintained that to absorb the culture of the majority isn't necessarily to answer children's greatest need. Children, she affirmed, should first study their own cultural backgrounds and should master basic skills for gathering information.

Generating Ideas

Start with any controversial topic that interests you. To understand it better, you may need to find out more about it. Turn to some of your trusty resources. Observe, if you can. Converse. What do others think? Do some reading in a library. In gathering material, you will discover more exactly where you stand.

As she strove to discover ideas for her paper, Susan Fendel kept a free-flowing notebook in which she recorded thoughts as they came to her. Her notes reveal interesting facets of her writing processes. Many of the ideas she wrote down never actually made it into her final draft. Still, when she began writing, she had more than enough material to choose from. Part of her notebook is reproduced on the next page.

State your claim. It will help you focus your view if you state it in a sentence: a thesis or statement of your claim. *Make your claim narrow enough.* For a paper due a week from now, "The city's waterfront has become a stodgy, run-down disgrace" can probably be supported by your own observations. But the claim "The welfare program in this country has become a disgrace" would take much digging, perhaps the work of years. (For more advice on this important point, see "Stating a Thesis," p. 491.)

Your claim stated, you'll need evidence to support it. This matter is crucial, so let's take time right now to examine it.

Supply evidence. What is evidence? Anything that demonstrates the truth

11/14/87
AIDS
1) Frightening = consequence of sexual revolution
2) Frustrating = fatal, incurable, affecting "innocent groups"
3) Isolating = Instant ostracization, both physical and emotional distancing. Hard to overcome stigma.

Intro should have these three topics introduced

11/15/89
Heard on News:

Heterosexual couple found out that they had AIDS.
Made a suicide pact. He dies. She was discovered before she died, and recovered.

Man's autopsy revealed no sign of AIDS. The woman did not have AIDS either. She was arrested for attempted suicide (suicide is illegal) and for facilitating her lover's suicide.

Modern Romeo and Juliet ←

Usable in paper? Intro?

11/17/89
Rough draft completed, needs more detail, more expansion. Should I write it again or save it for first revision?

Language works well, must review for "tightening" aspects.

Hawthorne—The Scarlet Letter—is this too confusing a concept to begin and end paper with?

Some of Susan Fendel's preliminary notes

of your claim: facts and figures, expert opinions, illustrations and examples, reported experience. At this point, we won't discuss those tremendous sources of evidence you can obtain by *deeply* exploring a library or by doing field research: actual legwork and firsthand reporting to find evidence that no one has published before. We discuss such sources in detail in Part Three, "Investigating." For now, let's see how you select what will be trustworthy in supporting your claim. Evidence comes in several varieties:

1. *Facts.* Facts are statements that can be verified by objective means, such as reading a reliable account or going and looking. Of course, we take

many of our facts from the testimony of others. We believe that the Great Wall of China exists, though we have never beheld it with our own eyes.

A fact is usually stated in an impersonal way: "Algonquian Indians still live in Old Orchard Beach"; "If you pump all the air out of a five-gallon varnish can, it will collapse." Sometimes a small fact casts a piercing light. Claiming that strip-mining in his hometown had injured the environment, one student recalled taking a walk through local hills before a mining operation had moved in and being almost deafened by a din of birdcalls. The paper ended with a quiet statement of fact: "Yesterday, on that same walk, I heard no birds at all."

2. *Statistics.* Another valuable kind of evidence, statistics are facts expressed in numbers, gathered in answer to a question. What are the odds that you will be a murder victim? According to statistics compiled by the FBI in 1984, 1 in 100 if you are an American man, 1 in 323 if you are an American woman. (A student cited that statistic in an essay arguing that strict handgun control laws are desirable.)

Most writers, without trying to be dishonest, interpret statistics to help their causes. The statement "Fifty percent of the populace have incomes above the poverty level" might be used to back the claim that the government of an African nation is doing a fine job. Putting the statement another way, "Fifty percent of the populace have incomes below the poverty level" might use the same statistic to show that the government's efforts to aid the disadvantaged are inadequate. A writer, of course, is free to interpret a statistic; and it is only human to present a case in a favorable light. But statistics should not be used to mislead. On the wrapper of a peanut bar, we read that one one-ounce serving contains only 150 calories and 70 milligrams of sodium. The claim is true, but the bar weighs 1.6 ounces. Eat the whole thing, as you are more likely to do than serving yourself exactly 62½ percent of it, and you'll ingest 240 calories and 112 milligrams of sodium—a heftier amount than the innocent statistic on the wrapper leads you to believe.

Such abuses make some readers automatically distrust statistics. Use figures fairly, and make sure they are accurate. If you doubt a statistic or a fact, why not check it out? Compare it with facts and statistics reported by several other sources. A report that differs from every other report may well be true, but distrust it unless it is backed by further evidence.

3. *The testimony of experts.* By *experts,* we mean people with knowledge of a particular field gained from study and experience. The test of an expert is whether his or her expertise stands up to the scrutiny of others knowledgeable in that field. An essay by basketball player Akeem Olajuwon explaining how to play offense or by economist John Kenneth Galbraith setting forth the causes of inflation carries authority. But does your expert have any bias that would affect his or her reliability? Statistics on cases of lung cancer attributed to smoking might be better taken from government sources than from a representative of the tobacco industry.

4. *Memory and observation.* Obviously, firsthand experience and observation are persuasive. They add life to any paper. Perhaps in supporting the claim "It's foolish to exercise too strenuously" you might recall your own experience: "As a lifeguard for two summers, I watched hundreds of people exhaust themselves in jumping the waves and once had to rescue the victim of a heart attack." As readers, most of us tend to trust the writer who declares, "I was there. This is what I saw."

If you'd like any questions to stimulate your search for evidence, try these.

DISCOVERY CHECKLIST: TAPPING RESOURCES

- What do you already know about this topic? What convinces *you* of the truth of your claim?
- What testimony can you provide from your own firsthand experience?
- What have you observed, or what might you observe, that would probably support your stand?
- What have you read about this topic? What else might you read? For a start, consult the catalog of your library and the *Readers' Guide to Periodical Literature* (discussed on pp. 398 and 407–408).
- What expert might you talk with?
- What illustrations and examples to back up your claim can you imagine? (Don't claim that these are facts, of course!)
- Try to imagine yourself as your reader—what further evidence might persuade you?

For this assignment, you can expect to write a relatively short paper and complete it within a week. You assemble a mass of evidence in written form. You take notes, in a notebook or on large, 4-by-6-inch or 5-by-7-inch index cards. (Cards have the advantage of being shufflable, easily arranged in an order for writing a draft.) Perhaps you'll have clippings or photocopies. Spread all this stuff out on a table and choose the evidence that best supports your claim. Let's see how you decide.

Testing evidence   When is evidence useful and trustworthy? When—

It is accurate. A writer assumes all responsibility for verifying facts and figures. Statistics from ten-year-old encyclopedias, such as population figures, are probably out of date. Take facts from latest sources.

It is reliable. To decide whether you can trust it, you'll need to evaluate its source, as we have detailed. Whenever possible, do some reading. Compare information given in one source with information given in another.

It is to the point. It backs the exact claim you're making in your paper. This point may seem too obvious to deserve mention, but you'd be surprised how many writers get hung up on an interesting fact or opinion that has nothing to do with what they're trying to demonstrate. Sometimes a writer will leap from evidence to conclusion without reason, and the result is a *non sequitur* (Latin for "it does not follow"): "Benito Mussolini made the trains run on time. He was one of the world's leading statesmen." The evidence about trains doesn't support a judgment on Mussolini's statesmanship. (For more about errors in reasoning, see pp. 525–527.) If your evidence contradicts or belies your claim, your claim shouldn't be made.

It is representative. Any examples you select should be typical of all the things included in your claim. If you claim that, in general, students on your campus are well informed about their legal rights, don't talk just to prelaw majors, talk to an English major, an engineering major, a biology major, and others. Probably most writers, in the heat of persuading, can't help unconsciously stacking the evidence in their own favor. But the best writers don't deliberately suppress evidence to the contrary. The writer for an airline magazine who tried to sell package tours to India by declaring "India is an attractive land of sumptuous wealth and splendor" might give for evidence the Taj Mahal and a luxury hotel while ignoring the slums of Bombay and Calcutta. The result might be effective advertising but hardly a full and faithful view.

It is sufficient and strong enough to back the claim. How much evidence you use depends on the size of your claim. Evidently, it will take less evidence to claim that a downtown park needs better maintenance than to claim that the Department of the Interior needs reorganizing. How much evidence you need may depend, too, on how much your reader already knows. Who will be reading your paper? A group of readers, all from Washington, D.C., and vicinity, will not need much evidence to be persuaded that the city's modern Metro transit system is admirable in its efficiency, but more evidence may be needed to convince readers who don't know Washington.

As you try to comprehend another person's beliefs and feelings, you can try to imagine yourself in that person's place. If you do, you will probably think of more ideas—points to make, objections to answer—than if you think only of presenting your own view.

Beware of oversimplifying. Some writers fall into the error of *oversimplification,* supplying a too-easy explanation for a phenomenon that may be vast and complicated: "Of course our economy is in trouble. People aren't buying American-made cars." Both statements may be true, but the second seems insufficient to account for the first: obviously there is much more to the economy than cars alone. More information is called for. Whenever in doubt that you've given enough evidence to convince your readers, you are probably well advised to come up with more.

Not that mere quantity is enough. One piece of vivid and significant evidence—such as the firsthand testimony of an expert, given in that person's memorable words—may be more persuasive than a foot-high stack of statistics. In evaluating your evidence, you can ask yourself a few questions.

DISCOVERY CHECKLIST: TESTING EVIDENCE

- Does your evidence lead to the stand you want to take? (If it all leads you to a different opinion, then you'll want to revise your claim.)

- If you are writing about some current situation, is your evidence—especially any statistical information—up to date?

- Are facts and figures accurate? If you doubt a piece of information, try to check it against published sources. See reports by others and facts given in reference works.

- If an important point rests on your quoting an opinion or citing information you receive from an expert, do you know that the person is respected in his or her field?

- Is your evidence complete? Does it at least reflect the full range of your topic? If it leads to a general claim ("Nursing homes in this city are fire-traps"), does the general statement rest on a large and convincing number of examples?

- Do you have enough evidence to persuade a reader? (Talk with fellow students, show them your evidence.)

- If you were to read an argument based on this evidence, would you be convinced? Imagine your paper all written and yourself in a reader's place.

Shaping a Draft

Once you have looked over your written evidence and sifted out the useful part, you will probably find it falling into shape. If you have taken notes on cards, you can group them into the order you'll follow in writing your draft.

Build on your claim. Having written your statement of your claim, keep writing. Summarize your reasons for holding this view. List the supporting evidence. You will find this writing growing into an argument. The result may even be a condensed version of the essay you plan to write.

If you prefer, you might make an informal outline (for methods, see p. 499). Your claim—your statement of your view—will most likely come early in the paper. Then you might give your evidence and any further reasons for holding your view. At the end of your paper, you will probably want to restate your claim firmly.

As you start to write your draft, make clear any questionable terms used in your claim. If your claim reads, "Humanists are dangerous," you had better give a short definition of *humanists* early on. Your terms need to be clear to you and to your reader, for they help determine the course of your argument. "At the very start," says Kenneth Burke, "one's terms leap to conclusions."

Spell out your beliefs. Sometimes in taking a stand you find yourself spelling out your personal beliefs, values, and assumptions. This is a fine idea.

WRITING WITH A COMPUTER: TAKING A STAND

If in taking your stand you'll be disputing the view of some other writer, start by creating a document. Type into it those passages from the book, magazine article, newspaper column, or editorial that has provoked you to dissent. Your time will be well spent: transcribing the other writer's very words will get you looking at them closely and will probably help you answer them. Besides, you'll have exact quotations at your fingertips. Then on the same disk create a second document to use in writing your draft.

When you want to cite the other writer's very words, just tell your computer to INSERT or MOVE or COPY (or whatever command your program uses to move text from one document and drop it into the one you're working on). Your computer thus enables you to add an exact quotation instantly in an appropriate place.

State them and you lay them out in the open for your reader to consider; the reader who accepts them is already on your side. If you declare, "I am against eating red meat because it contains fats and chemicals known to be harmful," you assert a claim and give evidence for it. The reader who responds, "That's right—I'm a vegetarian myself," is clearly in your camp. But even the reader who responds at first, "Oh, I don't know—a hamburger never killed anyone!" may warm to your view if you trouble to consider his or her assumptions. These might include the beliefs that a steak or a burger is delicious; that vegetables aren't; that red meat supplies needed protein; and that the chemicals haven't been proved dangerous. You could show that you are aware of these assumptions, and you might consider them seriously. You might even agree with some of them, perhaps accepting the first one—that meat tastes good. Then you might set forth, in a reasonable way, your own view. By spelling out your assumptions and by imagining those of a dissenting reader, you will win—at the very least—a respectful hearing.

Keep an eye on your reader. When you sense that your reader is likely to disagree, frankly acknowledge this fact. See how student Marty Reich does so in a paper in favor of limiting population growth in the city of Tucson, Arizona: "The reader may feel that I have grossly exaggerated the dangers of overpopulation, that the economy and biostructure of this desert city can easily support a few thousand more citizens. But let us consider the quantity of fresh water that each man, woman, and child consumes daily. . . ."

Credit your sources. As you write, make your sources of evidence clear. If an expert whom you quote has outstanding credentials, you may easily be able to put in a brief citation of those credentials: "Lewis Thomas, chancellor of the Memorial Sloan-Kettering Cancer Center," "Michael Scammell, author of the award-winning biography *Solzhenitsyn.*" If you have talked to your experts and are convinced of their authority, state why you believe your experts know their onions. "From conversation with Mr. Dworshak, who showed me six model wind tunnels he has built, I can testify to his extensive knowledge of aeronautics." In the opening sentence of "The First Person," Suzanne Britt refers to a convincing authority: a college freshman.

In supplying evidence, cite exact numbers whenever you can. To report that a condition holds true "in thirty-four cases out of fifty" is more convincing than to say "in many cases." At least it shows that you haven't taken a mere woolly-eyed gawp at a scene but have taken the trouble to count.

Rewriting

Does taking a stand seem harder than some earlier assignments? Most students find that it is. If you feel the need for special help with this assignment, enlist a couple of other students to read your draft critically and tell you whether they accept your arguments. They can use the questions in the peer editing checklist.

PEER EDITING CHECKLIST: TAKING A STAND

- Describe what you understand the writer's claim to be.
- How persuasive is the writer's evidence? Do you have any questions about that evidence?
- Can you suggest some good evidence the writer has overlooked?
- Describe the reader that the writer has written to. Is there anything more that the writer needs to know about his or her audience to improve the essay?
- Do you have any problems following or accepting the reasons for the writer's claim? Would you make any changes in any of the reasoning?
- Circle on the manuscript any spelling, punctuation, grammar, or word choice that impeded you in reading and understanding the writer's views.

A temptation, when you're writing a paper taking a stand, is to fall in love with the evidence you have gone to such trouble to collect. Some of it won't help your case; some may just seem boring and likely to persuade nobody. If so, pitch it. Sometimes you can have too much evidence, and if you throw some out, a stronger argument will remain. Sometimes you can become so attached to old evidence that, when new evidence or new thoughts come along, you won't want to discard what you have on hand. But in taking a stand, as in any other writing, second thoughts often surpass the thoughts that come at first. Be willing to revise not only your words but your view.

When you're taking a last look over your paper, proofread with care. Wherever you have given facts and figures as evidence, check for errors in names and numbers. This advice may seem trivial, but there's a considerable difference between "10,000 people" and "100,000 people." To refer to Sigmund Frued or Alvin Einstein won't persuade a reader that you know what you're talking about.

As you rewrite, here are some points to consider.

REVISION CHECKLIST: TAKING A STAND

- Does your view convince you? Or do you think you need still more evidence?
- In your paper, have you tried to keep in mind your readers and what would appeal to them?
- Might the points in your argument seem stronger if arranged in a different sequence?
- Have you unfairly omitted any evidence that would hurt your case? If so, you might make your paper more persuasive if you acknowledge it.
- In rereading your paper, do you have any excellent, fresh thoughts? If so, make room for them.

Other Assignments

1. Write a letter to the editor of your local newspaper or of a national news magazine (*Time, Newsweek, U.S. News & World Report*) in which you disagree with the publication's editorial stand on a current question or with the recent words or actions of some public figure. Be sure to make clear your reasons for holding a different view.

2. Write a paragraph or two in which you agree or disagree with one of the following suggestions—or some other you have lately read that interests you. You need not propose an alternative action; just give your opinion of the suggestion.

> Creationism and evolution should be given equal importance in high school science courses.
> Public television should be allowed to die a natural death.
> To protect certain endangered species of ocean fish, fish rationing should be imposed on consumers.
> The United States should invade Cuba.

3. Write a short paper in which you express your view on one of the following topics or another that comes to mind. Make clear your reasons for believing as you do.

> Bilingual education
> Smokers' rights
> The Miss America contest
> Chemical castration for rapists
> The fitness movement
> The minimum wage
> Mandatory drug testing for athletes

4. Write a short comment in which you agree or disagree with the following quotation from Gilbert and Sullivan's musical comedy *Ruddigore.* Use examples and evidence to support your view.

> If you wish in this world to advance
> Your merits you're bound to enhance;
>   You must stir it and stump it,
>   And blow your own trumpet,
> Or, trust me, you haven't a chance.

5. Writing in *Weekly World News,* columnist Ed Anger (with tongue in cheek?) headlines his claim "Junk Food Made Our Country Great." After all, he reasons, American heroes have grown up on hamburgers, french fries, potato chips, beer, Twinkies, Snickers, and Coke. "You never saw The Duke [John Wayne] strolling around munching a pita bread sandwich stuffed with alfalfa sprouts."

> Ever see one of those parsley puffs punching a herd of cattle, operating an endloader, putting up a roof, or doing some other kind of he-man's work? Every one of them is skinny, beady-eyed, and yellow-skinned. You call that healthy? I call it sick. If all Americans looked as washed-out and wimpy as those broccoli Bruces, the Ruskies would be dropping down on us and taking over right now.

And he concludes:

> If American foods are so bad, how come all those foreign countries are building McDonald's and Burger Kings in their countries? Because they want their people to get tough and smart too—by eating like Americans.

Write a paragraph or two in reply to Ed Anger, discovering evidence for your own view, whatever it may be. If you care to dissent with Anger and analyze his remarks, the catalog of logical fallacies on page 525 may be of help to you.

FOR GROUP LEARNING

Here is a situation in which your writing group is likely to prove particularly valuable. Allow a day or two for members of the group to decide, at least tentatively, the positions they wish to take in their individual papers. Then hold a meeting at which each member takes a few minutes to set forth his or her position and to support it. Other members of the group may be invited to argue or to suggest any useful supporting evidence that may occur to them. One tremendous advantage of this activity is that, before you write, you'll probably hear some of the objections your readers are likely to raise. You'll be kept busy during this discussion; ask your group's recording secretary to list all the objections you get so that you'll remember them when writing your paper. If you can't answer any of the counterarguments, ask other members of the group to help you generate a reply. Of course, this group discussion might change your mind, make you aware that your ideas are half-baked, and cause you to alter your whole stand. If this happens, give thanks: it will be easier to revise your ideas now than to revise your paper later.

APPLYING WHAT YOU LEARN:
SOME USES OF TAKING A STAND

As you may have found out by now, not only paper assignments but also college examination questions sometimes ask you to take a stand on a controversy:

> Criticize the statement "There's too much science and not enough caring in the modern practice of medicine."

> Respond to the view that "there's no need to be concerned about carbon dioxide heating up the earth's atmosphere because a warmer climate, by increasing farm production, would be preferable to the one we have now."

Your answers to such questions indicate clearly to your instructor how firm a grasp you have on the material.

In your daily life, too, you'll sometimes feel the need to advance a view in writing. You never know when you'll be called on to represent your fellow tenants by writing a letter of protest to a landlord who wants to raise your rent or when you'll feel moved to write to a store manager complaining about the treatment you received. As an active citizen, you'll wish from time to time to write a letter to the editor of your local newspaper or of a national news magazine. You may want to write to those who represent you in Congress and in the presidency, making clear your view of some current issue you feel strongly about.

When you enter the working world, you'll be glad you can state your views clearly in writing. Newspaper editors are called on every day to take a stand on the editorial page. In fact, there is hardly a professional position you can hold in which you won't be invited from time to time to state and support your views about some important matter, often for the benefit of others in your profession. Here is a sample of such writing, in which Mary Anne Raywid, in the *Journal of Teacher Education* (Sept.–Oct. 1978) defends professors of education against the constant charge that they use jargon when ordinary English would do:

> This is not to deny that educators speak a language of their own. Indeed they do; and it is very much a part of their specialized knowledge. These words become a way first to select out certain qualities, events, and phenomena for attention; and they expedite communication via shorthand references to particular combinations of these. To cite a familiar example, when an educationist talks about a *meaningful learning experience,* s/he is not just spouting jargon, but distinguishing out of all the events and phenomena of a given time and place, a particular set. Moreover, a substantial list of things is being asserted about what is going on—e.g., the words *learning experience* suggest that it is, or it is meant to be, an episode from which learning results. The term *meaningful* is not superfluous but does a specific job: it adds that it is likely to be or was (depending on temporal perspective) a successful exercise in learning—which not all learning experiences proffered by teachers can claim. To qualify as *meaningful* in advance—in other words, well calculated to succeed—a number of conditions must be met, ordi-

narily including learner comprehension, interest, motivation, capacity, and likely retention.

Scientists who do original research face the task of persuading the scientific community that their findings are valid. Routinely, they write and publish accounts of their work in scientific journals for evaluation by their peers. In such articles they report new facts as well as state opinions. Some scientists and medical people, to be sure, write not only for their professional peers but for us general readers. Here, for instance, is Gerald Weissmann, in an essay called "Foucault and the Bag Lady," airing his views on the recent trend to deinstitutionalize the mentally ill:

> It has always seemed to me to constitute a fantastic notion that the social landscape of our large cities bears any direct relationship to that kind of stable, nurturing community which would support the fragile psyche of the mentally ill. Cast into an environment limited by the welfare hotel or park bench, lacking adequate outpatient services, prey to climatic extremes and urban criminals, the deinstitutionalized patients wind up as conscripts in an army of the homeless. Indeed, only this winter was the city of New York forced to open temporary shelters in church basements, armories, and lodging houses for thousands of half-frozen street dwellers. A psychiatrist of my acquaintance has summarized the experience of a generation in treating the mentally deranged: "In the nineteen-fifties, the mad people were warehoused in heated public hospitals with occasional access to trained professionals. In the sixties and seventies, they were released into the community and permitted to wander the streets without access to psychiatric care. In the eighties, we have made progress, however. When the mentally ill become too cold to wander the streets, we can warehouse them in heated church basements without supervision."

Weissmann's statement is a good illustration of a specialist writing for the rest of us—and forcefully taking a stand.

A Philosopher Takes a Stand

Nobel Prize-winner Bertrand Russell was an eminent British mathematician and philosopher. The following essay, written in 1936 and published in a book called *The Mysteries of Life and Death,* sets forth one of the controversial opinions for which Russell was famous. In it, he replies to an article by the Bishop of Birmingham, Dr. Barnes, that appeared in the same book.

DO WE SURVIVE DEATH?
Bertrand Russell

Before we can profitably discuss whether we shall continue to exist 1 after death, it is well to be clear as to the sense in which a man is the same person as he was yesterday. Philosophers used to think that there were definite substances, the soul and the body, that each lasted on from day to day, that a soul, once created, continued to exist throughout all

future time, whereas a body ceased temporarily from death till the resur-
rection of the body.

The part of this doctrine which concerns the present life is pretty cer-   2
tainly false. The matter of the body is continually changing by processes
of nutriment and wastage. Even if it were not, atoms in physics are no
longer supposed to have continuous existence; there is no sense in saying:
this is the same atom as the one that existed a few minutes ago. The
continuity of a human body is a matter of appearance and behavior, not of
substance.

The same thing applies to the mind. We think and feel and act, but   3
there is not, in addition to thoughts and feelings and actions, a bare entity,
the mind or the soul, which does or suffers these occurrences. The mental
continuity of a person is a continuity of habit and memory: there was yesterday one person whose feelings I can remember, and that person I regard
as myself of yesterday; but, in fact, myself of yesterday was only certain
mental occurrences which are now remembered and are regarded as part
of the person who now recollects them. All that constitutes a person is a
series of experiences connected by memory and by certain similarities of
the sort we call habit.

If, therefore, we are able to believe that a person survives death, we   4
must believe that the memories and habits which constitute the person will
continue to be exhibited in a new set of occurrences.

No one can prove that this will not happen. But it is easy to see that it   5
is very unlikely. Our memories and habits are bound up with the structure
of the brain, in much the same way in which a river is connected with the
riverbed. The water in the river is always changing, but it keeps to the same
course because previous rains have worn a channel. In like manner, previous events have worn a channel in the brain, and our thoughts flow along
this channel. This is the cause of memory and mental habits. But the brain,
as a structure, is dissolved at death, and memory therefore may be expected to be also dissolved. There is no more reason to think otherwise
than to expect a river to persist in its old course after an earthquake has
raised a mountain where a valley used to be.

All memory, and therefore (one may say) all minds, depend upon a   6
property which is very noticeable in certain kinds of material structures but
exists little if at all in other kinds. This is the property of forming habits as
a result of frequent similar occurrences. For example: a bright light makes
the pupils of the eyes contract; and if you repeatedly flash a light in a man's
eyes and beat a gong at the same time, the gong alone will, in the end,
cause his pupils to contract. This is a fact about the brain and nervous
system—that is to say, about a certain material structure. It will be found
that exactly similar facts explain our response to language and our use of
it, our memories and the emotions they arouse, our moral or immoral habits
of behavior, and indeed everything that constitutes our mental personality,
except the part determined by heredity. The part determined by heredity is
handed on to our posterity but cannot, in the individual, survive the disin-

tegration of the body. Thus both the hereditary and the acquired parts of a personality are, so far as our experience goes, bound up with the characteristics of certain bodily structures. We all know that memory may be obliterated by an injury to the brain, that a virtuous person may be rendered vicious by encephalitis lethargica, and that a clever child can be turned into an idiot by lack of iodine. In view of such familiar facts, it seems scarcely probable that the mind survives the total destruction of brain structure which occurs at death.

It is not rational arguments but emotions that cause belief in a future life. 7

The most important of these emotions is fear of death, which is instinctive and biologically useful. If we genuinely and wholeheartedly believed in the future life, we should cease completely to fear death. The effects would be curious, and probably such as most of us would deplore. But our human and subhuman ancestors have fought and exterminated their enemies throughout many geological ages and have profited by courage; it is therefore an advantage to the victors in the struggle for life to be able, on occasion, to overcome the natural fear of death. Among animals and savages, instinctive pugnacity suffices for this purpose; but at a certain stage of development, as the Mohammedans first proved, belief in Paradise has considerable military value as reinforcing natural pugnacity. We should therefore admit that militarists are wise in encouraging the belief in immortality, always supposing that this belief does not become so profound as to produce indifference to the affairs of the world. 8

Another emotion which encourages the belief in survival is admiration of the excellence of man. As the Bishop of Birmingham says, "His mind is a far finer instrument than anything that had appeared earlier—he knows right and wrong. He can build Westminster Abbey. He can make an airplane. He can calculate the distance of the sun. . . . Shall, then, man at death perish utterly? Does that incomparable instrument, his mind, vanish when life ceases?" 9

The Bishop proceeds to argue that "the universe has been shaped and is governed by an intelligent purpose," and that it would have been unintelligent, having made man, to let him perish. 10

To this argument there are many answers. In the first place, it has been found, in the scientific investigation of nature, that the intrusion of moral or aesthetic values has always been an obstacle to discovery. It used to be thought that the heavenly bodies must move in circles because the circle is the most perfect curve, that species must be immutable because God would only create what was perfect and what therefore stood in no need of improvement, that it was useless to combat epidemics except by repentance because they were sent as a punishment for sin, and so on. It has been found, however, that, so far as we can discover, nature is indifferent to our values and can only be understood by ignoring our notions of good and bad. The Universe may have a purpose, but nothing that we know suggests that, if so, this purpose has any similarity to ours. 11

Nor is there in this anything surprising. Dr. Barnes tells us that man   12
"knows right and wrong." But, in fact, as anthropology shows, men's views
of right and wrong have varied to such an extent that no single item has
been permanent. We cannot say, therefore, that man knows right and
wrong, but only that some men do. Which men? Nietzsche argued in favor
of an ethic profoundly different from Christ's, and some powerful governments have accepted his teaching. If knowledge of right and wrong is to
be an argument for immortality, we must first settle whether to believe
Christ or Nietzsche, and then argue that Christians are immortal, but Hitler
and Mussolini are not, or vice versa. The decision will obviously be made
on the battlefield, not in the study. Those who have the best poison gas
will have the ethic of the future and will therefore be the immortal ones.

Our feelings and beliefs on the subject of good and evil are, like every-   13
thing else about us, natural facts, developed in the struggle for existence
and not having any divine or supernatural origin. In one of Aesop's fables,
a lion is shown pictures of huntsmen catching lions and remarks that, if he
had painted them, they would have shown lions catching huntsmen. Man,
says Dr. Barnes, is a fine fellow because he can make airplanes. A little
while ago there was a popular song about the cleverness of flies in walking
upside down on the ceiling, with the chorus: "Could Lloyd George do it?
Could Mr. Baldwin do it? Could Ramsay Mac do it? Why, NO."° On this basis
a very telling argument could be constructed by a theologically minded fly,
which no doubt other flies would find most convincing.

Moreover, it is only when we think abstractly that we have such a high   14
opinion of man. Of men in the concrete, most of us think the vast majority
very bad. Civilized states spend more than half their revenue on killing each
other's citizens. Consider the long history of the activities inspired by moral
fervor: human sacrifices, persecutions of heretics, witch-hunts, pogroms
leading up to wholesale extermination by poison gases, which one at least
of Dr. Barnes's episcopal colleagues must be supposed to favor, since he
holds pacifism to be un-Christian. Are these abominations, and the ethical
doctrines by which they are prompted, really evidence of an intelligent
Creator? And can we really wish that the men who practiced them should
live forever? The world in which we live can be understood as a result of
muddle and accident; but if it is the outcome of deliberate purpose, the
purpose must have been that of a fiend. For my part, I find accident a less
painful and more plausible hypothesis.

"Could Lloyd George . . . Ramsay Mac do it?": The song chides three successive British prime
ministers of the 1920s: Lloyd George, Stanley Baldwin, and James Ramsay MacDonald.

Questions to Start You Thinking

1. In paragraph 5, Russell admits the impossibility of proving that people do not
   survive death. To what extent does this admission weaken his argument?

2. What does the essay gain from the author's quoting Bishop Barnes's article in paragraphs 9 and 10?

3. Point to statements in which Russell employs humor, irony, or sarcasm. (Consider especially his last three paragraphs.) Do you find these devices effective? Why or why not?

4. Cite examples of the evidence Russell uses to support his stand. Where is he most convincing? Where is he least so?

An Economist Takes a Stand

Milton Friedman, an influential conservative economist, is well known for his numerous scholarly articles, a regular column that he wrote for *Newsweek,* and his teaching at the University of Chicago. In this essay he takes a stand on a controversial issue of vital concern to businesspeople and laypeople alike.

THE SOCIAL RESPONSIBILITY OF BUSINESS IS TO INCREASE ITS PROFITS
Milton Friedman

When I hear businessmen speak eloquently about the "social respon- 1 sibilities of business in a free-enterprise system," I am reminded of the wonderful line about the Frenchman who discovered at the age of seventy that he had been speaking prose all his life. The businessmen believe that they are defending free enterprise when they declaim that business is not concerned "merely" with profit but also with promoting desirable "social" ends; that business has a "social conscience" and takes seriously its responsibilities for providing employment, eliminating discrimination, avoiding pollution and whatever else may be the catchwords of the contemporary crop of reformers. In fact they are—or would be if they or anyone else took them seriously—preaching pure and unadulterated socialism. Businessmen who talk this way are unwitting puppets of the intellectual forces that have been undermining the basis of a free society these past decades.

The discussions of the "social responsibilities of business" are notable 2 for their analytical looseness and lack of rigor. What does it mean to say that "business" has responsibilities? Only people can have responsibilities. A corporation is an artificial person and in this sense may have artificial responsibilities, but "business" as a whole cannot be said to have responsibilities, even in this vague sense. The first step toward clarity in examining the doctrine of the social responsibility of business is to ask precisely what it implies for whom.

Presumably, the individuals who are to be responsible are business- 3 men, which means individual proprietors or corporate executives. Most of the discussion of social responsibility is directed at corporations, so in what follows I shall mostly neglect the individual proprietors and speak of corporate executives.

In a free-enterprise, private-property system, a corporate executive is 4 an employee of the owners of the business. He has direct responsibility to his employers. That responsibility is to conduct the business in accordance with their desires, which generally will be to make as much money as possible while conforming to the basic rules of the society, both those embodied in law and those embodied in ethical custom. Of course, in some cases his employers may have a different objective. A group of persons might establish a corporation for an eleemosynary purpose—for example, a hospital or a school. The manager of such a corporation will not have money profit as his objectives but the rendering of certain services.

In either case, the key point is that, in his capacity as a corporate 5 executive, the manager is the agent of the individuals who own the corporation or establish the eleemosynary institution, and his primary responsibility is to them.

Needless to say, this does not mean that it is easy to judge how well 6 he is performing his task. But at least the criterion of performance is straightforward, and the persons among whom a voluntary contractual arrangement exists are clearly defined.

Of course, the corporate executive is also a person in his own right. As 7 a person, he may have many other responsibilities that he recognizes or assumes voluntarily—to his family, his conscience, his feelings of charity, his church, his clubs, his city, his country. He may feel impelled by these responsibilities to devote part of his income to causes he regards as worthy, to refuse to work for particular corporations, even to leave his job, for example, to join his country's armed forces. If we wish, we may refer to some of these responsibilities as "social responsibilities." But in these respects he is acting as a principal, not an agent; he is spending his own money or time or energy, not the money of his employers or the time or energy he has contracted to devote to their purposes. If these are "social responsibilities," they are the social responsibilities of individuals, not of business.

What does it mean to say that the corporate executive has a "social 8 responsibility" in his capacity as businessman? If this statement is not pure rhetoric, it must mean that he is to act in some way that is not in the interest of his employers. For example, that he is to refrain from increasing the price of the product in order to contribute to the social objective of preventing inflation, even though a price increase would be in the best interests of the corporation. Or that he is to make expenditures on reducing pollution beyond the amount that is in the best interests of the corporation or that is required by law in order to contribute to the social objective of improving the environment. Or that, at the expense of corporate profits, he is to hire "hard-core" unemployed instead of better qualified available workmen to contribute to the social objective of reducing poverty.

In each of these cases, the corporate executive would be spending 9
someone else's money for a general social interest. Insofar as his actions
in accord with his "social responsibility" reduce returns to stockholders, he
is spending their money. Insofar as his actions raise the price to customers,
he is spending the customers' money. Insofar as his actions lower the
wages of some employees, he is spending their money.

The stockholders or the customers or the employees could separately 10
spend their own money on the particular action if they wished to do so. The
executive is exercising a distinct "social responsibility," rather than serving
as an agent of the stockholders or the customers or the employees, only
if he spends the money in a different way than they would have spent it.

But if he does this, he is in effect imposing taxes, on the one hand, 11
and deciding how the tax proceeds shall be spent, on the other.

This process raises political questions on two levels: principle and con- 12
sequences. On the level of political principle, the imposition of taxes and
the expenditure of tax proceeds are governmental functions. We have established elaborate constitutional, parliamentary, and judicial provisions
to control these functions, to assure that taxes are imposed so far as
possible in accordance with the preferences and desires of the public—
after all, "taxation without representation" was one of the battle cries of
the American Revolution. We have a system of checks and balances to
separate the legislative function of imposing taxes and enacting expenditures from the executive function of collecting taxes and administering
expenditure programs and from the judicial function of mediating disputes
and interpreting the law.

Here the businessman—self-selected or appointed directly or indirectly 13
by stockholders—is to be simultaneously legislator, executive, and jurist.
He is to decide whom to tax by how much and for what purpose, and he is
to spend the proceeds—all this guided only by general exhortations from
on high to restrain inflation, improve the environment, fight poverty, and
so on and on.

The whole justification for permitting the corporate executive to be se- 14
lected by the stockholders is that the executive is an agent serving the
interests of his principal. This justification disappears when the corporate
executive imposes taxes and spends the proceeds for "social" purposes.
He becomes in effect a public employee, a civil servant, even though he
remains in name an employee of a private enterprise. On grounds of political principle, it is intolerable that such civil servants—insofar as their
actions in the name of social responsibility are real and not just window-
dressing—should be selected as they are now. If they are to be civil
servants, then they must be elected through a political process. If they are
to impose taxes and make expenditures to foster "social" objectives, then
political machinery must be set up to make the assessment of taxes and
to determine through a political process the objectives to be served.

This is the basic reason why the doctrine of "social responsibility" in- 15 volves the acceptance of the socialist view that political mechanisms, not market mechanisms, are the appropriate way to determine the allocation of scarce resources to alternative uses.

On the grounds of consequences, can the corporate executive in fact   16 discharge his alleged "social responsibilities"? On the other hand, suppose he could get away with spending the stockholders' or customers' or employees' money. How is he to know how to spend it? He is told that he must contribute to fighting inflation. How is he to know what action of his will contribute to that end? He is presumably an expert in running his company—in producing a product or selling it or financing it. But nothing about his selection makes him an expert on inflation. Will his holding down the price of his product reduce inflationary pressure? Or, by leaving more spending power in the hands of his customers, simply divert it elsewhere? Or, by forcing him to produce less because of the lower price, will it simply contribute to shortages? Even if he could answer these questions, how much cost is he justified in imposing on his stockholders, customers, and employees for this social purpose? What is his appropriate share and what is the appropriate share of others?

And, whether he wants to or not, can he get away with spending his   17 stockholders', customers', or employees' money? Will not the stockholders fire him? (Either the present ones or those who take over when his actions in the name of social responsibility have reduced the corporation's profits and the price of its stock.) His customers and his employees can desert him for other producers and employers less scrupulous in exercising their social responsibilities.

This facet of "social responsibility" doctrine is brought into sharp relief   18 when the doctrine is used to justify wage restraint by trade unions. The conflict of interest is naked and clear when union officials are asked to subordinate the interest of their members to some more general purpose. If the union officials try to enforce wage restraint, the consequence is likely to be wildcat strikes, rank-and-file revolts, and the emergence of strong competitors for their jobs. We thus have the ironic phenomenon that union leaders—at least in the U.S.—have objected to Government interference with the market far more consistently and courageously than have business leaders.

The difficulty of exercising "social responsibility" illustrates, of course,   19 the great virtue of private competitive enterprise—it forces people to be responsible for their own actions and makes it difficult for them to "exploit" other people for either selfish or unselfish purposes. They can do good— but only at their own expense.

Many a reader who has followed the argument this far may be tempted   20 to remonstrate that it is all well and good to speak of Government's having the responsibility to impose taxes and determine expenditures for such "social" purposes as controlling pollution or training the hard-core unemployed, but that the problems are too urgent to wait on the slow course of political processes, that the exercise of social responsibility by business-men is a quicker and surer way to solve pressing current problems.

Aside from the question of fact—I share Adam Smith's skepticism about   21 the benefits that can be expected from "those who affected to trade for the public good"—this argument must be rejected on grounds of principle. What it amounts to is an assertion that those who favor the taxes and expenditures in question have failed to persuade a majority of their fellow citizens to be of like mind and that they are seeking to attain by undemo-cratic procedures what they cannot attain by democratic procedures. In a free society, it is hard for "evil" people to do "evil," especially since one man's good is another's evil.

I have, for simplicity, concentrated on the special case of the corporate   22 executive, except only for the brief digression on trade unions. But precisely the same argument applies to the newer phenomenon of calling upon stock-holders to require corporations to exercise social responsibility. . . . In most of these cases, what is in effect involved is some stockholders trying to get other stockholders (or customers or employees) to contribute against their will to "social" causes favored by the activists. Insofar as they suc-ceed, they are again imposing taxes and spending the proceeds.

The situation of the individual proprietor is somewhat different. If he   23 acts to reduce the returns of his enterprise in order to exercise his "social responsibility," he is spending his own money, not someone else's. If he wishes to spend his money on such purposes, that is his right, and I cannot see that there is any objection to his doing so. In the process, he, too, may impose costs on employees and customers. However, because he is far less likely than a large corporation or union to have monopolistic power, any such side effects will tend to be minor.

Of course, in practice the doctrine of social responsibility is frequently   24 a cloak for actions that are justified on other grounds rather than a reason for those actions.

To illustrate, it may well be in the long-run interest of a corporation   25 that is a major employer in a small community to devote resources to providing amenities to that community or to improving its government. That may make it easier to attract desirable employees, it may reduce the wage bill or lessen losses from pilferage and sabotage or have other worthwhile effects. Or it may be that, given the laws about the deductibility of corporate charitable contributions, the stockholders can contribute more to charities they favor by having the corporation make the gift than by doing it them-selves, since they can in that way contribute an amount that would other-wise have been paid as corporate taxes.

In each of these—and many similar—cases, there is a strong tempta-   26 tion to rationalize these actions as an exercise of "social responsibility." In the present climate of opinion, with its widespread aversion to "capitalism," "profits," the "soulless corporation," and so on, this is one way for a corporation to generate goodwill as a byproduct of expenditures that are entirely justified in its own self-interest.

It would be inconsistent of me to call on corporate executives to refrain   27 from this hypocritical window-dressing because it harms the foundations of a free society. That would be to call on them to exercise a "social responsibility"! If our institutions and the attitudes of the public make it in their self-interest to cloak their actions in this way, I cannot summon much indignation to denounce them. At the same time, I can express admiration for those individual proprietors or owners of closely held corporations or stockholders of more broadly held corporations who disdain such tactics as approaching fraud.

Whether blameworthy or not, the use of the cloak of social responsi-   28 bility, and the nonsense spoken in its name by influential and prestigious businessmen, does clearly harm the foundations of a free society. I have been impressed time and again by the schizophrenic character of many businessmen. They are capable of being extremely far-sighted and clear-headed in matters that are internal to their businesses. They are incredibly short-sighted and muddle-headed in matters that are outside their businesses but affect the possible survival of business in general. This short-sightedness is strikingly exemplified in the calls from many businessmen for wage and price guidelines or controls or income policies. There is nothing that could do more in a brief period to destroy a market system and replace it by a centrally controlled system than effective governmental control of prices and wages.

The short-sightedness is also exemplified in speeches by businessmen   29 on social responsibility. This may gain them kudos in the short run. But it helps to strengthen the already too prevalent view that the pursuit of profits is wicked and immoral and must be curbed and controlled by external forces. Once this view is adopted, the external forces that curb the market will not be the social consciences, however highly developed, of the pontificating executives; it will be the iron fist of Government bureaucrats. Here, as with price and wage controls, businessmen seem to me to reveal a suicidal impulse.

The political principle that underlies the market mechanism is una-   30 nimity. In an ideal free market resting on private property, no individual can coerce any other, all cooperation is voluntary, all parties to such cooperation benefit or they need not participate. There are no values, no "social" responsibilities in any sense other than the shared values and responsibilities of individuals. Society is a collection of individuals and of the various groups they voluntarily form.

The political principle that underlies the political mechanism is con-   31 formity. The individual must serve a more general social interest—whether that be determined by a church or a dictator or a majority. The individual may have a vote and say in what is to be done, but if he is overruled, he must conform. It is appropriate for some to require others to contribute to a general social purpose whether they wish to or not.

Unfortunately, unanimity is not always feasible. There are some re- 32 spects in which conformity appears unavoidable, so I do not see how one can avoid the use of the political mechanism altogether.

But the doctrine of "social responsibility" taken seriously would extend 33 the scope of the political mechanism to every human activity. It does not differ in philosophy from the most explicitly collectivist doctrine. It differs only by professing to believe that collectivist ends can be attained without collectivist means. That is why, in my book *Capitalism and Freedom*, I have called it a "fundamentally subversive doctrine" in a free society, and have said that in such a society, "there is one and only one social responsibility of business—to use its resources and engage in activities designed to increase its profits so long as it stays within the rules of the game, which is to say, engages in open and free competition without deception or fraud."

Questions to Start You Thinking

1. Do you agree with Friedman that businessmen who say that business has social responsibilities are "preaching pure and unadulterated socialism"? Where else in his essay does the author use loaded words to attack what he decries? Is he fair in using such words?

2. What objections does Friedman raise to the doctrine of social responsibility for business?

3. To what practices does Friedman point in declaring that he "cannot summon much indignation to denounce them" (paragraph 27)? How does he reconcile this view with his reference to these same practices later in the paragraph as "approaching fraud"?

4. Write a paragraph in which you agree or disagree with the stand Friedman takes in paragraphs 20 and 21. Share it with the class.

CHAPTER 8

Proposing a Solution

Sometimes when you learn of a problem such as acid rain, nuclear fallout, or famine, you say to yourself, "Something should be done about that." This chapter will show you one way to do something constructive yourself: by the powerful and persuasive activity of writing.

Your purpose in such writing, as political leaders and advertisers well know, is to rouse your audience to action. Thomas Jefferson and his cohorts who wrote the Declaration of Independence proved as much, and even in your daily life at college you find chances to demonstrate this truth often. Does some policy of your college administrators irk you? Would you urge students to attend a rally for a cause or a charity? Write a letter to your college newspaper or to someone in authority, and try to stir your readers to action.

The uses of such writing go far beyond these immediate applications, as we will see. Accordingly, a college course (of any kind) will sometimes ask you to write a *proposal*: a recommendation that an action be taken. In the previous chapter, you took a stand and backed it up with evidence. Now go a step farther. If, for instance, you have made the claim "Our national parks are in sorry condition," you might urge readers to write to their representatives in Congress or donate funds to save endangered species or visit a national park and pick up trash. Or instead you may want to suggest that the Department of the Interior be given a budget increase to hire more park rangers, purchase additional park land to accommodate the increasing horde of visitors to the national parks, and buy more clean-up equipment. The first paper would be a call to immediate action on the part of your readers; the second, an attempt to forge a consensus about what needs to be done.

In making a proposal you set forth a solution, and you urge action by using words like *should, ought,* and *must*: "This city ought to have a Bureau of Missing Persons"; "Small private aircraft should be banned from flying closer than one mile to a major commercial airport"; "Every consumer must refuse to buy South African apples." Then you lay out, clearly and concisely, all the reasons you can muster to persuade your readers that your proposal deserves to be implemented.

LEARNING FROM OTHER WRITERS

In recent years, some people have complained that certain rock lyrics incite listeners to violence. Rock singers and composers and listeners have protested against any attempt at censorship. In an article from the *Boston Globe,* Caryl Rivers, novelist and professor of journalism at Boston University, sets forth her own view of the question, together with pointed suggestions for action.

WHAT SHOULD BE DONE ABOUT ROCK LYRICS?
Caryl Rivers

After a grisly series of murders in California, possibly inspired by the lyrics of a rock song, we are hearing a familiar chorus: don't blame rock and roll. Kids will be kids. They love to rebel, and the more shocking the stuff, the better they like it. 1

There's some truth in this, of course. I loved to watch Elvis shake his torso when I was a teenager, and it was even more fun when Ed Sullivan wouldn't let the cameras show him below the waist. I snickered at the forbidden "Rock with Me, Annie" lyrics by a black rhythm and blues group, which were deliciously naughty. But I am sorry, rock fans, that is not the same thing as hearing lyrics about how a man is going to force a woman to perform oral sex on him at gunpoint in a little number called "Eat Me Alive." It is not in the same league with a song about the delights of slipping into a woman's room while she is sleeping and murdering her, the theme of an AC/DC ballad that allegedly inspired the California slayer. 2

Make no mistake, it is not sex we are talking about here, but violence. Violence against women. Most rock songs are not violent—they are funky, sexy, rebellious, and sometimes witty. Please do not mistake me for a Mrs. Grundy. If Prince wants to leap about wearing only a purple jock strap, fine. 3

Let Mick Jagger unzip his fly as he gyrates, if he wants to. But when either one of them starts garroting, beating, or sodomizing a woman in their number, that is another story.

I always find myself annoyed when "intellectual" men dismiss violence   4
against women with a yawn, as if it were beneath their dignity to notice. I wonder if the reaction would be the same if the violence were directed against someone other than women. How many people would yawn and say, "Oh, kids will be kids" if a rock group did a nifty little number called "Lynchin," in which stringing up and stomping on black people were set to music? Who would chuckle and say, "Oh, just a little adolescent rebellion" if a group of rockers went on MTV dressed as Nazis, desecrating synagogues and beating up Jews to the beat of twanging guitars?

I'll tell you what would happen. Prestigious dailies would thunder on   5
editorial pages; senators would fall over each other to get denunciations into the *Congressional Record*. The president would appoint a commission to clean up the music business.

But violence against women is greeted by silence. It shouldn't be.   6

This does not mean censorship, or book (or record) burning. In a society   7
that protects free expression, we understand a lot of stuff will float up out of the sewer. Usually, we recognize the ugly stuff that advocates violence against any group as the garbage it is, and we consider its purveyors as moral lepers. We hold our nose and tolerate it, but we speak out against the values it proffers.

But images of violence against women are not staying on the fringes   8
of society. No longer are they found only in tattered, paper-covered books or in movie houses where winos snooze and the scent of urine fills the air. They are entering the mainstream at a rapid rate. This is happening at a time when the media, more and more, set the agenda for the public debate. It is a powerful legitimizing force—especially television. Many people regard what they see on TV as the truth; Walter Cronkite once topped a poll as the most trusted man in America.

Now, with the advent of rock videos and all-music channels, rock music   9
has grabbed a big chunk of legitimacy. American teenagers have instant access, in their living rooms, to the messages of rock, on the same vehicle that brought them Sesame Street. Who can blame them if they believe that the images they see are accurate reflections of adult reality, approved by adults? After all, Big Bird used to give them lessons on the same little box. Adults, by their silence, sanction the images. Do we really want our kids to think that rape and violence are what sexuality is all about?

This is not a trivial issue. Violence against women is a major social   10
problem, one that's more than a cerebral issue to me. I teach at Boston University, and one of my most promising young journalism students was raped and murdered. Two others told me of being raped. Recently, one female student was assaulted and beaten so badly she had $5,000 worth of medical bills and permanent damage to her back and eyes.

It's nearly impossible, of course, to make a cause-and-effect link be- 11
tween lyrics and images and acts of violence. But images have a tremendous power to create an atmosphere in which violence against certain
people is sanctioned. Nazi propagandists knew that full well when they
portrayed Jews as ugly, greedy, and powerful.

The outcry over violence against women, particularly in a sexual con- 12
text, is being legitimized in two ways: by the increasing movement of these
images into the mainstream of the media in TV, films, magazines, albums,
videos, and by the silence about it.

Violence, of course, is rampant in the media. But it is usually set in 13
some kind of moral context. It's usually only the bad guys who commit
violent acts against the innocent. When the good guys get violent, it's
against those who deserve it. Dirty Harry blows away the scum, he doesn't
walk up to a toddler and say, "Make my day." The A Team does not shoot
up suburban shopping malls.

But in some rock songs, it's the "heroes" who commit the acts. The 14
people we are programmed to identify with are the ones being violent, with
women on the receiving end. In a society where rape and assaults on
women are endemic, this is no small problem, with millions of young boys
watching on their TV screens and listening on their Walkmans.

I think something needs to be done. I'd like to see people in the industry 15
respond to the problem. I'd love to see some women rock stars speak out
against violence against women. I would like to see disc jockeys refuse air
play to records and videos that contain such violence. At the very least, I
want to see the end of the silence. I want journalists and parents and critics
and performing artists to keep this issue alive in the public forum. I don't
want people who are concerned about this issue labeled as bluenoses and
bookburners and ignored.

And I wish it wasn't always just women who were speaking out. Men 16
have as large a stake in the quality of our civilization as women do in the
long run. Violence is a contagion that infects at random. Let's hear something, please, from the men.

Questions to Start You Thinking

1. Does Rivers persuade you that action is necessary? Do you think she takes rock lyrics too seriously?

2. Can you recall from your own experience any other evidence that might support her argument?

3. Where in her essay does Rivers present, even sympathize with, views opposed to her own? By doing so, does she strengthen or weaken her case?

4. What unspoken values and assumptions do you discern in Rivers that make her argue as she does?

5. Where in her essay does Rivers use the resource of imagination? For what purpose?

After pondering an old problem—people who mix drinking and driving—
Jeffrey Ting came up with an original solution. For a freshman writing seminar
called Contemporary Social Problems, he wrote the following proposal.

Student Essay

THE DRINKING AGE:
HOW WE SHOULD DETERMINE IT
Jeffrey Ting

Recent history has shown that the big problem when the   1
driver mixes alcohol and gasoline comes from people between
the ages of sixteen and twenty. The reason for this problem
is not that young people are irresponsible. After the Vietnam War an old point was popularly raised: "Well, if a person
can be old enough to fight in a war why isn't he old enough
to drink?" So in the 1970s the drinking age was lowered in
most states to eighteen. This proved an experiment that
failed. Fatalities rose on the highways. That is why the
federal government in 1984 passed the law requiring states to
raise the drinking age to twenty-one or else lose federal
funding for their highways. Many states promptly reacted and
in early 1985 raised the drinking age to twenty-one.

Some individuals will be ready to drink at seventeen,   2
and others never will be if they live to be ninety. Instead
of penalizing all the twenty-one-year-olds who have been
spoiling for a beer ever since they were seventeen and who
would be perfectly well qualified to handle it, I would like
to propose a completely new solution to the problem. It is a
drinking license.

We have a driver's license now, which is given out to   3
persons who demonstrate their ability to drive, and this has
proven an effective system. Why then do we not license
drinking to those who can prove their competence? I do not
suggest that, to win one's drinking license, it should be
necessary to chug-a-lug a pitcher of beer and then walk a

straight line. It seems to me that the best way to determine the ability to handle alcohol would be to relate this ability to the ability to drive.

Let me imagine the plan like this. Let us say that the 4 driver's license, in a certain state, may be obtained at seventeen. Then should follow a period of eighteen months in which the young driver proves that he can keep an unblemished record--no drinking-related accidents. This caution would be necessary, for you may be sure that seventeen-year-olds who drive can find someone to buy beer for them. If at the end of that eighteen months the driver's record is clean, he can apply for a drinking license. A written test should be administered, like the one most states require for a driving license, to determine that the applicant has at least a basic knowledge of alcohol and its effects. Questions should be included such as "How many drinks does it take to get a person weighing 150 pounds over the point at which he can be declared legally inebriated?" "How long does it take, after that many drinks, to sober up?" "What is the best cure for a hangover?" (Answer: Honey.) And "How many people were killed last year in alcohol-related car accidents?" The applicant, if he can pass all this, receives a temporary drinking license good for six months of beer and wine, with hard liquor not yet permitted. If at the end of that six months he can both drink and drive and not have any accidents, he gets a permanent drinking license. I say "permanent," but this license can always be revoked. If the person is involved in a drinking-related accident he loses both driver's license and drinking license. No drinking license will be required for people over twenty-one.

At least two objections, I realize, can be leveled 5 against this plan. It will require more paperwork and more bureaucracy. I don't see this as a serious problem. Indeed, compared to the work that the present unworkable system creates for our courts, what with the charging of people for violating the drinking laws and the crushing burden of trials resulting from accidents, I believe this extra work would be relatively small. The states could charge a small fee for a drinking license, which the teenager would pay willingly, thus making money for the state.

A more serious objection is that this plan would tie 6 drinking licenses to drivers' licenses, and what about people who don't drive? Would they never be able to drink? That is a good objection, and I propose that, for those individuals without wheels, a different means be created for them to prove their ability to drink without causing any problems for society. They would be required to affirm that they are not going to obtain drivers' licenses. They would have to keep this pledge or else have to fall subject to the usual requirements for drivers. They would have an eighteen-month period following their seventeenth birthdays, during which they would be required to keep a clean police record. At the end of this eighteen months, if they had shown themselves to be good citizens, they could apply for and receive their drinking licenses. They would be required to take the same written test as anyone else.

While, like all official attempts to regulate unpredict- 7 able humans, the plan I suggest would not work perfectly, I expect that it would work much more efficiently in keeping drunken drivers off the roads than the present confusion of laws and drinking ages. It would view the growing individual as going through a series of gauntlets in taking his or her rightful place as a responsible member of adult society. Right now the law unfairly discriminates against those who are willing and able to assume responsibility early. My plan would trust those individuals who can show society that they are ready to be trusted.

Questions to Start You Thinking

1. What, to your mind, is Ting's most convincing point in favor of his proposal? Which is least convincing?

2. Are there other objections to Ting's plan that he fails to deal with? If so, what are they?

3. Which of the writer's five resources—recalling, observing, reading, conversing, imagining—does Ting use in his essay? On which one does he rely most heavily?

4. What other possible solutions to this same problem can you imagine?

LEARNING BY WRITING

The Assignment: Arguing for an Action

In this essay, you're going to accomplish two things. First, you'll carefully describe a social, economic, political, civic, environmental, or administrative problem—a problem you care about, one that irritates you or angers you, one that you strongly wish to see resolved. The problem may be large or small, but it shouldn't be trivial. (No comic essays about the awful problem of catsup that squirts from Big Macs, please. For this assignment you'll want to probe deeper and engage your thinking with other people's real concerns.) The problem may be one that affects the whole country, or it may be one that affects mainly people in your locality: your city, your campus, or your dormitory. Show your readers that this problem really exists and that it matters to them. Write for an audience who, once made aware of the problem, may be expected to help do something about it.

After setting forth the problem, go on to propose a way to solve it or at least alleviate it. What should be done? Supply evidence that your proposal is reasonable, that it can work, that a way to improve the existing state of affairs is within our grasp.

Some recent student papers that cogently argued for actions include the following.

A woman argued that SAT, ACT, and achievement test scores should be abolished as criteria for college acceptance. She demonstrated that the tests favor aggressive students from affluent families, who can afford to take courses and buy software programs designed to improve their scores.

A woman made a case for drafting all eighteen-year-olds for a year and putting them to work at such tasks as feeding the homeless, tutoring students who need special help, eliminating litter and graffiti, teaching the illiterate to read, planting trees and flowers, helping patients in nursing homes, and staffing day care centers.

A student of education, suggesting that students in sixth through ninth grades are ill served by the big, faceless middle schools and junior high schools they now attend, proposed a return to small, personal elementary schools that teach children from kindergarten through eighth grade.

A man, stressing the humanizing influence of light, sunshine, and green space, argued for a moratorium on the construction of all high-rise buildings.

A woman, setting forth her belief in the importance of new frontiers, advocated more and better-funded research into space travel.

Generating Ideas

In selecting a topic, your five familiar resources may supply you with knowledge of a problem that needs to be cured. Here are a few questions to help ideas start flowing.

DISCOVERY CHECKLIST: DRAWING FROM RESOURCES

- Can you recall any problem you have encountered in your own experience that you think needs a solution? If your topic is a problem you are well acquainted with, your writing task will be easier by far. Ask yourself what problems you meet every day or occasionally or what problems concern people near you.

- Consider how to improve systems (or ways of doing things) that you believe to be flawed. Can you think of a better way for your college to run its course registration? A better way for your state or community to control dangerous drugs?

- Have you observed a problem recently? What conditions in need of improvement have you seen on television or on your daily rounds? What action is called for?

- Have you read of any such problem in a newspaper or news magazine?

- Have you heard of any problem in recent conversation or class discussion?

- By trying to put yourself in the position of another person, perhaps someone of a different ethnic background, someone with fewer advantages, can you imagine some problem that no doubt exists? (This last suggestion invites you also to do some reading about it.)

Scan the news. One of the most convenient sources of information about real and current problems is a daily newspaper or a news magazine such as *Time, Newsweek,* or *U.S. News & World Report.* Any issue will abound with the cares of multitudes. In a single newspaper published on the morning we wrote these words, we found discussions of the problems of acid rain, teenage pregnancy, the high school dropout rate, famine in the Sudan, hunger in America, a spurt in the highway death toll due to drunken drivers, unemployment, cases of crack abuse, the difficulty of apprehending parents suspected of child abuse, traffic congestion, a surplus of wine produced by California vintners, terrorist hijackings of airliners, swindlers who sell worthless franchises, the disposal of toxic waste, a sharp increase in severe injuries in professional football (prompting debate over whether the rules of the game need to be changed), and the problem of how the United States and the Soviet Union can agree to reduce their nuclear missile stockpiles.

Brainstorming—compiling a list of possible writing topics—is another good way to begin. (See p. 471 for more advice on this useful strategy.)

Think about solutions. Once you've chosen a problem, try to come up with solutions. Some problems—such as that of reducing international tensions—present no easy solutions. Still, give some thought to any problem that you feel seriously concerned with. You can't be expected to solve, in one college writing assignment, a problem that may have thwarted teams of scientists and government experts. But sometimes a solution to a problem will reveal itself to a novice thinker. And for some problems, like the problem of reducing armaments, even a small contribution to a partial solution will be worth offering. Here are a few questions to help you think about the problem critically.

DISCOVERY CHECKLIST: UNDERSTANDING A PROBLEM

- How urgent is the problem? Does something need to be done about it immediately?
- For how long has this problem been going on?
- What causes for this problem can you find? What have been its effects? (For more ideas, glance ahead to Chapter 10.)
- In the past, have any problems like this been solved or eliminated?
- How does this problem affect the reader's health, well-being, conscience, or pocketbook?
- How many possible solutions can you imagine?

Consider your readers. Think of your audience—the readers you seek to persuade. If you are addressing your fellow students, maybe they haven't had occasion to think about the problem before. If you can discover any way to bring it home to them, any evidence to show that it affects and concerns them, your paper is likely to be effective. Do some more brainstorming. Try *freewriting,* the useful strategy of starting out to write steadily, thinking as you write (see p. 474 for more advice about freewriting.) As you write preliminary notes, consider the following points.

DISCOVERY CHECKLIST: UNDERSTANDING YOUR AUDIENCE

- Why should your readers care? Why is this a problem that concerns them personally?
- In the past, have they expressed any interest in this problem that you can recall?
- Do they belong to any organization, religious group, minority, or other segment of society that might make them especially likely to agree or disagree? What assumptions and values do they hold that you should be aware of?
- What attitudes have you in common with them? Do you and your readers already agree on anything?

Gather evidence. To show that the problem really exists, you'll need evidence and examples. Again, draw on your five familiar resources. While you think, scribble notes to yourself. Keep your pencil moving. If you feel that further reading in the library will help you know what you're talking about, now is the time. The *Readers' Guide to Periodical Literature* and the library catalog are trusty sources of relevant reading—the former to locate magazine articles on a subject, the latter to locate books. (For advice on using these aids, see Chapter 12.)

Shaping a Draft

Start with your proposal. A basic way to approach your paper is to state your proposal in a sentence: "A law should be passed enabling couples to divorce without having to go to court"; "The United States should secede from the United Nations." From such a statement, the rest of the argument may start to unfold. Usually a paper of this kind falls naturally into a simple two-part shape.

1. A claim that a problem exists. This is a long introductory part, describing the problem and supplying evidence to suggest that it is intolerable.
2. A claim that something ought to be done about it. This part is the proposal.

You can make your proposal more persuasive by including some or all of the following elements.

The knowledge or experience you have or the thinking you have done that qualifies you to propose a solution to the problem.

The values, beliefs, or assumptions that have caused you to feel strongly about the need for action. (Sample statement: "I believe that persons of fifteen are old enough to chart their own destinies and that it is morally wrong for them to remain under their parents' control with no say in the matter.")

WRITING WITH A COMPUTER: PROPOSING A SOLUTION
Your computer's wonderful ability to lift and move blocks of words has a special usefulness for this assignment. It gives you the power to play around, arranging the points of your argument in whatever sequence seems most effective. You might place first whatever you expect to be your readers' most powerful objection to your proposal and then answer it right away. Place the second strongest objection next, and so on. But who knows? Try different sequences until you find the one that works best. Your most convincing point might stand last—for a clincher.

What will be required—an estimate of money, people, skills, material. This part might include a list or enumeration of what is readily available now and what else will have to be obtained.

Exactly what must be done, step by step, to enact your solution.

How long the solution is likely to take.

What possible obstacles or difficulties may need to be overcome.

Why your solution to the problem is better than others that have been proposed or tried already.

What tests, controls, or quality checks might be used to make sure that your solution is proceeding as expected.

Any other evidence to show that what you suggest is practical, reasonable in cost, and likely to be effective.

Imagine your readers' objections. Perhaps you can think of possible objections your readers might raise: reservations about the high cost, the complexity, or the workability of your plan, for instance. It is wonderfully persuasive to anticipate the very objection that might occur to members of your audience and to deal with it and lay it to rest. Jonathan Swift, in "A Modest Proposal," is aware of this rhetorical strategy. After arguing that it will greatly help the poor of Ireland to sell their babies to rich landlords for meat (he's being ironic, savagely condemning the landlords' lack of feeling), Swift goes on:

> I can think of no one objection that will possibly be raised against this proposal, unless it should be urged that the number of people will be thereby much lessened in the kingdom. This I freely own, and it was indeed one principal design in offering it to the world.

When you come to set forth your proposal, you will increase the likelihood of its acceptance if you make the first step simple and inviting. A claim that national parks need better care might begin by suggesting that the reader head for such a park and personally size up the situation.

If as you go along you find you don't know enough about a certain point, don't hesitate to backtrack to the library, or to converse with others, or to give your memory another rummage, or to go out and observe, or to do some more imagining.

Cite sources carefully. When you collect ideas and evidence from outside sources, whether books and periodicals or nonprint sources, you'll need to document your evidence, that is, tell where you got everything. Check with your instructor on the documentation method he or she wants you to use. Chapter 14 contains extensive information on documentation systems, but for a short paper like the one assigned in this chapter, it will probably be enough to introduce brief lines and phrases to identify sources:

According to <u>Newsweek</u> correspondent Josie Fair . . .

As 1980 census figures indicate . . .

In his biography <u>FDR: The New Deal Years</u>, Kenneth S.

Davis reports . . .

While working as a Senate page in the summer of 1986, I observed . . .

Rewriting

Try your draft on other students. Are they convinced that the problem you are writing about is of vital concern to them? If not, why don't they care? Are they persuaded that your solution is likely and workable? You can ask them to consult the peer editing checklist as they comment on your draft.

PEER EDITING CHECKLIST: PROPOSING A SOLUTION

- What is your overall reaction to this proposal?
- Restate what you understand to be the major points.
  Problem:
  Formal proposal:
  Explanation of proposal:
      Criteria for evaluation:
      Process:
      Duration:
      Advantages:
      Disadvantages:
  Disqualification of other solutions:
  Recommendation:
- Has the writer carefully enough disqualified the other solutions?
- List any additional solutions you think the writer should disqualify.
- Describe what you think makes the writer trustworthy as a proposer.
- Describe the reader whom the paper seems to be addressing. Has the writer paid enough attention to the reader?
- Has the writer been persuasive?
- Would you recommend any changes?
- Circle on the manuscript any spelling, punctuation, grammar, or word choice that impeded your reading and understanding.

In drafting his essay, Jeffrey Ting encountered problems near the end. He wanted to come to an effective conclusion but, looking over the draft, he realized that he had not done so. After showing his paper to a friend and then studying it carefully, he made the following changes.

End with this!

~~The law I suggest~~ *It* would view the growing individual as going through a series of gauntlets in taking his or her rightful place as a responsible member of adult society. ~~While~~ *R*ight now the law *unfairly* discriminates against those who are willing and able to assume responsibility early. *M*y plan, ~~at least,~~ would trust those individuals who can show society that they are ready to be trusted.

~~What objections might be raised to the plan I have suggested?~~ At least two objections, I realize, can be leveled against this plan. *It will require* ~~M~~ore paperwork and more bureaucracy ~~will be required.~~ *I don't see this as* ~~This is not~~ a serious problem. Indeed, compared to the work that the present unworkable system creates for our courts, what with the charging of people for violating the drinking laws and the crushing burden of trials resulting from accidents, I believe this extra work would be relatively small. The states could charge a small fee for a drinking license, *which* ~~the~~ teenager would *pay willingly, thus making* ~~make~~ money for the state. ~~by paying willingly.~~

A more serious ~~Another~~ objection is that this plan would tie drinking licenses to drivers' licenses, and what about people who don't drive? *Would they never be able to drink? That is* ~~Being~~ a good objection, *and* I propose that, for *those* ~~these~~ individuals without wheels, a different means be created for them to prove their ability to drink without causing *any* problems for society. ~~in any way.~~ Some individuals will be ready to drink at seventeen, and others never will be if they live to be ninety. *Put in ¶ 2* They would be required to affirm that they are not going to obtain drivers' licenses. They would have to keep this pledge or else have to fall subject to the usual requirements for drivers. They would have an eighteen-month period following their seventeenth birthdays, during which ~~time~~ they would be required to keep a clean ~~and unblemished~~ police record. At the end of this eighteen months, if

```
they had shown themselves to be good citizens, they could

apply for and receive their drinking licenses.  They

would be required to take the same written test as anyone

else. 𝓗 While, like all official attempts to regulate hu-
                             would not
mans, the plan I suggest could never work perfectly, I
                              much more efficiently
expect that it would work really better in keeping drunk-

en drivers off the roads than the present confusion of

laws and drinking ages.  ⟨Insert 𝓗⟩
```

With the corrections, the paper was better organized. In going over his draft, Ting was also able to eliminate unnecessary words and, in general, improve the style. What emerged was the effective conclusion he wanted.

Be reasonable. Exaggerated claims for your solution will not persuade. Don't be afraid to express your own reasonable doubts that your solution will root out the problem forever. If you have ended your draft with a sort of resounding trumpet call or a horrific vision of what will happen if your plea should go unheard, ask yourself whether you have gone too far and whether a reader might protest, "Aaah, this won't mean the end of the world."

A temptation in writing a paper that proposes a solution is to simplify the problem so that the solution will seem all the more likely to apply. In looking back over your draft, if you have proposed an easy, three-step way to end war, famine, or pestilence, perhaps you have fallen into oversimplification. (For help in recognizing this and other errors in reasoning, see "Looking for Logical Fallacies," p. 525.) You may need to rethink both the problem and the solution.

In looking back over your draft once more, review these points.

REVISION CHECKLIST: PROPOSING A SOLUTION

- Have you made the problem clear?
- Have you made it of immediate concern to your readers, so that they will feel it is their business?
- Have you anticipated the doubts they may have?
- Have you made clear the steps that must be taken?
- Have you demonstrated that your solution to the problem will confer benefits?
- Have you considered other possible solutions to the problem before rejecting them in favor of your own?
- Have you come on as the well-meaning, reasonable writer that you are, one willing to admit, "I don't know everything"?

• Have you made a reasonable claim, not promised that your solution will do more than it can possibly do? Have you made believable predictions for the success of your plan, not wild ones?

Other Assignments

1. If in Chapter 7 you followed the assignment and took a stand, now write a few additional paragraphs extending the paper you have already written, going on to argue for an action.

2. Write an editorial in which you propose to your town or city officials an innovation you think would benefit the whole community. Here are a few suggestions to get your own thoughts working:

> A drug and alcohol education program in the schools
> A network of bicycle paths
> Conversion of a vacant lot into a park
> After-school programs for children of working parents
> A neighborhood program for crime prevention
> Low- or moderate-income housing
> A drop-in center for old people
> More recreational facilities for teenagers
> Tests of the local water supply
> A law against the dumping of hazardous wastes
> An adult education program

3. Write a letter to your congressional representative or your senator in which you object to some government policy with which you disagree. End your letter with a proposal for righting the wrong that concerns you.

4. Choose from the following list a practice that seems to you to represent an inefficient, unethical, unfair, or morally wrong solution to a problem. In a few paragraphs, give reasons for your objections. Then propose a better solution. (You might prefer not to choose a topic from the list, but let the list prompt you to think of another, different wrong solution.)

FOR GROUP LEARNING
Here is a one-on-one activity. Exchange with some other student the papers you both have written for an assignment in this chapter. Then, instead of writing the brief comments you might ordinarily write on another student's paper, write each other at least a few hundred words of reactions and suggestions. Exchange comments and then sit down together to discuss your experiences. What did you find out about proposing a solution? About writing? About peer editing?

Censorship
Corporal punishment for children
Laboratory experiments on animals
Strip-mining
Surrogate motherhood
State lotteries
The arms buildup

APPLYING WHAT YOU LEARN: SOME USES OF PROPOSALS

In college we often think of a proposal as a specific thing: as a written plan submitted to someone in authority who must approve it before we go ahead. Students embarking on a research project may be required to submit a proposal to an adviser or a committee in which they set forth what they intend to investigate and how they will approach their topic. Students who want academic credit for an internship or permission to carry on independent study often have to write a proposal laying out why they deserve it. Like writers of persuasive essays, they state a claim and supply evidence in its support. Seniors and postgraduates who apply for a grant or fellowship from a federal or private agency have to write proposals that will persuade the agency to support their work or research.

In business, too, proposals for action are often useful: for persuading a prospective customer to buy a product or service, recommending a change in procedure, suggesting a new project, or urging a purchase of new equipment. An office manager might use a proposal as a means to achieve harmony with co-workers: first discussing with the staff a certain problem—poor morale, a conflict between smokers and nonsmokers—and then writing a proposal to outline the solution on which the group has agreed. Copies of the proposal are given to the people who agreed on it so they can put it into action.

Throughout this chapter, we have looked at proposals as more general than plans in need of okaying. We have seen them as any arguments with which we try to influence readers to act on our ideas or, at the very least, to agree with them. Most of us have ideas for doing something more effectively than it has been done in the past, for improving a situation in which we discern some annoying fault, for abolishing a practice that strikes us as unfair or outmoded. We are often given opportunities, in college and beyond, to propose a solution to a problem. Sometimes we're given such an opportunity when we answer a question on an exam or when we are assigned to write a paper arguing for an action. "How can environmentalists change people's attitudes and therefore their actions toward the natural world?" "What suggestions can you make to alleviate the plight of women who want to work but cannot afford day care for their children?"

Thoughtful, imaginative answers to such questions can be the first crucial step toward solving some of the world's knottiest problems. By laying out possible solutions, writers can at the very least encourage fruitful debate. Every day in the world around us, we encounter proposals—on the editorial pages of newspapers and magazines, in books new and old. For example, in this paragraph from an editorial written for a 1979 textbook to urge more funding for research on alternative energy sources, nuclear physicist David Rittenhouse endorses the value and practicality of harnessing the wind:

> As another example of inadequate effort, no one is building a giant windmill. One prototype, built on a limited experimental basis during World War II, fed 1,000 kilowatts into the electricity grid in Vermont. That experiment came just at the dawn of the atomic age and was not followed up, probably because of early rosy hopes for infinite, cheap, and trouble-free nuclear power. Now that those early dreams have faded, it is high time to follow up on wind power development. The potential is enormous—almost limitless. Modern engineering stands ready, without awaiting further research and development, to build large numbers of giant windmills either in the sparsely settled parts of the Great Plains or offshore near the edge of the continental shelf, where they will bother almost no one. They can generate hydrogen to be stored and provide a steady source of power. The immediate need is for a few million dollars to build the first full-scale prototypes to convince decision makers that thousands of windmills would provide as much power as the nuclear plants that are being proposed.

Sometimes an entire article, essay, or other document is devoted to arguing for an action. In other cases, a writer's chief purpose may be to explain something or perhaps to express an opinion. Such an article can *end* with a proposal, a call to action. Carl Sagan, David Duncan Professor of Astronomy and Space Sciences at Cornell University, in an article for the September 1985 issue of *Discover,* gives his reasons for believing that the Strategic Defense Initiative (nicknamed Star Wars), proposed by the Reagan administration in 1983, will not work. Near the end of his article, Sagan proposes an alternative.

> But if strategic defense isn't the solution, what is? The only alternative for the U.S. and the U.S.S.R. is to act in what is clearly their mutual interest: to negotiate both a moratorium on the development and deployment of new nuclear weapons systems and to make massive, bilateral, and verifiable reductions in the present nuclear arsenals. Because the arsenals are so bloated—a single American missile-carrying submarine can destroy 192 Soviet cities—deep cuts can be made without compromising strategic deterrence. This is a task that does not require, as Star Wars does, a whole series of technological breakthroughs; it requires only political will. The two nations can take major steps now and create a climate for subsequent joint action to reduce the peril in which they have placed our species.

Like many proposals that you will read during your college years and beyond, Sagan's is controversial. Whether Sagan persuades or fails to persuade his readers, he performs a useful service. By giving us a thoughtful proposal on this crucial issue, he challenges us to think, too.

In time, some calls to action that at first are controversial become generally accepted. This has certainly been true of Dr. Elisabeth Kübler-Ross's views about how dying patients and their loved ones ought to be treated. Before she wrote her landmark book *On Death and Dying* (1969), terminally ill patients in hospitals were seldom told when they were close to death, and little was done to help them die with dignity. Their families felt uncomfortable about the silences and deceptions imposed on the dying. After studying the problem, Kübler-Ross evolved a number of suggestions that would ease a patient's transition into death—easing pain for the caregivers as well as for the patient. Among them is this one.

> There is a time in a patient's life when the pain ceases to be, when the mind slips off into a dreamless state, when the need for food becomes minimal and the awareness of the environment all but disappears into darkness. This is the time when the relatives walk up and down the hospital hallways, tormented by the waiting, not knowing if they should leave to attend the living or stay to be around for the moment of death. This is the time when it is too late for words, and yet the time when the relatives cry the loudest for help—with or without words. It is too late for medical interventions (and too cruel, though well meant, when they do occur), but it is also too early for a final separation from the dying. It is the hardest time for the next of kin as he either wishes to take off, to get it over with; or he desperately clings to something that he is in the process of losing forever. It is the time for the therapy of silence with the patient and availability for the relatives.
>
> The doctor, nurse, social worker, or chaplain can be of great help during these final moments if they can understand the family's conflicts at this time and help select the one person who feels most comfortable staying with the dying patient. This person then becomes in effect the patient's therapist. Those who feel too uncomfortable can be assisted by alleviating their guilt and by the reassurance that someone will stay with the dying until his death has occurred. They can then return home knowing that the patient did not die alone, yet not feeling ashamed or guilty for having avoided this moment which for many people is so difficult to face.

At their best, like Kübler-Ross's pioneering recommendations for facing death and dying, proposals are often the advance guard that comes before useful action.

Two Psychologists Make a Proposal

Clinical psychologist Edward Teyber and developmental psychologist Charles D. Hoffman, two professors at California State University, San Bernardino, published the following essay in April 1987 in *Psychology Today*. In it they not only define a contemporary problem—the frequent absence of divorced fathers from their children's lives—but also propose fresh solutions.

MISSING FATHERS
Edward Teyber and Charles D. Hoffman

The shared act of conception entitles children to both a mother and a father. In an unspoken tragedy, however, the natural birthright to two parents is lost to most children in the aftermath of divorce. In nine of ten cases of divorce, mothers take primary physical custody of the children, and the restriction of fathers' visits to every other weekend is still commonplace. In the years following divorce, fathers tend to see less and less of their children: some estimates suggest that about half of all divorced fathers have no regularly scheduled contact with their children, and about three out of four see their children less than once a week.

Social critics, witnessing this massive abandonment of responsibility, have tended to blame fathers exclusively, charging that they are simply too selfish and uncaring to follow through on their childrearing obligations. At times this is true, and it is distressing indeed when fathers give up on parenting. But there is far more to understanding this complex social problem than a simple, one-sided blaming of men. Divorced fathers who do want to take an active parenting role face formidable, though often unrecognized, obstacles.

There are two major reasons why many divorced fathers are absent from their children's lives. First, they tend not to be involved because our society's inadequate sex role prescriptions for both men and women lead to competing power bases within the family. Many parents still believe that children "belong" more to their mothers than to their fathers, even though there is no empirical evidence that women are better suited for childrearing than men. Mothers are presumed to be the "real" parent, the nurturant parent, while the father's role is limited to financial support and, perhaps, discipline. As a result of this, most fathers are not prepared to take on an active parenting role at the time of divorce. Although women's sex roles have expanded over the past decade to include success in the work world, there has not been a corresponding expansion of men's traditional roles to include competent and committed child care.

Mothering was institutionalized in the early 1900s by the Industrial Revolution, which established mutually exclusive and competing power bases in the family. While fathers have wielded much more power in the work world, mothers have held an equal but more covert power base in the realm of child care. But men's resistance to women's achievement in the work world has been more fully articulated than women's corresponding concerns over men's equal parenting status. Sure, many mothers would like to have their husbands change more diapers and fix more lunches. Fewer mothers, however, really want their children to be as emotionally close to their fathers as to themselves. Most of us continue to suffer the effects of these sex-role inadequacies, and that will change only when a future generation relinquishes these competing power bases. Mothers must support—indeed, insist on—fathers' equal involvement in parenting, just as men must support women's equality outside the home.

The second cause for divorced fathers' lack of involvement with their children is continuing conflict with the children's mothers. In Euripides' version of the classic Greek myth *Medea*, Jason leaves Medea for a beautiful young princess. Contemplating the ultimate revenge, Medea swears, "He shall never see alive again the sons he had from me . . . this is the way to deal Jason the deepest wound." The breakup of a modern marriage often arouses bitterness and distrust between ex-spouses that do not end with the divorce decree, and the mother's primary means of venting her bitterness is to align the children with her against their father. Responding in kind, many fathers retaliate by withholding financial support. 5

In many divorcing families, both mothers and fathers embroil the children in their continuing conflicts by pressuring them to take sides. They create "loyalty conflicts," either by being overtly angry and disparaging, or subtly sad and hurt when children wish to be close to the other parent. Unfortunately, few children of divorce have unencumbered permission from both parents to be equally involved with the other parent. 6

The mother is usually the primary caretaker before the divorce, and as a rule children live with her afterwards. As a result, children tend to be closer to their mothers than to their fathers. When subtly pressured to choose between their parents, most children's emotional allegiance goes to their mothers. In this way, the father's continuing involvement requires, in effect, his former wife's permission. Feeling powerless and controlled in this situation, many a father simply departs, abandoning parenting altogether. 7

Many mothers and fathers seem untroubled by divorced fathers' absence from parenting. Although there has been increased pressure recently to force fathers' compliance with child support and alimony payments, there appears to be little corresponding interest in involving fathers personally with their children. Ironically, one of the strongest determinants of a child's healthy adjustment to divorce is the extent of the father's continued participation as a parent. Children of divorce suffer socially, emotionally, and intellectually when their fathers are not actively involved as parents. They appear to internalize responsibility for the father's departure and suffer a precipitous loss of self-esteem and initiative that is reflected in depression, poor school performance and failure in peer relationships. Adolescent girls offer an especially poignant example: when their fathers are not around, they are more likely than girls with an available father to become sexually promiscuous. They have sex at an earlier age and with more partners, and they are more likely to marry young, to find their own marriage unsatisfying, and eventually to divorce themselves. 8

Furthermore, boys at every age suffer more from divorce than do girls— in part because they usually live with their mothers and have little time with their same-sex parent. Divorce is also more problematic for boys because mothers tend to be more critical and angry toward their sons than their 9 daughters, and when the father is absent mothers discipline daughters more effectively than sons. Research also suggests that when shared parenting arrangements are not workable, boys adjust better in the custody of their father, girls better in mother's custody. The best adjusted children of divorce, however, have frequent access, without conflict, to both parents.

Currently, about one million children experience a parental divorce every year. What can be done to help provide these children with both the fathering and mothering they continue to need? The first thing is to stop assigning blame. If you ask divorced mothers why fathers are uninvolved in parenting, the typical reply is, "I've done everything I can to keep him involved with the kids, but he doesn't want anything to do with them. He never has. The kids don't really want to visit him either. They only go because I tell them they must. Actually, they would rather be home with their friends." 10

In sharp contrast, if you ask divorced fathers why they are disengaged, they predictably respond, "She makes it really hard for me to be with the children. It's little things—like being late whenever I go to pick them up. I don't think she ever really wanted me to have my own relationship with the kids. She believes, like she told the judge, that 'children just ought to be with their mothers.' " Fathers also complain about pressure from their new wives, who often resent the money and attention the children receive. 11

Both sides have legitimate concerns, of course, but these radically differing viewpoints really reflect poor communication between angry ex-spouses. Polarized arguments over mothers' and fathers' rights and responsibilities must cease. The only solution is for children of divorce to have a dependable relationship with both parents—one allowing for frequent, regularly scheduled, and conflict-free access to both mother and father. There are many practical ways to achieve this. 12

Both divorcing parents must realize that the most loving gift they can give their children is permission to be as close to the other parent as to themselves. Parents need to disentangle their own lingering hostility from the child's need for a continuing relationship with the other parent. Grandparents can help by not taking sides against their former son- or daughter-in-law and instead discouraging both parents from embroiling children in parental battles and wrenching loyalty conflicts. Friends can support the father's identity as a parent by emphasizing both the importance of his contribution to his children's lives and the importance of his children to the quality of his life. A new woman in a man's life needs to support his efforts to remain involved with his children and not interpret his commitment as a threat. Therapists must help divorcing parents make concrete plans for custody and visitation, beginning at the time of separation, that ensure the father's active participation. Family lawyers must discourage litigious parents from fighting over children in court; rather, they should take an active role in impressing upon clients that whenever only one parent wins custody or visitation rights are limited, it is the children who lose. Judges must 13 examine their own sexist biases and discard the "tender years" doctrine and other myths about the primacy of motherhood. Instead, they must routinely decide on joint legal custody so that, by law, children belong equally to their mothers and their fathers. And visitation schedules should be written to guarantee equal participation of fathers and mothers in parenting. In cases where the father prefers to let the mother have primary physical custody, judges must provide visitation schedules that include overnight stays with the father every week.

Many fathers recognize, and welcome, their continuing responsibility 14 to care for their children following divorce. Yet without concerted efforts such as these, most divorced fathers simply will not take on an effective parenting role on their own. It is time to work together and ensure that all children can have both a mother and a father in the aftermath of divorce.

Questions to Start You Thinking

1. According to the authors, what are the reasons for the absence of many divorced fathers from the lives of their children?

2. What appears to be the authors' purpose for writing this essay? How completely do they fulfill it?

3. Sum up the authors' proposals. Are they worth considering? Are they realistic? Discuss.

4. Come up with some proposals of your own to solve the problem this essay deals with. How might your ideas be implemented? How can you convince others that your proposal would be worth implementing?

A Physician Makes a Proposal

The following essay, first published in the *New York Times Magazine,* grew out of a talk delivered at a scientific conference. Lewis Thomas is a distinguished physician, researcher, educator, and medical administrator who since 1984 has been president emeritus of the prestigious Memorial Sloan-Kettering Cancer Center in New York City. Thomas is also an engaging and thought-provoking writer of articles both in scientific journals and in three collections of essays. Clearly what he loves most about science are its unsolved mysteries.

THE ART OF TEACHING SCIENCE
Lewis Thomas

Everyone seems to agree that there is something wrong with the way 1 science is being taught these days. But no one is at all clear about when it went wrong or what is to be done about it. The term "scientific illiteracy" has become almost a cliché in educational circles. Graduate schools blame the colleges; colleges blame the secondary schools; the high schools blame the elementary schools, which, in turn, blame the family.

I suggest that the scientific community itself is partly, perhaps largely, to blame. Moreover, if there are disagreements between the world of the humanities and the scientific enterprise as to the place and importance of science in a liberal arts education and the role of science in twentieth-century culture, I believe that the scientists are themselves responsible for a general misunderstanding of what they are really up to.

During the last half-century, we have been teaching the sciences as though they were the same collection of academic subjects as always, and—here is what has really gone wrong—as though they would always be the same. Students learn today's biology, for example, the same way we learned Latin when I was in high school long ago: first, the fundamentals; then, the underlying laws; next, the essential grammar and, finally, the reading of texts. Once mastered, that was that: Latin was Latin and forever after would always be Latin. History, once learned, was history. And biology was precisely biology, a vast array of hard facts to be learned as fundamentals, followed by a reading of the texts.

Furthermore, we have been teaching science as if its facts were somehow superior to the facts in all other scholarly disciplines—more fundamental, more solid, less subject to subjectivism, immutable. English literature is not just one way of thinking; it is all sorts of ways; poetry is a moving target; the facts that underlie art, architecture, and music are not really hard facts, and you can change them any way you like by arguing about them. But science, it appears, is an altogether different kind of learning; an unambiguous, unalterable, and endlessly useful display of data that only needs to be packaged and installed somewhere in one's temporal lobe in order to achieve a full understanding of the natural world.

And, of course, it is not like this at all. In real life, every field of science is incomplete, and most of them—whatever the record of accomplishment during the last two hundred years—are still in their very earliest stages. In the fields I know best, among the life sciences, it is required that the most expert and sophisticated minds be capable of changing course—often with a great lurch—every few years. In some branches of biology the mind-changing is occurring with accelerating velocity. Next week's issue of any scientific journal can turn a whole field upside down, shaking out any number of immutable ideas and installing new bodies of dogma. This is an almost everyday event in physics, in chemistry, in materials research, in neurobiology, in genetics, in immunology.

On any Tuesday morning, if asked, a good working scientist will tell you with some self-satisfaction that the affairs of his field are nicely in order, that things are finally looking clear and making sense, and all is well. But come back again on another Tuesday, and the roof may have just fallen in on his life's work. All the old ideas—last week's ideas in some cases—are no longer good ideas. The hard facts have softened, melted away and vanished under the pressure of new hard facts. Something strange has happened. And it is this very strangeness of nature that makes science engrossing, that keeps bright people at it, and that ought to be at the center of science teaching.

The conclusions reached in science are always, when looked at closely, 7 far more provisional and tentative than are most of the assumptions arrived at by our colleagues in the humanities. But we do not talk much in public about this, nor do we teach this side of science. We tend to say instead: These are the facts of the matter, and this is what the facts signify. Go and learn them, for they will be the same forever.

By doing this, we miss opportunity after opportunity to recruit young 8 people into science, and we turn off a good many others who would never dream of scientific careers but who emerge from their education with the impression that science is fundamentally boring.

Sooner or later, we will have to change this way of presenting science. 9 We might begin by looking more closely at the common ground that science shares with all disciplines, particularly with the humanities and with social and behavioral science. For there is indeed such a common ground. It is called bewilderment. There are more than seven times seven types of ambiguity in science, all awaiting analysis. The poetry of Wallace Stevens is crystal clear alongside the genetic code.

One of the complaints about science is that it tends to flatten every- 10 thing. In its deeply reductionist way, it is said, science removes one mystery after another, leaving nothing in the place of mystery but data. I have even heard this claim as explanation for the drift of things in modern art and modern music: nothing is left to contemplate except randomness and senselessness; God is nothing but a pair of dice, loaded at that. Science is linked somehow to the despair of the twentieth-century mind. There is almost nothing unknown and surely nothing unknowable. Blame science.

I prefer to turn things around in order to make precisely the opposite 11 case. Science, especially twentieth-century science, has provided us with a glimpse of something we never really knew before, the revelation of human ignorance. We have been accustomed to the belief, from one century to another, that except for one or two mysteries we more or less comprehend everything on earth. Every age, not just the eighteenth century, regarded itself as the Age of Reason, and we have never lacked for explanations of the world and its ways. Now, we are being brought up short. We do not understand much of anything, from the episode we rather dismissively (and, I think, defensively) choose to call the "big bang," all the way down to the particles in the atoms of a bacterial cell. We have a wilderness of mystery to make our way through in the centuries ahead. We will need science for this but not science alone. In its own time, science will produce the data and some of the meaning in the data, but never the full meaning. For perceiving real significance when significance is at hand, we will need all sorts of brains outside the fields of science.

It is primarily because of this need that I would press for changes in 12
the way science is taught. Although there is a perennial need to teach the
young people who will be doing the science themselves, this will always be
a small minority. Even more important, we must teach science to those
who will be needed for thinking about it, and that means pretty nearly
everyone else—most of all, the poets, but also artists, musicians, philosophers, historians, and writers. A few of these people, at least, will be able
to imagine new levels of meaning which may be lost on the rest of us.

In addition, it is time to develop a new group of professional thinkers, 13
perhaps a somewhat larger group than the working scientists and the working poets, who can create a discipline of scientific criticism. We have had
good luck so far in the emergence of a few people ranking as philosophers
of science and historians and journalists of science, and I hope more of
these will be coming along. But we have not yet seen specialists in the
fields of scientific criticism who are of the caliber of the English literary
and social critics F. R. Leavis and John Ruskin or the American literary critic
Edmund Wilson. Science needs critics of this sort, but the public at large
needs them more urgently.

I suggest that the introductory courses in science, at all levels from 14
grade school through college, be radically revised. Leave the fundamentals,
the so-called basics, aside for a while, and concentrate the attention of all
students on the things that are not known. You cannot possibly teach quantum mechanics without mathematics, to be sure, but you can describe the
strangeness of the world opened up by quantum theory. Let it be known,
early on, that there are deep mysteries and profound paradoxes revealed
in distant outline by modern physics. Explain that these can be approached
more closely and puzzled over, once the language of mathematics has been
sufficiently mastered.

At the outset, before any of the fundamentals, teach the still impon- 15
derable puzzles of cosmology. Describe as clearly as possible, for the
youngest minds, that there are some things going on in the universe that
lie still beyond comprehension, and make it plain how little is known.

Do not teach that biology is a useful and perhaps profitable science; 16
that can come later. Teach instead that there are stuctures squirming inside
each of our cells that provide all the energy for living. Essentially foreign
creatures, these lineal descendants of bacteria were brought in for symbiotic living a billion or so years ago. Teach that we do not have the ghost
of an idea how they got there, where they came from, or how they evolved
to their present structure and function. The details of oxidative phospho-
rylation and photosynthesis can come later.

Teach ecology early on. Let it be understood that the earth's life is a 17
system of interdependent creatures, and that we do not understand at all
how it works. The earth's environment, from the range of atmospheric gases
to the chemical constituents of the sea, has been held in an almost un-
believably improbable state of regulated balance since life began, and the

regulation of stability and balance is somehow accomplished by the life itself, like the autonomic nervous system of an immense organism. We do not know how such a system works, much less what it means, but there are some nice reductionist details at hand, such as the bizarre proportions of atmospheric constituents, ideal for our sort of planetary life, and the surprising stability of the ocean's salinity, and the fact that the average temperature of the earth has remained quite steady in the face of at least a 25 percent increase in heat coming in from the sun since the earth began. That kind of thing: something to think about.

18   Go easy, I suggest, on the promises freely offered by science. Technology relies and depends on science these days, more than ever before, but technology is far from the first justification for doing research, nor is it necessarily an essential product to be expected from science. Public decisions about the future of technology are totally different from decisions about science, and the two enterprises should not be tangled together. The central task of science is to arrive, stage by stage, at a clearer comprehension of nature, but this does not at all mean, as it is sometimes claimed to mean, a search for mastery over nature.

19   Science may someday provide us with a better understanding of ourselves, but never, I hope, with a set of technologies for doing something or other to improve ourselves. I am made nervous by assertions that human consciousness will someday be unraveled by research, laid out for close scrutiny like the workings of a computer, and then—and *then* . . . ! I hope with some fervor that we can learn a lot more than we now know about the human mind, and I see no reason why this strange puzzle should remain forever and entirely beyond us. But I would be deeply disturbed by any prospect that we might use the new knowledge in order to begin doing something about it—to improve it, say. This is a different matter from searching for information to use against schizophrenia or dementia, where we are badly in need of technologies, indeed likely one day to be sunk without them. But the ordinary, everyday, more or less normal human mind is too marvelous an instrument ever to be tampered with by anyone, science or no science.

20   The education of humanists cannot be regarded as complete, or even adequate, without exposure in some depth to where things stand in the various branches of science, particularly, as I have said, in the areas of our ignorance. Physics professors, most of them, look with revulsion on assignments to teach their subject to poets. Biologists, caught up by the enchantment of their new power, armed with flawless instruments to tell the nucleotide sequences of the entire human genome, nearly matching the physicists in the precision of their measurements of living processes, will resist the prospect of broad survey courses; each biology professor will demand that any student in his path master every fine detail within that professor's research program.

The liberal arts faculties, for their part, will continue to view the scientists with suspicion and apprehension. "What do the scientists want?" asked a Cambridge professor in Francis Cornford's wonderful "Microcosmographia Academica." "Everything that's going," was the quick answer. That was back in 1912, and scientists haven't much changed.

But maybe, just maybe, a new set of courses dealing systematically with ignorance in science will take hold. The scientists might discover in it a new and subversive technique for catching the attention of students driven by curiosity, delighted and surprised to learn that science is exactly as the American scientist and educator Vannevar Bush described it: an "endless frontier." The humanists, for their part, might take considerable satisfaction in watching their scientific colleagues confess openly to not knowing everything about everything. And the poets, on whose shoulders the future rests, might, late nights, thinking things over, begin to see some meanings that elude the rest of us. It is worth a try.

I believe that the worst thing that has happened to science education is that the fun has gone out of it. A great many good students look at it as slogging work to be got through on the way to medical school. Others are turned off by the premedical students themselves, embattled and bleeding for grades and class standing. Very few recognize science as the high adventure it really is, the wildest of all explorations ever taken by human beings, the chance to glimpse things never seen before, the shrewdest maneuver for discovering how the world works. Instead, baffled early on, they are misled into thinking that bafflement is simply the result of not having learned all the facts. They should be told that everyone else is baffled as well—from the professor in his endowed chair down to the platoons of postdoctoral students in the laboratories all night. Every important scientific advance that has come in looking like an answer has turned, sooner or later—usually sooner—into a question. And the game is just beginning.

If more students were aware of this, I think many of them would decide to look more closely and to try and learn more about what *is* known. That is the time when mathematics will become clearly and unavoidably recognizable as an essential, indispensable instrument for engaging in the game, and that is the time for teaching it. The calamitous loss of applied mathematics from what we might otherwise be calling higher education is a loss caused, at least in part, by insufficient incentives for learning the subject. Left by itself, standing there among curriculum offerings, it is not at all clear to the student what it is to be applied to. And there is all of science, next door, looking like an almost-finished field reserved only for chaps who want to invent or apply new technology. We have had it wrong, and presented it wrong to class after class for several generations.

An appreciation of what is happening in science today, and how great a distance lies ahead for exploring, ought to be one of the rewards of a liberal arts education. It ought to be good in itself, not something to be acquired on the way to a professional career but part of the cast of thought needed for getting into the kind of century that is now just down the road. Part of the intellectual equipment of an educated person, however his or her time is to be spent, ought to be a feel for the queernesses of nature, the inexplicable thing, the side of life for which informed bewilderment will be the best way of getting through the day.

Questions to Start You Thinking

1. What faults does the author find with the way science is taught? Whom does he blame?

2. List the parts of Thomas's proposal. Which seem to you the most original or surprising?

3. In paragraph 22 Thomas the scientist speaks not of scientists but of poets as those "on whose shoulders the future rests." What do you understand from this remark?

4. What areas of your own expertise can you tap for proposals to reform the way something is now done?

CHAPTER 9

Evaluating

Evaluating means judging. You do it when you decide what candidate to vote for, when you pick which camera to buy from among several on the market, when you watch a game and size up a team's prowess. All of us find ourselves passing judgments continually, as we move through a day's routine.

Often, in everyday situations, we make quick snap judgments. A friend asks, "How was that movie you saw last night?" and you reply, "Terrific—don't miss it," or maybe, "Pretty good, but it had too much bloodletting for me." Those off-the-cuff opinions are necessary and useful. But to *write* an evaluation calls on a person to think more critically. Sometimes the writer first decides on *criteria*, or standards for judging, and practically always comes up with evidence to back up any judgment.

A written evaluation zeroes in on a definite subject. You inspect the subject carefully and come to a considered opinion. The subject might be a film, a book, a piece of music, a sports team, a group of performers, a concert, a product, a scientific theory, a body of research—the possibilities are wide.

LEARNING FROM OTHER WRITERS

Here are two good evaluations, the first by a professional writer.

The man who gave the world *Tom Sawyer* and *Huckleberry Finn* here casts a cold eye on the work of James Fenimore Cooper (1789–1851), the first and foremost American novelist to try to capture the vanishing frontier.

Cooper's Leatherstocking Tales (*The Pioneers, The Last of the Mohicans, The Prairie, The Pathfinder,* and *The Deerslayer*), recounting the adventures of woodsman Natty Bumppo and his Indian companion Chingachgook, reached a vast audience. You don't have to know Cooper's works to appreciate Twain's devastating (if unfair) case against him. Whatever Twain condemns, he will carefully illustrate.

FENIMORE COOPER'S LITERARY OFFENSES
Mark Twain

The Pathfinder and *The Deerslayer* stand at the head of Cooper's novels as artistic creations. There are others of his works which contain parts as perfect as are to be found in these, and scenes even more thrilling. Not one can be compared with either of them as a finished whole.

The defects in both of these tales are comparatively slight. They were pure works of art.—*Prof. Lounsbury*

The five tales reveal an extraordinary fullness of invention.

. . . One of the very greatest characters in fiction, Natty Bumppo. . . .

The craft of the woodsman, the tricks of the trapper, all the delicate art of the forest, were familiar to Cooper from his youth up.—*Prof. Brander Matthews*

Cooper is the greatest artist in the domain of romantic fiction yet produced by America. —*Wilkie Collins*

1   It seems to me that it was far from right for the Professor of English Literature in Yale, the Professor of English Literature in Columbia, and Wilkie Collins to deliver opinions on Cooper's literature without having read some of it. It would have been much more decorous to keep silent and let persons talk who have read Cooper.

2   Cooper's art has some defects. In one place in *Deerslayer*, and in the restricted space of two-thirds of a page, Cooper has scored 114 offenses against literary art out of a possible 115. It breaks the record.

3   There are nineteen rules governing literary art in the domain of romantic fiction—some say twenty-two. In *Deerslayer* Cooper violated eighteen of them. These eighteen require:

1. That a tale shall accomplish something and arrive somewhere. But the *Deerslayer* tale accomplishes nothing and arrives in the air.

2. They require that the episodes of a tale shall be necessary parts of the tale and shall help to develop it. But as the *Deerslayer* tale is not a tale and accomplishes nothing and arrives nowhere, the episodes have no rightful place in the work, since there was nothing for them to develop.

3. They require that the personages in a tale shall be alive, except in the case of corpses, and that always the reader shall be able to tell the corpses from the others. But this detail has often been overlooked in the *Deerslayer* tale.

4. They require that the personages in a tale, both dead and alive, shall exhibit a sufficient excuse for being there. But this detail also has been overlooked in the *Deerslayer* tale.

5. They require that when the personages of a tale deal in conversation, the talk shall sound like human talk, and be talk such as human beings would be likely to talk in the given circumstances, and have a discoverable meaning, also a discoverable purpose and a show of relevancy, and remain in the neighborhood of the subject in hand, and be interesting to the reader, and help out the tale, and stop when the people cannot think of anything more to say. But this requirement has been ignored from the beginning of the *Deerslayer* tale to the end of it.

6. They require that when the author describes the character of a personage in his tale, the conduct and conversation of that personage shall justify said description. But this law gets little or no attention in the *Deerslayer* tale, as Natty Bumppo's case will amply prove.

7. They require that when a personage talks like an illustrated, gilt-edged, tree-calf, hand-tooled, seven-dollar Friendship's Offering in the beginning of a paragraph, he shall not talk like a Negro minstrel in the end of it. But this rule is flung down and danced upon in the *Deerslayer* tale.

8. They require that crass stupidities shall not be played upon the reader as "the craft of the woodsman, the delicate art of the forest," by either the author or the people in the tale. But this rule is persistently violated in the *Deerslayer* tale.

9. They require that the personages of a tale shall confine themselves to possibilities and let miracles alone; or, if they venture a miracle, the author must so plausibly set it forth as to make it look possible and reasonable. But these rules are not respected in the *Deerslayer* tale.

10. They require that the author shall make the reader feel a deep interest in the personages of his tale and in their fate, and that he shall make the reader love the good people in the tale and hate the bad ones. But the reader of the *Deerslayer* tale dislikes the good people in it, is indifferent to the others, and wishes they would all get drowned together.

11. They require that the characters in a tale shall be so clearly defined that the reader can tell beforehand what each will do in a given emergency. But in the *Deerslayer* tale this rule is vacated.

In addition to these large rules there are some little ones. These require   4
that the author shall

12. *Say* what he is proposing to say, not merely come near it.

13. Use the right word, not its second cousin.

14. Eschew surplusage.

15. Not omit necessary details.

16. Avoid slovenliness of form.

17. Use good grammar.

18. Employ a simple and straightforward style.

Even these seven are coldly and persistently violated in the *Deerslayer* 5 tale.

Cooper's gift in the way of invention was not a rich endowment but such 6 as it was he liked to work it, he was pleased with the effects, and indeed he did some quite sweet things with it. In his little box of stage-properties he kept six or eight cunning devices, tricks, artifices for his savages and woodsmen to deceive and circumvent each other with, and he was never so happy as when he was working these innocent things and seeing them go. A favorite one was to make a moccasined person tread in the tracks of the moccasined enemy, and thus hide his own trail. Cooper wore out barrels and barrels of moccasins in working that trick. Another stage-property that he pulled out of his box pretty frequently was his broken twig. He prized his broken twig above all the rest of his effects, and worked it the hardest. It is a restful chapter in any book of his when somebody doesn't step on a dry twig and alarm all the reds and whites for two hundred yards around. Every time a Cooper person is in peril and absolute silence is worth four dollars a minute, he is sure to step on a dry twig. There may be a hundred handier things to step on but that wouldn't satisfy Cooper. Cooper requires him to turn out and find a dry twig, and if he can't do it, go and borrow one. In fact, the Leatherstocking Series ought to have been called the Broken Twig Series.

I am sorry there is not room to put in a few dozen instances of the 7 delicate art of the forest, as practiced by Natty Bumppo and some of the other Cooperian experts. Perhaps we may venture two or three samples. Cooper was a sailor, a naval officer; yet he gravely tells us how a vessel, driving toward a lee shore in a gale, is steered for a particular spot by her skipper because he knows of an *undertow* there which will hold her back against the gale and save her. For just pure woodcraft, or sailorcraft, or whatever it is, isn't that neat? For several years Cooper was daily in the society of artillery and he ought to have noticed that when a cannon-ball strikes the ground it either buries itself or skips a hundred feet or so, skips again a hundred feet or so, and so on till finally it gets tired and rolls. Now in one place he loses some "females"—as he always calls women—in the edge of a wood near a plain at night in a fog, on purpose to give Bumppo a chance to show off the delicate art of the forest before the reader. These mislaid people are hunting for a fort. They hear a cannon-blast, and a cannon-ball presently comes rolling into the wood and stops at their feet. To the females this suggests nothing. The case is very different with the admirable Bumppo. I wish I may never know peace again if he doesn't strike out promptly and follow the track of that cannon-ball across the plain through the dense fog and find the fort. Isn't it a daisy? If Cooper had any real knowledge of Nature's ways of doing things, he had a most delicate art in concealing the fact. For instance: one of his acute Indian experts, Chingachgook (pronounced Chicago, I think), has lost the trail of a person he is tracking through the forest. Apparently that trail is hopelessly lost. Neither you nor I could ever have guessed out the way to find it. It was very different with Chicago. Chicago was not stumped for long. He turned a running stream out of its course and there, in the slush in its old bed, were that person's moccasin tracks. The current did not wash them away, as it would have done in all other like cases—no, even the eternal laws of Nature have to vacate when Cooper wants to put up a delicate job of woodcraft on the reader.

We must be a little wary when Brander Matthews tells us that Cooper's 8 books "reveal an extraordinary fullness of invention." As a rule, I am quite willing to accept Brander Matthews's literary judgments and applaud his lucid and graceful phrasing of them, but that particular statement needs to be taken with a few tons of salt. Bless your heart, Cooper hadn't any more invention than a horse, and I don't mean a high-class horse, either, I mean a clotheshorse. It would be very difficult to find a really clever "situation" in Cooper's books, and still more difficult to find one of any kind which he has failed to render absurd by his handling of it. Look at the episodes of "the caves"; and at the celebrated scuffle between Maqua and those others on the tableland a few days later; and at Hurry Harry's queer water-transit from the castle to the ark; and at Deerslayer's half-hour with his first corpse; and at the quarrel between Hurry Harry and Deerslayer later; and at—but choose for yourself, you can't go amiss.

If Cooper had been an observer his inventive faculty would have worked 9 better: not more interestingly but more rationally, more plausibly. Cooper's proudest creations in the way of "situations" suffer noticeably from the absence of the observer's protecting gift. Cooper's eye was splendidly in-accurate. Cooper seldom saw anything correctly. He saw nearly all things as through a glass eye, darkly. Of course a man who cannot see the com-monest little everyday matters accurately is working at a disadvantage when he is constructing a "situation." In the *Deerslayer* tale Cooper has a stream which is fifty feet wide where it flows out of a lake; it presently narrows to twenty as it meanders along for no given reason, and yet when a stream acts like that it ought to be required to explain itself. Fourteen pages later the width of the brook's outlet from the lake has suddenly shrunk thirty feet and become "the narrowest part of the stream." This shrinkage is not ac-counted for. The stream has bends in it, a sure indication that it has alluvial banks and cuts them, yet these bends are only thirty and fifty feet long. If Cooper had been a nice and punctilious observer he would have noticed that the bends were oftener nine hundred feet long than short of it.

Cooper made the exit of that stream fifty feet wide in the first place for 10 no particular reason; in the second place, he narrowed it to less than twenty to accommodate some Indians. He bends a "sapling" to the form of an arch over this narrow passage and conceals six Indians in its foliage. They are "laying" for a settler's scow or ark which is coming up the stream on its way to the lake; it is being hauled against the stiff current by a rope whose stationary end is anchored in the lake; its rate of progress cannot be more than a mile an hour. Cooper describes the ark, but pretty obscurely. In the matter of dimensions "it was little more than a modern canal-boat."

Let us guess, then, that it was about one hundred and forty feet long. It was of "greater breadth than common." Let us guess, then, that it was about sixteen feet wide. This leviathan had been prowling down bends which were but a third as long as itself and scraping between banks where it had only two feet of space to spare on each side. We cannot too much admire this miracle. A low-roofed log dwelling occupies "two-thirds of the ark's length"—a dwelling ninety feet long and sixteen feet wide, let us say, a kind of vestibule train. The dwelling has two rooms, each forty-five feet long and sixteen feet wide, let us guess. One of them is the bedroom of the Hutter girls, Judith and Hetty; the other is the parlor in the daytime, at night it is papa's bed-chamber. The ark is arriving at the stream's exit now, whose width has been reduced to less than twenty feet to accommodate the Indians—say to eighteen. There is a foot to spare on each side of the boat. Did the Indians notice that there was going to be a tight squeeze there? Did they notice that they could make money by climbing down out of that arched sapling and just stepping aboard when the ark scraped by? No, other Indians would have noticed these things but Cooper's Indians never notice anything. Cooper thinks they are marvelous creatures for noticing but he was almost always in error about his Indians. There was seldom a sane one among them.

The ark is one hundred and forty feet long; the dwelling is ninety feet long. The idea of the Indians is to drop softly and secretly from the arched sapling to the dwelling as the ark creeps along under it at the rate of a mile an hour, and butcher the family. It will take the ark a minute and a half to pass under. It will take the ninety-foot dwelling a minute to pass under. Now, then, what did the six Indians do? It would take you thirty years to guess and even then you would have to give up, I believe. Therefore, I will tell you what the Indians did. Their chief, a person of quite extraordinary intellect for a Cooper Indian, warily watched the canal-boat as it squeezed along under him and when he had got his calculations fined down to exactly the right shade, as he judged, he let go and dropped. And *missed the house!* That is actually what he did. He missed the house and landed in the stern of the scow. It was not much of a fall, yet it knocked him silly. He lay there unconscious. If the house had been ninety-seven feet long he would have made the trip. The fault was Cooper's, not his. The error lay in the construction of the house. Cooper was no architect.

There still remained in the roost five Indians. The boat has passed under and is now out of their reach. Let me explain what the five did—you would not be able to reason it out for yourself. No. 1 jumped for the boat but fell in the water astern of it. Then No. 2 jumped for the boat but fell in the water still farther astern of it. Then No. 3 jumped for the boat and fell a good way astern of it. Then No. 4 jumped for the boat and fell in the water *away* astern. Then even No. 5 made a jump for the boat—for he was a Cooper Indian. In the matter of intellect, the difference between a Cooper Indian and the Indian that stands in front of the cigar-shop is not spacious.

The scow episode is really a sublime burst of invention but it does not thrill, because the inaccuracy of the details throws a sort of fictitiousness and general improbability over it. This comes of Cooper's inadequacy as an observer.

The reader will find some examples of Cooper's high talent for inac-   13
curate observation in the account of the shooting-match in *The Pathfinder.*

> A common wrought nail was driven lightly into the target, its head having been first touched with paint.

The color of the paint is not stated—an important omission, but Cooper   14
deals freely in important omissions. No, after all, it was not an important omission, for this nail-head is *a hundred yards from* the marksmen and could not be seen by them at that distance, no matter what its color might be. How far can the best eyes see a common house-fly? A hundred yards? It is quite impossible. Very well, eyes that cannot see a house-fly that is a hundred yards away cannot see an ordinary nail-head at that distance, for the size of the two objects is the same. It takes a keen eye to see a fly or a nail-head at fifty yards—one hundred and fifty feet. Can the reader do it?

The nail was lightly driven, its head painted, and game called. Then   15
the Cooper miracles began. The bullet of the first marksman chipped an edge of the nail-head; the next man's bullet drove the nail a little way into the target—and removed all the paint. Haven't the miracles gone far enough now? Not to suit Cooper, for the purpose of this whole scheme is to show off his prodigy, Deerslayer-Hawkeye-Long-Rifle-Leatherstocking-Pathfinder-Bumppo before the ladies.

> "Be all ready to clench it, boys!" cried out Pathfinder, stepping into his friend's tracks the instant they were vacant. "Never mind a new nail; I can see that, though the paint is gone, and what I can see I can hit at a hundred yards, though it were only a mosquito's eye. Be ready to clench!"
>
> The rifle cracked, the bullet sped its way, and the head of the nail was buried in the wood, covered by the piece of flattened lead.

There, you see, is a man who could hunt flies with a rifle, and command   16
a ducal salary in a Wild West show today if we had him back with us.

The recorded feat is certainly surprising just as it stands, but it is not   17
surprising enough for Cooper. Cooper adds a touch. He has made Pathfinder do this miracle with another man's rifle; and not only that, but Pathfinder did not have even the advantage of loading it himself. He had everything against him, and yet he made that impossible shot, and not only made it but did it with absolute confidence, saying, "Be ready to clench." Now a person like that would have undertaken the same feat with a brickbat, and with Cooper to help he would have achieved it, too.

Pathfinder showed off handsomely that day before the ladies. His very   18
first feat was a thing which no Wild West show can touch. He was standing with the group of marksmen, observing—a hundred yards from the target,

mind; one Jasper raised his rifle and drove the center of the bull's-eye. Then the Quartermaster fired. The target exhibited no result this time. There was a laugh. "It's a dead miss," said Major Lundie. Pathfinder waited an impressive moment or two, then said in that calm, indifferent, know-it-all way of his, "No, Major, he has covered Jasper's bullet, as will be seen if anyone will take the trouble to examine the target."

Wasn't it remarkable! How *could* he see that little pellet fly through the   19 air and enter that distant bullet-hole? Yet that is what he did, for nothing is impossible to a Cooper person. Did any of those people have any deep-seated doubts about this thing? No; for that would imply sanity and these were all Cooper people.

> The respect for Pathfinder's skill and for his *quickness and accuracy of sight* [the italics are mine] was so profound and general, that the instant he made this declaration the spectators began to distrust their own opinions, and a dozen rushed to the target in order to ascertain the fact. There, sure enough, it was found that the Quartermaster's bullet had gone through the hole made by Jasper's, and that, too, so accurately as to require a minute examination to be certain of the circumstance, which, however, was soon clearly established by discovering one bullet over the other in the stump against which the target was placed.

They made a "minute" examination; but never mind, how could they   20 know that there were two bullets in that hole without digging the latest one out? for neither probe nor eyesight could prove the presence of any more than one bullet. Did they dig? No; as we shall see. It is the Pathfinder's turn now; he steps out before the ladies, takes aim, and fires.

But, alas! here is a disappointment, an incredible, an unimaginable   21 disappointment—for the target's aspect is unchanged; there is nothing there but that same old bullet-hole!

> "If one dared to hint at such a thing," cried Major Duncan, "I should say that the Pathfinder has also missed the target!"

As nobody had missed it yet, the "also" was not necessary, but never   22 mind about that for the Pathfinder is going to speak.

> "No, no, Major," said he, confidently, "that *would* be a risky declaration. I didn't load the piece, and can't say what was in it; but if it was lead, you will find the bullet driving down those of the Quartermaster and Jasper, else is not my name Pathfinder."
>
> A shout from the target announced the truth of this assertion.

Is the miracle sufficient as it stands? Not for Cooper. The Pathfinder   23 speaks again, as he "now slowly advances toward the stage occupied by the females":

> "That's not all, boys, that's not all; if you find the target touched at all, I'll own to a miss. The Quartermaster cut the wood, but you'll find no wood cut by that last messenger."

The miracle is at last complete. He knew—doubtless *saw*—at the dis- 24
tance of a hundred yards—that his bullet had passed into the hole *without
fraying the edges*. There were now three bullets in that one hole, three
bullets embedded processionally in the body of the stump back of the
target. Everybody knew this, somehow or other, and yet nobody had dug
any of them out to make sure. Cooper is not a close observer but he is
interesting. He is certainly always that, no matter what happens. And he is
more interesting when he is not noticing what he is about than when he is.
This is a considerable merit.

The conversations in the Cooper books have a curious sound in our 25
modern ears. To believe that such talk really ever came out of people's
mouths would be to believe that there was a time when time was of no
value to a person who thought he had something to say, when it was the
custom to spread a two-minute remark out to ten, when a man's mouth was
a rolling-mill and busied itself all day long in turning four-foot pigs of
thought into thirty-foot bars of conversational railroad iron by attenuation,
when subjects were seldom faithfully stuck to but the talk wandered all
around and arrived nowhere, when conversations consisted mainly of irrel-
evancies with here and there a relevancy, a relevancy with an embarrassed
look, as not being able to explain how it got there.

Cooper was certainly not a master in the construction of dialogue. In- 26
accurate observation defeated him here as it defeated him in so many other
enterprises of his. He even failed to notice that the man who talks corrupt
English six days in the week must and will talk it on the seventh, and can't
help himself. In the *Deerslayer* story he lets Deerslayer talk the showiest
kind of book-talk sometimes, and at other times the basest of base dia-
lects. For instance, when some one asks him if he has a sweetheart, and
if so where she abides, this is his majestic answer:

> "She's in the forest—hanging from the boughs of the trees, in a soft rain—in
> the dew on the open grass—the clouds that float about in the blue heavens—
> the birds that sing in the woods—the sweet springs where I slake my thirst—
> and in all the other glorious gifts that come from God's Providence!"

And he preceded that, a little before, with this:

> "It consarns me as all things that touches a fri'nd consarns a fri'nd."

And this is another of his remarks:

> "If I was Injin born, now, I might tell of this, or carry in the scalp and boast of
> the expl'ite afore the whole tribe; or if my inimy had only been a bear"—[and
> so on].

We cannot imagine such a thing as a veteran Scotch Commander-in- 27
Chief comporting himself in the field like a windy melodramatic actor, but
Cooper could. On one occasion Alice and Cora were being chased by the
French through a fog in the neighborhood of their father's fort:

"Point de quartier aux coquins!" cried an eager pursuer, who seemed to direct the operations of the enemy.

"Stand firm and be ready, my gallant 60ths!" suddenly exclaimed a voice above them; "wait to see the enemy; fire low, and sweep the glacis."

"Father! father," exclaimed a piercing cry from out the mist; "it is I! Alice! thy own Elsie! spare, O! save your daughters!"

"Hold!" shouted the former speaker, in the awful tones of parental agony, the sound reaching even to the woods, and rolling back in solemn echo. " 'Tis she! God has restored me my children! Throw open the sally-port; to the field, 60ths, to the field! pull not a trigger, lest ye kill my lambs! Drive off these dogs of France with your steel!"

Cooper's word-sense was singularly dull. When a person has a poor ear 28
for music he will flat and sharp right along without knowing it. He keeps near the tune, but it is *not* the tune. When a person has a poor ear for words, the result is a literary flatting and sharping; you perceive what he is intending to say but you also perceive that he doesn't *say* it. This is Cooper. He was not a word-musician. His ear was satisfied with the *approximate* word. I will furnish some circumstantial evidence in support of this charge. My instances are gathered from half a dozen pages of the tale called *Deerslayer*. He uses "verbal" for "oral"; "precision" for "facility"; "phenomena" for "marvels"; "necessary" for "predetermined"; "unsophisticated" for "primitive"; "preparation" for "expectancy"; "rebuked" for "subdued"; "dependent on" for "resulting from"; "fact" for "condition"; "fact" for "conjecture"; "precaution" for "caution"; "explain" for "determine"; "mortified" for "disappointed"; "meretricious" for "factitious"; "materially" for "considerably"; "decreasing" for "deepening"; "increasing" for "disappearing"; "embedded" for "inclosed"; "treacherous" for "hostile"; "stood" for "stooped"; "softened" for "replaced"; "rejoined" for "remarked"; "situation" for "condition"; "different" for "differing"; "insensible" for "unsentient"; "brevity" for "celerity"; "distrusted" for "suspicious"; "mental imbecility" for "imbecility"; "eyes" for "sight"; "counteracting" for "opposing"; "funeral obsequies" for "obsequies."

There have been daring people in the world who claimed that Cooper 29
could write English but they are all dead now—all dead but Lounsbury. I don't remember that Lounsbury makes the claim in so many words, still he makes it for he says that *Deerslayer* is a "pure work of art." Pure, in that connection, means faultless—faultless in all details—and language is a detail. If Mr. Lounsbury had only compared Cooper's English with the English which he writes himself—but it is plain that he didn't, and so it is likely that he imagines until this day that Cooper's is as clean and compact as his own. Now I feel sure, deep down in my heart, that Cooper wrote about the poorest English that exists in our language and that the English of *Deerslayer* is the very worst that even Cooper ever wrote.

I may be mistaken, but it does seem to me that *Deerslayer* is not a 30
work of art in any sense; it does seem to me that it is destitute of every

detail that goes to the making of a work of art; in truth, it seems to me that *Deerslayer* is just simply a literary *delirium tremens*.

A work of art? It has no invention; it has no order, system, sequence, or result; it has no lifelikeness, no thrill, no stir, no seeming of reality; its characters are confusedly drawn and by their acts and words they prove that they are not the sort of people the author claims that they are; its humor is pathetic; its pathos is funny; its conversations are—oh! indescribable; its love-scenes odious; its English a crime against the language. 31

Counting these out, what is left is Art. I think we must all admit that. 32

Questions to Start You Thinking

1. For what reason does Twain reject the evaluations by Wilkie Collins and by the two professors? How does he demonstrate his own qualifications to judge Cooper's novels?

2. Describe the tone of Twain's essay. (By *tone* we mean a writer's attitude.) What is the effect of Twain's prefacing his sentence about the character tracking the cannon-ball, "I wish I may never know peace again . . ." (paragraph 7)? of his addressing Brander Matthews, "Bless your heart" (paragraph 8)? of his saying, "There have been daring people in the world who claimed that Cooper could write English but they are all dead now—all dead but Lounsbury (paragraph 29); of his summing up in paragraph 31?

3. Look up the passage about the ark (in Chapter 4 of *The Deerslayer*) and decide for yourself if Twain's criticism is fair or if, in calculating the ark's measurements, Twain is guilty of hairsplitting.

4. What is the allusion in Twain's statement "He saw nearly all things as through a glass eye, darkly" (paragraph 9)?

5. What do you infer to be Twain's purpose in writing his essay? How would you sum it up?

In a lively paper written for a composition class, Matthew Munich examines a familiar form of entertainment and gives his opinion of it.

Student Essay

I WANT MY MTV
Matthew A. Munich

The concept of the music video, a short film in which 1
video images interpret a song, is not a new one. The beginnings date as far back as the 1960s in the Beatles' full-length film A Hard Day's Night or later in the Rolling

Stones' movie <u>Gimme Shelter</u>. With cable television and some
of its subsidiary channels, however, the music video has received a tremendous amount of attention and popularity. MTV,
a channel devoted solely to showing music videos twenty-four
hours a day, has made the music video not only a new medium
but also a new form of art. While it may not be fair to
judge the popularity of the music video as a cultural step
backward, neither can we consider it, in its display of violence and sexist attitudes, a cultural step forward. Music
video can be thought of as a step timed to society, a form
that meets a new criterion of entertainment.

Music video did for music what television did to radio;   2
in fact, MTV is a television station for videos. Before music video, listening was a more active process. The listener
created a personal image of the song. With MTV, however, so
compelling is the visual image that it imprints on the brain;
the song cannot be divorced from the video. This phenomenon
resembles television's "laugh tracks" in that not only is the
television showing us a picture but it's telling us what we
should think is funny. In this sense, music videos do not
require the viewer's active attention or imagination.

Music video does provide a place where new and important   3
film techniques can be tried and developed. The Cars' video,
which won best video of 1984, exemplifies this stage of technological advancement. This video employed some of the most
recent discoveries in film computer graphics. Music video
can help exploit new ways of using film as an artistic
expression.

While the methods used by music videos might be new and   4
innovative, the content seems stereotypical and trite. The
figure of women in music videos is a large part of this
stereotyped content. The "Spellbound" video by the group
Triumph is a good example of the treatment of women. The
video shows a man driving at night, and as he approaches a
nebulous figure his car starts to break apart. When he sees
that the figure is a woman with fluffed-out hair, wearing
ripped white fabric, the car falls completely apart. He

emerges from the wreckage and follows her in a trance. She
stops to let him reach her, kisses him, and turns him into a
statue. The video ends with the band playing the song on
stage with the statue. The video suggests that, while women
may be beautiful, they possess evil powers that will be the
downfall of men. Modern props notwithstanding, this woman is
a version of the Medusa who has been turning men to stone for
centuries.

Regressing to an earlier stage than classical myth, peo-   5
ple in music video frequently dress in tribal garb. We see
people in tattered clothing, nonhuman hair styles, jungle
skins, and face paint. Although the medium is new, then,
these painted creatures portray the primitive thrust of music
video. A typical example is the "Talk to Me" video by the
group Iam Siam, which shows a young girl taken by force to
some tribal ritual where she is encircled by natives wearing
face paint and loincloths. Watching this happen is a bald
person painted blue and white from top to bottom. He decides
to rescue this woman from the ceremony and, once he gets her
back to safety, he touches her, instantly transforming her to
a creature with the same paint job. Although music video
advances technologies, it returns ideologically to a primitive state.

The concept of the music video invades our lives in   6
other ways than just on television. Movies that appear to be
nothing more than two-hour music videos are becoming popular.
The Talking Heads' movie Stop Making Sense is nothing more
than an extended music video. Clearly the toleration for
this new art form reflects popular taste; Flashdance and
Footloose are other immense successes that reflect the music
video mode. Who is the audience for the hard-imaged, fan-
tastical, and sometimes amusing but always loud and rhythmic
sounds? What, if anything, does the form tell us about our
culture?

If music video is art, it is art you can do your home-   7
work to. It speaks of a culture that loves gimmicks and
quick fixes and noise. MTV has a mesmerizing effect, almost

hypnotizing us and offering a visual counterpart to a drugged state. Like a dope peddler, the video station fosters addiction by promising total coverage: we can watch it all the time; we never have to give it up. It reflects our culture's fascination with and, more ominously, return to a more primitive state. There is no subtlety; every idea and theme is spelled out, not once but many times. Natives beat drums, beat their chests, and beat women. Women, conversely, are the stereotypical downfall of men. Music video is quintessentially modern because it's so thin: quickly replaced, dispassionate, disposable. In the nuclear age, MTV is us.

Questions to Start You Thinking

1. What is Munich's final judgment on MTV? Do you think it too extreme?
2. How convincing is the evidence the author marshals to support his evaluation?
3. What knowledge other than an acquaintance with music videos does Munich bring to his essay?

LEARNING BY WRITING

The Assignment: Writing an Evaluation

Pick a subject to evaluate, one with which you have some personal experience and which you feel reasonably competent to evaluate. This might be a play or a film, a TV program, a piece of music or a concert, a work of graphic art, a product new on the market, a government agency (such as the Postal Service), or—what else? Then, in a thoughtful essay, evaluate your subject.

In writing your evaluation, you will have a twofold purpose to fulfill: (1) to set forth your assessment of the quality of your subject and (2) to convince your reader that your judgment is reasonable—that is, based on your having considered evidence.

Among the lively and instructive student-written evaluations we've seen recently are these:

A music major, asked to evaluate the work of American composer Aaron Copland, found Copland a trivial and imitative composer "without a tenth of the talent or inventiveness that George Gershwin or Duke Ellington had in his little finger." To support his negative view, he critically analyzed Copland's *Appalachian Spring, Rodeo,* and other works.

A man planning a career in business management evaluated a computer firm in whose main office he had worked one summer, using the criteria of efficiency, productivity, ability to appeal to new customers, and degree of employee satisfaction.

A woman from Brazil, whose family included two scientists and who had herself visited the Amazon rain forest and had seen at first hand the effects of industrial development, critically evaluated the efforts of the U.S. government to protect the ozone layer, comparing them with efforts being made (or advocated) by environmentalists in her own country.

A student of history, assigned the task of evaluating the long-term effects of the Volstead Act of 1919 (prohibiting the manufacture and distribution of alcoholic beverages), found in favor of the maligned Prohibition law, giving evidence in its support.

For an English course, a man writing an evaluation of *Going after Cacciato,* Tim O'Brien's novel of American soldiers in Vietnam (1978), favorably compared it, point by point, with Ernest Hemingway's much-praised novel of World War I, *A Farewell to Arms.*

Generating Ideas

For a start, why not do a little *freewriting,* setting down ideas as fast as they come to mind? (This strategy is discussed in detail on p. 474.) Think of the features of your subject worth considering: in the case of a popular singer such as Tracy Chapman or Michelle Shocked, perhaps her on-stage manner, her rapport with her audience, her musicianship, her selection of material, her originality. How well does she score on these points?

You'll want to spend time finding evidence to back your judgment. You might observe (as you would do if you were evaluating a performance or the prowess of a sports team); or read in a library, checking out reviews by other critics; or converse, to see what others think.

Establish your criteria. In evaluating, you may find it helpful to set up *criteria,* standards to apply to your subject. In evaluating the desirability of Atlanta as a home for a young careerist, you might ask: Does it provide an ample choice of decent-paying entry-level positions in growth firms, suitable for a college graduate? The availability of such jobs would be one criterion for testing Atlanta. Evidently, any criterion you use to judge has to fit your subject, your audience, and your purpose. Ample entry-level jobs might not matter to the writer of an article in *Modern Maturity* evaluating Atlanta as a place to live, addressing an audience of retirees. Criteria more appropriate for that article might be the clemency of the weather and the quality and cost of medical care. To take another example of useful and specific criteria: in a review of a new automobile for *Car & Driver,* addressed to a readership of serious car buffs, a writer might evaluate the car by criteria such as styling and design, handling, fuel efficiency, value, safety features, and quality of the ride.

Early on, you might try jotting down a list of your criteria. If you can think of any, they will greatly help you evaluate. For each point you plan to consider, note any evidence that springs to mind. If none springs, or not enough, you can readily see where you'll need more material.

Try comparing and contrasting. Although not all writers of evaluations compare or contrast, doing so may be useful for evaluating. (When you *compare,* you point to similarities; when you *contrast,* differences.) Often, you can readily size up the worth of a thing by setting it next to another of its kind. Which city—Dallas or Atlanta—holds more advantages for a young single person looking for a job? (The purpose of such a paper might be to recommend settling in one city or the other.) How does an IBM personal computer stack up against a Macintosh for word processing? (Purpose: to decide which to buy.) Such questions invite you to set two subjects side by side so that one may throw the other into sharp relief. To be comparable, of course, your two subjects need to have plenty in common. The quality of a sports car might be judged by comparing it with a racing car, but not by comparing it with a Sherman tank.

If you want to try this method, ask yourself: What would be comparable to my subject? When a likely thing occurs, make a list of points you wish to compare. What similarities and differences leap to mind? If you get interested in any of these points and feel the urge to keep on writing, do. Your list might turn into a scratch outline you can use in drafting your paper.

WRITING WITH A COMPUTER: EVALUATING

If in writing your evaluation you plan to compare and contrast your subject with another of its kind, your computer just might be your best friend. Surely it will be if it has split-screen capability and can display what you write in double columns. You can put this feature to excellent use when you draw up your rough outline. Split the screen into two columns and type a heading for each: Subject A, Subject B. In the left-hand column list each point to be compared. Add notes indicating whatever evidence you have for Subject A. Then in the right-hand column do the same for Subject B, so that your outline will look like the following (for a paper for a film history course, comparing and contrasting a classic German horror movie, *The Cabinet of Dr. Caligari,* with the classic Hollywood movie *Frankenstein*).

```
       CALIGARI                 FRANKENSTEIN

1. sets and lighting:

       dreamlike,               realistic, but with heavy
       impressionistic          Gothic atmosphere (as in
       (deliberately angular    climax: a nighttime scene,
       and distorted; deep      torches highlighting
       shadows throw figures    monster's face)
       into relief)
```

And so on, point by point. By displaying each point and each bit of evidence side by side, you can outline your comparison with great efficiency.

Try defining your subject. Another way to evaluate is to *define* your subject, to indicate its nature so clearly that your readers can easily tell it from others of its kind. In defining, you help your readers understand your subject: its structure, its habitat, its functions. Evaluating MTV, Matthew Munich does some *extended* defining: he discusses the nature of the popular video channel, its techniques, its content, its view of women, its effects on its audience. This kind of defining isn't the same as writing a *short definition,* such as you'd find in a dictionary. (For how to do that, see "Strategies," p. 512.) Munich's purpose is to judge MTV. So you might ask, What is the nature of my subject? Or, put differently, What qualities make it unique, unlike others of its sort? Scribble down any qualities that occur to you. As you can see, this is a demanding question. But write out your answer and you may find that you have written most of your paper and that you have formed an opinion of your subject as you went along.

To help you zero in on a promising subject and some likely material, you might ask yourself a few questions.

DISCOVERY CHECKLIST: EVALUATING

- What evidence can you recall to back up your judgments? If not from memory, from what other resource might you draw it?
- What criteria, if any, do you plan to use in making your evaluation? Are they clear? Will they be reasonably easy to apply?
- Would comparing and contrasting help in evaluating your subject? If so, with what might you compare or contrast your subject?
- What specific qualities set your subject apart from all the rest of its general class?

Shaping a Draft

Reflect a moment: what is your purpose in this evaluation? What main point do you wish to make? Keep this point in mind as you write, and you'll be more likely to arrive at it.

You might want to make that point at the beginning of your paper, then demonstrate it by looking at specific evidence, and finally hark back to it again in your closing lines. Organizing your paper differently, you might open by wondering, "How good a film is *The Rainmaker*?" or "Is Keynes's theory of inflation still valuable, or is it hopelessly out of date?" or "Are organically grown vegetables worth their higher price?"—raising some such question about your subject to which your paper will reply. You then consider the evidence, a piece at a time, and conclude with your overall judgment.

Consider your criteria. Some writers like to spell out criteria to apply to whatever they're evaluating. Many find that a list of criteria gives them confidence and provokes ideas. But we should admit that that isn't the only possible way to approach your draft. To be a good evaluator, you don't absolutely have to have foreordained criteria. You can, of course, just move into your subject and thoughtfully sniff around. T. S. Eliot said that, in criticizing literature, criteria, standards, and touchstones (great works to hold lesser works up to) don't help all that much. In a statement that sounds snobbish but isn't when you think about it, he declared that all a good critic needs is to be very intelligent.

Consider outlining. If you plan to compare your subject to something else, here is a little more advice. Most writers find that, in comparing and contrasting, an outline—even a rough list—facilitates writing a draft. An outline will help you keep track of points to make. One way to put together an outline is *subject by subject.* You have your say about subject A and then do the same for subject B. In writing a short paper comparing Atlanta and Dallas, you would complete your remarks about Atlanta and then head west. This method is workable for a short essay of two or three paragraphs, but for a longer essay it has drawbacks. In an essay of, say, a thousand or two thousand words, your reader might find it hard to remember all your points about Atlanta, ten paragraphs ago, while reading about Dallas.

A better way to organize a longer comparison is *point by point.* You take up one point at a time and apply it first to one subject, then to the other:

1. Job opportunities
   a. Dallas
   b. Atlanta
2. Recreation possibilities
   a. Dallas
   b. Atlanta

And so on, for however many points you want to compare.

Keep your outline simple, and don't be ruled by it. If, while you write your draft, good thoughts come to you, by all means let them in. (If you need a quick refresher course in outlining, see "Strategies," p. 498.)

Rewriting

Be fair. Make your judgments reasonable, not extreme. Few things on earth are all good or all evil. You need not find Atlanta or Dallas a paradise in order to recommend it to a career-minded young settler. A reviewer can find fault with a film and conclude that nevertheless it is worth seeing. There's nothing wrong, of course, with passing a fervent judgment ("This is the trashiest excuse for a play I have ever suffered through"), but consider your readers and their likely reactions.

However strongly you word your judgments, make sure that no one will fail to see what you think. Enlist the help of a peer editor, who can read your draft and consider these questions.

- When you finish reading the essay, can you tell exactly what the writer thinks of the subject?
- What is your overall reaction to this essay? Does the writer make you agree with his or her evaluation?
- Does the writer give you sufficient evidence for his or her judgment?
- Are there any places in the essay where the writer ignores his or her readers, when it might have helped to be aware of them? Point out such places.
- Look at the way the writer has arranged his or her points. Would you recommend any changes in how the essay is organized?
- Circle any instances where you think grammar, spelling, punctuation, or usage may need a polish.
- What did you like best about the essay? Suggest any revisions that might make it more successful.

If you do any comparing and contrasting, look back over your draft with special care. Make sure that, all along, you keep discussing the same points about each subject. It might confuse your reader to compare, say, job opportunities in Dallas with sports facilities in Atlanta. Make sure you haven't fallen into a monotonous drone: A does this, B does that; A looks like this, B looks like that. Compare and contrast with feeling, and the result may be a lively paper. And it won't be mechanical in its symmetry, like two salt and pepper shakers.

In thinking critically about your draft, you might find this checklist handy.

REVISION CHECKLIST: EVALUATING

- In each paragraph, or almost every one, have you given your readers evidence to support your view? Have you recalled, observed, read, or picked up from conversation any definite facts that your readers might go and verify? If your draft looks a little thin for lack of evidence, from which resource or resources might you draw more?
- Have you been fair to both your subject and your readers? If you are championing something, have you deliberately skipped over any of its damning disadvantages or glaring faults? If condemning your subject, have you omitted any of its admirable traits?
- Do any of your judgments need rewording, to tone them down or qualify them? Consider your readers. Is your conclusion likely to make them think that you are a wild-eyed nut?

- If you anticipate that readers will make any objections to your views, can you insert any answers to their objections?

- Is the judgment you pass on your subject unmistakably clear? Reread like a reader. Rewrite, if need be, to give your evaluation more emphasis.

- If you compared one thing with another, do you look consistently for the same points in both?

Other Assignments

1. Write an evaluation of a college course you are now taking. (So that you can be completely objective, we suggest you work on some course other than your writing course.) Consider its strengths and weaknesses. Does the instructor present the material clearly, understandably, and interestingly? Can you confer with the instructor if you need to? Is there any class discussion or other feedback? Are the assignments pointed and purposeful? How is the textbook: helpful, readable, easy to use? Does this course give you your money's worth?

2. If you disagree with Matthew Munich in his evaluation of MTV, write an essay setting forth your own evaluation. If you agree with Munich, you might instead read some reviews of films, recordings, television, and books in recent magazines (*Time, Newsweek, Rolling Stone, The New Yorker,* or others) until you find a review you think quite wrong-headed. Write a reply to it, giving your own evaluation.

3. Analyze a story, poem, or play (as we discussed in Chapter 6), and you will be in a good position to evaluate it. Here are two poems on a similar theme. Read them critically, seeing what you find in them, and decide which seems to you the better poem. Then, in a paragraph or two, set forth your evaluation. Some criteria to apply might be the poet's choice of concrete, specific words that appeal to the senses instead of vague generalities and his awareness of his audience. (Does anything in either poem prompt you to object to it?)

> PUTTING IN THE SEED
> You come to fetch me from my work tonight
> When supper's on the table, and we'll see
> If I can leave off burying the white
> Soft petals fallen from the apple tree
> (Soft petals, yes, but not so barren quite,   5
> Mingled with these, smooth bean and wrinkled pea),
> And go along with you ere you lose sight
> Of what you came for and become like me,
> Slave to a springtime passion for the earth.
> How Love burns through the Putting in the Seed   10
> On through the watching for that early birth
> When, just as the soil tarnishes with weed,
> The sturdy seedling with arched body comes
> Shouldering its way and shedding the earth crumbs.
> —Robert Frost (1874–1963)

FOR GROUP LEARNING
Before you write to an assignment in this chapter, get together with your writing group or your customary peer editors. Discuss the subject you plan to evaluate and see whether the group can help you arrive at a sound judgment of it. They will need to see what it is you're evaluating or hear your detailed report about it. If you are evaluating a short literary work or an idea expressed in a reading, it might be an excellent idea to read that short work or excerpt aloud to the group so that they all may be familiar with it. Ask your listeners to supply reasons for their own evaluations. Maybe they'll suggest reasons that hadn't occurred to you.

BETWEEN OUR FOLDING LIPS
Between our folding lips
God slips
An embryon life, and goes;
And this becomes your rose.
We love, God makes: in our sweet mirth   5
God spies occasion for a birth.
Then is it His, or is it ours?
I know not—He is fond of flowers.
          —T. E. Brown (1830–1897)

APPLYING WHAT YOU LEARN: SOME USES OF EVALUATING

In your college writing you'll be called on over and over to evaluate. On an art appreciation exam, you might be asked to evaluate the relative merits of Norman Rockwell and Andrew Wyeth as realistic painters. Speech pathology students, after considering the long-standing controversy that rages in education for the deaf, might be called on to describe and then evaluate three currently disputed teaching methods: oral/aural, signing, and a combination of the two. Students of language and linguistics may be asked to decide which of two methods of articulation therapy is more valuable: Skinner's behaviorist theory or Chomsky's theory of innate language acquisition. Outside of class, students on some campuses are invited to write comments for a student-run survey to evaluate their college courses.

In life beyond campus, every executive or professional needs to evaluate. An editor accepts and rejects manuscripts. A personnel director selects people to hire. A lawyer sizes up the merits of a case and decides whether to take it. A retailer chooses the best product to sell. A speech pathologist evaluates the speech and language skills of prospective patients. You can think of endless other examples of evaluating, a kind of critical thinking we do every day of our lives.

Familiar kinds of *written* evaluation abound. Daily newspapers and magazines contain reviews of films, books, TV programs, records, and videos. Many sports writers, columnists, and political commentators evaluate. The magazine *Consumer Reports* contains detailed evaluations of products and services, like this one from "Is There a DAT [digital audio tape] in Your Future?" (January 1989).

> While prices will surely decline over time, we don't think DATs are going to make CDs obsolete anytime soon. First, while DAT players are much faster than conventional cassette decks at locating song tracks, they'll never be able to hop from track to track as quickly as a CD player.
>
> Second, digital audio tapes aren't as impervious to wear as compact discs. The tape comes into physical contact with a rotating recording head similar to a VCR's, and that will eventually degrade sound quality on the tape.
>
> Finally, recording quality might not be quite as close to perfect as DAT makers have implied—and record companies feared. When we tried out the *Sony DTC 1000 ES* DAT recorder last year, we found that it didn't match the low background noise performance of CD players. Unless that noise was a problem unique to our tested machine, DAT sound doesn't equal the quality of CD sound.
>
> For all of those reasons—price, durability, convenience, quality of sound, and the reluctance of the recording industry—we think that DAT will coexist with, rather than supplant, the compact disc in the years ahead.

Like many general magazines, professional journals contain book reviews that not only give a brief rundown of a book's contents but also indicate whether the reviewer considers the book worth reading. In the March 13, 1989, issue of *Chemical & Engineering News,* Deborah C. Andrews reviews the second edition of a textbook by H. J. Tichy called *Effective Writing for Engineers, Managers, Scientists.* Included in the review is an evaluation:

> What this text does well is to use words to talk about words. Pages are heavy with text, and visuals are exceedingly rare. Tichy writes within the framework of English (and French) literature as well as the literature of science, often calling upon the masters for clever phrases and telling anecdotes, some of them somewhat arcane—like a reference to an address before the French Academy by the 18th century naturalist Count Georges-Louis Leclerc de Buffon. In a section on figures of speech, she includes mention of some, like metonymy and litotes, that would stymie many English majors.

For a final example, Howard Gardner, in *Artful Scribbles,* an inquiry into what children's drawings mean, makes a sharp contrast between the drawings of younger children and those of older children.

> When drawings made by eight- or nine-year-olds are juxtaposed to those produced by younger children, a striking contrast emerges. There is little doubt about which came from which group: works by the older children feature a kind of precision, a concern for detail, a command of geometrical form which are lacking in the attempts by younger artists. Schemas for familiar objects are readily recognized, and attempts at rendering less familiar objects can initially be decoded. And yet one hesitates to call the drawings by the older children "better"—

indeed, most observers and sometimes even the youngsters themselves feel that something vital which is present at the age of six or seven has disappeared from the drawings by the older children. A certain freedom, flexibility, *joie de vivre* [zest for life], and a special fresh exploratory flavor which mark the childlike drawings of the six-year-old are gone; and instead of being replaced by adult mastery, this loss has merely been supplanted by a product that is at once more carefully wrought yet also more wooden and lifeless.

As you'll notice, Gardner, while giving the strong points of each age group of artists, apparently favors the work of the young, for all its faults.

A Film Critic Evaluates

Pauline Kael, influential motion picture critic for *The New Yorker,* brings to her work erudition, a sprightly style, and demanding criteria. In this review, written in 1976 when *Rocky* first appeared and collected in *When the Lights Go Down* (1980), Kael passes judgment on an enormously popular film that most of us know—one she manages to enjoy, whatever its faults.

ROCKY
Pauline Kael

Chunky, muscle-bound Sylvester Stallone looks repulsive one moment, noble the next, and sometimes both at once. In *Rocky,* which he wrote and stars in, he's a thirty-year-old cub fighter who works as a strong-arm man, collecting money for a loan shark. Rocky never got anywhere, and he has nothing; he lives in a Philadelphia tenement, and even the name he fights under—the Italian Stallion—has become a joke. But the world heavyweight champion, Apollo Creed (Carl Weathers), who's a smart black jester, like Muhammad Ali, announces that for his Bicentennial New Year's fight he'll give an unknown a shot at the title, and he picks the Italian Stallion for the racial-sexual overtones of the contest. This small romantic fable is about a palooka gaining his manhood; it's Terry Malloy finally getting his chance to be somebody. *Rocky* is a threadbare patchwork of old-movie bits (*On the Waterfront, Marty, Somebody Up There Likes Me,* Capra's *Meet John Doe,* and maybe even a little of Preston Sturges's *Hail the Conquering Hero*), yet it's engaging, and the naive elements are emotionally effective. John G. Avildsen's directing is his usual strictly-from-hunger approach; he slams through a picture like a poor man's Sidney Lumet. But a more painstaking director would have been too proud to shoot the mildewed ideas and would have tried to throw out as many as possible and to conceal the others— and would probably have wrecked the movie. *Rocky* is shameless, and that's why—on a certain level—it works. What holds it together is innocence.

In his offscreen bravado, Stallone (in Italian *stallone* means stallion) has claimed that he wrote the script in three and a half days, and some professional screenwriters, seeing what a ragtag of a script it is, may think that they could have done it in two and a half. But they wouldn't have been able to believe in what they did, and it wouldn't have got the audience cheering, the way *Rocky* does. The innocence that makes this picture so winning emanates from Sylvester Stallone. It's a street-wise, flowers-blooming-in-the-garbage innocence. Stallone plays a waif, a strong-arm man who doesn't want to hurt anybody, a loner with only his pet turtles to talk to. Yet the character doesn't come across as maudlin. Stallone looks like a big, battered Paul McCartney. There's bullnecked energy in him, smoldering; he has a field of force, like Brando's. And he knows how to use his overripe, cartoon sensuality—the eyelids at half-mast, the sad brown eyes and twisted, hurt mouth. Victor Mature also had this thick sensuality, but the movies used him as if it were simple plushy handsomeness, and so he became ridiculous, until he learned—too late—to act. Stallone is aware that we see him as a hulk, and he plays against this comically and tenderly. In his deep, caveman's voice, he gives the most surprising, sharp, fresh shadings to his lines. He's at his funniest trying to explain to his boss why he didn't break somebody's thumbs, as he'd been told to; he's even funny talking to his turtles. He pulls the whiskers off the film's cliché situations, so that we're constantly charmed by him, waiting for what he'll say next. He's like a child who never ceases to amaze us.

Stallone has the gift of direct communication with the audience. 3
Rocky's naive observations come from so deep inside him that they have a Lewis Carroll enchantment. His unworldliness makes him seem dumb, but we know better; we understand what he feels at every moment. Rocky is the embodiment of the out-of-fashion pure-at-heart. His macho strut belongs with the ducktails of the fifties—he's a sagging peacock. I'm not sure how much of his archaism is thought out, how much is the accidental result of Stallone's overdeveloped, weight lifter's muscles combined with his simplistic beliefs, but Rocky represents the redemption of an earlier ideal— the man as rock for woman to cleave to. Talia Shire plays Adrian, a shy girl with glasses who works in a pet store; she's the Betsy Blair to Stallone's Marty.° It's unspeakably musty, but they put it over; her delicacy (that of a button-faced Audrey Hepburn) is the right counterpoint to his primitivism. It's clear that he's drawn to her because she isn't fast or rough and doesn't make fun of him; she doesn't make hostile wisecracks, like the other woman in the pet store, or talk dirty, like the kids in the street. We don't groan at this, because he's such a *tortured* macho nice-guy—he has failed his own high ideals. And who doesn't have a soft spot for the teenage aspirations congealed inside this thirty-year-old bum?

Stallone is the picture, but the performers who revolve around him are 4
talented. Carl Weathers, a former Oakland Raiders linebacker, is a real

---

Betsy Blair . . . Marty: In the film *Marty* (1955), Betsy Blair plays a gentle, lonely woman who falls for a roughneck, a butcher named Marty.

find. His Apollo Creed has the flash and ebullience to put the fairy-tale plot in motion; when the champ arrives at the ring dressed as Uncle Sam, no one could enjoy the racial joke as much as he does. Adrian's heavyset brother Paulie is played by Burt Young, who has been turning up in movies more and more frequently in the past three years and still gives the impression that his abilities haven't begun to be tapped. Young, who actually was a professional fighter, has the cracked, mottled voice of someone who's taken a lot of punishment in the sinuses; the resonance is gone. As Mickey, the ancient pug who runs a fighters' gym, Burgess Meredith uses the harsh, racking sound of a man who's been punched too often in the vocal cords. The director overemphasizes Meredith's performance (much as John Schlesinger did in *The Day of the Locust*); Meredith would look better if we were left to discover how good he is for ourselves. I found *Marty* dreary, because the people in it were sapped of energy. But Stallone and Talia Shire and the others here have a restrained force; you feel that they're being pressed down, that they're under a lid. The only one who gets a chance to explode is Paulie, when, in a rage, he wields a baseball bat, and it's a poor scene, out of tune. Yet the actors themselves have so much more to them than they're using that what comes across in their performances is what's under the lid. The actors—and this includes Joe Spinell as Gazzo, Rocky's gangster boss—enable us to feel their reserves of intelligence; they provide tact and taste, which aren't in long supply in an Avildsen film.

Rocky is the kind of movie in which the shots are underlighted, because 5 the characters are poor and it's wintertime. I was almost never convinced that the camera was in the right place. The shots don't match well, and they're put together jerkily, with cheap romantic music thrown in like cement blocks of lyricism, and sheer noise used to build up excitement at the climactic prizefight, where the camera is so close to the fighters that you can't feel the rhythm of the encounter. And the film doesn't follow through on what it prepares. Early on, we see Rocky with the street-corner kids in his skid-row neighborhood, but we never get to see how these kids react to his training or to the fight itself. Even the bull mastiff who keeps Rocky company on his early-morning runs is lost track of. I get the feeling that Avildsen is so impatient to finish a film on schedule (or before, as if it were a race) that he hardly bothers to think it out. I hate the way *Rocky* is made, yet better might be worse in this case. Unless a director could take this material and transform it into sentimental urban poetry—a modern equivalent of what Frank Borzage used to do in pictures such as *Man's Castle*, with Spencer Tracy and Loretta Young—we're probably better off with Avildsen's sloppiness than with careful planning; a craftsmanlike *Rocky* would be obsolete, like a TV play of the fifties.

Stallone can certainly write; that is, he can write scenes and dialogue. 6 But as a writer he stays inside the character; we never get a clear outside view of Rocky. For that, Stallone falls back on clichés, on an urban-primitive myth: at the end, Rocky has everything a man needs—his manhood, his woman, maybe even his dog. (If it were rural-primitive, he'd have some land, too.) In a sense, *Rocky* is a piece of innocent art, but its innocence doesn't sit too well. The bad side of *Rocky* is its resemblance to *Marty*—its folklorish, grubby littleness. Unpretentiousness shouldn't be used as a virtue. This warmed-over bum-into-man myth is unworthy of the freak macho force of its star; talking to turtles is too endearing. What separates Stallone from a Brando is that everything Stallone does has one purpose: to make you like him. He may not know how good he could be if he'd stop snuggling into your heart. If not—well, he may be to acting what Mario Lanza was to singing, and that's a form of bumminess.

Questions to Start You Thinking

1. Would you call this review favorable or unfavorable? If you have seen the film *Rocky* on TV, on videotape, or in a theater, do you agree with Kael's assessment?

2. What is the quality Kael most admires about the film? In her eyes, what are its principal faults?

3. In her essay Kael makes comparisons, mentioning other movies, other actors, other directors. What do these comparisons contribute to her assessment of *Rocky*? To appreciate her remarks, do you need to be familiar with these other movies and moviemakers?

4. When you first saw *Rocky*, which may have been several or many years ago, what early impressions did you carry away from the movie? After reading Kael's evaluation, would you change your own early opinion of the film or stick to it?

A Lawyer Evaluates

We all take for granted that no one is supposed to shout "Fire!" in a crowded theater, but what did Justice Oliver Wendell Holmes mean when he said that? In the following essay, eminent lawyer Alan Dershowitz looks closely at a classic analogy and finds it wanting.

SHOUTING "FIRE!"
Alan M. Dershowitz

When the Reverend Jerry Falwell learned that the Supreme Court had   1
reversed his $200,000 judgment against *Hustler* magazine for the emotional distress that he had suffered from an outrageous parody, his response was typical of those who seek to censor speech: "Just as no person may scream 'Fire!' in a crowded theater when there is no fire, and find cover

under the First Amendment, likewise, no sleazy merchant like Larry Flynt should be able to use the First Amendment as an excuse for maliciously and dishonestly attacking public figures, as he has so often done."

Justice Oliver Wendell Holmes's classic example of unprotected 2 speech—falsely shouting "Fire!" in a crowded theater—has been invoked so often, by so many people, in such diverse contexts, that it has become part of our national folk language. It has even appeared—most appropriately—in the theater: in Tom Stoppard's play *Rosencrantz and Guildenstern Are Dead* a character shouts at the audience, "Fire!" He then quickly explains: "It's all right—I'm demonstrating the misuse of free speech." Shouting "Fire!" in the theater may well be the only jurisprudential analogy that has assumed the status of a folk argument. A prominent historian recently characterized it as "the most brilliantly persuasive expression that ever came from Holmes's pen." But in spite of its hallowed position in both the jurisprudence of the First Amendment and the arsenal of political discourse, it is and was an inapt analogy, even in the context in which it was originally offered. It has lately become—despite, perhaps even because of, the frequency and promiscuousness of its invocation—little more than a caricature of logical argumentation.

The case that gave rise to the "Fire!"-in-a-crowded-theater analogy— 3 *Schenck v. United States*—involved the prosecution of Charles Schenck, who was the general secretary of the Socialist Party in Philadelphia, and Elizabeth Baer, who was its recording secretary. In 1917 a jury found Schenck and Baer guilty of attempting to cause insubordination among soldiers who had been drafted to fight in the First World War. They and other party members had circulated leaflets urging draftees not to "submit to intimidation" by fighting in a war being conducted on behalf of "Wall Street's chosen few." Schenck admitted, and the Court found, that the intent of the pamphlets' "impassioned language" was to "influence" draftees to resist the draft. Interestingly, however, Justice Holmes noted that nothing in the pamphlet suggested that the draftees should use unlawful or violent means to oppose conscription: "In form at least [the pamphlet] confined itself to peaceful measures, such as a petition for the repeal of the act" and an exhortation to exercise "your right to assert your opposition to the draft." Many of its most impassioned words were quoted directly from the Constitution.

Justice Holmes acknowledged that "in many places and in ordinary 4 times the defendants, in saying all that was said in the circular, would have been within their constitutional rights." "But," he added, "the character of every act depends upon the circumstances in which it is done." And to illustrate that truism he went on to say,

> The most stringent protection of free speech would not protect a man in falsely shouting fire in a theater, and causing a panic. It does not even protect a man from an injunction against uttering words that may have all the effect of force.

Justice Holmes then upheld the convictions in the context of a wartime 5 draft, holding that the pamphlet created "a clear and present danger" of hindering the war effort while our soldiers were fighting for their lives and our liberty.

The example of shouting "Fire!" obviously bore little relationship to the 6 facts of the Schenck case. The Schenck pamphlet contained a substantive political message. It urged its draftee readers to *think* about the message and then—if they so chose—to act on it in a lawful and nonviolent way. The man who shouts "Fire!" in a crowded theater is neither sending a political message nor inviting his listener to think about what he has said and decide what to do in a rational, calculated manner. On the contrary, the message is designed to force action *without* contemplation. The message "Fire!" is directed not to the mind and the conscience of the listener but, rather, to his adrenaline and his feet. It is a stimulus to immediate *action*, not thoughtful reflection. It is—as Justice Holmes recognized in his follow-up sentence—the functional equivalent of "uttering words that may have all the effect of force."

Indeed, in that respect the shout of "Fire!" is not even speech, in any 7 meaningful sense of that term. It is a *clang* sound—the equivalent of setting off a nonverbal alarm. Had Justice Holmes been more honest about his example, he would have said that freedom of speech does not protect a kid who pulls a fire alarm in the absence of a fire. But that obviously would have been irrelevant to the case at hand. The proposition that pulling an alarm is not protected speech certainly leads to the conclusion that shouting the word *fire* is also not protected. But the core analogy is the nonverbal alarm, and the derivative example is the verbal shout. By cleverly substituting the derivative shout for the core alarm, Holmes made it possible to analogize one set of words to another—as he could not have done if he had begun with the self-evident proposition that setting off an alarm bell is not free speech.

The analogy is thus not only inapt but also insulting. Most Americans 8 do not respond to political rhetoric with the same kind of automatic acceptance expected of schoolchildren responding to a fire drill. Not a single recipient of the Schenck pamphlet is known to have changed his mind after reading it. Indeed, one draftee, who appeared as a prosecution witness, was asked whether reading a pamphlet asserting that the draft law was unjust would make him "immediately decide that you must erase that law." Not surprisingly, he replied, "I do my own thinking." A theatergoer would probably not respond similarly if asked how he would react to a shout of "Fire!"

Another important reason why the analogy is inapt is that Holmes emphasizes the factual falsity of the shout "Fire!" The Schenck pamphlet, however, was not factually false. It contained political opinions and ideas 9 about the causes of the war and about appropriate and lawful responses to the draft. As the Supreme Court recently reaffirmed (in *Falwell v. Hustler*), "The First Amendment recognizes no such thing as a 'false' idea." Nor does it recognize false opinions about the causes of or cures for war.

A closer analogy to the facts of the Schenck case might have been 10 provided by a person's standing outside a theater, offering the patrons a leaflet advising them that in his opinion the theater was structurally unsafe, and urging them not to enter but to complain to the building inspectors. That analogy, however, would not have served Holmes's argument for punishing Schenck. Holmes needed an analogy that would appear relevant to Schenck's political speech but that would invite the conclusion that censorship was appropriate.

Unsurprisingly, a war-weary nation—in the throes of a know-nothing 11 hysteria over immigrant anarchists and socialists—welcomed the comparison between what was regarded as a seditious political pamphlet and a malicious shout of "Fire!" Ironically, the "Fire!" analogy is nearly all that survives from the Schenck case; the ruling itself is almost certainly not good law. Pamphlets of the kind that resulted in Schenck's imprisonment have been circulated with impunity during subsequent wars.

Over the past several years I have assembled a collection of in- 12 stances—cases, speeches, arguments—in which proponents of censorship have maintained that the expression at issue is "just like" or "equivalent to" falsely shouting "Fire!" in a crowded theater and ought to be banned, "just as" shouting "Fire!" ought to be banned. The analogy is generally invoked, often with self-satisfaction, as an absolute argument-stopper. It does, after all, claim the high authority of the great Justice Oliver Wendell Holmes. I have rarely heard it invoked in a convincing, or even particularly relevant, way. But that, too, can claim lineage from the great Holmes.

Not unlike Falwell, with his silly comparison between shouting "Fire!" 13 and publishing an offensive parody, courts and commentators have frequently invoked "Fire!" as an analogy to expression that is not an automatic stimulus to panic. A state supreme court held that "Holmes's aphorism . . . applies with equal force to pornography"—in particular to the exhibition of the movie *Carmen Baby* in a drive-in theater in close proximity to highways and homes. Another court analogized "picketing . . . in support of a secondary boycott" to shouting "Fire!" because in both instances "speech and conduct are brigaded." In the famous Skokie case one of the judges argued that allowing Nazis to march through a city where a large number of Holocaust survivors live "just might fall into the same category as one's 'right' to cry fire in a crowded theater."

Outside court the analogies become even more badly stretched. A 14 spokesperson for the New Jersey Sports and Exposition Authority complained that newspaper reports to the effect that a large number of football players had contracted cancer after playing in the Meadowlands—a sta-dium atop a landfill—were the "journalistic equivalent of shouting fire in a crowded theater." An insect researcher acknowledged that his prediction that a certain amusement park might become roach-infested "may be tan-tamount to shouting fire in a crowded theater." The philosopher Sidney Hook, in a letter to the *New York Times* bemoaning a Supreme Court de-cision that required a plaintiff in a defamation action to prove that the offending statement was actually false, argued that the First Amendment does not give the press carte blanche to accuse innocent persons "any more than the First Amendment protects the right of someone falsely to shout fire in a crowded theater."

Some close analogies to shouting "Fire!" or setting off an alarm are, of course, available: calling in a false bomb threat; dialing 911 and falsely describing an emergency; making a loud, gunlike sound in the presence of the President; setting off a voice-activated sprinkler system by falsely shouting "Fire!" In one case in which the "Fire!" analogy was directly to the point, a creative defendant tried to get around it. The case involved a man who calmly advised an airline clerk that he was "only here to hijack the plane." He was charged, in effect, with shouting "Fire!" in a crowded thea-ter, and his rejected defense—as quoted by the court—was as follows: "If we built fireproof theaters and let people know about this, then the shouting of 'Fire!' would not cause panic."   15

Here are some more-distant but still related examples: the recent in-cident of the police slaying in which some members of an onlooking crowd urged a mentally ill vagrant who had taken an officer's gun to shoot the officer; the screaming of racial epithets during a tense confrontation; shouting down a speaker and preventing him from continuing his speech.   16

Analogies are, by their nature, matters of degree. Some are closer to the core example than others. But any attempt to analogize political ideas in a pamphlet, ugly parody in a magazine, offensive movies in a theater, controversial newspaper articles, or any of the other expressions and ac-tions catalogued above to the very different act of shouting "Fire!" in a crowded theater is either self-deceptive or self-serving.   17

The government does, of course, have some arguably legitimate bases for suppressing speech which bear no relationship to shouting "Fire!" It may ban the publication of nuclear-weapon codes, of information about troop movements, and of the identity of undercover agents. It may crimi-nalize extortion threats and conspiratorial agreements. These expressions may lead directly to serious harm, but the mechanisms of causation are very different from that at work when an alarm is sounded. One may also argue—less persuasively, in my view—against protecting certain forms of public obscenity and defamatory statements. Here, too, the mechanisms of causation are very different. None of these exceptions to the First Amend-ment's exhortation that the government "shall make no law . . . abridging   18 the freedom of speech, or of the press" is anything like falsely shouting "Fire!" in a crowded theater; they all must be justified on other grounds.

A comedian once told his audience, during a stand-up routine, about   19 the time he was standing around a fire with a crowd of people and got in trouble for yelling "Theater, theater!" That, I think, is about as clever and productive a use as anyone has ever made of Holmes's flawed analogy.

Questions to Start You Thinking

1. What reasons does the author give for criticizing Justice Holmes's use of the fire analogy? What further criticism does he make of Holmes's handling of the Schenck case?

2. Can you think of an occasion on which Justice Holmes's fire analogy might be used without incurring Dershowitz's scorn?

3. What seems to you the strongest ammunition Dershowitz uses in support of his evaluation?

4. Does Dershowitz have a purpose beyond criticizing Holmes? If so, what is it?

CHAPTER 10

Seeking Causes
and Effects

When a house burns down, an insurance company assigns a claims adjuster to look into the disaster and answer the question Why? The answer—the *cause* of the fire, whether it be lightning, a forgotten cigar, or a match that the homeowner deliberately struck—is given in a written report. The adjuster also details the *effects* of the fire: what was destroyed or damaged, what repairs will be needed, how much they will cost.

In assigning you to write a paper tracing causes, no instructor will expect you to set forth a definitive explanation with absolute certainty. To ask why a huge phenomenon took place, such as continental drift or the Depression of the 1930s, is to propose long and serious toil. After decades, historians are still trying to account for that remarkable burst of intellectual energy called the Italian Renaissance. Taken seriously, the simple statement "Herbert Hoover became unpopular because the stock market crashed" would call for months of effort to demonstrate for sure that the president's unpopularity resulted from the crash and from no other cause. To seek causes, even if a writer has all the time in the world, is at best an uncertain pursuit. "Causality," says French philosopher of history Paul Veyne, "is always accompanied by mental reservation."

Still, in the process of seeking causes and effects, both you and your readers learn a good deal and understand the subject more clearly. To probe causes and to detail effects, you have to think about a subject critically, to gather information and ideas, and to marshal evidence. Effects, by the way, are usually easier to demonstrate than causes. The results of a fire are apparent to an onlooker the next day, although its cause may be obscure.

LEARNING FROM OTHER WRITERS

The following two essays explore causes and effects. "Why We Burned a Wilderness," a student-written paper, draws conclusions likely to surprise readers. A major in recreation management, Katie Kennedy had the opportunity to work for a season at a wildlife sanctuary near Naples, Florida. The experience changed one of her previous beliefs. You'll notice that she draws her material from all five basic resources: recalling, observing, reading, conversing, and imagining.

Student Essay

WHY WE BURNED A WILDERNESS
Katie Kennedy

Here I was, slogging through a Florida swamp with a lighted drip torch in my hand, leaving behind me a trail of fire. I was going against everything I believed about fires in the outdoors. It had been ingrained in me to take the utmost caution in using fire in the woods, lest a blaze rage out of control. Yet now I was purposely setting fire to the surrounding grasses, vines, and scrubby trees with the intent of burning them to the ground.

1

I imagined the upcoming scene: clouds of insects rising, birds and animals--snakes, frogs, turtles, deer, armadillos, raccoons, opossums, rabbits, and maybe a bobcat--fleeing the blaze. I tried not to think about the animals I was killing or leaving homeless. Smokey the Bear would be appalled.

2

Six of us had set out to do the day's burning, four naturalists including myself, Greg the warden-biologist, and Ed the sanctuary manager. First we did a small practice burn along the side of the road, where Ed told us about the drip torches and how to use them. Drip torches are three-gallon tanks of gas mixed with diesel fuel, with a long spout and nozzle. When inverted and lit, they emit a thin stream of fire, as a watering can spouts water. "Today we're going to try to use the wind," Ed explained. "We'll try to keep it at our backs. Then it will spread the fire in the direction we're walking."

3

I lit my torch and pulled a bandana over my nose and   4
mouth. We spread out and tried to head in the same direction, burning as we went along. The vegetation was very
thick, but I had to keep moving and rip through it, since the
fire was close behind. The heat was intense and the smoke
bothered my eyes. We couldn't see one another because of the
dense vines and shrubs but had to keep yelling back and forth
to make sure we were all still heading in the right direction
and, most important, not trapping someone inside a ring of
fire. Dry, crackling grass makes a lot of noise as it burns,
so we had to yell loudly. Sometimes I'd find a mucky ditch
in my way, or a thorny vine, but there wasn't time to ponder
an alternate route. I just had to forge ahead, sinking up to
my knees in cold, muddy water. I always found it nerve-
racking to be followed so closely by the fire, although after
my first ditch crossing I was somewhat comforted by the
thought that my soaked jeans and boots probably wouldn't
burn.

I never got over my uneasiness about being so close to   5
the fire. I didn't like going on controlled burns. Yet, as
a seasonal naturalist at the National Audubon Society's Corkscrew Swamp Sanctuary in the Big Cypress Swamp region of
South Florida, I soon learned that burns had to be done periodically to ensure the health of the swamp. One of my duties was to go along with the full-time staff to see how the
burns were done. Another duty, one I hadn't expected, was to
read books. I learned a lot from one of them, Fire in South
Florida Ecosystems, by the staff of the Southeast Forest Experiment Station in Asheville, North Carolina (Washington,
D.C.: U.S. Forest Service, 1980). It convinced me that trees
and plants of the swamp need fire to survive.

The interrelationship of vegetation with fire has   6
evolved over thousands of years. In the past, when South
Florida was covered with an unbroken canopy of vegetation,
fires would start naturally by lightning. Sometimes, they
would rage from one side of the Florida peninsula to the

other and die only on reaching the coast. Or they might
blaze until extinguished by the rains of the next wet season.
Yet, in as little as two weeks, fresh green growth would begin to cover the ground again. When people started to discover the beauty of South Florida and began to chop it down
to get to it, cutting through the wilderness with roads and
housing developments, they brought their prejudices against
fire with them. When natural fires were not allowed to take
their course, the delicate balance was upset, causing havoc
in the ecological system.

At Corkscrew Swamp Sanctuary, there are a diversity of   7
habitats, including pineland, marsh, wet prairie, bald cypress and pond cypress stands, and hardwood hammocks. What
makes each distinct are the species of trees and plants found
there, depending on how much water each area receives, its
elevation, and other factors. Therefore, there are different
animals associated with each habitat too. One goal of the
sanctuary management is to keep this diversity of habitats
available. Plant diversity ensures animal diversity, since
certain animals prefer one habitat over another for food and
shelter. Each habitat is burned on its own schedule. The
wet prairie, for example, is burned every one to three years,
while the pinelands, a more established plant community, are
burned every five to seven years. If fire were kept out of
an area, the natural progression would be toward hardwoods
such as oaks. Eventually, all the areas would end up looking
much the same, with the same plant composition. Burning ensures that areas such as marsh and wet prairie will remain
that way.

In a wilderness, fire has still other valuable effects.   8
Fire recycles nutrients. By reducing the vegetation to ash,
the nutrients locked up in growing trees and plants are returned to the soil so that they may be used again. Without
fire, some plants would not to be able to reproduce. The
seeds of certain plants must germinate through an ash layer.
Other plants are stimulated to drop seeds only after feeling

intense heat, ensuring that after a fire, new seeds are released to carry on the species.

Fire is a wonderful cleanser. It acts as a check on   9
various diseases: the heat and flames kill off harmful plant
parasites and bacteria. Another reason for burning is to get
rid of leaf litter. If all the fallen leaves and decaying
vegetation were allowed to pile up, a natural fire would be a
disaster for the sanctuary. Eliminating the extra fuel ensures that minimal damage will occur if an uncontrolled fire
should accidentally start.

Through their long association with fire, South Flori-   10
da's plants have evolved many adaptations to its recurrences.
Florida slash pines have a thick, spongy bark that contains
much moisture. When a fire passes by, the bark may be
singed, but the tree is protected. Saw palmettos have a long
thick stem or "runner" that hugs the ground, so that a fire,
unable to take hold from below, passes right over it. And I
have to admit that nothing is wasted in a fire, not even the
lives of the insects. Many birds come to a burned-over area
to feed. Red-shouldered hawks love toasted grasshoppers.

I learned to unlearn my belief that fire and plants are   11
enemies. Soaked to mid-thigh, muscles sore, face and arms
scratched, covered with seeds and burrs, I would emerge from
a tangle of vines with a fire close on my heels. Taking the
bandana from over my mouth and nose, I would gulp fresh air.
I had to tell myself that I was giving the plants a hand. I
was just helping a natural process that, until interrupted by
humans, had been going on for centuries. The trees needed
me. I looked across the fire lane at an area that had been
burned a few weeks before, and already the ground was covered
with light green. I'll have to have a talk with Smokey the
Bear. He may have to change a few of his ideas if he ever
retires to Florida.

Questions to Start You Thinking

1. What evidence do you find of the writer's critically rethinking an earlier belief
   and then revising it?

2. By beginning and ending with the writer's personal experience, what does this essay gain? Can it be charged that the memories recalled in the first four paragraphs and the last paragraph don't serve the main purpose of the paper—to explain the "why" behind the burns?

3. At any point, do you get the sense that the writer is criticizing human beings? If so, what is her point? Do you agree or disagree? For what reasons?

4. What phenomenon have you observed lately whose causes or effects might be worth exploring?

In the sixties and seventies Jonathan Kozol gained fame as a teacher, author, and stern critic of American education. With the publication of *Rachel and Her Children* (1988) he has also gained a reputation as an advocate for the homeless. Kozol's "Distancing the Homeless," which appeared in the Winter 1988 issue of the *Yale Review*, was the basis for this essay.

ARE THE HOMELESS CRAZY?
Jonathan Kozol

It is commonly believed by many journalists and politicians that the homeless of America are, in large part, former patients of large mental hospitals who were deinstitutionalized in the 1970s—the consequence, it is sometimes said, of misguided liberal opinion that favored the treatment of such persons in community-based centers. It is argued that this policy, and the subsequent failure of society to build such centers or to provide them in sufficient number, is the primary cause of homelessness in the United States.

Those who work among the homeless do not find that explanation satisfactory. While conceding that a certain number of the homeless are or have been mentally unwell, they believe that, in the case of most unsheltered people, the primary reason is economic rather than clinical. The cause of homelessness, they say with disarming logic, is the lack of homes and of income with which to rent or acquire them.

They point to the loss of traditional jobs in industry (two million every year since 1980) and to the fact that half of those who are laid off end up in work that pays a poverty-level wage. They point out that since 1968 the number of children living in poverty has grown by three million, while welfare benefits to families with children have declined by 35 percent.

And they note, too, that these developments have occurred during a time in which the shortage of low-income housing has intensified as the gentrification of our major cities has accelerated. Half a million units of low-income housing are lost each year to condominium conversion as well as to arson, demolition, or abandonment. Between 1978 and 1980, median rents climbed 30 percent for people in the lowest income sector, driving many of these families into the streets. Since 1980, rents have risen at even faster rates.

Hard numbers, in this instance, would appear to be of greater help than psychiatric labels in telling us why so many people become homeless. Eight million American families now use half or more of their income to pay their rent or mortgage. At the same time, federal support for low-income housing dropped from $30 billion (1980) to $7.5 billion (1988). Under Presidents Ford and Carter, 500,000 subsidized private housing units were constructed. By President Reagan's second term, the number had dropped to 25,000.

In our rush to explain the homeless as a psychiatric problem even the words of medical practitioners who care for homeless people have been curiously ignored. A study published by the Massachusetts Medical Society, for instance, has noted that, with the exceptions of alcohol and drug use, the most frequent illnesses among a sample of the homeless population were trauma (31 percent), upper-respiratory disorders (28 percent), limb disorders (19 percent), mental illness (16 percent), skin diseases (15 percent), hypertension (14 percent), and neurological illnesses (12 percent). Why, we may ask, of all these calamities, does mental illness command so much political and press attention? The answer may be that the label of mental illness places the destitute outside the sphere of ordinary life. It personalizes an anguish that is public in its genesis; it individualizes a misery that is both general in cause and general in application.

There is another reason to assign labels to the destitute and single out mental illness from among their many afflictions. All these other problems—tuberculosis, asthma, scabies, diarrhea, bleeding gums, impacted teeth, etc.—bear no stigma, and mental illness does. It conveys a stigma in the United States. It conveys a stigma in the Soviet Union as well. In both nations the label is used, whether as a matter of deliberate policy or not, to isolate and treat as special cases those who, by deed or word or by sheer presence, represent a threat to national complacence. The two situations are obviously not identical, but they are enough alike to give Americans reason for concern.

The notion that the homeless are largely psychotics who belong in institutions, rather than victims of displacement at the hands of enterprising realtors, spares us from the need to offer realistic solutions to the deep and widening extremes of wealth and poverty in the United States. It also enables us to tell ourselves that the despair of homeless people bears no intimate connection to the privileged existence we enjoy—when, for example, we rent or purchase one of those restored town houses that once provided shelter for people now huddled in the street.

What is to be made, then, of the supposition that the homeless are primarily the former residents of mental hospitals, persons who were carelessly released during the 1970s? Many of them are, to be sure. Among the older men and women in the streets and shelters, as many as one-third (some believe as many as one-half) may be chronically disturbed, and a number of these people were deinstitutionalized during the 1970s. But to operate on that assumption in a city such as New York—where nearly half the homeless are small children whose average age is six—makes no sense. Their parents, with an average age of twenty-seven, are not likely to have been hospitalized in the 1970s, either.

A frequently cited set of figures tells us that in 1955 the average daily census of nonfederal psychiatric institutions was 677,000, and that by 1984 the number had dropped to 151,000. But these people didn't go directly from a hospital room to the street. The bulk of those who had been psychiatric patients and were released from hospitals during the 1960s and early 1970s had been living in low-income housing, many in skid-row hotels or boardinghouses. Such housing—commonly known as SRO (single-room occupancy) units—was drastically diminished by the gentrification of our cities that began in the early '70s. Almost 50 percent of SRO housing was replaced by luxury apartments or office buildings between 1970 and 1980, and the remaining units have been disappearing even more rapidly.

Even for those persons who are ill and were deinstitutionalized during the decades before 1980, the precipitating cause of homelessness in 1987 is not illness but loss of housing. SRO housing offered low-cost sanctuaries for the homeless, providing a degree of safety and mutual support for those who lived within them. They were a demeaning version of the community health centers that society had promised; they were the de facto "halfway houses" of the 1970s. For these people too—at most half of the homeless single persons in America—the cause of homelessness is lack of housing.

Even in those cases where mental instability is apparent, homelessness itself is often the precipitating factor. For example, many pregnant women without homes are denied prenatal care because they constantly travel from one shelter to another. Many are anemic. Many are denied essential dietary supplements by recent federal cuts. As a consequence, some of their children do not live to see their second year of life. Do these mothers sometimes show signs of stress? Do they appear disorganized, depressed, disordered? Frequently. They are immobilized by pain, traumatized by fear. So it is no surprise that when researchers enter the scene to ask them how they "feel," the resulting reports tell us that the homeless are emotionally unwell. The reports do not tell us that we have *made* these people ill. They do not tell us that illness is a natural response to intolerable conditions. Nor do they tell us of the strength and the resilience that so many of these people retain despite the miseries they must endure.

A writer in the *New York Times* describes a homeless woman standing on a traffic island in Manhattan. "She was evicted from her small room in the hotel just across the street," and she is determined to get revenge. Until she does, "nothing will move her from that spot. . . . Her argumentativeness and her angry fixation on revenge, along with the apparent absence of hallucinations, mark her as a paranoid." Most physicians, I imagine, would be more reserved in passing judgment with so little evidence, but this reporter makes his diagnosis without hesitation. "The paranoids of the street," he says, "are among the most difficult to help."

Perhaps so. But does it depend on who is offering the help? Is anyone   14
offering to help this woman get back her home? Is it crazy to seek vengeance for being thrown into the street? The absence of anger, some psychiatrists believe, might indicate much greater illness.

"No one will be turned away," says the mayor of New York City, as   15
hundreds of young mothers with their infants are turned from the doors of shelters season after season. That may sound to some like a denial of reality. "Now you're hearing all kinds of horror stories," says the President of the United States as he denies that anyone is cold or hungry or unhoused. On another occasion he says that the unsheltered "are homeless, you might say, by choice." That sounds every bit as self-deceiving.

The woman standing on the traffic island screaming for revenge until   16
her room has been restored to her sounds relatively healthy by comparison. If three million homeless people did the same, and all at the same time, we might finally be forced to listen.

Questions to Start You Thinking

1. According to Kozol, what are the immediate causes of homelessness in America? What are the remote causes?

2. What reason does Kozol give for the widespread perception that the homeless are, by and large, mentally ill? To what extent does he agree with this perception?

3. Where in the essay does Kozol switch from searching out causes to detailing the effects of homelessness? Is he guilty of going around in circles? Explain.

4. Read one newspaper or magazine article that probes the causes of some contemporary problem: the shortage of reasonable day-care options, for instance, or the low academic scores of American students compared with students in other developed countries. Can you suggest additional causes that the article writer seems to have ignored?

LEARNING BY WRITING

The Assignment: Understanding a Change

Point to some definite change that has taken place in your lifetime and describe it briefly. That part of your paper is only an introduction. Make it no longer than two or three paragraphs.

Then, in the main part of your paper, do any one of the following tasks to show how the change came about and what followed as a result.

1. Explain the causes of this change.
2. Explain its subsequent effects.
3. Explain both.

By "change" we mean a noticeable, lasting transformation, an alteration produced by some event, some definite new force, some new invention or discovery, some deep-down shift in the structure of society—not a trend or a passing fad likely to burn out in a year, like Spuds McKenzie T-shirts, break dancing, or the grapefruit diet. The change might be one that has affected only you, such as a move to another location. It might be a change that has affected not only yourself but also many other people in a city or region (the growth of high technology in the Silicon Valley of California) or in society at large (the arrival of the personal computer).

Write for an audience of your fellow students. If you write about a change in your own life, assume that your readers will care to know more about you. If you write about some change in a region or in society at large, assume that they will want to compare their own impressions of this change with yours.

Papers written in response to this assignment have included the following.

A woman's recollection of having lived for a year in rural Mexico that detailed the effects of her stay on her outlook and opinions after her return to the United States.

A woman's view of a shift she has noticed in her lifetime: in male attitudes toward women. Now, she finds, women are treated with less "fake politeness" and with more respect. Her paper explores causes for this change besides the women's movement. One leading cause is that a shift in the economy from industry to service and technology has created more jobs in which women can shine.

A man's contention that, in quality of architectural design, new buildings constructed in Minneapolis have greatly improved over those designed before World War II. He surveys the reasons for this improvement, citing the influence of architects and city planners.

A woman's observation that America has seen a decline in popular interest in space travel. She arrays evidence to support this claim: children no longer want to be astronauts; the fact that people have walked on the moon is now rarely mentioned in the press. She then asks why and finds causes for the decline, including decreased funding for the space program and the Challenger disaster.

Generating Ideas

What change that has taken place in your lifetime would be enjoyable or instructive to explore? This assignment leaves you the option of writing either from personal experience or from what you know or can find out.

Search your memory. A random search of your memory may help get you started. You might let your thoughts wander back to how things were a few years ago or when you were a child. Then ask yourself: In what respects are things different today?

These changes might be any of the following kinds (or any others that occur to you).

- A change in how you live (caused by a new job; a fluctuation in income; personal or family upheaval caused by death, divorce, accident, illness, or good fortune; starting college).
- A change in where you live.
- A change in the environment (such as air pollution, natural events such as a flood or a storm, the coming of new industry to a locality, or the failure of an old industry).
- A change caused by growing up or gaining in maturity.
- A change caused by a new invention (computers, microchips, pocket calculators, VCRs) or discovery (a wonder drug, a better design for reeds for woodwinds).
- A change in social opportunities (women now more readily accepted as corporate executives, judges, governors, candidates for other high political office; blacks and Hispanics increasingly prominent in sports as coaches and managers or media commentators).

Soon, when a few thoughts percolate, reach for a pencil and brainstorm—jot down a list of likely topics that come to mind. (For more tips on brainstorming, see p. 471). Then choose the idea that you care most about, one that promises to be neither too large nor too small. A paper that confined itself to the causes of a family's move from New Jersey to Montana might be only one sentence long: "My father's company transferred him." But the subsequent effects of the move (on the writer and other family members) might require a whole paper. So the writer would probably choose to include both causes and effects. On the other hand, unless you are writing a very long term paper, the causes of a change in women's roles during the past twenty years are likely to prove too many and too profound even to begin to sketch in fewer than ten thousand words. Instead, can you narrow your topic? You might consider just one aspect of these changes, such as why more married women today hold full-time jobs.

List causes and effects. Your choice tentatively made, write for ten or fifteen minutes and set down likely causes and effects.

In looking for causes, look first for *immediate causes*—those evident and close at hand that clearly led to a situation or development. Then look for *remote causes:* underlying, more basic reasons for the situation, not always evident to an observing eye—perhaps causes that came earlier. The immediate cause of unemployment in a town might be the closing of a factory. But the more remote cause of unemployment might be competition from a foreign business, against which the local company couldn't survive. The immediate cause of an outbreak of sunburn cases might be a week of blazing sunshine. But the more remote cause of the problem might be the thinning of the ozone layer, causing a greater amount of harmful radiation to seep through the atmosphere.

Look back in time only as far as seems necessary. A paper on the causes of the sexual revolution that began with the fall of Adam would probably be going back too far. The writer might better confine the inquiry to what has been happening since 1970 or 1980.

Work with a pencil and check, star, or underline any causes that stand out as probable. Another way to rate the items on your list is to ask: Is this an *essential* cause? Is it something without which the change couldn't have happened? (Then it deserves a big star.) Or, without it, might the change have taken place nevertheless, for some other reason? (It might still matter, but less importantly.)

If you haven't figured out enough causes to explain the change to your satisfaction, you need to do some more digging. Remember, you have five major resources.

DISCOVERY CHECKLIST: USING BASIC RESOURCES

- *Recall.* Do you remember having lived through this change? Can you remember life before it, and after?
- *Observation.* Can you go out right now and see the effects of this change in the world nearby?
- *Conversation.* Whom might you ask about it?
- *Reading.* Have any books or magazine articles on this change been published lately? (You might check a library catalog and the *Readers' Guide to Periodical Literature.*)
- *Imagining.* Can you imagine possible causes or effects of this change and then test your imaginings against reality? For instance, if you are writing about why married women want jobs, try putting yourself in the place of such a woman when she stays home full-time. What is her situation? Then talk to such a woman, either a homemaker or an ex-homemaker now employed. See how well you have imagined.

If your topic calls on you to account for people's behavior, consider some suggestions from Kenneth Burke. A literary critic and philosopher, Burke has proposed a set of questions designed to discover the deep-down causes of a person's actions. For a writer, Burke's questions often generate insights, observations, and hunches worth pursuing. Take a look at "Seeking Motives" (p. 480).

Shaping a Draft

Katie Kennedy's "Why We Burned a Wilderness" follows a clear plan. In her first four paragraphs, Kennedy recalls the burning of the swamp; in the rest of the paper she shows why the swamp was burned. The essay was written from this brief scratch outline:

1. Going on the burn—I expected bad effects

2. Why was burn done?
   History of South Fla.—nature needs help
   Fire releases nutrients
   Some plants need fire to reproduce
   Diversify vegetation
   Check disease
   Get rid of leaf litter
   Guard against more serious fire

3. Bad effects not so bad at all
   Plants adapt
   Nothing wasted

The paper makes its point: it shows the reason for which professional naturalists act—to give nature a hand. And it shows that cause and effect are closely related: naturalists act in order to achieve desired effects. In paragraph 2, the writer *imagines* the disastrous effects of the fire: homeless creatures fleeing, some dying. Paragraph 6 sets forth the valuable effects of natural fires.

WRITING WITH A COMPUTER: SEEKING CAUSES AND EFFECTS
Whether you're looking for causes or effects, word processing can simplify your job. In setting forth causes, you can make a list of causes and, next to each item on the list, drop in your evidence for it. In writing a paper determining effects, you can make a similar list and flesh it out with evidence. ("The lowering of the tariff on Japanese-made cars worked havoc in the automotive industry"—that statement of an effect calls for evidence: a few facts to back it up).

Does your evidence seem substantial? You can tell from a glance at your screen exactly where you need to generate more material. Highlight any skimpy parts with **boldface** or underlining so you won't forget these needy places when you revise. With a couple of keystrokes, you can highlight a whole long passage. Later, after you've revised and strengthened the passage, you can delete the highlighting with a few more keystrokes.

If in following your assignment you've decided to look for causes, many possible causes may present themselves. In planning your paper, try to assign them relative importance: classify them as major causes or minor ones. If you are writing about why more married women hold jobs now than they did ten years ago, you might make a list that includes (1) boredom and (2) economic necessity—husbands don't earn enough. On reflection, you might decide that economic necessity is a major cause; boredom, probably a minor one. Plan to give economic necessity more room.

Having finished the first part of your paper, the description of the change, you prepare to fulfill one of the three tasks (to explain causes, explain effects, or explain both). Your next sentence will probably write itself. Let it be a sentence that will make clear to your reader which task you are going to perform. We don't mean you ought to say, in a flat and mechanical fashion, "Now I am going to explain the causes of this change." You can announce your task more casually, more naturally, as if you were talking to someone: "At first, I didn't realize that keeping six pet cheetahs in our backyard would bother the neighbors." Or, in a paper about your father's sudden move to a Trappist monastery: "The real reason for Father's decision didn't become clear to me for a long while."

Rewriting

As you know by now, ascertaining causes and effects takes hard thought. You'll want to set aside an especially generous amount of time to look back over, ponder, and rewrite this paper. Katie Kennedy wrote several drafts of "Why We Burned a Wilderness." As she approached the paper's final version, one of the problems she faced was making a smooth transition from recalling her own experience to probing causes.

belongs / ~~I always found it~~
the / ~~It always seemed~~ nerve-racking to be followed so
eding
it. \ closely by the fire., *although* ~~After~~ my first ditch crossing/ I was
somewhat comforted by the thought that my soaked jeans
and boots probably wouldn't burn. ¶I never got over my   *Start ¶*
here!
uneasiness about being so close to the fire. ~~Although~~ I
going on controlled burns. Yet,
didn't like ~~it,~~ as a seasonal naturalist at the National
Audubon Society's Corkscrew Swamp Sanctuary in the Big
learned
Cypress Swamp region of South Florida, I soon ~~was taught~~
that burns had to be done periodically to ensure the
swamp
health of the ~~sanctuary.~~ One of my duties was to go
along with the full-time staff to see how the burns were
done. ~~The heat was intense and the smoke bothered my~~ *Doesn't belong*
here. But
where?

~~eyes.~~ Another duty, ~~and this~~ one I hadn't expected, was to read books. I learned a lot from *one of them,* *Fire in South Florida Ecosystems*, by the staff of the Southeast Forest Experiment Station in Asheville, North Carolina (Washington, D.C.: U.S. Forest Service, 1980). *It* ~~I was~~ convinced *me* that trees and plants of the swamp need fire to survive. ¶ The interrelationship of *vegetation* ~~trees~~ with fire has *evolved* ~~been an evolving thing~~ over thousands of years. In the past, when South Florida was covered with *an* ~~un~~broken *canopy of* vegetation, fires would *start* ~~be started~~ naturally by lightning. Sometimes, *they would rage* ~~there would be fire~~ from one side of the Florida peninsula to the other *and die only on reaching the coast*. Or they might blaze until extinguished by the rains of the next wet season. Yet, in as little as two weeks, fresh green growth would begin to cover the ground again.

End ¶ here!

Kennedy started her revision on this troublesome section by eliminating a few lifeless passive constructions and unnecessary words. She also made some details more vivid, allowing the fires to *rage* and substituting *an unbroken canopy of vegetation* for *unbroken vegetation*. As she worked, she moved one sentence to a more appropriate spot earlier in the essay. Finally, she realized that paragraph 5 ought to be a tightly organized transition paragraph and that paragraph 6 ought to begin in a new place.

In revising a paper that traces causes, you might ask yourself the following questions.

REVISION CHECKLIST: ASKING WHY

- Why are you going to all the work of demonstrating causes? Have you shown your reader that your paper has a point to it?
- Have you given any evidence to convince a reader that the causes you find are the true ones?
- If not, where can you discover more evidence? Look to your five basic resources: recalling, observing, reading, conversing, and imagining.
- Have you claimed remote causes you can't begin to prove? That's all right, but do indicate sheer guesswork.
- Have you stated the causes with cocksure, swaggering certainty, when in all honesty you might admit that you're only guessing? ("Thus it is obvious, as I have proved conclusively, that unemployment in Ohio is entirely due to the activities of pro-environment lobbyists.")

- Have you fallen into any logical fallacies (see p. 525), such as *oversimplification*—assuming that there was only one small cause for a large phenomenon? A typical oversimplification: "The revolution in sexual attitudes began because Marilyn Monroe posed in the nude for a calendar."

  Another common mistake in logic is the *post hoc* fallacy, from the Latin *post hoc, ergo propter hoc*, meaning "after this, therefore because of this." In other words, don't assume that one thing caused another just because it preceded it. This is the error of a writer who declares, "Sandra Day O'Connor was appointed to the Supreme Court; in the following year, there was a noteworthy increase in the number of convicted rapists." (There seems no clear causal connection here: the Supreme Court doesn't try rapists.)

In revising a paper setting forth effects, you might ask yourself the following questions.

REVISION CHECKLIST: DETERMINING EFFECTS

- What possible further effects have you left out? Are any of them worth adding?
- Do you make clear that these effects have indeed occurred? Have you given any evidence—perhaps reported any observations or testimony, perhaps quoted any opinions from authorities?
- Could any effect you mention have resulted not from the change you describe but from some other cause?

Remember, unless you are writing a paper that sets forth exact scientific findings (reporting, say, the effects of combining two chemicals), your instructor won't expect you to write a definitive explanation. You'll be expected only to do what lies within your capacity: to write an explanation that is thoughtful, searching, and reasonable.

Before you type a final draft, why not let a peer reader check over your paper and answer the questions on one of the following checklists. The first applies to a paper seeking causes, the second to a paper concerned with effects.

PEER EDITING CHECKLIST: SEEKING CAUSES

- Describe your overall response to the paper.
- Does the writer present causes that seem logical and possible?

- Did other causes occur to you that you think the writer should consider? If so, list them.
- Circle on the manuscript any areas where spelling, punctuation, grammar, or word choice got in the way of your reading or understanding of the essay.
- If you were going to hand in this essay for a grade, is there anything you'd be sure to revise?

PEER EDITING CHECKLIST: DETERMINING EFFECTS

- Describe your first response to the paper.
- What seems to you to be the purpose of the essay? Does setting forth effects let the writer accomplish his or her purpose?
- Has the writer overlooked some effects that should be added? List any that occurred to you as you read the paper.
- Are you convinced by the logic used in the paper? Do all the effects the writer gives seem to be the result of the change he or she describes? Point out any effects that you found hard to accept as results of the change the writer describes.
- For the effects set forth as fact, has the writer given you enough evidence that they are fact? List any you don't believe really happened.
- Circle on the manuscript any areas where spelling, grammar, punctuation, or word choice got in the way of your reading or understanding of the essay.
- If you were going to hand in this paper for a grade, what would you be sure to revise?

Other Assignments

1. In a short paper, explain *either* the causes *or* the effects of a situation that exists today in our society. Draw on your reading, your conversation, your memory, your observations—on any useful resource.

    Some existing situations might be the difficulty of getting admitted to law school, the shortage of highly qualified elementary school teachers in some areas, the willingness of businesses to hire college graduates with degrees in the liberal arts—or whatever interests and concerns you.

    Your readers for this paper won't be sociologists or other professionals who would expect a profound explanation, but fellow students with interests similar to your own who might appreciate what you have to say.

2. Write an explanation of your own motives. Explore your reasons for taking some step or for doing something in a customary way. (All of us do some things without first reasoning. If you need help in pinning down reasons for your own behavior, some of Kenneth Burke's suggestions on pp. 480–482 may be useful.)

FOR GROUP LEARNING
Together in class or in your writing group, tell aloud a two-minute story
that you invent to explain the causes behind any surprising event that you
find reported in this morning's news. Either realistic explanations or tall
tales will be acceptable. You'll need to prepare your story carefully in
advance. Invite the others to comment on it and, with their reactions in
mind, set down your story on paper to turn in at the next class. In writing
it down, embellish and improve on your story as much as you desire.

Before you write *any* paper setting forth causes or effects, you will find
it particularly helpful to talk over with your fellow students what you plan
to say. Ask for their comments. Invite them to add to your list of causes
or effects if they can. In discerning causes and effects, always a complex
task, you will generally find that several heads are far better than one.

3. In an introductory philosophy course at Loyola College in Maryland, Frank J.
Cunningham asks his students to write, instead of a traditional research paper,
a short original essay exploring their own ideas and opinions. The assignment
calls for students first to describe an idea and then to ask themselves why they
hold it:

> Over the years, in the process of growing up and growing civilized, all
> of us have developed certain opinions about the way things happen, about
> what works and what doesn't work, about how things are. We have also
> developed certain expectations toward our world based on these opinions.
>
> Under ordinary circumstances, we live with these opinions and expec-
> tations unquestioningly, and, on the whole, we manage quite well with our
> lives. But . . . in philosophy we look at things we don't normally look at,
> question things we normally take for granted, analyze what we accept from
> day to day.
>
> As preparation for this somewhat unusual (some would say perverse)
> activity, I would like you to think about your own opinions. Think about your
> views of the world, your expectations, your certainties, and decide on some-
> thing of which you are absolutely certain. It may be a part of your normal
> life, a truth derived from your education, something that you have learned
> through your years of experience, something you were told, something you
> figured out on your own. Now write a short essay (no more than two pages)
> describing the one thing about which you are absolutely certain and why this
> thing commands such certainty.
>
> Remember that an essay such as this requires thought as preparation.
> You should not expect to sit down immediately at the typewriter and produce
> it. Remember too that there are at least two separate thinking tasks to be
> performed. First you must consider your stock of truths to find one in which
> you have utmost confidence. This will probably take some time and effort
> since we are willing to let a lot of truths pass without putting them to the
> test. Second, you must consider the reason for your certainty. In working
> out this part of the essay it might be useful to pretend that you are trying to
> convince a very reasonable but thoroughly doubting person of the truth of
> your position.

HELMUT CHECKED THE BOULDER AT TWELVE-
MINUTE INTERVALS THROUGHOUT THE NIGHT

"WE'LL HAVE NO ALLITERATION IN THIS
HERE BUNKHOUSE!" SNORTED McCULLOCH

IT WAS MRS. CRABTREE AND SHE WAS
IN NO MOOD FOR PLEASANTRIES

4. Glen Baxter, a humorous artist, specializes in the curious scene that cries out for an explanation. From the group of his drawings here, pick a drawing that interests you. In a paragraph, set forth the causes that might have led to the scene depicted in it. Then in a second paragraph, give at least one effect that might follow from it. Allow your imagination free rein.

APPLYING WHAT YOU LEARN: SOME USES OF SEEKING CAUSES AND EFFECTS

Examination questions often pose a problem in causality: "Trace the causes of the decline of foreign sales of American automobiles." Equally familiar is the exam question that calls for a survey of effects: "What economic effects of the repeal of Prohibition were immediately evident in the early 1930s?" Problems of that very same sort, you'll find, will frequently turn up as paper topics. In a child development course, you might be asked to research what makes some people become child abusers. In a speech pathology course you might be called on to investigate the causes and effects of head trauma, fetal alcohol syndrome, learning disabilities or dyslexia, Down's syndrome—all of which are relevant to impaired communication skills.

But in fulfilling any kind of college writing assignment, even one that doesn't ask you to look for causes or effects, you may wish to spend *part* of your paper exploring one or the other or both. For a chemistry assignment you would most likely do this in the discussion section of a paper that analyzes. In a paper that deals with any phenomenon—say, a sociology course assignment to write about an increase in teenage pregnancies among middle-class suburbanites—a paragraph or two that explores the causes of that phenomenon or its effects might add considerable depth to your paper.

At any moment in a book or article that deals with some current phenomenon, the writer may ask why—in only a paragraph or a few paragraphs. In *The Economics of Public Issues*, a college textbook, Douglass C. North and Roger Leroy Miller make the surprising claim that the ban of cigarette advertising on television has had effects injurious to your health:

> The banning of advertising has had dramatic effects in other industries too. In 1976, Congress banned the advertising of cigarettes on television in response to the Surgeon General's finding that cigarette smoking could lead to lung cancer. It was argued that captive TV watchers should not be subjected to the advertising of a hazardous product. The results of such a ban were just the opposite of the desired effect. The lack of cigarette advertising on TV has caused two distinct phenomena, both of which have led to possible increased health problems. Prior to the banning of cigarette advertising on TV, the American Cancer Society and the antismoking lobbyists succeeded in forcing free antismoking ads on TV. Under the Fairness Doctrine promulgated by the Federal Communications Commission, networks are supposed to air *both* sides of the story (as if there were only two sides to every argument). Thus, if TV networks were accepting money for cigarette advertisements, it was argued they must also accept antismoking ads (and for free). Thus, prior to 1976, there were several antismoking ads a day on each network. After the ban on TV advertising of cigarettes, however, the networks were no longer obligated under the Fairness Doctrine to show antismoking ads for free. Thus, the number of antismoking ads dropped dramatically. Apparently such ads were having an effect, especially among teenagers and women, for the percentage of teenagers and women who smoke has been rising since the time cigarette TV ads were banned. Perhaps that is coincidence, but perhaps not.
>
> The other phenomenon that may be leading to increased health hazards on the part of the American public results from the fact that TV advertising is a powerful, and perhaps the single most effective, means to introduce new cigarettes into the marketplace. Once people are set on smoking a particular brand of cigarette, it is hard to get them to change or to be aware of new brands; but TV advertising did just that—it made them aware of what was available. Professor Ben Klein has found that since the banning of advertising on TV, the introduction of new low tar, low nicotine cigarettes has dropped by 42 percent. Presumably, smokers benefit by switching to low tar, low nicotine cigarettes because they reduce the probability of lung disease in the future. Thus, the banning of such advertising has led consumers to stick with their old brands of cigarettes, which are likely to have higher levels of tar and nicotine and, hence, are more of a health hazard.

In less formal writing, too, the method is used continually. Stephen King, in *Danse Macabre*, his study of horror movies, asks why the average American, living a life without terror or violence, will pay four or five dollars to see a horror movie. In several paragraphs, King considers "simple and obvious" reasons: to show that we aren't afraid, to have fun, to feel comfortable in our own essential normality. Then he considers a deeper reason for the films' appeal:

> The mythic horror movie, like the sick joke, has a dirty job to do. It deliberately appeals to all that is worst in us. It is morbidity unchained, our most base instincts let free, our nastiest fantasies realized—and it happens, fittingly enough, in the dark. For these reasons, good liberals often shy away from horror films. For myself, I like to see the most aggressive of them—*Dawn of the Dead*, for instance—as lifting a trapdoor in the civilized forebrain and throwing a basket of raw meat to the hungry alligators swimming around in that subterranean river beneath. Why bother? Because it keeps them from getting out, man. It keeps them down there and me up here. It was Lennon and McCartney who said that all you need is love, and I would agree with that. As long as you keep the gators fed.

To be sure, King's suggested explanation doesn't end the inquiry, but it offers a provocative answer to the question Why?

In his article "Causation of Terror," social historian Feliks Gross seeks to explain a difficult, complex, and vitally important matter: the reasons for political assassinations and terrorism in Europe and Russia in the nineteenth and twentieth centuries. Gross recalls cases of political parties who have used terrorist tactics to overthrow moderate and democratic governments; he remembers the victims of oppressive rule who have used terrorist tactics to fight back: the histories of the Armenians and Bulgarians under Turkish rule, the Serbs under Croatian Ustasha government, the Polish underground fighters who resisted Nazi occupation. Tentatively, offering a vast generalization, Gross finds that economic hardship does not usually cause its victims to respond with terrorist tactics and political assassinations. Instead, the causes of terrorism appear to lie in ethnic tensions and clashes of political ideology.

"It is of paramount significance," Gross concludes, "to understand the conditions that are conducive to political assassination." By controlling such conditions, perhaps we might even prevent terrorism. Applied to such an end, exploring causes and effects is no mere game, but a way of seeking peace and ensuring it.

A Historian Seeks Causes

In this lively essay, now included in *Fasting Girls: The Emergence of Anorexia Nervosa as a Modern Disease* (1988), medical historian Joan Jacobs Brumberg writes of a disease that afflicts many young people today. She deals with it as a phenomenon in the nineteenth century, seeking out why it began.

THE ORIGINS OF ANOREXIA NERVOSA
Joan Jacobs Brumberg

Contrary to the popular assumption that anorexia nervosa is a peculiarly 1
modern disorder, the malady first emerged in the Victorian era—long before the pervasive cultural imperative for a thin female body. The first clinical

descriptions of the disorder appeared in England and France almost simultaneously in 1873. They were written by two well-known physicians: Sir
William Withey Gull and Charles Lasègue. Lasègue, more than any other
nineteenth-century doctor, captured the rhythm of repeated offerings and
refusals that signaled the breakdown of reciprocity between parents and
their anorexic daughter. By returning to its origins, we can see anorexia
nervosa for what it is: a dysfunction in the bourgeois family system.

Family meals assumed enormous importance in the bourgeois milieu,   2
in the United States as well as in England and France. Middle-class parents
prided themselves on providing ample food for their children. The abun-
dance of food and the care in its preparation became expressions of social
status. The ambience of the meal symbolized the values of the family. A
popular domestic manual advised, "Simple, healthy food, exquisitely prepared, and served upon shining dishes and brilliant silverware . . . a gentle
blessing, and cheerful conversation, embrace the sweetest communions
and the happiest moments of life." Among the middle class it seems that
eating correctly was emerging as a new morality, one that set its members
apart from the working class.

At the same time, food was used to express love in the nineteenth-   3
century bourgeois household. Offering attractive and abundant meals was
the particular responsibility and pleasure of middle-class wives and mothers. In America the feeding of middle-class children, from infancy on, had
become a maternal concern no longer deemed appropriate to delegate to
wet nurses, domestics, or governesses. Family meals were expected to be
a time of instructive and engaging conversation. Participation was expected
on both a verbal and gustatory level. In this context, refusing to eat was
an unabashedly antisocial act. Anorexic behavior was antithetical to the
ideal of bourgeois eating. One advice book, *Common Sense for Maid, Wife,
and Mother*, stated: "Heated discussion and quarrels, fretfulness and
sullen taciturnity while eating, are as unwholesome as they are un-
christian."

Why would a daughter affront her parents by refusing to eat? Lasègue's   4
1873 description of anorexia nervosa, along with other nineteenth-century
medical reports, suggests that pressure to marry may have precipitated the
illness.

Ambitious parents surely understood that by marrying well, at an ap-   5
propriate moment, a daughter, even though she did not carry the family
name, could help advance a family's social status—particularly in a bur-
geoning middle-class society. As a result, the issue of marriage loomed
large in the life of a dutiful middle-class daughter. Although marriage did
not generally occur until the girl's early twenties, it was an event for which
she was continually prepared, and a desirable outcome for all depended
on the ability of the parents and the child to work together—that is, to state
clearly what each wanted or to read each other's heart and mind. In the
context of marital expectations, a daughter's refusal to eat was a provoc-

ative rejection of both the family's social aspirations and their goodwill toward her. All of the parents' plans for her future (and their own) could be stymied by her peculiar and unpleasant alimentary nihilism.

Beyond the specific anxieties generated by marital pressure, the Victorian family milieu in America and in Western Europe harbored a mélange of other tensions and problems that provided the emotional preconditions for the emergence of anorexia nervosa. As love replaced authority as the cement of family relations, it began to generate its own set of emotional disorders.

Possessiveness, for example, became an acute problem in Victorian family life. Where love between parents and children was the prevailing ethic, there was always the risk of excess. When love became suffocating or manipulative, individuation and separation from the family could become extremely painful, if not impossible. In the context of increased intimacy, adolescent privacy was especially problematic: for parents and their sexually maturing daughters, what constituted an appropriate degree of privacy? Middle-class girls, for example, almost always had their own rooms or shared them with sisters, but they had greater difficulty establishing autonomous psychic space. The well-known penchant of adolescent girls for novel-reading was an expression of their need for imaginative freedom. Some parents, recognizing that their daughters needed channels for expressing emotions, encouraged diary-keeping. But some of the same parents who gave lovely marbled journals as gifts also monitored their content. Since emotional freedom was not an acknowledged prerogative of the Victorian adolescent girl, it seems likely that she would have expressed unhappiness in nonverbal forms of behavior. One such behavior was refusal of food.

When an adolescent daughter became sullen and chronically refused to eat, her parents felt threatened and confused. The daughter was perceived as willfully manipulating her appetite the way a younger child might. Because parents did not want to encourage this behavior, they often refused at first to indulge the favorite tastes or caprices of their daughter. As emaciation became visible and the girl looked ill, many violated the contemporary canon of prudent childrearing and put aside their moral objections to pampering the appetite. Eventually they would beg their daughter to eat whatever she liked—and eat she must, "as a sovereign proof of affection" for them. From the parents' perspective, a return to eating was a confirmation of filial love.

The significance of food refusal as an emotional tactic within the family depended on food's being plentiful, pleasing, and connected to love. Where food was eaten simply to assuage hunger, where it had only minimal aesthetic and symbolic messages, or where the girl had to provide her own nourishment, refusal of food was not particularly noteworthy or defiant. In contrast, the anorexic girl was surrounded by a provident, if not indulgent, family that was bound to be distressed by her rejection of its largess.

Anorexia nervosa was an intense form of discourse that honored the   10
emotional guidelines that governed the middle-class Victorian family. Refusing to eat was not as confrontational as yelling, having a tantrum, or
throwing things; refusing to eat expressed emotional hostility without being
flamboyant. And refusing to eat had the advantage of being ambiguous. If
a girl repeatedly claimed lack of appetite she might indeed be ill and therefore entitled to special treatment and favors.

In her own way, the anorexic was respectful of what historian Peter Gay   11
called "the great bourgeois compromise between the need for reserve and
the capacity for emotion." The rejection of food, while an emotionally
charged behavior, was also discreet, quiet, and ladylike. The unhappy adolescent who was in all other ways a dutiful daughter chose food refusal
from within the symptom repertoire available to her. Precisely because she
was not a lunatic, she selected a behavior that she knew would have some
efficacy within her own family.

Questions to Start You Thinking

1. What common assumption about anorexia nervosa does Brumberg challenge? On
   what evidence does she base her challenge?
2. According to Brumberg, what is the main underlying cause of anorexia?
3. What light do the immediate causes of anorexia in Victorian times shed on its
   causes today?
4. Where in her essay does the author rely on any of the five resources for writers
   (recalling, observing, reading, conversing, and imagining)?
5. What do you take to be Brumberg's purpose in writing?

An Astronomer Determines Effects

Carl Sagan, a noted astronomer and professor at Cornell University, has written more than four hundred articles for both popular magazines and professional journals. Of all of them, this one strikes us as the most essential for
every concerned citizen's reading list.

THE NUCLEAR WINTER
Carl Sagan

Into the eternal darkness, into fire, into ice.
—Dante, The Inferno

Except for fools and madmen, everyone knows that nuclear war would   1
be an unprecedented human catastrophe. A more or less typical strategic
warhead has a yield of 2 megatons, the explosive equivalent of 2 million
tons of TNT. But 2 million tons of TNT is about the same as all the bombs

exploded in World War II—a single bomb with the explosive power of the entire Second World War but compressed into a few seconds of time and an area 30 or 40 miles across. . . .

In a 2-megaton explosion over a fairly large city, buildings would be vaporized, people reduced to atoms and shadows, outlying structures blown down like matchsticks and raging fires ignited. And if the bomb were exploded on the ground, an enormous crater, like those that can be seen through a telescope on the surface of the Moon, would be all that remained where midtown once had been. There are now more than 50,000 nuclear weapons, more than 13,000 megatons of yield, deployed in the arsenals of the United States and the Soviet Union—enough to obliterate a million Hiroshimas.

But there are fewer than 3,000 cities on the Earth with populations of 100,000 or more. You cannot find anything like a million Hiroshimas to obliterate. Prime military and industrial targets that are far from cities are comparatively rare. Thus, there are vastly more nuclear weapons than are needed for any plausible deterrence of a potential adversary.

Nobody knows, of course, how many megatons would be exploded in a real nuclear war. There are some who think that a nuclear war can be "contained," bottled up before it runs away to involve many of the world's arsenals. But a number of detailed analyses, war games run by the U.S. Department of Defense and official Soviet pronouncements, all indicate that this containment may be too much to hope for: once the bombs begin exploding, communications failures, disorganization, fear, the necessity of making in minutes decisions affecting the fates of millions and the immense psychological burden of knowing that your own loved ones may already have been destroyed are likely to result in a nuclear paroxysm. Many investigations, including a number of studies for the U.S. government, envision the explosion of 5,000 to 10,000 megatons—the detonation of tens of thousands of nuclear weapons that now sit quietly, inconspicuously, in missile silos, submarines, and long-range bombers, faithful servants awaiting orders.

The World Health Organization, in a recent detailed study chaired by Sune K. Bergstrom (the 1982 Nobel laureate in physiology and medicine), concludes that 1.1 billion people would be killed outright in such a nuclear war, mainly in the United States, the Soviet Union, Europe, China, and Japan. An additional 1.1 billion people would suffer serious injuries and radiation sickness, for which medical help would be unavailable. It thus seems possible that more than 2 billion people—almost half of all the humans on Earth—would be destroyed in the immediate aftermath of a global thermonuclear war. This would represent by far the greatest disaster in the history of the human species and, with no other adverse effects, would probably be enough to reduce at least the Northern Hemisphere to a state of prolonged agony and barbarism. Unfortunately, the real situation would be much worse.

In technical studies of the consequences of nuclear weapons explo-   6
sions, there has been a dangerous tendency to underestimate the results.
This is partly due to a tradition of conservatism which generally works well
in science but which is of more dubious applicability when the lives of
billions of people are at stake. In the Bravo test of March 1, 1954, a 15-
megaton thermonuclear bomb was exploded on Bikini Atoll. It had about
double the yield expected, and there was an unanticipated last-minute shift
in the wind direction. As a result, deadly radioactive fallout came down on
Rongelap in the Marshall Islands, more than 200 kilometers away. Almost
all the children on Rongelap subsequently developed thyroid nodules and
lesions, and other long-term medical problems, due to the radioactive fallout.

Likewise, in 1973, it was discovered that high-yield airbursts will chem-   7
ically burn the nitrogen in the upper air, converting it into oxides of nitrogen;
these, in turn, combine with and destroy the protective ozone in the Earth's
stratosphere. The surface of the Earth is shielded from deadly solar ultraviolet radiation by a layer of ozone so tenuous that, were it brought down
to sea level, it would be only 3 millimeters thick. Partial destruction of this
ozone layer can have serious consequences for the biology of the entire
planet.

These discoveries, and others like them, were made by chance. They   8
were largely unexpected. And now another consequence—by far the most
dire—has been uncovered, again more or less by accident.

The U.S. Mariner 9 spacecraft, the first vehicle to orbit another planet,   9
arrived at Mars in late 1971. The planet was enveloped in a global dust
storm. As the fine particles slowly fell out, we were able to measure temperature changes in the atmosphere and on the surface. Soon it became
clear what had happened:

The dust, lofted by high winds off the desert into the upper Martian   10
atmosphere, had absorbed the incoming sunlight and prevented much of
it from reaching the ground. Heated by the sunlight, the dust warmed the
adjacent air. But the surface, enveloped in partial darkness, became much
chillier than usual. Months later, after the dust fell out of the atmosphere,
the upper air cooled and the surface warmed, both returning to their normal
conditions. We were able to calculate accurately, from how much dust there
was in the atmosphere, how cool the Martian surface ought to have been.

Afterwards, I and my colleagues, James B. Pollack and Brian Toon of   11
NASA's Ames Research Center, were eager to apply these insights to the
Earth. In a volcanic explosion, dust aerosols are lofted into the high atmosphere. We calculated by how much the Earth's global temperature
should decline after a major volcanic explosion and found that our results
(generally a fraction of a degree) were in good accord with actual measurements. Joining forces with Richard Turco, who has studied the effects of
nuclear weapons for many years, we then began to turn our attention to
the climatic effects of nuclear war. [The scientific paper, "Global Atmos-

pheric Consequences of Nuclear War," is written by R. P. Turco, O. B. Toon, T. P. Ackerman, J. B. Pollack, and Carl Sagan. From the last names of the authors, this work is generally referred to as "TTAPS."]

We knew that nuclear explosions, particularly groundbursts, would lift 12
an enormous quantity of fine soil particles into the atmosphere (more than 100,000 tons of fine dust for every megaton exploded in a surface burst). Our work was further spurred by Paul Crutzen of the Max Planck Institute for Chemistry in Mainz, West Germany, and by John Birks of the University of Colorado, who pointed out that huge quantities of smoke would be generated in the burning of cities and forests following a nuclear war.

Groundbursts—at hardened missile silos, for example—generate fine 13
dust. Airbursts—over cities and unhardened military installations—make fires and therefore smoke. The amount of dust and soot generated depends on the conduct of the war, the yields of the weapons employed, and the ratio of groundbursts to airbursts. So we ran computer models for several dozen different nuclear war scenarios. Our baseline case, as in many other studies, was a 5,000-megaton war with only a modest fraction of the yield (20 percent) expended on urban or industrial targets. Our job, for each case, was to follow the dust and smoke generated, see how much sunlight was absorbed and by how much the temperatures changed, figure out how the particles spread in longitude and latitude, and calculate how long before it all fell out of the air back onto the surface. Since the radioactivity would be attached to these same fine particles, our calculations also revealed the extent and timing of the subsequent radioactive fallout.

Some of what I am about to describe is horrifying. I know, because it 14
horrifies me. There is a tendency—psychiatrists call it "denial"—to put it out of our minds, not to think about it. But if we are to deal intelligently, wisely, with the nuclear arms race, then we must steel ourselves to contemplate the horrors of nuclear war.

The results of our calculations astonished us. In the baseline case, the 15
amount of sunlight at the ground was reduced to a few percent of normal— much darker, in daylight, than in a heavy overcast and too dark for plants to make a living from photosynthesis. At least in the Northern Hemisphere, where the great preponderance of strategic targets lies, an unbroken and deadly gloom would persist for weeks.

Even more unexpected were the temperatures calculated. In the base- 16
line case, land temperatures, except for narrow strips of coastline, dropped to minus 25° Celsius (minus 13° Fahrenheit) and stayed below freezing for months—even for a summer war. (Because the atmospheric structure becomes much more stable as the upper atmosphere is heated and the lower air is cooled, we may have severely *under*estimated how long the cold and the dark would last.) The oceans, a significant heat reservoir, would not freeze, however, and a major ice age would probably not be triggered. But because the temperatures would drop so catastrophically, virtually all crops and farm animals, at least in the Northern Hemisphere, would be destroyed,

as would most varieties of uncultivated or undomesticated food supplies. Most of the human survivors would starve.

In addition, the amount of radioactive fallout is much more than expected. Many previous calculations simply ignored the intermediate time-scale fallout. That is, calculations were made for the prompt fallout—the plumes of radioactive debris blown downwind from each target—and for the long-term fallout, the fine radioactive particles lofted into the stratosphere that would descend about a year later, after most of the radioactivity had decayed. However, the radioactivity carried into the upper atmosphere (but not as high as the stratosphere) seems to have been largely forgotten. We found for the baseline case that roughly 30 percent of the land at northern midlatitudes could receive a radioactive dose greater than 250 rads, and that about 50 percent of northern midlatitudes could receive a dose greater than 100 rads. A 100-rad dose is the equivalent of about 1,000 medical X-rays. A 400-rad dose will, more likely than not, kill you.

The cold, the dark, and the intense radioactivity, together lasting for months, represent a severe assault on our civilization and our species. Civil and sanitary services would be wiped out. Medical facilities, drugs, the most rudimentary means for relieving the vast human suffering, would be unavailable. Any but the most elaborate shelters would be useless, quite apart from the question of what good it might be to emerge a few months later. Synthetics burned in the destruction of the cities would produce a wide variety of toxic gases, including carbon monoxide, cyanides, dioxins, and furans. After the dust and soot settled out, the solar ultraviolet flux would be much larger than its present value. Immunity to disease would decline. Epidemics and pandemics would be rampant, especially after the billion or so unburied bodies began to thaw. Moreover, the combined influence of these severe and simultaneous stresses on life are likely to produce even more adverse consequences—biologists call them synergisms—that we are not yet wise enough to foresee.

So far, we have talked only of the Northern Hemisphere. But it now seems—unlike the case of a single nuclear weapons test—that in a real nuclear war, the heating of the vast quantities of atmospheric dust and soot in northern midlatitudes will transport these fine particles toward and across the Equator. We see just this happening in Martian dust storms. The Southern Hemisphere would experience effects that, while less severe than in the Northern Hemisphere, are nevertheless extremely ominous. The illusion with which some people in the Northern Hemisphere reassure themselves—catching an Air New Zealand flight in a time of serious international crisis, or the like—is now much less tenable, even on the narrow issue of personal survival for those with the price of a ticket.

But what if nuclear wars *can* be contained, and much less than 5,000 megatons is detonated? Perhaps the greatest surprise in our work was that even small nuclear wars can have devastating climatic effects. We considered a war in which a mere 100 megatons were exploded, less than one percent of the world arsenals, and only in low-yield airbursts over cities. This scenario, we found, would ignite thousands of fires, and the smoke from these fires alone would be enough to generate an epoch of cold and dark almost as severe as in the 5,000-megaton case. The threshold for what Richard Turco has called the Nuclear Winter is very low.

Could we have overlooked some important effect? The carrying of dust   21
and soot from the Northern to the Southern Hemisphere (as well as more local atmospheric circulation) will certainly thin the clouds out over the Northern Hemisphere. But, in many cases, this thinning would be insufficient to render the climatic consequences tolerable—and every time it got better in the Northern Hemisphere, it would get worse in the Southern.

Our results have been carefully scrutinized by more than 100 scientists   22
in the United States, Europe, and the Soviet Union. There are still arguments on points of detail. But the overall conclusion seems to be agreed upon: there are severe and previously unanticipated global consequences of nuclear war—subfreezing temperatures in a twilit radioactive gloom lasting for months or longer.

Scientists initially underestimated the effects of fallout, were amazed   23
that nuclear explosions in space disabled distant satellites, had no idea that the fireballs from high-yield thermonuclear explosions could deplete the ozone layer, and missed altogether the possible climatic effects of nuclear dust and smoke. What else have we overlooked?

Nuclear war is a problem that can be treated only theoretically. It is   24
not amenable to experimentation. Conceivably, we have left something important out of our analysis, and the effects are more modest than we calculate. On the other hand, it is also possible—and, from previous experience, even likely—that there are further adverse effects that no one has yet been wise enough to recognize. With billions of lives at stake, where does conservatism lie—in assuming that the results will be better than we calculate, or worse?

Many biologists, considering the nuclear winter that these calculations   25
describe, believe they carry somber implications for life on Earth. Many species of plants and animals would become extinct. Vast numbers of surviving humans would starve to death. The delicate ecological relations that bind together organisms on Earth in a fabric of mutual dependency would be torn, perhaps irreparably. There is little question that our global civilization would be destroyed. The human population would be reduced to prehistoric levels, or less. Life for any survivors would be extremely hard. And there seems to be a real possibility of the extinction of the human species.

It is now almost forty years since the invention of nuclear weapons. We   26
have not yet experienced a global thermonuclear war—although on more than one occasion we have come tremulously close. I do not think our luck can hold forever. Men and machines are fallible, as recent events remind

us. Fools and madmen do exist, and sometimes rise to power. Concentrating always on the near future, we have ignored the long-term consequences of our actions. We have placed our civilization and our species in jeopardy.

Fortunately, it is not yet too late. We can safeguard the planetary civilization and the human family if we so choose. There is no more important or more urgent issue.   27

Questions to Start You Thinking

1. How valid do the reasons Sagan gives for his skepticism about the possibility of "contained nuclear war" seem to you?

2. What is the apparent purpose of "The Nuclear Winter"?

3. Consider Sagan's statement "Nuclear war is a problem that can be treated only theoretically" (paragraph 24). To what extent does this fact affect the author's credibility?

4. Sagan's article first appeared in *Parade* magazine, a Sunday newspaper supplement. What constraints would writing for *Parade*'s audience have placed on the author? How well has he triumphed over these limitations?

PART THREE

INVESTIGATING

To do research is, in a sense, to venture into the unknown: to explore, to experiment, to discover facts and laws, to revise earlier thinking. When its object is to probe the mysterious recesses of the human brain or the far galaxies, research can be thrilling. That may be why some people devote their lives to such investigation—in libraries, in the field, in laboratories.

In one college research paper due in a month, you won't be expected to unfold the secrets of the brain or the Spiral Nebula. You may not make any earth-shaking discoveries. Even so, you just might find a little excitement as you become increasingly aware that in doing research you don't merely paste together information and opinions taken from other people; you use that material to think for yourself. You arrive at your own fresh view.

To help you find your own view and express it convincingly, our assignment for a library research paper in Chapter 11 is fairly simple. If you take our advice, you will make a short investigation, not an extremely deep one. But you *will* learn how to do research in a library, how to use various useful sources to fulfill a purpose, and how to bring together your findings in a readable, trustworthy paper.

The second chapter in this section, "Knowing Your Library," is merely informative. It explains the many sources available in a library.

Chapter 13 will take you into field research, often done by observing and conversing with people to find out something brand-new. This chapter includes a paper by a college student who broke new ground: he revealed new knowledge about a little-known, much-maligned, sometimes glamorized business—bail bonding.

Chapter 14, "Documenting Sources," need not be read through; it is merely there to be consulted when you type up your paper in finished form.

CHAPTER 11

Writing from Library Research

All around us, information keeps exploding. From day to day, software and the video screen, books, newspapers, and magazines shower us with facts and figures, statements and reports, views and opinions—some of them half-baked, some revealing and trustworthy. College gives you experience in sorting through this massive burst of wordage. It asks you to distinguish between data and opinion, off-the-wall claims and expert interpretations. To help you gain such skills is usually one purpose of writing a library research paper.

When you approach your assignment, you'll need to ask a question you really want to answer and then start living with that question, thinking about it. Otherwise, though your finished product may look neat and may keep all its notes in order, it will be just a stack of accurately despoiled paper. Some writers start writing a library research paper feeling like slaves to a library, obliged to squirrel up acorns of information for no reason except to make a tall pile. But a library isn't your boss; it exists to serve you. Regard your work as a meaningful chance to expand the frontiers of what you know already.

Back in Chapter 3, "Writing from Reading," if you did the main assignment, you read works by other writers and wrote a paper that one of your readings inspired. When you wrote, you gave credit to those other writers in an informal way. That experience will prove good preparation for writing a research paper. This new task, though, will be different in at least the following ways.

All your reading will point in one direction.

You'll do more interpreting, more piecing together, more evaluating, more throwing away of the unnecessary.

You'll learn to cite and list your sources in the exact form that many scholars and other professionals follow in writing research papers.

To be able to write a library research paper is a useful skill. This kind of writing is essential not only in an academic community but in business and the professions.

To give you a sense of what one student encountered in fulfilling a typical research paper assignment, we will tell you a true story. It's about a freshman who began her investigation with enthusiasm, found herself stopped in her tracks, and had to start out in a fresh direction. Her story will give you an idea of how a typical research paper is written.

LEARNING FROM ANOTHER WRITER: ONE STUDENT'S EXPERIENCE

At first, Lisa Chickos wasn't daunted to find herself taking English 102 that spring, even though it was a course many students dreaded. Its notorious requirement—a research paper—made some people register for it unhappily. But in high school back in Apollo, Pennsylvania, Chickos had coped with more than one writing assignment that had taken her into the library. Research, in her experience, hadn't been cause for despair.

Even so, the English 102 assignment presented challenges. As often happens in college, the nature of the course itself suggested a direction for its students' research papers. That spring, Ms. Miller's section was centered on a theme: the changing roles of men and women in contemporary society. To start their thinking along that broad and promising line, the students had been reading *On the Contrary*, a collection of essays on male and female role playing. Within the large area of that topic, the research paper assignment left the way wide open: "Write a paper of at least 1500 words on a subject that has its source in our discussions and on which we have agreed."

A month would be an awfully short time to go from a tentative topic to a finished research paper. But along the way, the instructor would meet with each student at least twice in conference to follow the student's progress and offer counsel.

Right at the start, Chickos's investigation ran head-on into its tallest obstacle. Chickos had decided on a general direction: to find out more about women who make movies, their roles as producers, directors, and workers behind the scenes. That subject keenly appealed to her, but it led to immediate discouragement. In her college library, she made a preliminary search of the catalog and the *Readers' Guide to Periodical Literature* but turned up very little recent material. It may have been that she wasn't looking in the right places or that the best sources weren't available to her. Had she consulted a specialized index, such as *Film Literature Index,* she might have found more leads. She did find articles on women filmmakers and skimmed through them, but they struck her as too slight—lacking in facts and figures, in clearly stated views. From them, she couldn't get a clear sense of the extent of women's influence on filmmaking. Besides, what could her conclusion be? Probably something obvious: "Hooray for women filmmakers—more power to them!" Disappointed, Chickos realized that in the time she had, she probably couldn't write a strong paper on that interesting subject.

All wasn't lost. In the reference room, she dug into indexes. In the *Readers' Guide* she found a promising article listed: "A Bright Woman Is Caught in a Double Bind." She looked up the article in *Psychology Today* and found it thought-provoking. Some women, said psychologist Matina Horner, won't aspire to administrative positions because they fear success: if they succeed, they might find themselves cast out from society. This point confirmed an idea Chickos had met in her introductory psychology course. The textbook contained a discussion about some women's feelings that to deviate from traditional sex roles is more frightening than to fail. Ideas were coinciding. Chickos began to take notes.

Although she was moving in a clearer direction, she didn't have a definite topic yet. Administration—that seemed a discouragingly broad subject to investigate. What particular field of endeavor for bright women might she concentrate on? She looked over the anthology of essays her English class had discussed, and she did some random thinking. In elementary and secondary schools, most teachers are women. But what about their administrators—the principals, the superintendents? She reasoned, "We tend to think that a school administrator has to be a man." But was that necessarily the case?

She decided to find out. With the aid of the library catalog, she tracked down two books that promised to light the way: collections of essays by various writers entitled *Women and Educational Leadership* and *Academic Women on the Move.* When she looked into them, she found helpful comments by the fistful. Her research began to soar in its new direction.

In the second book, she came across a passage that annoyed her and made her want to keep investigating. Patricia Albjerg Graham, a teacher of history and education at Columbia University, made a revealing comment:

> Administrators are expected to be independent and assertive, behaviors understood as "tough and bitchy" when displayed by women, but "clear-headed and attentive to detail" when found in a man.

Graham's remark indicated sex discrimination in the hiring of school administrators, and Chickos felt her resentment continue to rise. Just how prevalent was this attitude? She read further. By happenstance, a kind of luck that sometimes favors research paper writers, she soon met (in *Women and Educational Leadership*) another quotation that fruitfully irritated her. A male administrator frankly admitted, "It's easier to work without women. Principals and superintendents are a management team. . . . I wonder if we could hang together so well if some of us were women."

Chickos was beginning to feel involved personally. This paper would be well worth writing! Could she find out more about this outrageous situation, even suggest what might be done about it? If so, maybe the toil of shuffling note cards, outlining, and citing sources would all be justified. She set to work with confidence. A couple of times Ms. Miller met with Chickos to monitor her progress and offer advice. "But she didn't try to tell me what avenues to follow," Chickos recalls. "The direction of my research had to be original."

When Chickos did some early drafting, she set down her points as they occurred to her. As she reviewed her draft, one idea stood out from the rest. Educator Jacqueline Clement had posed a problem: "Administrators usually start out as teachers and move up through the ranks. Why, then, if women make up the pool of potential educational leaders, are so few of them at the top?" On her draft, Chickos penned a red star next to this thought. She had found her basic research question, and the remainder of her paper would try to answer it.

In this chapter, we'll show you some of the research materials Lisa Chickos consulted, some notes she took, and some of her experiences along the way. Finally, we'll give you her completed paper, "Educational Leadership: A Man's World."

LEARNING BY WRITING

Lisa Chickos's experience of getting momentarily stopped at the start could have happened to anyone at any college. As a rule, in any composition course a research paper is your most complicated job.

Some of our advice in this chapter may be old news to you. You may have learned in high school how to take research notes or how to make a working bibliography. At times, as we guide you through writing your paper, we'll pause to explain those special skills. To master them, if you haven't mastered them already, will speed you toward that triumphant day when you bang a final staple through your paper. But if at any moment you find us telling you more than you need to know, just skip over that part and go on. Later, should you want that information, you can always return to it.

The Assignment:
Writing from Library Research

Find a topic that intrigues you. To learn as much about it as you can, research that topic in the library. Then, based on your research, write a paper that calls on you to use one or all of the critical thinking skills you honed in Part Two of this book: analyzing, taking a stand, evaluating, seeking causes and effects, perhaps proposing a solution to a problem. Your purpose will be to come to some conclusions about your chosen topic. Assume that your audience is your instructor and your fellow students. Here's how you proceed, in more or less this order.

1. Choose a general subject you care to investigate.
2. Do a little reading around in it, to see exactly what aspects of the subject most keenly interest you.

(If you know, from early on, exactly what interests you, you can skip the first two steps.)

3. State, in the form of a question, exactly what you care to find out.
4. By means of library research, find an answer to your question. This answer may be tentative—just a healthy hunch—but if it is your best hunch, go ahead and stick up for it.
5. Then, in a paper of at least 1500 words, set forth your conclusions. Give evidence to support them, drawn from your research.

If you like, and if your topic seems to call for it, add a further step:

6. Propose some action that should be taken. Suggest to your readers what they might do, if it is an action in which they can effectively take part.

This paper, as you can see, will be more than a stack of facts. Reading and digesting the ideas of ten or twelve other writers is just the first step. In the process of writing your paper, you'll be called on as well to bring your own intelligence to bear on what you have read.

Among student research papers we have seen recently, the following were the most informative.

A woman researched and then praised the British system of supplying drug addicts with drugs, thus making business for drug dealers less profitable.

A man analyzed the process through which an unpublished song by an unknown composer might be recorded and go on to hit the top of the charts. He concluded that if you are an unknown composer, your chances of such success are remote, but the odds aren't hopeless.

A man, after considering several possible solutions to the problem of America's national debt, came to the conclusion that the best solution would be a national lottery. He supported his proposal with evidence from his research into national lotteries held in other countries.

A woman researching the health problems of Vietnam veterans concluded that the ill effects of their exposure to Agent Orange would haunt them and their families well into the twenty-first century.

A Chinese-American student examined what he called "the myth of the model minority"—the perception in the United States that Asian immigrants generally succeed in spite of all obstacles—and found it to be little more than a justification for racism.

To define the poet's role in the society of his times, a man analyzed and evaluated the political poetry of Seamus Heaney.

A woman, seeking causes for what she perceived as the decline of our national parks, concluded that underfunding and understaffing were paramount.

A note on schedules Along with the assignment to write a research paper, some instructors will suggest a schedule. Lisa Chickos's instructor blocked out the students' obligations like this:

March 26: Topic due (the question to be answered)

April 3: Thesis statement due (a one-sentence statement of what the paper will demonstrate)

April 9: Preliminary outline due

April 18: Draft due

April 25: Completed paper due

But if your instructor doesn't give you a series of deadlines, you'll be wise to set some for yourself. You can depend on this: a research paper will require more time than you expect. When putting it into its final draft, you'll need hours to cite all your sources accurately. You'll need time, then, to look it all over and proofread it, not be forced to toss everything together in a desperate all-night siege. A clear-cut schedule will help.

Generating Ideas

How can we most effectively help long-term prisoners, on their release, to return to society?

Did Walt Disney make any admirable and original contributions to American art, or was he a mere imitator, a purveyor of slick schlock, as some of his critics have charged?

What should be done about acid rain?

Should the U.S. State Department act to prevent American soldiers of fortune—hired mercenaries—from fighting in Africa?

If you already have a narrowly defined research question in mind, such as the preceding examples—congratulations. You can just skip to the Discovery Checklist on page 351. But if you don't have a question yet, read on.

Choosing your territory To explore, you need a territory—a subject that interests you. Perhaps, as Lisa Chickos found, your work in this very course or in another course will suggest an appropriate territory. Chickos wrote a paper suggested by a theme that ran through all the readings and discussions in her writing course. A psychology course might encourage you to investigate mental disorders; a sociology course, labor relations.

You'll have an easier time from the start if you can make your territory smaller than "mental disorders" or "labor relations." "Schizophrenia" or "steelworkers' strikes" would be smaller, more readily explorable territories. But if you don't feel that you can make your topic so narrow and definite yet, go ahead, start with "mental disorders" or "labor relations."

For finding your general subject, the following questions may help you at the start. They'll send you back once more to every writer's five basic resources.

DISCOVERY CHECKLIST: CHOOSING YOUR TERRITORY

- Can you recall from your work or leisure experience, from travel or study, something you'd care to read more about?
- What have you observed recently that you could more thoroughly investigate with the aid of books and magazines? (Suggestion: try watching the evening news, taking notes as you watch.)
- What have you recently read that has left you still wondering?
- In recent conversation with friends, in class discussions, what topics have arisen that you'd care to explore?
- What can you imagine that might be confirmed or denied by your reading? If, for instance, you can imagine life as a peasant on a feudal manor or as a slave on a plantation, you might go to some history books to have your mental picture corrected and enlarged. If you can imagine yourself living on a space station in orbit, you might learn from recent science writers what such a space station will probably be like.

Your next move is to take an overall look at your subject, to see what's in it for you.

Taking an overview Before launching an expedition into a little-known territory, a smart explorer first makes a reconnaissance flight and takes an overview. Having seen the terrain, the explorer then chooses the very spot to set up camp: the point on the map that looks most promising. Research writers do something like that, too. Before committing themselves to a topic, they first look over a broader territory to see what parts of it look most attractive.

How do you take an overview? You might begin by looking up your subject in an encyclopedia and reading the general articles about it—*unions* or *labor relations, schizophrenia* or *mental illness* or (still more general) *psychiatry.* By now, you are a veteran reader of encyclopedias, but if you care for any tips on using both general encyclopedias and specialized ones, see Chapter 12 (pp. 404–405).

In your library's reference room, you might check the *Readers' Guide to Periodical Literature,* that green-bound index of recent articles in popular magazines. It will direct you to the latest information and opinion, classified by many subjects. Browsing in an introductory textbook, if any seems likely to help, is also a useful early step. For the general subjects we've been considering, labor relations and mental illness, you might go to a textbook in political science or psychology.

When Lisa Chickos began investigating women in school administration, she had only a large, vague subject in mind. But as she kept reading and thinking, she saw a smaller idea she wanted to concentrate on: "discrimination against women school and college administrators." That seemed plenty to consider in a 1500-word research paper. As you read, keep a lookout for any ideas that intrigue you and that you might like to explore.

How much time should you devote to your overview? Many students find that they can make such a reconnaissance flight in an evening or a few hours. At this point, your investigation need go only far enough to suggest a question you'd care to answer—one like Chickos's "In educational administration, why are so few women at the top?" Let's see what goes into a workable, researchable question.

Stating your question   Once you have zeroed in on part of a territory to explore, you can ask a definite question. Ask what you want to find out, and your task will leap into focus. Having begun with a broad, general interest in (let's say) social problems in large cities, a writer might then ask, "What happens to teenage runaways on the streets of Manhattan?" Or, if a writer has started with a general yen to know more about contemporary architecture, a definite question might be "Who in America today is good at designing sports arenas?"

Brainstorm. You might start with a brainstorming session. For fifteen or twenty minutes, let your thoughts revolve, and jot down whatever questions come to mind—even useless ones. Then, looking over your list, you may find one that appears promising.

Size up your question. A workable question has to be narrow enough to allow a fruitful investigation in the library. A question can be too immense and the research it would call for too overwhelming to complete in a month— "How is the climate of the earth changing?" "Who are the world's best living storytellers?" "Why are there poor among us?" "What's going on in outer space?"

On the other hand, a question can be too narrow. If a mere source or two could answer it, the resulting research paper may be thin and uninteresting. "How does the First Lady do her hair?" would be a shallow question to research. It would turn up facts but few opinions. All you would need to answer it would be one popular magazine interview with a White House hairdresser. But even if you were to find such an interview, you would lack sufficient material. The subject has provoked a lot of gossip, but little thought. Probably you could either search out an answer to that question in fifteen minutes or waste days and find nothing worth taking a note about. So instead, ask a question that will lead you to a lot of meaty books and articles. "How does the First Lady influence the politics of this administration?" That might be worth a research paper.

A caution: if you pick a topic currently in the news, you may have trouble finding valuable material—deep analysis, critical thought, ample historical background, intelligent controversy. For many current topics, the only printed sources may be recent newspapers and news magazines. The topic may be too new for anyone yet to have done a book or a really thorough magazine analysis about it.

Hone your question. Try to keep the wording of your question as simple as you can: set yourself one thing to find out, not several. A question that reads "How do current art and music still reflect the cultural revolution of the 1960s?" is too big. You could split such a question into two parts and then pick one of them: "How does art still reflect the cultural revolution of the 1960s?" or "How does music . . . ?" By qualifying the word *music*, you might cut the question still further down to size: "How does last year's rock music . . . ?" Focus on whatever you most keenly wish to learn.

A well-wrought research question suggests ways to answer it. Say the question is "What has caused a shortage of low-income housing in northeastern cities?" The wording suggests subject headings that may be found in the library catalog or the *Readers' Guide: housing, housing shortage, low-income housing, urban housing.*

Until you start working in the library, of course, you can't know for certain how fruitful your question will be. If it doesn't lead you to any definite facts, if it doesn't start you thinking critically, you'll need to reword it or throw it out and ask a new question. But at the very least, the question you first ask will give you a definite direction in which to start looking.

When you have tentatively stated your question, you can test it by asking other questions about it.

DISCOVERY CHECKLIST: QUESTIONING YOUR QUESTION

- Is this question answerable—at least partly answerable—in the time you have? Does it need to be reduced or expanded?

- Does the question refer to a matter that has been written about only lately? Or, like a more promising question for library research, will it send you to books and magazines of at least a year earlier?

- Have you worded your question as plainly and simply as you can? Do you understand exactly what you'll be looking for?

- Does the question ask for just one answer, not many?

- Does your question interest you? Do you honestly crave the answer to it? If so, your research is likely to cruise along at a great rate and you will find yourself enjoying a sense of discovery. Interest yourself and you are also likely to interest your reader.

Making a preliminary search You can quickly see whether your question is likely to lead to an ample research paper by conducting a short, fast search that shouldn't take you more than an hour. Just check the library catalog to see what books appear under your subject heading. If possible go into the stacks and look over the shelves. Take a quick check of magazine articles: consult the last annual *Readers' Guide,* looking under the subject heading closest to your special concern. Don't look up the articles yet; just see how many there are and whether their titles sound promising. If your subject is "Women: School Administrators," an article called "Iona Dawes Honored with Birthday Cake for Fourteen Years as Principal" is probably going to be too specific to help.

This preliminary search has a simple purpose: to ascertain that you'll have enough material to do the job. If the material looks so skimpy that you won't have anything to choose from, and you'll need to force every crumb of it into your paper to get 1500 words, you might better ask another question. If your first trip into the stacks reveals ten yards of books, alarm bells should start ringing. Did someone other than Shakespeare write Shakespeare's plays? A thousand books have dealt with that question. What caused the Civil War? Every United States history book offers a few explanations. You might want to ask a different question. Instead of a question that only two books might answer, or a question that a hundred books might answer, pick a question that a dozen or twenty might.

Making a working bibliography Before going on with your investigation, you need a working bibliography: a detailed list of books and articles you plan to consult.

Your overview and preliminary search may have given you a good rough notion of where your most promising material lies. Now you need titles and information. Some writers keep track of everything in a notebook small enough to fit a pocket. Others find that the most convenient way to compile such a working bibliography is on 3-by-5-inch note cards, one source to a card. Cards are handy to work with: you can arrange and shuffle them. The more care you take in listing your tentative sources, the more time you'll save later, when at the end of your paper you compile a list of works cited. At that point, you'll be grateful to find all the necessary information at your fingertips.

What should each source card contain? Everything necessary to write the final list of sources to be placed at the end of your paper. Include the following for books (see Figure 11.1).

1. The library call number, in the upper left corner of the card.
2. In the upper right corner, in uppercase letters, just the last name of the book's author so that you can identify the source at a glance.
3. The author's full name.
4. The book's title, including its subtitle if it has one.
5. The publication information: publisher, place, and year of publication.

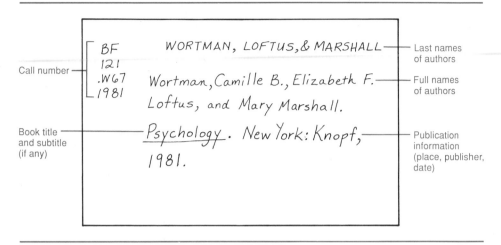

FIGURE 11.1 A bibliography card for a book in MLA style

For a magazine article, your source card need contain no library call number, but you'll need the following data (see Figure 11.2).

1. In the upper right corner, in uppercase letters, the last name of the person who wrote the article.
2. The author's full name.
3. The title of the article, in quotation marks, followed by the name of the publication, underlined.
4. For a scholarly journal, the series number (if there is one) and the volume number (sometimes followed by the issue number).

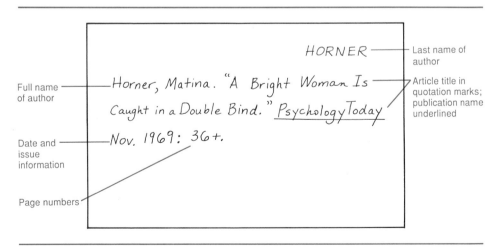

FIGURE 11.2 A bibliography card for an article in MLA style

5. The date of the issue: for a journal, the year in parentheses; for a monthly magazine, the month and year; for a weekly or daily publication, the month, day, and year.
6. The page numbers of the article (The " + " indicates that the article covers more than one page, but not consecutive pages.)

This may seem like a lot of record keeping. But now, as you begin your research, it will take you less time to jot down all this information in full than to make future trips to the library. As you will see, you'll need every last bit of this information. You will need it in citing your sources and in making your list of works cited. On the night before your paper is due, you will thank your stars you've got all this stuff.

To fill your bibliography cards with promising titles to look for, what sources do you consult? The following three are essential. You probably know them already, but if you don't, you will quickly get some hands-on experience. (They are also discussed in detail in the next chapter.)

1. *The library catalog,* for the titles and locations of books. Early on, you'll no doubt consult this master listing of every book and bound periodical in the library. Are you acquainted with the *Library of Congress Subject Headings*? This useful directory can help you find a particular subject in the catalog even if you don't know exactly what to call it. For more about this helpful aid, see page 399. For a basic description of the catalog, how it works, and how it can serve you, see pages 398–402.

2. *An index to periodicals,* for the titles of magazine articles. In high school, you probably used at least the *Readers' Guide to Periodical Literature,* which covers popular magazines, but if your subject falls into the category of art, music, theater, film, architecture, law, business, or education, other indexes can be helpful. Some cover specialized magazines and scholarly journals. If you'd like a short description of these indexes—there may be one just right for your project—see pages 407–409.

3. *A ready-made bibliography,* for a list of books and articles on a certain subject, often with a brief descriptive opinion of each item. Imagine what a big job you'll be spared if someone has already drawn up a bibliography for your subject. For more about such bibliographies, see page 407.

For your present short-range investigation, those three basic sources will probably lead to more books and articles than you can weave into 1500 or 2000 words. But what if they don't, and you need still more material? In that case, you can find thumbnail descriptions of other likely sources in Chapter 12. Whenever a college course calls on you to do a longer and deeper research paper, such as a term paper at the end of a course or an honors thesis, you will surely need more sources than the three basic ones suggested here. Your present task, though limited, is still large: to think with the aid of printed sources and, with their help, to speak your mind.

Evaluating your sources   With any luck, in making your working bibliography you will have turned up some books and articles by writers of deep knowledge and high integrity. You may also have turned up a few hasty hunks of verbiage written by hacks or some material written with biases—which may be perfectly good as long as you recognize the biases. How do you know what sources are trustworthy? Here are some questions to ask yourself:

Is the source timely? A good indication of a source's reliability is a recent date of publication. If you are using a book that has been revised, use the latest edition. Try to cite at least some material published in recent years.

Is the writer a recognized authority? See whether any credentials are given in a *blurb,* or biographical note, at the beginning or end of a book or article. If still in doubt, you might check whether the writer is listed in the library catalog as the author of other books on the subject and in *Who's Who, Contemporary Authors,* or reference works covering specialized fields, such as *American Men and Women of Science.* Inclusion in such works isn't a guarantee that the writer is absolutely trustworthy, but you may be able to get an idea of the author's background. Ask your reference librarian whether the writer's name is familiar. But ultimately, the best test of a writer's authority is whether his or her work meets the critical demands of other authorities. You might find some authorities on campus to talk with. Your instructor is an authority on some things. And you might do some more reading in the field and start becoming an authority yourself.

Is the source primary or secondary? In most research papers you'll need both primary and secondary sources. A *primary source* is an observer: someone, let's say, who witnessed a fire and writes an account of it. A primary source may also be the person who originally makes a statement: the fire chief who gives his report on the blaze. A *secondary source* is a writer or speaker who refers to primary sources—such as a newspaper reporter who writes of the fire after talking with eyewitnesses or a historian who has read the reporter's account in an old newspaper. If you quote a book written by child psychologist Jean Piaget, you quote a primary source; a secondary source might be a book by another writer discussing Piaget's theories.

Secondary sources aren't necessarily less trustworthy just because they are not firsthand reports. Eyewitnesses can be prejudiced, self-serving, or simply unable to know as much as a later writer who has talked with *many* eyewitnesses. In writing a history paper on the attitudes of American social workers toward World War I, you might quote a primary source: Jane Addams, founder of Chicago's Hull House, who was a pacifist. If you relied only on Addams's words, though, you might get the idea that social workers were unanimously opposed to the war effort. To put Addams's views into perspective you'd also need secondary sources, which would show that most of her peers didn't want to identify with her unpopular pacifism and publicly disagreed with her.

If your source is a weekly news magazine like *Time, Newsweek,* or *U.S. News & World Report,* the writer of an article is likely to be a reporter, not always a famous name, perhaps not a world-renowned authority. Such magazines do, however, feature some articles by experts; and all such magazines have a good reputation for checking their facts carefully. They try to present a range of opinions but sometimes *select* facts to mirror the opinions of their editors. In a serious, reputable periodical of general interest, other than a news weekly—a magazine such as *New York Review of Books,* the *Atlantic, Harper's,* or the *American Scholar*—articles are often written by well-known authorities.

Who are its readers? In testing another writer's statements, it helps to notice the audience for which they were written. Does the periodical have a predictable point of view? Is it written toward any special audience? *The Nation,* a magazine of commentary from a left-leaning political point of view, is likely to give you a different picture of the world from that found in the *National Review,* edited by conservative William F. Buckley, Jr. How can you find out, if you don't already know, the general outlook of the periodical you're examining?

Read the advertisements, if any. These are usually the surest guide to a magazine's audience. To whom are its editors trying to appeal? *Time, Newsweek,* and *U.S. News & World Report* address mostly college-educated professionals. A large part of this audience consists of businesspeople—as shown by the many ads for office copiers, delivery services, hotels that welcome the business traveler, and corporations trumpeting their own importance. Weekly tabloids such as the *National Enquirer,* the *Star,* and *Weekly World News* specialize in scandal and sensation, with headlines like SEX-CHANGE NUN TURNS TV WRESTLER and ELVIS ALIVE ON FLYING SAUCER. The ads offer fortune-telling rocks, courses in hypnosis, and cold creams that remove wrinkles with one quick smear. These tabloids probably appeal to two audiences: the gullible and people who like to say "My land! What will they think up next?"

Read more than one issue of the magazine. Browse, at least, through several issues—as many as necessary to understand the magazine's assumptions and its audience.

Read the editorials, in which the editors, making no pretense of being impartial, set forth their views. In most magazines, these will be in a front section and may not even be signed, since the name of the editor is on the masthead, near the contents. If you can find an editorial commenting on a familiar issue, you may soon know the magazine's bias.

Read any featured columnists who appear regularly. Usually their jobs depend on their voicing opinions congenial to the magazine's editors and publishers. But this test isn't foolproof. Sometimes a dissenting columnist is hired to lend variety.

Read with an analytic eye the lead features or news stories (those most prominently placed in the front of the issue), paying special attention to the last paragraph, in which the writer often declares what it all means. Sometimes this will betray assumptions that reveal where the magazine stands: "Despite the stern criticisms leveled at Centro Oil by environmentalists, the company has weathered this small storm and no doubt will outlast many to come." The voice is clearly that of a friend of the oil company.

Read the letters to the editor. Some magazines, like *Time,* strive to offer space to a diversity of opinion. (When *Time* prints two letters on a subject, one is generally pro and one is con.) You can often get a line on the level of schooling and intelligence shown by who writes the letters and thereby understand something about the magazine's readers.

A helpful work of reference that evaluates magazines is *Magazines for Libraries*. It mentions biases, tells what sort of material specific magazines customarily print, and gives circulation figures.

For still more advice on evaluating evidence, turn back to "Testing Evidence," on pages 231–233.

Setting out: note taking Once you have a working bibliography and have evaluated your sources and winnowed out any you don't trust, you need to begin reading and accumulating material. What will you look for? Examples and illustrations of the ideas you're pursuing as well as evidence to support them—and to refute them.

As you read, decide whether to take notes and, if so, how extensively. You can't always guess the usefulness of a source in advance. Sometimes a likely source turns out to yield nothing much, and a book that had promised to be a juicy plum shrivels to a prune in your hands.

Take thorough notes. If you do take notes while you read, take ample ones. Many a writer has come to grief by setting down sketchy jottings and trusting memory to fill in the blanks. You'll probably find that using note cards will work better than taking notes on pieces of paper. Then, when the time comes to organize the material you've gathered, you can shuffle your cards into an order that makes most sense to you. Roomy 4-by-6-inch or 5-by-8-inch cards will hold more than the 3-by-5-inch cards you used for your working bibliography. Even a meaty idea ought to fit on one card. Use one card per idea. Putting two or more ideas on the same card complicates your task when you reach the drafting stage.

Some research writers insist that the invention of photocopying has done away with the need to take notes. Indeed, judicious photocopying can save you time as you gather materials for your paper, but the key word here is *judicious*. Simply photocopying everything you read with the vague notion that some of it contains material valuable for your essay is likely in the end to cost you more time rather than less. Much of it won't be worth saving. Most important, you won't have digested and evaluated what was on the page; you will merely have copied it. Selecting what is essential, transcribing it by hand, perhaps nutshelling or paraphrasing it, helps make it yours. When later you start drafting, unless your paper is to be very short, it will take you longer to decode great bundles of photocopied material than to work from carefully thought-out note cards. Indiscriminate photocopying may also cost you a lot of money.

If, however, you're using a source that doesn't circulate, such as a reference book always kept in the reference room, you may want to photocopy the relevant pages so that you can use them whenever and wherever is convenient for you. Just make sure that the name of the source and the page number appear on your copy so that you can make a source card for it. If not, pencil it on the photocopy. When you start organizing your notes, you may find it convenient to scissor out of a photocopied page what you're going to use and stick it onto a note card.

A good rule is to make your notes and citations full enough so that, once they're written, you're totally independent of the source from which they came. That way you'll avoid having to rush back to the library in a panic trying to find again, in a book or periodical you returned weeks ago, some nugget of material you want to include in your paper. Good, thoughtful notes can sometimes be copied verbatim from note card to first draft. But often they will take rewriting to fit them in so they don't stand out like boulders in the stream of your prose.

A useful note card includes three elements:

An identifier, usually the last name of the author whose work you're citing, followed by the *page number or numbers* on which the information can be found

A subject heading, some key word or phrase you make up yourself to help you decide where in your paper the information will best fit

The fact, idea, or quotation you plan to use in your paper

You'll need all these elements so that later, when it's time to incorporate your notes into your paper or develop your ideas from multiple sources, you'll have an accurate record of what you found in each source. You'll also know exactly where you found it, and you will be able to cite every source without difficulty. (For sample note cards, see Figures 11.3, 11.4, and 11.5.)

While you're taking notes, you can keep evaluating. You can be deciding whether the stuff is going to be greatly valuable, fairly valuable, or only a little bit valuable. Some note takers put a star at the top of any note they assign great value to, a question mark on a note that might or might not be useful. Later, when they're organizing their material, they can see what especially stands out and will need emphasis.

Bristle while you work. In reading the material you are collecting, if you can look at it a little sourly and suspiciously, that might be to your advantage. Mary-Claire van Leunen, author of *A Handbook for Scholars* (New York: Knopf, 1978), has advised researchers who must read much scholarly writing: "Do not smile sweetly as you read through pages of graceless, stilted, maundering bombast. Fume, fuss, be angry. Your anger will keep you up to the mark when you turn to writing yourself."

How many notes are enough? When you find that the sources you consult are mostly repeating what you've learned from previous sources, you have probably done enough reading and note taking. But before you reach that point, we'd like to remind you of three ways of setting down notes that will help you write a good, meaty paper. (You have met them before in Chapter 3, "Writing from Reading.")

Writing from sources: quoting, nutshelling, paraphrasing   Preparing to write her paper on women in educational administration, Lisa Chickos found a thought-provoking paragraph in Patricia Albjerg Graham's "Status Transitions of Women Students, Faculty, and Administrators," a chapter in *Academic Women on the Move*:

> Violation of cultural stereotypes may be another factor working against women faculty members moving into upper-level administrative positions. It generally is assumed that women can make their best contributions in positions subordinate to men. Hence the university administrator's job description is almost invariably drawn with a man in mind, particularly a married man whose wife can provide auxiliary social support. Moreover, administrators are expected to be independent and assertive, behaviors understood as "tough and bitchy" when displayed by women, but "clear-headed and attentive to detail" when found in a man. Tolerance for men's behavior is a good deal broader than it is for that of women. Men are permitted their idiosyncracies of whatever sort, but women are expected to maintain a much more precarious balance between conspicuous competence and tactful femininity. Manifestations of independence and autonomy are expected in a male executive; their presence in women makes some male colleagues cringe.

Quoting. To quote selectively—to choose the words with life and pith in them—is one convincing way to demonstrate and refute ideas and to marshal evidence. To do so, you'll need to copy a brief quotation carefully onto a card, making sure to reproduce exactly the spelling and punctuation, even if they're unusual. Go back over what you've written to make sure that you've copied it correctly. Put quotation marks around the material so that when you come to include it in your paper, you'll remember that it's a direct quotation. You might also want to remind yourself in a bracketed note that you intend to use the author's words in a quotation. Lisa Chickos wrote herself the note card shown in Figure 11.3 to extract a lively quotation.

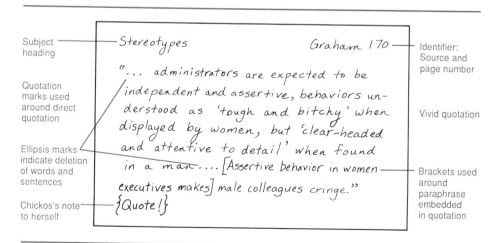

FIGURE 11.3 A sample note card giving a direct quotation from a source

Sometimes it doesn't pay to transcribe a quotation word for word. Parts may fail to serve your purpose, such as transitions ("as the reader will recall from Chapter 14"), parenthetical remarks ("which data slightly modifies the earlier view of Pflug"), and other information useless to you. Lisa Chickos, quoting a sentence on her note card shown in Figure 11.3, doesn't bother to take down the transition word "Moreover" with which the sentence begins. But she faithfully indicates the omission by using an ellipsis mark (. . .).

Nutshelling. Nutshelling, or summarizing, takes less room than quoting extensively. To give your reader just the sense of a passage from another writer, you can condense it in your own words. If Lisa Chickos had put into nutshell form the essential ideas she wished to take from the paragraph in Graham's article, her note card might have looked like Figure 11.4.

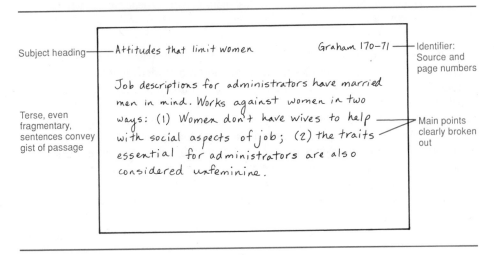

Subject heading—Attitudes that limit women   Graham 170–71—Identifier: Source and page numbers

Terse, even fragmentary, sentences convey gist of passage

Job descriptions for administrators have married men in mind. Works against women in two ways: (1) Women don't have wives to help with social aspects of job; (2) the traits essential for administrators are also considered unfeminine.

Main points clearly broken out

FIGURE 11.4   Nutshelling, or summarizing, a paragraph

Paraphrasing. A third strategy useful in taking research notes, paraphrasing also transforms an author's ideas into your own words. Unlike nutshelling, though, paraphrasing doesn't necessarily make your notes any briefer. Why paraphrase? It is especially helpful when the language of another writer isn't particularly vivid and memorable (unlike the phrase from Graham that Lisa Chickos quotes: "tough and bitchy"). When the writer's ideas look valuable but the words seem not worth preserving in the original, render them in paraphrase. Don't hover so close to the writer's very words that your paraphrase is merely an echo. If your source writes, "In staging an ancient Greek tragedy today, most directors do not mask the actors," and you write, merely changing the word order, "Most directors, in staging an ancient Greek tragedy today, do not mask the actors," you have stuck too closely to the original. Write instead: "Few contemporary directors of Greek tragedy insist that their actors wear masks." When you paraphrase, also avoid the temptation to merely substitute a synonym here and there. That way lies madness—and perhaps a charge of plagiarism. The style in paraphrasing, as in nutshelling, has to be yours. When you paraphrase, by the way, you aren't judging or interpreting another writer's ideas—you are simply trying to express them fairly and accurately in different words. If Lisa Chickos had chosen to paraphrase Graham, her note card might have looked like Figure 11.5.

Paraphrase is about half the length of original passage.

No interpretation or evaluation of original passage is included.

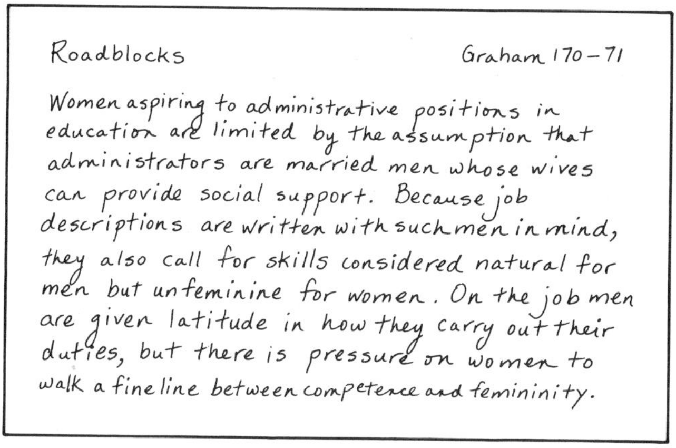

> Roadblocks   Graham 170-71
>
> Women aspiring to administrative positions in education are limited by the assumption that administrators are married men whose wives can provide social support. Because job descriptions are written with such men in mind, they also call for skills considered natural for men but unfeminine for women. On the job men are given latitude in how they carry out their duties, but there is pressure on women to walk a fine line between competence and femininity.

Although emphasis of original is maintained, word choice and order have been reworked to avoid the danger of plagiarism.

FIGURE 11.5   Paraphrasing the quotation from Graham's article

How do you abstract the main idea from another writer's thoughts? Before you nutshell or paraphrase, we'd suggest that you do the following.

1. Read the original passage over a couple of times.
2. Without looking at it, try to state its gist, the point it makes, the main sense you remember.
3. Go back and reread the original passage one more time, making sure you got its gist faithfully. Revise as necessary.

If you have dealt carefully with the material, you won't have to put quotation marks around anything in your paraphrase.

Unless an assignment strictly confines you to library sources, which it might, no law forbids your using any promising nonlibrary materials in your research paper. To make a point, you can recall your own experience, observations, conversations, past reading. And why park your imagination outside the library? You might want to bring together sources not usually related. One fine research paper we have read, by a prelaw student, compared gambling laws in ancient Rome with gambling laws in present-day Atlantic City. Placing Rome and Atlantic City cheek to cheek took imagination.

Honest borrowing. You have an obligation to repay the researchers, scholars, and writers who came before you. That is why, in doing research, you cite your source materials so carefully, mentioning the names of all other writers you borrow from. You do this not only for quotations you take but also for ideas, even though you have nutshelled or paraphrased them in your own words. Sometimes, because a student fails to acknowledge all sources, he or she is blamed for plagiarism. Or the writer fails to paraphrase but uses the original writer's words without quotation marks. The writer is suspected of a rip-off, when he or she merely failed to make a debt clear.

Chapter 14 offers information about how to cite and list sources so that, like any good scholar, you will know exactly how to pay your debts in full.

Shaping a Draft

You began gathering material with a question in mind. It asked what you wanted to find out. By now, if your research has been thorough and fruitful, you know the answer. The moment has come to weave together the material you have gathered. We can vouch for two time-proven methods.

The thesis method. Decide what your research has led you to believe. What does it all mean? Sum up that view in a sentence. It is your thesis, the one main idea your paper will demonstrate. Lisa Chickos's preliminary thesis sentence might be "The scarcity of women school administrators can be alleviated." (For more advice on composing such a sentence, see p. 491.) You then start writing your draft, including only material that supports your thesis, concentrating from beginning to end on making that thesis clear.

The answer method. Some writers have an easier time of writing if they plunge in and start writing without first trying to state any thesis at all. If you care to try this method, recall your original question and start writing with the purpose of answering it, lining up evidence as you go.

Evaluating your material   About now, you will probably wish to sift through all the evidence you have collected. If you've been taking notes on cards, the labor of sorting the cards into piles will be made easier. But thinking will be the hardest part of sorting: you'll need to reflect on each item, imagining it as a piece of your finished paper. You might classify your notes into three categories:

> essential material
> good but less important material
> material not worth the powder to blow it up

How to decide what is essential? *A useful note will plainly help answer your original question.* If that question was "How far advanced is Soviet computer technology?" then a comment by a Norwegian engineer who was permitted to use a large computer at the Soviet Academy of Sciences and who evaluated its performance would obviously be very valuable. Of lesser import might be an American tourist's recollection of seeing a large computer in Moscow being unloaded from a truck. Yet if for any reason the latter note seemed memorable, you should hang on to it, at least until writing a draft.

You aren't trying to impose your will on your material so that it proves only what you want to prove. Still, the rough rule we can offer for evaluating your material is this: *Does this note help you say what you now want to say?*

Organizing your ideas   If your material seems not to want to shape up, you may find it helpful to outline. You might arrange all your note cards in an order that makes sense. Then the stack of cards becomes your outline, and, as you write, turning over card after card, you follow it. Or you can make an informal outline on paper (see p. 499). That's what Lisa Chickos did at first. She made a rough preliminary listing of the points she planned to cover.

Introduction

Leadership in American education

Barriers to women who might go into administration
  Perceptions of women's ability
  Socialization
  "Fear of success"
  Departure from traditional roles
  Family and geographic ties
  Female stereotypes

Solutions
  Mutual support
  Support from male colleagues
  Encouragement of children
  Support from family
  Openness of employers
  Support from organizations and legislation

As you can see, Chickos included the heading "Fear of success," and at that point she found the outline prompting her ideas. Next to "Fear of success" she wrote, "Say something about deviating from prescribed roles." Obviously young women in educational administration might be afraid of being branded as "tough and bitchy" (to quote Graham again). "I may need another category," Chickos realized, noting to herself, "Women who have reached positions. Maybe a separate category for barriers that inhibit both women from rising in administration and employers from hiring them." Just looking over her rough outline proved stimulating: it made thoughts start to flow.

From notes to outline to draft   Note cards are only the raw material for a research paper. If they are to end up in a readable, unified whole, they need shaping and polishing. Much wordage in your notes probably won't need to go into your paper. When you draft, you'll find yourself summarizing your notes or selecting just the useful parts of them.

When you look over your outline, if you use one, compare each section with the notes you have on hand for it. If for a certain section you have no notes, or only a single note, your research has a gap to fill. Back to the library.

WRITING WITH A COMPUTER: LIBRARY RESEARCH

SHAPING A DRAFT

In writing a research paper, you'll find word processing a great boon. Any material you collect can be sorted and grouped on screen—laid in the very place it should go. Material can be shifted about, a wonderful power to have in organizing long blocks of copy. And especially in a research paper where everything has to be documented and chances to make mistakes abound, you'll appreciate the ease of making corrections. Then, too, word processing lets you easily add any stray material that may turn up late in the process of writing.

For taking notes in a library, by the way, nothing beats a portable computer—if you have one or can rent or borrow one. With your materials at hand, you can type in quotations, thus eliminating the need to recopy them later—and lessening the chance of making mistakes.

(For suggestions for rewriting with a computer, see p. 375.)

When you are satisfied that your notes fall into some kind of order and you have material for every part of your outline, you can start to write. If things don't fall into perfect order, start writing anyway. Get something down on paper so that you will have something to revise.

All the while you're writing, you keep citing: referring your reader exactly to the sources of your material. To cite your sources is easy—it just takes time and care. In the body of your paper, right after every fact, idea, or quotation you have borrowed, you tell your reader where you found it. In Chapter 14, we show you in detail how to cite. It's probably easiest to cite your sources carefully *while you're drafting your paper.* Although to do so takes a little extra time as you write, it saves fuss when you're putting your paper into final form.

Right now, probably all you need to do is to note in your draft, right after each borrowed item, the name of the author and the page of the book you took it from. If you're using two or more works by the same author, you need one more detail to tell them apart. Assign each one a short title—the first word or phrase of a title will do.

```
An assassin outrages us not only by his deed but also by
offering an unacceptable reason for violence.  Nearly as
offensive as his act of wounding President Reagan was
Hinckley's explanation that he fired in order to impress
screen star Jody Foster.  (Szasz, "Intentionality," 5)
```

The title in parenthesis is short for an article by Thomas Szasz, "Intentionality and Insanity," to distinguish it from another work by Szasz that the writer also cites: *The Myth of Mental Illness.*

When in writing a draft you include a direct quotation, you might as well save copying time. Just paste or tape in the whole note card bearing the quotation. Your draft may look sloppy, but who cares? You're going to recopy the quotation anyway when you type your final version.

If, when you lay the quotation into place, a few words to introduce it spring to mind, by all means put them in. A brief transition might go something like "A more negative view of standardized intelligence tests is that of Harry S. Baum, director of the Sooner Research Center." Then comes Baum's opinion, that IQ tests aren't very reliable. The transition announces why Baum will be quoted. Evidently, you have previously written about somebody else's praise of IQ tests; now Baum will cast cold water on them. And the transition, brief as it is, tells us a little about Baum: his professional title. Indicating that he is a recognized authority, this bit of information makes us more willing to accept his expert view. (For more suggestions on introducing ideas, see "Using Transitions," p. 513.)

But if no transition occurs at the moment, don't sit around waiting for it. Slap that card into place and keep writing while the spirit is moving you along. Later, when you rewrite, you can always add connective tissue. Just remember to add it, though—a series of slapped-in cards would make rough reading.

Using sources (not letting sources use you)   Sometimes you can get drawn into discussing something that really doesn't have anything much to do with your investigation, perhaps because the material is interesting and you happen to have a heap of it. It's a great temptation, when a note has cost you time and toil, to want to include it at all costs. Resist. Include only material that answers your research question. Your paper will be far stronger as a result. A note dragged in by force always sticks out like a pig in the belly of a boa constrictor.

Quoting needs to be done sparingly, and for good reason—to add support and authority to your assertions. Otherwise, it raises needless complications. Some writers of college research papers do much pointless quoting. This notion is understandable, but dubious. Mary-Claire van Leunen in *A Handbook for Scholars* gives cogent advice:

> Quote only the quotable. Quote for color; quote for evidence. Otherwise, don't quote. When you are writing well, your sentences should join each other like rows of knitting, each sentence pulling up what went before it, each sentence supporting what comes after. Quotation introduces an alien pattern—someone else's diction, someone else's voice, someone else's links before and afterward. Even necessary quotations are difficult to knit smoothly into your structure. Overquotation will result in something more like a bird's nest than like fine handiwork.

That quotation, by the way, seems to us worth quoting. Its words are memorable, worth taking to heart.

Nutshell and paraphrase again: using long passages   Nutshell and paraphrase are fine ways to avoid quoting excessively. We first talked about these useful methods on page 79, and earlier in this chapter we saw how Lisa

Chickos used them. Both methods translate another writer's ideas into your own words.

If, to save time in the library, you made photocopies of long passages, you now have to face the task of selecting from them, boiling them down, and weaving them into your paper. To illustrate once again how nutshelling and paraphrasing can serve you, let's first look at a passage from historian Barbara W. Tuchman. In *The Distant Mirror: The Calamitous 14th Century* (New York: Knopf, 1978), Tuchman sets forth the effects of that famous plague the Black Death. In her foreword to her study, she admits that any historian dealing with the Middle Ages faces difficulties. For one, large gaps exist in the supply of recorded information:

ORIGINAL

A greater hazard, built into the very nature of recorded history, is overload of the negative: the disproportionate survival of the bad side—of evil, misery, contention, and harm. In history this is exactly the same as in the daily newspaper. The normal does not make news. History is made by the documents that survive, and these lean heavily on crisis and calamity, crime and misbehavior, because such things are the subject matter of the documentary process—of lawsuits, treaties, moralists' denunciations, literary satire, papal Bulls. No Pope ever issued a Bull to approve of something. Negative overload can be seen at work in the religious reformer Nicolas de Clamanges, who, in denouncing unfit and worldly prelates in 1401, said that in his anxiety for reform he would not discuss the good clerics because "they do not count beside the perverse men."

Disaster is rarely as pervasive as it seems from recorded accounts. The fact of being on the record makes it appear continuous and ubiquitous whereas it is more likely to have been sporadic both in time and place. Besides, persistence of the normal is usually greater than the effect of disturbance, as we know from our own times. After absorbing the news of today, one expects to face a world consisting entirely of strikes, crimes, power failures, broken water mains, stalled trains, school shutdowns, muggers, drug addicts, neo-Nazis, and rapists. The fact is that one can come home in the evening—on a lucky day—without having encountered more than one or two of these phenomena.

This passage in a nutshell, or summary, might become as follows:

NUTSHELL

Tuchman reminds us that history lays stress on misery and misdeeds because these negative events attracted notice in their time and so were reported in writing; just as in a newspaper today, bad news predominates. But we should remember that suffering and social upheaval didn't prevail everywhere all the time.

As you can see, this nutshell merely abstracts from the original. Not everything in the original has been preserved: not Tuchman's thought about papal bulls, not the specific examples such as Nicolas de Clamanges and the modern neo-Nazis and rapists. But the gist—the summary of the main idea—echoes Tuchman faithfully.

Before you write a nutshell, or summary, an effective way to sense the gist of a passage is carefully to pare away examples, details, modifiers, offhand remarks, and nonessential points. Here is the original quotation from Tuchman as one student marked it up on a photocopy, crossing out elements she decided to omit from her paraphrase:

> ~~A greater hazard,~~ built into the ~~very~~ nature of recorded history, is ~~overload of the negative:~~ the disproportionate survival of the bad side ~~of evil, misery, contention, and harm. In history~~ this is exactly the same as in the daily newspaper. ~~The normal does not make news. History is made by the~~ documents that survive, ~~and these~~ lean heavily on crisis and calamity, crime and misbehavior, because such things are the subject matter of the documentary process ~~of lawsuits, treaties, moralists' denunciations, literary satire, papal Bulls. No Pope ever issued a Bull to approve of something. Negative overload can be seen at work in the religious reformer Nicolas de Clamanges, who, in denouncing unfit and worldly prelates in 1401, said that in his anxiety for reform he would not discuss the good clerics because "they do not count beside the perverse men."~~
>
> Disaster is rarely as pervasive as it seems from recorded accounts. ~~The fact of being on the record makes it appear continuous and ubiquitous whereas~~ it is more likely to have been sporadic both in time and place. Besides, persistence of the normal is usually greater than the effect of disturbance, as we know from our own times. ~~After absorbing the news of today, one expects to face a world consisting entirely of strikes, crimes, power failures, broken water mains, stalled trains, school shutdowns, muggers, drug addicts, neo-Nazis, and rapists. The fact is that one can come home in the evening—on a lucky day—without having encountered more than one or two of these phenomena.~~

Rewording what was left, she wrote the following nutshell version:

NUTSHELL

```
History, like a daily newspaper, reports more bad
than good.  Why?  Because the documents that have come
down to us tend to deal with upheavals and disturbances,
which are seldom as extensive and long-lasting as history
books might lead us to believe.
```

In filling her nutshell, you'll notice, the student couldn't simply omit the words she had deleted. The result would have been less readable and still long. She knew she couldn't use Tuchman's very words: that would look like a steal. To make a good, honest, compact nutshell that would fit smoothly into her research paper, she had to condense most of the original words into her own.

Now here is Tuchman's passage in paraphrase. The writer has put Tuchman's ideas into other words but retained her major points. Note that the writer gives Tuchman credit for the ideas.

PARAPHRASE

> Tuchman points out that historians find some distortion of the truth hard to avoid, for more documentation exists for crimes, suffering, and calamities than for the events of ordinary life. As a result, history may overplay the negative. The author reminds us that we are familiar with this process from our contemporary newspapers, in which bad news is played up as being of greater interest than good news. If we believed that newspapers told all the truth, we would think ourselves threatened at all times by technical failures, strikes, crime, and violence--but we are threatened only some of the time, and normal life goes on. The good, dull, ordinary parts of our lives do not make the front page, and praiseworthy things tend to be ignored. "No Pope," says Tuchman, "ever issued a Bull to approve of something." But in truth, social upheaval did not prevail as widely as we might think from the surviving documents of medieval life. Nor, the author observes, can we agree with a critic of the church, Nicolas de Clamanges, in whose view evildoers in the clergy mattered more than men of goodwill.

In that reasonably complete and accurate paraphrase, about three-quarters the length of the original, most of Tuchman's points have been preserved and spelled out fully, even though they have been rearranged. Paraphrasing enables the writer to emphasize the ideas important to his or her research, makes the reader more aware of them as support for the writer's thesis than if the whole passage had been quoted directly. But notice that Tuchman's great remark about papal bulls has been kept a direct quotation because the statement is short and memorable, and it would be hard to improve on her words. The writer, you'll observe, doesn't interpret or evaluate Tuchman's ideas—she only passes them on.

Make sure that, like the writer of the nutshell and the paraphrase just given, you indicate your original source. You can pay due credit in a terse phrase: "Barbara W. Tuchman believes that . . ." or "According to Barbara W. Tuchman. . . ."

Often you paraphrase to emphasize one essential point. Here is an original passage from Evelyn Underhill's classic study, *Mysticism*:

ORIGINAL

> In the evidence given during the process for St. Teresa's beatification, Maria de San Francisco of Medina, one of her early nuns, stated that on entering the saint's cell whilst she was writing this same "Interior Castle" she found her [St. Teresa] so absorbed in contemplation as to be unaware of the external world. "If we made a noise close to her," said another, Maria del Nacimiento, "she neither ceased to write nor complained of being disturbed." Both these nuns, and also Ana de la Encarnacion, prioress of Granada, affirmed that she wrote with immense speed, never stopping to erase or to correct, being anxious, as she said, to write what the Lord had given her before she forgot it.

Suppose that the names of the witnesses do not matter, but the researcher wishes to emphasize, in fewer words, the celebrated mystic's writing habits. To bring out that point, the passage might be paraphrased (and quoted in part) like this:

PARAPHRASE

> Evelyn Underhill has recalled the testimony of those who saw St. Teresa at work on The Interior Castle. Oblivious to noise, the celebrated mystic appeared to write in a state of complete absorption, driving her pen "with immense speed, never stopping to erase or to correct, being anxious, as she said, to write what the Lord had given her before she forgot it."

Avoiding plagiarism Here is a point we can't stress too strongly. When you paraphrase, never lift another writer's words or ideas without giving that writer due credit or without transforming them into words of your own. If you do, you risk being accused of plagiarism. You have seen in this chapter examples of honest nutshelling and paraphrasing. Introducing them into a paper, a writer would clearly indicate that they belong to Barbara Tuchman (or some other originator). Now here are a few horrible examples: paraphrases of Barbara Tuchman's original passage (on p. 366) that lift, without thanks, her ideas and even her very words. Finding such gross borrowings in a paper, an instructor might hear the ringing of a burglar alarm. First is an egregious example that lifts both thoughts and words.

PLAGIARIZED

> Sometimes it's difficult for historians to learn the truth about the everyday lives of people from past societies because of the disproportionate survival of the bad side of things. Historical documents, like today's news-

papers, tend to lean rather heavily on crisis, crime, and
misbehavior. Reading the newspaper could lead one to expect a world consisting entirely of strikes, crimes,
power failures, muggers, drug addicts, and rapists. In
fact, though, disaster is rarely so pervasive as recorded
accounts can make it seem.

A more subtle theft, lifting thoughts but not words:

PLAGIARIZED

It's not always easy to determine the truth about
the everyday lives of people from past societies because
bad news gets recorded a lot more frequently than good
news does. Historical documents, like today's newspapers, tend to pick up on malice and disaster and ignore
flat normality. If I were to base my opinion of the
world on what I see on the seven o'clock news, I would
expect to see death and destruction around me all the
time. Actually, though, I rarely come up against true
disaster.

Here is an example that fails to make clear which ideas belong to the writer
and which belong to Tuchman (although none of them belong to the writer):

Barbara Tuchman explains that it can be difficult
for historians to learn about the everyday lives of
people who lived a long time ago because historical
documents tend to record only the bad news. Today's
newspapers are like that, too: disaster, malice, and confusion take up a lot more room on the front page than
happiness and serenity. Just as the ins and outs of our
everyday lives go unreported, we can suspect that upheav-
als do not really play so important a part in the making
of history as they seem to do.

To avoid falling into such habits, whenever you make a paraphrase check
it against the original. Observe these cautions:

1. Quote no words from your original without placing them in quotation
   marks.
2. Take pains to identify the author of any quotation.
3. Credit by name the originator of any idea you use.

4. Make sure you indicate where another writer's ideas stop and where yours begin. (You might end your paraphrase with some clear phrase or phrases of transition: "—or so Tuchman affirms. In my own view. . . .")
5. If, all the way through, your paraphrase slavishly parallels the author's sentence structure (the author asks three questions, so you ask three questions), rewrite it and vary it.
6. If your paraphrase looks, at any place, close to the exact words of the original, carefully rewrite it in your own words.

Ending (also beginning)   Perhaps, as we have suggested, only after you have written the body of your paper will a good beginning and a concluding paragraph or paragraphs occur to you. The head and tail of your paper might then make clear your opinion of whatever you have found out. But that is not the only way to begin and end a research paper. Lisa Chickos begins with a short summary of what her investigation revealed:

> Whoever first said "It's lonely at the top" must
> have had the field of education in mind--more specifi-
> cally, women in education. Although women predominate at
> the lower levels in education, the "top" of the educa-
> tional field is overwhelmingly composed of men.

With facts and figures, Chickos goes on to support her view. That's a strong, concise beginning, and it makes the situation clear. A different opening paragraph might have answered the question she had investigated ("Why do so few women become educational leaders?").

> For a woman to become a school administrator, she
> must battle stereotyped attitudes. This obstacle defeats
> many teachers who try to rise in their profession and
> discourages many others from trying.

That opening may not be as lively as the one Chickos actually wrote, but it would do. Still another way to begin a research paper is to sum up the findings of other scholars. One research biologist, Edgar F. Warner, has reduced this kind of opening to a formula:

> First, in one or two paragraphs, you review everything that has been said about your topic, naming the most prominent earlier commentators. Next you declare why all of them are wrong. Then you set forth your own claim, and you spend the rest of your paper supporting it.

That pattern may seem cut and dried, but it is clear and useful. If you browse in specialized journals in many fields—literary criticism, social studies, the sciences—you may be surprised how many articles begin and go on in that very way. Of course, you don't need to damn every earlier commentator. One or two other writers may be enough to argue with. Erika Wahr, a student writing on the American poet Charles Olson, starts her research paper by disputing two views of him:

> To Cid Corman, Charles Olson of Gloucester, Massa-
> chusetts, is "the one dynamic and original epic poet
> twentieth-century America has produced" (116). To Allen
> Tate, Olson is "a loquacious charlatan" (McFinnery 92).
> In my opinion, the truth lies between these two extremes,
> nearer to Corman's view.

Whether or not you have stated your view in your beginning, you will certainly need to make it clear in your closing paragraph or paragraphs. A suggestion: before writing the last lines of your paper, read back over what you have written earlier. Then, without looking at your paper, try to put your view into writing. (For more suggestions on starting and finishing, see pp. 516 and 518.)

Rewriting

Because in writing a library research paper it is easy to lose sight of what you're saying, why not ask a fellow student to read over your draft and give you reactions? Ask your peer editor to answer the questions in the peer editing checklist.

PEER EDITING CHECKLIST: WRITING FROM LIBRARY RESEARCH

- What is your overall reaction to this paper?
- What do you understand the research question to be?
- What promises has the writer made that should be met in the paper?
- How interested were you in continuing to read the paper? If you didn't have to, would you have kept on reading? Why or why not?
- What changes might you make to the introduction that would wake up a sleepy instructor drinking coffee at 3:00 A.M. and enlist his or her careful attention?
- Does the conclusion merely restate the introduction? If so, suggest some specific changes.
- Is the conclusion too abrupt or too hurried? If so, suggest three specific revisions that would make the reader feel that the essay has ended exactly as it should.
- Are there any places where the essay becomes hard to follow? Star these.

When you set about the task of rewriting, you can work on binding your paper together by backtracking at the trouble spots your peer editor has starred and by briefly summarizing the discussion so far. By so doing, you remind your reader of what you have already said. This strategy might seem pompous in a paper of 500 words, when the reader has hardly had time to forget what you have said; but it can come in handy in a longer paper when, after a few pages, the reader's memory may need refreshing, and a summary of the argument so far will be welcome. Such a brief summary might go like this: "As we can infer from the previous examples, most veteran career counselors are reluctant to encourage women undergraduates to apply for jobs as principals in elementary schools."

When you look over your draft, here are a few other points you can inspect critically (and, if need be, try to improve).

REVISION CHECKLIST: LOOKING OVER EVERYTHING

- Do you honestly feel you have said something, not just heaped facts and statements by other writers that don't add up to anything? If your answer is no, a mere heap of meaningless stuff is all you've got, then you face a painful decision. Take a long walk and try to define what your research has shown you. Don't despair: talk to other students, talk to your instructor. It may be that you need a whole new question whose answer you care about. Or it may be that you need to do some harder thinking.

- Does your paper make clear the research question it began with? Does it reveal, early on, what you wanted to find out and why this might be important to the reader?

- Does it sum up your findings? Because your paper is short, perhaps it doesn't need a formal concluding summary. In that case, does it clearly present your findings as it goes along?

- Have you included only library materials that told you something and left out any that seem useless (even though you worked hard to look them up and take notes on them)?

- Have you digressed in any places from answering the question you set out to answer? If so, does the digression help your reader understand the nature of the problem, or does it add extraneous material that might simply be omitted? (Although it is a shock to discover you have written, say, six pages that don't advance your research, be brave—use those scissors, feed that wastebasket.)

- Does each new idea or piece of information seem to follow from the one before it? Can you see any stronger order in which to arrange things?

- Is the source of every quotation, every fact, every idea you have borrowed made unmistakably clear? If your readers cared to look up your sources, could they readily find them in a library?

Preparing your manuscript   A research paper calls on you to follow special rules in documenting your sources—in citing them as you write and in listing them at the end of your paper. At first, these rules may seem fiendishly fussy, but for good reason professional writers of research papers swear by them and follow them to a *T.* The rules will make sense if you imagine a world in which scholarly and professional writers could prepare their research papers in any old way they pleased. The result would be a new tower of Babel. Research papers go by the rules in order to be easily readable, easily set into type. The rules also ensure that all necessary information is there to enable any reader interested in the same subject to look up the original sources.

Style guides. In humanities courses and the social sciences, most writers of research papers follow the style of the Modern Language Association (MLA) or the American Psychological Association (APA). Your instructor will probably suggest which style to observe; if you are not told, use MLA. The first time you prepare a research paper according to MLA or APA rules, you'll need extra time to look up just what to do in each situation. Chapter 14 gives examples of most of the usual situations.

Quotation style. When you use a direct quotation from one of your sources, ordinarily you simply put into quotation marks, in the body of your paper, the words you're using, along with the name of the person who said them.

```
It was Patrick Henry who said, "Give me liberty or give
me death."

Johnson puts heavy emphasis on the importance of "giving
the child what she needs at the precise moment in her
life when it will do the most good."
```

When you include a quotation longer than four typed lines, you set it off in your text by indenting the whole quotation ten spaces from the margin if you're following MLA style, five for APA style. You double-space the quotation, just as you do the rest of your paper. Don't place quotation marks around an indented quotation and, if the quotation is a paragraph or less, don't indent its first line. (For detailed instructions about quoting sources, see Chapter 14.)

Works cited. At the very end of a library research paper, you supply a list of all the sources you have cited: books, periodicals, and any other materials. Usually this list is the last thing you write. It will be easy to make if, when you compiled your working bibliography, you included on each note card all the necessary information (as shown in Figures 11.1 and 11.2). If you did, you can now simply arrange those cards in alphabetical order and then type the information about each source, following the MLA or APA guidelines (given in Chapter 14, pp. 457 and 464). The MLA specifies that you entitle your list "Works Cited"; the APA, "References." Any leftover parts—cards for sources you haven't used after all—may now be sailed into the wastebasket. Resist the temptation to transcribe them, too, and impressively lengthen your list.

Last pass. Before you hand in your final revision, go over it one last time

---

WRITING WITH A COMPUTER: LIBRARY RESEARCH

REWRITING

If you plan to use traditional bottom-of-the-page footnotes, see if your word processing program will format them for you. A program that does so even figures out for you how much space to allow for the footnote at the bottom of each page.

Research papers, being rich in names and numbers, invite misspellings and other typographical errors. A great way to proofread your finished research paper, before you print it out, is to go to the bottom of the document you have been writing, scroll backward, and reread what you have written line by line. This technique prevents you from getting so interested in what you've written that you forget to notice mistakes. Instead, it keeps you looking at spelling, punctuation, and such mechanical matters, concentrating on one line at a time.

(For suggestions on shaping a draft with a computer, see p. 364.)

---

for typographical and mechanical errors. If you have written your paper on a word processor, it's an easy matter to correct errors right on the screen before you print it. If you find any mistakes in a paper you have typewritten, don't despair. Your instructor knows how difficult and frustrating it would be to retype a whole page to fix one flyspeck error. Correct it neatly in ink. (How to be neat? See p. 579.)

Manuscript form. A note following Chapter 20 tells you how to style a finished (typewritten or word-processed) manuscript. Its advice on proper formatting applies not only to library research papers but to any other college papers you may write.

A COMPLETED LIBRARY RESEARCH PAPER

Lisa Chickos's irritation at men who would call a hard-working woman school administrator "tough and bitchy" led her to write a paper she strongly cared about. The completed paper is more than a compilation of facts, more than a string of quotations. Chickos sets forth a problem that irritates her, and she proposes action.

To help her instructor follow her thoughts, she prefaced her paper with a formal outline. Written in complete statements, it is a *sentence outline*—a document not for the writer's own use but meant to be read. (If your instructor asks for such an outline, see the advice on formal outlines on p. 501.)

In her later college life, Chickos found, the training she acquired as a freshman researcher proved valuable. "Now that I'm a history major," she said, "I'm *always* doing research papers."

Title page contains, on separate lines, centered and double-spaced, the title of the paper, the writer's name, the course number, and the date.

Educational Leadership: A Man's World

Lisa Chickos

Professor Laura Miller

English 102

May 12, 198–

Outline

Thesis: To achieve fair representation in educational administration, women must change the
current system.

 I. Women make up most of the staff but men
  make up most of the administration of
  public school systems.

  A. In 1972, 62 percent of all teachers
   were women, but 99 percent of superintendents, 98 percent of high school
   principals, and 80 percent of elementary school principals were men.

  B. Today, two-thirds of teachers are
   women, but the great majority of administrators are men.

 II. Why do so few women become educational
  leaders?

  A. Women do not seem to have less ability than men to be effective leaders.

   1. One study showed that women prin-
    cipals were viewed as no less
    competent than men principals.

   2. Another study indicated that men
    in competitive situations become
    aggressive and self-interested
    while women consider the inter-
    ests of all involved.

   3. Women administrators have been
    described as "conscientious, sen-

All pages after the
title page are num-
bered in the upper
right corner half an
inch from the top.
The writer's name ap-
pears before the page
number. Outline
pages are numbered
with small roman nu-
merals (the title page
is counted but is not
numbered).

Type "Outline" cen-
tered, one inch from
the top. Double-space
to the first line of text.

The thesis states
the main idea of the
paper.

This outline is in sen-
tence form rather than
in the shorter topic
form.

Chickos iii

sitive . . . , reliable, adaptable, and tactful."

B. Women may have been socialized not to
aspire to positions of leadership.

1. Boys are encouraged to be competitive, whereas girls are taught
merely to look and act nice but
not to reach for high goals.

2. Women may fear success and the
social rejection that may accompany success.

3. Women may fear the consequences
of "unfeminine" behavior--that
is, independence and assertive-
ness, particularly in nontraditional professions such as
administration.

4. Women lack role models in positions of educational leadership;
men in such positions do not provide adequate role models for
young girls and women.

C. Family and geographic ties may prevent women from seeking or being offered high-level positions.

1. Women's jobs are seen as providing a second, not a primary, income for their families, so women
have less incentive to seek
higher-level positions.

2. Women are not considered as geo-

Chickos iv

graphically mobile as men and are
therefore overlooked for positions
that may require relocating.

D. The female stereotype, which catego-
rizes women as emotional and non-
task-oriented, prevents women from
advancing.

    1. Women are considered capable of
obeying rules and taking orders
but not of making rules and giving orders.

    2. Women are not offered administra-
tive positions because men control the hiring process.

    3. Women in responsible positions
are seen merely as tokens and are
inhibited from performing naturally and effectively, thereby
creating a negative image of
women administrators.

III. Women can break the negative stereotypes
and can try to change the system that
prevents them from advancing.

A. Women must provide support for other
women in administrative positions and
for women seeking to advance.

B. Women need the support of their male
colleagues, who are in positions of
power and are able to make changes.

C. Boys and girls need to be encouraged

Chickos v

to reach their own goals, even if
they include nontraditional careers.

D. Women need the cooperation of their
husbands and children so that they
are freer to pursue more responsible
positions.

E. Employers must not consider women applicants differently from men applicants and should include more women
in the hiring process.

F. Organizations and legislation can
support women seeking administrative
positions.

Educational Leadership: A Man's World

Whoever first said "It's lonely at the top" must have had the field of education in mind--more specifically, women in education. Although women predominate at the lower levels in education, the "top" of the educational field is overwhelmingly composed of men. If women are to be more fairly represented in educational administration, they must overcome the restrictions imposed by the current system, which is built on outdated ideas about women's work and on stereotypes about women's abilities.

In 1972, 62 percent of the professional staff of the public schools were female. Yet 99 percent of the superintendents, 98 percent of the high school principals, and 80 percent of the elementary school principals were male (Schmuck 244). Unfortunately, these figures haven't improved much. Today, two-thirds of the public school teachers are women, but the great majority of the administrative positions are still held by men (Truett 1).

Could it be that men have more ability than women to be effective leaders? This hardly seems the case. A research study conducted by Fischel and Pottker asking teachers to evaluate women principals showed no significant differences in the behavior of women principals compared with that of men principals, and the women

Chickos 2

Text pages are numbered with arabic numerals in the upper right corner preceded by writer's last name. Leave one-inch margins at the top, bottom, and sides of the paper. Place page number half an inch from the top.

were certainly viewed as competent leaders (qtd. in Biklen 10).

Biklen is a secondary source for the study by Fischel and Pottker, so citation reads "qtd. in."

In fact, some studies show that women are likely to be more effective educational leaders than men. One study, for example, indicated that when placed in competitive situations, men become very aggressive and tend to act in ways that are most advantageous for themselves. Women usually try to consider the interests of all those involved, not just their own (Conoley 39).

Writer uses transitional words and phrases (In fact, Furthermore, In another) to link paragraphs discussing various studies.

Furthermore, the study showed that in educational settings, groups accomplish more when they have a leader who works with them rather than ruling over them--someone who listens to the opinions of all the group members and tries to do what's best for all involved (Conoley 40).

Paraphrase and summary rather than direct quotation to discuss the results of most studies.

In another survey, which measured the attitudes toward women as school district administrators, "conscientious, sensitive to the needs of others, reliable, adaptable, and tactful" were some of the terms used to describe the most effective administrators (Temmen 9).

Direct quotation for the exact terms given by respondents in this study.

Clearly, women do have the ability to be effective educational leaders. Therefore, the reasons that more men reach higher positions must lie elsewhere.

Writer indicates that she will list other reasons and uses transitional words such as one, also, and others to highlight each new reason.

One possibility may be that women simply do not aspire to positions of leadership. From early childhood, boys are encouraged to be competitive. Organized sports and other games

Chickos 3

send young boys a clear message--be the best.
For young girls, however, the emphasis is placed
mainly on looks and personality. They are not
encouraged to reach high goals (Clement 134).
For this reason, a woman may not attach the same
importance to an administrative position as a
man would.

Women also may not aspire to administrative
positions because of a "fear of success." Society's concept of femininity tells young girls
that achievement is a masculine quality. It
doesn't mix with a pretty face and pleasant
personality. This gives many girls the fear
that they will be socially rejected if they
succeed in reaching a position of authority
(Horner 36).

Others have suggested that women may not
actually have a fear of success. Women who
were tested for fear of success showed a fear of
losing love or of being socially rejected. The
small number of men who showed some fear of
success questioned the value of the success
rather than showing any fears about possible
rejection (Johnson 176). For this reason, it
has been speculated that women have a fear of
what might happen if they deviated from traditional sex roles, not a fear of succeeding
(Wortman, Loftus, and Marshall 368).

Fear of the consequences of "unfeminine"
behavior is certainly legitimate. Society's
attitudes are unfavorable toward women in tra-

Citation of work by
two or three authors
gives the names of all
authors.

Chickos 4

ditionally male professions. As Dr. Patricia

Albjerg Graham, a member of the history and

education faculty at Barnard College and Teach-

ers College, Columbia University, states, "ad-

ministrators are expected to be independent and

assertive, behaviors understood as 'tough and

bitchy' when displayed by women, but 'clear-

headed and attentive to detail' when found in a

man" (170).

Obviously, no woman (or man, for that mat-

ter) would want to be described as "tough and

bitchy." Young girls need to see that they can

fill administrative positions and still gain

approval. What better place for this to start

than in the educational system? Unfortunately,

because there are so few women already in higher

positions, young girls have no role models to

follow. There are plenty of men for girls to

pattern themselves after, but it is easier for

children to model themselves after someone they

can identify with and, in most cases, a young

girl can most easily identify with a woman

(Antonucci 186).

Young women in college and entering the job

market also need role models. They need to see

that other women have succeeded and that they

too can succeed and thus strive to seek better

jobs (Antonucci 188).

Perhaps the major reason women don't reach

for administrative jobs is family. If a woman

is a wife and mother, she has added responsi-

Direct quotation rather than paraphrasing for the source's strong, effective language. Title and credentials establish the source as an authority.

Source's name mentioned at the beginning of the quotation, so the citation gives only the page number.

Chickos 5

bilities and may not be able to put as much time
as she would like into a demanding job (Graham
170).

Also, it is rare to find a family woman
working in the educational system who is the
sole or main breadwinner. In a survey of public school administrators, the working husbands
of the female administrators made more money
than their wives, while the working wives of
male administrators made less money than their
husbands (Truett 9). It can be speculated that
men see their jobs as the main source of family
income and, therefore, go after the highest-
paying positions, while some women view their
jobs as a second income and have no financial
need for a better position.

A woman's geographic mobility may also influence her decision not to advance in her
field. There is nothing strange about a family
relocating because of the father's job transfer,
but it is not commonplace for a family to move
to a new location for the mother's job. Not
only does the possibility of relocating keep
some women from pursuing jobs, but women's supposed immobility also keeps women who do pursue
such jobs from being hired. Employers assume
that a man would be able to relocate and a woman
would not and simply do not consider women for
certain positions. Interestingly, however, the
survey of public school administrators revealed
that the person who had moved the most (three

Chickos gives her
interpretation of some
data in sentence form
and then presents the
statistics themselves.

Chickos 6

times in the past five years) was a woman
(Truett 13). This same survey showed no real
difference between men and women in willingness
to relocate; 16.7 percent of the men anticipated
a future move to obtain a better job, as did 14
percent of the women (Truett 15). Actually,
neither men nor women seem very eager to relocate for a higher position, but women are certainly no less willing to relocate than men
(Truett 22).

Other factors keep women from reaching
higher positions that they desire and also
inhibit other women from pursuing similar
positions. The female stereotype, which cate-
gorizes women as being emotional and nontask-
oriented, can cause many problems. This stereotype holds that women can be part of the system, obeying its rules and taking orders, but
that they are not capable of running the system--
making the rules and giving the orders (Biklen
10). This societal attitude convinces some
women that they don't have what it takes to be a
leader. As Sari Knopp Biklen states, "People's
perceptions about their ability influence
achievement more than their actual ability or
level of aspiration" (8). But, as mentioned
earlier, women do have the ability to become
successful leaders.

The female stereotype also keeps women from
being hired. Many men have this image of all
women, and because the educational leaders are

primarily men, they may not even consider hiring women for administrative positions (Schmuck 248). An interview with male administrators revealed their feelings:

> It's easier to work without women. Principals and superintendents are a management team. It fosters interde-pendence and mutual support. We need each other for survival. It's no evil liaison--it's just pure poli-tics. I wonder if we could hang to-gether so well if some of us were women. (Biklen 12)

Quotation of more than four typed lines is indented ten spaces from the left margin and is double-spaced with no quota-tion marks. Citation is in parentheses fol-lowing the end punc-tuation of the quotation.

This brings up another difficulty that women must confront. Because there are so few women in educational administration, a woman who reaches such a position may see herself (and may be seen by others) as a token or representative of all women. This makes it very difficult to perform naturally (Biklen 16). Because she is in the spotlight and because she may feel like an outsider in a male-dominated profession, a woman may adopt a "female behavior" (passive, compromising, and so on), which in turn gives her role as a female administrator a negative image (Clement 136).

Women must work to break these negative stereotypes. Women who are already in adminis-trative positions must consciously try to project a positive image to their male col-leagues (Schmuck 249). The women in these po-

Chickos 8

sitions must also encourage women who are on the
way up, and they all need to support one another. One female administrator pointed out:

> It used to be when I walked into a
> room full of men and only one woman I
> would tend to ignore her. Now when I
> walk into a similar situation the
> woman and I at least have eye-contact.
> There's too damn few of us women; we
> found out we need to support each
> other. If there were more of us we
> would be free to act just as folks,
> but because there are so few of us,
> there is the common bond of being
> women. (Schmuck 254)

But women cannot just join forces and try
to overthrow the system. They need to have the
support of their male colleagues, too, because
the men are in the power positions and have the
ability to make changes. Also, if women banded
together and excluded men from their efforts,
that in itself would be discrimination, which is
exactly what must be overcome (Schmuck 251).

Outside forces can also aid in changing the
present situation. During the school years,
boys and girls can be taught that there is
nothing wrong with pursuing untraditional careers and can be encouraged to reach for their
own goals--not the goals society has set for
them (Johnson 180).

Chickos 9

In addition, family support can be a great help. If a career woman is also a wife and mother, she is actually carrying two jobs. Support from her husband and the independent behavior of her children may give a woman a chance to pursue a position she thought was not within her reach (Biklen 14).

The system also must change if women are ever to become an equal part of educational administrations. Those who review applications should not consider marital status and family because, as discussed earlier, employers often consider a family to be a burden for a woman's career but not for a man's. Also, since administrative staffs are essentially male, and they tend to hire men over women, some women need to be involved in selection processes (Weitzman 485).

A number of organizations and some legislation, such as Sex Equity in Educational Leadership (SEEL), the National Council of Administrative Women in Education (NCAWE), the Leadership and Learning Cooperative (LLC), and the Women's Educational Equity Act (WEEA), have been designed to facilitate the changes that are necessary to ensure equity in educational leadership.

Organizations are common knowledge, and no source is needed.

With the help of such groups and legislation, along with an enlightened public, perhaps equality in educational administration will soon be realized.

Chickos 10

Works Cited

Antonucci, Toni. "The Need for Female Role
Models in Education." Biklen and
Brannigan 185-195.

Biklen, Sari Knopp. "Introduction: Barriers to
Equity--Women, Educational Leadership, and
Social Change." Biklen and Brannigan
1-23.

Biklen, Sari Knopp, and Marilyn B. Brannigan.
Women and Educational Leadership. Lexington, MA: Heath, 1980.

Clement, Jacqueline. "Sex Bias in School
Administration." Biklen and Brannigan
131-137.

Conoley, Jane Close. "The Psychology of Leadership: Implications for Women." Biklen
and Brannigan 35-46.

Graham, Patricia Albjerg. "Status Transitions
of Women Students, Faculty, and Administrators." Academic Women on the Move. Ed.
Alice S. Rossi and Ann Calderwood. New
York: Russell Sage Foundation, 1973.
163-72.

Horner, Matina. "A Bright Woman Is Caught in a
Double Bind." Psychology Today Nov. 1969:
36+.

Johnson, Marilyn. "How Real Is Fear of Success?" Biklen and Brannigan 175-82.

Schmuck, Patricia A. "Changing Women's Representation in School Management: A Systems

---

Margin notes:

Works cited parenthetically in text of paper are listed here alphabetically by author's last name. Type "Works Cited" centered, one inch from top. Double-space to first entry and double-space within and between entries. Indent turn lines five spaces.

Book itself is not cited parenthetically in text of paper, but more than two entries in the list of works cited are taken from it. Publication information is given here, and short cross-references to it are used in the other entries.

Chapter in an edited book with publication information given in this entry.

Article in a monthly magazine.

Chapter in an edited book. Note cross reference to another book in the list of works cited.

Chickos 11

Perspective." Biklen and Brannigan 239-59.

Temmen, Karen.   "A Research Study of Selected
    Successful Women Administrators in the Ed-
    ucational Field."   St. Louis: CEMREL,
    1982.

Truett, Carol.   "Professional and Geographic
    Mobility of a Selected Sample of Nebraska
    Public School Administrators: Differences
    between Men and Women."   Paper.   Annual
    Meeting of the National Conference of Pro-
    fessors of Educational Administration.
    San Marcos, TX, 1982.

Weitzman, Lenore J.   "Affirmative Action Plans
    for Eliminating Sex Discrimination in Aca-
    deme."   Academic Women on the Move.   Ed.
    Alice S. Rossi and Ann Calderwood.   New
    York: Russell Sage Foundation, 1973.
    463-504.

Wortman, Camille B., Elizabeth F. Loftus, and
    Mary Marshall.   Psychology.   New York:
    Knopf, 1981.

Study sponsored by a corporation.

Paper presented at a conference.

Book with more than one author.

Questions to Start You Thinking

1. Which of the reasons given in this paper for women's failure to advance in the field of education seems to you the strongest? What makes it hard to refute?

2. Do any of the points that Chickos includes for support seem to you less convincing? What are they? If you were her peer editor, what suggestions would you make that might strengthen her main point?

3. What other professions can you name in which men hold most positions of leadership? Why do you think this is so?

Other Assignments

Using your library sources, write a short research paper, under 3000 words, in which you give a rough survey of the state of current knowledge on one of the following topics or on another that you and your instructor agree offers promising opportunities for research. Proceed as if you had chosen to work on the main assignment.

1. The health of the economy or the stability of the government in a third world country

2. Career opportunities in a certain line of work that interests you

FOR GROUP LEARNING

To write a collaborative essay from library research is a complex job, and we recommend that you attempt it only if your writing group has already had some success in writing a collaborative paper. If you do embark on such an endeavor, you will find that working as a research team can make your project advance with alacrity. After consulting with your instructor and getting a go-ahead, your group might develop a research paper following one of the assignments in this chapter. (An instructor who agrees to accept a collaborative research paper will give the same grade to all participants.)

You will need to fix a series of deadlines, parcel out the work, and meet faithfully according to a schedule. Here is a sample schedule that one group followed for an eight-week research project:

Week 1: Members individually seek a topic to suggest to the group and take overviews.

Week 2: The group meets and members agree on a topic: a research question. They choose a coordinator to keep the project moving, someone willing to make phone calls to keep in touch with people when necessary. The group clears the topic with the instructor.

Weeks 3–4: Assisted by two people, the coordinator makes a preliminary search and compiles a tentative bibliography. The group meets to divide up responsibilities: who will collect what material. Then, without further meetings, all begin work.

3. Another planet in the solar system, or comets, novas, black holes, perhaps even a neighboring star

4. Progress in the cure and prevention of a disease or syndrome

5. Treatment of drug abuse or the rehabilitation of users

6. The "greenhouse effect" (a phenomenon causing a change in worldwide climate)

7. The possibility of an accord between the United States and the Soviet Union in reducing stockpiles of nuclear weapons

8. Present methods of disposing of nuclear wastes and a comparison of their relative effectiveness

9. Attempts to ban smoking in public places

10. The growth of telecommuting: the tendency of people to work in their own homes, keeping in touch by phone and computer modem with the main office

APPLYING WHAT YOU LEARN: SOME USES OF LIBRARY RESEARCH

In many courses beyond your English course you will be asked to write papers from library research. The more deeply you move into core requirements and specialized courses for your major, the more independent research and think-

---

FOR GROUP LEARNING (Continued)

Week 5: Each member continues his or her assigned portion of the research.

Week 6: The group meets to evaluate the material and to see where any further information may be needed. Members collaborate on a rough outline or plan.

Week 7: Three writers divide up the outline and each writes part of a draft (if possible, with the aid of a word processor). The other group members read over the writing for at least one hour during this week and help solve any problems in it.

Week 8: All group members meet for one long evening session and carefully review the draft. All write comments and corrections on it. Then two fresh writers divide the criticized draft and type it up smoothly. Whoever has done the least work to date is designated the proofreader. The coordinator gives the whole paper another, final proofreading.

Obviously such a plan can succeed only if your group can work in a close, friendly, and responsible fashion. No one should enter into such an arrangement without first making sure of enough unobstructed time to meet all assigned responsibilities—or else the whole project can bog down in an awful mess. But if it succeeds, as it probably will, your research will generate excitement. You'll know the pleasure of playing your part on a dynamic, functioning team.

ing you will do. At some colleges, a long research paper is required of all seniors to graduate. Beyond college, the demand for writing based on library research is evident. Scholars explore issues that absorb and trouble them and the community of scholars to which they belong. In the business world, large companies often maintain their own specialized libraries since information and opinions are worth money and decisions have to be based on them. If you should take an entry-level job in the headquarters of a large corporation, don't be surprised to be told, "We're opening a branch office in Sri Lanka, and Graham (the executive vice-president) doesn't know a thing about the place. Can you write a report on it? Customs, geography, climate, government, state of the economy, political stability, religion, lifestyle, and all that?" In a large city newspaper, reporters and feature writers continually do library research (as well as field research), and the newspaper's library of clippings on subjects covered in the past (the "morgue") is in constant use. Many popular magazine articles were obviously researched in a library: "The Strangest Career in Movies" (for which the writer looked up all the biographies and biographical facts about Greta Garbo), "New Findings about Sunburn" (for which the writer went through the past year's crop of medical journals).

As one of the ways they become prominent in their disciplines, academics and professionals in many fields—law, medicine, English, geography, social studies, art and music history, the history of science—write and publish papers and whole books based on library research in specialized and scholarly journals. In an exciting study of urban architecture, *Spaces: Dimensions of the Human Landscape* (New Haven: Yale University Press, 1981), Barrie B. Greenbie draws connections between our notion of "self"—a personal universe bounded by the skin—and our sense of the kind of dwelling we feel at home in. In exploring this relationship (and the need to build dwellings that correspond to our psychic needs), Greenbie brings together sources in psychology, architecture, economics, and literature (the poetry of Emily Dickinson). This passage from the beginning of his book may give you a sense of his way of weaving together disparate materials:

> The psychoanalyst Carl Jung placed great emphasis on the house as a symbol of self, and many others have elaborated this idea.[1] Of course Jung considered "self" both in a social as well as individual sense, and in fact the concept of *self* has no meaning except in the context of *others*. Most of us share our houses with some sort of family group during most of our lives, and while parts of an adequately sized house may belong primarily to one or another individual, the boundaries of the home are usually those of a cluster of selves which form a domestic unit. Even people who by choice or circumstance live alone express in their homes the images and traditions formed at one time in a family group.
>
> The architects Kent C. Bloomer and Charles W. Moore view buildings as the projection into space of our awareness of our own bodies. Fundamental and obvious as this relationship might seem, it has been to a great extent ignored in contemporary architecture. Bloomer and Moore sum up the personal situation very well in their book, *Body, Memory, and Architecture:*

One tell-tale sign remains, in modern America, of a world based not on a Cartesian abstraction, but on our sense of ourselves extended beyond the boundaries of our bodies to the world around: that is the single-family house, free-standing like ourselves, with a face and a back, a hearth (like a heart) and a chimney, an attic full of recollections of *up,* and a basement harboring implications of *down.*[2]

Many North American tract houses fit this characterization less adequately than they might. But whatever the deficiencies of domestic and other kinds of contemporary architecture may be, they are as nothing compared to the short-comings of most urban design. . . . This book will focus on the hierarchical structures that extend from the "skin" of the family home to the street and beyond.

Notice that Greenbie uses endnote form (see p. 454) because the amount of information he has to put in his notes might have interrupted the flow of his prose. Endnote 1, for instance, reads:

[1] Carl G. Jung, *Memories, Dreams, and Reflections* (London: Fontana Library Series, 1969). For an exceptionally good summary and elaboration, see Clare Cooper, "The House as Symbol of the Self," in *Designing for Human Behavior,* ed. J. Lang et al. (Stroudsburg, Pa.: Dowden, Hutchinson, and Ross, 1974).

Earlier, we pointed out that unless your assignment confines you to library materials, your research paper may draw on any other sources you have: recall of your personal experience, observation, conversation, previous reading, even imagination. Here is a memorable example of two professional writers on biology, Anne and Paul Ehrlich, combining library materials with their own experience.

The direct benefits supplied to humanity by other species are often little appreciated, but nonetheless they can be very dramatic. In 1955 Paul's father died after a grim thirteen-year battle with Hodgkin's disease, a leukemia-like disorder of the lymphatic system. Just after his death, some Canadian scientists discovered that an extract of the leaves of a periwinkle plant from Madagascar caused a decrease in the white blood cell count of rats. Chemists at Eli Lilly and Company analyzed the chemistry of periwinkle leaves, and the analysis turned up a large number of alkaloids, poisonous chemicals that plants apparently have evolved to protect themselves from animals that eat them and parasites that infest them.[1] Two of these alkaloids, vincristine and vinblastine, have proven to be effective in treating Hodgkin's disease. Indeed, treatment with vincristine in combination with other chemical agents now gives a very high remission rate and long periods where no further treatment is required in patients even in the advanced stage of the disease.

Thus a chemical found in a plant species might have helped greatly to prolong Bill Ehrlich's life—and is now available to help the five to six thousand people in the United States alone who contract Hodgkin's disease annually. As some measure of its economic value, total sales of vincristine worldwide in 1979 were $35 million.[2] Vincristine also is used along with other compounds to fight a wide variety of cancers and cancerlike diseases, including one form of leukemia, breast cancer, and cancers that afflict children. Had the periwinkle plant been wiped out before 1950, humanity would have suffered a loss—even though no one would have realized it. (*Extinction: The Causes and Consequences of the Disappearance of Species* [New York: Random House, 1981], 53–54.)

---

[1]P. R. Ehrlich and P. H. Raven, "Butterflies and Plants: A Study of Coevolution," *Evolution* 18 (1964): 586–608.

[2]Information on origins of vincristine is from G. E. Trease and W. C. Evans, *Pharmacognosy,* 10th ed. (Baltimore: Williams and Wilkins, 1972). The figure on the value of sales is from Norman Myers, "What Is a Species Worth?" manuscript for *Science Digest,* 1980.

As you can see from that remarkable illustration, these writers care very much about a topic for library research. In a personal way, they combine what they discover with what they already know.

CHAPTER 12

Knowing Your Library: A Directory of Sources

In the previous chapter, we didn't want to bore you with anything you know already. Neither did we want to ply you with additional information, lest you lose sight of what library research is all about. But there is a good deal that most of us ordinary citizens not trained in library school don't know about a large library. Now that you have seen the process of thoughtful writing that goes into a library research paper, perhaps you would like to see in greater depth what your library has to offer.

Lately, public service announcements on television have urged us to find out what our libraries contain besides those dry old fossils, books. It is true: nowadays most libraries also lend recordings, software, videotapes, musical scores, works of art, and sometimes (as our hometown's public library lends to responsible children) even pet animals. Through a computer terminal, a library may have access to a data bank, bringing a world of information to your fingertips. Unfortunately, at the moment, to lay a hand on this world will cost you about $30 an hour.

Yet for all these changes, in a college library, books are still indispensable properties. Technology may have altered our methods of storing, retrieving, and transmitting ideas, but the book still remains a compact and relatively inexpensive source. It is also easier than a computer to curl up with.

Most libraries have a reference librarian who can find anything from a two-letter word for "ancient Egyptian sun god" (for a distraught crossword puzzle addict) to an 1898 news story stored on microfilm. Know your reference librarian. You might be surprised at the resources this learned specialist can reveal for you.

By the way, when you set out to do college research, don't forget your *local* library. In large towns and cities, it may be less busy than your college library. Some of its facilities—reference room, current newspapers, and popular magazines—may be just as extensive as your college's, if not more so.

Whatever library you use, you'll save time if you first know your way around. You'll need to locate the centers of action: circulation desk where you charge out books; reference room; catalog (drawers of cards or a computer terminal); microfilm projectors; special collections of materials on specific subjects; current newspapers and periodicals; back issues. Here are five small questions worth knowing the answers to. If any stumps you, ask a librarian.

DISCOVERY CHECKLIST: FIVE PRACTICAL MATTERS

- If another borrower has a book out, how can you get it held for you on its return?
- If this library doesn't have a certain book you need, can you order it on interlibrary loan?
- If you haven't previously taken a guided tour of your college library, is one available?
- Is there a pamphlet mapping the library's rooms and explaining its services?
- Are there any available study carrels—usually small cubicles with desks in the stacks—that you can use while working on your research paper?

CONSULTING THE LIBRARY CATALOG

Like the ignition key that starts the car, a library catalog starts your book search moving. You consult it for detailed information on every book in the library.

If your library's catalog is a traditional sort, it is housed in file drawers, on 3-by-5-inch cards. In many libraries nowadays, although a catalog still has cards, you view them on a screen. They are filed on microfilm or microfiche or on a computer, and you scroll through them.

The catalog lets you look up a book in any of three ways: (1) by author, (2) by title, or (3) by subject. Here's some special advice about subject headings.

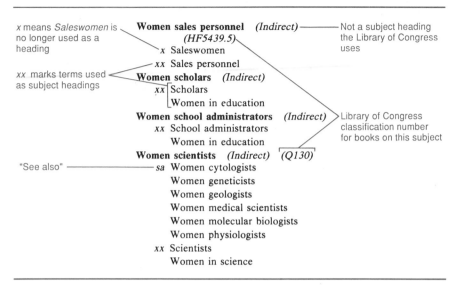

FIGURE 12.1   Entries from the *Library of Congress Subject Headings*

Library of Congress Subject Headings

Sometimes, if you go straight to the catalog, you can't find the subject heading you're after, or helpful books don't seem to be listed under the subject headings you do find. Suppose you look up "Women school administrators" in the catalog and there isn't any such subject. In fact, the library may own several books on the subject, but they are listed in the catalog under "School administrators" and "Women in education." Now how do you find out that useful information? You can look up "Women school administrators" in a copy of *Library of Congress Subject Headings,* a volume usually on hand near the catalog. (If your library is an older or smaller one that files books under the Dewey decimal system instead of the Library of Congress system, you can consult instead the *Dewey Decimal Classification and Relative Index.*) Figure 12.1 shows how entries look in the *Library of Congress Subject Headings.*

Finding a Book

In some libraries, author cards are contained in one file, title cards in a second, subject cards in a third. In other libraries, all cards are filed together alphabetically. On the author card, the main card for each book, you find the following information—which often will give you some ideas about the book before you look for it. (Figure 12.2 shows a typical author card.)

1.   The call number. The combination of letters and numbers tells you exactly where to find the book.

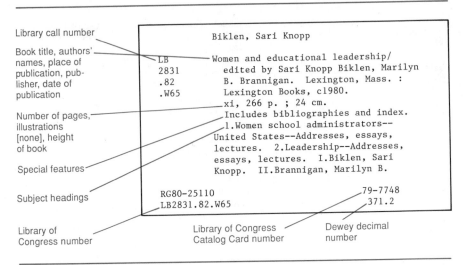

Library call number

Book title, authors' names, place of publication, publisher, date of publication

Number of pages, illustrations [none], height of book

Special features

Subject headings

Library of Congress number

    Biklen, Sari Knopp

LB   Women and educational leadership/
2831   edited by Sari Knopp Biklen, Marilyn
.82   B. Brannigan. Lexington, Mass. :
.W65   Lexington Books, c1980.
              xi, 266 p. ; 24 cm.
              Includes bibliographies and index.
              1.Women school administrators--
              United States--Addresses, essays,
              lectures. 2.Leadership--Addresses,
              essays, lectures. I.Biklen, Sari
              Knopp. II.Brannigan, Marilyn B.

    RG80-25110   79-7748
    LB2831.82.W65   371.2

Library of Congress
Catalog Card number

Dewey decimal
number

FIGURE 12.2   A Library of Congress author card

2. The author's full name, last name first, with birth and death dates (if known).
3. The title as it appears on the book's title page; the fact that the book has been revised in a second (or later) edition if that is the case.
4. Publication information: city, name of publisher, and date of publication.
5. The number of pages, the height of the book, and mention of any maps, charts, or illustrations the book may contain.
6. A list of whatever special features the book may have—bibliographies, appendices, indexes, illustrations.
7. All subject headings under which the book is filed in the library.
8. The International Standard Book Number used by librarians to order books. (You need pay no attention to it.)

   The title card looks like the main card except that it lists the book's title at the top, above the name of the author (see Figure 12.3).

   When you start your research, you may find subject cards more useful than author cards. They will often lead you to useful titles. Also, the subject you look under may direct you to related subjects and thus to still more titles. The subject card looks just like the author card except the author's name appears under a subject heading (see Figure 12.4).

   Assuming that the book you want is in the library, you can expect its call number to help you find it. The first letter or letters of the call number point you to its neighborhood. A book, for instance, whose call number starts with an *S* is about agriculture or forestry. (For a rundown of the Library of Congress system of classifying books, see the next section, or look for a location chart posted prominently in your library.)

```
LB          Women and educational leadership/
2831           edited by Sari Knopp Biklen, Marilyn
.82            B. Brannigan.  Lexington, Mass. :
.W65           Lexington Books, c1980.
               xi, 266 p. ; 24 cm.
               Includes bibliographies and index.
               1.Women school administrators--
            United States--Addresses, essays,
            lectures.  2.Leadership--Addresses,
            essays, lectures.  I.Biklen, Sari
            Knopp.  II.Brannigan, Marilyn B.

   RG80-25110                      79-7748
   LB2831.82.W65                    371.2
```

FIGURE 12.3   A Library of Congress title card

FIGURE 12.4   Library of Congress subject cards with subject subdivisions

```
            LEADERSHIP--ADDRESSES, ESSAYS,
               LECTURES.

   LB          Women and educational leadership/
   2831           edited by Sari Knopp Biklen, Marilyn
   .82            B. Brannigan.  Lexington, Mass. :
   .W65           Lexington Books, c1980.
```

```
               WOMEN SCHOOL ADMINISTRATORS--UNITED
                  STATES--ADDRESSES, ESSAYS, LECTURES.

      LB          Women and educational leadership/
      2831           edited by Sari Knopp Biklen, Marilyn
      .82            B. Brannigan.  Lexington, Mass. :
      .W65           Lexington Books, c1980.
                     xi, 266 p. ; 24 cm.
                     Includes bibliographies and index.
                     1. Women school administrators--
                  United States--Addresses, essays,
                  lectures.  2.Leadership--Addresses,
                  essays, lectures.  I.Biklen, Sari
                  Knopp.  II.Brannigan, Marilyn B.

         RG80-25110                      79-7748
         LB2831.82.W65                    371.2
```

If your library lets you wander freely in the stacks, you're lucky. Shelved near the book you've come for may be others by the same author or on the same subject. Browse around in the neighborhood. Lisa Chickos, who discovered *Women and Educational Leadership* in the catalog, might have found on the same shelf another title full of promise for her research: *Academic Women on the Move.* The golden rule for research in the stacks is this: *to do right unto others, don't put a book back in place hastily.* Replace it wrong and no one else will be able to locate it.

UNDERSTANDING SYSTEMS OF CLASSIFICATION

To help you find books easily, every library organizes its shelves by a system of classification. We will look at the two most prevalent. Some people claim that it pays to memorize these systems; then when you have to trek from one section of the library to another looking for books, your head will save your feet. At least, you may care to recognize the call numbers of books in the category of your investigation.

Library of Congress System

Most college libraries use the same system of book classification used by the Library of Congress in Washington, D.C. If your library does, you'll find that call letters and numbers direct you to books grouped in subject areas.

A	General Works	M	Music
B	Philosophy, Psychology, Religion	N	Fine Arts
		P	Language and Literature
C–D	Foreign History and Topography	Q	Science
E–F	America	R	Medicine
G	Geography, Anthropology, Sports and Games	S	Agriculture and Forestry
		T	Engineering, Technology
H	Social Sciences	U	Military Science
J	Political Science	V	Naval Science
K	Law	Z	Bibliography and Library Science
L	Education		

Dewey Decimal System

Small libraries often still use the older Dewey decimal system of classifying books. Other libraries, in transition, have some books filed according to the Dewey decimal system and some according to the Library of Congress method. The Dewey decimal system files books into large categories by numbers.

000–099 General Works

100–199 Philosophy

200–299 Religion

300–399 Social Sciences, Government, Customs

400–499 Philology

500–599 Natural Sciences

600–699 Applied Sciences

700–799 Fine and Decorative Arts

800–899 Literature

900–999 History, Travel, Biography

Incidentally, neither Admiral George Dewey, who took Manila, nor educator John Dewey started the Dewey decimal system. The credit goes to Melvil Dewey (1851–1931), founder of the American Library Association.

USING THE PERIODICALS ROOM

The periodicals room houses current and recent issues of magazines and newspapers. Many of the items on your working bibliography that you found listed in the latest *Readers' Guide to Periodical Literature* will be there. Older issues, bound into volumes for previous years, are shelved by call numbers. Some are kept on microfiche or microfilm (see p. 413). A list or file of periodicals' names and their call numbers is usually posted conspicuously in the periodicals room; if you can't find it, look up the name of the periodical in your library catalog.

In the periodicals room, too, current newspapers are available. Even in most small libraries, you'll find at least the *New York Times* and your nearest big city's daily, probably also the *Washington Post* and the *Christian Science Monitor,* two newspapers noted for their coverage of national and international affairs. Most libraries have back issues of the *New York Times* on microfilm and the *New York Times Index* (see "News Indexes," p. 410). The *Wall Street Journal,* an extremely well written and edited daily newspaper, not only covers business news but reviews films and books and often features articles of interest to the general public.

SURVEYING THE REFERENCE SECTION

Make your own tour of that treasure trove for researchers: the reference section. See what is available. Interesting reference books exist on subjects you may never have dreamed had been covered. You may find whole shelves devoted to general areas in which you plan to do research. A helpful listing is provided by the *American Library Association Guide to Reference Books,* edited by Eugene P. Sheehy.

Here is a short tour of a few groups of reference books.

Encyclopedias

Back in high school when you had to do a research paper, you shot like a comet straight to an encyclopedia. (Sometimes you read *two* encyclopedias, and that was all the research required.) An encyclopedia (the word comes from the Greek, meaning "a general education") can still help you get an overview of your subject and may be especially valuable when you are first casting around for a topic. But when you start investigating more deeply, you will need to go to other sources as well.

General encyclopedias are written for the reader who isn't a specialist, who wants a decent smattering of information, or who wants some fact he or she is missing. In all but the cheapest encyclopedias, notable experts write the longer and more important articles. The *New Encyclopaedia Britannica,* now published in Chicago, is the largest general (that is, unspecialized) encyclopedia on the shelves. More sprightly in style, and sometimes beating the *Britannica* to the shelves with recent information, are other popular encyclopedias: *Encyclopedia Americana, Collier's, New Columbia, World Book,* and several more.

All encyclopedias struggle with a problem: how to give a reader not only specific facts but a broader, more inclusive view. If you look something up, how do you find out that your subject relates to larger matters that also might interest you? If, for instance, you look up Marie Curie, how do you learn that she and her work are discussed under "Chemistry," "Curie, Pierre," "Physics," "Polonium," "Radiation," "Radioactivity," and "Uranium" as well? To help you find all the places where a topic is discussed, some encyclopedias offer an index in a separate volume referring to other articles. *World Book* gives cross-references after an article ("See also . . ."). The *Britannica* now comes in two parts. A ten-volume *Micropaedia* (which you consult first, like any other encyclopedia) offers a concise, pointed article and may also refer you to other places in a nineteen-volume *Macropaedia* containing longer articles, wider in scope.

Specialized Encyclopedias

Specialized encyclopedias are written for the searcher interested in a single area: art, movies, music, religion, science, rock and roll. How do you know that someone has prepared one in the very field you are investigating? Look up your subject in the catalog. If a specialized encyclopedia about your subject exists, you will find it indicated on a subject card. The *Encyclopedia of World Art,* for instance, is usually listed under "Art—Dictionaries." (Specialized encyclopedias are often classified as dictionaries, even though they contain much more than short definitions.) Better yet, dwell a while in the area of the reference room that involves your subject and glance at the books shelved there. If your subject is from science, see the *McGraw-Hill Encyclopedia of Science and Technology* or *Van Nostrand's Scientific Encyclopedia.* If you are writing about some aspect of life in a less industrialized, developing nation, the *Encyclopedia of the Third World* might be valuable. If existentialism is your subject, likely places to look might be the *Dictionary of the History of Ideas,* the *Encyclopedia of Philosophy,* and the *Harper Dictionary of Modern Thought.* The *Encyclopedia Judaica* and the *New Catholic Encyclopedia* concentrate on matters of faith, tradition, ritual, history, philosophy, and theology. Just to give you a notion of the variety of other specialized encyclopedias, here is a sampling of titles:

Black's Law Dictionary

Encyclopedia of Banking and Finance

Encyclopedia of Biochemistry

Encyclopedia of Pop, Rock, and Soul

Harper's Bible Dictionary

International Encyclopedia of the Social Sciences

New Grove Dictionary of Music and Musicians

Oxford Companion to American Literature

Oxford Dictionary of the Christian Church

Dictionaries

Besides desk dictionaries, of the kind on every college student's desk, your library's reference section stocks large and specialized dictionaries. You'll find dictionaries of foreign languages; dictionaries of slang; dictionaries of regionalisms; dictionaries of medical, scientific, and other specialized terms. If you don't know what NATO or RSVP stands for, a specialized dictionary such as the *Acronyms, Initialisms, and Abbreviations Dictionary* might help. An unabridged dictionary, such as *Webster's Third New International*—the kind so hefty it sits on a stand of its own, tied down with a chain—tries to include every word and phrase in current use in the language. The *New Century Cyclopedia of Names,* a dictionary of names of people and peoples, places, works of art, and other proper names of every kind, is useful for tracking down allusions—mentions of things that a writer believes are common knowledge but that you may not happen to know.

The massive and monumental *Oxford English Dictionary (OED)* is a historical dictionary: that is, it lists words with dated examples of their occurrences in the language, from the twelfth century to the twentieth, arranged in chronological order. Any shade of meaning an English word ever had is there, making it a beloved treasure for any word freak (who probably owns the two-volume edition in reduced print, which comes with a magnifying glass). It is invaluable if you are tracing the history of an idea through the centuries: you can see how the meaning of a word may have changed. Along with those changes, sometimes, go major changes in society and its people. One student, writing a paper on pollution in the environment, looked up the word *pollution* in the *OED* and as a result was able to reinvigorate the contemporary meaning of the word with earlier meanings of shame and sin. If, in defining terms used in your paper, you need a definition of *freedom,* consult the *OED* and an immense storehouse will swing open to you. You'll find quotations using this luminous word in a whole spectrum of ways, starting with its earliest recorded appearance in the language.

Because the original edition of this great dictionary was completed in 1933, it does not cover words that have recently entered the language. However, the second edition of the *Oxford English Dictionary,* published in 1989, includes (in handy *A*-to-*Z* sequence) material previously published in four supplementary volumes. It adds about five thousand new words or new meanings to the original *OED,* among them *slapstick* (see Figure 12.5) and *yuppie.* Look to see whether your library has this latest edition. If you like words, you'll enjoy browsing in it.

FIGURE 12.5   Entry from the *Oxford English Dictionary,* 2nd ed.

sla·pstick. orig. *U.S.* Also **slap-stick.** [f. SLAP *v.*¹ + STICK *sb.*¹] **1.** Two flat pieces of wood joined together at one end, used to produce a loud slapping noise; *spec.* such a device used in pantomime and low comedy to make a great noise with the pretence of dealing a heavy blow (see also quot. 1950).

1896 *N.Y. Dramatic News* 4 July 9/3 What a relief, truly, from the slap-sticks, rough-and-tumble comedy couples abounding in the variety ranks. **1907** *Weekly Budget* 19 Oct. 1/2 The special officer in the gallery, armed with a 'slap-stick', the customary weapon in American theatre galleries, made himself very officious amongst the small boys. **1925** M. W. DISHER *Clowns & Pantomimes* 13 What has caused the playgoers' sudden callousness? The slapstick. Towards the end of the seventeenth century Arlequin had introduced into England the double-lath of castigation, which made the maximum of noise with the minimum of injury. **1937** M. COVARRUBIAS *Island of Bali* iv. 77 Life-size scarecrows are erected, but soon the birds become familiar with them... Then watchmen circulate among the fields beating bamboo drums and cracking loud bamboo slapsticks. **1950** *Sun* (Baltimore) 10 Apr. 3/1 The 50-year-old clown..said that when he bent over another funnyman accidentally hit him with the wrong side of a slap-stick. He explained that a slap-stick contains a blank ·38-caliber cartridge on one side to make a bang. **2. a.** *attrib.* passing into *adj.* Of or pertaining to a slapstick; of or reminiscent of knockabout comedy.

1906 *N.Y. Even. Post* 25 Oct. 10 It required all the untiring efforts of an industrious 'slap-stick' coterie..to keep the enthusiasm up to a respectable degree. **1914** *Photoplay* Sept. 91 (*heading*) Making slap-stick comedy.

1923 *Weekly Dispatch* 4 Mar. 9 He likes good comedies.. but thinks the slapstick ones ridiculous. **1928** *Daily Sketch* 7 Aug. 4/3 The jokes..are rapier-like in their keenness, not the usual rolling-pin or slapstick form of humour. **1936** W. HOLTBY *South Riding* iv. v. 258 She took a one-and-threepenny ticket, sat in comfort, and watched a Mickey Mouse film, a slapstick comedy, and the tragedy of Greta Garbo acting Mata Hari. **1944** [see *POCHO]. **1962** A. NISBETT *Technique Sound Studio* x. 173 Decidedly unobvious effects, such as the cork-and-resin 'creak' or the hinged slapstick 'whip'. **1977** R. L. WOLFF *Gains & Losses* ii. iv. 296 The prevailing tone of the book is highly satirical, with strong overtones of slapstick farce.

b. *absol.* Knockabout comedy or humour, farce, horseplay.

1926 *Amer. Speech* I. 437/2 *Slap-stick,* low comedy in its simplest form. Named from the double paddles formerly used by circus clowns to beat each other. **1930** *Publishers' Weekly* 25 Jan. 420/2 The slapstick of 1929 was often exciting. The Joan Lowell episode was regarded as exposing the gullibility of the critics... The popularity of 'The Specialist' made the whole book business look cockeyed. **1955** *Times* 6 June 9/1 A comic parson (Mr. Noel Howlett) is added for good measure, mainly to play on the piano while other people crawl under it. Even on the level of slapstick the farce seemed to keep in motion with some difficulty and raised but moderate laughter. **1967** M. KENYON *Whole Hog* xxv. 253 A contest which had promised..to be short and cruel, had become slapstick. **1976** *Oxf. Compan. Film* 640/1 As it developed in the decade 1910–20..slapstick depended on frenzied, often disorganized, motion that increased in tempo as visual gags proliferated.

Bibliographies

It takes work to make a working bibliography. Wouldn't it be great if a bibliography came ready-made for you? Perhaps it does.

Each field of knowledge has its own bibliography, often more than one, which may appear in an issue of a learned journal or as a separate publication, like the *International Bibliography of Sociology*. Is there a bibliography in your area of interest? Consult the latest *Bibliographic Index: A Cumulative Bibliography of Bibliographies*. A quarterly, it is gathered into one volume each year. Turn to it for listings, by subject, of specialized bibliographies and also of books and articles that contain specialized bibliographies. Some bibliographies you track down will be *annotated*; that is, they will give you a short summary of what a book or article contains. Sometimes the bibliographer will venture a judgment about a book's worth.

Some encyclopedias, after the end of an article, will also give you a short list of relevant works worth reading. Often such a list will include the best-known and most popular books on a subject. Such lists are usually directed to a reader who knows nothing much about the subject rather than to a specialist, and they may be long out of date. We recommend that you look first into the *Bibliographic Index*. It's a wonderful instrument for the serious specialist.

Indexes to Periodicals

Magazines, because they can be published faster than books, often print the latest information and opinions months before they appear in book form. Look to them for the most up-to-date material.

To find recent articles on any subject you're investigating, start with the *Readers' Guide to Periodical Literature*, issued monthly, collected into thicker issues quarterly, and bound into a heavyweight volume in each new year. The *Readers' Guide* classifies, by author and subject, recent articles from popular magazines aimed toward general readers—*Time, The New Yorker, Psychology Today*—but not scholarly or professional magazines such as *American Zoologist, Harvard Business Review, Physics Today,* or *Journal of Music Theory,* which address specialized audiences. It gives cross-references so that with a little digging you can usually find headings that will lead you to useful articles. Under each heading, entries give you the title and author of an article and the name of the periodical, its volume number and date, and the pages on which the article can be found.

When you're making a working bibliography with the aid of the *Readers' Guide* and you want the most up-to-date material, begin with the most recent issue, then work backward through previous issues or annual volumes. If, like Lisa Chickos, you had decided to investigate why so few educational administrators are women, you would have found in the 1987 volume of the *Readers'*

Guide the headings "Women school administrators" and "Women school superintendents and principals." Under the first you would have found indexed an article from the January 1987 issue of a periodical called *Education Digest* that seemed promising enough to follow up (see Figure 12.6). After combing through earlier issues of the *Readers' Guide* for more leads, you would have amassed a list of perhaps seven or eight articles that seemed to promise valuable information on your topic. At that point, you'd be ready to check out your library's collection of periodicals to see how many of the listed articles you could find and read.

Naturally, the *Readers' Guide* falls short of including every periodical your investigation might call for. To supplement it, *Access: The Supplementary Index to Periodicals* has, since 1975, been listing the contents of many regional and city magazines not found in the *Readers' Guide*. It includes the following periodicals as well as dozens more.

> *Alaska*
>
> *Analog Science Fiction*
>
> *Horn Book*
>
> *Hot Rod*
>
> *Mother Jones*
>
> *Poetry*
>
> *Sporting News*
>
> *TV Guide*
>
> *Western Horseman*
>
> *Whole Earth Software Review*

Articles in more magazines than are included in either the *Readers' Guide* or *Access* are indexed in a database, *Magazine Index*. In some libraries, you

FIGURE 12.6 Entries from the *Readers' Guide to Periodical Literature*

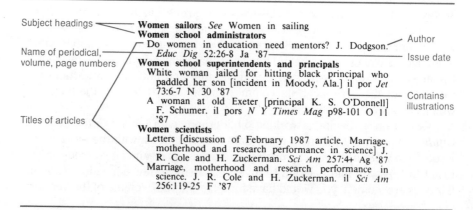

Subject headings — **Women sailors** *See* Women in sailing
Women school administrators
Do women in education need mentors? J. Dodgson. — Author
Name of periodical, — *Educ Dig* 52:26-8 Ja '87 — Issue date
volume, page numbers / **Women school superintendents and principals**
White woman jailed for hitting black principal who
paddled her son [incident in Moody, Ala.] il por *Jet*
73:6-7 N 30 '87 — Contains
A woman at old Exeter [principal K. S. O'Donnell] illustrations
F. Schumer. il pors *N Y Times Mag* p98-101 O 11
Titles of articles '87
Women scientists
Letters [discussion of February 1987 article, Marriage,
motherhood and research performance in science] J.
R. Cole and H. Zuckerman. *Sci Am* 257:4+ Ag '87
Marriage, motherhood and research performance in
science. J. R. Cole and H. Zuckerman. il *Sci Am*
256:119-25 F '87

can view it on a computer monitor. But you probably won't need it, and wouldn't want to pay its hourly fee, for usual college assignments. (Databases are discussed further on p. 414.)

If you find too few leads in the *Readers' Guide* or *Access* or not enough solid information in popular magazine articles, you may want to consult a selected subject index for more scholarly or professional materials. Here is a short list of some indexes widely available.

Art Index

Biological Abstracts RRM

Business Periodicals Index

Criminology Index

Education Index

Environment Index

Film Literature Index

General Science Index

Humanities Index

Social Sciences Index

Art Index is broader in scope than its name implies: it lists not only articles on graphic art but also many on archeology, architecture, city planning, crafts, films, industrial design, interior design, and photography. For a research paper on women as school and college administrators, the relevant section of *Education Index* for July 1986–June 1987 is illustrated in Figure 12.7.

FIGURE 12.7 Entry from *Education Index*

Women as criminals *See* Female offenders
Women as educators
   Academic woman: twenty-four years of progress? J. E. Stecklein and G. E. Lorenz. *Lib Educ* 72:63-71 Spr '86
   Academic women in science 1977-1984. L. Weis. il *Academe* 73:43-7 Ja/F '87
   Annie Mae in academe: professionalization as sabotage. S. Radford-Hill. *Women's Stud Q* 14:21-2 Spr/Summ '86
   Black, female college presidents declare they are leaders for 'entire institutions'. G. Evans. il *Chron Higher Educ* 32:25+ My 14 '86
   Career development and succession of women to the superintendency. B. K. Dopp and C. A. Sloan. bibl *Clearing House* 60:120-6 N '86
   Chief academic officers at black colleges and universities: a comparison by gender. L. E. Williams. bibl *J Negro Educ* 55:443-52 Fall '86
   Do women college administrators manage differently than men? S. W. Jones. *Educ Horiz* 64:118-19 Spr '86
   Do women in education need mentors? J. Dodgson. *Educ Dig* 52:26-8 Ja '87

News Indexes

To locate a newspaper account of virtually any recent event or development, your most likely printed aid is the *New York Times Index.* Most libraries subscribe to the *Times,* and many keep back years of it on microfilm. Its semimonthly *Index,* bound into a volume each year, directs you to stories in daily and Sunday issues all the way back to the newspaper's founding in 1851.

Say you're pursuing the question of why relatively few women hold top jobs as administrators in schools and colleges. "Women" might seem your largest, most central idea, so in the 1987 volume you look up "Women" and under it find the subheading "Education." This is a mere cross-reference that lists the dates of five stories about women in education; it doesn't have room to tell you what the stories are about. It directs you to a larger category, "Education and Schools," where you find listed and briefly summarized all the stories about education, in chronological order. You skim down the listing and check the five dates that interest you. For April 5, three stories about education are listed (see Figure 12.8). Clearly, the first one will be the most promising story for this topic. And the story will be easy to find. The legend "Ap 5, I, 23:1" indicates that it appeared on April 5 in section I of the newspaper, page 23, column 1. The length of the story is also indicated: "L" for a long story (more than three columns), "M" for a story of medium length (between one and three columns), "S" for a short item (less than a column long). This system points you to substantial stories especially worth looking up and (if your time is scarce) saves you from bothering with short items that might or might not prove worthwhile.

Other newspapers that publish indexes include the *Wall Street Journal,* the *Washington Post,* and the *Times* of London. *Facts on File* (discussed on p. 412) publishes an index twice a month to help readers locate its summaries of recent news. Also, some libraries now receive computerized indexes, such as *National Newspaper Index,* which lists the contents not only of the *New*

FIGURE 12.8 Entry from the *New York Times Index*

Report by National Organization for Women claims most American women are vulnerable to sex discrimination in schools and universities, as members of student body and faculty; report says only seven states and territory of Guam have adequate protection against sex discrimination in education; states are Alaska, California, Florida, Maine, Nebraska, Oregon and Rhode Island (M), Ap 5,I,23:1

Glenwood D Brogan, 18-year-old student at Hammond High School in Columbia, Md, is sentenced to six months in jail for spiking coffee of Janet Thurman, teacher of home economics, with derivative of cayenne pepper; Thurman has undergone minor surgery several times since she drank coffee (S), Ap 5,I,44:6

April 7 elections in 550 of New Jersey's 606 school districts will determine makeup of local school boards and also fate of budgets; remaining 56 districts have appointed school boards; education officials are hoping for greater voter turnout but most do not count on it (M), Ap 5,XI,8:4

York Times but also of the *Christian Science Monitor* and the *Wall Street Journal.* Ask your reference librarian whether your library makes any computerized index available without your having to pay a steep fee for it.

Abstracts

To cope with the information explosion, many collections of abstracts (or condensed versions) are available. Specialists can keep up with their changing territories with the aid of (for instance) *Abstracts of English Studies, Biological Abstracts, Chemical Abstracts, Journal of Economic Abstracts,* and *Sociological Abstracts.* Such periodicals can help you see, without much legwork, another researcher's principal findings and can direct you to sources worth consulting in their entirety.

For summaries of doctoral theses, see *Dissertation Abstracts.* Although these are usually read only by doctoral candidates looking for a topic that hasn't been exhausted, they could perhaps be useful for research on a specialized topic. A doctoral thesis not published in book form is generally available on microfilm.

Before you go to the trouble of searching for a book, *Book Review Digest* can give you a notion of what it is about and how good it is. This publication doesn't exactly abstract books—doesn't nutshell their kernels—but it does describe them briefly and then supply quotations from critics who reviewed the books in newspapers or magazines.

Biographical Sources

If you want to know about someone's life and work, you have a rich array of sources. To find quickly the names and dates of famous people now dead, *Webster's New Biographical Dictionary* can be handy. For more extensive treatment of outstanding Americans (dead ones only), see the *Dictionary of American Biography (DAB)* in 20 volumes (1928–36 and later supplements). The British equivalent is the *Dictionary of National Biography.* Lately, a four-volume set has filled many gaps in the *DAB: Notable American Women, 1607–1950. Who Was Who* (for Britain) and *Who Was Who in America* preserve facts on those cut down by the grim reaper.

For the lives of living celebrities of all nations, see *Current Biography* (published monthly and gathered together each year), a highly readable and entertaining compilation. Bare facts on the lives and works of celebrities and people prominent in their fields are listed in *Who's Who* (for Britain), *Who's Who in America,* and *Who's Who in the World.* Regional American editions (*Who's Who in the West* as well as volumes for the Midwest, South and Southwest, and East) and *Who's Who of American Women* encapsulate people not included in the nationwide volume. See if your library has the latest edition of *Who's Who Among Black Americans* (1988). Marquis, publisher of *Who's Who in America,* also offers specialized *Who's Who*'s: *Who's Who in American Law* and similar volumes for finance and industry, frontier science and technology, religion, and science.

The lives of writers are usually well documented. For early writers' biographies, see *American Authors, 1600–1900, British Authors before 1800, British Authors of the Nineteenth Century, Twentieth Century Authors* and its supplement, and *World Authors, 1950–1970.* Writers from all countries, including hundreds not found in encyclopedias, are usually to be found in *Contemporary Authors* and its revisions, a vast series that covers not just poets and fiction writers but popular writers in every field. *Contemporary Novelists, Contemporary Poets,* and *Contemporary Dramatists* contain not only biographies and bibliographies but critical estimates.

Yearbooks and Almanacs

Encyclopedia publishers, realizing that time gallops on and that their product rapidly becomes obsolete, bring out an annual yearbook of recent events and discoveries in an attempt to look up to date. We consider these to be rather cumbersomely organized sources, designed to extract more money from owners of encyclopedias. If you want a short account of a recent event or development, try *Facts on File.* Calling itself a "Weekly World News Digest, with Cumulative Index," it is a concise list of news events. Important events rate more space. Twice a month it publishes an index on blue paper, and then quarterly yellow indexes supersede the blue ones. The weekly issues are gathered into a binder every year and placed on the library's shelves.

Many miscellaneous facts—news events, winners of prizes, athletic records—are compiled in a yearly almanac such as the *World Almanac and Book of Facts,* a popular, variously useful work that many people like to have as a desk-top reference. In it you can find out everything from the population of Bloomington, Indiana, to information about job openings and current earnings, from the locations of hazardous waste sites to the time the moon rises on any given date—and much more. Your library may also offer specialized almanacs: *American Jewish Year Book, Catholic Almanac, Canadian Almanac and Directory.*

Gazetteers and Atlases

Gazetteers list places and give basic facts about them. Two popular gazetteers are the *Columbia Lippincott Gazetteer of the World* and *Webster's New Geographical Dictionary.*

For maps, see atlases such as *The Times Atlas of the World, National Atlas of the United States of America,* and (for maps that show political boundaries in the past—fascinating!) the *Historical Atlas.*

EXPLORING OTHER SOURCES

Besides reference books, your library may have other sources that will supply you with ideas and information not available elsewhere.

Microfilm and Microfiche

Most libraries now take advantage of microfilm to store newspapers and other materials that would otherwise take up acres of valuable shelf space. If you aren't acquainted with the stuff, if the projector in the reference room has looked like an intimidating mystery, you should get to know it, for marvelous research opportunities are available to you if you do. If, for instance, you are writing a paper on World War II, wouldn't it be great to see the front page of a newspaper for December 8, 1941, the day the U.S. Congress declared war? Or to quote from an editorial published on that fateful day? (To this question, one researcher, Professor John Ruszkiewicz, ruefully replied, "Sure—if the bulb works, the image will focus, the reels will take up the film, and the film is in the right box." Clearly, microfilm has problems that still need ironing out.)

Microfilm is small photographic film that contains the images of printed pages in reduced form. A whole week's file of daily newspapers can be preserved on a strip of microfilm two inches wide and seven or eight feet long. Wound into a roll and stashed in a small, labeled box, the microfilm can be stored in a few square inches of space. Microfilm saves books that otherwise might be lost: it crumbles more slowly than paper does. It also permits the publication of monographs and dissertations, which have small audiences, for less cost than printing.

Complete files of historically important magazines that are now practically impossible to obtain are currently at the service of a small library. In many reference rooms, files of the *New York Times* and other frequently consulted newspapers and periodicals sit in microfilm boxes next to a viewing projector. The machine bears instructions, but if you need help getting the thing to work, ask a librarian. Once you have the film on the machine, you crank till you come to the very page you are looking for. Some projection machines will print out a photocopy of any page.

A *microfiche* is a card containing a sheet of translucent microfilm bearing many frames: images of printed pages reduced 20:1. Sixty to a hundred book pages can fit on one microfiche. Copies of rare books and manuscripts can now be obtained cheaply and stored safely in a small space. While in the past only a library with $30,000 to spare could own a copy of Francis Bacon's *Novum Organum,* now any library can own a microfiche copy for a small fraction of that sum. One file cabinet can hold the contents of a rare-book room. A projector shows each frame of the microfiche on a viewing screen. A reader-printer can produce a photocopy of any page you require.

Databases

Databases, great troves of information obtainable over telephone wires and run on computers, are now available in many libraries. Particularly useful for research on a cross-curricular subject that spans several disciplines (such as medical ethics or legal language), computer searching may be used instead of rummaging through indexes, books, and periodicals by hand. There is a charge—generally $30–55 an hour—but by zeroing in on what you most want, this service might save your looking through hundreds of scattered sources.

On some campuses, you will find microcomputer centers whose computer terminals can be connected to hundreds of "banks" of periodicals all over the country. You can arrange an appointment with a librarian to observe (and offer advice) while you search a bank for articles relating to your subject. *End-user searching,* in which the librarian trains student users to conduct their own searches effectively, is becoming common practice on many campuses. Whether you search with the aid of a librarian or search on your own, first talk with the librarian about the search you have in mind, to determine which database will be most useful to you.

When you begin your search, you can ask a question—for instance, "What has been written about famine in Africa?" Or ask for rundowns on key words: *famine, Africa.* In a minute or so, the computer will list indexed words and phrases that are similar and the number of items it has titles for.

FAMINE, 346 ITEMS
FAMINE, IN CAMBODIA, 34 ITEMS
FAMINE, IN CONGO, 27 ITEMS
FAMINE, IN ETHIOPIA, 43 ITEMS
FAMINE, IN INDIA, 34 ITEMS
FAMINE, IN MIDDLE AGES, 4 ITEMS
FAMINE RELIEF, 63 ITEMS
FAMINE VICTIMS, MEDICAL STUDIES OF, 52 ITEMS

Your next move is to ask the computer to show you citations under any subject heading or headings (called *descriptors*) that look promising. Each cited item has an identifying number. Entered into the computer, this number brings you bibliographical facts on the book, article, or other printed source, a brief abstract (a summary of the item), and a list of all the various descriptors that identify it ("famine victims, medical studies; famine relief organizations; International Red Cross; Oxfam; India"). For an extra fee, some will supply a printout of the item itself.

To a serious researcher, a database can be a wonderful means of sifting through a world of information in a hurry. Still, a computer search has its limitations. Most databases, being recent innovations, go back no further than to books and articles published in the last ten or twenty years. To find earlier items, you will still need earlier printed volumes of specialized indexes.

A further problem in using databases is that unless you find the right descriptors, you can spend an enormous amount of money needlessly. If you are seeking nothing but items about famine relief in India, tell the computer to search only for items with two descriptors: "India" and "famine relief." You might then receive only twelve articles. Otherwise, the computer will deliver too much: the descriptor "famine relief" alone would bring you sixty-three descriptions, while "India" alone might bring you thousands. In using some databases, you need to instruct the computer to supply you only with items written in English or other languages you can read, or you may be overwhelmed with titles in languages you do not know.

At this writing, more than five hundred databases are available, with trade names like ERIC (for education topics), PsycINFO (for sources in psychology), ABI/Inform (for business and finance), and SCISEARCH (for biological and applied sciences). If you are interested in using one, first decide the exact subject of your investigation. To help you narrow your search, nearly every database supplies a current, alphabetical list of its own descriptors. You can inspect this list (called a *thesaurus*) before you begin searching. Unless you have money to burn, don't try using a database without the help of a patient librarian.

Nowadays many campus libraries own CD-ROM (short for "compact disk, read-only memory") versions of online databases such as ERIC, PsycINFO, InfoTrac, and Magazine Index. These products offer a few advantages over other databases: they cost you nothing to use, they often employ keywords similar to those in printed indexes, and you can print out your list of citations while you wait. However, relatively few specialized CD-ROM products are available so far, some of them less sophisticated and less flexible in their searching options than pay-as-you-go databases. InfoTrac, although a valuable guide to magazine articles, lists only articles published in the past three years. When in doubt about the best available database for your purpose, consult your reference librarian.

Government Documents

"A glance at the organization of our government documents," says Mary-Claire van Leunen, author of *A Handbook for Scholars,* "may suggest that the United States is neither a democracy nor a republic, but an anarchy. Writing a good reference to a federal document would be simple if only one of those brainy forefathers of ours had thought to write at the bottom of the Declaration of Independence, 'Serial #1,' but it's too late now." It is true that because government documents differ widely in format, depending on which branch of the government published them, they are sometimes hard to find; but often they contain valuable material worth searching for.

Among major American publishers is the United States Congress. Its primary publications include the *Congressional Record,* a daily transcript of what is said in both the House and the Senate, together with anything else members of Congress wish inserted; bills, acts, laws, and statutes (after a bill is enacted into law it is bound into *Statutes at Large*); and the minutes of congressional committee hearings. Most college libraries carry at least the *Congressional Record.*

The judicial branch of the government doesn't publish anything except cases. But other executive departments and state governments publish prolifically, as do various agencies of the United Nations. John L. Andriot's *Guide to U.S. Government Publications* lists and explains the printed products of most federal agencies. The U.S. Government Printing Office in Washington, D.C., publishes and distributes some popular works, including *Your Child From 1 to 6* and the *Government Manual,* an explanation of how the government is organized.

There is, by the way, a *Monthly Catalog of United States Government Publications,* compiled into one volume annually. Matthew Lesko's guidebook *Information U.S.A.* (New York: Viking, 1983) is valuable for both library and field research. It lists federal libraries open to the public (some offering free telephone reference service) and free government publications and how to order them. It also tells where and how to inquire for information (with phone numbers).

Brochures, Handouts, and Annual Reports

For other kinds of printed material, your library may be helpful—or you may need to round it up on your own. Often, on a visit to a museum or historic site, you are given (along with your ticket of admission) a pamphlet to carry with you, containing a terse history of the place and perhaps a map of its exhibits. This kind of material can prove valuable to researchers. Usually it is the work of curators and other dedicated experts who know their locales, and sometimes it is hard to find anywhere else. If, say, you are making a field trip to a computer museum before writing about the history of early computers, you might carefully save any handout. You might also peruse the gift shop or the pamphlet rack at the information desk, even if the offerings cost money. If you can't visit the museum or historic site, a phone call might tell you how to mail order its publications.

Many concerned organizations, such as the American Cancer Society, the American Heart Association, Physicians for Social Responsibility, and others, sometimes publish surveys and reports that they will send you on request. Some of their valuable handouts are made known through public service announcements on radio and television. For names, addresses, and telephone numbers of a variety of organizations and agencies, see the *Encyclopedia of Associations.* This useful guide includes a brief overview of each organization and lists its available publications and reports.

The U.S. Government's Consumer Information Center in Pueblo, Colorado, sends free pamphlets (*Occupations in Demand, Being Your Own Boss*) and sells larger brochures at low prices (*The Job Outlook in Brief, Exercise and Weight Control*). A list of publications with an order form is available on request; the zip code is 81002.

Most large corporations produce hefty annual reports, copies of which are yours for the asking. Few people except investors write to a corporation for an annual report, but the corporations are willing to give a copy to practically anyone seriously interested in their activities. You are likely to receive a vast, handsomely printed document favorably portraying the past year's operations and future expectations of the company so that present stockholders will be reassured and future investors will be attracted; the report usually contains graphs, charts, photographs, and other documents. Writing a research paper on recent developments in artificial intelligence, a student we know requested the annual reports of several computer and software firms. For the cost of a few postage stamps, he received hundreds of pages of up-to-date information and professional opinion that would have been difficult to find elsewhere.

CHAPTER 13

Writing from Research in the Field

Finding material in a library is only one way to do research. You can also generate your own ideas and information—in other words, tap your own primary sources.

Most often in college, field research is required in upper-level courses. For a term paper in the social sciences, education, or business studies, you may be expected to interview people or gather statistics. Usually, course assignments in field research are directed toward specific ends. A psychology assignment to test a hypothesis, for example, might ask you to observe people in a situation of stress and to report their behavior.

If you enjoy meeting and talking with people and don't mind what news reporters call "legwork," you will relish the fun and satisfaction of obtaining ideas and information at first hand. Perhaps you will even investigate matters that few researchers have investigated before. Many rich, unprinted sources of ideas and information lie beyond library walls. This chapter will reveal a few of them. It will show you how to write a research paper not only by reading but also by observing, conversing with people, recalling, and imagining—so that in the future, library researchers may be able to cite *you*.

Like library research, field research should be more than a squirreling-up of facts—or else you may end up with a great heap of rotting acorns and no nourishment. Field research (and kindly underline this sentence) has to be the sensitive, intelligent, and critical selection of *meaningful* ideas and information. As the chapter proceeds, we'll give you more specific suggestions for picking out what is meaningful from what isn't. Right now, it is sufficient to note that you can expect to change your initial hunches while at work out in the field. You'll be sifting evidence, revising and correcting your early thoughts, forming clearer ideas. When you begin a project on identical twins, say, you might seek evidence to back up your hunch that identical twins are likely to enter the very same line of work in later life. Perhaps, though, the evidence will refuse to march in the path you want it to follow. You might end up disproving your hunch and coming to a fresh realization: that some twins, perhaps, develop in independent directions.

LEARNING FROM ANOTHER WRITER: ONE STUDENT'S EXPERIENCE

To show you a student thinking and solving problems in the field, changing his mind while collecting material and coming to fresh realizations, let us tell the story of Jamie Merisotis. A political science major with an assignment to write an honors thesis, Merisotis became interested in studying the lives and work of people engaged in an unusual profession: bail bonding. He grew increasingly curious about this business of supplying bail money for suspected criminals who have been arrested.

Whatever your field research topic, you will probably have an easier time gathering ideas and information than Jamie Merisotis had. First, because he found little recent published research on his topic, he decided to try to interview every bondsman practicing in an East Coast state he knew well, where the bail bond system still thrives. His labors were complicated by the fact that while attending college in Maine, he pursued his research in another state. It took him most of a year to obtain his evidence, for he had only weekends and vacations for interviewing.

"The hardest part," Merisotis recalls, "was getting the bondsmen to talk to me." Busy people who shun publicity, many bondsmen flatly turned down the student's request for interviews. At first, Merisotis had trouble even getting in touch with the bondsmen, since many publish only their phone numbers, not their addresses. The phone numbers connect to an answering service that relays only calls from people in need of bail money. Luckily, a friendly bail commissioner took an interest in Merisotis's study and encouraged the bondsmen to talk to him. Even with this help, one bondsman had to be called ten times before he consented to an interview. "I think he finally broke down just to get rid of me," Merisotis says. In the end, he succeeded in interviewing eighteen bail bondsmen—about half of all those practicing in the state, perhaps the largest number ever interviewed by any researcher, student or professional.

Although the bail bondsman is a familiar figure in detective movies and fiction, surprisingly little about his life has been documented. A few facts may help you glimpse the nature of Merisotis's project. In effect, a bail bond is a promissory note stating that if the defendant does not appear in court to stand trial, he or she will forfeit a sum of money. When a person arrested and charged with a crime has to post bail, needs money to do so, and cannot raise it alone, he or she calls a bail bondsman. In some commentaries Merisotis read, the bondsmen are "mindless thugs," "moronic leeches," "cigar-chomping social parasites living off the misfortunes of others." Reports have circulated that bondsmen use guns and brass knuckles to whip their errant clients into submission. On television they are romanticized: in the series *The Fall Guy* (now in reruns), glamorous bondswoman Big Jack sometimes sends muscle man Lee Majors to track down missing clients for her.

Curious to learn the truth behind the stereotypes, Merisotis formulated his question for research: *What is an accurate description of the life and work of a typical bail bondsman?* As he interviewed practicing bondsmen, he found his preliminary ideas changing. In some cases, he learned, bondsmen do indeed threaten violence against clients they suspect will fail to appear ("I'll break your legs," "I'll get a gorilla over to take you in") or they threaten financial disaster ("Your mother will pay if you don't show"). Empowered to arrest clients who run out on them, they sometimes (but seldom) risk their necks tracking down a fugitive. Compared to their stereotypes on television, however, their lives are quiet. If some of their tactics are unpleasant, bondsmen do provide a useful service. Slow to risk their money, suspicious of some prospects, they nevertheless assist many low-income people who otherwise would languish in jail. They help make the legal system work. Because they assume responsibility for their clients' appearing in court, they often pester a client, browbeat him, and see that he shows up for trial.

In our legal system, then, bondsmen are valuable people. Yet to his surprise Merisotis found little recent literature on the topic in his college library. We'll continue to trace his story in this chapter and finally show you a chapter from his completed paper.

LEARNING BY WRITING

The Assignment: Researching a Subculture

Here is a typical *general* writing assignment for a field research paper, one that leaves up to you the task of finding a specific topic. Try to find a topic that, because you care about it, will elicit your desire to write.

Consider some group of people in our society about whose lives and activities you would like deeper knowledge. The group you choose should be one whose members you would be able to engage in conversation—vagrants, amateur rock musicians, members of the Society of Friends, aspiring painters, women construction workers, model railroad buffs, hospital patients, people who live in a certain locality, or any other group of people that for any reason keenly interests you. Find out as much as you can about the group by observing, by conversing with people, by questioning them, by seeking any other evidence that you do not find in print but discover for yourself.

From what you have learned, draw some conclusion or make some generalization. Present it in a paper, supporting it with evidence you have collected. Write for an audience of your fellow students, but, to keep your paper fair and accurate, write it so that it might also be read by members of the group you have observed.

Among successful papers we have seen written from this assignment are the following.

> Using her own observations, a questionnaire she had devised, and a series of interviews, a woman set out to test the validity of something she had read: that the tradition of the family dinner was fast disappearing from middle-class life. She wrote this paper for a freshman English course centering on the theme "The Way We Live Now."

> A man studying child development, after observing two- and three-year-olds at a day-care center and keeping a log of his observations for three weeks, wrote about the many ways the two groups of children differed from each other.

> In a sociology course, a man sought out and interviewed people in the helping professions who worked with street people in his city. He also talked with some of the homeless people themselves, in an effort to find out what forces had driven them to the streets and what was being done for them.

> A man conducted a survey among his fellow students to learn their reasons for choosing the college they attended. He sorted out their answers, emerging with a varied list and increased respect for his college's reputation.

> A woman who had recently moved from Baltimore to Portland, Oregon, relied on recall, observation, and conversation to record and interpret cultural differences between easterners and westerners. After writing the paper for an English class, she sold part of it to a newspaper as a feature article.

Generating Ideas

Before you set out on your field research, you first have to decide on a subject you want to investigate—the later lives of identical twins, say, or the methods of designing hang gliders. Start by casually looking into something that appeals to you, seeing whether to persist in further investigation. Those trusty resources for writers discussed in Part One may prove their usefulness. You might observe your subject in action (twins, hang gliders, or whatever) and recall what you already know about it. You might talk with anyone familiar with it, do some reading about it in a library, and imagine yourself doing field research into it (interviewing twins or builders of hang gliders). The more you look into a subject, the more it is likely to interest you.

Once you feel sure of your direction, state a research question—exactly what are you trying to find out? How to word such a question is discussed in Chapter 11 on page 350. The research question is the central question to ask yourself and to keep living with; the following are other, smaller ones.

DISCOVERY CHECKLIST: WEIGHING POSSIBILITIES

- Where will you find more ideas and information about this subject? Whom might you consult for suggestions?
- What places should you visit?
- Whom should you talk with?
- How much time and effort is this investigation likely to take? Is your project reasonable?

You may not be able to answer this last question accurately until you start investigating, but make a rough guess. Set yourself a schedule, with deadlines for completing your research, for drafting, for rewriting. For any project in which you interview people, an excellent rule of thumb is to allow 50 percent more time than you might reasonably think necessary. People may be out when you call or you may find that one interview didn't supply all you need and that you'll have to do a follow-up. For a college paper, a field research project has to be humanly possible. If you begin with the intention of interviewing all the identical twins in your county, you might take a look at your deadline (and your course load) and then decide to limit your research to a sampling of, say, twenty individuals. Robert A. Day, author of *How to Write and Publish a Scientific Paper* (Philadelphia: ISI Press, 1983), offers this sound advice: "Don't start vast projects with half-vast ideas." Don't start half-vast projects, either.

Reading for background   Jamie Merisotis didn't plunge blindly into field research. Even though it was slim, his reading gave him leads to follow up. Books such as Roy B. Flemming's *Punishment Before Trial: An Organizational Perspective of Felony Bail Processes* (New York: Longman, 1982) helped fill him in on how the bail bond business operates. He also found a few helpful articles on bail bonding in professional law journals, such as *Criminal Law Bulletin, Justice System Journal,* and *Law and Society Review.*

A useful question for you before you start to do field research is What helpful background material on your topic can you find first of all in your library?

Directing an interview   People in all walks of life are often willing, sometimes even eager, to talk to a college student writing a research paper. Many, you may find, will seem flattered by your attention. Interviews—conversations with a purpose—may prove to be your main source of material. In Chapter 4 (p. 104), we gave advice that once again may come in handy.

1. Make sure your prospect is willing to be quoted in writing.
2. Fix an appointment for a day when this person will have enough time—if possible, an hour—to have a thorough talk with you.

3. Appear promptly, with carefully thought-out questions to ask.
4. Really listen. Let the person open up.
5. If a question draws no response, don't persist and make a nuisance of yourself; just go on to the next question.
6. Make additional notes right after the interview ends to preserve anything you didn't have time to record during the interviews.

Despite bondsmen's initial reluctance to talk to him, in the end Jamie Merisotis came up with a trove of exciting material. His interviews were never shorter than forty-five minutes. Some bondsmen, apparently gratified by his taking their work seriously, opened up and talked candidly for as long as two hours. As is usual in studies of criminal justice, Merisotis's research paper gave the bondsmen anonymity. Because some bondsmen's activities (such as coercing clients to appear) hover on the borderline of the law, Merisotis had to assure them that he would not cite their names. He wouldn't even identify the state they practiced in. Some bondsmen, in fact, would agree to be interviewed only on the condition that their voices not be tape-recorded.

For his own guidance, Merisotis first made himself a list of questions he wanted to ask. To persuade the bondsmen to trust him, he began with questions that voiced his genuine interest in them as people:

Tell me about yourself—where you live, where you grew up, your personal background.

How long have you been working as a bondsman? Do you plan to stay in the business?

Let's suppose you're having an average day. Could you tell me what this average day as a bondsman is like? In other words, what happens that you consider "regular"?

Then he probed more deeply, pursuing his main interest in his paper: how the bondsman operates. He asked questions to zero in on the bondsman's activities and reveal certain parts of them in detail:

What do you consider when deciding to post bond for a defendant?
Do you consider his or her ties to the community?
His past record?
His financial situation?
The offense he is charged with?
Are there any other things you take into account?

To round out his view of the bondsmen's activities, Merisotis sought interviews with legal professionals. To his disappointment, although he asked them many times, no judges would consent to be interviewed. But Merisotis persisted. He talked with others in the legal system: police, prosecutors, public defenders, private attorneys, sheriffs, and bail commissioners. They confirmed, and sometimes supplemented, what the bondsmen had told him in confidence.

As Merisotis collected more and more evidence, not only his ideas changed but also the language he couched them in. From reading about bail bondsmen in legal journals, he had picked up the term *deposit bail,* which he used in his first interviews. But he soon found that the phrase belonged to classrooms and law offices, not to bondsmen in the field. He had to change it to *ten percent bail* so that the bondsmen would understand him.

Preparing a questionnaire   From each of the eighteen bail bondsmen who consented to talk with him, Jamie Merisotis sought even more evidence than his interview alone would bring. When the conversation came to an end, he would hand each person a questionnaire to fill out and return.

Questionnaires, as you know, are part of contemporary life. You probably filled out one the last time you applied for a job or for college. Many people, in our experience, enjoy having their knowledge tapped or their opinion solicited. Indeed, filling out a questionnaire has a gamelike appeal, as you can tell from the frequency with which self-quiz features appear in popular magazines: "How Rigid Are You?" followed by a thirty-question quiz to score yourself.

As a rule, when researching a particular question, professional pollsters, opinion testers, and survey takers survey thousands of individuals, chosen to represent a certain segment of society or perhaps a broad range of the populace (widely diversified in geography, income, ethnic background, and education). Their purpose may be to inform manufacturers who are test-marketing new products or trying to identify a new market. It may be to help a politician in planning a campaign. Questionnaires are widely used because they deliver large stores of useful information quickly and efficiently.

To make it easy for his interviewees to return his questionnaire, Merisotis provided each with a stamped, addressed envelope. Apparently, the bondsmen, after they opened up and talked, felt involved in his research and became willing also to reply to written questions.

Merisotis's questionnaire is reprinted in Figure 13.1. The questions call for short answers, easy to supply. He had used his most complicated questions in his interviews. This questionnaire asks for information revealing the bondsman's personal history, his family circumstances and background, his income, his education, his religious and political views. In keeping with his promise to the bondsmen to maintain their anonymity, Merisotis identified each questionnaire by a number and did not use the respondent's name.

Know your purpose. What is this questionnaire trying to discover? Since bail bondsmen often are asked to aid disadvantaged minorities, people who don't have personal lawyers or large bank accounts, Merisotis correctly guessed that the bondsmen's views, allegiances, education, and personal circumstances might well throw some light on their policies in deciding whether or not to take a risk on a client and write a bond. Why did Merisotis's questionnaire deliver good results? It addressed the questions its author wanted answered. It was directed to the people able to answer it.

WRITING WITH A COMPUTER: FIELD RESEARCH

GENERATING IDEAS

In compiling the results of your questionnaire, see whether you have access to software that includes an option enabling you to *sort* numbers and statistics. It might save you hours of tallying with pencil and paper. Like all ready-made computer programs, such software may be expensive, but you may find it available at your library or your campus computer center.

By using this questionnaire, Merisotis soon found a clear picture of typical bondsmen emerging—one quite different from the image in the popular mind. Most bondsmen, the responses indicated, are not lone wolves, glamorously racing around cornering fugitives, but are cautious middle-class citizens: most of them married, with children, people of more education than he had expected, churchgoers and templegoers involved in community activities. From the responses to his questionnaire, he concluded that most bondsmen are not pistol-packing vigilantes but "day-to-day businessmen determined to make a living within the limits of the law."

You too will want to define the purpose of your questionnaire and then thoughtfully invent questions to fulfill it. If, for instance, you want to know how effective a day-care center is in the eyes of working mothers who entrust their children to it, you might ask questions like these: Do your children report that they are happy there? Have you ever had reason to complain? If so, about what?

Keep it simple. Any questionnaire you design has to be one that people are willing to answer. The main point to remember in writing a questionnaire is to make it easy and inviting to fill out. If you make it too complex and time-consuming, the recipient will throw it away. Ask questions that call for a simple yes or no, for a word or a few words. Ask yourself as you write each question what information you want to acquire with the question. Then read it over to be sure that it will work the way it is written. It's a good idea to ask for just one piece of information per question. Like Merisotis, keep it simple: list alternative answers with blanks for your respondent to check.

Be flexible in approaching respondents. You'll be especially lucky if you can assemble a group of people (at, say, an evening coffee for parents or children in a day-care center) and have them fill out your questionnaire on the spot. Facing the group, you can explain the purpose of your research, and, to enlist their confidence, you can invite questions and answer them. If you must send your questionnaire to people, include a concise letter or note explaining what you are trying to do and what use you will make of the replies. You might say, "This questionnaire should take no more than ten minutes of your time to complete" or give some such estimate that will make the task look reasonable to the respondent. Some professional questioners offer a

---

Questionnaire

Interview number_____

Age:

Marital status:

Number of dependents:

Father's occupation:

Mother's occupation:

How old were you when you became a bondsman?

How did you learn to become a bondsman?

_____ family member was a bondsman   _____ taught myself
_____ friend was a bondsman   _____ other (Please explain)

How long, in months and years, would you estimate it took you to learn about
bail bonding?

How many days a week do you work as a bondsman?

Do you hold another job?

Estimate your earnings as a bondsman last year:

_____ less than $10,000   _____ $20,000 to $30,000
_____ $10,000 to $15,000   _____ more than $30,000
_____ $15,000 to $20,000

How many employees do you have (excluding other bondsmen)?

In what state were you born?

In what state have you lived the most number of years?

How long have you been a resident of this state?

Do you speak any foreign languages?

If so, which?

Estimate the percentage of your clients who do not speak English:

_____ less than 10 percent
_____ 10 percent to 50 percent
_____ more than 50 percent

Which best describes the education you have received?

_____ some high school   _____ some four-year college
_____ graduated high school   _____ graduated four-year college
_____ some two-year college   _____ post-college or graduate study

List the schools and colleges you have attended, starting with high school:

What newspapers and magazines do you read regularly?

FIGURE 13.1 Jamie Merisotis's questionnaire to bail bondsmen

---

morsel of bait: a small check or a coupon good for a free jar of pickles. You
might promise a copy of your finished paper or article, a brief report of the
results, or a listing of each respondent's name in an acknowledgment.

Even with such little enticements, professional poll takers and opinion

```
Questionnaire / page 2

Which of the following best describes your partisan political preference?

_____ sometimes vote Democrat          _____ always vote Republican
_____ usually vote Democrat            _____ independent
_____ always vote Democrat             _____ don't vote
_____ sometimes vote Republican        _____ usually vote for another
_____ usually vote Republican                party  (Please name)

Which word best describes your political beliefs?

_____ left-liberal                     _____ moderate conservative
_____ liberal                          _____ conservative
_____ middle-of-the-road

Are you a veteran of any U.S. wars?  If so, which ones?


How many of the following kinds of organizations do you belong to?

_____ veterans' organizations (VFW, American Legion, etc.)
_____ religious organizations (Knights of Columbus, etc.)
_____ fraternal and service organizations (Masons, Elks, etc.)
_____ service organizations (Kiwanis, Boy Scout leader, etc.)
_____ business organizations (Chamber of Commerce, etc.)
_____ advocate or lobbyist organizations (National Rifle Association,
      Greenpeace, Common Cause, etc.)

Please indicate any you contribute to or otherwise actively support.


What is your religious affiliation?

_____ Protestant                       _____ Muslim
_____ Roman Catholic                   _____ Other  (Please name)
_____ Eastern Orthodox                 _____ None
_____ Jewish

How often do you attend religious services?

_____ very regularly                   _____ infrequently
_____ fairly regularly                 _____ never


Please list any hobbies or special interests:
```

FIGURE 13.1   (Continued)

testers find that a 40 percent response to a mailed questionnaire is unusually high. That is why they often conduct surveys by telephone, with the phone caller filling in the questionnaire for the respondent. Better results will come if you distribute your questionnaire in person, laying a copy in your prospects' hands. In this regard, an especially valuable use for a questionnaire is to follow up an interview, as Jamie Merisotis found.

If you can't interview a person, you might find it worthwhile to add to your questionnaire some "open questions," questions that call for short written responses. Although you are likely to get a smaller response to these, they might supply you with something worth quoting or might suggest facts for you to consider when you mull over the findings. Urge your recipients to flip over the questionnaire and use the back side if they need more room.

Tally your responses. When you get back all your questionnaires, sit down and tally the results. That is easy enough to do if you are just counting short answers ("Republican," "Democrat"), but longer answers to open questions ("What is your goal in life?") will need to be summed up in paraphrase and then sorted into rough categories ("To grow rich," "To serve humanity," "To travel," "To save own soul"). By this means, you can count similar replies and accurately measure the extent of a pattern of responses.

Making a field trip   A visit to observe at first hand may well be essential in field research, as it certainly was in Jamie Merisotis's study. Merisotis visited four criminal courts, where he observed the bondsmen in action. In his paper, his observations supplied the evidence for his contention that the work of a bondsman has some socially redeeming use:

> In the crowded, often disorganized environment of a lower criminal court, bondsmen are a stabilizing influence. Their presence is unmistakable. They can be seen conferring with family and friends of defendants in courthouse corridors, speaking with prosecutors during a court recess, and keeping track of defendants still to be presented in court. Bondsmen help keep order in the courtroom, and they locate people. One bondsman was frequently observed assisting in translating for Spanish-speaking defendants when the official courtroom interpreter was unavailable.

Merisotis also observed the bondsmen on their daily rounds. He accompanied several as they made calls, observing them talking with clients and writing bonds. This firsthand experience supplied authentic details from which his writing profited.

In making an observational visit of your own, you may care to recall the suggestions we give in Chapter 4. You may need to make an appointment. Right away when you arrive, identify yourself and your business. Some receptionists will insist on identification. You might ask your instructor for a statement on college letterhead, declaring that you are a bona fide student doing field research. (If this document doesn't get you in, you can always return in overalls and say you have come to replace a fluorescent light. Seriously, unless your topic is bail bondsmen, you will probably be surprised at how helpful most people will be.) Follow-up field trips may be necessary if, while you are writing, you find gaps in your research or if new ideas occur that you'll need to test by further observation.

Inquiring by telephone   If you can't talk to an expert in person, your next best resource may be a telephone interview. A busy person whom you call during a working day may not be able to give you a half hour of conversation on the spur of a moment, and it is polite to ask for a time when you may call again. You will waste the person's time (and yours) if you try to wing your interview; have written questions in hand before you dial. Take notes.

Federal regulations, by the way, forbid recording an interview over the phone without notifying the person who is talking that you are recording his or her remarks and without using a recorder connector with a warning device that emits a beep signal every fifteen seconds. For a charge, some telephone companies will now make a beep-punctuated recording of your conversation and mail you a tape cassette; ask your operator whether this service is available.

The telephone, of course, has other uses besides interviewing. Early in his project Jamie Merisotis placed scores of phone calls to set up his face-to-face interviews. Later he checked some facts by making further calls.

Interviews, questionnaires, visits, and telephone inquiries are the sources of evidence you are likely to find most useful in field research. (To see how Jamie Merisotis drew from all these sources, see the chapter from his honors thesis beginning on p. 438.) But other sources of ideas and information will serve you, too, for other kinds of field research. Briefly, we'll run through them.

Letter writing   Do you know a person whose knowledge or opinions you need but who lives too far away to interview? Write him or her a letter. Make it short and polite, keep your questions brief and pointed, and enclose a stamped, self-addressed envelope for a reply.

Large corporations, huge organizations such as the Red Cross and the National Wildlife Federation, and branches of the military and the federal government are accustomed to getting such mail. In fact, many of them employ public relations officers whose duty is to answer you. Sometimes they will unexpectedly supply you with a bonus: free brochures, press releases, or other material that they think might interest you. Many such nuggets of material valuable for research are to be had for nothing, from people trying hard to give it away.

Using television and radio programs, films, and recordings Intriguing possibilities for writing lie in the media. If you ever care to do a research paper about television, radio, movies, or contemporary theater or music, you may find yourself doing field research as original as if you went out and interviewed eighteen bail bondsmen. Because your material lies close at hand (in the case of television, it may be yours at the twist of a knob), our only advice to you is to get plenty of it. Watch (or listen to) a large amount of it and draw conclusions.

Successful papers based on such research are legion. One student we know wrote an excellent research paper on public service commercials, free time devoted to good causes (like accident prevention and saving whales), which all television channels are required by law to make available. She classified the different causes being promoted and their different pitches or appeals, and she found an interesting correlation between the causes given air time and the presumed interests of a station's advertisers. For example, one station that aired many beer commercials rarely aired a public service message about the dangers of alcohol. Another student fruitfully compared the news coverage of an election by three major networks and the Public Broadcasting System by first recording a dozen televised newscasts with the aid of a VCR. Her main finding was that the networks seemed determined to cast the election into a more dramatic form—similar to a prizefight or a football game—than Public Broadcasting did, even though the outcome became clear very early.

Program guides (*TV Guide,* a station's own guide, or a daily newspaper) can save you time by directing you to the most relevant programs. For easy reference, the script of a broadcast or telecast may be available on request (or for a small charge) from a station or network; if an announcer does not proclaim that it is available, you can write to inquire.

In writing about movies or plays, don't forget to check out reviews in magazines and newspapers. In writing about a recording, inspect any information supplied on an insert or on the sleeve. Record labels, too, sometimes provide dates, names of members of a group, and song composers.

Using a camera or a videocamera Even if you are only an amateur photographer, taking pictures in the field may greatly advance your research. Some photographs may serve as illustrations to include in your paper; others may help you remember details while you write. One student of architecture, making a survey of the best-designed buildings in her city, carried a 35-mm camera and photographed each building she proposed to describe. A student of sociology, looking into methods used to manage large crowds, found it effective to carry a videocamera to a football game. Later, watching a few crowd scenes in slow motion, he felt better able to write lively and accurate accounts of how police and stadium guards performed their jobs.

Attending lectures and conferences Professionals in virtually every walk of life—and also special-interest groups—sometimes convene for a regional or national conference. Such conferences bring together doctors, lawyers, engineers, scientists, librarians, teachers, and assorted people bound together by some mutual concern (a conference to protest acid rain, a convention of science fiction fans). These meetings can be fertile sources of fresh ideas.

Fortunately, college campuses sometimes welcome such conferences, and if there are any of possible use to you, go take them in. An idea for a field research paper might result. At some conferences, lectures and panel discussions are open to the public. At others, to gain admission you might have to enroll in the conference, for a fee. This drawback might discourage a casual researcher, but if your honors thesis depends on material to be discussed at the conference, or if you are thinking of a possible career in that profession, you might find it worthwhile to pay the fee. To attend a professional conference, to meet and talk with speakers and fellow attendees, can be an excellent way to learn the language of a discipline. If you plan to be an ornithologist, start thinking and talking and writing like an ornithologist. Learn the vocabulary, the habits of mind. To steep yourself in the language of a specialized conference is one way to begin. You can take notes on the lectures, which are given by speakers who usually are distinguished in their specialties, and thus get some firsthand live opinions. You may even be able to ask questions from the audience or corner the speakers later for informal talk.

Proceedings of important conferences may be published later (unfortunately, often months or years later) and eventually can be tracked down in a library. A paper presented at one such conference of professors of educational administration is cited in the research paper by Lisa Chickos on page 381.

Check the weekly schedules of events listed on your college bulletin boards and in your campus newspaper. These may alert you to other lectures (besides those delivered at conferences) that may hold ideas and information useful to you.

Shaping a Draft

All the while you have been gathering material, you have been evaluating it, deciding what to trust, which evidence looks most likely to answer your basic research question. Presumably, you have been doing some heavy sifting and discarding along the way. If you have, you will have saved yourself much toil at the present moment, when you are ready to shape your material into a paper.

At this point, as you glance over what you have collected, you can again be critical of it. Do you have *enough* material to demonstrate what you hope to demonstrate? If not, you may need to go out and get more. How much is enough? To answer that, we can't lay down any hard-and-fast rule. But the larger the generalization you make from your evidence, the more evidence it calls for in support. Clearly, you cannot decide that all day-care centers in the state of Washington are safe, well-managed facilities from having visited

WRITING WITH A COMPUTER: FIELD RESEARCH

SHAPING A DRAFT

The ability of a computer to help you juggle and rearrange material greatly facilitates your task in organizing your field research. By now, your background reading, interviews, questionnaire, field trips, and telephone inquiries will probably have generated much material. If you have had time to transcribe your findings on software as you went along, your paper will be easier to organize; if you still need to transcribe your material, you will first want to winnow the best of it so as not to have to type up everything. When discarding any material, don't destroy it yet. You can't tell—perhaps it might still come in handy. With some word processing programs, you need not zap it out: you can block it off so that it won't print but will still remain visible on screen. If your program won't do that, no problem: just create another document to store your spare material. You may be glad you did.

only five of them in Seattle; and in a research project bounded by the limited time of a college course, you may need to trim down your generalization: "The day-care centers *I visited in Seattle* impressed me by their safety and professional management" [emphasis ours].

Most college writers find, at the moment they begin to shape a first draft, that they have collected a bewildering array of material. If you've done much legwork, the amount and variety of your evidence may dismay you. Do you feel frozen as you contemplate your difficulties? Don't know how you will ever pull this jumble into shape? Stop trying to plan; start writing. Don't worry about which part of your paper to write first—start with anything at all. If you just get something down on paper, then later you can decide where to place it. Absorb yourself in your task. Maybe your material will start falling into shape as you write.

Organizing your ideas   With any luck, your material may fall readily into shape, but if it is various and extensive, you may find you need to outline beforehand. In Chapter 16, we offer detailed advice on outlining (p. 498). For some writers, a dependable-looking outline inspires confidence.

In organizing your field research, remember that, as is true of most other kinds of writing, some intuitive art is called for. It is not enough to relate the steps you took in answering your research question: you aren't writing a memoir, you're reporting what you found out. And it may be that a reader will take in your material more readily if you try putting it together in various combinations until you find out what seems most engaging and clear. In a guidebook titled *How to Write and Publish Engineering Papers and Reports* (Philadelphia: ISI Press, 1982), Herbert B. Michaelson remarks:

Because there is no one best way to organize all engineering manuscripts, the role of the imagination cannot be overemphasized. Writing progress seldom follows the same sequence as progress on an engineering project. Designing a device or developing a process may get off to a false start, or may be sidetracked into a wrong approach, or may undergo modifications before the work is completed. A manuscript describing all these stages of the design or process would be difficult to read. After the problems have been solved in the laboratory, it is time for a new exercise of the imagination: the design of the manuscript.

If you began with a clear, carefully worded question for research (first discussed on pp. 350–351), you will generally have an easier time in organizing your evidence to answer it. Of course, research questions often may change and re-form while you're at work in the field. Don't be afraid, when the time comes to organize, to junk an original question that no longer works and to try to reorganize your material around a newly formed question. In the long run, you'll save both time and toil.

Interpreting your evidence To be sure, organizing the facts you collect is an important part of your task. You might easily mistake that part for the most important part of field research. But still more important is *interpreting* those facts. What do they indicate? In themselves, facts and statistics may not always make much sense. Much more likely to communicate meaning to your reader is what you make of your figures—your summaries of what statistics mean. Instead of reporting that 34.1 percent of your respondents favor capital punishment (with no further comment on the statistic), it might make more sense to write, "More than a third of the people I questioned said that they believe capital punishment is sometimes justified, although many of these people qualified their answers. They said they believed in it only to punish violent crimes such as murder and rape."

With pencil in hand, reread any notes you have taken. Think critically about the evidence that you have gathered. Try to answer the basic research question you began with. You will want to put this answer into the conclusion of your paper. Obviously, this final part of your paper is highly important. In it, you try to draw some generalization about what you have learned. An example: "I find, therefore, that sky divers, far from being reckless and suicidal as some people think, are responsible experts who carefully prepare for their jumps and observe every safety precaution."

Evaluate your sources. You can probably trust anyone you interviewed who has a good reputation among other experts in the same field. Did some person you interviewed seem indifferent, half asleep? Did he appear not to know what he was talking about? Discard his testimony or give it only a passing mention. Did any others impress you with their competence? Rely on them more heavily.

If you used a questionnaire and tabulated the replies, show them to fellow students whose opinions you respect. What conclusions do they draw? Test their interpretations against your own.

Here are some evidence-testing questions.

DISCOVERY CHECKLIST: EVALUATING EVIDENCE

- Is any of your evidence hearsay ("I understand she was a pretty reckless driver in her younger days")? If so, can you support or discount a speaker's view by comparing it with any other evidence?

- Was anyone who described an important event actually on the scene? Is it likely that the passage of time has distorted his or her memory?

- Does the testimony agree with published accounts—in books, magazines, and newspapers?

- Have you compared different people's opinions or accounts of the same thing? In general, the more people, the better.

- Do you base any large generalization on a single example, one fact, one individual opinion? If so, reconsider your claim.

- If you have tried to question a random sampling of people, do you feel they are truly representative?

- Did an interviewee exhibit prejudice or bias? Some remarks may need to be discounted.

- How detailed is your evidence? How extensive?

For more suggestions on evaluating facts and testimony, glance back over the section "Testing Evidence" in Chapter 7 (pp. 231–233).

Using sources (not letting sources use you)   While you write, it is easy to get distracted from your central inquiry—from your attempt to answer the research question you started out with. No doubt you will have collected experiences, comments from people, and miscellaneous delightful facts that you think you just have to include in your paper. Maybe they belong in an informal paper—a memoir, say, of your life as a field researcher—but be willing to omit them in writing up your field research. Some material that you may have taken great pains to collect may not prove useful when you draft. If it doesn't serve your inquiry, leave it out—don't yank it in by the heels.

A common danger, besides letting sources dominate a draft and receive undeserved prominence, is for a writer to swagger in triumph over what he or she discovered. Cultivate a certain detachment. Make no exorbitant claims for what you have discovered ("Thus I have shown that day-care centers universally deserve the trust of any parent in the state of Washington"). You have probably not answered your research question for all time; you need not claim to be irrefutable. Norman Tallent, in his guidebook *Psychological Report Writing* (Englewood Cliffs: Prentice-Hall, 1976), quotes a professional reader of reports in the field of psychology: "I have seen some reports which affected me adversely because of a tendency to sound pompous with the implication 'This is the final word!' rather than 'This is an opinion intended to be helpful in understanding the whole.' "

As you write, introduce pieces of evidence with transitions, such as "*Two other bail bondsmen disagreed* that first-time offenders make the best risks" or "*Elsewhere, in the southwest end, a more ethnically various part of the city,* few respondents felt that the problem of unemployment was serious." On the art of smoothly weaving quotations and other material into your paper, Chapter 11 makes a few suggestions (pp. 364–368).

Rewriting

As in writing a library research paper, you will probably find it easier to write the beginning and ending of your paper after you have done your research and written it up. You'll now better understand what you have demonstrated.

Looking over your evidence and your draft, you may quite possibly find your conclusion changing. Don't be afraid of making a whole new interpretation.

Not every spoken remark you've collected will be worth quoting, and if you faithfully introduce every one, word for word, the result may sound like drivel. In that case, summarize and paraphrase in your own words. To test whether a quotation is worth quoting, ask yourself:

Are these words memorable? Would you recall them if you hadn't written them down? If not, away with them!

Does the speaker's remark support any point you're trying to make? Or does it seem mere maundering chin music? If so, out with it!

When you sit down to rewrite, here are other, possibly useful questions to ask yourself.

REVISION CHECKLIST: LOOKING OVER YOUR RESULTS

- Have you put in only evidence that makes a point?
- Have you ever yielded to the temptation to put in some fact or quotation just because it cost effort to obtain?
- Are your sources of information trustworthy? Do you have lingering doubts about anything anyone told you? (If so, whom might you consult to verify it?)
- Did you take advantage of any library material that supplied background information or helped you test the validity of your evidence?
- Is your conclusion (or generalization) made clear?
- Do you spend much space announcing what you are going to do or repeating what you demonstrated? (If you do, consider whether such passages might be whittled down or done without.)

- If you include observations made on a field trip or visit, do you now need to make any follow-up visit?
- Do you need more evidence to back up any point? If so, where might you obtain it?

Once you have done all you can do by yourself to make your paper informative, tightly reasoned, and interesting to read, you might wish to take one last step: show it to one of your friends and ask for his or her criticisms. Answering your peer editor's comments will probably take extra time; but if you take this step seriously, the final result will almost surely be a better paper than the one you might otherwise have handed in. See if your peer reader will, in writing, answer the questions in the peer editing checklist.

PEER EDITING CHECKLIST: WRITING FROM RESEARCH IN THE FIELD

- Describe your overall reaction to the paper.
- What do you think about the conclusions the writer has drawn from his or her research? Do they seem fair and logical? Describe any problems you have with the conclusions.
- Does the writer need all the quotations he or she has used? Point out any that puzzled you or that you thought were not well incorporated.
- Do you have any questions about the writer's evidence? Point out any areas where the writer has not fully backed up his or her conclusions.
- Has the writer described the results of a survey or questionnaire clearly? Do you need any additional information or explanation?
- Look carefully at the conclusion. Does it clearly enough answer the writer's research question? Did you learn anything in the paper that you think should be somehow included in the conclusion?
- Please look carefully at transitions and put an asterisk anywhere you think the writer needs to work harder.

Preparing your manuscript   The form of your field research paper isn't much different from that of a library research paper (whose final preparation is discussed briefly on pp. 373–375). One difference may occur when, if you are following APA style, you come to prepare a list of your sources ("References") at the end of your paper. You do not list personal communications such as letters, interviews, and phone conversations. You need list only sources that a reader can verify: published works and public records. For specific advice on citing and listing your sources, see Chapter 14.

Proofreading a field research paper calls for checking information carefully—not against neatly printed sources, which are easier to check, but against your original notes and jottings. Allow yourself ample time to give your paper a final going-over. (For further instructions, see also "A Note on Manuscript Style and Computer Formatting," p. 577.)

A COMPLETED FIELD RESEARCH PAPER

When Jamie Merisotis completed his honors thesis, it caused a local stir. Friends and roommates who read it were greatly intrigued and impressed by it. As his academic department required, large parts of his thesis were devoted to explaining recent and pending legislation as it affected the bail bond business and to giving an account of his methods of research (which account we have already summarized). But let us show you one short, self-contained chapter of the paper, which illustrates how Merisotis put his field research to use. The paper is written in APA style, so both direct quotations and indirect quotations, taken from interviews, are dated. Unlike most field research papers, this one contains no names, for in order to persuade the bondsmen to talk freely, Merisotis had to agree to keep them all anonymous. In preserving anonymity, he followed the practice of *Law and Society Review,* a professional journal that sometimes publishes articles quoting criminals who want to conceal their identities. He dated all facts and quotations he obtained from interviews, but lest anyone see a pattern in the responses and try to identify the speakers, he did not distinguish one speaker from another.

Unlike a library research paper, this field research paper has no listing of its sources entitled "References." Merisotis's information came entirely from personal communications, mostly from interviews and responses to his questionnaire, which he distributed privately. But if, using the APA style, you were writing a field research paper that referred to public sources, such as a lecture to an audience or records in courthouses, which are open for anyone's inspection, then at the end of your paper you would add a list of "References."

How a Bondsman Decides to Post Bail
Jamie Merisotis

The bail bondsman's decision whether or not
to post bond for a defendant is probably the
single greatest power he wields in the legal
system. People who seek the services of a
bondsman normally do not have the means to raise
the full bond amount themselves. Thus the
bondsman is often the deciding factor in determining a defendant's pretrial status. Defendants unable to secure the services of a bondsman
often remain in the custody of the state until
the trial, which may be several months later.

When a bondsman is asked to write a bond,
he considers several factors. This decision-
making process is complex, and most bondsmen
stress that each client is considered on his own
terms. Nevertheless, from this research several clear patterns have emerged. (All evidence cited in this study is from personal
communications.)

By far the most important factor, at least
initially, is the amount of the bond. After
all, it is the bond amount that ultimately
yields the bondsman's fee. Of course, the
bondsman is also aware that the greater fee
carries the greater risk. One telltale sign of
the importance of the bond amount may be seen
from the bondsman's method of screening prospective clients. A defendant, or someone

2

close to him, can call the bondsman by looking
under "Bonds--Bail" in the telephone book or
requesting the list of bondsmen from the police
station. But a phone call does not bring direct access to the bondsman. In most cases, a
professional answering service fields calls for
the bondsman, then notifies him through an
electronic beeper. The bondsman then calls the
answering service and takes the message. What
is interesting is that the answering service
asks callers only three questions: (1) name, (2)
where they are at the moment, and (3) the bond
amount. Clearly this amount is of tantamount
importance to the bondsman, and he makes note of
it immediately when taking the message. Bondsmen concur that the bond amount is very important in their decision-making process, as these
comments reveal:

> Let's say I get a call at three
> o'clock a.m. I've just gotten into bed
> and the service beeps me with a call.
> It's late but I take the call and find out
> it's for a five hundred dollar bond out in
> [a town about 20 miles from the bondsman's
> house]. My answer to that is simple. No.
> There's no way I drag myself out of bed
> for a 50 dollar fee. As a matter of fact,
> I might even call the service back and
> tell them not to bother me with nickel
> fees. (November 29, 1985)

3

I don't write bonds for under five
hundred. Whether I'm taking a call or
sitting in court during arraignments, I
can't--won't--even sneeze at a guy who
wants my services on a two-fifty bond.
It's not worth my time. (December 27,
1985)

Do you know how much paperwork there
is on a bond? Do you? I'm not saying I
won't write a bond because of the paperwork, but any bondsman will tell you that
paperwork is the worst part of this job.
If I write only a few bonds a week, you
better believe they're good risks for good
money. (November 9, 1985)

Bondsmen who have a large bond volume, but deal
in very low bonds, rarely survive in the modern
bail bond business.

Bondsmen consider another important factor:
the alleged offense. It tells them something
about the defendant, which in turn gives them an
idea of the likelihood that he will appear.
Probably the single offense that causes greatest
apprehension to bondsmen is a failure to appear,
also referred to as FTA. Obviously, a defendant who did not face the court in a previous
case is not a good risk. Failing to appear is
a sin that many bondsmen will not forgive, and
thus recidivist criminals may often find that
they have no benefactors in the community of

4

bondsmen. In other cases, bondsmen have personal preferences for not wanting to bond out
certain defendants. Sample responses demonstrate this eclecticism:

>   I don't bond sex offenders. Perverts
> don't deserve to be free. (November 29,
> 1985)
>
>   I try to stay away from people who
> are charged with violent crimes, espe-
> cially if it involves a gun. Will he turn
> around and use it on me? I don't want to
> find out. (January 11, 1986)
>
>   No prostitutes, and no one that deals
> in heroin. You never know where those
> kind of people will be in the morning.
> (October 5, 1985)

Another factor that bondsmen take into account is the defendant's community ties. Most
bondsmen ask the defendant where he lives, what
kind of job he has, and how long he has lived in
the area. This information is important to a
bondsman because it gives him an idea of the
likelihood of a defendant's returning for trial;
it also gives him some information about how
difficult the client would be to trace if he
failed to appear in court. Bondsmen are wary
of out-of-state defendants because the costs of
retrieving a client from a long distance are
naturally higher. But information on community
ties can also be used to measure the client's

5

credibility. As one bondsman stated, "A guy
who's got a good job, wife, kids, whatever, is a
lot better risk than some chump with no address"
(October 5, 1985).

Some bondsmen express no apprehensions
about career criminals if they "know the guy or
his family" (November 16, 1985; January 4,
1986). Others, however, are unwilling to assume the risk for repeat offenders. "If I'm in
another business," one bondsman said, "steady
clients are great. In this business, steady
clients are bad news" (December 30, 1985).

Several bondsmen said they take the defendant's age into consideration because they
believe that young clients have high rates of
failure to appear. That the defendant is living with his parents, however, bondsmen take as
a sign of stability. One bondsman noted that
if a parent has "gone down" (engaged a bondsman
before), "you know the kid will have someone
around making sure he gets to court" (November
6, 1985).

It should be noted that a majority of
bondsmen denied that race is a factor in their
decisions. Others, quite vocal about their
racial preferences, said they do not bond out
black defendants. The reasons offered were
mostly stereotypes:

I'll bond out a black person if he
comes from a good neighborhood. But I

6

definitely check the address. A lot of
the time, I read [the name of a predomi-
nantly black area] and say to myself, "If
this guy skips, are you gonna go in there
and drag him out?" Unless I'm in a daring
mood, there's no way. (January 11, 1986)
Women defendants are also approached cautiously
by some bondsmen. One remarked that women are
sometimes difficult to trace because "once the
case comes up, months or even a year later, she
could be married and change her name. That
makes tracing difficult" (November 6, 1985).

In many cases the bondsman requires an indemnitor on the bond. This person is often a
relative or friend, usually the person who
called the bondsman. The indemnitor agrees to
compensate the bondsman for his losses in the
event of forfeiture or to deposit collateral
with the bondsman. The bondsman's decision to
post bond is often contingent on who the indemnitor is and what he has to offer as security
or collateral. Only in extenuating circum-
stances--if he knows the defendant well or is
feeling extraordinarily compassionate--will the
bondsman not require an indemnitor. Indeed,
the indemnitor in some ways plays a more important role in the bondsman's business than does
the defendant, as the following comments show:

I deal strictly with the indemnitor.
I want to know who this person is, how

7

much money he's got, and what he can offer
me for collateral. Otherwise, no deal.
(November 8, 1985)

Really, my financial leverage--you
know, how I'm gonna get my money back if
the client skips--is with the indemnitor.
As co-signer, they're putting their butt
on the line for this guy. . . . Most
times, I don't even see the defendant
until it's time to sign the papers.
(December 30, 1985)

Bondsmen accept an array of things as security or collateral: for example, stocks, savings account passbooks, real estate, and car
titles. A bondsman wants to know how much leverage he will have with a defendant in the event
of forfeiture. Clearly, a majority of this
leverage is with the indemnitor, the person who
has the most to lose (at least financially) if
the client absconds.

Whether any of these factors that bondsmen
consider really affects the defendant's likelihood of appearance for trial--a most important
question in every bondsman's mind--goes beyond
the scope of the present study. Nevertheless,
each bondsman perceives these factors and weighs
them differently. His analysis ultimately
yields the decision whether or not to assume the
risk for a defendant.

Questions to Start You Thinking

1. How does the life of a bail bondsman appear similar to the lives of any other businesspeople you know? In what ways is it strikingly different?

2. How does Merisotis demonstrate his opening contention that the bondsman wields great power within the legal system?

3. In his concluding paragraph, how does he separate his own view from the views of the bondsmen? With what opinions that the bondsmen have expressed (and which he has quoted) do you suppose he might disagree?

4. What other interesting, unusual, or unfamiliar occupations come to mind about which you might enjoy doing field research?

Other Assignments

1. As Jamie Merisotis did, investigate a job or profession. Interview people in this line of work, explain what they do, and try to characterize them. Your topic need not be as colorful and hard to research as bail bonding; just pick a profession you care to know more about, perhaps one that you consider a career possibility.

2. Write a portrait of life in your town or neighborhood as it was in the past from interviews with senior citizens. Any photographs or other visual evidence you can gather might be valuable to include. If possible, try to verify any testimony you receive by comparing it with a file of old newspapers (probably available at a local newspaper office) or by talking with a local historian.

3. Write a short history of your immediate family from interviews, photographs, scrapbooks, old letters, written but unpublished records, and any other sources.

4. Investigate a current trend you have noticed on television (collecting evidence by observing news programs, other programs, or commercials).

5. Write a survey of recent films of a certain kind (detective movies, horror movies, science fiction movies, comedies, love stories), making generalizations that you support with evidence from your own film watching.

6. Study the lyrics of contemporary popular songs and draw a conclusion about them, citing a dozen or more examples. (Suggestions: Your research might sup-

FOR GROUP LEARNING

While writing your field research paper, hold meetings with your writing group. At the outset, you can draw on the knowledge of others: perhaps they can suggest sources unknown to you. Later in the process, meet to talk over any problems you encounter and exchange drafts for reactions and criticism. Because this is likely to be a large project, you might want to team up with another student and write your field research paper in collaboration.

port the argument of Caryl Rivers, whose article "What Should Be Done about Rock Lyrics?" appears on pp. 251–253 — or it might enable you to argue with her.)

APPLYING WHAT YOU LEARN: SOME USES OF FIELD RESEARCH

Opportunities may arise to do field research in almost any college course, at any level, in which you are called on to collect evidence and to observe. If you happen to be a student of journalism, you may be sent out to cover news stories: one of the most practical applications of field research. In education and social studies courses, field trips and observational visits are commonplace. (Columbia College offers a well-known undergraduate course in the sociology of New York City that includes trips to police lockups, morgues, and charity hospitals.) In a course in psychology, medical care, or political science, you may have to observe people's behavior and interpret it.

In the world beyond the campus, to carry out useful field research is an enormous and bustling concern. Sociologists seek to explain the components of the population. Bankers and stockbrokers and businesspeople seek to predict trends in the economy. Businesspeople seek new products that will sell, or they try to learn why an established product isn't selling better. Often they seek to understand a potential market and how to appeal to it. Professionals who conduct research often set forth their findings in reports and articles — that is why specialized technical and professional journals abound. Anthropologists and sociologists study how people live, archeologists dig up evidence of how people lived in the past, biologists and students of the environment collect evidence about the behavior of species of wildlife.

Here, for instance, is the anthropologist E. Richard Sorenson reporting his observations of children of the Fore, a tribal people in New Guinea who live by agriculture. He published his findings in "Cooperation and Freedom Among the Fore in New Guinea" (in *Learning Non-Aggression: The Experience of Non-Literate Societies,* ed. Ashley Montague [New York: Oxford University Press, 1978]). Taking movies with a concealed camera that went unnoticed and taking still pictures without alerting the tribesmen in advance, Sorenson photographed growing children and their families in their daily activities. From the pictures and his notes, he formed several interesting generalizations about the Fore people's practices in childrearing.

> The core discovery was that young infants remained in almost continual bodily contact with their mother, her housemates, or her gardening associates. At first, mothers' laps were the center of activity, and infants occupied themselves there by nursing, sleeping, and playing with their own bodies or those of their caretakers. They were not put aside for the sake of other activities, as when food was being prepared or heavy loads were being carried. Remaining in close, un-

FIGURE 13.2 A generally practiced deference to the desires of the young in the choice of play objects permitted them to investigate and handle knives and other potentially harmful objects frequently. They were expected to make use of the tools and materials which belonged to their adult associates and were indulged in this expectation. As a result, use of knives was common, particularly for exploratory play.

interrupted physical contact with those around them, their basic needs, such as rest, nourishment, stimulation, and security, were continuously satisfied without obstacle. . . .

A second crucial thread running from infancy through childhood was the unrestricted manner in which exploratory activity and pursuit of interest were left to the initiative of the child. As the infant's awareness increased, his interests broadened to the things his mother and other caretakers did and to the objects and materials they used. Then these youngsters began crawling out to explore things nearby that attracted their attention. By the time they were toddling their interests continually took them on short sorties to nearby objects and persons. As soon as they could walk well, the excursions extended to the entire hamlet and its gardens, and then beyond with other children. Developing without interference or supervision, this personal exploratory quest freely touched on whatever was around, even axes, knives, machetes, and fire [Figure 13.2].

Initially astonished by the ability of young children to manage so independently without being hurt, I eventually began to see how this capability also emerged from the infants' milieu of close human physical proximity and tactile interaction. Touch and bodily contact lent themselves naturally to satisfying the basic needs of the babies and provided the basis for an early kind of communicative experience based on touch. In continual physical touch with people engaged in daily pursuits, infants and toddlers began to learn the forms of behavior and response characteristic of Fore life. Muscle tone, movement, and mood were components of this learning process; formal instruction was not. . . . Competence with the tools of life developed quickly, and by the time they were able to walk, Fore youngsters could safely handle axes, knives, fire, and so on.

The early pattern of exploratory activity included frequent return to one of the "mothers." Serving as a home base, the bastion of security, a woman might occasionally give the youngster a nod of encouragement, if he glanced in her direction with uncertainty. Yet rarely did anyone attempt to control or direct, nor did they participate in a child's quests or jaunts.

At first I found it quite remarkable that toddlers did not recklessly thrust themselves into unappreciated dangers, the way our own children tend to do. Eventually I came to see that they had no reason to do so. From their earliest days, they enjoyed a benevolent sanctuary from which the world could be confidently viewed, tested, and appreciated. These human bases were neither demanding nor restrictive, so there was no need to escape or evade them in the manner so frequently seen in Western culture. Confidently, not furtively, the youngsters were able to extend their inquiry, widening their understanding as they chose. There was no need to play tricks or deceive in order to pursue life. Nor did they have to act out impulsively to break through subliminal fears induced by punishment or parental anxiety. Such children could safely move out on their own, unsupervised and unrestricted.

Most of us may never go on a field research expedition to New Guinea, but the techniques that Sorenson demonstrates—patiently collecting evidence, laying aside his own unwarranted assumptions, and finally making generalizations about the behavior patterns he observed—may serve for any investigation of the unfamiliar. You might try emulating Sorenson's accuracy, patience, and open-mindedness the next time you write a paper about people or a lifestyle different from your own.

In the sciences, social sciences, and fields of business (such as marketing or advertising), writers of articles frequently report on still another kind of study: their observations of tests and practical inquiries they have made. People in the helping professions, after testing and observing their patients, interviewing their families, and studying information from other professionals who have known them, often write case studies, which they keep on file and sometimes share with their colleagues. Only rarely are case studies meant for publication. Here, from a mental health center, is an example of one such case study.

Debbie is a twelve and a half-year-old girl from a broken home (father deserted six years ago and continues to upset the family by calling to complain to Debbie's mother about his present wife). Debbie is thought to be underachieving in school. Her teachers see her as an angry, troubled child. Debbie herself complains that schoolwork overwhelms her, tires her out. The following report seeks to achieve an understanding of Debbie as a basis for taking further action.

Debbie's intellectual status is above average. Her observations are accurate and there is originality of thought. She is an insecure child who has many fears. She fears the loss of her integrity, attack from others, and her own impulses. Debbie has a great need for acceptance and affection, but is inhibited by an overpowering fear of being rejected and hurt. There seems to be hostility directed to the mother. The relationship has not been mutually satisfying, often leaving Debbie frustrated. It is my impression that the mother's inconsistencies in handling the child may be a source of anger. Now she wants her own way and is conflicted about her dependency. Her attitudes to men are also unwholesome. They are seen as weak and mutilated. And she is confused about herself. She feels inadequate, and having a specific learning disability she requires more guidance and love than most children her age. However, not being able successfully to reach out to others has only left her more frustrated. Since Debbie finds it difficult to relate to people and because her own feelings are threatening to her, she withdraws to an immature fantasy world that provides little refuge. Even her fantasy is fearful, involving aggression and fear of being injured emotionally. Debbie is a very unhappy child.

In one memorable college paper, a business student reported the results of his attempt to give out free samples of a new margarine to supermarket customers. When he spread globs of the stuff on soft white bread, he had very little luck trying to give away samples. But when he dabbed the stuff daintily on tempting-looking crackers studded with sesame seeds, it moved well. He then tried dainty dabs of margarine on bread (with a little more success, but not much) and sometimes fat globs on the crackers (which moved fairly well). His conclusion: the crackers were the catalyst that made the margarine move. But in margarine samples, he decided, smaller offerings had proved more appealing than generous ones. These findings may not seem earthshaking to you, but to a merchant of margarine they might prove worth their weight in butter.

Anybody, in practically any field, can conduct an experiment. You might even ask yourself, What experiment might I conduct that might produce interesting results? In fact, what experiments might you conduct in order to write an interesting paper *for this very course?* Once again, you'll need your imagination.

CHAPTER 14

Documenting Sources; Using a Style Book

In newspaper language, a *style book* is a list of usages that every writer for the paper observes. A style book might instruct reporters, for instance, to refer to women as *Ms.*, to use a lowercase letter and not a capital on names of the seasons (*spring*, not *Spring*), to put quotation marks around the title of a book, a film, or a song. Every newspaper makes up its own style book and every staff writer has a copy. The style book helps determine the personality of a newspaper. For years, the *Chicago Tribune* insisted on spelling *philosophy* "filosofy," while the New York *Daily News* referred to no woman as a *lady* unless she was a convicted prostitute. More important, a style book saves each writer from having to deliberate about every fussy little thing: to capitalize or not to capitalize? It keeps all the articles in a newspaper consistent and so makes the paper more easily readable.

A similar logic operates in scholarly writing. Writers of college research papers most often follow the rules from either of two handbooks, one compiled by the Modern Language Association (MLA), the other by the American Psychological Association (APA). The style of the MLA is generally observed in papers for English composition, literature, and foreign language courses. APA style usually prevails in papers for the social sciences and business. If your research takes you into any scholarly or professional journals in those special areas, you will probably find all the articles following a recognizable style.

In other disciplines, other handbooks prescribe style: the *CBE Style Manual* of the Council of Biology Editors (1983), for instance, is used in the biological sciences and medicine. You will need to familiarize yourself with it, or with other manuals, if you ever do much research writing in those or other disciplines.

This chapter is here for handy reference. We try to tell you no more than you will need to know to write a freshman research paper. You won't have to worry about many of these matters until you are typing your paper in finished form. Then you can refer to this advice. To know MLA style or APA style will be useful at these moments:

In citing while you write—at any time when you want to document, often on a note card, exactly where you obtained a fact, idea, opinion, or quotation.

In listing all your sources—that is, in adding a final bibliography, a list entitled "Works Cited" or "References."

The purpose of citing and listing your sources is to enable any interested reader to look them up and verify what you say. The mechanics of documentation may seem fussy, but the obligation to cite and list sources keeps research writers truthful and responsible.

CITING: MLA STYLE

As you write, you need to indicate what you borrowed and where you found it. The *MLA Handbook for Writers of Research Papers,* 3rd ed. (New York: MLA, 1988) has extensive and exact recommendations. If you want more detailed advice than that given here, you can purchase a copy of the *MLA Handbook* or see a copy in the reference room of your college library.

Citing Printed Sources

To cite a book or a periodical in the text of a paper, you usually place in parentheses the author's last name and the number of the page containing the information cited. You do this as close as possible to your mention of the information you have borrowed, as in the following examples.

A WORK BY A SINGLE AUTHOR

At least one critic maintains that Dean Rusk's exposure to Nazi power in Europe in the 1930s permanently influenced his attitude toward appeasement:

In contrast to Acheson, who had attended Groton, Yale, and Harvard despite his family's genteel

> poverty, Rusk was sheer Horatio Alger stuff.
> He had grown up barefoot, the son of a tenant
> farmer in Georgia's Cherokee county. . . .
> Then came the moment that transformed his life
> and his thinking. He won a Rhodes scholarship
> to Oxford. More important, his exposure to Eu-
> rope in the early 1930s, as the Nazis consoli-
> dated their power in Germany, scarred his mind,
> leading him to share Acheson's hostility to ap-
> peasement in any form anywhere. (Karnow 179)

> One reason we admire Simone de Beauvoir is that "she
> lived the life she believed" (Morgan 58).

For complete information about your source, the reader can then turn to the end of your paper and refer to your list entitled "Works Cited" (see p. 457). Notice that a long direct quotation is indented ten spaces and needs no quotation marks to set it off from the text of your paper.

For the sake of readability, you'll sometimes want to mention an author or authors in your text, putting only the page number in parentheses.

A WORK BY TWO OR MORE AUTHORS

> Taylor and Wheeler present yet another view (25).

A WORK BY A CORPORATE AUTHOR

> The American Red Cross lists three signs of oxygen depri-
> vation: blue tongue, lips, and fingernails; loss of con-
> sciousness; and dilated pupils (181).

A GOVERNMENT DOCUMENT

> The Department of Health and Human Services sets forth
> several methods for combating future outbreaks of
> mosquito-borne diseases (25).

AN ANONYMOUS WORK

When no author is mentioned on the title page of the work you're citing, refer to your source with a shortened version of the title (the first word or phrase).

> In Alcoholism, we find a list of questions people can ask
> themselves if they suspect their drinking has gotten out
> of hand (3).

MULTIPLE WORKS BY THE SAME AUTHOR

If you have used two works by the same author (or authors), you need to indicate with an abbreviated title which one you are citing in the text. In a paper that uses as sources two books by Iona and Peter Opie, *The Lore and Language of Schoolchildren* and *The Oxford Nursery Rhyme Book,* you would cite the first book as follows:

> The Opies found that the children they interviewed were
> more straightforward when asked about their "magic prac-
> tices" or their "ways of obtaining luck or averting ill-
> luck" than when asked about their "superstitions" (<u>Lore</u>
> 210).

MULTIPLE WORKS IN THE SAME CITATION

If you refer to more than one source, separate the two citations with a semicolon.

> The love between Aylmer and Georgiana, in Hawthorne's
> story "The Birthmark," has been called rare, pure, and
> beautiful (Matthiessen 254; Van Doren 131).

WORKS WITH EDITORS, TRANSLATORS, OR COMPILERS

When you cite a writer whose work appears in a book that has an editor, translator, or compiler, you need cite only the writer's name and the page number. Due credit to the editor, translator, or compiler will be given in your list of works cited.

> Critic Denis Donoghue refers to Randall Jarrell's
> "wonderful feeling for dreams and for the children who
> attend them" (57).

A MULTIVOLUME WORK

For a work with multiple volumes, show the author's name and the volume number followed by a colon and the page number.

> In ancient times, astrological predictions were sometimes
> used as a kind of black magic (Sarton 2: 319).

Citing Nonprint Sources

In both library and field research, it is likely that some of your material will be drawn from nonprint sources: interviews, questionnaires, phone calls, tapes and recordings, personal letters, films, filmstrips, slide programs, video-tapes, computer programs. Finding material in the field (as in an interview) means that *you* are the source. You should document all your material as faithfully as you credit books, newspapers, and periodicals. Probably the easiest way to do that is to weave your mention of each source into the body of your paper.

```
Hearing Yeats read "The Song of the Old Mother" on tape
sheds new light on several lines in the poem.

On the H. L. Mencken recording, journalist Donald Howe
Kirkley, Sr., was able to persuade the veteran writer to
talk about his defeats as well as his triumphs.
```

In your list of works cited you give complete information about each source. Transitions—phrases to introduce quotations, statistical tables, and other blocks of material—can also serve you well. (For weaving material in gracefully, see the suggestions in Chapter 11, p. 365.)

Using Endnotes to Cite Printed Sources

Some students and instructors continue to prefer notes rather than parenthetical citations for documentation, especially when the citations need to be long. The *MLA Handbook,* after giving detailed instructions for the newer, simpler way of citing sources that it now recommends, still contains instructions for doing it the old way.

If you use endnotes, you number your citations consecutively in the body of your text, like this.[1] You roll your typewriter platen up a notch or learn the command in your word processing program for superscripts. Then, at the end of the text, on a new page, you center the title "Notes," skip two spaces, and cite each source, in sequence, with a corresponding number. Double-space the entire list. Unless your instructor prefers otherwise, this method can eliminate the need for a "Works Cited" list since it contains the same publishing information, merely adding the specific page number for each citation. Only the form is slightly different. The note for the first sentence in this paragraph would look like this.

FIRST REFERENCE TO A BOOK

```
        1 Joseph Gibaldi and Walter S. Achtert, MLA Handbook
for Writers of Research Papers, 3rd ed. (New York: MLA,
1988) 183.
```

The first line of each note is indented five spaces from the left-hand margin. A comma separates the authors' names from the title. The publishing information is in parentheses, and the number of the page containing the borrowed information is not set off with a comma or any other punctuation. *Notice that this example also shows how to cite a book that is in a second or later edition.*

SUBSEQUENT REFERENCE

Should you cite the same work a second time, you use just the authors' last names and a page number.

2 Gibaldi and Achtert 181.

A WORK WITH A CORPORATE AUTHOR

3 American Red Cross, Lifesaving: Rescue and Water Safety (New York: Doubleday, 1974) 181.

A GOVERNMENT DOCUMENT

4 United States, Dept. of Health and Human Services, Mosquito Control Measures in Gulf Coast States (Washington: GPO, 1986) 25.

AN ANONYMOUS WORK

5 Alcoholism and You (Pearl Island: Okra, 1986) 3.

MULTIPLE WORKS BY THE SAME AUTHOR

If you have consulted more than one work by the same author (or authors), give full documentation for each one the first time it is mentioned. In subsequent references, include an abbreviated title after the author's name. For instance, if you have previously referred to both Opie books mentioned previously, your next citation might look like this:

6 Opie and Opie, Lore 192.

A WORK IN AN EDITED COLLECTION

When you document one item from a work in an edited collection, begin with the name of the author of the individual work. "The Example of *Billy Budd*" is the name of an article written by Warner Berthoff (*Billy Budd* is the title of a short novel by Herman Melville). *Twentieth Century Interpretations of* Billy Budd is the name of Howard P. Vincent's collection of essays about *Billy Budd*, written by various people.

7 Warner Berthoff, "The Example of Billy Budd," Twentieth Century Interpretations of Billy Budd: A Collection of Critical Essays, ed. Howard P. Vincent (Englewood Cliffs: Prentice, 1971) 58-60.

A MULTIVOLUME WORK

When you cite a multivolume work, indicate which volume contains the pages from which you have borrowed.

8 Francis James Child, ed., The English and Scottish Popular Ballads, 5 vols. (New York: Cooper Square, 1962) 2: 373-76.

A JOURNAL ARTICLE

The following is the usual form for citing information from a journal article.

⁹ Carol Cook, "'The Sign and Semblance of Her Honor': Reading Gender Difference in <u>Much Ado about Nothing</u>," <u>PMLA</u> 101 (1986): 200.

NEWSPAPER AND MAGAZINE ARTICLES

Newspaper and magazine articles are treated very much like journal articles.

¹⁰ Richard D. Lamm, "English Comes First," <u>New York Times</u> 1 July 1986, natl. ed.: A23.

¹¹ Robin Morgan, "The World without de Beauvoir," <u>Ms</u>. July 1986: 58.

Using Endnotes to Cite Nonprint Sources

The endnotes for nonprint sources appear in the same list, titled "Notes," as the printed sources.

AUDIOTAPES AND RECORDINGS

¹ H. L. Mencken, <u>H. L. Mencken Speaking</u>, Caedmon, TC 1082, 1960.

² William Butler Yeats, "The Song of the Old Mother," <u>The Poems of William Butler Yeats,</u> audiotape, read by William Butler Yeats, Siobhan McKenna, and Michael MacLiammoir, Spoken Arts, SAC 8044, 1974.

FILMSTRIPS, SLIDE PROGRAMS, VIDEOTAPES

Document a filmstrip, slide program, or videotape by including the name of the director or producer.

³ <u>Wildlife Conservation</u>, sound filmstrip, prod. Wildlife Research Group, 1986 (87 fr., 11 min.).

COMPUTER PROGRAMS

To document a computer program, include the name of the company that produced the program and the date.

⁴ <u>Business Systems</u>, computer software, Regis Software, 1985.

LECTURES

To cite a lecture, speech, or address, first give the speaker's name and the title of the talk (if any—see the official program), and then state where you heard it.

> 5 Lois DeBakey, "The Intolerable Wrestle with Words and Meaning," International Technical Communication Conference, Washington, 2 May 1971.

PERSONAL COMMUNICATIONS

You would document a personal letter received from one of your sources by including your correspondent's name and the date of the letter. The entries for a personal interview and a telephone interview are similar.

> 6 Helen Nearing, personal interview, 12 Nov. 1985.
>
> 7 John Bowlby, telephone interview, 3 June 1983.
>
> 8 Charles G. Sherwood, letter to the author, 29 Sept. 1986.

For more detailed information about citing nonprint sources, see the *MLA Handbook for Writers of Research Papers.*

LISTING: MLA STYLE

At the end of your paper, you will be expected to provide a list of sources from which you have gleaned ideas or information. The usual procedure in an English course is to follow the guidelines set forth by the Modern Language Association. We include here a brief rundown of the advice you are most likely to find useful as you set about the task of listing your sources.

Begin by starting a new page, continuing the page numbering of your paper. Under the title "Works Cited," skip two spaces and, starting flush with the left-hand margin, list your sources alphabetically by author, last name first; if there is no author, alphabetize by title. Double-space between entries and between lines within entries. When an entry exceeds one line, indent subsequent lines five spaces.

Listing Printed Sources

Notice that the information about each source appears in three sections, each followed by a period: author or agency's name (if there is one), title, and publishing information. Give the author's name and the title in full as they appear on the title page. If the publisher lists more than one city, include just the first. Use just the first name of a publisher with multiple names: not Holt,

Rinehart and Winston, but simply Holt. Omit initials too. For J. B. Lippincott Co., simply write Lippincott.

A WORK BY A SINGLE AUTHOR

```
Karnow, Stanley.  Vietnam: A History.  New York: Viking,
     1983.
```

A WORK BY TWO OR MORE AUTHORS

For a work with more than one author, reverse only the first author's name.

```
Taylor, Edwin F., and John A. Wheeler.  Spacetime
     Physics.  San Francisco: Freeman, 1966.
```

A WORK BY A CORPORATE AUTHOR

```
American Red Cross.  Lifesaving: Rescue and Water Safety.
     New York: Doubleday, 1974.
```

A GOVERNMENT DOCUMENT

To list a government document in accordance with MLA guidelines is much like listing any work that has a corporate author. Start with the name of the government, then the department or agency that put out the document, then the title of the publication, identifying information, and publication information (the place, publisher, and date).

```
United States.  Dept. of Health and Human Services.
     Mosquito Control Measures in Gulf Coast States.
     Washington: GPO, 1986.
```

AN ANONYMOUS WORK

```
Alcoholism and You.  Pearl Island: Okra, 1986.
```

MULTIPLE WORKS BY THE SAME AUTHOR

When listing successive books by the same author, put the titles in alphabetical order and include the author's name in full for the first entry only. In subsequent entries, indicate the author's name by using three hyphens and a period (or a comma if the person is an editor or translator).

```
Opie, Iona, and Peter Opie.  The Lore and Language of
     Schoolchildren.  Oxford: Clarendon-Oxford UP, 1960.
---, eds.  The Oxford Nursery Rhyme Book.  Oxford:
     Clarendon-Oxford UP, 1955.
```

A WORK WITH AN EDITOR, COMPILER, OR TRANSLATOR

Follow the name of an editor, compiler, or translator with a comma and a standard abbreviation (ed., comp., trans.). *Note too the standard way to list a multivolume work and the way to signal a university press.*

Child, Francis James, ed. The English and Scottish Popular Ballads. 5 vols. New York: Cooper Square, 1962.

Glen, Duncan, ed. Selected Essays of Hugh MacDiarmid. Berkeley: U of California P, 1970.

Williams, Miller, trans. Sonnets of Giuseppe Belli. Baton Rouge: Louisiana State UP, 1981.

A WORK IN AN EDITED COLLECTION

To quote a work that you find in an edited collection, begin with the name of the writer who wrote the individual work.

Berthoff, Werner. "The Example of Billy Budd." Twentieth Century Interpretations of Billy Budd: A Collection of Critical Essays. Ed. Howard P. Vincent. Englewood Cliffs: Prentice, 1971.

Donoghue, Denis. "The Lost World." Randall Jarrell: 1914-1965. Ed. Robert Lowell, Peter Taylor, and Robert Penn Warren. New York: Farrar, 1967.

AN ENTRY IN A REFERENCE BOOK

Most research at the college level moves quickly beyond encyclopedias. If for some good reason you do cite an entry from a reference book, enter it under the name of its author or, if it is unsigned, under the name of the article's title. If the reference book is well known, enter only its title and edition.

Fuller, R. Buckminster. "Geodesic Dome." Encyclopedia Americana. 1985 ed.

"Stichomythia." American Heritage Dictionary. 1979 ed.

A JOURNAL ARTICLE

Begin with the author's name, and place in quotation marks the title of a journal article. Follow with the journal's title, underlined, and the volume number (if there is one). The year of publication belongs in parentheses, followed by a colon and the page numbers.

Cook, Carol. "'The Sign and Semblance of Her Honor': Reading Gender Difference in Much Ado about Nothing." PMLA 101 (1986): 186-202.

A NEWSPAPER ARTICLE

List a newspaper article with the author's name first, then the title of the article, the name, date, and edition of the newspaper, and the page number. Notice that the day comes before the month.

> Lamm, Richard D. "English Comes First." New York Times
> 1 July 1986, natl. ed.: A23.

A MAGAZINE ARTICLE

The entry for a magazine article is similar to that for a journal article. If a newspaper or a magazine article is printed on more than one page and the pages are not consecutive, simply put a "+" after the first page number.

> Morgan, Robin. "The World without de Beauvoir." Ms.
> July 1986: 58+.

Listing Nonprint Sources

If you're using the MLA guidelines, your "Works Cited" page will list nonprint sources alphabetically along with print sources.

AUDIOTAPES AND RECORDINGS

For tapes and recordings, entries begin with the name of the speaker, the writer, or the production director, depending on what you want to emphasize.

> Mencken, H. L. H. L. Mencken Speaking. Caedmon, TC
> 1082, 1960.
> Yeats, William Butler. "The Song of the Old Mother."
> The Poems of William Butler Yeats. Audiotape. Read
> by William Butler Yeats, Siobhan McKenna, and Mi-
> chael MacLiammoir. Spoken Arts, SAC 8044, 1974.

FILMSTRIPS, SLIDE PROGRAMS, VIDEOTAPES

Citations for filmstrips, slide programs, and videotapes generally start with the title, underlined. Enter other information—writer, performers, producer—if it seems pertinent. Information about the size and length of the film or program follows the date.

> Wildlife Conservation. Sound filmstrip. Prod. Wildlife
> Research Group, 1986. 87 fr., 11 min.

COMPUTER PROGRAMS

> Business Systems. Computer software. Regis Software,
> 1985.

LECTURES

> Hurley, James. Address. Opening General Sess., American
> Bar Assn. Convention. Chicago, 17 Jan. 1987.

PERSONAL COMMUNICATIONS

Telephone interviews, interviews that you conduct in person, and comments you have obtained by letter are listed as follows.

```
Bowlby, John.  Telephone interview.  3 June 1983.
Nearing, Helen.  Personal interview.  12 Nov. 1985.
Sherwood, Charles G.  Letter to the author.  29 Sept.
      1986.
```

CITING: APA STYLE

The American Psychological Association (APA) supplies a guide to the style most commonly used in the social sciences. This style is set forth in its *Publication Manual,* 3rd ed. (Washington, DC: APA, 1983). As in the newest MLA style, APA citations are made in parentheses in the body of the text.

Citing Printed Sources

A WORK BY A SINGLE AUTHOR

```
A number of experts now believe that cognitive develop-
ment begins much earlier than Piaget had thought (Gelman,
1978).
```

Notice that, because it is often necessary to refer to a whole study, only the author's name and the publication year are generally included in the citation. If the author's name appears in the body of the text, only the date is given in parentheses.

```
As Gelman (1978) points out, a number of experts now be-
lieve that cognitive development begins much earlier than
Piaget had thought.
```

If you do refer to a specific page, use "p." and set it off with a comma.

```
Dean Rusk's exposure to Nazi power in Europe in the 1930s
seems to have permanently influenced his attitude toward
appeasement (Karnow, 1983, p. 179).
```

When the author's name appears in the text, the page number still belongs in parentheses after the cited material.

```
Karnow (1983) maintains that Dean Rusk's exposure to Nazi
power in Europe in the 1930s "scarred his mind" (p. 179).
```

If you set off a long quotation in a block, the author's name and the publication year can follow the quotation with no additional period. (These are Karnow's actual words about Dean Rusk, former U.S. secretary of state.)

> At least one critic maintains that Dean Rusk's exposure to Nazi power in Europe in the 1930s permanently influenced his attitude toward appeasement:
>
>> Then came the moment that transformed his life and his thinking. He won a Rhodes scholarship to Oxford. More important, his exposure to Europe in the early 1930s, as the Nazis consolidated their power in Germany, scarred his mind, leading him to share Acheson's hostility to appeasement in any form anywhere.   (Karnow, 1983)

A WORK WITH TWO AUTHORS

Refer to coauthors by their last names, in the order in which they appear in the book or article you cite. (This is especially important in the sciences, where the person whose name comes first is generally the main researcher.) Join the names by "and" if they appear in the body of the text, by an ampersand ("&") if they are in parentheses.

> Ex-mental patients released from institutions but given no follow-up care will almost surely fail to cope with the stresses of living on their own (Bassuk & Gerson, 1978).

> Bassuk and Gerson (1978) hold out little hope for ex-mental patients who are released from institutions but are given no follow-up care.

A WORK WITH MULTIPLE AUTHORS

When a book or article you cite has three or more authors (but fewer than six), include all the last names in your first reference only. In referring to the same source again, use the first author's name only, followed by "et al.," which means "and others." For *more* than six authors, use "et al." even in the first reference.

> In one study, the IQs of adopted children were found to correlate more closely with the IQs of their biological mothers than with those of their adoptive mothers (Horn, Loehlin, & Wellerman, 1975).

```
Later studies have challenged the genetic view advanced
by Wesson et al. (1978) by citing, among other things,
selective placement on the part of adoption agencies.
```

A WORK BY A CORPORATE AUTHOR

In the first citation, use the full name of the corporate author in parentheses.

```
There are three signs of oxygen deprivation (American Red
Cross, 1974).
```

A GOVERNMENT DOCUMENT

A citation in your text, at the end of a sentence, would simply identify the document by originating agency, as given in the reference list, followed by its abbreviation (if any) and year of publication (and page number, if appropriate).

```
Clearly, it is of paramount importance to stop the spread
of mosquito-borne diseases (Department of Health and
Human Services [DHHS], 1986, p. 25).
```

Later citations would use just the abbreviation for the agency and the date (DHHS, 1986).

AN ANONYMOUS WORK

When you cite an anonymous work, such as a pamphlet or an unsigned newspaper article, identify it with a short title and a date.

```
There are questions people can ask themselves if they
suspect their drinking has gotten out of hand
(Alcoholism, 1986).
```

MULTIPLE WORKS BY THE SAME AUTHOR

Identifying sources with dates is especially useful when you need to cite more than one work by the same author.

```
One nuclear energy proponent for years has insisted on
the importance of tight controls for the industry (Wein-
berg, 1972). . . . He goes so far as to call on utility
companies to insure each reactor with their own funds
(Weinberg, 1977).
```

When citing two or more sources written by the same author during the same year, arrange the titles alphabetically in the reference list (see pp. 465–466) and identify each with a lowercase letter placed after the date (1976a, 1976b, 1976c, and so on). Identify them the same way in your text. Here the book referred to is Stephen H. Schneider's *The Genesis Strategy*.

```
Those who advocate the "genesis strategy" would have the
world store up food in preparation for future climatic
changes (Schneider, 1976b).
```

MULTIPLE WORKS IN THE SAME ENTRY
Refer to works by different authors in alphabetical order, and include the
dates of the studies you cite.

```
Several studies (Bassuk & Gerson, 1978; Miller, 1977;
Thompson, 1980) blame society for the plight of homeless
mental patients.
```

Citing Nonprint Sources

Mention nonprint sources in the same style as print sources.

PERSONAL INTERVIEWS
Personal communications are not given in the reference list according to
APA style. But in the text of your paper, you should include the initials and
surname of your communicator, with the date remembered as exactly as
possible.

```
C. G. Sherwood (personal communication, September 29,
1986) has specific suggestions about the market in
Belgium.
```

```
It is important to keep in mind the cultural differences
between countries, especially in this case the differ-
ences between the United States and Belgium (C. G. Sher-
wood, personal communication, September 29, 1986).
```

LISTING: APA STYLE

If you're using APA guidelines (which you might do in listing both field and
library materials), each entry should contain most of the same information
given in an MLA citation, but the format is slightly different. In the APA style,
the list of works cited is called "References" and appears at the end of the
text. For entries that run past the first line, indent subsequent lines three
spaces.

Listing Printed Sources

Organize your list alphabetically by author. The year appears immediately
following the author's name, in parentheses. In the title only the first word,

proper names, and the word following a colon are capitalized. For the author's first and middle names, only initials are used. Note that APA style uses a more complete name for a publisher (including "Press") than does MLA style.

A WORK BY A SINGLE AUTHOR

```
Karnow, S. (1983).  Vietnam: A history.  New York: Viking
     Press.
```

A WORK WITH TWO OR MORE AUTHORS

In a work with multiple authors, all authors' names are inverted and they are separated by commas.

```
Miller, G. A., Galanter, E., & Pribram, K. H.  (1960).
     Plans and the structure of behavior.  New York: Holt,
     Rinehart and Winston.
```

A WORK BY A CORPORATE AUTHOR

Books with corporate authors are treated very much like books with individual authors.

```
American Red Cross.  (1974).  Lifesaving: Rescue and
     water safety.  New York: Doubleday.
```

A GOVERNMENT DOCUMENT

To list a government publication in your reference list in accord with APA style, start with the name of the department and then give the date of publication, the title (and author, if any), identifying number, and publisher.

```
Department of Health and Human Services.  (1986).
     Mosquito control measures in Gulf Coast states (DHHW
     Publication No. F 82-06000): Washington, DC: U.S. Gov-
     ernment Printing Office.
```

AN ANONYMOUS WORK

List an anonymous book, pamphlet, or news article by its full title.

```
Alcoholism and you.  (1986).  Pearl Island: Okra Press.
```

MULTIPLE WORKS BY THE SAME AUTHOR,
PUBLISHED DURING THE SAME YEAR

Arrange the titles alphabetically and identify their order with lowercase letters beginning with "a."

```
Schneider, S. H.  (1976a).  Climate change and the world
     predicament: A case study for interdisciplinary
     research.  Boulder, CO: National Center for Atmos-
     pheric Research.
```

Schneider, S. H.   (1976b).   The genesis strategy: Climate
    and global survival.   New York: Plenum Press.

A WORK IN AN EDITED COLLECTION

For one selection from a book with an editor, proceed as follows.

Lewontin, R. C.   (1976).   Race and intelligence.   In
    N. J. Block & G. Dworkin (Eds.), The IQ controversy
    (pp. 78-92).   New York: Pantheon.

AN ARTICLE IN A PERIODICAL

If in your paper you cited an article from a periodical that paginates
continuously throughout a single year, the reference listing looks as follows.
Note that the volume number is underlined.

Gelman, R.   (1978).   Cognitive development.   Annual
    Review of Psychology, 29, 297-332.

If a periodical paginates each issue separately, the listing should be as follows.

Bassuk, E. L., & Gerson, S.   (1978, February).   Deinsti-
    tutionalization and mental health services.
    Scientific American, pp. 46-53.

A NEWSPAPER ARTICLE

Auerbach, J. D.   (1986, June 22).   Nuclear freeze at a
    crossroads.   The Boston Globe, p. A19.

Listing Nonprint Sources

Nonprint sources appear alphabetically in your "References" along with
printed works.

RECORDINGS

Mencken, H. L.   (Interviewee), with Donald Howe Kirkley,
    Sr. (Interviewer).   (1960).   H. L. Mencken speaking
    (Record No. TC 1082).   New York: Caedmon.

VIDEOTAPES, AUDIOTAPES, SLIDES

Wildlife Research Group (Producer).   (1986).   Wildlife
    conservation.   [Sound filmstrip].

The location and name of the distributor, if they are known, appear at the
end of the citation.

COMPUTER PROGRAMS

When documenting computer programs, include the same information as in the MLA citations, with the addition of the city of origin. If the author is known, his or her name appears first, and the title of the software appears after the date, followed immediately (without an intervening period) by the bracketed description of the source.

```
Business systems.  (1985).  [Computer program].  Barton,
     CA: Regis Software.
```

PERSONAL COMMUNICATIONS

The newest APA guidelines suggest omitting personal communications (interviews, letters, memos, phone conversations, and so on) from the reference list because they do not provide recoverable data. You would of course mention such sources in the body of your paper—even if you do so simply, as Jamie Merisotis does in reporting his conversations with bail bondsmen ("One bondsman stated . . .").

PART FOUR

STRATEGIES:
A REFERENCE
MANUAL

The following six chapters constitute a manual offering special advice on strategies. The word *strategy* may remind you of warfare: in the original Greek sense of the word, it is a way to win a battle. Writing a college paper, you'll probably agree, is a battle of a kind. In this manual you'll find an array of small weapons to use—perhaps some heavy artillery.

Here are techniques you can learn, methods you can follow, good practices you can observe in writing more effectively. Earlier in this book, you saw many of these strategies briefly mentioned. At moments when we didn't want to slow you down by explaining them in detail, we gave them a mere passing glance. We would now like to give them the discussion they deserve.

No strategy will appeal to every writer, and no writer uses every one for every writing task. Outlining is a strategy that has rescued many a writer from getting lost, but we know writers who never outline except to make (sometimes) the roughest of lists.

You won't need to read this manual all the way through. It is meant only to refer to when you need it. If you care to browse in it, we trust you'll find reward—especially if you try out some of these strategies.

CHAPTER 15

Strategies for Generating Ideas

First, here are two useful techniques for starting ideas flowing and recalling information: brainstorming and freewriting. Then comes advice on the valuable habit of journal keeping, a great way to ensure a constant supply of ideas. Last in this chapter, "Asking a Reporter's Questions" and "Seeking Motives" suggest ways to probe deeply into events, phenomena, and human acts.

BRAINSTORMING

When you brainstorm, you start with a word or phrase that might launch your thoughts in some direction. For a set length of time, putting the conscious, analytical part of your mind on hold, you scribble a list of ideas as rapidly as possible. Then you look over the often surprising results.

For a college writing assignment, you might brainstorm to find a specific topic for a paper. If at any time in writing you need to generate some needed piece of material such as an illustration or example, you can brainstorm. If you have already written a paper, you can brainstorm to come up with a title for it.

Brainstorming can be a group activity. In the business world, brainstorming sessions are common strategies to fill a specific need: a name for a product, a corporate emblem, a slogan for an advertising campaign. Members of a group sit facing one another. They designate one person as the recording secretary to take down on paper or a blackboard whatever suggestions the others offer. If the suggestions fly too thick and fast, the secretary jots down the best one in the air at that moment. For several minutes, people call out ideas. Then they look over the secretary's list in hopes of finding useful results.

You can try group brainstorming like that with a few other students. But you may find brainstorming also useful when, all by yourself, you need to shake an idea out of your unconscious. Here is how one student did just that. On the opening day of a writing course, Martha Calbick's instructor assigned a paper from recall: "Demonstrate that the invention of the computer has significantly changed our lives." Following the instructor's advice, Calbick went home and brainstormed. First, she wrote the key word *computer* at the top of a sheet of paper. Then she set her alarm clock to sound in fifteen minutes and began to scribble away. The first thing she recalled was how her kid brother sits by the hour in front of a home computer playing Wizardry, a Dungeons and Dragons kind of game. The first recollection quickly led, by free association, to several more.

> Wizardry
> my kid bro. thinks computers are for kids
> always trading games with other kids—
>   software pirates
> Mother says it's too bad kids don't play
>   Wiffle Ball anymore
> in 3rd grade they teach programming
> hackers
> some get rich
> Ed's brother-in-law—wrote a program for
>   accountants
> become a programmer? big future?
> guided missiles
> computers in subway stations—print tickets
> banks—shove in your plastic card
> a man lucked out—deposited $100—computer
>   credited him with $10,000
> sort mail—zip codes
> computers print out grades
> my report card showed a D instead of a B—
>   big fight to correct it
> are we just numbers now?

When her alarm clock rang, Calbick dropped her pencil and took a coffee break. When she returned to her desk, she was pleased to find that a few of her random thoughts suggested directions that interested her. Much of the list she immediately discarded, going through it with a pencil and crossing out most entries. She didn't have any interest in Wizardry, and she didn't feel she knew enough to write about missiles. She circled the question "are we just numbers now?" It looked promising. Maybe some of the other ideas she had listed might express that very idea, such as the mindlessness of the computer that had credited the man with $10,000. As she looked over the list, she began jotting down more thoughts, making notes on the list and adding to it. "Dealing with computers isn't dealing with people," she wrote next to the circled question. From her rough-and-ready list, an idea was beginning to emerge.

Calbick was later to write a whole paper on the simple computer error in her high school office that had momentarily robbed her of a good grade. She recalled how time-consuming it had been to have that error corrected. She mentioned a few other cases of computer error, including that of the man who had struck it rich at the bank. Her conclusion was a wry complaint about computerized society: "A computer knows your name and number, but it doesn't know who you are."

You can see how brainstorming typically works and how it started one student going. Whenever you try brainstorming, you might follow these bits of advice.

1. *Start with a key word or phrase*—one that will head your thoughts in the direction you wish to pursue.

2. *Set yourself a time limit.* Fifteen or twenty minutes is long enough—brainstorming can be strenuous.

3. *Write rapidly.* List any other words, any thoughts, phrases, fragments, or short sentences that surface in connection with your key word. Keep your entries brief.

4. *Don't stop.* While you're brainstorming, don't worry about misspelling, repetition, absurdity, or irrelevance. Write down whatever comes into your head, as fast as your pencil will go. Now is not the time to analyze or to throw any suggestion away. Let your unconscious run free. Never mind if it comes up with ideas that seem crazy or far out. Don't judge, don't arrange—just produce. If your mind goes blank, keep your pencil moving, even if you are only repeating what you've just written.

When you finish, look over your list to see what may be interesting. Circle or check anything you want to think about further. If anything looks useless, scratch it out.

Look over your edited list. You can now do some conscious organizing. Do any of the thoughts you have generated link together? Can you group them? If so, maybe they will suggest a topic. If you succeed in finding a topic from your brainstorming session, you might then wish to try another technique—*freewriting* (the next strategy we discuss).

If you are writing and you need an example—some specific thing—you can brainstorm at any time. In writing her paper on computers Martha Calbick couldn't think of a name for a typical computer store. She wrote down some real names she knew (Computer World, Computerland, OnLine Computers Plus), and those triggered a few imaginary ones. Within three minutes, she hit on one she liked: Byte City.

Whether you brainstorm at your writing desk or in a lounge with a group of friends, you will find this strategy calling up a rich array of thoughts from knowledge, memory, and imagination. Try it and see.

FREEWRITING

Like brainstorming, freewriting is a way to fight writer's block by tapping your unconscious. To freewrite, you simply begin writing in the hope that good ideas will assert themselves. You write without stopping for fifteen or twenty minutes, trying to keep words pouring forth in a steady flow. Freewriting differs from brainstorming: in freewriting you write not a list but a series of sentences. They don't have to be grammatical or coherent or stylish sentences; just let them leap to the paper and keep them flowing along. When you have just the beginning of an idea, freewriting can help open it up and show you what it contains. When you have an assignment that looks difficult, freewriting can get you under way.

Generally, freewriting is most productive if it has an aim. You have in mind—at least roughly—some topic, a purpose, or a question you want answered. Before you begin, you write a sentence or two summing up the idea you're starting out with. Martha Calbick, who found a topic by brainstorming (p. 472), headed the page on which she freewrote with the topic she had decided to pursue: "How life in the computer age seems impersonal." Then, exploring some of the rough ideas she had jotted down in her brainstorming session, she let words flow rapidly.

> Computers—so how do they make life impersonal? You push in your plastic card and try to get some cash. Just a glassy screen. That's different—not like looking at a human teller behind a window. When the computer tells you you have no money left in your account, that's terrible, frightening. Worse than when a person won't cash your check. At least the person looks you in the face, maybe even gives you a faint smile. Computers make mistakes, don't they? That story in the paper about a man—in Utica, was it?—who deposited a hundred dollars to his account and the computer misplaced a decimal point and said he had put in $10,000.

The result, as you can see, wasn't polished prose. It was full of false starts down distracting alleys and little asides to herself that she later crossed out. Still, in twenty minutes she produced a rough draft that served (with much rewriting) as the basis for her finished essay.

If you want to try freewriting for yourself, here's what you do.

1. *Write a sentence or two at the top of your page:* the idea you plan to develop by freewriting.

2. *For at least ten minutes, write steadily without stopping.* Start by expressing whatever comes to mind, even if it is only "I don't want to write a paper because I have nothing at all to say about any subject in the universe." If your mind goes blank, write, "My mind is blank, I have nothing to say, I don't know where to go next," and keep at it until some new thought floats into view.

3. *Don't censor yourself.* Don't stop to cross out false starts, misspellings, or grammatical errors. Never mind if your ideas have gaps between them. Later, when you look them over, some of the gaps may close. If you can't think of the word that perfectly expresses your meaning, put in a substitute. At least it will keep your pencil moving.

4. *Feel free to explore.* That sentence (or those sentences) you started with can serve as a rough guide, but they shouldn't be a straitjacket. If as you write you stray from your original idea, that change in direction may possibly be valuable. Sometimes, you may discover a more promising idea.

Some writers prepare for freewriting. They find it pays to spend a few prior minutes in thought. While you wait for the moment when your pencil is to start racing, some of these questions may be worth asking yourself.

What interests you about this topic? What aspects of it do you most care about?

What does this topic have to do with you?

What do you recall about it from your own experience? What do you know about it that the next person doesn't?

What have you read about it?

What have you observed about it for yourself?

Have you ever talked with anyone about it? If you have, what did you find out?

How might you feel about this topic if you were someone else? (You might try thinking about it from the imagined point of view of a friend, a parent, an instructor, a person of the opposite sex, a person from another country.)

At the very least, your freewriting session may give you something to rewrite and make stronger. You can prod and poke at the parts that look most interesting to see if they will further unfold. In expanding and developing what you have produced by freewriting, here are a few questions you might ask.

What do you mean by that?

What interests you in that idea?

If that is true, what then?

What other examples or evidence does this statement call to mind?

What objections might your reader raise to this?

How might you answer them?

KEEPING A JOURNAL

If you are already in the habit of keeping a journal, consider yourself lucky. If not, now is a good time to begin. Journal writing offers rich rewards to anyone who engages in it every day or several times a week. All you need is a notebook, a writing implement, and a few minutes for each entry; and you can write anywhere. There are students whose observations, jotted down during a bus ride, turned into remarkable journal entries. Not only is journal writing satisfying in itself, a journal can also be a storehouse of material to write about.

What do you write? The main thing to remember is that a journal is not a diary. When you make a journal entry, the emphasis is less on recording what happened than on *reflecting* about what you do or see, hear or read, learn or believe. A journal is a record of your thoughts, for an audience of one: yourself.

In a journal you can plan your life, try out ideas, vent fears and frustrations. The following passage, from *The Journals of Sylvia Plath* (New York: Doubleday, 1982), was written in the early 1950s when the poet was a college freshman. Uncommonly sensitive and colorful, her journal exhibits the freedom and frankness of a writer who was writing for only her own eyes. In this entry she contrasts the happy fantasy world she inhabited as a child with the harsher realities of college life.

> After being conditioned as a child to the lovely never-never land of magic, of fairy queens and virginal maidens, of little princes and their rosebushes, of poignant bears and Eeyore-ish donkeys, of life personalized as the pagans loved it, of the magic wand, and the faultless illustrations—the beautiful dark-haired child (who was you) winging through the midnight sky on a star-path . . . of the Hobbit and the dwarves, gold-belted with blue and purple hoods, drinking ale and singing of dragons in the caverns of the valley—all this I knew, and felt, and believed. All this was my life when I was young. To go from this to the world of grown-up reality. . . . To feel the sex organs develop and call loud to the flesh; to become aware of school, exams (the very words as unlovely as the sound of chalk shrilling

on the blackboard), bread and butter, marriage, sex, compatibility, war, economics, death, and self. What a pathetic blighting of the beauty and reality of childhood. Not to be sentimental, as I sound, but why the hell are we conditioned into the smooth strawberry-and-cream Mother Goose world, Alice-in-Wonderland fable, only to be broken on the wheel as we grow older and become aware of ourselves as individuals with a dull responsibility in life? To learn snide and smutty meanings of words you once loved, like "fairy." To go to college fraternity parties where a boy buries his face in your neck or tries to rape you if he isn't satisfied with burying his fingers in the flesh of your breast. To learn that there are a million girls who are beautiful and that each day more leave behind the awkward teenage stage, as you once did, and embark on the adventure of being loved. . . . To be aware that you must compete somehow, and yet that wealth and beauty are not in your realm.

Like Plath, to write a valuable journal you need only the honesty and the willingness to set down what you *genuinely think and feel.* When you first face that blank journal page, plunge boldly into your task by writing down whatever observation or reaction comes to mind, in any order you like. No one will criticize your spelling or punctuation, the way you organize or the way you express yourself. A journal entry can be a list or an outline, a paragraph or a full-blown essay.

To know what to put into your journal, you have only to *un*cover, *re*cover, *dis*cover what is happening both inside and outside your head. Describe a person or a place. As accurately as you can, set down a conversation you have heard, complete with slang or dialect or colloquialisms. Record any insights you have gained into your actions or those of others. Make comparisons. Respond to something you have read or to something mentioned in a class. Do you agree with it? Disagree? Why? What was wrong with the last movie or television show you watched? What was good about it? Have you or has someone you know faced a moral dilemma? Was it resolved? If so, how?

Perhaps you have some pet peeves. List them. What do you treasure? Have you had an interesting dream or daydream? What would the world be like if you were in charge? What are your religious convictions? What do you think about the current political scene or about this nation's priorities? Have you visited any foreign countries? Did you learn anything of worth from your travels?

On days when your mind is sluggish, when you can come up with no observations or insights to record, do a stint of freewriting or of brainstorming in your journal, or just describe a scene, an object, or a person present before you. Any of those activities may result in at least a few good thoughts to follow up in future entries.

One further benefit rewards the faithful journal keeper. Well done, a journal is a mine studded with priceless nuggets: thoughts and observations, reactions and revelations that are yours for the taking. When you have an essay to write, chances are you will find that a well-stocked journal is a treasure indeed. Rifle it freely—not only for writing topics, but for insights and material. It can make your writing assignments far easier to fulfill. "This book is my savings bank," wrote Ralph Waldo Emerson in his journal. "I grow richer because I have somewhere to deposit my earnings; and fractions are worth more to me because corresponding fractions are waiting here that shall be made integers by their addition." Emerson refers to his personal writing process. In many of his lectures and essays, he would combine thoughts that had begun as disconnected entries. From the savings bank of his journal, the nineteenth-century Yankee philosopher made heavy withdrawals.

Your journal can also be used for the warm-up writing you do when you start collecting your thoughts in preparation for any assignment, whether short or long. In it you can group ideas, scribble outlines, sketch beginnings, capture stray thoughts, record relevant material from any one of the writer's five resources (recalling, observing, reading, conversing, imagining) that bear on your assignment.

A journal can be a catch-all or miscellany, like Emerson's, or it can be a focused, directed thing. Some instructors assign students to keep journals of their readings in a certain discipline. Faced with a long paper to write, and weeks or months to do it in, you might wish to assign *yourself* to keep a specialized journal. If, say, you were going to write a survey of current economic theories or an account of the bird life of your locality, you might keep a journal of economists whose work you read or the birds you are able to observe. Then, when the time comes to write your paper, you will have plenty of material to quarry.

ASKING A REPORTER'S QUESTIONS

News reporters, assembling facts with which to write the story of a news event, ask themselves six simple questions, the five *W*'s—

Who?
What?
Where?
When?
Why?

—and an *H:* How? In the *lead,* or opening (and most important) paragraph of a good news story, where the writer tries to condense the whole story into a sentence, you will find simple answers to all six questions:

The ascent of a giant homemade fire balloon (*what*)
startled residents of Costa Mesa (*where*)
last night (*when*)
as Ambrose Barker, 79, (*who*)

in an attempt to set a new altitude record, (*why*)
zigzagged across the sky at a speed of nearly 300 miles per hour. (*how*)

Such answers don't go deep. In a few words, they give only the bare bones of the story. If readers want to learn more, they keep reading. But answering the questions enables the writer to seize all the essentials of the story and give them to us in brief.

Later in a news story, the reporter will relate in greater detail what happened. He or she can dig and probe and make the story more interesting. With a little thought on the reporter's part, the six basic questions can lead to further questions, generating more to write about than space will allow.

WHO is Ambrose Barker, anyway? (An amateur balloonist? A jack-of-all-trades? A retired professional aeronautical engineer?) Is he a major figure in balloonist circles? (Call a professional balloonist and ask, "Who is this Ambrose Barker? Ever hear of him?") What kind of person is he: a serious student of ballooning or a reckless nitwit? What do his neighbors and his family think of him? (Interview them.) What words spoken by Barker himself will show the kind of person he is? Is he proud of his flight? Humble? Disappointed? Determined to try again? What was his mental state at the moment he took off? (Elated and determined? Crazed? Inebriated?)

WHAT happened, exactly? Was Barker or anyone else hurt? What did his craft look like from close up? (How big was it? Any distinguishing features?) What did it look like to a spectator on the ground? (Did it resemble a shooting star? A glowing speck? Did it light up the whole sky?) Did Barker's flight terrify anybody? Did the police receive any phone calls? Did the nearest observatory? What has happened since the flight? (Will anyone sue Barker for endangering life and property? Will the police press charges against him? Has he received any threats, any offers to endorse products?)

WHERE did Barker take off from? (A ballfield? A parking lot? His back yard? What is his exact street address?) From where to where did he fly? Where did he land? Where did the onlookers live? In what neighborhoods? How far off was the most distant observer who sighted Barker's balloon? (Was it visible, say, from forty miles?)

WHEN, by the clock, did the flight take place? (What time did Barker take off? How long was he aloft? Exactly when did he touch down again?) Was the choice of evening for the flight deliberate? (Barker could have gone up in the daytime. Did he want to fly by night to be more noticeable?) Did he deliberately choose this particular time of year? When did Barker first conceive his plan to tour Costa Mesa in a fire balloon? (Just the other day? Or has he been planning his trip for thirty years?)

WHY did Barker want to set a record? What impelled him? What reasons did he give? (And might he have had any reasons other than the ones he gave?) Why did he wait till he was seventy-nine to take off? Was making such a flight a lifelong dream? Did he feel the need to soar above the crowd? Did he want his neighbors to stop laughing at him ("That thing will never get off the ground . . .")? Why did his balloon zigzag across the sky, not sail in a straight line? Why were spectators terrified (if they were)?

HOW did Barker make his odd craft airborne? What propelled it into the sky? (A bonfire? Jet fuel? Gunpowder?) Did he take off without aid, or did his wife or a friend assist? How did he construct the balloon: where did he get the parts? Did he make the whole thing with his own two hands or have help? How did he steer the craft? How did he land it? Was the landing smooth or did he come down in a heap? How was he greeted when he arrived?

Your topic in a college writing task may be less spectacular than a fire balloon ascent: a team winning or losing a pennant, an experience of your own, an ancestor's arrival in America. It might be what happened at some moment in history (the firing on Fort Sumter at the start of the Civil War) or in social history (the rise of rock music). The six basic questions will work in discovering how to write about all sorts of events and phenomena; and, given thought, your six basic questions can lead to many more.

Don't worry if some of the questions lead nowhere. Just try answering any that look promising: jot down any thoughts and information that come to you. At first, you can record these unselectively. You are just trying to gather a big bunch of ideas and material. Later, before you start to write, you'll want to weed out the bunch and keep only those buds that look as though they might just open wide.

SEEKING MOTIVES

In a surprisingly large part of your college writing, you try to explain human behavior. In a paper for history, you might show why Lyndon Baines Johnson decided not to seek a second full term as president. In a report for a psychology course, you might try to explain the behavior of people in an experimental situation. In a literature course, writing of Nathaniel Hawthorne's *The Scarlet Letter,* you might analyze the motives of Hester Prynne: why does she conceal the name of her illegitimate child's father? Because people, including characters in fiction, are so complex, this task is challenging. But here is a strategy useful in seeking out human motives.

If you want to better understand any human act, according to philosopher-critic Kenneth Burke, you can analyze its components. To do so, you ask five questions. (To produce useful answers, your subject has to be an act performed for a reason, not a mere automatic reaction like a sneeze.)

What was done?
Who did it?
What means did the person use to make it happen?
Where and when did it happen and in what circumstances?
What possible purpose or motive can you attribute to the person?

Answering those questions starts a writer generating ideas. Burke names the five components as follows.

1. The *act.*
2. The *actor:* the person who acted.
3. The *agency:* the means or instrument the actor used to make the act happen. (If the act is an insult, the agency might be words or a slap in the face; if it is murder, the agency might be a sawed-off shotgun.)
4. The *scene:* where the act took place, when, and in what circumstances.
5. The *purpose:* the motive for acting.

As you can see, Burke's *pentad,* or set of five categories, covers much the same ground as the news reporter's five *W*'s and an *H.* But Burke's method differs in that it can show how these components of a human act affect one another. This line of thought can take you deeper into the motives for human behavior than most reporters' investigations ever go.

How might the method be applied? Say you are writing a paper to explain your own reasons for taking some action. Burke's list of the components of an act may come in handy. Let's take, for example, the topic "Why I Enrolled in Prelaw Courses." You might analyze it like this:

1. The *act* is your decision.
2. The *actor*—that's you.
3. The *agency* is your enrolling in college and beginning a program of study.
4. The *scene* is your home last spring (where the circumstances might have included many earnest, knock-down, drag-out discussions with your family on the subject of what you should study in college).
5. The *purpose* is at least twofold: to make comfortable money and to enter a career you expect to find satisfying.

What happens when you start thinking about what each of these factors had to do with any other? What if you ask, say, "How did the *scene* of my decision influence the *actor* (me)?"

You may then recall that your father, who always wanted to be a racing car driver himself, tried to talk you out of your decision and urged you to hang around racetracks instead. In arguing with him you were forced to defend your notion of studying law. You came to see that, yes, by George, being a lawyer would be a great life for you. Maybe your brother was on the scene, too, and he said, "Why don't you go to law school? You always were a hard-liner in arguments." Maybe that was a factor in your decision. You can pursue this line of thought. Then maybe you can try making another link: between scene and purpose. Ask, "How did my home motivate me?" Maybe then you realize that your brother gave you a real purpose: to show the world how well you can argue. Maybe you realize that your decision to go to law school was a way to prove to your father that you don't need to be a racing car driver—you can make good in a different career.

This example, to be sure, may not fit you personally. Perhaps you don't live with a father or a brother, and you can't stand the thought of studying law. But the point is that you can begin all sorts of fruitful lines of inquiry simply by asking questions that team up these components. Following Burke's method, you can pair them in ten ways:

actor to act	act to scene	scene to agency
actor to scene	act to agency	scene to purpose
actor to agency	act to purpose	agency to purpose
actor to purpose		

If you wish to understand this strategy, try writing one question for each pair; for example, for the first pair, "What does the actor have to do with the scene?" If you were writing about your move to study law, this question might be put: "Before I made my move, what connection existed, if any, between me and this college?" Try to answer that question and you may sense ideas beginning to percolate. "Why," you might say, "I came here because I know a good lawyer who graduated from the place." You'll get a head start on your writing assignment if, while trying to answer the questions, you take notes.

The questions will serve equally well for analyzing someone else's motives. If you were trying to explain, for a history course, why President Johnson chose not to run again, the five elements might perhaps be these.

Act: Announcing the decision to leave office without standing for reelection.

Actor: President Johnson.

Agency: A televised address to the nation.

Scene (including circumstances at the time): Washington, D.C., March 31, 1968. Protesters against the nation's involvement in Vietnam were gaining in numbers and influence. The press was increasing its criticism of the president's escalation of the war. Senator Eugene McCarthy, an antiwar candidate for president, had made a strong showing against Johnson in the New Hampshire primary election.

Purpose: Think of any *possible* purposes: to avoid a probable political defeat, to escape further personal attacks, to spare his family, to make it easier for his successor to pull the country out of the war, to ease bitter dissent among Americans.

If you started asking questions such as "What did the actor have to do with the agency?" you might come up with an answer like "Johnson apparently enjoyed facing the nation on television. Commanding the attention of a vast audience, he must have felt he was in control—even though his ability to control the situation in Vietnam was slipping."

Do you see the possibilities? The value of Burke's questions is that they can start you writing. Not all the questions will prove fruitful, and some may not even apply. But one or two might reveal valuable answers. Try them and see.

CHAPTER 16

Strategies for Shaping a Draft

Starting to write often seems a chaotic activity, but when you shape a draft, you try to reduce the chaos and create order. In doing so, you can use the strategies in this chapter.

In general, especially when writing a paper that calls for critical thinking, you'll shape your draft around one central point (see "Stating a Thesis"). In nearly any kind of writing task, you can organize your thoughts by various strategies (see "Grouping Your Ideas" and "Outlining"). You can develop good, meaty, well-unified paragraphs, trying for an opening that will enlist your readers' attention and a conclusion that will satisfy them. You can supply clear, pointed examples. (All these matters will be dealt with under "Paragraphing.") Another way to give an example will be briefly discussed in "Telling a Story."

STARTING TO WRITE

For most writers, the hardest part of writing comes first: the moment when they confront a blank sheet of paper. Fortunately, you can do much to get ready for it. Sometimes a simple trick or a playful change of your writing circumstances will ease you over that hard part and get you smoothly rolling along.

Experienced writers have many tested techniques to get moving. Many of the suggestions that follow may strike you as useless and far-out, even silly, but all have worked for some writers. Some work for us, and we hope a few will work for you.

Unless getting started is never a problem for you, we invite you to browse through this list. We've sorted the suggestions into three kinds:

1. Setting up circumstances in which you feel comfortable and ready to write
2. Preparing your mind
3. Making the start of a writing job gamelike and enjoyable

You may care to check or underline or highlight any suggestions that look useful. You're the only writer who can know which ideas might work for you.

Setting up Circumstances

Get comfortable.   We don't just mean turn on a bright light because it's good for your eyes; why not create an environment? If you can write only with your shoes off or with a can of Orange Crush, by all means set yourself up that way. Some writers need a radio blaring heavy metal, others need quiet. Circumstances that put you in the mood for writing can encourage you.

Exhaust your excuses.   Most writers are born experts at coming up with reasons not to write; and if you are one of those writers, you might find that it helps to run out of reasons. Is your room annoyingly jumbled? Straighten it. Drink that can of soda, sharpen those pencils, throw out that trash, make that phone call home. Then, your mind swept clean, you might have to give in and write. (If, after you go through all these steps, you still have good excuses not to write, jot down a list of them. At least you will then be writing.)

Yield to inspiration.   Classical Greek and Roman critics held that a goddess called a Muse would gently touch a poet and leave him inspired. Whether or not you believe in divine inspiration, sometimes ideas, images, metaphors, or vague but powerful urges to write will arrive like sudden miracles. Good writers stay alert for them. When they come, even if you are taking a shower or getting ready to go to a movie, you are wise to yield to impulse and set aside everything else and write. You will find, then, that words will flow with little exertion. Don't feel guilty if friends think you a hermit for declining that movie date. You may be a hermit, but at least you'll be a hermit with a finished paper. If that movie is irresistible, jot down enough notes to rekindle your idea later when you can go back to it.

Relocate.   Try writing in an unfamiliar place: a bowling alley, a bar, a bus station. Passers-by will wonder what you are doing there, scribbling away. Their curiosity might cause you to concentrate hard on your writing, just to show them that you aren't crazy but know what you're doing. We have heard of whole novels written in a cafeteria in midtown Manhattan.

Write in the library. See if you can find a quiet corner where you can work surrounded by heads bowed in concentration. These good examples may start you concentrating too. Keep away from any corner of the library where a bull session is raging.

Write on a schedule. Many writers find that it helps to have a certain predictable time of day to write. This method won't work for all, but it worked marvels for English novelist Anthony Trollope, a crack-of-dawn writer. Each day at 5:30 A.M., Trollope, before he dressed, would seat himself at his writing table, place his watch before him, spend half an hour rereading his work of the previous day, and then write 250 words every fifteen minutes until he had done his daily stint of 2500 words. His literary labors over at 8:30, he would then set off to his job at the General Post Office. "I have found," he noted dryly, "that the 250 words have been forthcoming as regularly as my watch went." (He wrote more than sixty books.) Trollope may have been a compulsive scheduler, but there is much to be said for forming the habit of writing daily. Over the desk of John Updike, a prolific writer of our own day, hangs the motto *Nulla dies sine linea* ("Never a day without a line"), a saying of the Roman writer Pliny. Even if you can't write every day, it may help to declare, first thing in the morning, "All right, today from 11 to 12 I'll sit down and write."

Defy a schedule. On the other hand, if you write on a schedule and your work isn't going well, break out of your usual time frame. If you are an afternoon writer, write at night.

Write early in the morning. Try writing in the small hours when the world is still. Before you are wholly awake, your stern self-critic might not be awake yet either. (When you edit and proofread, though, you might want to be fully awake.) Poet Donald Hall likes to get up at dawn and start writing poems. He says that, his mind being closer to dream, the results are often more surprising and intriguing. Perhaps you might just find yourself staring at blank paper wishing for breakfast, but this technique is worth at least one try.

Write in bed. This technique might help you relax and get more work done— provided you can keep your eyes open. At the helm of Britain during World War II, Winston Churchill usually did a morning's work in bed, reading dispatches and answering them, conducting an extensive correspondence with his generals. Marcel Proust, the French novelist, also liked to write while horizontal.

Change activities. When words won't come, do something quite different from writing for a while. Walk, run, throw a Frisbee, work out at the gym. Exercise refreshes a tired brain with a shot of brand-new oxygen. Sometimes it helps to eat lunch, take in a movie, check out an art exhibit, listen to music, take a nap, or go down to the corner store and watch the cold cut slicer. Sometimes while you're not even thinking about the writing task before you, your unconscious mind will be working on it.

Switch instruments. Change the way your writing feels, looks, and sounds when it hits paper. Are you a typist? Try writing in longhand. If you are an inveterate pen user, type for a change. Try writing with a different kind of pencil or pen: a colored felt-tip, say, or an erasable pen. Try writing on note cards (which are easy to shuffle and rearrange) or on colored paper (yellow second-sheets, by the way, are cheaper than typing paper). Perhaps you'll hit upon a new medium you'll enjoy much more. (Have you tried writing with a word processor?)

Preparing

Discuss your plans. Collar any nearby listener: roommate, student down the hall, spouse, parent, friend. Tell the other person why you want to write this particular paper, what you're going to put into it, how you're going to lay out your material. If the other person says, "That sounds good," you'll be encouraged; but even if the reaction is a yawn, at least you will have set your own thinking in motion.

Shrink your immediate job. Break the writing task into several smaller parts and oblige yourself (for now) to do only the first one. It would look hard to hike cross-country, less hard if you knew you had to go only twenty miles by the first night. Similarly, writing a 750-word paper, you might get going faster if you vow to turn out, say, just the first three paragraphs.

Freewrite. That is, just start out writing a bunch of stuff nonstop. You might start by writing your topic (if you have one) at the top of your paper and then listing the thoughts about it that first come to mind. Or you might just start writing any old thing. Because you will find yourself thinking as you freewrite, any old thing will often find that it wants to head in a certain direction. Novelist Philip Roth once said that when he starts a new book, he has to write many pages before he comes to "a paragraph that's alive." At that moment he tells himself, "Okay, that's your beginning, start there," and he discards all he had previously written: just a warm-up exercise. This method of writing is somewhat like the method that Spanish artist Joan Miró said he practiced in his work: "Rather than starting out to paint something, I begin painting and as I paint, the picture begins to assert itself, or suggest itself under my brush." (For more advice about freewriting and how you can use it to generate ideas, see p. 474.)

Write an angry letter to your instructor.   Tell that (you can think of a name) just what you think of him or her for making you write a piece of foolish trash you don't want to write, that you're never going to write, that you wouldn't write in a million years. Tell that instructor and indeed the whole college what to do with their crummy college degree. Then, having vented your ire, keep writing. (When you turn in your finished paper, leave that letter out of it.)

State your purpose.   In a sentence or a few lines, set forth what you want your paper to achieve. Are you trying to tell a story? If so, what is that story trying to do—prove a point or perhaps simply entertain? Are you trying to explain something? Win a reader over to your way of thinking? Sometimes doing this will define your job and bring blurred thoughts into focus. (For more about stating your purpose, see "Stating a Thesis" on p. 491.)

Read for fun.   Read whatever you feel like reading. The step from reading to writing is a short one. Even when you're just reading for kicks, you start to involve yourself with words. Who knows, you might by pure accident (which tends to happen to some writers) hit upon something useful to your paper.

Read purposefully.   If you have a topic, or an area to search for one, set out to read what's being written about it. As you read, take notes. Naturally, the more you know about your topic, the more securely you will feel on top of it and ready to write.

Try the carrot-and-stick.   This method may work when inspiration is on strike. Like a donkey encouraged to plod toward his destination by a juicy carrot suspended in front of his teeth, promise yourself a reward. Keep it simple: a trip to the vending machine, a walk in the open air, a phone call to a friend, a fifteen-minute visit to a neighbor, a TV show—but only when you arrive at some moment in your labors at which you will truly feel you have earned your reward.

Seek a provocative title.   Write down ten or twenty possible titles for your paper and then, looking over them, decide if any one sounds strikingly good to you. If so, you will probably be encouraged to write something rather than let such a promising title go to waste.

Keep a daily journal.   Use the journal to record your experiences as a writer. You don't want to make this a huge project; we know you have other things to do. But you might be surprised how scribbling in a journal for fifteen minutes a day will nourish your writing. A small (5-by-7-inch) spiral-bound or looseleaf notebook is a nice, unintimidating size. Setting words down on a page becomes an everyday routine. In this, your writer's journal, you might note any writing problems you run into (and overcome), any ideas for things you'd like to write, any reactions to your writing you get from other people, any writing strategies that work well for you, anything about how to write that dawns on you. Journals can be kept for many purposes: a journal to record your reading and your reactions to it, a journal to track your progress in any course you take, a journal in which to save any stray thoughts you care to remember. (For more detailed suggestions about journals, see p. 476.) For a student paper that emerged from a journal kept for a biology class, see Sandy Messina's "Footprints: The Mark of Our Passing" (p. 36).

Doodle. At least you'll be pushing a pencil, even if you are only drawing rabbits, stick figures, or goofy faces. Who can tell? As you sit with pencil in hand, words might start to flow.

Making a Start Enjoyable

Some writers find that if they can just make the art of writing start out playfully, like a game, they will find themselves at work before they know it.

Time yourself. Try being an Anthony Trollope: set out your watch, alarm clock, or egg timer and vow to finish a page of draft before the buzzer sounds or your time expires. Don't stop for anything—if you find yourself writing drivel, which you can always cross out later, just push on. This is a way to prompt yourself to hurry, if your natural bent is to dawdle.

Slow to a crawl. If such speed quotas don't work for you—and some people might find them a source of sheer paralysis—time yourself to write with exaggerated laziness, completing, say, not a page every fifteen minutes, but a sentence. Maybe your speed will improve. At least you'll have a sentence.

Begin badly—on purpose. For fun, begin by writing a deliberately crummy sentence, full of mistakes and misspellings and fuzzy mush-headedness. Then cross it out and write another, better sentence. This technique may help you clear the false starts out of the way quickly so that from then on, your paper can only improve.

Begin on scrap paper. There is something intimidating about a blank white sheet of paper that may have cost two or three cents. Some writers feel reluctant to mess up such a beautiful item. A bit of advice on that score comes from John Legget, novelist, biographer, and former director of the Writer's Workshop at the University of Iowa. To write preliminary notes, he uses the back of an old envelope or other scrap paper from his wastebasket. In this way, he told an interviewer, he is able to get started, feeling no guilt about "spoiling a nice piece of paper with my thoughts."

Tape-record yourself.   Talk a first draft of your paper into a tape recorder. Then play it back. Then write. Unless you are a skilled stenographer (and you have one of those tape recorders with a stop pedal that may be turned off and on easily while you type), you probably would find it hard to transcribe your spoken words, but this technique can sometimes set your mind in motion.

Imagine you're giving a speech.   On your feet, in front of an imaginary cheering crowd, spontaneously utter an opening paragraph. Then—quick!— write it down.

Write in a role.   Pretend you are someone else (your instructor? your best friend? a screen star? some writer whose work you know well?) and write in that person's voice. Or invent an imaginary character and write as that character would. (Be careful to invent a character who might naturally write about your topic. An essay for an economics course, on supply and demand, might well be written in the person of a farmer or a small businessperson but might not go well if written from a punk rocker's point of view.) William York Tindall, a literary scholar and critic, once confided that he had been unable to write his doctoral dissertation, couldn't get a handle on it, until one day he hit upon the notion of writing it as though he were Edward Gibbon, cool and cynical author of *The Decline and Fall of the Roman Empire*. Once he tried on Gibbon's voice, Tindall said, his own writing took off at a brisk clip.

Try the Great Chef method.   According to the legend, the great French chef Escoffier, by smelling a dish of food, could analyze it for its ingredients and then go into his kitchen and duplicate it. In similar fashion, analyze a paragraph by another writer—pick a paragraph you admire—and cook up a new paragraph of your own from its ingredients. Substitute your words for the other writer's, but keep the same number of sentences and keep each about the same length. If the other writer starts with a question, you start with a question. If the other writer uses a quotation, you use a quotation at the same place. The result will smell somewhat like the original, only different.

Write with excessive simple-mindedness.   Do a whole paragraph or a whole paper the way a six-year-old talks: in plain, short, simple sentences. Karin Mack and Eric Skjei, in *Overcoming Writing Blocks*, call this technique "Dick-and-Janing":

> Remember the first books of childhood, with their familiar characters and simple declarative sentences? "See Spot run. Hear Jane laugh. See Zeke rake leaves." Entire stories told in sentences of less than five words each. When you face an especially delicate or difficult writing assignment, you can get the skeleton of a rough draft started by reducing the first few paragraphs to Dick-and-Janese.

Dick-and-Janing works like this. Let's suppose you're writing an essay on some complex topic, say, "Television: Its Influence on Family Life." You might begin: "Television is fun. It brings families together. They all watch *The Cosby Show*. Television is bad. Nobody talks. Nobody says how was your day. They watch the Huxtables' day . . ." and so on. Now, you wouldn't want to turn in a paper written like that; your readers would think you were still in third grade. But you have something down on paper that you can retool.

Address a sympathetic reader.   Write as if you were writing to a close friend. You might even begin, "Dear Friend, How's the hometown treating you? I am writing a paper for an English class that I think you might like to read"—and so on. (You can always cross out that beginning later.) If you have a picture of that friend, place it in front of you.

Begin writing the part you find most appetizing.   Novelist Bill Downey, in a book of advice on writing, *Right Brain . . . Write On!*, urges writers to tackle jobs for which they feel the most excitement. "This makes writing different from childhood," he observes, "when we were forced to eat our vegetables first and then get our dessert. Writers are allowed to have their dessert first." When you begin a writing task, try skipping the tough-looking steak for a while and start with the brownie. Set down the thoughts that come most readily to mind.

RESTARTING

When you have to write a long or demanding essay that you can't finish at one sitting, a special challenge often will arise. If a writing task drags on and on, sometimes you may return to it only to find yourself stalled. You tromp your starter and nothing happens. Your engine seems reluctant to turn over. In such a fix, don't call AAA for a jump-start—try the following suggestions for getting back on the road.

Reread what you have written.   When you return to work, spend a few minutes rereading what you have already written. This method was a favorite of Ernest Hemingway, who, even when writing a novel, would begin a day's work by rereading his manuscript from page 1. Trollope urged this technique on any beginning writer: "By reading what he has last written, just before he recommences his task, the writer will catch the tone and spirit of what he is then saying, and will avoid the fault of seeming to be unlike himself." (Just don't let rereading become a way to evade the writing itself.)

Try snowplowing.   *Snowplowing* is the term invented by Jacqueline Jackson in her book about writing (and other things) *Turn Not Pale, Beloved Snail.*

When you reach a point in a writing job that stops you cold—an obstinate passage or paragraph that won't come right—you imitate a snowplow and charge ahead through the difficulty:

> The plow gets to the bank and can't push it any farther. Then it goes back, revs up, comes barreling along the plowed snow, hits the bank and goes through—or at least a little farther.
>
> I reread the earlier paragraphs . . . and approach the impasse pretending it isn't there. I want to take it by surprise. Then when I'm suddenly upon it, I swerve. I don't reread it, for this would keep me in the same old rut. Instead I start writing madly, on the strength of the new thrust. This often gets me a few sentences farther, sometimes right through the bank.

Pause in midstream.   End a writing session by breaking off in mid-sentence or mid-paragraph. Just leave a sentence trailing off into space, though you may know perfectly well what its closing words should be. That way, when you return to your task, you can sit down and start writing again immediately.

Leave yourself hints for how to continue.   Maybe you're tired—it's been a long day, and you can't write any more. Quit, but if your head still holds any notions you have not yet expressed, jot down quick notes for them. In a few words, tell yourself what you think might come next. Then, when you come back to work, you will face not a blank wall but some rich and suggestive graffiti.

STATING A THESIS

Most pieces of effective writing make one main point. In "What Is a Hunter?" (p. 12), Robert G. Schreiner maintains that anyone who knows no more than how to fire a rifle makes a cruel and stupid hunter. In "The First Person" (p. 221), Suzanne Britt advances the view that writers may use the pronoun *I* without apology. After you have read such an essay, you could sum up its writer's main point in a sentence or (if the idea is large and complicated) in two or three sentences. You might call your summary a *thesis statement.*

Often a thesis—the writer's main point—will be plainly stated in the piece of writing itself. In her defense of the first person, Britt clearly spells out her thesis in her opening paragraph:

> The admonition against "I" is absurd and will, I hope, come to an end in the waning decades of the twentieth century.

Such a thesis statement, which often comes at the beginning or at the end of an essay, helps the reader see the main point unmistakably. In some writing, though, a thesis may simply be implied. Nowhere in David Quammen's "A Republic of Cockroaches" (p. 65) will you find it said that, to survive, the human race must avert nuclear holocaust. But Quammen's whole essay, in demonstrating that cockroaches could inherit the earth, makes the main point painfully evident. You too can imply rather than state your main point in what you write. If you can keep your main idea clearly posted on the bulletin board of your mind, you need not set it down, even for yourself.

At some moment in the writing process, though, many writers find it helpful to jot down a thesis statement. The statement may help them clarify a main idea in their own minds. It may help guide them as they write by reminding them of the point they're driving at. Sometimes, before even setting a word on paper, writers know what main point they intend to make. Such writers feel reassured to know where they are going; for them, to state a thesis may be a good way to break the ice and start words flowing. Other writers will not know their main point until they write. For them, writing is in part an act of discovering a thesis.

Often, during the interplay of a writer's mind, the English language, and a piece of paper, an insight will appear. If this discovery occurs to you, you might wish—at that moment when in the midst of your work your thesis becomes clear to you—to set it down in a statement, even post it over your desk as a friendly reminder. Then it won't get away; and when you finish your draft, the thesis statement will make it easier for you to evaluate what you have written. As you revise, you can reconsider your thesis statement and ask yourself, "Have I made that main point clear?"

Not all writing tasks call for a thesis statement. You may not need one in recalling, say, a memorable personal experience. In telling an entertaining story, writing a letter to a friend, reviewing a book, analyzing a process into its stages, you are not necessarily driving toward a single point. In writing "If I Could Found a College" (p. 127), Jennifer Bowe has no thesis; she simply describes her imagined ideal.

But stating a thesis will often be a useful strategy in explaining and arguing. A thesis statement can help you stay on track and, incorporated into your essay, can help your reader readily see your point. Most writers of research papers find that they can clearly organize their thoughts and their material if they state a thesis (at least to themselves) just as soon as they can decide what their research demonstrates.

Often a good, clear, ample statement of thesis will suggest to you an organization for your ideas. Say you plan to write a paper from the thesis "Despite the several disadvantages of living in a downtown business district, I wouldn't live anywhere else." That thesis statement suggests how to organize an essay. You might start with several paragraphs, each discussing a disadvantage of living in the business district, and then move on to a few paragraphs that discuss advantages. Then close with an affirmation of your fondness for downtown city life.

How do you arrive at a thesis? You have heard a similar question before, worded differently: How do you discover what you want to say? We are back to the age-old problem of college writers that Part One of this book tries to resolve. In every writer's resources—recalling, observing, conversing, reading, and imagining—you can find ideas, including likely main ideas for papers. We have traced the variable, not entirely predictable ways in which you can turn a rough idea into a draft and on into finished writing (in Chapters 1 through 5). For specific techniques to start ideas flowing, you'll find more suggestions in Chapter 15, "Strategies for Generating Ideas."

If you decide to write on the topic "The decline of old-fashioned formal courtesy toward women," you indicate the area to be explored. Still, that topic doesn't really tell you the main point of your paper. What will you try to do in your paper, anyhow? Will you perhaps affirm something, or deny, or recommend? If you stick with that topic about old-fashioned formal courtesy—how women don't need coats or chairs held for them anymore—then (at some point in your writing) you might state a thesis like this: "The new, less formal manners make men respect women more." Or "The new, less formal manners make women respect themselves more because they no longer need to pretend to be helpless." Or (taking a personal view) "I miss the old formal courtesy."

If, to change topics, you plan to describe an old hotel, what possible point will you demonstrate? If you have one already in mind when you start to write, perhaps a thesis sentence might read: "I love the old Raccoon Racket Club: it's quaint and funny, even if it is falling apart, as my description will show." If you are going to compare and contrast two things—for instance, two local newspapers in their coverage of a Senate election—what is the point of that comparison and contrast? One possible thesis statement might be "The *Herald*'s coverage of the Senate elections was more thorough than the *Courier*'s."

As you write, you don't have to cling to a thesis for dear life. Neither must you force every fact to support your thesis, if some facts are reluctant to. You might want to change your thesis while you write. A thesis statement can be tentative. Just to put your *trial* thesis into words can help you to stake out the territory you need to know better. Before you look up more information about wolves, you might guess that you're probably going to maintain the thesis "Wolves are a menace to people and farm animals and ought to be exterminated." Suppose, though, that further reading and conversation don't support that statement at all. Suppose what you learn contradicts it. Your thesis statement isn't chiseled in marble. You can change it to "The wolf, a relatively peace-abiding animal useful in nature's scheme of things, ought to be protected and encouraged to multiply." That's what a thesis is for: to guide you on a quest, not to steer you on a foolish and unheeding march to doom. You can restate it at any time: as you write, as you rewrite, as you rewrite again.

As Suzanne Britt's "The First Person" demonstrates, if you insert your thesis statement into your paper it will alert your reader to your main idea. Perhaps you will want to state your thesis in your opening sentence: "Computers are the greatest help for bashful lovers since Cupid first shot darts."

Or you might want to place this main idea at the very end: "As we have seen, without computer networks, which have proven to be a tremendous boon to shy intellectuals, some poor hackers would probably never find their soulmates at all."

Here are four suggestions for writing a workable thesis statement.

1. *State it exactly* in as detailed and down-to-earth a way as you can. The thesis statement "There are a lot of troubles with chemical wastes" is too huge and general. Are you going to deal with all chemical wastes, through all of history, all over the world? Make the statement more specific: "Careless dumping of leftover paint is to blame for a recent skin rash in Georgia."

2. *State just one central idea.* This proposed thesis sentence has one idea too many: "Careless dumping of leftover paint has caused a serious problem in Georgia, and a new kind of biodegradable paint now looks promising." Either the first half (before the *and*) or the second half of the statement would suffice.

3. *State your thesis positively.* Write "The causes of breast cancer remain a challenge for medical scientists" instead of "Medical scientists do not know what causes breast cancer." The former statement might lead to a paper about an exciting quest. But the latter statement seems to reflect a halfhearted attitude by the writer toward the subject. Besides, to demonstrate that some medical scientists are still working on the problem would be relatively easy: you could show that after an hour doing research in a library. To prove the negative statement, that no medical scientist knows the answer, would be a harder task.

4. *Limit your thesis statement to what it is possible to demonstrate.* A thesis statement should stake out enough territory for you to cover thoroughly inside the assigned word length, and no more. To maintain throughout a 700-word paper the thesis "My favorite tune is 'Good Thing' by Fine Young Cannibals" would be a difficult task unless you could go into voluminous (and interesting) detail. "For centuries, popular music has been indicative of vital trends in Western society" wouldn't do for a 700-word paper either: that thesis would be large enough to inform a whole encyclopedia of music in twelve volumes. "In the past two years, a rise in the number of preteenagers has resulted in a comeback for heavy metal on our local concert scene"—now, that idea sounds much more likely.

To take a few more examples of thesis statements:

"Indian blankets are very beautiful." That statement seems too vague and hard to demonstrate for a usual college writing assignment of 400 to 1000 words.

"American Indians have adapted to modern civilization." That sounds too large, unless you plan to write a 5000-word term paper in sociology.

"Members of the Apache tribe have become celebrated as skilled workers in high-rise construction." All right; you could probably find support for that thesis by spending two hours doing research in a library.

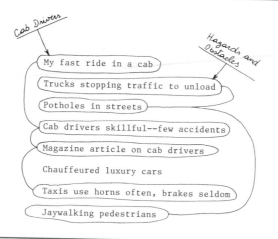

FIGURE 16.1   The linking method for grouping ideas

GROUPING YOUR IDEAS

In any bale of scribblings you have made while exploring a topic, you will usually find a few ideas that seem to belong together. They make the same point ("Just what I need," you think, "*two* examples of how New Yorkers drive"). They might follow one another ("Here are facts on the frequency of New York traffic jams—from this, I can go to the point that New York drivers are frustrated").

As you look over your preliminary notes, you'll want to indicate to yourself any connections you find between your materials. You'll need to sort your notes into groups, arrange them in sequences. Here are six common ways to work.

1. *Rainbow connections.* Some writers list on a sheet of paper all the main points they're going to express. (They don't recopy all their material—they just list each main point briefly.) Then, taking colored pencils, they circle with the same color any points that seem to go together. When they write, they can follow the color code and deal with similar ideas at the same time.

2. *Linking.* Other writers, though they work in black and white, also start by making a list of major points. They draw lines that link similar ideas. Then they number each linked group, to remember in what sequence to deal with it. Figure 16.1 is an illustration of a linked list. This particular list was produced in a one-person brainstorming session. It is nothing but a brief jotting-down of points the writer wants to make in an essay to be called "Manhattan Driving." The writer has drawn lines between points that seem to go together.

He has numbered each linked group in the order he plans to follow when writing and has supplied each with an outline heading. When he writes his draft, each heading will probably inspire a topic sentence or a few lines to introduce each major division of his essay. One point failed to relate to any other: "Chauffeured luxury cars." In the finished paper, it probably will be left out. This rough plan, if expanded three or four times, would make a workable outline for a short paper. It sifts out useless material; it arranges what remains.

3. *Solitaire.* Some writers, especially scholars, collect notes and ideas on roomy (5-by-8-inch) file cards. When they organize, they spread out the cards and arrange them in an order, as in a game of solitaire. When the order looks worth keeping, when each idea seems to lead to the next, they gather all the cards into a deck once more and wrap a rubber band around them. Then when they write, they deal themselves a card at a time and translate its contents into readable writing.

4. *Scissors and tape.* Other writers swear by scissors and Scotch tape. They lay out their rough notes before them. Then they group any notes that refer to the same point and that probably belong in the same vicinity. With scissors, they separate items that don't belong together. They shuffle the pieces around, trying for the most promising order. After throwing out any ideas that don't belong anywhere, they lock up the material into a structure. They join all the parts with tape. They may find places in the grand design where ideas and information are lacking. If so, they make a note of what's missing and tape that note into place. Although this taped-together construction of cards or slips of paper may look sloppy, it can serve as a workable outline to follow.

Some writers use this strategy not merely for planning, but for planning and drafting simultaneously. They tape together not just notes, but passages they have written separately. If you follow this method, you write whatever part you want to write first, then write the next most tempting part, and so on until you have enough rough stuff to arrange into a whole piece of writing. You'll need to add missing parts and to supply transitions (discussed on p. 513).

5. *Clustering.* Novelist and historian William Manchester describes this planning technique: "I write a word in the center of the page. Then I circle it with other words until a pattern appears." If you want to try clustering, take a piece of paper and in the middle of it write your topic in one or a few words. Put a circle around the topic. Then think of the major divisions into which this topic might be sliced. For an essay called "Manhattan Drivers," the major divisions might be (1) taxi drivers, (2) bus drivers, (3) truck drivers, (4) drivers of private cars—New Yorkers, and (5) drivers of private cars—out-of-town visitors. Write these divisions on your page, clustering them around your topic, and circle them, too. You now have the beginning of a rough plan for an essay.

Now, around each division, make another cluster of points you're going to include: examples, illustrations, facts, statistics, bits of evidence, opinions,

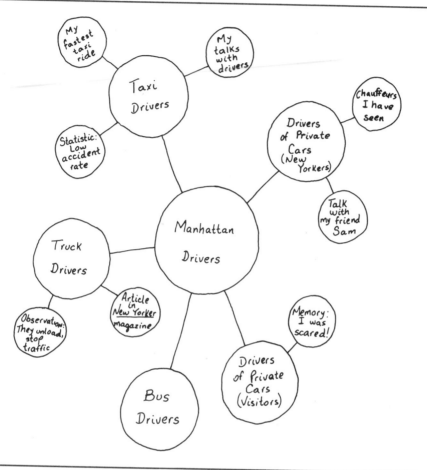

FIGURE 16.2 The clustering method for generating ideas

whatever. On your page, identify each item with a brief label ("My taxi ride," "Talk with New York friend," "Statistic on accidents").

What makes clustering especially useful is that when you cluster, you don't just plan. Your chart shows you at a glance where you need to generate ideas and information. If any major divisions look lonesome, evidently you need to come up with more material to surround them.

Clustering is a particularly valuable strategy for any writing assignment that calls for much evidence, such as a persuasive essay or a research paper. Figure 16.2 presents a cluster for "Manhattan Drivers." For a long paper (of, say, 1000 words), it would need more material. The division "Bus Drivers" hasn't any.

6. *The electronic game.* With the advent of word processing, many writers now arrange their rough notes into groups right on a computer screen, mov-

ing items from place to place until they like the resulting plan. Much computer software is dedicated to outlining, making it possible for the user to try out different schemes of organization before deciding on any one of them. (For detailed suggestions on writing with the aid of a computer, see Chapter 19, "Strategies for Writing with a Computer.")

OUTLINING

Some writers start writing without any plan. "When I work," says novelist Norman Mailer, "I don't like to know where I'm going." In college, you are often obliged to write with little advance planning—as when, on a final exam, you are given fifteen minutes to discuss the effects of World War II on patterns of world trade. Yet whether they lay out extensive plans on paper or arrange ideas in their heads as they go along, good writers organize what they write.

In the previous section, "Grouping Your Ideas," we set forth ways to bring related thoughts together. Another perhaps more familiar means to organize ideas is to outline. For most writing, most of the time, most college writers find it enough to make a scratch outline—perhaps just a list of points to make. A written outline, whether brief or greatly detailed, serves as guide and friend. If you forgot where you are going or what you are trying to say, you can always pause to consult it. An outline can be like a map that you make before setting out on a journey. It shows where to set out from, where to stop along the way, and where at last to arrive. Unlike highway maps, outlines can be flexible. While you drive along, occasionally consulting your map, you can easily revise your route.

How detailed an outline will you need? The answer depends in part on the kind of writer you are. Some writers feel most comfortable when writing with a highly detailed outline: buoyed up as though by a pair of water wings. Others feel inhibited by such a thing, as though they were trying to swim in a straitjacket. Some writers like to lay out the job very carefully in advance; others prefer to lay it out more loosely and follow an outline more casually. Do people tell you your writing isn't well organized and that they can't follow you? Then maybe you need a more detailed outline. Do they tell you your writing sounds tired and mechanical, as if you're ticking off your note cards in numerical order? Maybe your outline is constricting you and you should keep it brief.

Sometimes, when you have written the first draft of a paper that you suspect doesn't quite make sense, outlining can help you apply first aid. If you can't easily make an outline of what you have written, then probably your reader will have a hard time following you. Something is wrong with the paper's basic construction. Perhaps the main points don't follow clearly. Maybe the sequence of ideas needs rearranging. Maybe too many ideas are jammed into too few paragraphs. It is often easier to operate on your outline than on your ailing paper. Work on the outline until you get it into strong shape and then rewrite the paper to follow it.

An outline, even a detailed one, shouldn't say *everything* you plan to write in your paper. You shouldn't use up all your thought and energy on your outline. If yours gets too detailed, stop and set it aside with your notes.

Informal Outlines

For in-class-writing and for brief essays, often a *short* or *informal outline,* also called a *scratch outline,* will serve your needs. It is just a brief list of points to make, in the order you plan to make them. The short outline is only for your own eyes. When the writing job is done, you pitch the outline into the trash basket.

The following is an informal outline for a 600-word paper on the topic "Los Angelenos versus New Yorkers: Who Are Better Drivers?" Its thesis statement reads, "Los Angelenos are better drivers than New Yorkers because they are healthier, more skillful, and more considerate." (You'd need plenty of facts, observations, and other specific evidence to back up *those* claims, of course!) One obvious way to proceed would be to list the three points you want to compare (physical fitness, skill, and consideration). Then, for each quality, you might plan to discuss (1) New Yorkers and (2) Los Angelenos: how they do or don't exhibit it. You could put this plan in simple outline form, like this:

1. An old controversy
2. Physical fitness
   — New Yorkers: less time and space in which to exercise
   — Los Angelenos: outdoor lifestyle conducive to physical and mental ease
3. Skill at the wheel: both highly skilled
   — New Yorkers: more small, crowded streets
   — Los Angelenos: a lot of freeway driving
4. Consideration for others
   — New Yorkers: tendency to vent their aggressions at the wheel
   — Los Angelenos: laid-back attitude toward life reflected in driving habits
5. Conclusion: Los Angelenos win.

A simple five-point outline like that could easily fall into a five-paragraph essay. If you have a great deal to say about New Yorkers and Los Angelenos, though, the essay might well run longer—perhaps to eight paragraphs: introduction, conclusion, and three pairs of paragraphs in between. But outline and essay won't always correlate neatly. You may not know until you write exactly how many paragraphs you'll need.

An informal outline can be even less formal than the preceding one. If you were writing an in-class essay, an answer to an examination question, or a very short paper, your outline might be no more than three or four phrases jotted down in a list.

> Physical fitness
> Skill
> Consideration for others

Often a clear thesis statement (discussed on p. 491) will suggest a way to outline. Let's say you are assigned, for an anthropology course, a paper on the people of Melanesia. A thesis statement reads, "The Melanesian pattern of family life may look strange to westerners, but it fosters a degree of independence that rivals our own." Laying out ideas in the same order as they follow in that thesis statement, you might make a short, simple outline like this:

> 1. Features that appear strange:
>   A woman supported by her brother, not her husband
>   Trial marriages usual
>   Divorce from her children possible for any mother
> 2. Admirable results of system:
>   Wives not dependent on husbands for support
>   Divorce between mates uncommon
>   Greater freedom for parents and children

This informal outline might result in an essay that naturally falls into two parts: strange features, admirable results. In writing and thinking further, you might want to flesh out that outline with more material. The outline might expand accordingly.

Say you plan to write a "how-to" essay on buying a used car. Your thesis statement might read: "Despite traps that lie in wait for the unwary, you can get a good deal if you first read car magazines and *Consumer Reports*, check ads in the papers, make phone calls to several dealers, test-drive critically, and take along a friend who's a mechanic." Follow this same sequence of ideas in your outline, and you will probably start out your paper with some horror stories about people who get taken by car sharks and then proceed to list, point by point, your bits of advice. Of course, you can always change the sequence or revise your thesis statement if you find it makes sense to do so as you go along.

Formal Outlines

A *formal outline* is the Mercedes-Benz of outlines: an elaborate job built with time and care and meant for showing off. As a plan to be used for everyday writing jobs, it would take too much time—probably more than it would be worth.

In college, a formal outline is occasionally used for term papers, research papers, honors theses, doctoral dissertations, and other ambitious projects. As a rule, it isn't meant for a writer's own guidance, but for an instructor or a committee to ponder before (or after) the writer writes. Because research papers and theses require so much work, some academic departments ask a writer to submit a formal outline before going ahead and toiling for months, perhaps in vain. Some instructors in assigning a research paper ask for a special kind of formal outline—a sentence outline—to make the paper's organization easier to appreciate and to discuss. For an example, see Lisa Chickos's sentence outline on page 377. Writing such a detailed outline can pay off: with only a little more work, it can turn into a finished paper. In business, a formal outline for a research project (or for a program of matters to be discussed) might be offered to a meeting of a board of directors—meant to impress the top brass with how logical the bottom brass can be.

A formal outline offers the greatest amount of guidance that an outline can give. In a clear, logical way, it spells out where you are going to go. It shows how ideas relate, one to another: how large points lead to smaller. It ranks the points to be made according to their importance and inclusiveness: a point labeled with a roman numeral is a major point that takes in more territory than the letter A point under it.

When you make a formal outline, you place your thesis statement at the beginning. Then you list your most important points—those that most directly bear upon your thesis—in roman numerals: I, II, III. These points support and develop the main idea of your whole paper. Then you break down these points into divisions that take capital letters: A, B, C. You subdivide those into divisions with arabic numbers—1, 2, 3—and you further subdivide those into divisions with small letters: a, b, c. Be sure to cast all headings in parallel grammatical form: phrases or sentences but not both. If you have so much material that you have to subdivide still further, arabic numerals and small letters, both in parentheses, are commonly used. But it will take a hugely complicated writing project to need subdividing that far.

A formal outline for a long, thoroughly researched paper about New York and Los Angeles drivers might start like this:

```
Thesis statement:  Driving habits in New York City and
Los Angeles reflect basic cultural and behavioral differ-
ences between easterners and westerners.
  I.  New York drivers aggressive and impatient
      A.  Manifestations of these traits
          1.  Horn-blowing and shouting
```

```
        2.  Running red lights
        3.  Disregard for pedestrians
    B.  Reasons for their behavior
        1.  New York an old city
        2.  Population density
            a.  Limited contact with nature for most
                people
            b.  Little time and space for exercise
        3.  Fast-paced lifestyle
        4.  Traffic laws not rigidly enforced
            a.  Not enough police
            b.  General acceptance of status quo
            c.  A certain pride in survival skills--
                pedestrians and drivers alike

II.  Los Angeles drivers laid-back and relaxed
    A.  Contributing factors
        1.  Los Angeles a comparatively new and
            sprawling city
            a.  More room for cars
            b.  Fewer pedestrians
            c.  Vast network of freeways--little need to
                drive far on narrow streets
        2.  Outdoor living year-round
            a.  Fewer frustrations
            b.  A slower-paced life
    B.  Less frenzy on L.A. roads
        1.  Laws generally enforced and obeyed
        2.  Consideration on the part of most drivers
            for pedestrians and other drivers
```

This outline would continue, but from this much of it you can see how a formal outline unfolds. Some readers will grow wrathful if you list only one lonesome item in a subcategory, as in this formal outline for an essay on earthquakes:

```
    D.  Probable results of an earthquake
        1.  Houses stripped of their paint
```

If that point is all you have to say, then why not just combine your categories?

```
    D.  Houses stripped of paint during an earthquake
```

But more likely, the lack of more than one subpoint indicates that more thinking needs to be done, more evidence discovered. With a little more thought or reading, the outline might grow:

```
    D.  Probable results of an earthquake
        1.  Broken water mains
        2.  Collapsed bridges
        3.  Gaps in road surfaces
```

```
     4.   Cracks in foundations
     5.   Houses stripped of their paint
```

Not only has this writer come up with more points, she has ranked them in an order of diminishing importance. This careful planning will save her some decisions when she comes to write ("Now, which of these results do I deal with first?").

Often written after the paper, meant for the benefit of the reader and not the writer, a formal outline can also be a planning strategy. If you do write it in advance for your own guidance, let it be tentative. You will want to revise it to include any new ideas you may discover as you go along.

PARAGRAPHING

Even your most willing readers need occasionally to pause, to digest what you tell them. This is why essays are written not in large, indigestible lumps of prose but in *paragraphs*—small units, each indented, each more or less self-contained, each contributing something new in support of your essay's main idea.

Paragraphs can be as short as one sentence or as long as a page. Sometimes their length is governed by the audience for whom they are written or by the medium in which they appear. News writers, for instance, tend to write in brief, one- or two-sentence paragraphs to make their stories easy to cut to fit a page. Newspaper readers, consuming facts like popcorn, seem not to mind this style of skimpy paragraphing. (To find long, meaty paragraphs in a newspaper, you have to read the editorials.) Academic writers, on the other hand, assume some willingness on the part of their colleagues to read through long paragraphs in a specialized treatise.

Most paragraphs are organized around one idea or event and form sections of a larger whole. As we will show on page 515, sometimes a paragraph serves as a bridge, a *transition,* between the paragraph preceding and the one following. Effective paragraphs are both well organized and unified. They seem to go somewhere.

Ideally, a paragraph indentation signifies a pause, as if the writer were taking a breath, finished making one point and ready to begin another. In real life, when they slice their thoughts into paragraphs, probably no two writers work by exactly the same principles. Certain writers dwell on one idea at a time. They state a point and develop it amply: illustrate it with an example or a story, perhaps give a few facts to support it. Then, finished with that point, they indent and start making a further point in a fresh paragraph. Their prose seems to fall into paragraphs naturally. At the opposite extreme are those writers who don't even think about where to break their paragraphs until they finish a first draft. Then they go back over their work and mark a paragraph at each place where an important new point starts. Such slicing isn't always logical. Inspect the articles in some current magazine and, indeed, you'll meet writers who begin a new paragraph for no apparent reason except that they feel the old paragraph has run on long enough. As for readers, they tend not even to notice where a writer's paragraph breaks fall. Readers care only about whether the writer's thoughts follow in a sensible line and interest them.

Why, then, pay attention to paragraphs? You have to keep your readers with you every step of the way. This involves developing each of your main points fully and clearly, using examples and abundant evidence, before going on to the next. It means taking your readers by the hand and not only telling but *showing* them, with plenty of detailed evidence, exactly what you mean.

Using Topic Sentences

One tried-and-true way to draft an effective paragraph is to write down in advance one sentence that spells out what the paragraph's central point is to be. We call such a sentence a *topic sentence.* It supplies the foundation on which to build the rest of the paragraph.

Often when you read good clear prose, especially writing that explains or argues, you can pick out a given paragraph's topic sentence. Usually, as in this example from James David Barber's *The Presidential Character: Predicting Performance in the White House,* it appears first in the paragraph, followed by sentences that illustrate and support what it says. (In all the following examples, we have put the topic sentences in *italics.*)

> *The first baseline in defining Presidential types is activity-passivity.* How much energy does the man invest in his Presidency? Lyndon Johnson went at his day like a human cyclone, coming to rest long after the sun went down. Calvin Coolidge often slept eleven hours a night and still needed a nap in the middle of the day. In between, the Presidents array themselves on the high or low side of the activity line.

Here the topic sentence clearly shows at the outset what the paragraph is to be about. The second sentence defines *activity-passivity.* The third and fourth sentences, by citing extremes at either end of the baseline, supply illustrations: active Johnson, passive Coolidge. The final sentence makes a generalization that reinforces the central point.

Not every topic sentence stands at the beginning of its paragraph. Sometimes the first sentence of a new paragraph functions as a transition, linking what is to come with what has gone before, as in the following illustration from the essay "On Societies as Organisms" by science writer and physician Lewis Thomas. In such a paragraph the *second* sentence might be the topic sentence. The paragraph quoted here follows one about insects that ends, ". . . and we violate science when we try to read human meanings in their arrangements."

> It is hard for a bystander not to do so. *Ants are so much like human beings as to be an embarrassment.* They farm fungi, raise aphids as livestock, launch

armies into wars, use chemical sprays to alarm and confuse enemies, capture slaves. The families of weaver ants engage in child labor, holding their larvae like shuttles to spin out the thread that sews the leaves together for their fungus gardens. They exchange information ceaselessly. They do everything but watch television.

Occasionally a writer, especially one attempting to persuade the reader to agree, piles detail upon detail throughout a paragraph. Then, with a dramatic flourish, the writer *concludes* with the topic sentence. You can see this technique in the following paragraph, from Heidi Kessler's paper in response to a writing assignment in sociology: to report on a contemporary social problem and voice an opinion on it.

> A fourteen-year-old writes to an advice columnist in my hometown newspaper that she has "done it" lots of times and sex is "no big deal." At the neighborhood clinic where my aunt works, a hardened sixteen-year-old requests her third abortion. A girl-child I know has two children of her own, but no husband. A college student in my dorm now finds herself sterile from a "social disease" picked up during casual sexual encounters. Multiply these examples by thousands. *It seems clear to me that women, who fought so hard for sexual freedom equal to that of men, have emerged from the battle not as joyous free spirits but as the sexual revolution's walking wounded.*

By the time you come to the end of the paragraph, you might be ready to accept the conclusion in the topic sentence. Reversing the most usual order of paragraph development (to make a general statement and back it up with particulars), this paragraph moves instead from the particular to the general: from the examples of individual girl-children and women to the larger statement about American women made in the topic sentence.

The topic sentence, then, can appear anywhere in the paragraph. It is also possible to find a perfectly unified, well-organized paragraph that has no topic sentence at all, like this one from "New York" by Gay Talese.

> Each afternoon in New York a rather seedy saxophone player, his cheeks blown out like a spinnaker, stands on the sidewalk playing *Danny Boy* in such a sad, sensitive way that he soon has half the neighborhood peeking out of windows tossing nickels, dimes and quarters at his feet. Some of the coins roll under parked cars, but most of them are caught in his outstretched hand. The saxophone player is a street musician named Joe Gabler; for the past thirty years he has serenaded every block in New York and has sometimes been tossed as much as $100 a day in coins. He is also hit with buckets of water, empty beer cans and eggs, and chased by wild dogs. He is believed to be the last of New York's ancient street musicians.

No one sentence neatly sums up the writer's idea. Like most effective paragraphs that lack a topic sentence, Talese's paragraph contains something just as good: a topic idea. The author doesn't allow his paragraph to wander aimlessly. He knows exactly what he wants to achieve: a description of how Joe Gabler, a famous New York street musician, plies his trade. Because Talese succeeds in keeping this main purpose firmly in mind, the main point—that Gabler meets both reward and abuse—is clear to the reader as well.

A paragraph is likely to have a strong topic idea, too, if you begin it with a question. You'll probably find it easy to organize the rest of the paragraph around the answer to that question. Here is a paragraph, by psychoanalyst Erik Erikson, organized by the question-and-answer method.

> Is the sense of identity conscious? At times, of course, it seems only too conscious. For between the double prongs of vital inner need and inexorable outer demand, the as yet experimenting individual may become the victim of a transitory extreme identity consciousness, which is the common core of the many forms of "self-consciousness" typical for youth. Where the processes of identity formation are prolonged (a factor which can bring creative gain), such preoccupation with the "self-image" also prevails. We are thus most aware of our identity when we are just about to gain it and when we (with that startle which motion pictures call a "double take") are somewhat surprised to make its acquaintance; or, again, when we are just about to enter a crisis and feel the encroachment of identity confusion.

Evidently to write by the topic sentence method won't help every writer; some find it inhibiting. But if you generally have trouble organizing an essay, you might try it. One foolproof way to plan is to make a sentence outline (see Lisa Chickos's outline on pp. 377–380) and then write a paragraph enlarging on every sentence.

With practice, organizing a paragraph around one main point can become almost second nature. A writer accustomed to this method can see exactly where more examples and illustrations are called for: if a paragraph looks skimpy and consists of little besides the topic sentence, then it probably needs more beef.

The more pointed and lively your topic sentence, the more interesting the paragraph that is likely to surround it. If your topic sentence leads off your paragraph, think of it as bait to hook your readers and tow them along with you. "There are many things wrong with television" may be a little dull and vague, but at least it's a start for a paragraph. Zero in on one specific fault, change the sentence to "Of all television's faults, the one I can't stand is its nightly melodramatization of the news" and go on to illustrate your point with two or three melodramatic newscasts that you remember. An arresting paragraph—and an arresting paper—will probably result from that topic sentence.

Giving Examples

An example—the word comes from the Latin *exemplum,* meaning "one thing chosen from among many"—is a typical instance that illustrates a whole type or kind. Here's an example, from *In Search of Excellence* by Thomas J. Peters and Robert H. Waterman, Jr., explaining why America's top corporations are so successful:

Although he's not a company, our favorite illustration of closeness to the customer is car salesman Joe Girard. He sold more new cars and trucks each year, for eleven years running, than any other human being. . . . Why start with Joe? Because his magic is the magic of IBM and many of the rest of the excellent companies. It is simply service, overpowering service. Joe noted, "There's one thing that I do that a lot of salesmen don't, and that's believe the sale really begins after the sale—not before. The customer ain't out the door, and my son has made up a thank-you note."

Had a writer in love with generalities written that paragraph, he might have begun in the same way, with a generalization about "closeness to the customer." But then, instead of giving the example of Joe the car salesman and a sample of his speech, he might have gone on, still staying up in the clouds: "The need to consider the customer as an individual is very important to the operation of a successful business. The retailer is well advised to consider the purchaser as a person with whom he will have a continuing relationship," and so on, vaguely and boringly. Not only do examples make your ideas clear, they also interest your reader. Writers who stay up in the clouds of generality may have bright ideas, but in the end a reader may not care.

Giving examples, as Peters and Waterman do, is one way to back up a general statement of the sort you make in a topic sentence. On page 504 James David Barber illustrates the main idea of his paragraph (that "activity-passivity" characterizes presidents) with examples of different presidential types: the drowsy Coolidge, the energetic Johnson.

To find your own examples, do a little brainstorming or thinking. Review whatever you know. You can begin with your own experience, with whatever is near you. When you set out to draft a paragraph on a topic that you think you know nothing about—the psychology of gift giving, let's say—revolve it slowly in your mind. Maybe you will find yourself an expert on it. Did you ever know a person who gave large gifts people didn't want and felt uncomfortable accepting? Now why do you suppose he or she behaved that way? Was the gift giver looking for gratitude? A feeling of importance? Power over the recipient? How might you tell? If necessary, you might discover still more examples from conversation with others, from your reading, from digging in the library. By using examples, you make an idea more concrete and tangible. Examples aren't trivial doodads you add to a paragraph for decoration; they are what holds your readers' attention and shows them that your writing makes sense.

In truth, examples are only one kind of *evidence*—the factual basis for an argument or an explanation. Besides pointing to the example of President Coolidge, James David Barber gives a little evidence to show that Coolidge was sleepy: the report that he would sleep eleven hours a night and then take a nap in midday besides. To back up your general statements, you would do well to supply such statements of fact, bits of historical record, your own observations. Mary Harris "Mother" Jones in old age published the story of her life as a labor organizer, *The Autobiography of Mother Jones*. In this view of a Pennsylvania coal miner's lot at the turn of the century, she makes a general statement and then with ample evidence lends conviction to her words.

> Mining at its best is wretched work, and the life and surroundings of the miner are hard and ugly. His work is down in the black depths of the earth. He works alone in a drift. There can be little friendly companionship as there is in the factory; as there is among men who build bridges and houses, working together in groups. The work is dirty. Coal dust grinds itself into the skin, never to be removed. The miner must stoop as he works in the drift. He becomes bent like a gnome.
>
> His work is utterly fatiguing. Muscles and bones ache. His lungs breathe coal dust and the strange, damp air of places that are never filled with sunlight. His house is a poor makeshift and there is little to encourage him to make it attractive. The company owns the ground it stands on, and the miner feels the precariousness of his hold. Around his house is mud and slush. Great mounds of culm [the refuse left after coal is screened], black and sullen, surround him. His children are perpetually grimy from playing on the culm mounds. The wife struggles with dirt, with inadequate water supply, with small wages, with overcrowded shacks.
>
> The miner's wife, who in the majority of cases worked from childhood in the nearby silk mills, is overburdened with child bearing. She ages young. She knows much illness. Many a time I have been in a home where the poor wife was sick in bed, the children crawling over her, quarreling and playing in the room, often the only warm room in the house.

Mother Jones, who was not a learned writer, wrote these memoirs in her mid-nineties. Her style may be heavy with short, simple sentences ("She ages young. She knows much illness"), but her writing is clear and powerful. She knows the strength of a well-chosen verb: "Coal dust *grinds* itself into the skin." Notice how she opens her description by making two general statements: (1) "Mining is wretched work" and (2) the miner's life and surroundings are "hard and ugly." Then she supports these generalizations with an overwhelming barrage of facts from her own experience. The result is a moving, convincingly detailed portrait of the miner and his family.

Here's a revealing experiment you can easily make to test your skill at using examples. Glance back over the last essay you wrote for your writing course. How long are its paragraphs? Are they solid and stout? Or are they skimpy, undernourished: is there hardly a paragraph longer than three sentences? If indeed you find your paragraphs tending toward frailty, ask why. Maybe you need to be more generous in giving examples.

To give plenty of examples is one of the writer's chief tasks. We can't stress this truth enough. Most beginning writers don't give a reader enough examples. You'll want to cultivate the habit of example giving. Do something to remember its importance. Put a ring around this paragraph, or star it, or paint this motto over your writing desk: USE EXAMPLES! Or engrave it on your brain screen in letters of gold.

Other Ways of Developing a Paragraph

In earlier chapters of this book, you have seen the usefulness of certain strategies, valuable when you're writing a whole essay with a particular purpose in mind: the strategies of *analyzing, comparing and contrasting, seeking causes and effects,* and *defining.* In developing a paragraph, too, these strategies can serve you well.

Analyzing   You'll recall from Chapter 6 that analyzing means breaking a subject into its parts. You do so to understand your subject better. It's far easier to take in a subject, especially a complex subject, one piece at a time. In a common kind of analysis, *dividing,* a writer slices a subject into its components. This subject may be as concrete and definite as Manhattan (which a writer might divide into neighborhoods), or as abstract as, say, a person's knowledge of art (which the writer might divide into knowledge of sculpture, painting, drawing, and other forms). In the following paragraph from his college textbook *Wildlife Management,* Robert H. Giles, Jr., analyzes an especially large, abstract subject: the management of forest wildlife in America. To explain which professional environmentalists in America assume which duties and responsibilities, Giles divides forest wildlife management into six levels or areas of concern, arranged roughly from large to small. To a nonspecialist, this subject may seem head-stoppingly complicated. But see how neatly Giles divides it and explains it in a paragraph of less than 175 words.

> There are six scales of forest wildlife management: (1) national, (2) regional, (3) state or industrial, (4) county or parish, (5) intra-state region, management unit, or watershed, and (6) forest. Each is different. At the national and regional levels, management includes decisions on timber harvest quotas, grazing policy in forested lands, official stance on forest taxation bills, cutting policy relative to threatened and endangered species, management coordination of migratory species, and research fund allocation. At the state or industrial level, decision types include land acquisition, sale, or trade; season setting; and permit systems and fees. At the county level, plans are made, seasons set, and special fees levied. At the intra-state level, decisions include what seasons to recommend, what stances to take on bills not affecting local conditions, the sequence in which to attempt land acquisition, and the placement of facilities. At the forest level, decisions may include some of those of the larger management unit but typically are those of maintenance schedules, planting stock, cutting rotations, personnel employment and supervision, road closures, equipment use, practices to be attempted or used, and boundaries to be marked.

(For more about this kind of analysis, as you might use it in essay writing, see p. 181.)

Analyzing a process   You can also analyze an action or a phenomenon: how a skyscraper is built, how a political revolution begins, how sunspots form on the sun's surface. Analyzing a process is one of the most useful kinds of writing: telling step by step how something is done or how to do something. This strategy will be familiar if you have ever followed directions in a cookbook, but it is also useful in writing about more complex processes. It can explain large, long-ago happenings that a writer couldn't possibly have witnessed, such as the formation of the Grand Canyon or the solar system. Here, for instance, is a paragraph of collaborative writing by a team of botanists, Peter H. Raven, Ray F. Evert, and Helena Curtis (from their college textbook, *Biology of Plants*).

> About 127 million years ago—when angiosperm pollen first appears in the fossil record—Africa and South America were directly linked with one another and with Antarctica, India, and Australia in a great southern supercontinent called Gondwanaland. Africa and South America began to separate at about this time, forming the southern Atlantic Ocean, but they did not move completely apart in the tropical regions until about 90 million years ago. India began to move northward at about the same time, colliding with Asia about 45 million years ago and thrusting up the Himalayas in the process. Australia began to separate from Antarctica about 55 million years ago, but their separation did not become complete until about 40 million years ago.

Notice the writers' use of *time markers*—phrases of transition such as *about 127 million years ago, at about this time, until about 90 million years ago.* (Few of us will clearly imagine such vast extents of time, but at least the time markers make clear to us the sequence of events.) This paragraph illustrates the kind of process analysis that sets forth how something happens: an *informative* process analysis. Another familiar kind is the *directive* or "how-to" process analysis, which you often meet in the printed directions that come with merchandise in need of assembling. A directive process analysis instructs us in doing something—how to box, how to invest for retirement, how to clean a painting—or in making something—how to draw a map, blaze a trail, or put together a simple computer. (For more extended use of these strategies in longer papers, see p. 192.)

Comparing and contrasting   Often, if your purpose is to explain or define or evaluate a subject, you can develop a paragraph effectively by setting a pair of subjects side by side and *comparing and contrasting* them. (Comparing is indicating similarities; contrasting, differences.) Working together, these twin strategies use one subject to clarify another. The dual method works well for a pair of things similar in nature: two cities, two films, the theories of two economists. It can show that a writer has clearly observed and thoroughly understood both. For this reason, college examiners will often ask you to compare and contrast (sample exam question: "Discuss the chief similarities and differences between nineteenth-century French and English colonial policies in West Africa"). In a travel essay, "Venezuela for Visitors," written for the well-educated (and well-off) readers of *The New Yorker,* novelist John Updike sees Venezuelan society as polarized: it consists of rich people and

Indians. In the following paragraph, Updike compares and contrasts the two classes.

> Missionaries, many of them United States citizens, move among the Indians. They claim that since Western civilization, with all its diseases and detritus, must come, it had best come through them. Nevertheless, Marxist anthropologists inveigh against them. Foreign experts, many of them United States citizens, move among the rich. They claim they are just helping out, and that anyway the oil industry was nationalized five years ago. Nevertheless, Marxist anthropologists are not mollified. The feet of the Indians are very broad in front, their toes spread wide for climbing avocado trees. The feet of the rich are very narrow in front, their toes compressed by pointed Italian shoes. The Indians seek relief from tension in the use of *ebene,* or *yopo,* a mind-altering drug distilled from the bark of the ebene tree and blown into the user's nose through a hollow cane by a colleague. The rich take cocaine through the nose, and frequent mind-altering discotheques, but more customarily imbibe cognac, *vino blanco,* and Scotch, in association with colleagues.

For most of this paragraph, you'll notice, Updike simply sets the two side by side: the feet of the poor, the feet of the rich; how the poor get high, how the rich do. But merely by doing so, he throws the two groups of people into sharp relief. (For more about comparing and contrasting, as they may be useful especially in writing an evaluation, see p. 294.)

Seeking causes and effects   To divide the flow of reasons and results into *causes* and *effects* is a familiar, often-encountered kind of analysis. Although to search out causes and effects will often take a writer a whole book or at least an essay, at times in writing a paper you may wish to explore these matters more briefly. You may then find yourself setting forth causes and/or effects in a paragraph. Here are examples of two such paragraphs from a longer essay (one paragraph dealing with effects, the other with causes). Sheila Tobias, a university teacher and administrator, in a study called *Overcoming Math Anxiety,* deals with a compelling problem: fear of mathematics. Finding this fear especially prevalent in female students from elementary school through college, Tobias sets forth its effects on their academic performances and shows how a reluctance to study math limits many in their choice of a career. She sums up some possible causes for girls' performing less well in math than boys of the same age.

> One reason for the differences in performance . . . is the amount of math learned and used at play. Another may be the difference in male-female maturation. If girls do better than boys at all elementary school tasks, then they may compute better only because arithmetic is part of the elementary school curriculum. As boys and girls grow older, girls are under pressure to become less competitive academically. Thus, the falling off of girls' math performance from age 10 to 15 may be the result of this kind of scenario: (1) Each year math gets harder and requires more work and commitment. (2) Both boys and girls are pressured, beginning at age 10, not to excel in areas designated by society as

outside their sex-role domain. (3) Girls now have a good excuse to avoid the painful struggle with math; boys don't.

In succeeding paragraphs, Tobias offers still more reasons for the phenomenon, and she gives convincing evidence. (For more illustrations and more pointers on seeking causes and effects, see Chapter 10.)

Defining   Often, in writing any paper that calls for critical thinking, you'll need to do some defining. (*Define,* from the Latin, means "to set bounds to.") You can define a thing, a word, or a concept. Sometimes in writing you stop to define a standard word not often used. You define it to save your readers a trip to the dictionary. It might be a word or phrase you've coined yourself. Then you have to explain it or your readers won't know what you're talking about. Prolific word coiner and social prophet Alvin Toffler, in *The Third Wave,* for instance, invents (among many others) the word *techno-sphere,* which he defines as follows:

> All societies—primitive, agricultural, or industrial—use energy; they make things; they distribute things. In all societies the energy system, the production system, and the distribution system are interrelated parts of something larger. This larger system is the *techno-sphere.*

Scientists all over the world, if they didn't agree on the meaning of a word or an idea, would find it difficult to share knowledge. Here is a technical writer making his subject clear (to readers who can follow him): Gessner G. Hawley in an article, "A Chemist's Definition of pH." Though Hawley goes on to write an extended definition, he begins with a short definition:

> pH is a value taken to represent the acidity or alkalinity of an aqueous solution; it is defined as the logarithm of the reciprocal of the hydrogen-ion concentration of a solution:

$$pH = \ln \frac{1}{[H^+]}$$

What is equality? What is intelligence, socialism, preventive medicine, brand loyalty, a minimum wage, a holding corporation? Whenever in your writing you need to indicate the nature of an idea, a thing, a movement, a phenomenon, an organization—then you'll find yourself defining. (For more about this useful skill, see p. 295 in Chapter 9.)

Classifying   Let us add one more rhetorical strategy not previously dealt with in this book, worth having in your personal artillery: *classifying.* To classify is to make sense of a complicated and potentially bewildering array of things—works of literature, mental illnesses, this year's movies—by sorting them into categories you can deal with one at a time. A literature book customarily arranges works of literature into three genres or classes: stories, poems, and plays. One paragraph in a discussion about movies might sort them by audience (children's movies, movies for teenagers, movies for mature audiences) or by subject matter (love-romance, mystery, science fiction, sports, exotic places) and then go on to deal separately with each category. In a textbook lesson on how babies develop, Kurt W. Fischer and Arlyne Lazerson (writing in *Human Development*) take a paragraph to describe a research project that classified individual babies into three types:

> The researchers also found that certain of these temperamental qualities tended to occur together. These clusters of characteristics generally fell into three types—the easy baby, the difficult baby, and the baby who was slow to warm up. The *easy infant* has regular patterns of eating and sleeping, readily approaches new objects and people, adapts easily to changes in the environment, generally reacts with low or moderate intensity, and typically is in a cheerful mood. The *difficult infant* usually shows irregular patterns of eating and sleeping, withdraws from new objects or people, adapts slowly to changes, reacts with great intensity, and is frequently cranky. The *slow-to-warm-up infant* typically has a low activity level, tends to withdraw when presented with an unfamiliar object, reacts with a low level of intensity, and adapts slowly to changes in the environment. Fortunately for parents, most healthy infants—40 percent or more—have an easy temperament. Only about 10 percent have a difficult temperament, and about 15 percent are slow to warm up. The remaining 35 percent do not easily fit one of the three types but show some other pattern.

When you classify, you try to make order out of a jumble of stuff: you take many things and, to simplify your view of them, group them *by their similarities*. The simplest method is *binary* (or *two-part*) classification, in which the writer sorts things into two piles: things that possess a feature, things that don't possess that feature, as a chemist does in classifying solutions as either acids or bases. This method ignores fine gradations between two extremes, but sometimes it is clearly the right approach. You might classify people as scientists and nonscientists, literate and illiterate. In short, whenever you need to reduce complexity to an understandable order, don't be surprised to find yourself classifying.

Using Transitions

Effective writing is well organized. It proceeds in some sensible order, each sentence following naturally from the one before it. Yet even well-organized prose can be hard to read unless it contains *transitions:* devices that tie together words in a sentence, sentences in a paragraph, paragraphs in an essay.

You already use transitions every day, in both your writing and your speech. You can't help it. Instinctively you realize that certain words and phrases help your audience follow your line of thought. But some writers, in a rush to get through what they have to say, omit important linkages between thoughts. Hastily, they assume that because a connection is clear to them it will automatically be clear to their readers.

If your readers sometimes have trouble following you, you may find it useful to pay attention to transitions. Often just a word, phrase, or sentence of transition inserted in the right place will transform a seemingly disconnected passage into a coherent one.

Back in Chapter 6, we discussed time markers, those transitions especially useful for telling a story or analyzing a process because they make clear *when* one thing happens in relation to another. Time markers include words and phrases like *then, soon, the following day,* and *in a little while.* (For that discussion, see p. 192.) But not all transitions mark time. The English language contains many words and phrases that make clear other connections between or within sentences. Consider choosing one of the following transitions to fit your purpose. (We group them here by purposes.)

SUMMARIZE OR RESTATE	in other words, to put it another way, in brief, in simpler terms, on the whole, in fact, in a word, to sum up, in short, in conclusion
RELATE CAUSE AND EFFECT	therefore, accordingly, hence, thus, thereupon, consequently, as a result, because of, for
AMPLIFY OR COMPARE	and, also, too, besides, as well, in addition, moreover, furthermore, likewise, similarly, in effect
CONCEDE OR CONTRAST	on the other hand, whereas, but, however, nevertheless, still, and yet, or, even so, although, unlike, in spite of, on the contrary, at least
GIVE EXAMPLES	in particular, for instance, for example
QUALIFY	for the most part, by and large, with few exceptions, mainly, in most cases, sometimes
LEND EMPHASIS	it is true, indeed, of course, certainly, to be sure, obviously, without doubt, evidently, clearly, understandably
MARK THE PLACE	in the distance, close by, near at hand, far away, above, below, to the right, on the other side, opposite, to the west, next door

Occasionally a whole sentence serves as a transition. Often, but not always, it is the first sentence of a new paragraph. When the transitional sentence appears in that position, it harks back to the contents of the previous paragraph while simultaneously hinting at the direction the new paragraph is to take. Here is a sample, excerpted from an essay by Marsha Traugot about adopting older and handicapped children, in which the transitional sentence (*in italics*) begins a new paragraph.

> . . . Some exchanges hold monthly meetings where placement workers looking for a match can discuss waiting children or families, and they also sponsor parties where children, workers, and prospective parents meet informally.
>
> *And if a match still cannot be made?* Exchanges and other child welfare organizations now employ media blitzes as aggressive as those of commercial advertising. . . .

By repeating the key word *match* in her transitional sentence and by inserting the word *still,* Traugot makes clear that in what follows she will build on what has gone before. At the same time, by making the transitional sentence a rhetorical question, Traugot promises that the new paragraph will introduce fresh material, in this case answering the question.

As we see in Traugot's passage about adoption, still another way to make clear the relationship between two sentences, two paragraphs, or two ideas is to *repeat* a key word or phrase. Such repetition, purposefully done, almost guarantees that the reader will understand how all the parts of even a complicated passage fit together. Note the transitional force of the word *anger* in the following paragraph, from *Of Woman Born* by poet Adrienne Rich, in which the writer explores her relationship with her mother:

> And I know there must be deep reservoirs of anger in her; every mother has known overwhelming, unacceptable anger at her children. When I think of the conditions under which my mother became a mother, the impossible expectations, my father's distaste for pregnant women, his hatred of all that he could not control, my anger at her dissolves into grief and anger *for* her, and then dissolves back again into anger at her: the ancient, unpurged anger of the child.

The repetition of the one word in several contexts—those of a mother's anger toward her children and a child's anger, past and present, toward her mother—holds all the parts of this complex paragraph together, makes clear the unity and coherence of its ideas. Repetition of the word *mother* performs the same binding function.

Pronouns, too, because they always refer back to nouns or other pronouns, serve as transitions by making the reader refer back as well. Note how certain pronouns (indicated by *italics*) hold together the following paragraph by columnist Ellen Goodman.

> I have two friends who moved in together many years ago. *He* looked upon this step as a trial marriage. *She* looked upon *it* as, well, moving in together. *He* was sure that in a matter of time, after *they* had built up trust and confidence, *she* would agree that marriage was the next logical step. *She,* on the other hand, was thrilled that here at last was a man *who* would never push *her* back to the altar.

Goodman's paragraph contains transitions other than pronouns, too: time markers like *many years ago, in a matter of time,* and *after they had built up trust; on the other hand,* which makes clear that what follows will represent a contrast from what has gone before; and repetition. All serve the main purpose of transitions: keeping readers on track.

Transitions may be even longer than sentences. When you write an essay, especially one that is long and complicated, you'll find that to move clearly from one idea to the next will sometimes require an entire paragraph of transition:

```
    So far, we have been dwelling on the physical and
psychological effects of driving nonstop for more than
```

```
two hundred miles. Now let's reflect on causes. Why do
people become addicted to their steering wheels?
```

Usually, such a paragraph will be shorter than its neighbors, but you'll want to allow it whatever space it may require. Often, as in the preceding example, it makes a comment on the structure of the essay. The writer is taking time out to explain what she is doing so that her readers may readily follow her.

Let a transition paragraph come to your aid, too, whenever you go off on one branch of argument and then return to your main trunk. Here's an example from a masterly writer, Lewis Thomas, in an essay, "Things Unflattened by Science." A medical doctor, Thomas has been complaining in his essay that biologists keep expecting medical researchers to come up with quick answers to intractable problems: cancer, schizophrenia, stress. He takes most of a paragraph to explain why he doesn't think medical science can solve the problem of stress: "Stress is simply the condition of being human." Now, to turn again to the main idea of his essay—what biological problems he would like to see solved—Thomas inserts a transition paragraph:

> But I digress. What I wish to get at is an imaginary situation in which I am allowed three or four questions to ask the world of biomedical science to settle for me by research, as soon as possible. Can I make a short list of top-priority puzzles, things I am more puzzled by than anything else? I can.

In a new paragraph, he continues: "First, I want to know what goes on in the mind of a honeybee." He wonders if a bee is just a sort of programmed robot or if it can think and imagine, even a little bit. Neatly and effectively, the transition paragraph has led to this speculation and to several further paragraphs that will come.

If you can do without transition paragraphs, do. Sometimes a question at the start of a paragraph will supply enough connection: "Why do people become addicted to their steering wheels?" That question neatly introduces a whole new idea. If the essay is short and clear, the question saves a whole transition paragraph. Use such a paragraph only when you sense that your readers might get lost if you don't patiently lead them by the hand.

Writing an Opening

Even writers with something to say occasionally find it hard to begin. Often they are so intent on writing a brilliant opening paragraph that they freeze, unable to write anything at all. Brilliant beginnings are fine if you can get them, but they may be gifts of God. "Start with a bang," Richard Strauss advised his fellow composers, and he opened his symphonic poem *Thus Spake Zarathustra* with a sunrise: the whole orchestra delivers a tremendous explosion of sound. But in most writing, brilliance and orchestral explosions are neither expected nor required. In truth, when you sit down to draft an essay, you can ease your way into the job by simply deciding to set words— any words—on paper, without trying at all for an arresting or witty opening.

A time-honored approach to your opening paragraphs is to write them *last,* after you have written the body of your essay and know exactly in what direction it is headed. Some writers like to write a first draft with a long, driveling beginning and then in rewriting cut it down to the most dramatic, exciting, or interesting statement, discarding everything that has gone before.

At whatever point in the writing process you set about fashioning an opening paragraph of your own, remember that your chief aim is to persuade your readers to lay aside their preoccupations and enter, with you as guide, the world set forth in your essay. Often a simple anecdote, by capturing your readers' interest, serves as a good beginning. Here is how Harry Crews opens his essay "The Car":

> The other day, there arrived in the mail a clipping sent by a friend of mine. It had been cut from a Long Beach, California, newspaper and dealt with a young man who had eluded police for fifty-five minutes while he raced over freeways and through city streets at speeds up to 130 miles per hour. During the entire time, he ripped his clothes off and threw them out the window bit by bit. It finally took twenty-five patrol cars and a helicopter to catch him. When they did, he said that God had given him the car, and that he had "found God."

Most of us, reading such an anecdote, want to read on. What will the author say next? What has the anecdote to do with the essay as a whole? Crews has aroused our curiosity.

In some essays, the author introduces a subject and then turns momentarily away from it to bring in a vital bit of detail, as in this opening paragraph by A. Alvarez from "Shiprock," an essay about climbing a mountain:

> I suppose the first sight of a mountain is always the best. Later, when you are waiting to start, you may grow to hate the brute, because you are afraid. And when, finally, you are climbing, you are never aware of the mountain as a mountain: it is merely so many little areas of rock to be worked out in terms of hand-holds, foot-holds and effort, like so many chess problems. But when you first see it in the distance, remote and beautiful and unknown, then there seems some reason for climbing.

That paragraph establishes the author as someone with firsthand knowledge. Alvarez proceeds smoothly from the opening paragraph about mountain climbing in general to the heart of his essay, with a sentence of transition at the start of his second paragraph: "I first saw Shiprock on a midsummer day."

A well-written essay can also begin with a short definition, as James H. Austin begins "Four Kinds of Chance":

> What is chance? Dictionaries define it as something fortuitous that happens unpredictably without discernible human intention. Chance is unintentional and capricious, but we needn't conclude that chance is immune from human intervention. Indeed, chance plays several distinct roles when humans react creatively with one another and with their environment.

To ask a question like that is often an effective way to begin. The reader will expect the essay to supply an answer.

To challenge readers, a writer may begin with a controversial opinion.

> Unlike any other sport, football is played solely for the benefit of the spectator. If you take the spectator away from any other game, the game could still survive on its own. Thus tennis players love tennis, whether or not anyone is watching. Golfers are almost churlish in their dedication to their game. Ping-Pong players never look around. Basketball players can dribble and shoot for hours without hearing a single cheer. Even baseball might survive the deprivation, despite the lack of parks. Softball surely would. But if you took away the spectators, if you demolished the grandstands and boarded up the stadium, it is inconceivable to think that any football would be played in the eerie privacy of the field itself. No football team ever plays another team just for the fun of playing football. Army plays Navy, Michigan plays Purdue, P.S. 123 plays P.S. 124, only with the prospect of a loud crowd on hand.

After his first, startling remark, the writer, Wade Thompson, generalizes about games unlike football: "If you take the spectator away from any other game, the game could still survive on its own." Then the author backs up his generalization with examples of such games: tennis, golf, Ping-Pong, basketball, baseball, softball. Finally Thompson returns to his original point, thus emphasizing the direction his essay will take.

An effective opening paragraph often ends, as does Thompson's, with a statement of the essay's main point. To end your opening paragraph this way, after first having captured your readers' attention, is to take your readers by the hand and lead them in exactly the direction your essay is to go. No one can ask more of any introduction. Such a statement can be brief, as in the second sentence of this powerful opening of an essay by educator George B. Leonard called "No School?":

> The most obvious barrier between our children and the kind of education that can free their enormous potential seems to be the educational system itself: a vast, suffocating web of people, practices and presumptions, kindly in intent, ponderous in response. Now, when true educational alternatives are at last becoming clear, we may overlook the simplest: no school.

If you find it difficult to write an opening paragraph, try these suggestions.

1. Don't worry *too* hard about capturing and transfixing your readers with your opening. It is enough to introduce an idea.
2. Open with an anecdote, a description, a comparison, a definition, a quotation, a question, or some vital background.
3. Set forth your thesis (as discussed on p. 491).
4. Hint in advance what you will say in paragraph two.

Writing a Conclusion

The final paragraphs of an essay linger longest in the reader's mind. Here is a conclusion that certainly does so. In "Once More to the Lake," about returning with his young son to a vacation spot the author had known and loved as a child, E. B. White conveys his confused feeling that he has gone back in time to his own childhood, that he and his son are one. Then, at the end of the essay, in an unforgettable image, he remembers how old he really is:

> When the others went swimming my son said he was going in, too. He pulled his dripping trunks from the line where they had hung all through the shower and wrung them out. Languidly, and with no thought of going in, I watched him, his hard little body, skinny and bare, saw him wince slightly as he pulled up around his vitals the small, soggy, icy garment. As he buckled the swollen belt, suddenly my groin felt the chill of death.

White's concluding paragraph is a classic example of an effective way to end. It begins with a sentence of transition that points back to what has gone before and at the same time looks ahead. (He might just as easily have put a transitional sentence at the end of the preceding paragraph.) After the transition, White leads us quickly to his final, chilling insight. Then he stops.

Yet even a quiet ending can be effective, as long as it signals clearly that the essay is finished. Sometimes the best way to conclude a story, for instance, is simply to stop when the story is over. This is what Martin Gansberg does in his true account of the fatal beating of a young woman, Kitty Genovese, in full view of residents of a Queens, New York, apartment house, who, unwilling to become involved, did nothing to interfere. Here is the last paragraph of his account, "38 Who Saw Murder Didn't Call Police":

> It was 4:25 A.M. when the ambulance arrived to take the body of Miss Genovese. It drove off. "Then," a solemn police detective said, "the people came out."

For an essay that traces causes or effects, analyzes, evaluates, or argues, a deft concluding thought performs the worthy function of reinforcing your main idea. Notice the definite click with which former heavyweight champion Gene Tunney closes the door on "The Long Count," an analysis of his two victorious fights with Jack Dempsey, whose boxing style differed markedly from Tunney's own.

> Jack Dempsey was a great fighter—possibly the greatest that ever entered a ring. Looking back objectively, one has to conclude that he was more valuable to the sport or "The Game" than any prizefighter of his time. Whether you consider it from his worth as a gladiator or from the point of view of the box office, he was tops. His name in his most glorious days was magic among his people, and today, twenty years after, the name Jack Dempsey is still magic. This tells a volume in itself. As one who has always had pride in his profession as well as his professional theories, and possessing a fair share of Celtic romanticism, I wish that we could have met when we were both at our unquestionable best. We could have decided many questions, to me the most important of which is whether "a good boxer can always lick a good fighter."
>
> I still say yes.

It's easy to suggest what *not* to do at the end of an essay. Don't leave your readers suspended in midair, half expecting you to go on. Don't introduce a brand-new topic that leads away from the true topic of your essay. And don't feel you have to introduce your final paragraph with an obvious signal that the end is near. Words and phrases like "In conclusion," "As I have said," or "So, as we see," have their place, but do without them and your essay is likely to end more gracefully. In a long, complicated paper, a terse summation of your main points right before your concluding sentences may help your reader grasp your ideas; but a short paper usually requires either no summary at all or little more than a single sentence.

"How *do* you write an ending, then?" you might well ask. An apt quotation can neatly round out an essay, as Malcolm Cowley demonstrates at the end of an essay in *The View from Eighty,* his discussion of the pitfalls and compensations of old age.

> "Eighty years old!" the great Catholic poet Paul Claudel wrote in his journal. "No eyes left, no ears, no teeth, no legs, no wind! And when all is said and done, how astonishingly well one does without them!"

In a sharp criticism of American schools, humorist Russell Baker uses another technique for ending his essay "School vs. Education": that of stating or restating his claim. Baker's main point is that schools do not educate, and he concludes:

> Afterward, the former student's destiny fulfilled, his life rich with Oriental carpets, rare porcelain and full bank accounts, he may one day find himself with the leisure and the inclination to open a book with a curious mind, and start to become educated.

It is also possible to introduce at the end of your essay not new topics that you haven't time to go into, but a few new implications concerning the topic you *have* covered. As you draw to a close and are restating your main point, ask yourself, "What now?" Why not try to leave your reader with one or two provocative thoughts to ponder? Obstreperous 1920s debunker H. L. Mencken uses this technique in "The Libido for the Ugly," an essay about the ugliness of American cities and towns.

> Here is something that the psychologists have so far neglected: the love of ugliness for its own sake, the lust to make the world intolerable. Its habitat is the United States. Out of the melting pot emerges a race which hates beauty as it hates truth. The etiology of this madness deserves a great deal more study than it has got. There must be causes behind it; it arises and flourishes in obedience to biological laws, and not as a mere act of God. What, precisely, are the terms of those laws? And why do they run stronger in America than elsewhere? Let some honest *Privat Dozent°* in pathological sociology apply himself to the problem.

Privat Dozent: A lecturer at a German university.

TELLING A STORY

Telling a story is a vivid and convincing way to give an example or to illustrate what a writer is saying. Mahatma Gandhi, in *An Autobiography,* makes the point that a truly independent man tends to his own personal needs. To illustrate this principle, he tells a story: an incident that happened when he was a young lawyer in South Africa.

> In the same way as I freed myself from slavery to the washerman, I threw off dependence on the barber. All people who go to England learn there at least the art of shaving, but none, to my knowledge, cut their own hair. I had to learn that too. I once went to an English hair-cutter in Pretoria. He contemptuously refused to cut my hair. I certainly felt hurt, but immediately purchased a pair of clippers and cut my hair before the mirror. I succeeded more or less in cutting the front hair, but I spoiled the back. The friends in the court shook with laughter—"What's wrong with your hair, Gandhi? Rats have been at it?" "No, the white barber would not condescend to touch my black hair," said I, "so I preferred to cut it myself, no matter how badly."

A simple story. Why is it so powerful? In his opening sentence, Gandhi promises to tell us about some kind of revolution ("I threw off dependence on the barber"). Out of curiosity, we read on. We soon find the writer telling us of something even more gripping: a confrontation with a racial bigot. We sympathize with the writer, with his attempts to cut his own hair, with his experience of ridicule (especially if we have ever had friends make fun of us). The clincher of the story comes in the last line: Gandhi, with an apt comeback, turns humiliation into triumph. Bigotry has taught him something.

Effective writers, like Gandhi, often tell stories to illustrate their ideas. They know that *narration,* or storytelling, is a powerful means to engage and hold a reader's interest. They know that, with the aid of a story, a general point can become more persuasively clear.

Narratives come in all lengths, from hefty novels like Leo Tolstoy's *War and Peace* to this ghost story in a sentence: "Before going to bed one night, a man hung his wig on the bedpost; in the morning, he found it had turned white." But in most essay writing, a story will take only a paragraph. Like Gandhi's haircutting story, it may be just an *anecdote:* a brief, entertaining account of a single incident.

Whatever its length, every good story has a purpose, even if the purpose is simply to entertain. As in Gandhi's story, this purpose may be to illustrate a point. It may be to supply evidence to clinch an argument; it may be—if the story is a joke—merely to amuse. To think for a moment, "Why do I want to tell this story? What am I trying to achieve?" may repay you when you come to write.

Let's say you're writing a paper for a psychology course. Your central idea is "Few people, witnessing some swift, unexpected event, can remember it accurately without adding to it." You could go on about that in an abstract way ("The natural tendency is to reinforce our memories with additional elements by which we make sense out of our perceptions"). But the point might come across much more memorably, clearly, and effectively if you could tell the story of three witnesses to a car accident, all of them honest and well intentioned, who gave wildly different accounts of it.

Before you write a story, make sure you have a whole story to tell. Like a newspaper reporter, you can ask yourself certain questions: What happened? Who took part? When? Where? Why did these events take place? How did they happen? (See p. 478.)

If you have plenty of time and space, you can tell a story by *scene* (or scenes), like a fiction writer. To do so, you first imagine each event and the persons involved in it so clearly and fully and in such great detail that you might be watching the event in a movie. You then try to draw the scene or scenes in words. You don't merely mention people, you portray them. You can include dialogue and description.

A more concise method is to tell the story by *summary*. You sum up what happened, briefly, just telling of events in general rather than presenting them in detail. Summary, though it may produce writing with less detail and vividness, isn't an inferior method to the method of drawing scenes. Most stories are told by this method, for it takes less time and fewer words. Novelists, writing to keep readers enthralled, can afford to draw detailed scenes in the hundreds of pages at their disposal; someone telling several stories in the course of a short essay will want instead to summarize them. If you tell your story in a single paragraph, then most likely you'll use the method of summary.

Some storytellers change methods in mid-story. They'll begin by drawing elaborate scenes and then they'll say, "Well, to make a long story short . . ." and wrap up everything in a hasty summary. They would be well advised to stick to one method or the other.

A usual way to tell a story, an easy one for a writer to follow, is to tell it in chronological order — that is, in the same sequence the events followed in time. But when you see some good reason not to stick to chronology, you can depart from it. You might, for instance, return to earlier events by *flashback,* departing from chronology to hark back to an earlier scene. That earlier scene, you might decide, is more vivid and arresting than later scenes, and you would be more likely to capture your reader's interest if you started with it. A rule of thumb is to tell a story in chronological order *unless* a different order would make a better story.

CHAPTER 17

Strategies for Rewriting

The advice in this chapter is meant to lend you support in revising your paper, whether you change all its main ideas or only polish its words and phrases.

Some of these strategies will prove useful to you in doing a thorough, top-to-bottom revision. Sometimes a first draft needs to be entirely rethought and recast into a new mold. In "Stressing What Counts," we suggest how you can emphasize important ideas. That advice surely applies to rewriting whole essays; the section also gives hints for rewriting just *parts* of essays: sentences and paragraphs.

REVISING DEEPLY

When you look back over your draft, how do you know what you need to rewrite? In previous chapters of this book, in the "Rewriting" sections, you found specific advice for such decision making. Here now are three *general* checklists of questions you might ask yourself in preparing to rewrite. You can use these questions in revising drafts written for practically any paper assignment. But the questions will prove useful only if you allow time to give your work a thorough going-over. When you have a few hours to spare, they will help you find opportunities to make not just slight, cosmetic touchings-up, but major improvements.

- Have you accomplished what you set out to do? If not, what still needs doing?
- Has your paper said everything that you believe needs to be said?
- Do you still believe everything you say? In writing the paper, have you changed your mind, rethought your assumptions, made a discovery? Do any of your interpretations or statements of opinion now need to be revised?
- Have you tried to take in too much territory, with the result that your coverage of your topic seems too thin? How might you—even now—reduce the scope of your paper? Could you cut material, perhaps write a new introduction making clear exactly what you propose to do?
- Do you know enough about your subject? Does more evidence seem called for? If so, try recalling, observing, reading, conversing, and imagining.
- If you have taken ideas and information from other writers, have you always given credit where it is due?
- If you have written to persuade readers, can you sum up in a sentence the claim your paper sets forth? (For help, see "Stating a Thesis," p. 491.)
- Have you emphasized what matters most? Have you kept the essential idea or ideas from being obscured by a lot of useless details and distracting secondary thoughts? (For help, see "Stressing What Counts," p. 528.)

- Would any paragraphs make more sense or follow better if arranged in a different order? Try imagining how a paragraph might look and sound in a new location. Scissor it out and stick it into a different place; reread and see whether it works well there.
- Does your topic make itself clear early in the paper, or must the reader plow through much distracting material to come to it? Later in the draft, is there any passage that would make a better beginning?
- Can you cut any long-winded asides?
- Does everything follow clearly? Does one point lead to the next? If connections aren't clear, see "Using Transitions," page 513.
- Does the conclusion follow from what has gone before? It doesn't seem arbitrarily tacked on, does it? (See "Writing a Conclusion," p. 518.)
- Do you suspect your paper is somewhat confused? If you suspect it, you are probably right. Suggestion: Make an informal outline of the paper as it now stands. Then look over the outline and try to spot places to make improvements. Revise the outline, then revise the paper. (For advice on outlining, see p. 498.)

- Who will read this paper? Does the paper tell them what they will want to know? Or does it tell them only what they probably know already?
- Does the beginning of the paper promise your readers anything that the paper never delivers?
- Are there any places where readers might go to sleep? If so, can such passages be shortened or deleted? Do you take ample time and space to unfold each idea in enough detail to make it both clear and interesting? Would more detailed evidence help—perhaps an interesting brief story or a concrete example? (See "Giving Examples," p. 506.)
- Are there places where readers might raise serious objections? How might you recognize these objections, maybe even answer them?
- Have you used any specialized or technical language that your readers might not understand? If so, can you work in brief definitions?
- What attitude toward your readers do you seem to take? Are you overly chummy, needlessly angry, cockily superior, apologetic? Do you still feel that way?
- From your conclusion, and from your paper as a whole, will your readers be convinced that you have told them something worth knowing?

LOOKING FOR LOGICAL FALLACIES

Logical fallacies are common mistakes in thinking—often, the making of statements that lead to wrong conclusions. Here are a few of the most familiar, to help you recognize them when you see or hear them and so guard against them when you write. If when you look back over your draft you discover any of these, cut them, think again, and come up with a different argument.

Non sequitur (From the Latin, "It does not follow.") This is the error of stating a claim that doesn't follow from your first premise (the statement you begin with): "Marge should marry Jergus. Why, in high school he got all A's." Come up with stronger reasons for Marge's decision—reasons that have to do with getting good grades *as a husband.*

Oversimplification This fallacy is evident when a writer offers neat and easy solutions for large, complicated problems: "If we want to do away with drug abuse, let's get tough—let's sentence every drug user to life imprisonment." (Even users of aspirin?)

Either/or reasoning This logical fallacy is a special brand of oversimplified thinking: assuming that there are only two sides to a question, that all statements are either true or false, that all questions demand either a yes or a no answer. "The nonbiologist," comments Eric B. Lenneberg, "mistakenly thinks of genes as being directly responsible for one property or another; this leads him to the fallacy of dichotomizing everything as being dependent on either genes or environment." Other adherents to the either/or principle divide reality into either mind or body, sense or intellect, intelligence or stupidity, public or private, finite or infinite, humanity or nature, good or evil, competence or incompetence. An either/or reasoner assumes that a problem has only two possible solutions, only one of which is acceptable. "What are we going to do about acid rain? Either we shut down all the factories that cause it or we just forget about acid rain and learn to live with it. We've got no choice, right?" Consider more than two choices.

Argument from dubious authority   An unidentified authority can be used unfairly to shore up a quaking argument: "According to some of the most knowing scientists in America, smoking two packs a day is as harmless as eating a couple of oatmeal cookies. So let's all smoke." A reader should also doubt an authority whose expertise lies outside the subject being considered: "TV personality Ed McMahon calls this insurance policy the lowest-priced and most comprehensive available."

Argument ad hominem   (From the Latin, "against the man") This fallacy consists of attacking people's opinions by attacking their character. "Carruthers may argue that we need to save the whales, but Carruthers is the kind of person who always gets excited over nothing." A person's circumstances can also be turned against him: "Carruthers would have us spend millions to save whales, but I happen to know that he owns a yacht from which he selfishly enjoys watching whales."

Argument from ignorance   This fallacy involves maintaining that, because a claim has not been disproved, it has to be accepted. "Despite years of effort, no one has conclusively proved that ghosts don't exist; therefore, we should expect to see them at any time." The converse is also an error: that because a conclusion has not been proved it should be rejected. "No one has ever shown that there is life on any other planet. Evidently the notion of other living things in the universe is unthinkable."

Begging the question   Set out to prove a statement already taken for granted, and you beg the question. When you reason in a logical way, you state that because something is true, then another truth follows as a result. But when you beg the question, you repeat that what is true is true. If, for instance, you argue that rapists are a menace because they are dangerous, you don't prove a thing. Beggars of questions just repeat what they already believe, in different words. Sometimes this fallacy takes the form of *arguing in a circle*, demonstrating a premise by a claim and a claim by a premise: "He is a liar because he simply isn't telling the truth."

Post hoc ergo propter hoc ("After this, therefore because of this") This fallacy confuses cause and effect: "Because Jimmy Carter was obliged to leave the White House, the problem of inflation has been alleviated." (In a way, this is another form of oversimplification: attributing huge effects to just one simple cause.)

Arguing by analogy The writer who does this uses a *metaphor* (a figure of speech that points to a similarity: "Her speech was a string of firecrackers") as though it were evidence to support a claim. In explaining, an analogy may be useful. It can set forth a complex idea in terms of something familiar and easy to imagine. For instance, shooting a spacecraft to a distant planet is like sinking a golf ball with uncanny accuracy into a hole a half mile away. But if forced into an argument, an analogy will be logically weak, though it may sound neat and clear. Dwelling only on similarities, a writer doesn't consider differences—since to admit them would only weaken the analogy. "People were born free as the birds. It's cruel to expect them to work." Hold on— human society and bird society have more differences than similarities. Because they are alike in one way doesn't mean they're alike in *every* way. In 1633, Scipio Chiaramonti, professor of philosophy at the University of Pisa, made this leaky analogy in arguing against Galileo's claim that the earth orbits the sun: "Animals, which move, have limbs and muscles. The earth has no limbs and muscles, hence it does not move."

Further Reading about Logic

When you state a claim and back it with evidence, you reason logically (as we saw in Chapter 7, in the section "Generating Ideas"). Lately, the study of logic, or systematic reasoning, has seen exciting developments. If you care to venture more deeply into its fascinating territory, a good, lively, and challenging introductory textbook is Albert E. Blumberg's *Logic* (New York: Knopf, 1976).

Recently, a practical method of reasoning has been devised by the British philosopher Stephen Toulmin. In *The Uses of Argument* (Cambridge, Eng.: Cambridge University Press, 1969), Toulmin sets forth his system in detail. A clear, explicit argument needs three parts: the *data* (or evidence), the *claim* (what you are proving), and the *warrant* (the thinking that leads from data to claim). Toulmin's own example of such an argument is this:

Harry was born in Bermuda ————┬———— Harry is a British subject
        (*Data*)   (*Claim*)

Since a man born in Bermuda
will be a British subject
(*Warrant*)

Toulmin's views are fully explained and applied by Douglas Ehninger and Wayne Brockriede in *Decision by Debate,* 2nd ed. (New York: Harper & Row, 1978) and by Toulmin himself, with Richard Rieke and Allan Janik, in *Introduction to Reasoning,* 2nd ed. (New York: Macmillan, 1984).

STRESSING WHAT COUNTS

A boring writer writes as though every idea is no more important than any other. An effective writer cares what matters, decides what matters most, and shines a bright light on it.

You can't emphasize merely by underlining things or by throwing them into CAPITAL LETTERS. Such devices soon grow monotonous, and a writer who works them hard ends up stressing nothing at all, like a speaker whose every second word is a curse. One Navy boatswain's mate, according to folklore, couldn't talk without emphasizing every noun with an obscene adjective. To talk that way cost him great effort. By the time he could get out an order to his crew to bail, the boat had swamped. Emphasis wasn't all that was lost.

An essential of good writing, then, is to emphasize things that count. How? This section offers four suggestions.

Stating First or Last

One way to stress what counts is to put important things first or last. The most emphatic positions in an essay, or in a single sentence, are two: the beginning and the end. Let's consider each.

Stating first   In an essay, you might state in your opening paragraph what matters most. Writing a paper for an economics course in which students had been assigned to explain the consequences of import quotas (such as a limit on the number of foreign cars allowed into a country), Donna Waite began by summing up her findings:

> Although an import quota has many effects, both for the nation imposing the quota and the nation whose industries must suffer it, I believe that the most important is generally felt at home. A native industry gains a chance to thrive in a marketplace of lessened competition.

Her paper goes on to illustrate her general observation with evidence. Summing up the most important point right at the start is, by the way, a good strategy for answering a question in an essay examination. It immediately shows the instructor that you know the answer.

A paper that takes a stand or makes a proposal might open with a statement of what the writer believes.

```
Our state's antiquated system of justices of the
peace is inefficient.
```

```
For urgent reasons, I recommend that the United
States place a human observer in temporary orbit around
the planet Mars.
```

The body of the paper would set forth the writer's reasons for holding the view, and probably the writer would hammer the claim or thesis again at the end.

That advice refers to whole essays. Now let's see how in a single sentence you can stress things at the start. Consider the following unemphatic sentence,

```
When Congress debates the Hall-Hayes Act removing
existing legal protections for endangered species, as now
seems likely to occur on May 12, it will be a consider-
able misfortune if this bill should pass, since the ex-
tinction of many rare birds and animals would certainly
be the result.
```

The coming debate, and its probable date, take up the start of the sentence. The writer might have made better use of this emphatic position.

```
The extinction of many rare birds and animals will
follow passage of the Hall-Hayes Act.
```

Now the writer stresses what he most fears: dire consequences. (In a further sentence, he might add the date of the coming debate in Congress and his opinion that passage of the legislation would be a misfortune.)

Consider these further examples (a sentence in rough draft and in a revision):

```
It may be argued that the best way to choose soft-
ware for a small business is to call in a professional
consultant, who is likely to be familiar with the many
systems available and can give helpful advice.
```

```
The best way to choose software for a small business
is to call in a professional consultant.
```

In the second version, the paper might go on: "Familiar with the many systems available, such an expert can give helpful advice." Notice that in the revision, the two most important ingredients of the idea are placed first and last. *Best way* is placed up front, and *professional consultant,* standing last in the sentence, is also given emphasis.

Stating last In your reader's mind, an explosion of silence follows the final statement in your paper. To place an idea last can throw weight on it. One way to assemble your ideas in an emphatic order is to proceed from least important to most important.

This order is more dramatic: it builds up and up. Not all writing assignments call for drama, of course. In the papers on import quotas and justices of the peace, any attempt at a big dramatic buildup might look artificial and contrived. Still, this strategy is worth considering. Perhaps in an essay on city parks and how they lure shoppers to the city, the claim or thesis sentence— summing up the whole point of the essay—might stand at the very end: "For the inner city, to improve city parks will bring about a new era of prosperity." Ask yourself: "Just where in my essay have I made my one main point, the point I most want to make?" Once you find it, you see if you can place it last by cutting or shifting what comes after it.

Repeating

In general, it's economical to say a thing once. But at times a repetition can be valuable. One such time is when a repetition serves as a transition: it recalls something said earlier. (We discuss such repetition on p. 515.)

Repetition can be valuable, too, when it lends emphasis. When Robert Frost ends his poem "Stopping by Woods on a Snowy Evening" by repeating a line, he does so deliberately:

> The woods are lovely, dark and deep,
> But I have promises to keep,
> And miles to go before I sleep,
> And miles to go before I sleep.

The effect of this repetition is to lay weight on the fact that, for the speaker, a long, weary journey remains.

This device—repeating the words that most matter—is more often heard in a speech than found in writing. Recall Lincoln's Gettysburg Address, with its promise that "government of the people, by the people, and for the people" will endure; and Martin Luther King's famous speech with the insistent refrain "I have a dream." This is a powerful device for emphasis. Break it out only when an occasion calls for it.

CUTTING AND WHITTLING

Like pea pickers who throw out dirt and pebbles, good writers remove need-less words that clog their prose. They like to. One of the chief joys of revising is to watch 200 paunchy words shrink to a svelte 150. To see how saving words helps, let's first look at some wordiness. In what she imagined to be a gracious, Oriental style, a New York socialite once sent this dinner invitation to Hu Shi, the Chinese ambassador:

> O learned sage and distinguished representative of the numerous Chinese nation, pray deign to honor my humble abode with your noble presence at a pouring of libations, to be followed by a modest evening repast, on the forthcoming Friday, June Eighteenth, in this Year of the Pig, at the approximate hour of eight o'clock, Eastern Standard Time. Kindly be assured furthermore, O most illustrious sire, that a favorable reply at your earliest convenience will be received most humbly and gratefully by the undersigned unworthy suppliant.

In reply, the witty diplomat sent this telegram:

CAN DO. HU SHI.

Hu Shi's reply disputes a common assumption: that the more words an idea takes, the more impressive it will seem. Most good contemporary writers know that the more succinctly they can state an idea, the clearer and more forceful it will be.

Since the sixteenth century, some English writers have favored prolixity and, like the woman who invited Hu Shi, have deliberately ornamented their prose. George Orwell, a more recent writer who favored concision, thought English writing in his day had set a new record for wind. Perhaps the verbosity he disliked has been due in part to progress in the technology of writing. Quill pens that had to be dipped have given way to pens with ball points or felt tips, to electric typewriters and word processors. These strides have made words easier to seize and perhaps have made them matter less. As a printer-reporter in Virginia City, Nevada, Mark Twain sometimes wrote while he set type, transferring letters of lead from a case to a composing stick in his hand. An editorial might weigh ten pounds. Twain said the experience taught him the weight of a word. He soon learned to use no word that didn't matter.

Some writers may begin by writing a long first draft, putting in every scrap of material, spelling out their every thought in detail. They know that later it will be easier to trim away the surplus than to add missing essentials. But they mean to work back through the jungle of their prose with a merciless machete. In their revising habits, such writers may be like sculptor Auguste Rodin, who when an admirer asked, "Oh, Monsieur Rodin, is sculpture difficult?" answered lightly, "Not at all! I merely behold the statue in the block of stone. Then I chip away everything else." Let us see how writers chip away.

WORDY

```
As far as getting ready for winter is concerned, I put
antifreeze in my car.
```

REVISED

```
To get ready for winter, I put antifreeze in my car.
```

Some writers can't utter an idea without first sounding trumpets before it.

WORDY

```
The point should be made that . . .
I might hasten to add that . . .
Let me make it perfectly clear that . . .
```

Cut the fanfare. Why bother to announce that you're going to say something? We aren't, by the way, attacking the usefulness of transitions that lead a reader along. You wouldn't chop a sentence like "Because, as we have seen, Chomsky's theory fails to account for the phenomenon of stuttering, let us consider the work of speech psychologist Wendell Johnson."

The phrases *on the subject of, in regard to, in terms of, as far as . . . is concerned,* and their ilk often lead to wind.

WORDY

```
He is more or less a pretty outstanding person in regard
to good looks.
```

Write instead, "He is strikingly handsome" or "In looks, he stands out." Here's an especially grim example of corporate prose (before cutting and after):

WORDY

```
Regarding trainees' personal life in relation to domestic
status, it is not the intention of the management to ob-
ject to the marriage of any of its trainees at their own
individual discretions.
```

REVISED

```
Trainees may marry if they like.
```

Words can also tend to abound after *There is* or *There are.*

WORDY

```
There are many people who dislike flying.
```

This construction provides an easy way to open a sentence, but it takes words. You can cut it.

REVISED

```
Many people dislike flying.
```

Here's another instance:

WORDY

```
There is a lack of a sense of beauty in Wallace.
```

Make this "Wallace lacks a sense of beauty" or "Wallace is insensitive to beauty." Indeed, the verb *to be* can make a statement wordy when a noun or an adjective follows it.

WORDY

```
The Akron game was a disappointment to the fans.
```

Replace *to be* by an active verb and revise the sentences:

REVISED

```
The Akron game disappointed the fans.
```

Not only do such changes save words, they strengthen a verb and enliven a sentence.

Often, when a clause begins with a relative pronoun (*who, which, that*), you can whittle it to a phrase:

WORDY

```
Venus, which is the second planet of the solar system, is
called the evening star.
```

REVISED

```
Venus, the second planet of the solar system, is called
the evening star.
```

WORDY

```
Bert, who is a prize-winning violist, played a work of
Brahms.
```

REVISED

```
Bert, a prize-winning violist, played a work of Brahms.
```

The more you revise, the more shortcuts you'll discover. The following sentences have words that can just be cut (indicated in *italics*). Try reading each sentence without them.

Howell spoke for the sophomores and Janet *also spoke* for the seniors.
Professor Lombardi is *one of the most* amazing *men.*
He is *somewhat of* a clown, but *sort of the* lovable *type.*

As a major in *the field of* economics, I plan to concentrate on *the area of* international banking.
The decision as to whether *or not* to go is up to you.
The vice-chairman *very much* regrets that he is *very* busy.

Adjectives and adverbs are often dispensable. Consider the difference between these two versions.

WORDY

```
Johnson's extremely significant research led to highly
important major discoveries.
```

REVISED

```
Johnson's research led to major discoveries.
```

While sometimes a long word conveys a shade of meaning that its shorter synonym doesn't, in general it's a good idea to shun a long word or phrase when you can pick a short one. Instead of *the remainder,* try to write *the rest;* instead of *activate, start* or *begin;* instead of *expedite, rush;* instead of *adequate* or *sufficient, enough.* Wordiness, to be sure, doesn't always come from slinging overlarge words. Sometimes it comes from not knowing a right word — one that wraps an idea in a smaller package. The cumbersome expression *persons who are new to the sport of skiing* could be replaced by *novice skiers.* Consider these two remarks about a boxer:

WORDY

```
Andy has a left fist that has a lot of power in it.
```

REVISED

```
Andy has a potent left.
```

By the way, it pays to read. From reading, you absorb words like *potent* and *novice* and set them to work for you.

Here is a student essay that gained from cutting and whittling. John Martin, a business administration major, wrote this economics paper to fulfill the assignment "Set forth and briefly discuss a current problem in international trade. Venture an opinion or propose a solution." You can see the thoughtful cuts and condensations that Martin made with the help of his English instructor and his peer editor. Following the edited draft, you'll find the paper (p. 536) as he resubmitted it — in fewer words.

FIRST DRAFT

Japan's Closed Doors: Should the U.S. Retaliate?

~~There is currently~~ A serious problem *is* brewing in ~~the world of~~ international trade~~;~~ *a cliché to cut* ~~which may turn out to be a real tempest in a teapot, so to speak.~~ According to the latest National Trade Estimates report, several ~~of the countries that the~~ U.S. *trading partners* ~~has been doing business with~~ deserve to be condemned for ~~what the report has characterized as~~ "unfair trade practices." The government has said it will use the report to single out ~~specific~~ countries ~~which it is then going to go ahead and~~ *to* punish under the Super 301 provisions of the trade law.

The Super 301 section ~~of the trade law~~ requires *attack* Carla Hills, ~~who is~~ the U.S. trade representative, to ~~try~~ *calls* ~~to get rid of~~ what she ~~has officially designated to be~~ "priority unfair practices." She will be slashing at the *same thing as impediments* ~~whole~~ web of impediments ~~and obstacles~~ that have ~~slowed down or~~ denied *American* ~~the various products of the many United States~~ firms ~~much~~ *fast* access to Japanese markets.

~~It is important for the reader to note here that for a long time, longer than anyone can remember,~~ Japan has *long* been the ~~leading~~ prime candidate for a dose of Super 301. Over the past decade~~,~~ ~~there have been many years of negotiations and battering by different~~ *have battered* industry groups at the ~~unyielding~~ doors of ~~the~~ Japanese markets, *with* ~~which have yielded~~ some success~~es~~, but ~~have pretty much~~ failed ~~miserably to~~ *make them swing wide.* ~~dent the invisible trade barriers that stand looming between us and the Japanese markets, preventing the free access of U.S. goods to Japanese consumers. As far as~~ The U.S. trade deficit with Japan~~, is concerned, it was somewhat~~ more than $50 billion last year~~, and it~~ shows ~~very~~ little sign of *improving* ~~getting significantly much better~~ in 1990.

Some American businesspeople would ~~like to~~ take aim at Japan immediately. However, Clyde Prestowitz, ~~who is~~

a former Commerce Department official, ~~seriously~~ doubts
that ~~in the last analysis~~ it would be ^wise to^ ~~a good idea to come
out and~~ name Japan ~~to feel the terrible effects of~~ ^for^ retaliation under Super 301 : ~~in view of the fact that in his
opinion,~~ "It's hard to negotiate with guys you are calling cheats." No doubt ~~there are~~ many other observers ~~who~~
share his view.

Evidently ~~it is the task of~~ the administration ^has^ to
try to ^help^ ~~pave the way for~~ U.S. exports ~~to~~ wedge their way
into ~~the~~ protected Japanese markets while keeping ~~it
firmly~~ in mind that the interests of both ~~the United
States and the Japanese~~ nations call for ^stronger^ ~~a strengthening
of the~~ economic and military ties. ~~that bind both countries into a sphere of friendly relationship. It is my
personal conclusion that~~ If the administration goes ahead ,
~~with this,~~ it will ~~certainly~~ need to plan ~~ahead for the
future~~ carefully.

"ties" will
suffice.

REVISED VERSION

Japan's Closed Doors: Should the U.S. Retaliate?

A serious problem is brewing in international trade.
According to the latest National Trade Estimates report,
several U.S. trading partners deserve to be condemned for
"unfair trade practices." The government has said it
will use the report to single out countries to punish
under the Super 301 provisions of the trade law.

The Super 301 section requires Carla Hills, the U.S.
trade representative, to attack what she calls "priority
unfair practices." She will be slashing at the web of
impediments that have denied American firms fast access
to Japanese markets.

Japan has long been the prime candidate for a dose
of Super 301. Over the past decade, industry groups have
battered at the doors of Japanese markets, with some success, but failed to make them swing wide. The U.S. trade

deficit with Japan, more than $50 billion last year, shows little sign of improving in 1990.

Some American businesspeople would take aim at Japan immediately. However, Clyde Prestowitz, a former Commerce Department official, doubts that it would be wise to name Japan for retaliation under Super 301: "It's hard to negotiate with guys you are calling cheats." No doubt many other observers share his view.

Evidently the administration has to try to help U.S. exports wedge their way into protected Japanese markets while keeping in mind that the interests of both nations call for stronger economic and military ties. If the administration goes ahead, it will need to plan carefully.

Here is a final list of questions to use in slimming your writing.

REVISION CHECKLIST: CUTTING AND WHITTLING

- Do you announce an idea before you utter it? If so, consider giving the announcement a chop.
- Can you recast any sentence that begins *There is* or *There are*?
- What will happen if, wherever you use *to be*, you substitute an active verb?
- Can you reduce to a phrase any clause beginning with *which is, who is,* or *that is*?
- Do you see any useless words that might go? Try omitting them.

CHAPTER 18

Strategies for Working with Fellow Writers:

Collaborative Learning

Some people imagine the writer all alone in an ivory tower, toiling in perfect solitude. But in the real world, writing is often a collaborative effort. In business firms, reports are sometimes written by teams and revised by committees before being submitted to top-level managers. People sit around a table throwing out ideas, which a secretary transcribes and someone else writes up. A crucial letter, an advertisement, or a company's annual report embodies the thinking and writing of many. Research scientists and social scientists often work in teams of two or more and collaborate on articles for professional journals. In Chapter 8, we presented an essay by Edward Teyber and Charles D. Hoffman, two psychologists writing in collaboration for a general audience. Even this book is the result of collaborative writing.

In more and more colleges today, instructors are encouraging students to work together on their writing. Students, to be sure, can give one another help and support that an instructor can't begin to provide. That is why, in the body of this book, we include peer editing checklists and suggest activities for group learning (in Chapters 1–10, 11, and 13). Whether or not your instructor finds time to use them, they may supply ideas you can use on your own.

Forming a writing community In some courses, instructors encourage a class to divide into smaller groups. Sometimes these groups encourage and inspire one another, getting together for definite reasons: to discuss reading, to generate ideas for each student's paper, or to supply constructive criticism of drafts and finished papers. In some courses, student groups are invited to collaborate on one piece of writing. Group members spend some time at the start of the course getting to know one another; all are given a list of names, addresses, and phone numbers of everyone in the group.

Naturally these groups don't always work in harmony. Some members may become dictatorial, others may slack off. If you find yourself in a group that develops problems, don't let them snowball—try to thrash them out as soon as they arise. From the start, all members of a group should agree clearly on what needs doing and how to go about doing it. Taking part in a group calls for patient give-and-take, much as you are likely to do later as a member of a business firm, medical team, academic committee, theater group, research team, social agency, or other professional organization. Oftener than not, the results from writing groups have been so encouraging that more and more instructors are making them part of a composition course.

Breaking away   Whether or not your instructor formally organizes you into a group, you will want to break out of your ivory tower now and again to develop your own writing community. You'll want to show what you write to other students, read their work, talk over your work in your courses and any writing you're planning. Students, we realize, have tight schedules. Besides, at many colleges all live off-campus, making it hard to hold casual get-togethers. Writing laboratories and writing centers are one response to this problem. Inquire whether your college has such a facility and, if it does, investigate. Drop by and see what it has to offer you.

Peer tutors   Writing centers usually function with peer tutors, students who have some experience (and usually some training) in helping other students to write. Typically, a student comes into the writing center with a problem: "My sociology teacher has assigned a term paper and I don't have the foggiest notion how to go about it." Student and peer tutor sit down together and try to get the project under way. The peer tutor, of course, doesn't write the paper for the student, but only helps the student to fulfill the assigned task. What makes peer tutors effective is that they aren't professors, able to decree and empowered to grade; they're helpful friends of your own generation. To be such a peer tutor, as many have testified, can be a major learning experience.

PEER EDITING

Your first draft written, you face the task of shaping your paper into its final, most readable form. How do you know what needs improving and changing? You may be quite pleased with your draft as it stands and feel reluctant to think it needs anything more done to it. But at this point you may be wise to submit your paper to other student writers—your peers.

For many student writers, it comes as a pleasant surprise to find how genuinely helpful fellow students can be. Asked to read an early draft, they respond to a paper, signal strengths in it, and offer constructive suggestions. In doing so, they explicitly guide a writer in revising. When you are the writer, this process gives you a very real sense of having a living, breathing, supportive audience nearby.

Some instructors make peer evaluation a regular part of a course. They ask students to form small groups—often three or four people—and to read and respond to one another's writing in class. Other instructors ask that the reading and responding be done at home. In some classes, each member of the small group receives a photocopy of the writer's first draft, marks it up, and returns it to the instructor. By this system the instructor monitors the whole process, collects all the comments, and passes them on to the writer to use in revising the draft. Giving reactions to other writers becomes part of each student's process of learning to write better. In fact, students are graded not only on their writing but also on their skill as editors. Often the instructor will ask the student who gets the comments to grade the commentators or at least give them written responses in return. As a rule, all comments on a paper are set down in writing, not merely discussed in class. And so, when the author of the paper goes home to revise it, she or he has a record of the suggestions and can think each one over carefully.

If your instructor does not require peer editing, you can arrange it on your own. Enlist one or more peers to read your work and comment on it. You can provide the same service in return. Should the students you recruit be willing to read and react but reluctant to write comments for you, at least you can have them go through your draft with you, pointing out what they distrust—and admire. If you work that way, be sure you write down any suggestions any reader makes. Otherwise you may forget them by the time you're ready to revise.

Before you show a draft to your peer editor, you might take a few minutes to write down the two or three chief questions about your draft that you'd like him or her to answer. What do you want to know, the better to proceed with your rewrite? Attach your questions to your draft. Anyone who reads it will first read your questions about it and will try to come up with brief written answers for you. To discuss after your paper is done: how helpful was it to write out these questions? If it proves worth doing, you may want to do it for any future paper you show to a peer editor.

SERVING AS A READER

What does it take to be a helpful, supportive peer editor? Once you see what such a peer editor goes through and serve as a reader and commentator yourself, perhaps you'll better appreciate any reactions you get to your own writing.

Be tactful. It might go without saying, but we'll say this anyway: approach your fellow writer's work in a friendly way. Remember, you aren't out to pass godlike judgment on your peer's effort ("What confused garbage!"). Your purpose is to give honest, intelligent appreciation—to help make the other writer aware of what's written right, not only what's written wrong. When you find fault, you can do so by making impartial observations—statements that nobody can deny. A judgmental way to criticize might be "This paper is confused. It keeps saying the same thing over and over again." But a more useful comment might be more specific: "Paragraph 5 makes the same point as paragraphs 2 and 3" (which observation suggests that two of the three paragraphs might be eliminated).

Look at the big picture. Your job isn't merely to notice misspelled words or misused semicolons (although it can't hurt to signal any that you see). Bend your mind to deeper matters: to what the writer is driving at, to the sequence of ideas, to the apparent truth or falsehood of the observations, to the quantity and quality of any evidence, to the coherence or unity of the paper as a whole.

Ask questions. For help in looking for things like that, skim the following checklist of reader's questions. Not all these points will apply to every paper. We've given more questions here than you'll usually want to ask.

FIRST QUESTIONS

What is my first reaction to this paper?

What is this writer trying to tell me? What does he or she most want me to learn?

What are this paper's greatest strengths?

Does it have any major weaknesses?

QUESTIONS ON MEANING

Do I understand everything? Is there any information missing from this draft that I still need to know?

Is what this paper tells me worth saying, or does it only belabor the obvious? Does it tell me anything I didn't know before?

Is the writer trying to cover too much territory? Too little?

Does any point need to be more fully explained or illustrated?

When I come to the end, do I find that the paper has promised me anything it hasn't delivered?

Could this paper use a down-to-the-ground revision? Would it benefit from a different topic altogether—one the writer perhaps touches but doesn't deal with in this paper?

QUESTIONS ON ORGANIZATION

Has the writer begun in such a way that I'm interested? Am I quickly drawn into the paper's main idea? Or can I find, at some point later in the paper, a better possible beginning?

Does the paper have one main idea, or does it struggle to handle more than one? Would the main idea stand out better if anything were removed?

Might the ideas in the paper be more effectively rearranged in a different order? Do any ideas belong together that now seem too far apart?

Does the writer keep to one point of view—one angle of seeing? (If he starts out writing as a college student, does he switch to when he was a boy without telling me? If he starts out as an enemy of smoking, does he end up as an advocate?)

Does the ending seem deliberate, as if the writer meant to conclude at this point? Or does the writer seem merely to have run out of gas? If so, what can the writer do to write a stronger conclusion?

QUESTIONS ON LANGUAGE AND WRITING STRATEGIES

Do I feel this paper addresses *me*? Or does the writer appear to have no idea who might be reading the paper?

At any point in the paper, do I find myself disliking or objecting to a statement the writer makes, to a word or a phrase with which I'm not in sympathy? Should this part be kept, whether or not I object, or should it be changed?

Does the draft contain anything that distracts me, that seems unnecessary, that might be struck?

Do I get bored at any point and want to tune out? What might the writer do to make me want to keep reading?

Can I follow the writer's ideas easily? Does the paper need transitions (words and phrases that connect), and, if it does, at what places?

Does the language of this paper stay up in the clouds of generality, referring always to *agricultural commodities* and *legality,* never to *pigs' feet* and *parking tickets*? If so, where and how might the writer come down to earth and get specific?

Do I understand all the words the writer uses, or are there any specialized words (such as scientific words or dialect) whose meaning needs to be made clearer?

LAST QUESTION

Now that I have lived with this paper for a while and looked at it closely, how well does it work for me?

To show the writer just where you had a reaction, write comments in the margins of the paper. Then at the end write some overall comment, making any major, general suggestions. Let your final comment sum up the paper's strong and weak points. It can hardly be all good or all bad. Vague blame or vague praise won't help the writer. Don't say, "I liked this essay a lot because I can relate to it." True, such a response might be better than nothing: it might make the writer feel glad. But "That example in paragraph 9 clarified the whole point of the paper for me" might make the author feel glad for good reason.

What does a helpful overall comment look like? Here is the way Maria Mendez responded to a draft of a paper by Jill Walker that ended up being titled "Euthanasia and the Law":

> Jill—
> The topic of this paper interested me a lot, because we had a case of euthanasia in our neighborhood. I didn't realize at first what your topic was—maybe the title "Life and Death" didn't say it to me. Your paper is full of good ideas and facts—like the Hemlock Society to help mercy-killing. I got lost when you start talking about advances in modern medicine (paragraph 6) but don't finish the idea. To go into modern medicine thoroughly would take a lot more room. Maybe euthanasia is enough to cover in five pages. Also, I don't know everything you're mentioning ("traditional attitudes toward life and death"). I could have used an explanation there—I'm from a different tradition. On the whole, your paper is solid and is going to make us agree with you.
> Maria

WRITING WITH A COMPUTER: SERVING AS A READER

If the writer wrote with a word processor, the two of you might sit down in front of the monitor screen together. You can scroll slowly through the document, commenting on the draft line by line. But if the writer doesn't want to stick around and watch you edit, you can put your comments and suggestions in brackets at whatever places in the draft they need to be made. Thanks to word processing, it will be easy for the writer, after reading all the comments, to search for every first bracket and delete each comment.

```
Harry S Truman had a folksy way of expressing
himself, which makes us remember many of his
sayings.  [Can you give an example?]  He was a
folksy speaker [Cut this repetition.] and de-
veloped his style in the rough-and-tumble of
Mississippi politics.  [You mean Missouri.]
```

LEARNING AS A WRITER

You, the writer whose work is in the spotlight, will probably find you can't just sit back and enjoy your fans' reactions. To extract all the usefulness from the process of peer reviewing, you'll need to play an active part in discussing your work. Probably your readers will give you many more specific reactions if you question them, directing their attention to places in your paper where you especially want insights. This will help them do a good job for you. Get at specific issues, get at the *whys* behind their responses. Ask pointed questions like these *in writing* for your critics to think about:

> When you read my conclusion, are you convinced that I'm arguing for the one right solution to this problem? Can you imagine any better solution?

> Paragraph four looks skimpy—only two short sentences. What could I do to make it longer?

> How clear is my purpose? Can you sum up what I'm trying to say? What steps can I take to make my point hit home to you?

You may already know that something is wrong with your early draft. Express any doubts you have. Point out to your readers what parts you found difficult to write. Ask them what *they* would do about any deficiencies.

The best editors are sympathetic but tough. Ask yours not to be too easy on you. Let them know that when you go back to your paper it will not be merely to make cosmetic repairs but, if need be, to make deep structural changes in what you have written. You might even get, from their reactions, new ideas you didn't have before. They may also have some tips about where to find more, and more valuable, material.

Take what's helpful. Occasionally students worry that asking another student, no wiser or brighter than themselves, to criticize their work is a risk not worth taking. It's true that you have to accept such help judiciously. Sometimes it will strike a reader that something is wrong with a piece of writing. Not wanting to seem unhelpful, the reader—although not knowing a surefire remedy—will make a suggestion anyway to show that he or she is trying to help. You want to be wary about following all the suggestions you receive. While some of them may help, others may lead down a dead-end street. At times when a reader finds fault with your work, you may want to make some change but not necessarily the very change your critic suggests.

Make a list of the suggestions you receive. You may find that some will cancel out others. Let your instincts operate: do any of the suggestions seem worth trying? The important thing in taking advice and suggestions is to listen to your critics but not be a slave to them. You have to feel that, after all, you're the boss.

It takes self-trust to take criticism with profit. The final decision about whether or not to act on the advice you get from your fellow students is solely up to you. If you feel that one person's suggestions have not helped at all, you would be wise to get a second opinion, and maybe a third. When several of your readers disagree, only you can decide whose suggestions to follow.

PEER EDITORS IN ACTION

The following brief histories point out how effectively fellow students can help a revision. First, consider this early draft of an opening paragraph for the essay "Why Don't More People Donate Their Bodies to Science?" by Dana Falk, written in a tandem course in English and sociology.

```
     The question of why more organs and body parts are
not donated "to science"--that is, for the use of organ
transplants, medical research, and college education--is
a puzzling one.  As I have learned through my research,
it is also a multidetermined one.  There are a plethora
of reasons that prevent there from being enough organs to
go around, and in this paper I shall examine a number of
the reasons I have uncovered, trying to evaluate the ef-
fectiveness of efforts to alleviate the shortage and sug-
gest possible alternate approaches myself.  Primarily,
though, we will simply look at the factors that prevent
health professionals from being able to supply body parts
each and every time a donor is needed.
```

Falk showed the paper to a fellow student, Pamela Kong, who jumped at once on the opening sentence. "This could be rephrased as a question," she suggested, and she wrote "AWKWARD" next to the sentence that begins "There are a plethora of reasons that prevent there from being. . . ." "That sentence was pretty bad!" Falk later realized. Kong zeroed in on the stilted word *multidetermined* (apparently meaning "having several causes") and called for a clearer announcement of where the paper was going. After reading Kong's comments and doing some hard thinking, Falk recast the opening paragraph to read:

```
     The gap between the demand for human organs and
their current supply is ever-widening.  With the intro-
```

```
duction of cyclosporine, an immunosuppressant, the suc-
cess rate of transplants is way up, yet this bright spot
is clouded by the fact that many potential donors and
their families resist giving away their body parts, cre-
ating an acute shortage.  Why is it that people so fear
giving their bodies to science?  My goal is to examine
the causes of the shortage of transplantable organs and
to review some possible solutions.
```

As you'll see if you compare the two passages, Falk's language becomes more concrete and definite with the use of two figures of speech. Now we have an "ever-widening gap" and a "bright spot" that is "clouded." The added detail about the newly successful drug lends the paper fresh authority—and no longer does the writer have to trumpet "my research." Pam Kong's suggestion to turn the question into an actual one (with a question mark) lends life to the sentence that now begins "Why is it that people so fear. . . ." The announced plan for the rest of the paper, now placed at the end of the paragraph, points toward everything that will follow. This hard-working job of rewriting (which continued throughout the whole paper) drew Falk's English instructor, Jeff Skoblow, to remark: "Your revising powers have grown formidable." No doubt some of the credit belonged to Pam Kong as well.

Now let's see how a peer editor helped a fellow student strengthen an entire paper. Kevin Deters wrote the following short essay for his English composition course. The assignment asked for a "reflective" essay in response to his own reading. Even in this early draft, you'll find, Deters's paper treats a challenging subject, and it comes to a thoughtful conclusion. But as the paper stands, what does it lack?

FIRST DRAFT

Where Few Men Have Gone Before

Kevin Deters

Space: the final frontier. This is the subject
addressed by the renowned writer Isaac Asimov in "Into
Space: The Next Giant Step," a short piece published in
the St. Louis Post-Dispatch. Asimov, the author of over
four hundred science and science fiction books, writes
about the space station that will be built in orbit
around the earth in the near future. He examines the advantages and numerous possibilities of space travel that
such a station would allow. This space station will give
people the opportunity to be explorers, help conserve resources on earth, and unite the nations of the world as
they forge the common goal of discovering knowledge of
outer space.

"It is absolutely necessary that we build a base
other than earth for our ventures into space. . . . The
logical beginning is with a space station," Asimov says.
The space station would serve as a stepping stone to future permanent bases on the moon and Mars. Adventurous
settlers would pave the spaceways just as Daniel Boone
and his followers blazed trails through the Kentucky
wilderness. It is these space travelers "who will be the
Phoenicians, the Vikings, the Polynesians of the future,
making their way into the 21st century through a space-
ocean far vaster than the water-ocean traversed by their
predecessors."

These spacefarers will also find ways to help conserve valuable energy on earth. Asimov suggests that,
using the space station as a base, lunar materials could
be excavated from the moon to construct power stations to
direct solar energy toward the earth. Thus, energy and
money are saved, and this conservation could serve as a
deterrent to the use of nuclear energy.

With this new surplus of energy, nuclear energy and

all its applications such as power plants and missiles would become unnecessary. A major threat to world safety would be removed. The sun's never-ending supply of solar energy could be harnessed to become the chief energy source on earth, and dangerous forms of energy could be done away with.

As a result, expensive heating bills and the like would be unheard of. Energy costs would plummet as earth's populace took advantage of the sun's plentiful rays. The price decrease would snowball, affecting other aspects of life, eventually resulting in a cheaper cost of living.

The construction of such a space station could also help unify the countries of the world. A massive project like this enterprise would cost billions of dollars and take a massive amount of time and hard work. Asimov suggests that if the United States and the Soviet Union were to work together, costs and time could be considerably lessened. Such joint U.S./U.S.S.R. missions are not unheard of. The Apollo-Soyuz venture, which linked together a satellite from each nation, was a success.

This joint effort could help promote global togetherness as well. If the world's nations could unite to explore space, surely problems back home on earth could be easily solved. Such quibbles as the nuclear arms race and foreign trading disputes seem trivial and inconsequential when compared to the grandeur of space exploration.

And so, this space station will serve as a valuable tool for humanity. Man must now reach for the heavens above him, because if the earth's population keeps increasing, the planet will soon be too small to accommodate everyone. Space exploration is the only logical answer. Space is indeed the final frontier that lies before us. We only have to take advantage of it.

Kevin Deters's classmate, Jennifer Balsavias, read his reflective essay and filled out a peer editing questionnaire. Here are the questions and her responses to them.

PEER EDITING CHECKLIST

1. First, sit on your hands and read the essay through. Then describe your first reaction.

This was a well-written report. The only time I really noticed any reflection on the reading was in the last paragraph.

2. What is "reflective" about this essay? What is the purpose of the essay and the major reflection?

The purpose of the essay was to show the importance of space to humans and their expansion into that final frontier. In the last paragraph, he lets us know his feelings on the information given. He doesn't reflect about the reading throughout the paper.

3. How skillfully has the writer used reading? Look at the way quotations or paraphrases are inserted. Is it clear when the writer is using reading and when the ideas are the writer's? Comment on any areas that were problematic to you.

He uses quotes and information from the reading very well. The writer is definitely using the reading and adds only a few thoughts of his own. Needs to reflect more!

4. Is the paper informed enough by reading? Where could the paper improve by more careful or detailed use of "secondary" (not personal) materials?

It's not very personal. His own feelings and reflections should be involved. There is enough about the reading. Maybe he shouldn't expand so much on the subject. Maybe stop after the first or second paragraph and REFLECT!

5. Who's the essay written to? Describe the audience.

I feel it is written to those interested in space and the new space programs. I found it interesting.

6. List any terms or phrases that are too technical or specialized or any words that need further definition.

7. If you were handing the essay in for a grade, what
    would you be sure to revise?

I'd put some of my own reflections in, not just facts.

8. Circle on the manuscript any problems with spelling,
    punctuation, grammar, or usage.

None that I saw!

In reading Jennifer Balsavias's evaluation, Deters was struck by her main criticism: "The only time I really noticed any reflection on the reading was in the last paragraph." "Needs to reflect *more*!" Deters's paper seemed more like a report on an article than an essay analyzing the article with some original thinking. It was difficult for the reader to tell Isaac Asimov's opinions from Deters's own. Perhaps Deters needed to express his views more clearly and not shun the first-person *I*. He reworked his draft, trying to set forth his own opinions, trying also to tighten and sharpen his prose. Here is his revised essay.

REVISED VERSION

Where Few Have Gone Before

Kevin Deters

Space: the final frontier. The renowned writer
Isaac Asimov addressed this subject in "Into Space: The
Next Giant Step," a short piece published in the <u>St.
Louis Post-Dispatch</u>. Asimov, the author of over four
hundred science and science fiction books, writes about
the space station that will be built in orbit around the
earth in the near future. He examines the advantages and
numerous possibilities of space travel that such a station would allow. From this article, I gathered that
this space station will give people the opportunity to be
explorers, help conserve resources on earth, and unite
the nations of the world as they forge the common goal of
discovering knowledge of outer space. I'm intrigued by
each of these possibilities.

Asimov tells us, "It is absolutely necessary that we
build a base other than earth for our ventures into
space. . . . The logical beginning is with a space station." A space station would serve as a stepping stone to
future permanent bases on the moon and Mars. I can imagine adventurous settlers who would pave the spaceways
just as Daniel Boone and his followers blazed trails
through the Kentucky wilderness. These space travelers
Asimov describes as "the Phoenicians, the Vikings, the
Polynesians of the future, making their way into the 21st
century through a space-ocean far vaster than the water-
ocean traversed by their predecessors."

The spacefarers will also find ways to help conserve
valuable energy on earth. Asimov suggests that, with the
space station as a base, lunar materials could be excavated from the moon to construct power stations that
could direct solar energy toward the earth. Thus, energy
and money could be saved along with our diminishing fos-

sil fuels. I believe that this conservation could possibly serve as a deterrent to the use of nuclear energy. With this new surplus of energy, it is my belief that nuclear energy and all its applications such as power plants and missiles would become unnecessary. The sun's never-ending supply of solar energy could be harnessed to become the chief energy source on earth, and dangerous forms of energy could be done away with.

As a result, I suggest that undoubtedly expensive heating bills and the like would be unheard of. Energy costs would plummet as earth's populace would take advantage of the sun's plentiful rays. The price decrease would snowball, affecting other aspects of life, eventually resulting in a cheaper cost of living.

The construction of the space station that Asimov suggests could also help unify the countries of the world. A project like this would cost billions of dollars and take a massive amount of time and hard work. No one country could afford the project. Asimov suggests that if the United States and the Soviet Union were to work together, costs and time could be considerably lessened.

I conclude that without a doubt this joint effort could help promote global togetherness as well. If the world's nations could unite to explore space, surely problems back home could be easily solved. Such quibbles as the nuclear arms race and foreign trading disputes seem trivial and inconsequential when compared to the grandeur of space exploration.

Such joint U.S./U.S.S.R. missions are not unheard of. Although it was before my time, I know that the Apollo-Soyuz venture, which linked together a satellite from each nation, was a success. Also, I enjoyed the science fiction film 2010, partly because it detailed a

future manned flight to Mars by a crew consisting of both
American and Soviet astronauts.

And so, as Asimov suggests, this space station will
serve as a valuable tool for humanity. I concur, for I
believe the human race must now reach for the heavens.
If the earth's population keeps increasing, the planet
will soon be too small to accommodate everyone; it will
need "elbow room" like Daniel Boone. For me, space exploration is the only logical answer. Space is indeed
the final frontier that lies before us. We have only to
take advantage of it.

You'll notice that, as Jennifer Balsavias suggested, Deters seems to reflect harder in his revised version. And by speaking out in his own voice, he makes clear (as he didn't do in the earlier version) that many of his thoughts are his own, not Isaac Asimov's. Notice, too, Deters's smaller but highly effective alterations. At the end, he returns to his earlier, original comparison between pioneers in space and Daniel Boone. In the next-to-last paragraph, he brings in a further bit of evidence: a science fiction film he had recently seen, *2010.* All his changes produce a more concise, readable, and absorbing paper, one that goes a little deeper—thanks in part to the services of an honest, helpful peer editor.

As your writing skills continue to develop, you may find yourself relying less on your peers and more on your own ability to analyze your early drafts. When you ask yourself what is right or wrong with your own paper, you can use the very same list of questions you used in evaluating other writers' papers. And when you learn to answer those questions searchingly, you'll become your own most valuable reader.

CHAPTER 19

Strategies for Writing with a Computer

"I love being a writer," declares novelist Peter De Vries. "What I can't stand is the paperwork."

If you have ever felt this way, you can appreciate the modern miracle of the word processor—a computer with the software necessary for writing. Some writers think word processing the greatest thing since Gutenberg invented movable type. Many find that, for the first time, writing becomes fun—like playing a video game, setting down ideas in bursts like gunfire, zapping out any that seem unnecessary.

Have you not yet tried word processing and do you want to know more about it? Then read on.

Are you, on the other hand, a practiced veteran who already writes with a computer? Then skip over to page 559 for some practical tips on making word processing work more effectively for you.

As you have probably noticed, earlier chapters of this book also contain suggestions for computer-assisted writing. And for particulars on how to format and print out a word-processed manuscript, please see page 580.

WHAT WORD PROCESSING CAN DO

By enabling your work-in-progress to take shape on screen instead of on paper and by storing what you write, word processing does away with much of the mechanical work of rewriting. No more typing and retyping draft after draft. No more retyping a page just because you wish to switch around the order of two sentences. You can make changes neatly, right on screen, before the document is printed out. You can lift out words, sentences, and paragraphs and set them down somewhere else. You can readily add material or take it out. You can play around with the sequence of ideas, rearranging them into an order you like.

This tremendous advantage—ease of rewriting—is probably what enchants most writers. But revision isn't the only stage of writing in which a computer will be useful: it can help you quickly set down rough ideas and organize material; it can even do some of the work of editing and proofreading for you. Word processing lets you—

insert documents into other documents

search for and replace a word or phrase you wish to change

correct mistakes easily

print many copies, all equally legible

store a hundred or more pages of documents in a small space: on a disk no larger than a compact disc

Certain software programs can lend still greater assistance: they can check your spelling and grammar, feed you questions to prompt your ideas, help you organize your material. In a moment, we'll tell you more about some of these.

WHAT IT'S LIKE TO WRITE WITH A WORD PROCESSOR

"Everything you write comes out in a state of flux!" one writer complained, on first trying word processing, and went back to his typewriter. At first, for a writer accustomed to typing or pushing a pen, word processing may seem unnerving. You don't place marks directly on paper, where they stay put, to be corrected only by erasing or crossing out and rewriting or retyping. You arrange words in easily altered structures visible on a screen—or only partially visible. Because most screens display only about twenty-four lines at a time, some as few as sixteen, you won't be able to reread parts of what you write without "scrolling" your work backward or forward. What you directly produce is a long and detailed set of instructions for a printer to obey.

Word processing might seem ideal for a writer like paperwork-hating Peter De Vries. But paper is still an essential element in the process—it is where the words end up.

In word processing, you can throw down thoughts in whatever order they come to mind. Then you can move them around and arrange them as seems best. Of course, you can do this kind of planning and revising with paper and scissors, too, but word processors encourage it. They enable you to write an outline, then flesh it out on screen, working on it until it turns into a finished essay before your eyes. The process is a little like making a stew, adding an ingredient at a time, stirring and blending and cooking everything to a consistent thickness, all in the same pot. When you come across additional material, you can squeeze it right in where you want it, again without recopying. If you want to change a word throughout what you are writing, you tell the computer to search out that word and replace it each time it occurs. When you come to the end of a line, you don't have any typewriter carriage to return: the computer automatically begins a new line when it fills the old one to capacity. Unlike people who type on typewriters, writers who write with word processors may become more willing to draft quickly, less fearful of making mistakes.

And yet some college writers testify that a word processor makes them care more about getting things letter-perfect. Computers are sticklers for accuracy. Some students also find that to write in front of a glowing screen helps concentrate their attention. Fascinated, as if playing a video game, they stay aboard a train of thought for miles.

Writers who use word processors have widely different writing styles. Many prefer to write, rewrite, and edit entirely on screen, not even touching a piece of paper until they print out their finished product. Some like to set down alternative versions of a sentence or paragraph and look at them, decide which to keep, and destroy the rest. Others use some combination of word processing and more conventional technology. These writers still write a first draft in longhand and then copy over their stuff on a word processor for revising or editing. Others write on screen, print out the product, see what it looks like in black and white, then revise in pen or pencil, and finally go back to the word processor to make alterations. If you do all your work on screen, it may be wise to create a copy of the old document or print it out before beginning to edit it. Then, if you ever want to go back to something you've revised, you have a spare copy of it. If you like to revise a printout in pencil, you can triple-space or print it out with an unnaturally wide margin and give yourself plenty of revising room.

Even while you read, you can take notes. Instead of transcribing them laboriously on index cards, you can put them right on the disk—lay them right into what you're writing or make a separate file of them on the same disk (from which you can summon them at will). Some computers and software programs enable you to produce graphs and even graphic illustrations quickly and efficiently.

Disadvantages   Despite all these benefits, word processing has drawbacks. Some writers, according to author William Zinsser, miss the satisfaction of being able to rip a page out of the typewriter "and crumble it in a fit of frustration or rage." A trouble with writing with a stream of electrons is that the stream may dry up, if, say, your roommate plugs in a hair dryer while you have your word processor going and blows a fuse. Poof!—there goes your term paper. Some people worry terribly about accidentally erasing what they have written, and this makes them fearful of writing with a computer. These fears may be greatly exaggerated, unless you live in some place where the power is continually failing, like a Caribbean island, or where fuses continually blow, like a college dormitory. The answer to this problem, if it worries you, is to keep filing (or "saving") your work frequently. Whenever you come to a blank moment and want to knock off writing and vegetate for a while, save what you've written: transfer it out of the computer's memory to the disk. In five years of writing with word processors, we have lost only three pieces of copy—two of these because of human blunders, the other because of a momentary power failure.

So literal-minded is a computer that it will follow instructions any sensible human being would know enough to ignore. Hit a wrong key and you can transform a whole page to CAPITAL LETTERS—an obvious mistake, but the computer merely does what you tell it to. More devastating blunders are possible. You can lift out a paragraph or a page and save it in the computer's memory, fully intending to set it down in another place. Then you can get so absorbed in working on some other paragraph that you forget what you have lifted out. On some systems it is even possible, when you store something new, to erase by accident the piece you have previously lifted out and stored in memory. Because (unlike writing on paper) any words you remove become invisible, you are usually wise, any time you move something, to deliver it promptly to its destination.

Some writers become garrulous blabbers when they take to word processing. Finding to their surprise that they are enjoying writing, they run on and on. At one business firm, after word processors had been provided for the whole staff, the management found the people happily writing not brief memoranda but endless dissertations. Will a word processor turn you into a blabber? We suspect that it only makes you a more extreme case of the kind of writer you are already. If you are the sort who likes to fuss, word processing makes fussing easier. If you tend to jaw on and on, it will make you more loquacious by the yard, leading you to grind out vapid passages of word processorese. If you love concision, it will spur you to zap out the fat, make you all the more terse. You may have to keep yourself from sounding like a telegram.

WHAT IT TAKES

Hardware   At the outset, you will need a computer with at least 64 kilobytes of memory. This hardware is costly, but on many campuses nowadays you can cut costs. Some colleges can arrange for you to buy a PC (personal computer) at a deep discount or rent one. You will also need word processing software (a disk containing a program enabling you to write), sold under trade names such as WordStar, WordPerfect, Screenwriter II, Bank Street Writer— this last a program simple enough for schoolchildren to use. To make the program work, you must learn a series of commands, but don't fret: anyone who can learn to type can learn to use a word processor. You will also need a blank disk to write on and an electronic printer—one that will connect to your computer. (Not all brands of printers and computers get along together.)

An alternative: some writers use not a PC but a dedicated word processor or "small office system" such as the IBM Displaywriter. Such a computer is more limited in what it can do, but if all you want to do is write, then it will make life easy. Its program, generally simpler to learn than most programs designed for PCs, keeps supplying instructions that lend you support: it is a little like riding a bicycle with training wheels.

Computer centers At many colleges, you can reserve time to write at a computer center. There, you will probably compose at a keyboard that connects to a mainframe system—a powerful computer. Within its mighty brain, this collegewide behemoth stores (among other things) a word processing program. What facilities does your college offer? Ask around.

SPECIAL HELP FOR WRITERS

For most brands of computer, programs are now available to provide writers with special kinds of assistance. A cliché detector will automatically comb through prose and pick out stale phrases for freshening. Some programs will even check your spelling for you: these work by matching what you write against words in a dictionary stored in the computer's memory. Unfortunately, they are no substitute for human proofreading. Even the wisest spelling-check program won't complain about certain errors: if you accidentally type *her* instead of *here,* the program won't see it as a mistake, for in its dictionary *her* is a perfectly good word. Still other programs will check your grammar, show you what you did wrong, and suggest what to do about it. On the user's screen, IBM's word processing program Epistle will indicate a poorly structured sentence in red, alert the writer to the problem (or the broken grammatical rule) in blue, and suggest a correction in green. Such aids may help take the weight of editing and proofreading off the writer and free the mind for more essential things. Some instructors continue to expect a research paper to have endnotes (although the recent *MLA Handbook,* followed in this book, shows how to document sources without endnotes). Software can format endnotes and print them at the end of the paper where they belong.

Many word processing programs include an abbreviation feature—useful, say, if you will need to mention the name Peter Ilyich Tchaikovsky fifteen times in your essay. Instead of typing all those letters each time, you just type a special key followed by a *T* or an asterisk (or anything you've chosen) whenever you want it, and—presto!—the whole name will appear.

Some programs count words, so you can tell whether you are up to your assigned quota. Most programs will automatically drop in an identifying title at the top of each page, at the same time numbering the pages for you. One word processing program, called Nota Bene, will see that what you write conforms to any of five manuals of style, including the *MLA Handbook,* and will automatically format it for you. In practically every word processing program, you can search and replace—a feature useful if, in revising or editing, you think of a better word and want to substitute it at each place where a particular word occurs.

Other programs will even help you organize your rough ideas. Called "thought processors" or "idea processors," these have been developed under trade names such as Framework, ThinkTank, and Freestyle. They allow you to enter ideas and information at random and then help you organize your material into outline form. Of course, you still have to do the hard part yourself—come up with the ideas.

Computers now make it possible for writers to draw from vast realms of information available on *databases.* (On using a database in your research, see p. 414.)

A FEW PRACTICAL TIPS

For a change, if your word processing program lets you reverse the image on the screen of your monitor, try writing in white on black. The fresh look that all your words take on may render it a pleasure to write a draft.

A temptation, when your work isn't going well, is to spend your time editing: tinkering with the surface of your work and trying to prettify it instead of coping with the large and demanding revisions that may be necessary. One way to get around this temptation is to switch off your screen or twist up the darkness control until the words you write become unreadable. Keep writing even though you can't see your words. When you want to reread (and edit), then and only then take a look at them.

Because your screen will probably display only about twenty-four lines at a time, you may find it hard to hold in mind an entire piece of writing. In a long composition, large changes that involve several paragraphs may be harder to envision than if you had before you a stack of typed pages, which you could glance over in a flash. Of course, when you want to ponder several parts of your long document, you can scroll backward and forward; but then you have to hold in mind all that becomes invisible. The remedy for this problem (if you find it a problem) is to print out everything. Then you can ponder structural changes and other possible deep revisions much more easily and indicate with a pencil where you have work to do.

As people know who work all day at computer terminals in offices, watching a monitor can tire you out. Adjust the angle of your monitor and also its level of brightness for reading comfort. Take breaks now and then for exercise and light refreshments. The quality of your prose just might improve.

Have trouble thinking up a title for your paper? Rapidly freewrite a long list of titles at the top of your essay. Then delete all but the best.

Write out a short paper in three very different versions, starting a separate document for each of them. Then combine the best parts from all three versions.

Does your draft seem ill organized? Go through it and highlight in **bold** the main idea in each paragraph. You can then tell at a glance whether any ideas are missing or need rearranging into a different order.

Make a backup copy of the disk you're writing on, especially if you're not going to print out your work immediately. If you leave a disk lying around, one carelessly placed magnet—even a scissors or stapler that has become magnetized—can render parts of the disk unreadable. A telephone, stereo receiver, or TV set that makes contact with a disk will sometimes scramble it. Park a disk on a blazing hot radiator or spill a Coke on it and it can grow forgetful on you. Making a backup takes only minutes and can save hours.

Another good way to guard against accidental loss of words: print out a copy of everything you write.

Desktop publishing   Lately, desktop publishing has been working a revolution by making it cheaper and easier to produce newsletters, brochures, and small magazines all from the computer on your desk. With training, a single operator can produce good-looking pages resembling those of printed magazines in makeup quality and design. These may incorporate different styles and sizes of type, charts, graphs, and other computer-generated art. If anyone in your class has the skill and access to the hardware and software necessary, desktop publishing might transform what you and your fellow students write into a strikingly professional-looking magazine for local circulation.

THE LIMITS OF TECHNOLOGY

Enthusiasts of word processing sometimes argue that to write with a computer is a more congenial way to think in language than to write with a typewriter or a pen. The latter, they charge, tends to direct the flow of words in a straight line, through the slow, laborious recopying of draft after draft. The latter process requires a writer to retype or recopy good passages left unchanged as well as those that need rewriting—a process that differs from that of the mind, which corrects only things that need correcting. The human mind seems to think in a nonlinear way. It stores up odd fragments of information at any old time, on any old subject; it leaps like a grasshopper from one idea to another idea far removed. Word processing seems tailor-made for such a mind. It enables a writer to shape easily the amorphous blob of a first thought. All these arguments may hold true, but it is still hard to carry a word processor and a printer around in your pocket.

No computer will ever do all your thinking for you. The mind of a computer remains relatively simple compared with the human mind. Computer programs have been developed that will roughly translate simple scientific prose (after a fashion), but these programs often stumble, especially over any figurative language, such as metaphors ("Life is a bowl of cherries" or "Life is a can of worms"). One computer, told to translate the English proverb "Out of sight, out of mind" into literal Russian, dutifully complied. But when translated back into English, the proverb came out with an entirely different sense: "Invisible and insane."

If we regard computers with respect but not with slavish devotion, then with their aid we may be able to think—by writing—more swiftly and easily. More readily able to recall information, we may more readily deal with ideas of greater complexity. But the ideas have to be ours. A computer has no mind, no power to originate, no imagination at all—even though we call its spacious files a memory.

CHAPTER 20

Strategies for Writing in Class

So far, we've been considering how you write when *you* control your writing circumstances. We've assumed that in writing anything from a brief account of a remembered experience to a hefty research paper, you can write lying down or standing up, write in the quiet of a library or in a clattering cafeteria. Although an instructor may have handed you a deadline to meet, nobody has been timing you with a stopwatch.

But as you know, often in college you do need to write on the spot. You face quizzes to finish in twenty minutes, final exams to deliver in three or four hours, an impromptu essay to dash off in one class period. Just how do you discover, shape, and put across your ideas in a limited time, with the least possible agony?

First let's consider the techniques of writing an essay exam—in most courses the most important kind of in-class writing. Although lately multiple choice tests, scored by computer, have been whittling down the number of essay exams that college students write, still the tradition of the essay exam endures. Instructors believe that such writing shows that you haven't just memorized a bale of material but that you understand it, can think with it, and can make your thoughts clear to someone else. To prepare for an essay exam and to write it are seen as ways to lift knowledge out of textbook or notebook and bring it alive.

ESSAY EXAMINATIONS

The days before an examination offer you a chance to review what you have learned, to fill in any blank spots that remain. Such reviewing enables you to think deeply about your course work, to see how its scattered parts all fit together. Sometimes the whole drift and purpose of a course may be invisible until you look back over it.

As you review your reading and any notes gleaned from lectures and class discussion, it's a good idea—if the exam will be closed book—to fix in memory any vitally important names, dates, and definitions. We said "vitally important"—you don't want to clutter your mind with a lot of spare parts selected at random. You might well be glad, on the day of the exam, to have a few apt quotations at your command. But preparation isn't merely a matter of decorating a vast glacier of ignorance with a few spring flowers of dates and quotations. When you review, look for the main ideas or themes in each textbook chapter. Then ask yourself: What do these main ideas have to do with each other? How might they be combined? This kind of thinking is a practical form of imagining.

Some instructors favor open-book exams, in which you bring your books to class for reference, and perhaps your notes as well. In an open-book exam, ability to memorize is less important than ability to reason and to select what matters most. In such a writing situation, you have more opportunity than in a closed-book exam to generate ideas and to discover material on the spot.

When you study for either type of exam, you generate ideas. After all, what are you doing but discovering much more material than you'll be asked to use? The chief resource for most essay exams is your memory. What you remember may include observations, conversation, reading (usually important), and perhaps some imagination.

A good way to prepare in advance for any exam, whether the books are to be closed or open, is to imagine questions you might be asked. Then plan answers. We don't mean to suggest that you should try to psyche out your instructor. You're only slightly more likely to guess all the questions in advance than you are to clean out a slot machine in Las Vegas, but by thinking up your own questions, you review much material, imaginatively bring some of it together, and gain valuable experience in shaping answers. Sometimes, to help you get ready for an exam, the instructor will supply a few questions asked in former years. If you are given such examples, you can pattern new questions after them.

As you probably don't need to be told, trying to cram by going without sleep and food, consuming gallons of coffee, and reducing yourself to a wreck with red-rimmed eyes is no way to prepare. You can learn more in little bites than in huge gulps. Psychologists testify that if you study something for fifteen minutes a day for eight days, you'll remember far more than if you study the same material in one unbroken sprint of two hours.

Learning from Another Writer

To start looking at techniques of answering *any* exam question, let's take one concrete example. A final exam in developmental psychology posed this question:

> What evidence indicates innate factors in perceptual organization? You might find it useful to recall any research that shows how infants perceive depth and forms.

In response, David Ian Cohn sat back in his chair for ten minutes and thought over the reading he'd done for the course. What perception research had he heard about that used babies for subjects? He spent another five minutes jotting down ideas, crossed out a couple of weak ones, and drew lines connecting ideas that went together. (For an illustration of this handy technique, see "Linking," p. 495.) Then he took a deep breath and, without revising (except to cross out a few words of a sentence that seemed a false start), wrote this straightforward grade A answer:

Research on infants is probably the best way to demonstrate that some factors in perceptual organization are innate. In the cliff box experiment, an infant will avoid what looks like a drop-off, even though its mother calls it and even though it can feel glass covering the drop-off area. The same infant will crawl to the other end of the box, which appears (and is) safe. Apparently infants do not have to be taught what a cliff looks like.

Psychologists have also observed that infants are aware of size constancy. They recognize a difference in size between a 10-cm box at a distance of one meter and a 20-cm box at a distance of two meters. If this phenomenon is not innate, it is at least learned early, for the subjects of the experiment were infants of sixteen to eighteen months.

When shown various patterns, infants tend to respond more noticeably to patterns that resemble the human face than to those that appear random. This seemingly innate recognition helps the infant identify people (such as its mother) from less important inanimate objects.

Infants also seem to have an innate ability to match sight with sound. When simultaneously shown two television screens, each depicting a different subject, while being played a tape that sometimes matched one screen and sometimes the other, infants looked at whichever screen matched what they heard—not always, but at least twice as often.

Questions to Start You Thinking

1. If you were the psychology instructor, how could you immediately see from this answer that Cohn had thoroughly dealt with the question and only with the question?

2. In what places is his answer concrete and specific, not vague and general?

3. Suppose Cohn had tacked on a concluding paragraph: "Thus I have conclusively proved that there are innate factors in perceptual organization, by citing much evidence showing that infants definitely can perceive depth and forms." Would that have strengthened his answer?

4. Do you have any tried-and-true exam-answering techniques of your own that might have worked on that question or one like it? If so, why not share them with your class?

Generating Ideas

When, seated in the classroom, you begin your neck-and-neck race with the clock, you may feel tempted to start scribbling away frantically. Resist the temptation. First read over all the questions carefully. Notice whether you are expected to make any choices, and decide which questions to answer. Choices are luxuries: they let you ignore questions you are less prepared to answer in favor of those you can tackle with more confidence. If you are offered a choice, just X out any questions you are *not* going to answer so you don't waste time answering them by mistake. And if you don't understand what a question calls for, ask your instructor right away.

Few people can dash off an excellent essay exam answer without first taking time to discover a few ideas. So take a deep breath, get comfortable, sit back, and spend a few moments in thought. Instructors prefer answers that are concrete and specific to answers that stay up in the clouds of generality. To come up with specific details may first take thought. David Cohn's answer to the psychology question cites evidence all the way through: particular experiments in which infants were subjects. A little time taken to generate concrete examples—as Cohn did—may be time wisely spent.

Some people have a rare talent for rapidly putting their thoughts in order. Many, however, will start writing an exam with a burst of speed, like race horses sprinting out of a paddock, only to find that, although they are moving fast, they don't know which way to run. Your pen will move more smoothly if you have a few thoughts in mind. These thoughts don't have to be definitive—only something to start you writing. You can keep thinking and shaping your thoughts while you write.

Often a question will suggest a way to start your answer. Thought-provoking essay questions, to be sure, call for more than a regurgitation of your reading, but they often contain directive words that help define your task for you: *evaluate, compare, discuss, consider, explain, describe, isolate, summarize, trace the development of.* You can put yourself on the right track if you incorporate such a directive word in your first sentence.

Typical Exam Questions

Most examination questions fall into recognizable types, and if you can recognize them you will know how to organize them and begin to write. Here are specimens.

The cause-and-effect question In general, these questions are easy to recognize: they usually mention *causes* and *effects*.

> What were the immediate causes of the stock market crash of 1929?
>
> Set forth the principal effects on the economy commonly noticed as a result of a low prime rate of interest.

The first question invites you to recall specific forces and events in history; the second question (from an economics course) invites an account of what usually takes place. For specific advice on writing to show cause or effect, see Chapter 10.

The compare-and-contrast question One of the most popular types of examination questions, this calls on a writer to throw into sharp relief not one subject but two subjects. By pointing out similarities (comparing) and discussing differences (contrasting), you can explain both.

> Compare and contrast *iconic memory* and *eidetic imagery*. (1) Define the two terms, indicating the ways in which they differ, and (2) state the way or ways in which they are related or alike.

After supplying a one-sentence definition of each term, a student proceeded first to contrast and then to compare, for full credit:

> Iconic memory is a picturelike impression that lasts for only a fraction of a second in short-term memory. Eidetic imagery is the ability to take a mental photograph, exact in detail, which later can be recalled and studied in detail, as though its subject were still present. But iconic memory soon disappears. Unlike an eidetic image, it does not last long enough to enter long-term memory. IM is common, EI is unusual: very few people have it. Both iconic memory and eidetic imagery are similar, however: both record visual images, and every sighted person of normal intelligence has both abilities to some degree.

A question of this kind doesn't always use the words *compare* and *contrast*. Consider this question from a midterm exam in basic astronomy:

Signal at least three differences between Copernicus's and Kepler's models of the solar system. In what respects was Kepler's model an improvement on that of Copernicus?

What is that question but good old comparing and contrasting? The three differences all point to the superior accuracy of Kepler's model, so all a writer would need to do is list each difference and, in a few words, indicate Kepler's superiority.

Distinguish between *agnosia* and *receptive aphasia*. In what ways are the two conditions similar?

Again, without using the words *comparison* and *contrast,* the question asks for both. When you distinguish, you contrast, or point out differences; when you tell how two things are similar, you compare.

Briefly explain the duplex theory of memory. What are the main differences between short-term memory and long-term memory?

In this two-part question, the second part calls on the student to contrast (but not compare).

Which bryophyta resemble vascular plants? In what ways? How do these bryophyta *differ* from the vascular plants?

Writers of comparison-and-contrast answers sometimes fall into a trap: in this case, they might get all wound up about bryophyta and fail to give vascular plants more than a few words. When you compare and contrast two things, pay attention to both.

The demonstration question   In this kind of question, you are given a statement and asked to back it up.

Demonstrate the truth of Freud's contention that laughter may contain elements of aggression.

In other words, supply evidence to support Freud's claim. You might refer to crowd scenes you have experienced, perhaps quote and analyze a joke, perhaps analyze a scene in a TV show or film. Or use examples from your reading.

The discussion question   A discussion question may tempt an unwary writer to shoot the breeze.

Name and discuss three events that precipitated Lyndon B. Johnson's withdrawal from the 1968 presidential race.

This question looks like an open invitation to ramble aimlessly about Johnson and Vietnam, but it isn't. Whenever a question says "discuss," you will be wise to plan your discussion. What it asks is "Why did President Johnson decide not to seek another term? List three causes and explain each a little."

Discuss the economic uses of algae.

Here you might write a sentence or two on every use of pond scum you can think of ("Algae, when processed with yogurt cultures, become a main ingredient for a palatable low-calorie mayonnaise"). To deepen the discussion you might also tell how or why that use is important to the economy ("Last year, the sale of such mayonnaise increased by about thirty percent").

Sometimes a discussion question won't announce itself with the word *discuss,* but with *describe* or *explore:*

> Describe the national experience following passage of the Eighteenth Amendment to the Constitution. What did most Americans learn from it?

Provided you knew that the Eighteenth Amendment (Prohibition) banned the sale, manufacture, and transportation of alcoholic drinks and that it was finally repealed, you could discuss its effects—or perhaps the reasons for its repeal. (You might also assert that the amendment taught many Americans how to make whiskey out of rotten potatoes or how to fold a complete jazz band into a suitcase when the police raided a speakeasy, but probably that isn't what the instructor is after.)

The divide-or-classify question Sometimes you are asked to slice a subject into parts, or sort things into kinds.

> Enumerate the ways in which each inhabitant of the United States uses, on the average, 1595 gallons of water a day. How and to what degree might each person cut down on this amount?

This two-part question invites you, for a start, to divide up water use into several parts: drinking, cooking, bathing, washing clothes, brushing teeth, washing cars, and so on. Then after you divide them, you might go on to give tips for water conservation and tell how effective they are ("By putting two builder's bricks inside a toilet tank, each household would save 15–20% of the water required for a flush").

> What different genres of film did King Vidor direct? Name at least one outstanding example of each kind.

In this classification question, you sort things into categories—films into general kinds—possibly comedy, war, adventure, mystery, musical, western.

The definition question You'll often be asked to write an extended definition on an essay exam.

> Explain the three dominant styles of parenting: *permissive, authoritarian-restrictive,* and *authoritative.*

This question calls for a trio of definitions. It might help to illustrate each definition with an example, whether recalled or imagined.

Define the Stanislavsky method of acting, citing outstanding actors who have followed it.

As part of your definition, again you'd give examples.

The evaluation question   This is another favorite kind of question, much beloved by instructors because it calls on students to think critically. Here's a short example:

Set forth and evaluate the most widely accepted theories to account for the disappearance of the dinosaurs.

Here's a longer example:

Evaluate *two* of the following suggestions, giving reasons for your judgments:
a.   Cities should stop building highways to the suburbs and instead build public monorail systems.
b.   Houses and public buildings should be constructed to last no longer than twenty years.
c.   Freeways leading to the core of the city should have marked express lanes for buses and carpooling drivers and narrow lanes designed to punish with long delays individual commuters who drive their cars.

This last three-part question calls on you to argue for or against. Other argument questions might begin "Defend the idea of . . ." or "Show weaknesses in the idea of . . ." or otherwise call on you to take a stand.

The respond-to-the-quotation question   "Test the validity of this statement," a question might begin, and then it might go on to supply a quotation for close reading. In another familiar form, such a question might begin:

Discuss the following statement: High-minded opposition to slavery was only one cause, and not a very important one, of the animosity between North and South that in 1861 escalated into civil war.

The question asks you to test the writer's opinion against what you know. You would begin by carefully reading that statement a couple of times and then seeing whether you can pick a fight with it. It's a good idea to jot down any contrary evidence you can discover. If you end up agreeing with the statement, try to supply evidence to support it. (Sometimes the passage is the invention of the instructor, who hopes to provoke you to argument.)

Another illustration is the following question from an examination in women's literature:

Was the following passage written by Gertrude Stein, Kate Chopin, or Tillie Olsen? On what evidence do you base your answer?

She waited for the material pictures which she thought would gather and blaze before her imagination. She waited in vain. She saw no pictures of solitude, of hope, of longing, or of despair. But the very passions themselves were aroused within her soul, swaying it, lashing it, as the waves daily beat upon her splendid body. She trembled, she was choking, and the tears blinded her.

The passage is taken from a story by an earlier writer than either Stein or Olsen: Kate Chopin (1851–1904). If you knew Chopin, who specializes in physical and emotional descriptions of impassioned women, you would know the answer to the examination question, and you might point to language (*swaying, lashing*) that marks it as her own.

The process analysis question   Often, you can spot this kind of question by the word *trace*:

Trace the stages through which a bill becomes a federal law.

Trace the development of the medieval Italian city-state.

Both questions invite you to tell how something occurs or occurred. The other familiar type of process analysis, the "how-to" variety, is called for in this question:

An employee has been consistently late for work, varying from fifteen minutes to a half hour daily. This employee has been on the job only five months but shows promise of learning skills that your firm needs badly. How would you deal with this situation?

For pointers on writing a process analysis, see Chapter 5. In brief, you divide the process into steps and detail each step.

The far-out question   Sometimes, to invite you to use your imagination, an instructor will throw in a question that at first glance might seem bizarre.

Imagine yourself to be a trial lawyer in 1921, charged with defending Nicola Sacco and Bartolomeo Vanzetti, two anarchists accused of murder. Argue for their acquittal on whatever grounds you can justify.

On second glance, the question will be seen to reach deep. It calls on a prelaw student to show familiarity with a famous case (which ended with the execution of the defendants). In addition, it calls for knowledge of the law and of trial procedure. Such a question might be fun to answer; moreover, in being obliged to imagine a time, a place, and dramatic circumstances, the student might learn something. The following is another far-out question, this time from a philosophy course:

What might an ancient Roman Stoic philosopher have thought of Jean-Paul Sartre's doctrine of anguish?

In response, you might try to remember what the Stoics had to say about enduring suffering, define Sartre's view and define theirs, compare their views with Sartre's, imagine how they would agree (or, more probably, differ) with him.

Shaping a Draft (or the Only Version)

When the clock on the wall is ticking away, generating ideas and shaping an answer are seldom two distinct, leisurely processes: they often take place pretty much at the same time, and on scratch paper. Does your instructor hand you your own copy of the exam questions? If so, see if there's room on it to jot down ideas and roughly put them in order. If you can do your preliminary work right on the exam sheet, you'll have fewer pieces of scratch paper rattling around. Besides, you can annotate questions, underline points you think important, scribble short definitions. Write reminders that you will notice while you work: TWO PARTS TO THIS QUES.! or GET IN EXAMPLE OF ABORIGINES. To make sure that you include all necessary information without padding or repetition, you may care to jot down a brief, informal outline before setting pen to examination booklet. This was David Cohn's outline:

> cliff box— kid fears drop despite glass, mother, knows
>   shallow side safe
> size constancy — learned early if not intrinsic
> shapes— infants respond more/better to face shape than nonformed
> match sound w/sight— 2 TVs, look twice as much
>   at right one

Budget your time. When you have two or more essay questions to answer, block out your time at least roughly. Sometimes your instructor will suggest how many minutes to devote to each question or will declare that one question counts twenty points, another ten, and so on. Obviously a twenty-point question deserves twice as much time and work as a ten-pointer. If the instructor doesn't specify, then after you have read the questions, decide for yourself how much time each question is worth. Make a little schedule so that you'll know that at 10:30 it's time to wrap up question 2 and move on. Allot extra minutes to a question that looks complicated (such as one with several parts: a, b, c . . .) and fewer minutes to a simpler one. Otherwise, give every answer equal time. Then pace yourself as you write. A watch with an alarm you can set to buzz at the end of twenty or thirty minutes, alerting you that it's time to move on, might help—unless it would prompt your neighbors to start beating on you for buzzing.

Begin with the easy questions. Many students find it helps their morale to start with the question they feel best able to answer. Unless your instructor specifies that you have to answer the questions in their given order, why not skip around? Just make sure you clearly number the questions and begin each answer in such a way that the instructor will immediately recognize which question you're answering. If the task is "Compare and contrast the depression of the 1930s with the recession of the 1970s," an answer might begin:

> *Compared to the paralyzing depression that began in 1929, the recession of the 1970s seems a bad case of measles.*

The instructor would recognize that question, all right, whether you answered it first or last. If you have a choice of questions, you can label your answer *a* or *b* or restate the question at the start of your essay so that your instructor will have no doubt which alternative you have chosen, as in the following example:

> Question: Discuss *one* of the following quotations from the writings of Voltaire:
> a.   "The truths of religion are never so well understood as by those who have lost the power of reasoning."
> b.   "All roads lead to Rome."
>
> **ANSWER:**

> *When in September 1750, Voltaire wrote in a letter to Mme. de Fontaine, "All roads lead to Rome," his remark referred to more than the vast network of roads the ancient Romans had built—and built so well—throughout Europe....*

Try stating your thesis at the start. Some students find it useful to make their opening sentence a thesis statement—a sentence that makes clear right away the main point they're going to make. Then they proceed in the rest of the answer to back that statement up. This method often makes good sense. With a clear thesis statement to begin with, you will be unlikely to ramble into byways that carry you miles away from your main point. (See "Stating a Thesis," p. 491). That's how David Cohn opens his answer to the psychology question. One easy way to write such a thesis statement is to begin with the question itself.

> Can adequate reasons for leasing cars and office equipment, instead of purchasing them, be cited for a two-person partnership?

You might turn that question around, make it into a declarative statement, and *transform it into the start of an answer:*

> *I can cite at least four adequate reasons for a two-person partnership to lease cars and office equipment. For one thing, under present tax laws, the entire cost of a regular payment under a leasing agreement may be deducted....*

Stick to the point of the question. It's a temptation to want to throw into your answer everything you have learned in the course. But to do so defeats the purpose of the examination: not to parade your knowledge, but to put your knowledge to use. So when you answer an exam question cogently, you select *what matters* from what you know, at the same time shaping it.

Answer the whole question. Often a question will have two parts: it will ask you, say, to name the most common styles of contemporary architecture and then to evaluate one of them. Or it might say, "List three differences between the landscape paintings of Monet and those of Van Gogh" and then add, "Which of the two shows the greater influence of eighteenth-century neoclassicism?" When the dragon of a question has two heads, make sure you cut off both.

Stay specific. Pressed for time, some harried exam takers think, "I haven't got time to get specific here—I'll just sum up this idea in general." Usually that's a mistake. Every time you throw in a large, general statement ("The Industrial Revolution was a beneficial thing for the peasant"), take time to include specific examples ("In Dusseldorf, as Taine tells us, the mortality rate from starvation among displaced Prussian farm workers now dropped to nearly zero, although once it had reached almost ten percent a year").

Leave room to revise. Incidentally, it's foresighted to write on only one side of the page in your examination booklet. Leave space between lines. Then later, should you wish to add words or sentences or even a whole paragraph, you can do so with ease. Give yourself room for second thoughts and last-minute inspirations. As you write and as you revise, you may well do further discovering.

Rewriting

If you have paced yourself, you'll have at least a few minutes left at the end of your examination period when, while some around you are still agonizingly trying to finish, you can relax a moment and look over your work with a critical eye.

Even if you should stop writing with an hour to spare, it probably won't be worth your time to recopy your whole exam. Use any time you have left not merely to improve your penmanship but to test your ideas and how well they hang together. Add any large points you may have overlooked in writing your draft.

Your foresight in skipping every other line will now pay off. You can add sentences wherever you think new ones are needed. Cross out any hopelessly garbled sentences and rewrite them in the blank lines. (David Cohn crossed out and rewrote part of his last sentence. Originally it read, "When simulta-neously shown two television screens, each depicting a different subject, while being played *a tape that oscillated between which TV it was in time with. . . ."* He rethought the last words, which we have italicized, found them confusing, crossed them out, and instead wrote on the line above: "a tape that sometimes matched one screen and sometimes the other.") If you recall an important point you forgot to put in, you can add a paragraph or two on a left-hand page that you left blank. So the grader will not miss it, draw an arrow indicating where it goes. If you find that you have gone off on a big digression or have thrown in knowledge merely to show it off, boldly X out that block of wordage. Your answer may look sloppier, but your instructor will think the better of it.

Naturally, errors occur oftener when you write under pressure than when you have time to edit and proofread carefully. Most instructors will take into consideration your haste and your human fallibility. On an exam, what you say and how forcefully you say it matter most. Still, to get the small details right will just make your answer look all the sharper. No instructor will object to careful corrections. You can easily add words with carets:

$$\text{Israeli} \overset{\text{foreign}}{\wedge} \text{policy}$$

Or you can neatly strike out a word by drawing a line through it. Some students like to use an erasable pen for in-class writing. With the aid of this wonder of writing technology, they can hand in an exam of amazing cleanliness: a little smeary, maybe, but free of crossed-out words.

We don't expect you to memorize the following questions and carry them like crib notes into an examination. But when you receive your paper or blue book back and you look it over, you might learn more about writing essay exams if you ask them of yourself.

DISCOVERY CHECKLIST: EVALUATING YOUR PERFORMANCE

- Did you understand the question and what was expected?
- Did you answer the whole question, not just part of it?
- Did you stick to the point, not throw in information the question doesn't call for?
- Did you make your general statements clear by citing evidence or examples?
- Does your answer sprawl, or does it look shaped?
- Does your answer, at any place, show a need for more knowledge and more ideas? Did you inflate your answer with hot air, or did you stay close to earth, giving plenty of facts, examples, and illustrations?
- On what question or questions do you feel you did a good job that satisfies you, no matter what grade you received?
- If you had to write this exam over again, how would you *now* go about the job?

Let's end with a few tips on two other common kinds of in-class writing.

SHORT-ANSWER EXAMINATIONS

Requiring answers much terser than an essay exam does, the *short-answer exam* may call on you to identify names or phrases from your reading, in a sentence or less.

> Identify the following: Clemenceau, Treaty of Versailles, Maginot line, Dreyfus affair.

You might begin your answer to such a question:

> <u>Clemenceau</u>— premier of France in World War I.

Or, if a fuller identification is called for:

> <u>Georges Clemenceau</u>—This French premier, nicknamed The Tiger, headed a popular coalition cabinet during World War I and at the Paris Peace Conference demanded stronger penalties against Germany.

Writing a short identification is much like writing a short definition. Be sure to mention the general class to which a thing belongs:

> <u>Clemenceau</u>— French premier who....
> <u>Treaty of Versailles</u>—pact between Germany and the Allies that....
> <u>Maginot line</u>—fortifications which....

If you do so, you won't lose points for an answer like this, which fails to make clear the nature of the thing being identified:

> <u>Maginot line</u>—The Germans went around it.

IN-CLASS ESSAYS

Some instructors, to give you laboratory experience in writing on demand, may assign an impromptu essay to be written in class. The topic might be assigned in advance or at the start of the class. Being obliged to write such an impromptu essay, after getting used to a deadline a week or a month away, is a little like being told to drive a subcompact car when you're accustomed to a Lincoln Continental. But the way you write an essay in class need not differ greatly from the way you write anywhere else. Your usual methods of working can serve you well, even though you may have to apply them in a hurry.

If you have forty-five minutes to write an in-class essay, a good rule of thumb is to spend ten minutes preparing, thirty minutes writing, and five minutes rereading and making last-minute changes and additions. In the act of writing, you may find new ideas occurring to you and perhaps those exact proportions of time will need to change. Even so, a rough schedule like that will help you to allocate your time.

Those last few minutes you leave yourself to review your work may be the best-spent minutes of all.

A Note on Manuscript Style and Computer Formatting

Some instructors are sticklers in detailing how your paper ought to look; others maintain a benign indifference to such commonplaces. In writing for an instructor of either stripe, it is only considerate to turn in a paper easy to read and to comment on.

In case you have received no particular instructions for the form of your paper, here are some general, all-purpose specifications.

1. If you handwrite your paper, make sure your handwriting is legible. If you type, keep your typewriter keys clean.

2. Write or type on just one side of standard letter-size paper (8½-by-11 inches). Erasable typing paper, however helpful to a mistake-prone typist, may be irksome to an instructor who needs to write comments. The paper is easily smeared, and it won't take certain brands of pen.

3. If you handwrite your paper, use 8½-by-11 paper with smooth edges (not torn from a spiral-bound notebook).

4. Use a black ribbon if you type, blue or black ink if you write. If you use a machine that lets you change type styles, don't do your paper entirely in italics or extrafine characters. Pick an easy-to-read typeface.

5. For a paper without a separate title page, place your name, together with your instructor's name, the number and section of the course, and the date in the upper left corner of the first page, each item on a new line even with the left margin. Double-space between lines. Double-space again and center your title. Don't underline the title; don't put it in quotation marks or type the title all in capital letters; and don't put a period after it. Capitalize the first and last words, the first word after a colon or semicolon, and all other words except prepositions, conjunctions, and articles. Double-space twice between the title and the first line of your text.

6. Number your pages consecutively (do not type a page number on the first page). For a paper of two or more pages, put your last name in the upper right corner of each sheet after page 1 along with the page number. Do not type the word *page* or the letter *p* before the number and do not follow the number with a period or parenthesis.

7. Make sure you give your instructor plenty of room to write in, if need be. Leave ample margins—at least an inch—left and right, top and bottom. If you type, double-space your manuscript; if you write, use wide-ruled paper or skip every other line.

8. Indent each new paragraph five spaces.

9. Leave two spaces after every period or other end stop, one after a comma or semicolon.

10. Try not to break words at the ends of lines.

11. Long quotations should be double-spaced like the rest of your paper but indented from the left margin—ten spaces if you're following Modern Language Association (MLA) guidelines, five if you're using American Psychological Association (APA) guidelines. Citations appear in parentheses two spaces after the final punctuation mark of the block quotation. (For more about citing sources, see Chapter 14.)

12. Label all illustrations, and make sure they are bound securely to the paper.

13. Covering a short essay—one of, say, five pages—in a hefty binder or giving it a title page with a blank sheet or two after it is unnecessary. Title pages are generally reserved for research papers and other bulky works.

14. Staples are the best bet; paper clips quit their posts. By the way, don't ever try to bind your pages together by ripping a little tab in them and folding it. This method never works; the pages always come apart. Also, do not staple your pages all the way down the side; this makes it hard to turn the pages.

15. For safety's sake and peace of mind, make a copy of your paper.

Additional Suggestions for Research Papers

For research papers the format is the same with the following additional specifications.

1. Type a title page, with the title of your paper centered about a third of the way down the page. Then go down two to four more spaces and type your name, then the instructor's name, the number and section of the course, and the date, each on a separate line. Repeat your title on the first page of your paper.

2. Do not number your title page; your outline, if you submit one with your paper, is numbered with small roman numerals (ii, iii, and so on).

3. Don't put a number on the first page of your text (page 1); all subsequent pages through your notes and works cited pages are numbered consecutively with arabic numerals in the upper right corner of the page.

4. Double-space your notes and your list of works cited. (For more instructions for making such a list, see Chapter 14.)

5. If you are asked to hand in your note cards along with your paper, be
sure that they are in order and securely bound with a rubber band or placed
in an envelope.

How to Make a Correction

Although you will want to make any large changes in your rough draft, not
in your final copy, don't be afraid to make small corrections in pen when you
give your paper a last once-over. No writer is error-free; neither is any typist.
In making such corrections, you may find it handy to use certain symbols
used by printers and proofreaders.

A transposition mark (∿) reverses the positions of two words or two
letters:

        The nearby star Tau Ceti closely resmebles our sun.

Close-up marks (◝) bring together the parts of a word accidentally split
when a typewriter stutters. A separation mark (◞) inserts a space where one
is needed:

        The nearby star Tau Ceti closely re͡sembles our͟sun.

To delete a letter or a punctuation mark, draw a slanted line through it:

        The nearby star Tau Ceti closely res⁄embles our sun.

When you insert a word or letter, use a caret (∧) to indicate where the
insertion belongs:

                                            s
        The nearby star Tau Ceti closely reembles our sun.
                                          ∧

The symbol ¶ before a word or a line means "start a new paragraph":

        But lately, astronomers have slackened their efforts to

        study dark nebulae. ¶ That other solar systems may support

        life as we know it makes for still another fascinating

        speculation.

You can always cross out a word neatly, with a single horizontal line, and
write a better one over it (*never* type a correction right over a mistake).

                                    closely
        The nearby star Tau Ceti ~~somewhat~~ resembles our sun.

Finally, if a page has many errors on it, type or write it over again.
(Repairing mistakes is, of course, child's play if you're writing with a word
processor.)

Formatting Your Manuscript with a Word Processor

Writing with a computer encourages neatness: you can make all your corrections before you print out your final copy—or as many as you can spot while your work is still on screen. Here are some points to remember in formatting a word-processed manuscript.

Breaking lines Although when you write with a computer you don't need to keep watching for lines to end (there being no typewriter carriage to return), your computer may automatically break a few lines awkwardly. This tends to happen where you have an unusually long word or a phrase strung together with hyphens:

```
Speaking of his sociology classes, Professor Campbell

declared that he often met a

don't-give-a-damn-if-I-know-it-or-not attitude on the part

of some upperclassmen.   This attitude annoyed him greatly.
```

Check through each page before printing it out for similar awkward breaks. Some word processing programs include a *hyphen-push* or *word-break* command that enables you to instruct the computer where to split a word.

```
Speaking of his sociology class, Professor Campbell

declared that he often met a don't-give-a-damn-if-I-know-

it-or-not attitude on the part of some upperclassmen.
```

Leaving margins Allow the same generous margins you'd use if you typed or used pen. To get these margins you will have to make sure that your page breaks are accurate and instruct your printer carefully. Print out a sample page or two on scratch paper and, if the margins aren't right, give your computer fresh instructions.

Spacing Before you break your document into pages, make sure it is set for double-space.

To justify or not to justify? Many writers think it looks especially neat to use the power of a computer to *justify* their copy—that is, to make each line the same length, like lines in a printed book. Some feel, though, that shaggy right-hand margins look more like typewriting and are actually slightly more readable. Unless your instructor states any wishes on this score, we recommend not showing off the power of your computer but leaving the lines shaggy.

Choosing your printer If you can, print out your paper on a laser printer or a letter-quality printer. Crisp black copy will enhance the readability of what you write. Some instructors dislike reading papers printed on a dot matrix printer, which produces each letter with a series of tiny dots. They claim that such manuscripts look like tapes from supermarket cash registers. Still, late-model dot matrix printers produce much sharper copy than the early models did. Even an old dot matrix printer may produce good dark copy if you use a fresh ribbon and instruct your computer to print each line boldface. If you have any doubts about the legibility of your copy, show your instructor a sample of your printer's work and make sure it will be acceptable.

Checking the ribbon   If you're using a letter-quality printer, a single-loop ribbon will produce the sharpest copy. If using a continuous-loop ribbon (one that keeps working until you change it), make sure it's fresh enough to produce a good black printout.

Choosing paper   Some printers print on continuous-form paper with a detachable perforated strip (*tractor feed*) at either edge. Cheaper grades of such paper (15-pound and 18-pound weight) may not take ink well. For a better-looking manuscript, use 20-pound continuous-form paper designated for word processing. For still handsomer results, use single sheets of bond paper, even if you have to feed them in by hand. But if you do use continuous-form paper, don't turn in a manuscript that looks like a strip of wallpaper. Take the pages apart. If only low-grade continuous-form paper is available, it might improve the looks of your manuscript to photocopy it and submit the photocopy instead.

Experimenting with typefaces   Some printers offer an array of several *fonts,* or typefaces, enabling you to use different styles of type for different purposes. You might use, say, one kind of type for quotations from books, another for quotations from conversation. To experiment not only might be fun but also might provide helpful guidance for your reader. But resist the temptation to produce a four-ring circus of various typography. In the end, the words you write are what matter, not the typeface you print them in.

PART FIVE

HANDBOOK

Introduction: Grammar, or the Way Words Work

21. Basic Grammar

22. Grammatical Sentences

23. Effective Sentences

24. Punctuation

25. Mechanics

26. Word Choice

A Glossary of Troublemakers

583

HANDBOOK

Introduction: Grammar, or
the Way Words Work   585

CHAPTER 21
Basic Grammar   **589**
  1. Parts of Speech, 589
  2. Parts of Sentences and
     Sentence Patterns, 598
  3. Phrases and Clauses, 604
  4. Types of Sentences, 611

CHAPTER 22
Grammatical Sentences   **615**
  5. Verbs, 615
  6. Subject-Verb Agreement, 630
  7. Pronoun-Antecedent
     Agreement, 635
  8. Pronoun Reference, 638
  9. Pronoun Case, 641
  10. Sentence Fragments, 646
  11. Comma Splices and Fused
      Sentences, 652
  12. Adjectives and Adverbs, 657

CHAPTER 23
Effective Sentences   **662**
  13. Misplaced and Dangling
      Modifiers, 662
  14. Incomplete Sentences, 665
  15. Mixed Constructions and
      Faulty Predication, 670
  16. Parallel Structure, 673
  17. Coordination and
      Subordination, 677

CHAPTER 24
Punctuation   **685**
  18. End Punctuation, 685
  19. The Comma, 688
  20. The Semicolon, 699
  21. The Colon, 702
  22. The Apostrophe, 705
  23. Quotation Marks, 709
  24. The Dash and the
      Slash/Virgule, 713
  25. Parentheses, Brackets,
      and the Ellipsis Mark, 716

CHAPTER 25
Mechanics   **722**
  26. Abbreviations, 722
  27. Capital Letters, 726
  28. Numbers, 730
  29. Italics, 733
  30. The Hyphen, 736
  31. Spelling, 740

CHAPTER 26
Word Choice   **750**
  32. Appropriateness, 750
  33. Avoiding Sexism, 757
  34. Exact Words, 760
  35. Wordiness, 765

**A Glossary of
Troublemakers**   **769**

INTRODUCTION: GRAMMAR, OR THE WAY WORDS WORK

KIND LADY: Little boy, it's cold out! Where's your coat?

BOY: I ain't got none.

LADY: "Ain't got none?" My stars, boy, where's your grammar?

BOY: She's home settin' by the TV watchin' *Dallas*.

In this dialogue, the lady speaks of *grammar* as a set of rules for using language, like chalk-drawn lines that writers and speakers of English must toe. She seems more shocked by the boy's uttering the forbidden word *ain't* than by his running around coatless in the cold. We can describe her approach as *prescriptive*: there are right ways and wrong ways to use the English language.

An alternative is a *descriptive* approach: **grammar** is that study of language concerned with the regular, systematic, and predictable ways in which words work together. How do speakers of English create sentences? How do they understand each other's sentences? In the last fifty years, grammarians haven't been laying down strict rules so much as they have been listening, observing, and trying to define those implicit rules by which the language operates.

From this point of view, the boy in the street speaks according to a grammar, just as the lady does. His grammar may be less complex than hers, or less efficient as a means of communication, but it too consists of regular, predictable patterns of usage. Indeed, every speaker of English, even a child or a mentally retarded person, commands a grammatical system of tremendous complexity.

Take the sentence "A bear is occupying a telephone booth while a tourist impatiently waits in line." In theory, there are nineteen billion different ways to state the idea in that sentence.[1] (Another is "A tourist fumes while he waits for a bear to finish yakking on a pay phone.") How do we understand a unique sentence like that one? For we do understand it, even though we have never heard it before—not in those very same words, not in the very same order.

To begin with, we recognize familiar words and we know their meanings. Just as significantly, we recognize a grammatical structure. As we read or hear the sentence, we know that it contains a familiar pattern of **syntax**, or word order: This meaningful order helps the sentence make sense to us.

Ordinarily, we aren't even conscious of such an order, for we don't need

---

[1]Richard Ohmann, "Grammar and Meaning," *The American Heritage Dictionary* (Boston: Houghton Mifflin, 1979), pp. xxxi–xxxii.

to think about it; but it is there. To notice it, all we need do is rearrange the words of our sentence:

Telephone a impatiently line in waits tourist bear a occupying is a booth while.

The result is nonsense: it defies English grammar. The would-be sentence doesn't follow familiar rules or meet our expectations.

Hundreds of times a day, with wonderful efficiency, we perform tasks of understanding and of sentence construction more complex than any computer designed can even try. (Were artificial intelligence equally far advanced, a computer could not only scan books but make sense of them for you, and it could put together words sensitively enough to write your papers.) Indeed, linguist Noam Chomsky has suggested that the human brain probably contains some kind of language-grasping structure. Built into us before birth, it enables us to understand what we hear (whether that is English, Chinese, or Swahili) and equips us to put together our own sentences. Certainly some kind of language-grasping ability is part of our makeup. For we can understand and create sentences even as babbling toddlers, though we have never cracked a handbook and couldn't state one grammatical rule to save our lives.

Why, then, ever think about grammar in college? Isn't it entirely possible to write well without contemplating grammar at all? Yes. If your innate sense of grammar is reliable, you can write clearly and logically and forcefully without knowing a predicate nominative from a handsaw. Many of the writers featured in current magazines and newspapers would be hard pressed to name all the parts of speech they use. Most successful writers, though, have been practicing for so many years that grammar has become second nature to them. Few students we know have a built-in sense so infallible. When you doubt a word or a construction, a glance at a grammatical rule in a book can clear up your confusion and restore your confidence—just as referring to a dictionary can help your spelling.

Besides helping us to solve problems and bolstering our self-confidence, the study of grammar can be unexpectedly satisfying. Some students enjoy knowing, for instance, exactly why it makes more sense to say "Our soccer team is better than any other" than to say "Our soccer team is better than any." (For a grammatical reason, see p. 667.) After all, to write without knowledge of grammar is a little like driving a car without caring what goes on under the hood. Most of the time, you can drive around without knowing a thing except how to steer and brake and tromp on the gas; but at times you may thank your stars you know how a carburetor works and, when it won't work, what to do about it.

More complex than a car, the English language provides subtler challenges. For one thing, merely following rules doesn't guarantee good writing. The so-called grammatical rules you'll find in this handbook are not mechanical specifications, but accepted ways in which skilled writers and speakers put words together. They come from observations of what educated, accomplished users of English actually do—how they utilize the language to communicate their ideas successfully. The amateur writer can learn by following their example, just as an amateur athlete, artist, or even auto mechanic can learn by watching the professionals. Knowing how the English language works, and how its parts get along together, is of enormous value to you as a writer. Once you understand what goes on under the hood, so to speak, you will have a keener sense of words and of why at times they won't go—so that when you write, you drive smoothly to your destination.

CHAPTER 21

Basic Grammar

1. Parts of Speech   **589**
2. Parts of Sentences and Sentence Patterns   **598**
3. Phrases and Clauses   **604**
4. Types of Sentences   **611**

1 PARTS OF SPEECH

Grammar deals with the elements that make up sentences. These elements may be single words or whole phrases and clauses. Let's look first at the simplest building blocks of sentences: words.

We sort words into eight classes: the **parts of speech**. We tell them apart by their functions (the jobs they do in sentences), by their forms, and by their meanings. Like most classifications, the parts of speech are a convenience: it is easier to refer to *an adjective modifying a noun* than "that word there that tells something about that thing." Here is a quick review of the celebrated eight.

1a Nouns

A **noun** names. A **common noun** names a general class of person (*clergyman, believer*), place (*town, dormitory*), thing (*car, dog*), or concept (*freedom, industrialization*). A **proper noun** names a specific person, place, thing, or concept: *Billy Graham, Milwaukee, Cadillac, New Deal.*

589

1b Pronouns

A **pronoun** stands in place of a noun. Without pronouns, most writing would be top-heavy with repeated nouns. Imagine writing an essay on Martin Luther King, Jr., in which you had to say "Martin Luther King, Jr." or the "clergyman and civil rights leader" every time you mentioned your subject. Instead, you can handily use *personal pronouns* (*he* and *him*) and the *possessive pronoun* (*his*).

There are nine types of pronouns.

1. **Personal pronouns** (*I, you, it*) stand for nouns that name persons or things. "Mark awoke slowly, but suddenly *he* bolted from the bed."

2. **Possessive pronouns** (*his, our/ours*) are a form of personal pronoun showing ownership. They are used in place of nouns or as adjectives modifying nouns. "*His* trophy is on the left; *hers* is on the right."

3. **Intensive pronouns** (*yourself, themselves*) emphasize a noun or another pronoun. "Michael Jackson *himself* opened the door."

4. **Relative pronouns** (*who, that, which*) start a subordinate clause (see p. 609) that functions as an adjective modifying a noun or pronoun in another clause. "The gift *that* you give them ought to be handsome."

5. **Reflexive pronouns** have the same form as intensive pronouns but are used as objects referring back to subjects. "She helped *herself*."

6. **Interrogative pronouns** (*who, what*) ask or introduce questions. "*What* did you give them?"

7. **Indefinite pronouns** (*any, no one*) stand for persons or things not specified. "*No one* ran because of the rain."

PRONOUNS

	SINGULAR	PLURAL
PERSONAL PRONOUNS		
First person	I, me	we, us
Second person	you	you
Third person	he, she, it, him, her	they, them
POSSESSIVE PRONOUNS		
First person	my, mine	our, ours
Second person	your, yours	your, yours
Third person	his, her, hers, its	their, theirs
INTENSIVE AND REFLEXIVE PRONOUNS		
First person	myself	ourselves
Second person	yourself	yourselves
Third person	himself, herself, itself	themselves

8. **Demonstrative pronouns** (*this, those*) point to nouns. "*That*'s the man, officer!"

9. **Reciprocal pronouns** (*each other, one another*) express relationship between two or more nouns or other pronouns. "Joe and Donna looked at *each other* with complete understanding."

Exercise 1–1

Underline the nouns and pronouns in the following sentences. Identify each noun as common or proper. Identify the type of each pronoun (personal, possessive, relative, and so on). Answers for the lettered sentences appear in the back of the book. Example:

Little Boy Blue, come blow your horn.

Little Boy Blue [proper noun], come blow your [possessive pronoun] horn.

a. If Lois sells two paintings, her husband will be delighted.
b. The price seems high, but Lois herself makes only a small profit.
c. The bulk of the money that she earns pays for her supplies.
d. Lewis wants to sell his Corvette to someone who appreciates it.
e. I can't help myself; I love you and no one else.

1. Which do you yourself prefer?
2. Is that the woman to whom Mr. Snopes spoke on the phone?
3. I heard that Linda plans to buy herself the first pair of jeans that fits her.
4. Why don't you give her the old Calvin Kleins that don't fit you anymore?
5. The members of the task force congratulated one another for meeting the deadline.

RELATIVE PRONOUNS
that, what, whatever, which, who, whoever, whom, whomever, whose

INTERROGATIVE PRONOUNS
what, which, who, whom, whose

INDEFINITE PRONOUNS
all, another, any, anybody, anyone, anything, both, each, either, everybody, everyone, everything, few, many, neither, nobody, none, no one, nothing, one, several, some, somebody, someone, something

DEMONSTRATIVE PRONOUNS
such, that, these, this, those

RECIPROCAL PRONOUNS
each other, one another

1c *Verbs*

A **verb** shows action ("The cow *jumped* over the moon") or a state of being ("The cow *is* brown," "The cow *felt* frisky").

Verbs like *is* or *felt* often show a state of being by linking the sentence's subject with another word that renames or describes it, as in the last two examples. Such verbs are called **linking verbs**. (See also 5a.)

A verb that shows action is called **transitive** when it takes a direct object.

> VT   DO
> Jim *hit* the *ball* hard.

>   VT   DO
> *Does* she *resemble* her *mother?*

A transitive verb must have an object to complete its meaning. You can't write just *Jim hit* or *Does she resemble?* But if a verb is complete in itself and needs no object, we call it **intransitive**.

> The surgeon *paused.*

> Sally *lives* on Boilermaker Street.

Look up a verb in your dictionary and you will probably find it classified *vt* (for "verb, transitive") or *vi* (for "verb, intransitive"). Many verbs can work either way.

> The bus *stopped.*

> The driver *stopped* the bus.

Not all verbs consist of just one word. The **main verb** in a sentence identifies the central action (*hit, stopped*). We can show variations on this action by adding **helping verbs**, such as *can, have,* or *will.*

> HV   MV
> Alan *did* not *hit* the ball.

> HV   MV
> The bus *will have stopped* six times before we reach Main Street.

HELPING VERBS

There are twenty-three helping verbs in English. Fourteen of them can also function as main verbs:

be, is, am, are, was, were, being, been
do, does, did
have, has, had

The other nine can function only as helping verbs, never as main verbs:

can, could, should, would, may, might, must, shall, will

Exercise 1–2

Underline the verbs in the following sentences and identify each one as transitive (VT), intransitive (VI), linking (LV), or helping (HV). For each transitive verb, underline and mark its direct object (DO). Answers for the lettered sentences appear in the back of the book. Example:

> Underline and mark its direct object.

> VT   VT   DO
> <u>Underline</u> and <u>mark</u> its <u>direct object</u>.

a. When Jorge goes to Providence, Jim will accompany him.

b. Our coach dislikes players who are arrogant.

c. Never give yellow roses to a French friend: they symbolize infidelity.

d. The president should have spent more time on our proposal.

e. Harry dreams of becoming a famous novelist, but he rarely reads fiction.

1. If your letter comes in today's mail, I will mail you an answer tomorrow.

2. Louise introduced herself to Leon while he was walking his dog.

3. Leon is the musician whose band she likes so much.

4. Woodpeckers must have a padded lining inside their skulls.

5. If the sky were not so cloudy, would the ocean look blue?

1d Adjectives

An **adjective** adds information to a noun or a pronoun; we say that an adjective *modifies* the person or thing it describes. In modifying a noun or pronoun, an adjective often answers the question Which? or What kind? Usually an adjective is a single word.

> War is a *primitive* activity.
>
> *Young* men kill other *young* men.
>
> The *small brown* cow let out a *lackluster* moo.

ARTICLES

In the preceding examples, some grammarians would classify *the* and *a* as adjectives. Others would call them by a special name: *articles. The* is called the **definite article** because it indicates one particular item.

> I need to borrow *the* car.

A and *an* are the **indefinite articles** because they indicate any old whatever-it-is.

> I need to borrow *a* car.

1e *Adverbs*

An **adverb** modifies a verb, an adjective, or another adverb.

> The cow bawled *loudly.* [The adverb *loudly* modifies the verb *bawled.*]
>
> The cow bawled *very loudly indeed.* [Three adverbs in a row: *loudly* modifies the verb *bawled,* while *very* and *indeed* modify the adverb *loudly.*]

Adverbs often flesh out thoughts by showing how, when, or where an action happens.

> The cow *quickly* [how] galloped *outside* [where] and *immediately* [when] kicked the farmer.

Exercise 1–3

Underline and identify the adjectives, definite articles, indefinite articles, and adverbs in the following sentences. For each adverb, underline the word it modifies and mark that word as a verb, adjective, or adverb. Answers for the lettered exercises appear in the back of the book. Example:

> The opera was too long, but Judith sang beautifully.
>
>   ADV ADJ   V   ADV
> The opera was too long, but Judith sang beautifully.

a. After such a mild winter, the environmental experts greatly fear a drought.

b. James's elderly grandparents are incredibly mobile for their years.

c. The wildly beautiful Natasha often made wise men act foolishly.

d. She had a very short life, but she lived it fully.

e. We were absolutely delighted to get tickets to such a lovely play.

1. The character of Mercutio is not bad; the actor just played him badly.

2. The part of Juliet, in contrast, was remarkably well acted.

3. With someone so young in the role of Juliet, Romeo probably should have been younger.

4. My favorite parts are the romantic scenes.

5. Angela prefers the many comical scenes.

1f *Prepositions*

A **preposition** is a transitional word, usually short, that leads into a phrase. The preposition and its object (a noun or pronoun), plus any modifiers, form a prepositional phrase: *in the bar, under a rickety table, with you.*

A prepositional phrase can function as an adjective or an adverb. When it modifies a noun or pronoun, a prepositional phrase is called an **adjective phrase**.

> I want a room *with a view.* [The adjective phrase *with a view* modifies the noun *room.*]

Everybody *in Hillsdale* knows Big Jake. [The adjective phrase *in Hillsdale* modifies the pronoun *Everybody*.]

When it modifies a verb, an adjective, or an adverb, a prepositional phrase is called an **adverb phrase**.

Jarvis, the play reviewer, always leaves *after the first act*. [The adverb phrase *after the first act* modifies the verb *leaves*.]

Alice is miserable *without you*. [The adverb phrase *without you* modifies the adjective *miserable*.]

Ken works far *from home*. [The adverb phrase *from home* modifies the adverb *far*.]

There are dozens of prepositions in English. The chart includes the most common ones. Notice that some (not many) prepositions consist of more than one word. Also, some prepositions occasionally play other roles: *since*, for example, can be a preposition (*I've known him since childhood*), or an adverb (*He has since left town*), or a conjunction (*Let's go, since there's nothing to do here*).

COMMON PREPOSITIONS

about	below	except for	on	to
above	beneath	for	onto	toward
according to	beside	from	opposite	under
across	besides	in	out	underneath
after	between	in addition to	outside	unlike
against	beyond	inside	over	until
along	but (except)	in spite of	past	up
among	by	instead of	plus	upon
around	concerning	into	regarding	with
as	considering	like	since	within
at	despite	near	than	without
because of	down	next to	through	
before	during	of	throughout	
behind	except	off	till	

Exercise 1–4

Underline each prepositional phrase in the following sentences and identify it as an adjective or adverb phrase. Answers for the lettered sentences appear in the back of the book. Example:

In the beginning was the Word.

In the beginning was the Word. [Adverb phrase.]

a. Rarely has anyone ever behaved so rudely to me.

b. The muffin on the table was supposed to be Jeffrey's.

c. Ann warned us before the meeting that her proposal might cause trouble.

d. She presented it strictly according to the rules, but some committee members tried to block the discussion.

e. My belief is that all but a few troublemakers will be reasonable once they understand her position.

1. The politicians at City Hall would welcome a chance to intervene.

2. Let's stop beating around the bush and make some decisions.

3. Luis wants to go to the game this afternoon.

4. From his seat beyond the foul pole he can hardly see the batter.

5. I hope he can find an apartment in this neighborhood so we can see him more often.

1g Conjunctions

A **conjunction** links words or groups of words and connects them in sense.

A **coordinating conjunction** is a one-syllable word that joins elements with equal or near-equal importance: "Jack *and* Jill," "Sink *or* swim."

COORDINATING CONJUNCTIONS
and, but, for, nor, or, so, yet

A word used to make one clause dependent on, or subordinate to, another is called a **subordinating conjunction**.

Before we left the party, six people had fainted.

They passed out *because* Roger had spiked the punch.

I heard *that* they went looking for him the next day.

COMMON SUBORDINATING CONJUNCTIONS

after	even if	so	whenever
although	even though	so that	where
as	if	than	wherever
as if	in order that	that	whether
as soon as	once	though	while
as though	provided that	unless	why
because	rather than	until	
before	since	when	

Some conjunctions consist of paired words, such as *either ... or,* that appear separately but work together to join elements of a sentence. Such a pair is called a **correlative conjunction**.

Not only for her money *but also* for her cooking, Augustus courted Serena.

Neither his friends *nor* hers thought the marriage would last.

But *whether* from true love *or* mere laziness, they stayed together for sixty years.

CORRELATIVE CONJUNCTIONS		
as . . . as	just as . . . so	not only . . . but also
both . . . and	neither . . . nor	whether . . . or
either . . . or	not . . . but	

Certain adverbs also can function as conjunctions. Called *conjunctive adverbs,* these linking words show a relationship between two ideas, such as addition (*also, besides*), comparison (*likewise, similarly*), contrast (*instead, however*), emphasis (*namely, certainly*), cause and effect (*thus, therefore*), or time (*finally, subsequently*).

COMMON CONJUNCTIVE ADVERBS			
accordingly	furthermore	meanwhile	similarly
also	hence	moreover	still
anyway	however	nevertheless	then
besides	incidentally	next	thereafter
certainly	indeed	nonetheless	therefore
consequently	instead	now	thus
finally	likewise	otherwise	undoubtedly

1h *Interjections*

An **interjection** inserts an outburst of feeling at the beginning, middle, or end of a sentence.

I'd go, but, *oh,* I don't want to.

Ow! What torture it was to read that essay!

There are pigeons on the grass, *alas.*

An entire phrase can work as an interjection.

Who *the dickens* are you?

What *in the world* is my term paper doing in the waste basket?

Exercise 1–5

Underline and identify the conjunctions and interjections in the following sentences. Mark each conjunction as coordinating, subordinating, or correlative. Answers for the lettered sentences appear in the back of the book. Example:

Do we have to eat liver and onions again, for heaven's sake?

               COORD CONJ   **INTERJ**
Do we have to eat liver <u>and</u> onions again, <u>for heaven's sake</u>?

  a. Oh, well, the team will do better when Smoots gets back in the game.

  b. According to Polonius and many others, neither borrowing nor lending is wise.

  c. Geraldine and her sister took both piano and ballet lessons.

  d. Holy mackerel, what a big fish!

  e. Although time and tide wait for no man, Juan is taking hours to launch his boat.

  1. I'll dive in if you will, but, oh, that water's cold!

  2. Neither Larry's father nor Kevin's is tall, yet both boys grew up to be over six feet.

  3. How in the world are you and Elwood going to patch up your differences if neither of you will talk to the other?

  4. While I can't eat either potato chips or pretzels, I love peanuts.

  5. Susan and Lee enjoy their Spanish class more than they expected.

2   PARTS OF SENTENCES AND SENTENCE PATTERNS

PARTS OF SENTENCES

Every sentence has two basic parts: a subject and a predicate. The *subject* names something—a person, an object, an idea, a situation. The *predicate* makes an assertion about the subject. Any word group that is missing either of these elements is not a complete sentence.

SENTENCE PARTS AT A GLANCE

The **subject** of a sentence identifies some person, place, thing, activity, or idea.

The **predicate** of a sentence makes an assertion about the subject.

An **object** is the target or recipient of the action described by a verb.

A **complement** renames or describes a subject or object.

For basic sentence patterns, see page 602.

Both subject and predicate may consist of either one word or a group of words. A one-word subject is always a noun or pronoun; a one-word predicate is always a verb.

SUBJ PRED
Birds fly.

Many subjects and most predicates contain other elements as well, such as modifiers, objects, and complements. A modifier (such as an adjective or adverb) provides more information about the subject or some part of the predicate. A *direct* or *indirect object*, which always appears in the predicate, is the target or recipient of the action described by the verb. A *complement*, which also appears in the predicate, renames or describes the sentence's subject or object.

Let's look more closely at subjects, predicates, objects, and complements. Then we can explore the various ways of combining these elements in sentences.

2a *Subject*

The **subject** of a sentence identifies some person, place, thing, activity, or idea. Often the subject is the agent of the action described by the predicate ("*Jill* hit the ball"). Sometimes the subject is simply the topic of the predicate's action ("The *ball* was hit by Jill"; "*Baseball* came up for discussion"). Because the subject names something, it almost always is (or includes) a noun or pronoun. That noun or pronoun is the **simple subject**.

Queen Elizabeth waved to the crowd.

I waved back.

Often a subject includes additional nouns or pronouns, modifiers, or both. A subject that consists of two or more nouns or pronouns linked by a conjunction is called a **compound subject**.

The Queen and I exchanged waves.

Prince Charles, Princess Diana, and Princes William and Henry stood behind the Queen.

The **complete subject** consists of the simple or compound subject plus any words that modify it.

The imposing, world-famous Queen smiled at me.

A stern-looking bobby to her left scowled suspiciously.

Occasionally a subject is a phrase or clause that contains no nouns at all.

Whether or not to smile back was the question.

In a command, the subject is understood to be *you*, even though it does not appear in the sentence.

Don't [*you*] stand so close to me.

2b Predicate

The **predicate** of a sentence makes an assertion about the subject. This assertion can involve an action ("Birds *fly*"), a relationship ("Birds *have* feathers"), or a state of being ("Birds *are* cold-blooded"). The **simple predicate** consists of the main verb plus any helping verbs that accompany it (*will fly, should have flown*). (For a full list of helping verbs, see 1c.) The **complete predicate** consists of the verb plus any other words that help it to make its assertion, such as modifiers, objects, and complements.

Geese normally *can fly* more gracefully than chickens. [Simple predicate.]

Geese *normally can fly more gracefully than chickens*. [Complete predicate.]

Hiram *showed* me a goose that bites. [Simple predicate.]

Hiram *showed me a goose that bites*. [Complete predicate.]

In many sentences, the subject appears between two parts of the predicate.

When I visited his farm, Hiram *showed* me a goose that bites. [Simple predicate.]

When I visited his farm, Hiram *showed me a goose that bites*. [Complete predicate.]

You can tell that the opening clause *When I visited his farm* is part of the predicate because it modifies the verb (*showed*), not the subject (*Hiram*).

Exercise 2–1

Identify each simple subject (SS), complete subject (CS), simple predicate (SP), and complete predicate (CP) in the following sentences. Answers for the lettered sentences appear in the back of the book. Example:

Does your brother George really dye his hair?

Does your <u>brother</u> George really <u>dye</u> his hair?

a. Most wild animals do not make good pets.

b. War, that curse of the human race, has plagued civilizations throughout history.

c. Even after he became deaf, the composer Beethoven continued to write music.

d. One cup of coffee in the morning keeps me awake all day.

e. John Updike's mother, who had been a writer herself, always encouraged her son's literary aspirations.

1. Until the 1850s, the city now known as San Francisco was a tiny outpost with few human inhabitants.
2. The Golden Gate Bridge was named after the harbor entrance, long known as the Golden Gate.
3. The introduction of the telegraph enabled San Franciscans to find out when a ship was approaching the city.
4. San Francisco, like many California cities, was given its name by Spanish missionaries.
5. It was the Gold Rush that brought a flood of easterners and other outsiders to northern California.

2c Objects

An **object** is the target or recipient of the action described by a verb. Whereas the subject of a sentence does something, the object has something done to it or for it. Objects, like subjects, usually are (or include) nouns or pronouns.

Some geese bite *people*.

A sentence can have two types of objects: direct and indirect. A **direct object** completes the action performed by the subject or asserted about the subject; it is the verb's target. (Not all verbs take direct objects. Those that do are called *transitive verbs*; see 1c.)

She sells *seashells* by the seashore.

Birds have *feathers*.

Give me *your tired, your poor. . . .*

An **indirect object** names a person or other entity that is affected by the subject's action. Usually an indirect object is the recipient of the direct object, via the action described by the verb. Only certain transitive verbs take indirect objects. Among them are *ask*, *bring*, *buy*, *get*, *lend*, *offer*, *pay*, *promise*, *sell*, *show*, *tell*, and *write*.

She sells *the tourists* seashells.

Give *me* your tired, your poor. . . .

As you can see, the word *to* is implied before an indirect object. Often you can identify an indirect object by rearranging the sentence and inserting *to*.

She sells seashells *to the tourists*.

Give your tired and your poor *to me*.

2d Complements

A **complement** renames or describes a subject or object. It consists of a word or group of words in the predicate that completes the assertion in a sentence.

A complement that renames or describes a sentence subject is called a **subject complement**. It always follows a linking verb (see 1c, 5a). A subject complement can be a noun, an adjective, or a group of words that functions as a noun or adjective.

> S   SC
> That *dog* looks *friendly.*

> S   ┌────────────────SC────────────┐
> *Manute Bol* must be *the tallest basketball player in the NBA.*

A complement that renames or describes a direct or indirect object is called an **object complement**. Like a subject complement, an object complement can be a noun, an adjective, or a group of words that function as a noun or adjective.

> DO ┌──────────OC──────────┐
> Leroy calls *Julie the hostess with the mostest.*

> ┌────DO────┐ OC
> This new computer will keep *Professor Mutt happy.*

SENTENCE PATTERNS

With a subject, a verb, an object or two, a complement or two, and some modifiers, you can build virtually any English sentence. As complex as our language is, most sentences that we recognize as grammatical follow one of five patterns. Sometimes the order of the ingredients changes, and sometimes the pattern is obscured by modifying words and phrases. Here are the five basic sentence patterns, with examples. (Only simple subjects, verbs, objects, and complements are marked.)

1. **subject/verb**

> S   V
> The *king lives.*

> S   V
> The former *king* now *lives* in a cottage on the palace grounds.

> V   S
> Long *live* the *king*!

2. **subject/verb/subject complement**

> S   V   SC
> This *plum tastes ripe.*

> S   V   V V SC
> When this plum was picked, *it* probably *would* not *have tasted ripe.*

```
     SC          S   V
How ripe does this plum taste to you?
```

3. subject/verb/direct object

```
S      V            DO
I photographed the sheriff.
```

```
S  V              V        DO
I did not, however, photograph the deputy.
```

```
  V    S  V        V        DO
Would I have photographed Sheriff Brown if he were a kinder man?
```

4. subject/verb/indirect object/direct object

```
  S     V   IO    DO
Charlene asked you a question.
```

```
 V   IO           DO
Ask me no more questions than you wish to hear answered. [The subject you is
understood.]
```

```
 V      S     V  IO     DO
Didn't Charlene ask you a question?
```

5. subject/verb/direct object/object complement

```
    S     V    DO            OC
The judges rated Hugo the best skater.
```

```
    S               V   DO             OC
Six judges out of seven rated Hugo the best figure skater in the competition.
```

```
    S                     V   V  V    DO           OC
The judges, who may be biased, should have rated Hugo the second best of all
the skaters.
```

Exercise 2–2

Underline and identify the subject complements (SC), indirect objects (IO), direct objects (DO), and object complements (OC) wherever they appear in the following sentences. Mark the whole complement or object, not just its key noun or pronoun. Answers for the lettered sentences appear in the back of the book. Example:

Venus, the goddess of love, considered Adonis her equal.

```
                                      DO     OC
Venus, the goddess of love, considered Adonis her equal.
```

a. You are an educated person; how can you believe such a story?

b. By meowing, Timothy tells Judith his needs.

   c. Elizabeth, a cynical observer, believes that the president is an evasive man.

   d. Holography is an interesting art, but it requires expensive equipment.

   e. Many people call Chicago the windy city.

   1. Greyhounds are the dogs most often used for racing, which involves chasing a mechanical rabbit around a track.

   2. The scorers named Magic Johnson most valuable player in last week's game.

   3. The outfielder's agent negotiated him a new contract.

   4. Within a month, Juanita had become the toast of San Clemente.

   5. My friend Alicia calls her yellow Volkswagen Buttercup.

3 | PHRASES AND CLAUSES

Grammar deals not only with single words but with phrases and clauses as well. A **phrase** consists of two or more related words that work together: *my uncle Zeke*, *in the attic*, *will have been*. Words that do not work together do not make up a phrase: *Zeke uncle my*, *in attic the*, *been have will*.

Notice that a phrase doesn't make complete sense the way a sentence does. Useful as it may be, it is lacking. It may lack a subject (*will have been*), a verb (*my uncle Zeke*), or both (*in the attic*).

A **clause** has more going for it than a phrase: it contains both a subject and a verb. It too is a group of related words that work together. Clauses come in two forms: main and subordinate. A *main clause* needs only end punctuation to make it a complete sentence.

>   S   V
> *Uncle Zeke likes* solitude.

A *subordinate clause* contains a subject and a verb, but it cannot stand alone; it depends on a main clause to help it make sense.

>   S   V
> *who plays* the oboe

Only in combination with a main clause does a subordinate clause work as a sentence.

> Uncle Zeke, who plays the oboe, likes solitude.

TYPES OF PHRASES

Phrases, being incomplete by themselves, are versatile. They can function as nouns, verbs, adjectives, or adverbs. Every compound subject or object is a phrase by definition: *Zeke and Jake, my father and I*. So is every verb that consists of more than one word: *will have played, sang and danced.* Other types of phrases can play varied roles in sentences.

Playing the oboe is Uncle Zeke's favorite pastime. [Noun phrase—subject.]

He really enjoys *making music.* [Noun phrase—object.]

Uncle Zeke plays an oboe *custom-made for him.* [Adjective phrase modifying *oboe.*]

My music teacher says he plays *like a professional.* [Adverb phrase modifying *plays.*]

To determine whether a phrase functions as a noun, adjective, or adverb in a sentence, you can ask yourself what question the phrase answers. If it answers the question Who? or What?, it is a noun phrase. If it answers the question What kind?, it is an adjective phrase. If it answers the question When? or Where? or How?, it is usually an adverb phrase.

We can name phrases by the roles they play in a sentence: noun phrase, adjective phrase, adverb phrase. We can also name them by their form: prepositional phrase, verbal phrase, absolute phrase, appositive phrase. Because a phrase's form determines the roles it can play, our discussion of phrases will classify them by form.

3a *Prepositional Phrases*

What do the following sentences have in common?

Doesn't Lew have other friends besides Pat?

Over the next sand dune lies the ocean.

To understand his comments you must read between the lines.

Each sentence contains a **prepositional phrase**, so named because it starts with a preposition: *besides Pat, Over the next sand dune, between the lines.* (See the prepositions chart in 1f.)

Prepositional phrases are a common and very useful sentence ingredient. Most often, they function as adjectives or adverbs. When a prepositional phrase does the work of an adjective—that is, when it modifies a noun—we call it an **adjective phrase**.

Joyce wanted to live in a city *without smokestacks.* [Adjective phrase modifying *city.*]

Tyrone is a man *of honor.* [Adjective phrase modifying *man.*]

When a prepositional phrase does the work of an adverb—that is, when it modifies a verb, an adjective, or another adverb—we call it an **adverb phrase**.

She writes *with vigor.* [Adverb phrase modifying the verb *writes.*]

Jake feels indebted *to his coach.* [Adverb phrase modifying the adjective *indebted.*]

Mr. Francis phoned early *in the morning.* [Adverb phrase modifying the adverb *early.*]

Some prepositional phrases function as nouns; we call them **noun phrases.**

Over the river and through the woods is the long way to Grandmother's house.

3b *Verbal Phrases*

A **verbal** is a form of a verb that cannot stand by itself in a sentence. To function as the main verb of a sentence or clause, it needs a hand from another verb. Verbals include infinitives (*to live, to dream*), present participles (*falling, dancing*), and past participles (*lived, fallen*).

A verbal and its modifiers, if any, constitute a **verbal phrase.** The three types of verbal phrases are infinitive phrases (*to live alone, to dream vividly*); participial phrases (*falling behind, written in stone*); and gerund phrases (*smoking in the boys' room, slow dancing*). Verbal phrases (and verbals) can operate as nouns, adjectives, and adverbs.

INFINITIVE PHRASES

An **infinitive phrase** consists of the infinitive form of a verb preceded by *to* (*to quit*) plus any modifiers or objects (*to quit suddenly; to quit the job*). Infinitive phrases function as nouns, adjectives, and adverbs.

To err is human. [Noun phrase used as subject.]

Their goal is *to stop the pipeline project.* [Noun phrase used as subject complement.]

Jennifer is the candidate *to watch.* [Adjective phrase modifying *candidate.*]

Melvin lives *to eat.* [Adverb phrase modifying *lives.*]

He is too fat *to play tennis.* [Adverb phrase modifying *fat.*]

He moves too sluggishly *to return even the slowest serves.* [Adverb phrase modifying *sluggishly.*]

PHRASES AT A GLANCE

A **prepositional phrase** contains a preposition and its object(s) and any modifiers: "*In the old mansion* we found a stack *of books* hidden *behind the fireplace.*" (3a)

A **verbal phrase** consists of a verbal (a form of verb that cannot stand by itself in a sentence) and its modifiers: "All she wanted was *to attend college someday*" (**infinitive phrase**); "*Swimming in cold water,* we hardly noticed that the air temperature was 101 degrees" (**participial phrase**); "*Combing the dog's hair* took at least thirty minutes every other day" (**gerund phrase**). (3b)

An infinitive phrase is easy to distinguish from a prepositional phrase starting with *to:* in an infinitive phrase, *to* is followed first by a verb (*to row*) and only then by an object, if any (*to row a boat*). In a prepositional phrase, *to* is followed directly by its object, a noun or pronoun (*to me, to the lighthouse*).

PARTICIPIAL PHRASES

A **participial phrase** is an adjective phrase that opens with the present or past participle of a verb. Here are examples of the infinitive and participial forms of a few common verbs:

INFINITIVE	PRESENT PARTICIPLE	PAST PARTICIPLE
(to) find	finding	found
(to) fly	flying	flown
(to) go	going	gone
(to) see	seeing	seen
(to) walk	walking	walked

All participial phrases share two characteristics: they start with participles, and they function as adjectives.

> *Leading the pack,* Michael sprinted into the final straightaway. [Modifies *Michael.*]
>
> He made the most of the few seconds *remaining in his race.* [Modifies *seconds.*]
>
> *Worn out by the intensity of his effort,* Michael fell. [Modifies *Michael.*]

GERUND PHRASES

A **gerund phrase** is a noun phrase that opens with the present participle of a verb. It can serve as the subject of a sentence, a direct object, a subject complement, or the object of a preposition.

> *Giving blood* is a valuable public service. [Subject.]
>
> Audrey loves *performing in plays.* [Direct object.]
>
> Phil's job is *making doughnuts.* [Subject complement.]
>
> My mother is nervous about *traveling by herself.* [Object of a preposition.]

An **absolute phrase** is a verbal phrase that does not modify any one word in a sentence but rather modifies the entire sentence: "*Barring any unforeseen delay,* the space shuttle will be launched at noon." "*Given the umpire's obvious bias,* the game should be replayed." (3c)

An **appositive phrase** is a group of words that adds information about a subject or object by identifying it in a different way: "Magali, *a student from France,* learned colloquial English by living with an American family." (3d)

3c *Absolute Phrases*

An **absolute phrase** is one that contains a gerund, a participle, or an infinitive and adds information to a sentence. It does not modify any one word; rather, it modifies a whole main clause. Usually it stands at the beginning of a sentence.

> *To be perfectly frank,* your plan is ill conceived.
>
> *Considering this book's importance,* our library ought to contain several copies.

3d *Appositive Phrases*

An appositive is a word that adds to what we know about a subject or object simply by identifying it in a different way ("my dog *Rover*," "Harvey's brother *Fred*"). An **appositive phrase** is a group of words that provides the same kind of amplification.

> Bess, *the landlord's daughter,* had long black hair.
>
> I walked across the field, *a golden sea of wheat flecked with daisies,* to the stone wall.

Exercise 3–1

Underline and identify the prepositional, verbal (infinitive, participial, and gerund), absolute, and appositive phrases in the following sentences. For each prepositional and verbal phrase, also identify its role in the sentence (noun, adjective, adverb). Answers for the lettered sentences appear in the back of the book. Example:

> The hero of the movie *Robocop* is half human, half machine.
>
> The hero of the movie *Robocop* is half human, half machine. [Prepositional; adjective.]

a. Identifying parts of speech has never been my strong point.

b. The fellow in the beret is a fourth-generation Californian.

c. Given the situation, the children should be returned to their mother.

d. I heard their astonishing news through the grapevine.

e. The Confederacy, gone with the wind, remains a cherished Southern memory.

1. The North, Civil War victor, is less nostalgic.

2. Looking out on the morning rain, Carole used to feel uninspired.

3. Raymond's Las Vegas escapade gave playing blackjack a bad name.

4. Elsa didn't want to get on the plane, but Rick insisted.

5. Geoff's only accomplishment has been rebuilding that boat.

6. The money stolen from Gene's wallet would have paid his rent.

7. Cordelia, her father's favorite, loved King Lear the most.

8. Your loud music having interrupted my concentration, I can't finish my essay right now.

9. Blinded by the light, Bruce waved to his invisible audience.
10. Steve's dream is to ride his motorcycle across the country.

TYPES OF CLAUSES

A clause's main distinction from a phrase is that it has both a subject and a verb. Some clauses, indeed, can stand alone as complete sentences. They are called **main clauses** (or **independent clauses**).

My *sister has* a friend.

The *flowers were* beautiful.

Clauses that cannot stand alone are called **subordinate clauses** (or **dependent clauses**).

who comes from Lebanon

that *Dan gave* Nicola

A subordinate clause must be linked with a main clause for its meaning to be entirely clear.

My sister has a friend who comes from Lebanon.

The flowers that Dan gave Nicola were beautiful.

Subordinate clauses, like phrases, are versatile: they can function as nouns, adjectives, and adverbs. You can generally tell noun, adjective, and adverb clauses apart by asking, "What question does this clause answer?" A clause that answers the question What? or Who? is a noun clause. One that answers the question What kind? or Which one? is an adjective clause. One that answers the question When? or How? or Where? is usually an adverb clause.

3e *Noun Clauses*

A subordinate clause that serves as a sentence subject, object, or complement is called a **noun clause**. Usually a noun clause begins with *how, what, when, where, whether, who* (or *whom*), *whoever* (or *whomever*), or *that*.

What I believe is none of their business. [Noun clause as subject.]

James doesn't know *whom he should blame*. [Noun clause as direct object.]

In both of these examples, the relative pronoun that opens the subordinate clause (*What, whom*) is followed by the clause's subject and verb.

    S   V

what *I believe*

       S   V

whom *he should blame*

> **SUBORDINATE CLAUSES AT A GLANCE**
>
> A **noun clause** serves as a sentence subject, object, or complement. It answers the question What? or Who? (3e)
>
> An **adjective clause** serves as an adjective by modifying a noun or pronoun. It answers the question What kind? or Which one? (3f)
>
> An **adverb clause** plays the role of an adverb, modifying a verb, an adjective, or another adverb. It answers the question When? or How? or Where? (3g)

Sometimes, however, the relative pronoun that opens the subordinate clause also serves as the subject of the clause.

$$\overset{\text{S}\quad\text{V}}{}$$

James doesn't know *who did it*. [Noun clause as direct object.]

$$\overset{\text{S}\qquad\text{V}}{}$$

Sarah tells *whoever will listen* her complaints about Mrs. Quigley. [Noun clause as indirect object.]

In these two sentences, no additional noun or pronoun comes between *who* or *whomever* and the verb of the clause. The relative pronoun links the subordinate clause to the main clause, and it also functions as the subordinate clause's subject.

3f Adjective Clauses

Subordinate clauses can serve as adjectives by modifying nouns or pronouns. Usually an adjective clause is introduced by one of the relative pronouns: *who, which,* or *that.* Sometimes the relative pronoun is implied: "I got the letter [*that*] you sent me." You can tell an adjective clause from a noun clause by its role in a sentence.

I like people *who are optimistic.* [Adjective clause modifying *people.*]

I plan to major in psychology, *which has always interested me.* [Adjective clause modifying *psychology.*]

Science is a tide *that can only rise.* —Jonathan Schell. [Adjective clause modifying *tide.*]

3g Adverb Clauses

An adverb clause plays the role of an adverb in a sentence, modifying a verb, an adjective, or another adverb.

Larry left *before I could explain my mistake.* [Adverb clause modifying the verb *left.*]

He was sure *that I had insulted him.* [Adverb clause modifying the adjective *sure.*]

He loses his temper faster *than most people do*. [Adverb clause modifying the adverb *faster*.]

Generally, subordinate clauses acting as adverbs are introduced by one of the common subordinating conjunctions, such as:

after	so that	when
although	than	whenever
as	that	where
because	though	wherever
before	unless	while
if	until	why
since		

(For a complete list of subordinating conjunctions, see 1g.) As with adjective clauses, the subordinating conjunction in an adverb clause sometimes is implied rather than stated: "You paint so well [*that*] you could be a professional."

Exercise 3–2

Underline the subordinate clauses in the following sentences, and identify each one as a noun, adjective, or adverb clause. Answers for the lettered sentences appear in the back of the book. Example:

The man whose toe Susan had stepped on yelped in pain.

The man <u>whose toe Susan had stepped on</u> yelped in pain. [Adjective clause]

a. My grandfather was a rolling stone; wherever he lived at the moment was his home.
b. While we were still arguing about its value, the statue was removed from the gallery.
c. The shirt that I took to the cleaner's came back with a ripped sleeve.
d. Ann did so badly on the exam that she may fail the course.
e. Lee can't decide whether he should invite James.

1. Before you leave for the summer, we should discuss plans for the fall semester.
2. The man who we all thought was so charming has been arrested for fraud.
3. Sailing, which is Charlie's favorite summer pastime, has been banned in Rock Harbor.
4. Lewis sent us more postcards than we had time to read.
5. Blame John's death on the cocaine he refused to give up.

4 TYPES OF SENTENCES

What is a **sentence**? There is more than one answer. In conversation, the single word *Where?* can be a sentence. But in striving to write clear, readable prose, you will find it useful to think of a sentence as the expression of a complete thought containing at least one *main clause*—that is, a subject and a verb (see p. 609). So defined, sentences come in four varieties.

4a Simple Sentences

Any sentence that contains only one clause is a **simple sentence**, even if it includes modifiers, objects, complements, and any number of phrases in addition to its subject and verb.

> Even amateur stargazers can easily locate the Big Dipper in the night sky.
>
> George Washington exhibited courage and leadership during a crucial period in our country's history.
>
> Fred and Sandy have already applied for summer jobs.
>
> The spectators laughed and cried at the same time.

Notice in the last two examples that a simple sentence may have a compound subject (*Fred and Sandy*) or a compound verb (*laughed and cried*). Still, it remains a simple sentence, for it contains only one main clause. Sometimes the subject of a simple sentence is not stated but is clearly understood. In the command "Run!," the subject is evidently *you*.

4b Compound Sentences

A **compound sentence** consists of two or more main clauses joined by a coordinating conjunction such as *and*, *but*, or *for* or by a semicolon. Sometimes the semicolon is followed by a *conjunctive adverb* such as *however*, *nevertheless*, or *therefore*. (For complete lists of coordinating conjunctions and conjunctive adverbs, see 1g.)

```
                                       MAIN
         ┌─────────MAIN CLAUSE────────┐  ┌CLAUSE┐
         I would like to accompany you, but I can't.

         ┌─MAIN CLAUSE─┐ ┌─MAIN CLAUSE─┐
         Two's company; three's a crowd.

         ┌──────────MAIN CLAUSE────────────┐            ┌────────────────────────MAIN
         Henry Kissinger was born in Europe; therefore, he cannot be a candidate for the
         CLAUSE─────────────────────────┐
         presidency of the United States.
```

4c Complex Sentences

A **complex sentence** consists of one main clause and one or more subordinate clauses.

```
                              SUBORDINATE
         ┌──MAIN CLAUSE──┐ ┌───CLAUSE────┐
         I will be at the airport when you arrive.
```

┌──SUBORDINATE CLAUSE──┐ ┌────MAIN CLAUSE────┐
Since Amy bought a computer, she has been out of circulation.

┌───────SUBORDINATE CLAUSE───────┐ ┌MAIN CLAUSE┐ ┌────────SUBORDINATE
Because George has to travel widely, he is grateful whenever his far-flung

CLAUSE────────────────────────────┐
acquaintances invite him to a home-cooked meal.

In some sentences, the relative pronoun linking the subordinate clause to the main clause is implied rather than stated.

MAIN   SUBORDINATE
┌CLAUSE┐┌──CLAUSE──┐
I know [that] you saw us.

Sometimes the relative pronoun linking the main and subordinate clauses serves as the subject of the subordinate clause.

SUBORDINATE
┌──MAIN CLAUSE──┐ ┌──CLAUSE──┐
Paulette likes men *who* flatter her.

SUBORDINATE
┌──MAIN CLAUSE──┐ ┌──CLAUSE──┐
Don't bite the hand *that* feeds you.

4d Compound-Complex Sentences

As it name implies, **a compound-complex sentence** shares the attributes of a compound sentence (it contains two or more main clauses) and a complex sentence (it contains at least one subordinate clause).

┌──SUBORDINATE CLAUSE──┐ ┌────MAIN CLAUSE────┐   ┌────────MAIN
Where politics is concerned, Michael seems indifferent and Joanne seems ill

CLAUSE┐
informed.

SUBORDINATE   MAIN
┌────────MAIN CLAUSE────────┐ ┌CLAUSE┐┌──CLAUSE──┐
I'd gladly wait until you're ready; but if I do, I'll miss the boat.

Exercise 4–1

Identify each of the following sentences as simple, compound, complex, or compound-complex. Don't just pin labels on them: briefly explain what elements each sentence contains that make you classify it as you do. Answers for the lettered sentences appear in the back of the book. Example:

If a bullfrog had wings, he wouldn't bump his tail so much, but he'd have a hard time swimming.

┌─ SUBORDINATE CLAUSE ─┐┌────── MAIN CLAUSE ──────┐   ┌────── MAIN

If a bullfrog had wings, he wouldn't bump his tail so much, but he'd have a hard

CLAUSE ──────┐

time swimming. [Compound-complex.]

a. Not only women but also men and children benefit from society's increasing resistance to sex-role stereotypes.

b. Even in a life-or-death emergency, I know you can count on Marlene.

c. Biology is interesting, but I prefer botany as it is taught by Professor Haines.

d. Do you prefer bacon and eggs or cereal and toast for breakfast this morning?

e. Most people believe that poverty begets poverty; however, recent studies have shown that, more often than not, when children from welfare families reach adulthood, they achieve economic independence.

1. Geraldine believes that the sexual revolution, without compensating women for their losses, has robbed them of all the advantages automatically bestowed by old-fashioned marriage.

2. In my favorite television series, the detective invariably sends his assistant on some mysterious errand.

3. Do you want to dance, or would you rather take time out for pizza?

4. Since Jennifer moved to the city, her attendance at concerts, plays, and museum shows has increased markedly; and she dines out at least once a week.

5. As a boy, Mike couldn't wait to qualify for the Little League baseball team; a few weeks after joining, he wanted only to quit.

6. Executives who promote incompetent workers can drive a corporation to the brink of disaster.

7. In the Virgin Islands the sun shines every day, the temperature drops to a comfortable level every night, and the breeze rustles through the palm trees at all hours.

8. No one can say exactly how long ago it was that dinosaurs ceased to walk the earth.

9. At some point in the long and surprisingly complex history of popular music, rock-'n'-roll acquired its present identity as the music of youth and rebellion.

10. If a man makes a better mousetrap, the world will beat a path to his door.
—Ralph Waldo Emerson

CHAPTER 22

Grammatical Sentences

5. Verbs	**615**
6. Subject-Verb Agreement	**630**
7. Pronoun-Antecedent Agreement	**635**
8. Pronoun Reference	**638**
9. Pronoun Case	**641**
10. Sentence Fragments	**646**
11. Comma Splices and Fused Sentences	**652**
12. Adjectives and Adverbs	**657**

5   VERBS

All verbs are either *transitive* (in need of a direct object to receive the verb's action) or *intransitive* (complete in themselves). (See pp. 592–593.) This is one useful way to classify verbs, but not the only way.

Most verbs, whether transitive or intransitive, show action (*swim*, *fight*, *eat*, *hide*, *pay*, *sleep*, *win*). Some verbs indicate a state of being by linking the subject of a sentence with a word that renames or describes it; they are called *linking verbs*. A few verbs work with a main verb to give more information about its action; they are called *helping verbs* or *auxiliary verbs*.

VERB FORMS

5a Use a linking verb to connect the subject of a sentence with a subject complement.

Rather than tell what a sentence's subject does, a **linking verb** indicates what it *is* or *is like*. Some common linking verbs are *be*, *appear*, *feel*, and *grow*. A linking verb creates a sort of equation, either positive or negative, between the subject and its complement (see p. 601). The subject complement can be a noun, a pronoun, or an adjective.

> LV   SC
> Julia will *make* a good *doctor*. [Noun.]

> LV   SC
> George *is* not the *one*. [Pronoun.]

>   LV   SC
> London weather *seems foggy*. [Adjective.]

A verb may be a linking verb in some sentences and not in others.

> I often *grow* sleepy after lunch. [Linking verb with subject complement *sleepy*.]
> I often *grow* tomatoes in my garden. [Transitive verb with direct object *tomatoes*.]

If you pay attention to what the verb means, you can usually tell whether it is functioning as a linking verb.

COMMON LINKING VERBS
Some linking verbs tell what a noun is, was, or will be.

> *be, become, remain*
> *grow*: The sky *is growing* dark.
> *make*: One plus two *makes* three.
> *prove*: His warning *proved* accurate.
> *turn to*: The snow *has turned* to rain.

Some linking verbs tell what a noun might be.

> *appear, seem, look*

Most verbs of the senses can operate as linking verbs.

> *feel, smell, sound, taste*

5b Choose the right helping verb to give more information about a main verb's action or state of being.

A simple verb (*go*, *shoot*, *contemplate*) is limited. We can expand the range of information it conveys by adding a **helping** or **auxiliary verb**: *am going, did shoot, have contemplated.*

All the forms of *be*, *do*, and *have* can function as helping verbs. The other helping verbs are *can, could, may, might, must, shall, should, will,* and *would.* These last nine can function only as helping verbs, never as main verbs.

A main verb plus one or more auxiliaries is called a **verb phrase**. The parts of a verb phrase need not appear together but may be separated by other words.

> I probably *am going* to France this summer.
>
> You *should* not *have shot* that pigeon.
>
> This change *may* well *have been* seriously *contemplated* by the governor even before the election.

5c Know when to use each of the principal parts of a verb.

Verbs have three principal parts: the infinitive, the past tense, and the past participle. The principal parts are the forms the verb can take—alone or with helping verbs—to indicate the full range of times when an action or state of being does, did, or will occur.

The **infinitive** is the simple or dictionary form of the verb (*go, sing, laugh*) or the simple form preceded by *to* (*to go, to sing, to laugh*). (See p. 606.)

The **past tense** signals that the verb's action is completed (*went, sang, laughed*).

The **past participle** is combined with helping verbs to indicate action occurring at various times in the past or future (*have gone, had sung, will have laughed*). It is also used with forms of *be* to make the passive voice. (See pp. 626–627.)

In addition to the three principal parts, all verbs have a present participle, which consists of the infinitive plus *-ing*. The present participle is used to make the progressive tenses. (See 5j and 5k.) It also can modify nouns and pronouns ("the *leaking* bottle"); and, as a gerund, it can function as a noun ("*sleeping all day* pleases me"). (See p. 607.)

5d To form the past tense and past participle of a regular verb, add -d or -ed to the infinitive. For an irregular verb, memorize the principal parts.

Most verbs in English are *regular verbs*: they form the past tense and past participle in a standard, predictable way. Regular verbs that end in *-e* add *-d* to the infinitive; those that do not end in *-e* add *-ed*.

INFINITIVE	PAST TENSE	PAST PARTICIPLES
(to) smile	smiled	smiled
(to) act	acted	acted
(to) please	pleased	pleased
(to) trick	tricked	tricked

The English language has at least two hundred *irregular verbs*, which form their past tense and past participle in some other way than by adding *-d* or *-ed*. Most irregular verbs are familiar to native English speakers and pose no problem, although they can be a torment to people trying to learn the language. The principal parts chart lists just the most troublesome irregular verbs.

PRINCIPAL PARTS OF COMMON IRREGULAR VERBS

INFINITIVE	PAST TENSE	PAST PARTICIPLE
be	was	been
become	became	become
begin	began	begun
blow	blew	blown
break	broke	broken
bring	brought	brought
burst	burst	burst
catch	caught	caught
choose	chose	chosen
come	came	come
do	did	done
draw	drew	drawn
drink	drank	drunk
drive	drove	driven
eat	ate	eaten
fall	fell	fallen
fight	fought	fought
freeze	froze	frozen
get	got	got, gotten
give	gave	given
go	went	gone
grow	grew	grown
have	had	had
hear	heard	heard
hide	hid	hidden
know	knew	known
lay	laid	laid
lead	led	led
let	let	let
lie	lay	lain
make	made	made

INFINITIVE	PAST TENSE	PAST PARTICIPLE
raise	raised	raised
ride	rode	ridden
ring	rang	rung
rise	rose	risen
run	ran	run
say	said	said
see	saw	seen
set	set	set
sit	sat	sat
sing	sang	sung
slay	slew	slain
slide	slid	slid
speak	spoke	spoken
spin	spun	spun
stand	stood	stood
steal	stole	stolen
swim	swam	swum
swing	swung	swung
teach	taught	taught
tear	tore	torn
think	thought	thought
throw	threw	thrown
wake	woke, waked	woken, waked
write	wrote	written

For the appropriate form of any irregular verb not on this list, consult your dictionary. (Some dictionaries list principal parts for all verbs, some just for irregular verbs.)

5e *Learn the principal parts of the verbs* **lie** *and* **lay** *and* **sit** *and* **set.**

Among the most troublesome verbs in English are *lie* and *lay*. If you have difficulty choosing between them, you can forever eliminate confusion by taking two easy steps. The first is to memorize the principal parts and present participles of both verbs (see the chart).

The second step in deciding whether to use *lie* or *lay* is to fix in memory that *lie*, in all its forms, is intransitive. *Lie* never takes a direct object: "The island *lies* due East," "Jed *has lain* on the floor all day." *Lay*, on the other hand, is a transitive verb. It always requires an object: "*Lay* that pistol down."

The same distinction exists between *sit* and *set*. Usually, *sit* is intransitive: "He *sits* on the stairs." *Set*, on the other hand, almost always takes an object: "He *sets* the bottle on the counter." There are, however, a few easily memorized exceptions. The sun *sets*. A hen *sets*. Gelatin *sets*. You *sit* a horse. You can *sit* yourself down at a table that *sits* twelve.

PRINCIPAL PARTS AND PRESENT PARTICIPLES
OF *LIE* AND *LAY*, *SIT* AND *SET*

lie: recline

PRESENT TENSE	I lie	we lie
	you lie	you lie
	he/she/it lies	they lie
PAST TENSE	I lay	we lay
	you lay	you lay
	he/she/it lay	they lay
PAST PARTICIPLE	lain (We have *lain* in the sun long enough.)	
PRESENT PARTICIPLE	lying (At ten o'clock he was still *lying* in bed.)	

lay: put in place, deposit

PRESENT TENSE	I lay	we lay
	you lay	you lay
	he/she/it lays	they lay
PAST TENSE	I laid	we laid
	you laid	you laid
	he/she/it laid	they laid
PAST PARTICIPLE	laid (Having *laid* his clothes on the bed, Mark jumped into the shower.)	
PRESENT PARTICIPLE	laying (*Laying* her cards on the table, Lola cried, "Gin!")	

Exercise 5–1

Underline each incorrectly used irregular verb in the following sentences and substitute the verb's appropriate form. Some sentences may be correct. Answers for the lettered sentences appear in the back of the book. Example:

Lie your books on the windowsill near the spot where the flowers are setting.

<u>Lay</u> your books on the windowsill near the spot where the flowers are <u>sitting</u>.

a. When Joe's mother catched him laying around the house during school hours, she throwed him out.

b. We woke soon after the sun rose, and then we swam to the raft.

c. He lay his cards triumphantly on the table but soon found that he was not setting in a lucky chair after all.

d. Wendy knew how much Roger had drank, but she gone with him anyway.

e. I have laid awake, tossing and turning, every night since exams begun.

1. Why don't you lay down for a while after you have lain a fire in the fireplace?

sit: be seated

PRESENT TENSE	I sit	we sit
	you sit	you sit
	he/she/it sits	they sit
PAST TENSE	I sat	we sat
	you sat	you sat
	he/she/it sat	they sat
PAST PARTICIPLE	sat (I have *sat* here long enough.)	
PRESENT PARTICIPLE	sitting (Why are you *sitting* on that rickety bench?)	

set: place

PRESENT TENSE	I set	we set
	you set	you set
	he/she/it sets	they set
PAST TENSE	I set	we set
	you set	you set
	he/she/it set	they set
PAST PARTICIPLE	set (Paul has *set* the table for eight.)	
PRESENT PARTICIPLE	setting (Jerry has been *setting* pins at the Bowl-a-drome.)	

2. How could Ricardo have knew that Cindy drunk his coffee?

3. I have laid in an ample supply of groceries for tonight's birthday dinner, which we should have eaten yesterday.

4. Frank throwed a rock through the window and then teared down the curtains climbing inside.

5. I have set here for so long my legs won't move.

TENSES

The **tense** of a verb is the *time* when its action did, does, or will occur. With the *simple tenses* we can indicate whether the verb's action took place in the past, takes place in the present, or will take place in the future. The *perfect tenses* enable us to narrow the timing even further, specifying that the action was or will be completed by the time of some other action. The *progressive tenses* let readers know that the verb's action does, did, or will continue.

5f *Use the simple present tense for an action that takes place once, recurrently, or continuously in the present.*

The simple present tense is the infinitive form of the verb plus *-s* or *-es* for the third person singular.

I like, I go	we like, we go
you like, you go	you like, you go
he/she/it likes, he/she/it goes	they like, they go

(Notice that irregular verbs, such as *go*, form their simple present tense following the same rules as regular verbs.)

You can use the simple present tense for an action that is happening right now ("I *welcome* this news"), an action that happens repeatedly in the present ("Judy *goes* to church every Sunday"), or an ongoing present action ("Wesley *likes* ice cream"). In some cases, usually to ask a question or intensify the action, the helping verb *do* appears before the simple present verb.

I *do think* you should take the job.

Does Andy *want* it?

Besides present action, you can use the simple present for future action: "Football season *starts* Wednesday."

Use the simple present for a general truth, even if the rest of the sentence is in a different tense:

Columbus proved in 1492 that the world *is* round.

Mr. Hammond will argue that people *are* basically good.

5g *Use the simple past tense for actions already completed.*

Jack *enjoyed* the party.

Suzie *went* home early.

VERB TENSES AT A GLANCE

Note: the examples show first person only.

SIMPLE TENSES	REGULAR	IRREGULAR
Present	I cook	I see
Past	I cooked	I saw
Future	I will cook	I will see

PERFECT TENSES		
Present perfect	I have cooked	I have seen
Past perfect	I had cooked	I had seen
Future perfect	I will have cooked	I will have seen

Indicate the simple past tense with the verb's past tense form. Regular verbs form the past tense by adding -d or -ed to the infinitive; the past tense of irregular verbs must be memorized. If you add the helping verb *do,* use the past tense (*did*) with the infinitive form of the main verb.

I went, I did go	we went, we did go
you went, you did go	you went, you did go
he/she/it went, he/she/it did go	they went, they did go

5h Use the simple future tense for actions that are expected to happen but have not happened yet.

George *will arrive* in time for dinner.

Will you please *show* him where to park?

To form the simple future tense, add *will* to the infinitive form of the verb.

I will go	we will go
you will go	you will go
he/she/it will go	they will go

You can also use *shall* for first person or (for any person) to inject a tone of determination: "We *shall overcome!*"

Although the present tense can indicate future action ("We *go* on vacation next Monday"), most actions that have not yet taken place are expressed in the simple future tense ("Surely it *will snow* tomorrow").

5i Use the present perfect, past perfect, or future perfect tense for an action completed at the time of another action.

All three perfect tenses of a verb consist of the past participle plus a form of the helping verb *have.* The tense of *have* determines the tense of the whole verb phrase.

PROGRESSIVE TENSES	REGULAR	IRREGULAR
Present progressive	I am cooking	I am seeing
Past progressive	I was cooking	I was seeing
Future progressive	I will be cooking	I will be seeing
Present perfect		
progressive	I have been cooking	I have been seeing
Past perfect		
progressive	I had been cooking	I had been seeing
Future perfect		
progressive	I will have been cooking	I will have been seeing

The action of a *present perfect* verb was completed before the sentence is uttered. Its helping verb is in the present tense: *have* or *has.*

> I *have* never *been* to Spain, but *I have been* to Oklahoma.
>
> Mr. Grimaldi *has gone* home for the day.
>
> *Have* you *seen* John Sayles's new film?

You can use the present perfect tense either for an action completed before some other action ("I *have washed* my hands of the whole affair") or for an action begun in the past and still going on ("Max *has worked* in this office for twelve years").

The action of a *past perfect* verb was completed before some other action in the past. Its helping verb is in the past tense: *had.*

> The concert *had ended* by the time we found a parking space.
>
> Until I met her, I *had pictured* Jenna as a redhead.
>
> *Hadn't* you *wanted* to clean the house before Mother arrived?

The action of a *future perfect* verb will be completed by some point (specified or implied) in the future. Its helping verb is in the future tense: *will have.*

> The builders *will have finished* the house by June.
>
> When I get the Dutch Blue, I *will have collected* every stamp I need.
>
> *Won't* the store *have closed* by the time we get there?

5j Use the present progressive, past progressive, or future progressive tense for an action in progress.

All three progressive tenses of a verb consist of the present participle plus a form of the helping verb *be.* (You can form the present participle of any verb, regular or irregular, by adding *-ing* to the infinitive.) The tense of *be* determines the tense of the whole verb phrase.

The *present progressive* expresses an action that is taking place now. Its helping verb is in the present tense: *am, is,* or *are.*

> I *am thinking* of a word that starts with *R.*
>
> *Is* Joe *babysitting* while Marie *is* off *visiting* her sister?

You can also express future action with the present progressive of *go* plus an infinitive phrase:

> I *am going to read* Tolstoy's *War and Peace* some day.
>
> *Are* you *going to sign up* for Professor Blaine's course on the sixties?

The *past progressive* expresses an action that took place continuously at some time in the past, whether or not that action is still going on. Its helping verb is in the past tense: *was* or *were.*

The old men *were sitting* on the porch when we passed.

Lucy *was planning* to take the weekend off.

The *future progressive* expresses an action that will take place continuously at some time in the future. Its helping verb is in the future tense: *will be*.

They *will be answering* the phones while she is gone.

Will we *be dining* out every night on our vacation?

5k *Use the present perfect progressive, the past perfect progressive, or the future perfect progressive tense for an action that started in the past and did, does, or will continue.*

The *present perfect progressive* indicates an action that started in the past and is continuing in the present. Form it by adding the present perfect of *be* (*has been* or *have been*) to the main verb's present participle.

All morning Fred *has been singing* the blues about his neighbor's wild parties.

Have you *been reading* Janine's postcards from England?

The *past perfect progressive* expresses a continuing action that was completed before another past action. Form it by adding the past perfect of *be* (*had been*) to the main verb's present participle.

By the time Dave finally arrived, I *had been waiting* for twenty minutes.

The *future perfect progressive* expresses an action that is expected to continue into the future beyond some other future action. Form it by adding the future perfect of *be* (*will have been*) to the main verb's present participle.

By 1995 Joanne *will have been attending* school longer than anyone else I know.

The main thing to remember about verb tenses is to avoid changing from one to another without reason. Studying tenses can improve your writing by making you aware of the variety of verb forms at your disposal and by giving you practice at using them effectively.

Exercise 5–2

Underline and identify the tense of each verb phrase in the following sentences. Answers for the lettered sentences appear in the back of the book. Example:

John is living in Hinsdale, but he prefers Joliet.

John is living [present progressive] in Hinsdale, but he prefers [simple present] Joliet.

a. Yesterday Joan broke her leg because she was skiing too fast.

b. Bill sleeps for nine hours every night; even so, he is always yawning.

c. Until last weekend, Josh had never seen a whale, except on those nature specials the public television station runs.

d. The upcoming tour represents the first time the band will have performed together since they split up.

e. After I finish college, I probably will attend graduate school.

1. When they had eaten breakfast, Kate and Matthew strapped on their snowshoes.

2. As of December 1, Ira and Sandy will have been going together for three years.

3. I was thinking about all the fun we've had since we met in third grade.

4. Dan will have embarked on his career by the time his brother starts college.

5. Have you been hoping that Carlos will come to your party?

6. If so, you should know that he will not yet have returned from Chicago.

7. His parents had been expecting him home any day until they heard that he was still waiting for the bus.

8. Probably he is sitting in the depot right now, unless he has switched to the train.

9. I will be keeping my ears open for further news, since I know how much you had counted on Carlos.

10. Still, by the time the party has ended, you will have had so much fun that you won't be holding his absence against him.

VOICE

Intelligent students read challenging books.

Challenging books are read by intelligent students.

These two statements convey similar information, but their emphasis is different. In the first sentence, the subject (*students*) perform the verb's action (*read*); in the second sentence, the subject (*books*) receives the verb's action (*are read*). One sentence states its idea directly, the other indirectly. We say that the first sentence is in the *active voice* and the second is in the *passive voice*.

5l Use the active voice rather than the passive voice whenever practical.

Verbs in the **active voice**, or **active verbs**, consist of principal parts and helping verbs as described in this chapter so far. Verbs in the **passive voice**, or **passive verbs**, consist of the past participle preceded by a form of *be* ("you *are given*," "I *was given*," "she *will be given*"). Most writers prefer the active to the passive voice because it is clearer and simpler, requires fewer words, and identifies the actor and the action more explicitly.

ACTIVE VOICE *Sergeants give* orders. *Privates obey* them.

Normally a sentence's subject is the focus of our attention. If that subject is not the agent of the verb's action, but a passive recipient, we may find ourselves asking: What did the writer mean to emphasize? Just what is his or her point?

PASSIVE VOICE   *Orders are given* by sergeants. *They are obeyed* by privates.

The passive voice is often misused to lend pomp to a humble truth (or would-be truth). A preacher, at the funeral of a man about whom he could recall little good, intoned in his eulogy, "Cold pie was much esteemed by the remains." The preacher may have known that to say directly, in the active voice, "The departed liked cold pie," would have displayed in neon lights the poverty of his thought.

Some writers use the passive voice deliberately to obscure the truth—a contradiction of the very purpose of writing. One of the witnesses in the congressional Iran-Contra hearings tried to dodge a key question by replying, "Whether full knowledge had been attained by us at that time is uncertain." If he had answered in the active voice—"I don't know whether we knew everything then or not"—his listeners easily would have recognized an evasion.

This is not to say that you should cut the passive voice entirely from your writing. In some contexts the performer of the verb's action in a sentence is unknown or irrelevant. With a passive verb, you can simply omit the performer, as in "Many fortunes were lost in the stock market crash of 1929" or "The passive voice is often misused." It's a good idea, though, as you comb through a rough draft, to substitute the active voice for the passive unless you have a good reason for using the passive.

Exercise 5–3

Change the following sentences to the active voice unless you can justify keeping the passive. (You may change more than the verb if doing so improves the sentence.) Example:

> Only lip service is paid to moral values by too many of us.
>
> Too many of us pay only lip service to moral values.

a. The *World Book Encyclopedia*'s article about opossums was recently read by me.

b. A resemblance can be noted between the rat and the opossum.

c. Food is hunted at night by the opossum.

d. Like all marsupials, the young are carried in a stomach pouch by their mothers.

e. From fifteen to eighteen newborn opossums can be fitted into a teaspoon.

1. They are carried by their mothers for two months after birth.

2. Almost any kind of animal or vegetable food is eaten by the opossum.

3. Because opossums have long toes, their tracks are easily recognized.

4. Both North America and South America are lived in by these interesting animals.

5. "Playing possum" (pretending to be dead) was invented by these ingenious animals to fool their predators.

MOOD

Still another characteristic of verbs is their mood. Every verb is in one of three **moods**: the **indicative**, the **imperative,** or the **subjunctive**. Most of the verbs considered so far have been in the indicative mood. The imperative mood and subjunctive moods, though less common, add valuable versatility to the English language.

5m *Use the indicative mood to state a fact, to ask a question, or to express an opinion.*

The vast majority of verbs in English are in the indicative mood; they follow the rules for principal parts, tense, voice, and so forth that have been presented in this chapter.

FACT   Pat *left* home two months ago.

QUESTION *Will* she *find* happiness as a go-go dancer?

OPINION   I *think* not.

5n *Use the imperative mood to make a request or to give a command or direction.*

The understood but usually unstated subject of a verb in the imperative mood is *you.* The verb's form is the infinitive.

REQUEST   Please *be* there before noon.

COMMAND   *Hurry!*

DIRECTION To reach my house, *drive* east on State Street.

5o *Use the subjunctive mood in a subordinate clause that spells out a wish, a requirement, a suggestion, or any condition that is contrary to fact.*

The subjunctive mood suggests uncertainty: the action expressed by the verb may or may not actually take place as specified. In any clause opening with *that* and expressing a requirement, the verb is in the subjunctive mood and its form is the infinitive.

Professor Avery requires that every student *deliver* his or her work promptly.

She asked that we *be* on time for all meetings.

One way to distinguish between *that* clauses requiring the indicative mood and *that* clauses requiring the subjunctive mood is to insert *should* before the verb in the clause: if *should* fits, use the subjunctive.

Professor Avery requires that every student [should] *deliver* his or her work promptly.

She asked that we [should] *be* on time for all meetings.

When you use the subjunctive mood to describe a condition that is contrary to fact, use *were* if the verb is *be;* for other verbs, use the simple past tense. (Wishes, whether present or past, follow these rules.)

If I *were* rich, I would be happy.

If I *had* a million dollars, I would be happy.

Elissa wishes that Ted *were* more goal-oriented.

Elissa wished that Ted *knew* what he wanted to do.

For a condition that was contrary to fact at some point in the past, use the past perfect tense.

If I *had been* awake, I would have seen the meteor showers.

If Jessie *had known* you were coming, she would have cleaned her room.

Although use of the subjunctive mood has grown scarcer over the years, it still sounds crude to write "If I *was* you. . . . " If you ever feel that the subjunctive mood makes a sentence sound stilted, you can rewrite it, substituting an infinitive phrase.

Professor Avery wants every student *to deliver* his or her work promptly.

Exercise 5–4

Correct any errors in mood you find in the following sentences. Identify the mood of the incorrect verb as well as of its correct replacement. Some sentences may be correct. Answers for the lettered sentences appear in the back of the book. Example:

If a wish was a horse, then a beggar could ride.

If a wish *were* a horse, then a beggar could ride. [*Was* indicative; *were* subjunctive.]

a. When Janet cooks, she insists that Tom washes the dishes.

b. If Pete want me to help him, he can call and ask me himself.

c. If I was a licensed plumber, I could install the washing machine myself.

d. The IRS recommends that tax forms are filled out as soon as they become available.

e. If that man do not go away, call the police.

1. My sister's teacher insists that every girl wear a skirt to class.

2. You are at my house at six or we'll leave you behind.

3. I would feel more comfortable about leaving if someone was watching my things.

4. Courtesy demands that Jill returns your call.

5. I will pay him only if he give me the book by Friday.

6 SUBJECT-VERB AGREEMENT

What does it mean for a subject and a verb to agree? Practically speaking, it means that their forms are in accord: plural subjects take plural verbs, third-person subjects take third-person verbs, and so forth. Creating agreement in a sentence is like making sure that all the instruments in a song are playing in the same key. When your subjects and verbs agree, you prevent a discord that could distract readers from your message.

6a Make sure that your subject and your verb agree in person (first, second, or third) and in number (singular or plural).

Subject and verb agree in person:

I write my research papers on a typewriter. [Subject and verb in first person.]

Jim writes his research papers on a word processor. [Subject and verb in third person.]

Subject and verb agree in number:

Susan has enjoyed college. [Subject and verb singular.]

She and Jim have enjoyed their vacation. [Subject and verb plural.]

The present tense of most verbs is the infinitive form, with no added ending except in the third-person singular. (See 5f–5k.)

I enjoy	we enjoy
you enjoy	you enjoy
he/she/it enjoys	they enjoy

Forms of the verb *be* vary from this rule.

I am	we are
you are	you are
he/she/it is	they are

6b A verb agrees with its subject, not with any words that intervene.

My *favorite* of O. Henry's short stories *is* "The Gift of the Magi."

Dollars, once the dominant currency in international trade, *have* fallen behind the yen.

A singular subject linked to another noun or pronoun by a prepositional phrase such as *as well as, along with,* or *in addition to* remains a singular subject and takes a singular verb.

My cousin *James* as well as his wife and son *plans* to vote for the Democratic candidate.

6c Subjects joined by and usually take a plural verb.

Two or more nouns or pronouns linked by *and* constitute a *compound subject.* (See 2a.) In most cases, a compound subject counts as plural and takes a plural verb.

"Howl" and *"Gerontion" are* Barry's favorite poems.

Sugar, salt, and fat adversely *affect* people's health.

However, for phrases like *each man and woman* or *every dog and cat,* where the subjects are considered individually, use a singular verb.

Each man and woman in the room *has* a different story to tell.

Use a singular verb for two singular subjects referring to the same thing.

Lime juice and soda quenches your thirst and *tastes* good, too.

6d With subjects joined by or or nor, the verb agrees in number and person with the part of the subject nearest to it.

Either they or *Max is* guilty.

Neither Sally nor *I am* willing to face the truth.

Subjects containing *not . . . but* follow this rule also.

Not we but *George knows* the whole story.

You can remedy the awkwardness of such constructions by rephrasing the offending sentences.

Either they are guilty or Max is.

Sally and I are unwilling to face the truth.

We do not know the whole story, but George does.

6e With a collective noun, use a singular verb unless the meaning is clearly plural.

What do you do when the number of a subject is not obvious? Collective nouns, such as *committee, congregation, family, group, jury,* and *trio,* are singular in form, yet they represent more than one person. When a collective noun refers to a group of people acting in unison, it takes a singular verb.

The *jury finds* the defendant guilty.

My *family upholds* traditional values.

It is all right, though awkward, to use a plural verb with a collective noun when the members act individually.

The *jury do* not yet *agree* on a verdict.

Alice's *family* rarely *eat* together.

If you feel that using a plural verb with a collective subject results in an awkward sentence, reword the subject so that it refers to members of the group individually. (Also see 7e.)

The *jurors do* not yet *agree* on a verdict.

The *members* of Alice's family rarely *eat* together.

6f *With the indefinite pronouns* each, either, neither, anyone, anybody, anything, everyone, everybody, everything, one, no one, nobody, nothing, someone, somebody, *and* something, *use a third-person singular verb.*

Someone is bothering me.

Even when one of these subjects is followed by a phrase containing a noun or pronoun of a different person or number, use a singular verb.

Each of you *is* here to stay.

One of the pandas *seems* dangerously ill.

6g *With the indefinite pronouns* all, any, *and* some, *use a singular or a plural verb depending on how the pronoun is used.*

I have no explanation. *Is any* needed?

Any of the changes that really needed to be made *have* been made already.

All is lost.

All of the bananas *are gone*.

Some of the blame *is* mine.

Some of us *are* Democrats.

Many people who care about language still insist that *none* always takes a singular verb.

None of you *is* exempt.

Increasingly, though, *none*—like *all*, *any*, and *some*—appears as the subject of either a singular or a plural verb, depending on the sense in which the pronoun is used. (See also 7d, 7f.)

> *None* of his wives *were* blond.

6h When the subject of a subordinate clause is who, which, or that, the person and number of its antecedent determine the person and number of its verb.

When you are writing a subordinate clause that modifies a noun, the subject may be a relative pronoun: *who*, *which*, or *that*. To determine the person and number of the verb in the clause, look back at the pronoun's antecedent, the word to which the pronoun refers. (See 7a–7f.) The antecedent is usually (but not always) the noun closest to the relative pronoun.

> I have a friend *who studies* day and night. [The antecedent of *who* is the third-person singular noun *friend*. Therefore the verb in the subordinate clause is third-person singular, *studies*.]

> Unfortunately, I bought one of the two hundred recently manufactured cars *that have* defective upholstery. [The antecedent of *that* is *cars*, so the verb is third-person plural, *have*.]

> This is the only one of the mayor's new ideas *that has* any worth. [Here *one*, not *ideas*, is the antecedent of *that*. Thus the verb in the subordinate clause is third-person singular, *has*, not *have*.]

6i A verb agrees with its subject even when the subject follows the verb.

A writer need not necessarily place the subject of a sentence before the verb. In some sentences, an introductory phrase or a word such as *there* or *here* changes the ordinary subject-verb order. If a sentence opens with such a phrase or word, look for the subject after the verb. Remember that verbs agree with subjects, and that *here* and *there* are never subjects.

> Here *is* a *riddle* for you.

> There *are* forty *people* in my law class.

> Under the bridge *were* a broken-down *boat* and a worn *tire*.

6j A linking verb agrees with its subject, not its subject complement.

In some sentences, a form of the verb *be* is used to link two or more nouns ("Matthew *is* the composer"). The linking verb's subject is the noun that precedes it. Nouns that follow the linking verb are subject complements. (See 2d.) Take care to make a linking verb agree with the subject of the sentence, whether or not the verb agrees with the subject complement.

> *Jim is* a gentleman and a scholar.

> Amy's *parents are* her most enthusiastic audience.

6k *When the subject is a title, use a singular verb.*

When I was younger, *James and the Giant Peach* by Roald Dahl *was* my favorite book.

The Witches of Eastwick depicts a modern devil in New England.

6l *If your subject is a singular noun that is plural in form, use a singular verb.*

Some nouns look plural even though they refer to a singular subject: *news, measles, logistics, mathematics, physics, electronics, economics*. Such nouns take singular verbs.

The *news is* that *economics has become* one of the most popular majors.

Exercise 6–1

Find and correct any errors of subject-verb agreement in the following sentences. Some sentences may be correct. Answers for the lettered sentences appear in the back of the book. Example:

Addressing the audience tonight is the nominees for club president.

Addressing the audience tonight *are* the nominees for club president.

a. Our foreign policy in Cuba, Nicaragua, El Salvador, and Panama have not been as successful as most Americans had hoped.

b. The large amount of metal and chlorine in our water makes it taste funny.

c. I read about a couple who is offering to trade their baby for a brand-new Chevrolet.

d. A shave, a haircut, and a new suit has turned Bill into a different person.

e. Neither the fruit nor the vegetables is fresh.

1. Each of us, including Alice, want this to be a successful party.

2. The police force, after the recent rash of burglaries, have added more patrols in this neighborhood.

3. More disturbing than John's speech was the gestures that accompanied it.

4. Samantha is one of those women who never wear shoes indoors.

5. Nearly everybody who traveled by air during the last six weeks were aware of increased security precautions.

6. The bad news about interest rates have been widely publicized.

7. Most of the class believed that both the private sector and the government was taking appropriate action on homelessness.

8. Lee's sister, as well as his brothers, show great affection for their grandmother.

9. Ron Wood is not the only member of the Rolling Stones who have played in the band Faces.

10. Here among the geraniums lie the other rosebush you and Lois planted last spring.

7 PRONOUN-ANTECEDENT AGREEMENT

A pronoun's job is to fill in for a noun, much as an actor's double fills in for the actor. Pronouns are a short, convenient way for writers to avoid repeating the same noun over and over. The noun that a pronoun stands for is called its **antecedent**.

> The sheriff drew a six-shooter; he fired twice.

This action-packed sentence unfolds in a familiar order. First comes a noun (*sheriff*), and then a pronoun (*he*) that refers back to it. *Sheriff* is the antecedent of *he*.

Just as verbs need to agree with their subjects, pronouns need to agree with the nouns they stand for. A successful writer takes care not to shift number, person, or gender in mid-sentence ("The *sheriff* and the *outlaw* drew *their* six-shooters; *he* fired twice"). Rather, the writer starts each sentence with nouns clearly in mind and picks appropriate pronouns to refer to them.

7a *Make pronouns agree with their antecedents in person and number.*

Especially when a string of intervening words separates pronoun and antecedent, be sure that each pronoun matches its antecedent in person (first, second, or third) and in number (singular or plural). (See the pronouns chart in 1b.)

> **FAULTY**   All *campers* should bring *your* knapsacks.

Here, noun and pronoun disagree in person: *campers* is third person, but *your* is second person.

> **FAULTY**   Every *camper* should bring *their* knapsack.

Here, noun and pronoun disagree in number: *camper* is singular, but *their* is plural.

> **REVISED**   All *campers* should bring *their* knapsacks.
>
> **REVISED**   Every *camper* should bring *his or her* knapsack.

(See also 7f.)

PRONOUN AGREEMENT AT A GLANCE
Make a personal pronoun agree with its antecedent in

1. Number: singular or plural.
2. Person: first, second, or third.
3. Gender: masculine, feminine, or neuter.

7b *Use a plural pronoun with most antecedents joined by* and.

What if the subject of your sentence is two nouns (or a noun and a pronoun) connected by *and?* Such a compound subject is plural; use a plural pronoun to refer to it.

> *George,* who has been here before, *and Susan,* who hasn't, should bring *their* knapsacks.

However, if all the nouns in a compound subject refer to the same person or thing, they make up a singular antecedent. In that case, the pronoun too is singular:

> The *owner and founder* of this camp carries *his* own knapsack everywhere.

7c *Make a pronoun agree with the closest part of an antecedent joined by* or *or* nor.

If your subject is two or more nouns (or a combination of nouns and pronouns) connected by *or* or *nor,* look closely at the subject's parts. Are they all singular? If so, your pronoun should be singular.

> Neither *Joy nor Jean* remembered *her* knapsack last year.
>
> If *Sam, Arthur, or Max* shows up, tell *him* I'm looking for *him.*

If the part of the subject closest to the pronoun is plural, the pronoun should be plural.

> Neither *Joy nor her sisters* remembered *their* knapsacks last year.
>
> If you see *Sam, Arthur, or their friends,* tell *them* I'm looking for *them.*

7d *Use a singular pronoun for an antecedent that is an indefinite pronoun.*

An indefinite pronoun is one that does not refer to any specific person, place, or thing: *anybody, each, either.* (For a complete list, see the pronoun chart in 1b.) Indefinite pronouns are usually singular in meaning, so a pronoun referring to any of them is also singular.

> *Either* of the boys can do it, as long as *he's* on time.
>
> Warn *anybody* who's still in *her* swimsuit that a uniform is required for dinner.

Sometimes the meaning of an indefinite pronoun is plural. To avoid awkwardness, try not to use such a pronoun as an antecedent.

> Tell *everyone* in Cabin B that I'm looking for *him.*

This sentence works better if it is phrased differently.

> Tell *all the campers* in Cabin B that I'm looking for *them.*

(See also 6f, 7f.)

7e Use a singular or a plural pronoun to refer to a collective noun, depending on meaning.

A collective noun is a singular word for a group of people or items: *army, band, committee, jury.* When the members of such a group act as a unit, use a singular pronoun to refer to them.

> The *cast* for the camp play will be posted as soon as our theater counselor chooses *it.*

When the group members act individually, use a plural pronoun.

> The *cast* will go *their* separate ways when summer ends.

(See also 6e.)

7f Make pronouns agree with their antecedents in gender.

> If *one of your parents* brings you to camp, invite *him* to stay for lunch.

While technically correct (the singular pronoun *he* is used to refer to the singular antecedent *one*), this sentence overlooks the fact that some parents are male, some female. To make sure the pronoun refers to both, a writer has two choices.

> If *one of your parents* brings you to camp, invite *him or her* to stay for lunch.
>
> If your *parents* bring you to camp, invite *them* to stay for lunch.

Exercise 7–1

If any nouns and pronouns disagree in number, person, or gender in the following sentences, substitute pronouns that will get along better. If you prefer, strengthen any sentence by rewriting it. Some sentences may be correct. Possible improvements for the lettered sentences appear in the back of the book. Example:

> A cat expects people to feed them often.
>
> A *cat* expects people to feed *it* often.
>
> *Cats* expect people to feed *them* often.

  a. All students are urged to complete your registration on time.

  b. When a baby doesn't know their own mother, they may have been born with some kind of vision deficiency.

  c. Each member of the sorority has to make his own bed.

  d. If you don't like the songs the choir sings, don't join them.

  e. Selfish people always look out for oneself.

  1. Everyone is expected to keep their own clothes clean.

  2. Bill refuses to kill spiders because he says it eats other bugs.

  3. Neither Melissa nor James has received their application form yet.

4. He is the kind of man who gets their fun out of just sipping one's beer and watching his Saturday games on TV.

5. Many an architect finds work their greatest pleasure.

6. Although a business executive may work long hours, he should try to spend time with his family.

7. When our players heard the other team's jeers, they jumped to their feet.

8. Both they and Joyce have said she regrets the argument.

9. When one enjoys one's work, it's easy to spend all your spare time thinking about it.

10. If you love someone, set them free.

8 PRONOUN REFERENCE

Look hard at just about any piece of writing—this discussion, if you like—and you'll find that practically every pronoun in it points to some noun. This is the main use of pronouns: to refer in a brief, convenient form to some **antecedent** that has already been named. A pronoun usually has a noun or another pronoun as its antecedent. Often the antecedent is the subject or object of the same clause in which the pronoun appears.

> Josie hit the *ball* after *its* first bounce.
>
> Smashing into *Greg*, the ball knocked off *his* glasses.

The antecedent also can appear in a different clause or even a different sentence from the pronoun.

> *Josie* hit the *ball* when *it* bounced back to *her*.
>
> The *ball* smashed into *Greg*. *It* knocked off *his* glasses.

A pronoun as well as a noun can be an antecedent.

> My *dog* hid in the closet when *she* had *her* puppies. [*Dog* is the antecedent of *she*; *she* is the antecedent of *her*.]

PRONOUN REFERENCE AT A GLANCE

1. Name your antecedent—don't just imply it. (8a)
2. Give the pronouns *it, this, that,* and *which* clear antecedents. (8b)
3. Indicate clearly which of two or more nouns or pronouns is a pronoun's antecedent. (8c)
4. Place a pronoun close enough to its antecedent to make the relationship clear. (8d)

8a *Be sure your antecedents are named, not implied.*

In editing, in combing over what you write, be sure you have identified clearly the antecedent of each pronoun. A writer who leaves a key idea unsaid is likely to confuse readers.

> **VAGUE** Ted wanted a Norwegian canoe because he'd heard that *they* produce the lightest canoes afloat.

What does *they* refer to? Not to *Norwegian*, which is an adjective; the antecedent of a pronoun has to be a noun or pronoun. We may guess that this writer has in mind Norwegian canoe builders, but no such noun has been mentioned. To make the sentence work, the writer must supply an antecedent for *they*.

> **CLEAR** Ted wanted a Norwegian canoe because he'd heard that Norway produces [or *Norwegians produce*] the lightest canoes afloat.

Watch out for possessive nouns. They won't work as antecedents.

> **VAGUE** On William's canoe *he* painted a skull and bones. (For all we know, *he* might be some joker named Fred.)

> **CLEAR** On his canoe William painted a skull and bones.

8b *Clearly identify the antecedent of* it, this, that, *or* which.

Vagueness arises, thick as fog, whenever *it, this, that,* or *which* points to something a writer assumes he or she has said but indeed hasn't. Is the reference of a pronoun fuzzy? Might a reader get lost in the fog? Often the best way out of the fog is to substitute a specific noun or phrase for the pronoun.

> **VAGUE** I was an only child, and *it* was hard.

> **CLEAR** I was an only child, and *my solitary life* was hard.

> **VAGUE** Ruth majored in economics and applied for a job in a broker's office, *which* caused her father to exult. Still, *it* was not what she desired.

> **CLEAR** Ruth majored in economics and applied for a job in a broker's office, *steps* that caused her father to exult. Still, *a career in finance* was not what she desired.

8c *Indicate clearly which noun or pronoun is the pronoun's antecedent.*

Confusion strikes again if the antecedent of a pronoun is ambiguous—that is, if the pronoun seems to point in two or more directions. In such a puzzling situation, there's no lack of antecedent; the trouble is that more than one antecedent looks possible. Baffled, the reader wonders which the writer means.

> **CONFUSING** Rob shouted to Jim to take off his burning sweater.

Whose sweater does *his* mean—Jim's or Rob's? Simply changing a pronoun won't clear up the confusion. The writer needs to revise the sentence drastically enough to move the two antecedents out of each other's way.

CLEAR   "Help, Rob!" Jim shouted. "My sweater's on fire! Take it off!"

CLEAR   "Jim!" shouted Rob. "Your sweater's on fire! Take it off!"

CLEAR   Flames were shooting from Jim's sweater. Rob shouted to Jim to take it off.

As you can tell from that first fogbound sentence, pronouns referring to nouns of the same gender are particular offenders. How would you straighten out this grammatical tangle?

CONFUSING   Linda welcomed Lee-Ann's move into the apartment next door. Little did she dream that soon she would be secretly dating her husband.

Let meaning show the way. If you had written these sentences, you would know which person is the sneak. One way to clarify the antecedents of *she* and *her* is to add more information.

CLEAR   In welcoming Lee-Ann to the apartment next door, Linda didn't dream that soon her own husband would be secretly dating her former sorority sister.

Instead of *her own husband*, you can identify that philanderer by name if you have previously identified him as Linda's husband: "Ned would be secretly dating. . . ." (Grammatical tangles are easier than human tangles to straighten out.)

8d *Place your pronouns close enough to their antecedents to keep the relationship clear.*

Watch out for distractions that slip in between noun and pronoun. If, before your readers come to a pronoun in your sentence, they meet other nouns—interesting nouns—that might look like antecedents, they may become bewildered.

CONFUSING   Harper steered his dinghy alongside the polished mahogany cabin cruiser that the drug smugglers had left anchored under an overhanging willow in the tiny harbor and eased it to a stop.

What did Harper ease to a stop? By the time readers reach the end of the sentence, they are likely to have forgotten. To avoid confusion, keep the pronoun and its antecedent reasonably close together.

CLEAR   Harper steered his dinghy into the tiny harbor and eased it to a stop alongside the polished mahogany cabin cruiser that the drug smugglers had left anchored under an overhanging willow.

Never force your readers to stop and think, "What does that pronoun stand for?" You, the writer, have to do this thinking for them.

Exercise 8–1

Remedy any vagueness or puzzling ambiguity that you find in the following sentences. Rewrite each sentence or group of sentences so that any pronoun needing an antecedent clearly points to one. Possible revisions for the lettered sentences appear in the back of the book. Example:

> If your dog tries to bite your guest, tie him up in the yard.
>
> If your dog tries to bite your guest, tie the dog up in the yard.

a. When computers cost the same as television sets, every American will own one.

b. After Prime Minister Thatcher's meeting with Prime Minister Bhutto, she reported that she wasn't sure if she agreed with her position on freedom of speech.

c. I cannot speak of epileptic seizures with firsthand knowledge because I have never had any.

d. Marsha didn't know Russian and had allergies, but this didn't stop her from summering on a Soviet kelp farm.

e. Swaying gently in his parachute, floating lazily to earth, Edgar felt pure joy. It had been the finest thing he'd ever tried, and he was all for it.

1. Glancing down, Edgar saw the cactus loom and heard the rattlesnake hiss, which promised an uncertain landing.

2. The delicacy of the statue's carving, which obviously dates from a period when sculptors were highly respected, is what makes it valuable.

3. American auto workers and their Japanese counterparts differ in that they place less emphasis on quality. Detroit car manufacturers, however, are taking steps to solve this.

4. Casper told Damon he was an embezzler and he had been doing it for several years. It was, he added, none of his business; and he would thank him to keep quiet about it.

5. Beachcombing, picking up shells, bottles, and driftwood, I found one containing a yellowed message dated 1792. "Why," he pleaded, "has no one answered the message I launched in 1789?"

9 PRONOUN CASE

As you know, pronouns come in distinctive forms. The first-person pronoun can be *I*, or it can be *me, my, mine, we, us, our,* or *ours.* Which form do you pick? It depends on what job you want the pronoun to do. Filling these jobs may sound easy, but now and again every writer has a hard time hiring the pronoun that is properly qualified.

To choose correctly, it may help you to know the three *cases* used to classify pronouns. Depending on a pronoun's function in a sentence, we say that it is in the **subjective case,** the **objective case,** or the **possessive case.**

> PRONOUN CASES
>
> | SUBJECTIVE | OBJECTIVE | POSSESSIVE |
> |---|---|---|
> | I | me | my, mine |
> | you | you | your, yours |
> | he, she, it | him, her, it | his, her, hers, its |
> | we | us | our, ours |
> | you | you | your, yours |
> | they | them | their, theirs |
> | who | whom | whose |

Some pronouns change form when they change case and some do not. The personal pronouns *I, he, she, we,* and *they* and the relative pronoun *who* have different forms in the subjective, objective, and possessive cases. Other pronouns, such as *you, it, that,* and *which,* have only two forms: the plain case (which serves as both subjective and objective) and the possessive case.

We can pin the labels *subjective, objective,* and *possessive* on nouns as well as on pronouns. Nouns, after all, do the same jobs as pronouns. However, like the pronouns *you, it, that,* and *which,* nouns shift out of their plain form only in the possessive case (*teacher's* pet, the *Joneses'* poodle).

Beware, when you are not sure which case to choose, of the temptation to fall back on a reflexive pronoun (*myself, himself*). Reflexive pronouns have limited, specific uses in writing (see 1b). They do not take the place of subjective or objective pronouns. If you catch yourself writing, "You can return the form to John or *myself*" or "John and *myself* are in charge," replace the reflexive pronoun with one that is grammatically correct: "You can return the form to John or *me*"; "John and *I* are in charge."

> SUBJECTIVE PRONOUNS
> I, you, he, she, it, we, they, who, whoever, that, which

9a Use the subjective case when a pronoun is the subject of a sentence or clause.

I ate the granola.

Who cares?

Mark recalled that *she* played jai alai.

Election officials are the people *who* count.

Sometimes a compound subject will lead a writer astray: "Jed and *me* ate the granola." *Me,* an objective pronoun, is the wrong one for this job. Use the subjective form, *I,* instead.

A pronoun serving as subject for a verb is subjective even when the verb isn't written but is only implied:

Jed is hungrier than *I* [am].

Don't be fooled by a pronoun that appears immediately after a verb, as if it were a direct object, but that functions as the subject of a clause. The pronoun's case is determined by its role in the sentence, not its position.

The judge didn't believe *I* hadn't been the driver.

I think *she* likes me.

9b Use the subjective case when a pronoun serves as a subject complement.

A pronoun can function as a subject complement after a linking verb such as *is, seems,* or *appears.* (See 2d for more on subject complements, 5a for more on linking verbs.) Because it plays essentially the same role as the subject, the pronoun's case is subjective.

The phantom graffiti artist couldn't have been *he.* It was *I.*

9c Use the subjective case when a pronoun is in apposition to a subject or subject complement.

A pronoun placed in apposition to a subject or subject complement is like an identical twin to the noun it stands beside. It has the same meaning and the same case. (See also 3d.)

The class *officers*—Jed and *she*—announced a granola breakfast.

OBJECTIVE PRONOUNS
me, you, him, her, it, us, them, whom, whomever, that, which

9d Use the objective case when a pronoun serves as a direct object, an indirect object, or the object of a preposition.

The custard pies hit *him* and *me.* [Direct object.]

Whom do you love? [Direct object.]

Mona threw *us* towels. [Indirect object.]

Tell *her* your feelings. [Indirect object.]

Mona threw towels to *him* and *us.* [Object of a preposition.]

Binks is the professor of *whom* I hear glowing reports. [Object of a preposition.]

9e **Use the objective case when a pronoun is in apposition to a direct or indirect object or the object of a preposition.**

> Mona helped *us* all—Mrs. Van Dumont, *him*, and *me*. [*Him* and *me* are in apposition to the direct object *us*.]
>
> Binks gave his favorite *students*, Tom and *her*, an approving nod. [*Her* is in apposition to the indirect object *students*.]
>
> Yelling, the persistent pie flingers ran after *us*—Mrs. Van Dumont, Mona, *him*, and *me*. [*Him* and *me* are in apposition to *us*, the object of the preposition *after*.]

> **POSSESSIVE PRONOUNS**
> my, mine, our, ours, his, her, hers, its, your, yours, their, theirs

9f **Use the possessive case for pronouns that show ownership.**

Possessive pronouns can function as adjectives or as nouns. The pronouns *my, your, his, her, its, our,* and *their* function as adjectives by modifying nouns or pronouns.

> *Their* apartment is bigger than *our* house.
>
> *My* new bike is having *its* first road test today.

Notice that the possessive pronoun *its* does not contain an apostrophe. *It's* with an apostrophe is not a possessive pronoun, but a contraction for *it is*, as in "*It's* a beautiful day." If you want to write about the day and *its* beauty, be sure to omit the apostrophe.

The possessive pronouns *mine, yours, his, hers, ours,* and *theirs* can discharge the whole range of noun duties. These pronouns can serve as subjects, subject complements, direct objects, indirect objects, or objects of prepositions.

> *Yours* is the last vote we need. [Subject.]
>
> This day is *ours*. [Subject complement.]
>
> Don't take your car; take *mine*. [Direct object.]
>
> If we're honoring requests in chronological order, give *hers* top priority. [Indirect object.]
>
> Give her request priority over *theirs*. [Object of a preposition.]

9g **Use the possessive case when a pronoun modifies a gerund.**

A possessive pronoun (or a possessive noun) is the appropriate escort for a gerund, a form of verb that functions as a noun: *griping, being, drinking*. (See

3b.) As a noun, a gerund requires an adjective, not another noun, for a modifier.

> Mary is tired of *his griping*. [The possessive pronoun *his* modifies the gerund *griping*.]

> I can stand *their being* late every morning, but not *his drinking* on the job. [The possessive pronoun *their* modifies the gerund *being*; the possessive pronoun *his* modifies the gerund *drinking*.]

Gerunds can cause confusion when you edit your writing because they look exactly like participles. (See 3b.) Whereas a gerund functions as a noun, a participle often functions as an adjective modifying a noun or pronoun.

> Mary heard *him griping* about work. [The participle *griping* modifies the direct object *him*.]

If you are not sure whether to use a possessive or an objective pronoun with a word ending in *-ing*, look closely at your sentence. Which word—the pronoun or the *-ing* word—is the object of your main verb? That word functions as a noun; the other word modifies it.

> Mr. Phipps remembered *them* smoking in the boys' room.

> Mr. Phipps remembered *their* smoking in the boys' room.

In the first sentence, Mr. Phipps's memory is of *them*, those naughty students. *Them* is the object of the verb, so *smoking* is a participle modifying *them*. In the second sentence, Mr. Phipps remembers *smoking*, that nasty habit. The gerund *smoking* is the object of the verb, so the possessive pronoun *their* is the right choice to modify it.

In everyday speech, the rules about pronoun case apply less rigidly. Someone who correctly asks in conversation, "To whom are you referring?" is likely to sound affected. You are within your rights to reply, as did the comic-strip character Pogo Possum, "Youm, that's whom!" Say, if you like, "It's *me*," but write "It is *I*." Say, if you wish, "*Who* did he ask to the party?" but write "*Whom* did he ask?"

Exercise 9–1

Replace any pronouns that seem unfit for their jobs. (Consider all these examples as written—not spoken—English, and so apply the rules strictly.) Explain why each pronoun was unqualified for its position. Some sentences may be correct. Answers for the lettered sentences appear in the back of the book. Example:

> In the photograph, that's him at the age of seven.

> In the photograph, that's *he* at the age of seven. [*He* is a subject complement.]

a. She can run faster than me.

b. Mrs. Van Dumont awarded the prize to Mona and I.

c. Jud laughed at both of us—she and I.

d. Were you referring to we?

e. Jerry, myself, and the pizza chef regard you and she as the very women who we wish to get acquainted with.

1. I like to watch them swimming in the hotel pool.

2. Whoever you wish to invite along is acceptable to Jeff and I.

3. The waiters and us busboys are highly trustworthy.

4. I won't tolerate you whistling in the courtroom.

5. Strictly platonic affairs suit us—Biff, the Flipper, and me.

6. Dean Fitts and them, who I suspect of being the pie throwers, flung crusty missiles at Mona, Mrs. Van Dumont, he, and myself.

7. Have I reached the party who I spoke to yesterday?

8. I didn't appreciate you laughing at her and I.

9. They—Jerry and her—are the troublemakers.

10. It was him asking about the clock that started me suspecting him.

11. Juliana isn't as old-fashioned in her views as them.

12. She gave Jed and I some bad advice.

13. There is a lack of communication among you and he and Dean.

14. The counterattack was launched by Dusty and myself.

15. Whomever this anonymous letter writer is, I resent him lying about Jules and me and the cabbages.

10 SENTENCE FRAGMENTS

A **complete sentence** is one that has both a subject and a predicate and can stand alone. (See 2a, 2b.) A **sentence fragment** lacks a subject or a predicate or both or for some other reason fails to express a complete thought. We all use fragments in everyday speech, where their context and the way they are said make them understandable and therefore acceptable.

That bicycle over there.

Good job.

Not if I can help it.

In writing, sentence fragments like these fail to communicate complete, coherent ideas. Notice how much more effective they are when we turn them into complete sentences.

I'd like to buy that bicycle over there.

Hal did a good job sanding the floor.

Nobody will steal your seat if I can help it.

Advertisers are fond of sentence fragments because short, emphatic fragments command attention, like a series of quick jabs to the head.

> Seafood special. Every Tuesday night. All you can eat. Specially priced at $6.95. For seafood lovers.

Talkers and advertisers aren't the only users of sentence fragments. Reputable writers use them, too, especially in journals, descriptions, and fiction—often to good effect, as in this passage from the beginning of Vladimir Nabokov's novel *Lolita*:

> Lolita, light of my life, fire of my loins. My sin, my soul. Lo-lee-ta: the tip of the tongue taking a trip of three steps down the palate to tap, at three, on the teeth. Lo. Lee. Ta.

In your college writing, though, it is good practice to express your ideas in complete sentences. Writing a paper or a report is a more formal, less experimental activity than writing fiction. Besides, complete sentences usually convey more information than fragments—a big advantage in expository writing. Sprinkling sentence fragments through your work, unless you do so with

---

RECOGNIZING SENTENCE FRAGMENTS

Ask yourself when you reread your first draft:

1. Does every sentence have a subject?

   FRAGMENT   The *Voyager* spacecraft relayed clear pictures of Neptune. *And showed the planet's atmosphere violent with storms.*

   REVISED   The *Voyager* spacecraft relayed clear pictures of Neptune that showed the planet's atmosphere violent with storms.

2. Does every sentence have a verb?

   FRAGMENT   The little spacecraft proceeded on its way out of the solar system. *Its task at an end.*

   REVISED   Its task at an end, the little spacecraft proceeded on its way out of the solar system.

   REVISED   The little spacecraft proceeded on its way out of the solar system. Its task was at an end.

3. Does every sentence that contains a subordinate clause contain a complete main clause, too?

   FRAGMENT   *Which may make any alien spacefarers who find the Voyager wonder.*

   REVISED   Any alien spacefarers who find the *Voyager* may wonder over it.

great skill and style, tends to make readers wonder if you can tell a piece of thought from a whole thought completely thought through.

If you sometimes write sentence fragments without recognizing them, learn to edit your work. Luckily, fragments are fairly easy to correct. Often you can attach a fragment to a neighboring sentence with a comma, a dash, or a colon. Sometimes you can combine two thoughts without adding any punctuation at all.

10a *If your sentence fragment is a phrase, use punctuation or a conjunction to link it to an adjoining sentence.*

A freestanding phrase is a sentence fragment because it lacks a subject or a verb or both.

> FRAGMENT   Malcolm has two goals in life. *Wealth and power.*
>
> FRAGMENT   *To stamp out the union.* That was the bosses' plan.
>
> FRAGMENT   Schmidt ended his stories as he mixed his martinis. *With a twist.*

Wealth and power is a phrase rather than a sentence because it has no verb. *To stamp out the union* has a verbal, which cannot be used as the main verb of a sentence, and it has no subject. *With a twist* has neither a subject nor a verb. You can make each phrase express a complete thought by linking it with a neighboring sentence. In each case there are several ways to do this. Here is one set of possibilities:

> REVISED   Malcolm has two goals in life: wealth and power. [Colon links *wealth and power* to *goals*.]
>
> REVISED   To stamp out the union was the bosses' plan. [The infinitive phrase *To stamp out the union* becomes the subject of the sentence.]

REVISING SENTENCE FRAGMENTS

1. If your sentence fragment is a phrase, use punctuation or a conjunction to link it to an adjoining sentence. (10a)
2. If your sentence fragment is a clause, link it to an adjoining sentence or eliminate its subordinating conjunction. (10b)
3. If your sentence fragment uses *being* or another participle as its verb, either change the verb or join the fragment to a neighboring sentence. (10c)
4. If your fragment is a part of a compound predicate, reunite it with its other half to create a complete sentence. (10d)

REVISED Schmidt ended his stories as he mixed his martinis, with a twist. [Prepositional phrase *with a twist* is connected to a main clause with a comma.

10b If your sentence fragment is a subordinate clause, link it to an adjoining sentence or get rid of its subordinating conjunction.

Some sentence fragments are missing neither subject nor verb. Instead, they are subordinate clauses, unable to express complete thoughts unless linked with main clauses. (See 3e–3g, 4c.) As you examine your writing for sentence fragments, be on the lookout for *subordinating conjunctions*. (Some of the most common subordinating conjunctions are *although, because, if, since, unless, until,* and *while*; for a complete list, see 1g.) When you find a subordinating conjunction at the start or in the middle of a word group that looks like a sentence, that word group may be a subordinate clause and not a sentence at all.

FRAGMENT The new law will stem the tide of inflation. *If it passes.*

FRAGMENT Wealth doesn't guarantee happiness. *Whereas poverty does guarantee unhappiness.*

FRAGMENT George loves winter in the mountains. *Because he is an avid skier.*

If you find that you have treated a subordinate clause as if it were a complete sentence, you can correct the problem in one of two ways. You can combine the fragment with a main clause nearby; or you can make the subordinate clause into a complete sentence by dropping the subordinating conjunction.

REVISED The new law will stem the tide of inflation, if it passes.

REVISED Wealth doesn't guarantee happiness, whereas poverty does guarantee unhappiness.

REVISED George loves winter in the mountains. He is an avid skier.

A sentence is not necessarily a fragment just because it opens with a subordinating conjunction. Some perfectly legitimate complex or compound-complex sentences have their conjunctions up front instead of in the middle. (See 4c–4d.)

If you leave early, say good-bye.

Because of rain, the game was canceled.

10c If your sentence fragment uses being or another participle as its verb, either change the participle to a main verb or join the fragment to a neighboring sentence.

A participle (the principal part of the verb ending in *-ing*, such as *being, writing, looking*) can serve as the main verb in a sentence only when it is accompanied by another form of *be* ("Jeffrey *is being* nicer than usual"). When a writer mistakenly uses a participle alone as a main verb, the result is a sentence fragment.

> FRAGMENT   *Sally being the first athlete on the team to compete in a national contest.* She received many congratulatory telegrams.

One solution is to turn the fragment into a complete sentence by choosing a form of the verb other than the participle.

> REVISED   Sally *was* the first athlete on the team to compete in a national contest. She received many congratulatory telegrams.

Another solution is to combine the fragment with an adjoining sentence.

> REVISED   Being the first athlete on the team to compete in a national contest, Sally received many congratulatory telegrams.

Notice that *being* really isn't needed once you have a complete sentence. In fact, the sentence reads better without it.

> REVISED   The first athlete on the team ever to compete in a national contest, Sally received many congratulatory telegrams.

10d   *If your fragment is part of a compound predicate, reunite it with its other half to create a complete sentence.*

> FRAGMENT   In spite of a pulled muscle, Jeremy ran the race. *And won.*

A fragment such as *And won* sounds satisfyingly punchy. Still, it cannot stand on its own. "Ran . . . and won" is a compound predicate—two verbs with the same subject. You can create a complete sentence by linking the verbs.

> REVISED   In spite of a pulled muscle, Jeremy *ran* the race *and won.*

If you want to keep more emphasis on the second verb, you can turn the fragment into a full clause by adding punctuation and another subject.

> REVISED   In spite of a pulled muscle, Jeremy ran the race—and *he* won.

(For a review of the rules about punctuating linked phrases and clauses, see 17a-3.)

Exercise 10–1

Eliminate sentence fragments where they appear in the following examples. Some examples may be correct. Suggested revisions of the lettered exercises appear in the back of the book. Example:

Bryan hates parsnips. And loathes squash.

Bryan hates parsnips and loathes squash.

a. Polly and Jim plan to see the new Woody Allen movie. Which was reviewed in last Sunday's *New York Times*.

b. For democracy to function at all, two elements are crucial. An educated populace and a firm collective belief in people's ability to chart their own course.

c. Scholastic achievement is important to Alex. Being the first person in his family ever to attend college.

d. Does our society rob children of their childhood? By making them aware too soon of adult ills?

e. It was one of those days. Complete chaos. Friends coming over in an hour. A term paper to write.

1. If the German people had known Hitler's real plans. Would they have made him führer?

2. Lisa advocated sleeping no more than four hours a night. Until she started nodding through her classes.

3. Have you ever noticed that most children's books seem to be written for girls? With some notable exceptions, of course.

4. Jack seemed well qualified for a career in the air force. Except for his tendency to get airsick.

5. Illness often accompanies stress. After the death of a loved one, for example, catching a cold is common.

6. None of the board members objected to Butch's proposal at the time. Only afterward, when they realized its implications.

7. Michael volunteered to build the wall. Having nothing better to do over the weekend.

8. Richard III supposedly had the young princes murdered. No one has ever found out what really happened to them.

9. They met. They talked. They fought. They reached agreement.

10. I can't think about modern philosophy. Especially in hot weather.

Exercise 10–2

Rewrite the following paragraph, eliminating all sentence fragments.

When I was about eleven years old. I played on a Little League baseball team. Played, that is, when I wasn't sitting on the bench. Which was most of the time. I got into the lineup only because the rules said every kid had to get a chance at bat. A rule my coach didn't like. Because he wanted our team to win every game. I rarely got to play in the field. Only when a shortage of players made my presence there necessary. Then always right field. Unless there were a lot of lefties coming up to bat on the opposing team. Believe me when I say that, for me, Little League baseball was no fun.

11 | COMMA SPLICES AND FUSED SENTENCES

Splice two ropes, or two strips of movie film, and you join them into one. Splice two main clauses by putting only a comma between them, however, and you get an ungainly construction called a **comma splice**. Here, for instance, are two perfectly good main clauses, each separate, each able to stand on its own as a sentence:

> The detective wriggled on his belly toward the campfire. The drunken smugglers didn't notice him.

Now let's splice those sentences with a comma.

> COMMA SPLICE   The detective wriggled on his belly toward the campfire, the drunken smugglers didn't notice him.

The resulting comma splice makes for difficult reading.

Even more confusing than a comma splice is a **fused** (or **run-on**) **sentence**: two main clauses joined without any punctuation.

> FUSED SENTENCE   The detective wriggled on his belly toward the campfire the drunken smugglers didn't notice him.

Lacking clues from the writer, a reader cannot tell where to pause. To understand the sentence, he or she must halt and reread.

Even writers who know better can fall at times into fusing and comma splicing. Temptation may overwhelm them when, having written one sentence, they want to add some further thought. Either they simply jam the two thoughts together or they push in a comma, like a thumbtack, to stick on the second thought.

Here are five simple ways to repair both comma splices and fused sentences. Which one to choose depends on the length and complexity of your main clauses and the effect you want to achieve.

REVISING COMMA SPLICES AND FUSED SENTENCES
Try any of these five strategies:

1. Make each main clause a separate sentence. (11a)
2. Link the two main clauses with a comma and a coordinating conjunction. (1g); (11b)
3. Link the two main clauses with a semicolon or, if appropriate, a colon. (11c)
4. Subordinate one clause to the other. (11d)
5. Link the two main clauses with a semicolon, a conjunctive adverb, and a comma. (11e)

11a *Repair a comma splice or fused sentence by making each main clause a separate sentence.*

COMMA SPLICE   Sigmund Freud has been called an enemy of sexual repression, the truth is that he is not a friend of free love.

FUSED SENTENCE   Sigmund Freud has been called an enemy of sexual repression the truth is that he is not a friend of free love.

Neither sentence yields its meaning without a struggle. To point readers in the right direction, separate the clauses.

REVISED   Sigmund Freud has been called an enemy of sexual repression. The truth is that he is not a friend of free love.

11b *Repair a comma splice or fused sentence by linking the two main clauses with a comma and a coordinating conjunction.*

Is it always incorrect to join two main clauses with a comma? No. If both clauses are of roughly equal weight, you can use a comma to link them—as long as you add a coordinating conjunction (*and, but, for, nor, or, so, yet*) after the comma.

COMMA SPLICE   Hurricane winds hit ninety miles an hour, they tore the roof from every house on Paradise Drive.

REVISED   Hurricane winds hit ninety miles an hour, *and* they tore the roof from every house on Paradise Drive.

11c *Repair a comma splice or fused sentence by linking the two main clauses with a semicolon or colon.*

Joining two clauses with a comma and a coordinating conjunction usually yields a smooth, grammatically correct sentence. Smoothness, however, is not always the writer's goal. If two clauses are unequal in weight, or if the writer wants to emphasize both, a different option may work better.

A semicolon can keep two thoughts connected while giving full emphasis to each one.

COMMA SPLICE   Hurricane winds hit ninety miles an hour, they tore the roof from every house on Paradise Drive.

REVISED   Hurricane winds hit ninety miles an hour; they tore the roof from every house on Paradise Drive.

If the second thought clearly illustrates or explains the first, add it on with a colon.

The hurricane caused extensive damage: it tore the roof from every house on Paradise Drive.

Remember that the only punctuation powerful enough to link two main clauses single-handedly is a semicolon, a colon, or a period. A lone comma won't do the job.

11d Repair a comma splice or fused sentence by making one clause subordinate to the other.

If one main clause is more important than the other, or if you want to give it more importance, you can subordinate the less important clause to it. Using subordination helps your reader more than simply dividing a fused sentence or comma splice into two sentences. When you make one clause subordinate, you throw weight on the main clause. In effect, you show your reader how one idea relates to another—you decide which matters more.

FUSED SENTENCE Hurricane winds hit ninety miles an hour they tore the roof from every house on Paradise Drive.

REVISED *When hurricane winds hit ninety miles an hour*, they tore the roof from every house on Paradise Drive.

REVISED Hurricane winds *that hit ninety miles an hour* tore the roof from every house on Paradise Drive.

For a run-down of different ways to use subordination, see 3e–3g.

11e Repair a comma splice or fused sentence by linking the two main clauses with a semicolon, a conjunctive adverb, and a comma.

A writer who is sharp enough to beware of fused sentences and comma splices but who still wants to cram more than one clause into a sentence may join two clauses with a *conjunctive adverb*. Some common conjunctive adverbs are *also, besides, consequently, even so, finally, furthermore, however, indeed, moreover, nevertheless,* and *therefore*. (See 1g.) These transitional words and phrases can be a useful way of linking clauses—but only if used with the right punctuation.

COMMA SPLICE Sigmund Freud has been called an enemy of sexual repression, however the truth is that he is not a friend of free love.

The writer might consider a comma plus the conjunctive adverb *however* glue enough to combine the two main clauses; but that cheap fish glue won't hold. Stronger binding is called for.

REVISED Sigmund Freud has been called an enemy of sexual repression; however, the truth is that he is not a friend of free love.

A writer who fuses and comma splices sentences is like a man trying to join two boards. If he comma splices, he tries to put them together with only one nail; if he fuses, he puts them together with no nail at all. But most thoughts, to hang together, need plenty of hammering.

EXCEPTION: Certain very short, similar main clauses can be joined with a comma.

Only if you now feel sure that you can tell a comma splice or a fused sentence when you see one, read on: here comes a fine point. We hate to admit it, lest it complicate life, but once in a great while you'll see a competent writer joining main clauses with nothing but a comma between them.

Jill runs by day, Tom walks by night.

I came, I saw, I conquered.

Commas are not obligatory with short, similar clauses. If you find this issue confusing, you can stick with semicolons to join all main clauses, short or long.

Jill runs by day; Tom walks by night.

I came; I saw; I conquered.

Exercise 11–1

In the following examples, repair each comma splice or fused sentence in two ways and decide which way you believe works best. Be creative—don't revise every sentence in the same ways. Some sentences may be correct as written. Possible revisions for the lettered sentences appear in the back of the book. Example:

The castle looked eerie from a distance, it filled us with nameless fear as we approached.

1. The castle looked eerie from a distance. It filled us with nameless fear as we approached.

2. The castle looked eerie from a distance; it filled us with nameless fear as we approached.

3. The castle, which looked eerie from a distance, filled us with nameless fear as we approached.

a. Everyone had heard alarming rumors in the village about strange goings-on, we hesitated to believe them.

b. Bats flew about our ears as the carriage pulled up under a stone archway an assistant stood waiting to lead us to our host.

c. We followed the scientist down a flight of wet stone steps at last he stopped before a huge oak door.

d. From a jangling keyring Dr. Frankenstein selected a heavy key, he twisted it in the lock.

e. The huge door gave a groan it swung open on a dimly lighted laboratory.

1. Our guide turned, with a lopsided smile, silently he motioned us into the room.

2. Before us on a dissecting table lay a form with closed eyes to behold it sent a quick chill down my spine.

3. With glittering eyes the scientist strode to the table, he lifted a white-gloved hand.

4. The form lying before us seemed an obscenely large baby in disbelief I had to rub my eyes.

5. It resembled no human child instead it seemed constructed of rubber or clay.

6. With a hoarse cry Frankenstein flung a power switch, blue streamers of static electricity crackled about the table, the creature gave a grunt and opened smoldering eyes.

7. "I've won!" exclaimed the scientist in triumph he circled the room doing a demented Irish reel.

8. The creature's right hand strained, the heavy steel manacle imprisoning his wrist groaned in torment.

9. Like a staple wrenched from a document, the manacle yielded.

10. The creature sat upright and tugged at the shackles binding his ankles, Frankenstein uttered a piercing scream.

Exercise 11–2

Identify each of the following errors as either a fused sentence or a comma splice. Revise each, using either subordination or a conjunctive adverb. Some sentences may be correct. Possible revisions for the lettered sentences appear in the back of the book. Example:

The scientist's shriek echoed through the cavernous cellar, it roused a flapping cloud of frightened bats.

[Comma splice.] The scientist's shriek echoed through the cavernous cellar, rousing a flapping cloud of frightened bats.

a. The creature lumbered toward its terrified creator, Frankenstein shrank back against a wall.

b. To defend himself the scientist grabbed a wooden mallet it had been sitting on a cabinet nearby.

c. Frankenstein wore a smile of contemptuous superiority, his triumph proved brief in duration.

d. With one sweep of an arm the creature dashed aside the mallet its wooden head splintered on the stone floor.

e. What followed is engraved upon my dreams, I hesitate to disclose it lest it trouble your own.

1. Many psychologists believe fantasy stories can be valuable they are a means of exploring our secret fears.

2. We identify with the characters and situations, this helps us to face threatening experiences without going through them.

3. The hero is good, the villain is evil, and virtue triumphs.

4. We all carry around our own monsters some of them we created ourselves.
5. We fear an inner Frankenstein, otherwise why would we shiver whenever we enter a dark cellar?

Exercise 11–3

Write six or eight sentences, illustrating both fused sentences and comma splices. Then trade papers with a classmate and repair each other's deliberate errors in whatever ways yield the best results.

12 ADJECTIVES AND ADVERBS

An adjective is a word that modifies a noun or pronoun. (See 1d.) A phrase also can function as an adjective. (See 3a–3b, 3f.) An adjective's job is to provide information about the person, place, object, or idea named by a noun or pronoun. It typically answers the question Which? or What kind?

> Karen bought a *small red* car.
> The radios *on sale* are an *excellent* value.

An adverb is a word (or a phrase) that modifies a verb, an adjective, or another adverb. (See 1e, 3a–3b, 3g.) An adverb typically answers the question How? or When? or Where? Sometimes it answers the question Why?

> Karen bought her car *quickly*.
> The radios arrived *yesterday*; Max put them *in the electronics department*.
> Karen needed her new car *to commute to school*.

The most common problems that writers have with adjectives and adverbs involve mixing them up: sending an adjective to do an adverb's job or vice versa.

12a Use an adverb, not an adjective, to modify a verb, adjective, or adverb.

> **FAULTY**   Karen bought her car *quick*.
>
> **FAULTY**   It's *awful* hot today.

Although an informal speaker might be able to get away with these sentences, a writer cannot. *Quick* and *awful* are adjectives, so they can modify only nouns or pronouns. To modify the verb *bought* we need the adverb *quickly*; to modify the adjective *hot* we need the adverb *awfully*.

> **REVISED**   Karen bought her car *quickly*.
>
> **REVISED**   It's *awfully* hot today.

ADJECTIVES AND ADVERBS AT A GLANCE

ADJECTIVES

- Typically answer the question Which? or What kind?
- Modify nouns or pronouns

ADVERBS

- Answer the question How?, When?, Where?, or, sometimes, Why?
- Modify verbs, adjectives, and other adverbs

12b Use an adjective, not an adverb, as a subject complement or object complement.

If we write, "Her old car looked awful," *awful* is a subject complement: it follows a linking verb and modifies the subject, *car*. (See 2d, 5a.)

> **FAULTY** Her old car looked *awfully*.
> **REVISED** Her old car looked *awful*.

An object complement is a word that renames a direct object or completes the sentence's description of it. (See 2d.) Object complements can be adjectives or nouns, but never adverbs.

> Early to bed and early to rise makes a man *healthy, wealthy,* and *wise.* [Adjectives modifying the direct object *man*].

When you are not sure whether you're dealing with an object complement or an adverb, look closely at the word's role in the sentence. If it modifies a noun, it is an object complement and therefore should be an adjective.

> The coach called the referee *stupid* and *blind.* [*Stupid* and *blind* are adjectives modifying the direct object *referee.*]

If it modifies a verb, you want an adverb instead.

> In fact, though, the ref had called the play *correctly.* [*Correctly* is an adverb modifying the verb *called.*]

12c Use good *as an adjective and* well *as an adverb.*

A common adjective-adverb mix-up occurs when writers confuse *good* and *well* as subject complements. *Good* is almost always an adjective; *well* is almost always an adverb.

This sandwich tastes *good*. [The adjective *good* is a subject complement following the linking verb *tastes* and modifying the noun *sandwich*.]

Heloise's skin healed *well* after surgery. [The adverb *well* modifies the verb *healed*.]

Only if the verb is a linking verb (see list in 5a) can you safely follow it with *good*. Other kinds of verbs do not take subject complements. Instead, they need adverbs to modify them.

FAULTY   That painting came out *good*.

REVISED   That painting came out *well*.

Complications arise when we write or speak about health. It is perfectly correct to say *I feel good*, using the adjective *good* as a subject complement after the linking verb *feel*. However, generations of confusion have nudged the adverb *well* into the adjective category, too. A nurse may speak of "a well baby"; and greeting cards urge patients to "get well"—meaning, "become healthy." Just as *healthy* is an adjective here, so is *well*.

What, then, is the best answer when someone asks, "How do you feel?" If you want to duck the issue, reply, "Fine!" Otherwise, in speech either *good* or *well* is acceptable; in writing, use *good*.

12d *Form comparatives and superlatives of most adjectives with* -er *and* -est *and of most adverbs with* more *and* most.

Comparatives and superlatives are special adjective and adverb forms that allow us to describe one thing in relation to another. You can put most adjectives into their comparative form by adding *-er* and into their superlative form by adding *-est*.

The budget deficit is *larger* than the trade deficit.

This year's trade deficit is the *largest* ever.

We usually form the comparative and superlative of long adjectives with *more* and *most* rather than with *-er* and *-est*, to keep them from becoming cumbersome.

Our national debt is *enormous*.

It may become *more enormous* over the next few years.

For short adverbs that do not end in *-ly*, usually add *-er* and *-est* in the comparative and superlative forms. With all other adverbs, use *more* and *most*.

Spending *faster* than one earns will plunge a person into debt *sooner* than any other way I know.

The *more indiscriminately* we import foreign goods, the *more rapidly* the trade deficit grows.

It grows *fastest* and *most uncontrollably* when exports are down.

For negative comparisons, use *less* and *least* for both adjectives and adverbs.

Michael's speech was *less interesting* than Louie's.

Paulette spoke *less interestingly* than Michael.

Bud's speech was the *least interesting* of all.

The comparative and superlative forms of *bad* and *badly* are irregular, and so must be used with special care.

Tom's golf is *bad*, but no *worse* than George's.

Tom plays golf *badly*, but no *worse* than George does.

COMPARISON OF IRREGULAR ADJECTIVES AND ADVERBS

POSITIVE	COMPARATIVE	SUPERLATIVE
ADJECTIVES		
good	better	best
bad	worse	worst
little	less, littler	least, littlest
many, some, much	more	most
ADVERBS		
well	better	best
badly	worse	worst
little	less	least

12e *An adjective or adverb that is already comparative or superlative does not need* **more,** **most,** *or another helping word.*

Some words become comparative or superlative when we tack on *-er* or *-est*. Others, such as *top*, *favorite*, and *unique*, mark whatever they modify as one-of-a-kind by definition. Neither category requires further assistance to make its point. To say "a *more worse* fate" or "my *most favorite* movie" is redundant—"a *worse* fate" or "my *favorite* movie" does the job.

FAULTY   Lisa is *more uniquely* qualified for the job than any other candidate.

REVISED   Lisa is *better* qualified for the job than any other candidate.

REVISED   Lisa is *uniquely* qualified for the job.

12f *Use the comparative form of an adjective or adverb to compare two people, items, actions, or situations, and the superlative form to compare more than two.*

No matter how fantastic, wonderful, and terrific something is, we can call it the *best* only when we compare it with more than one other thing. Any comparison between two things uses the comparative form, not the superlative.

FAULTY   Their chocolate and vanilla are both good, but I like the chocolate *best*.

REVISED   Their chocolate and vanilla are both good, but I like the chocolate *better*.

FAULTY   Of his two dogs, he treats Bonzo *most affectionately*.

REVISED   Of his two dogs, he treats Bonzo *more affectionately*.

Exercise 12–1

Find and correct any improperly used adjectives and adverbs in the following sentences. Some sentences may be correct. Answers for the lettered sentences appear in the back of the book. Example:

Nobody on our team pitches as good as Jesse.

Nobody on our team pitches as *well* as Jesse.

a. Which of your two brothers is the oldest?

b. Since Mrs. Fox developed arthritis, she can't move as quick as she used to.

c. Using adjectives correct is tricky, but using adverbs correct is trickiest.

d. Among spring's greatest joys are the birds that sing so sweet every morning.

e. Judy talks a lot about Scott, but she spends all her time with Todd, so she must like Todd the most.

1. Hank's science project didn't work out as bad as he had feared.

2. Implanting the electrodes proved to be less harder than regulating the dosage.

3. That song sounds great when the drummer plays real loud.

4. After Luke's dog bit a skunk, the house didn't smell very good.

5. Would Snow White and her prince have lived happier ever after with the Seven Dwarfs out of the picture?

6. Even more worse than marrying a woman with seven jealous male friends would be having a witch for a mother-in-law.

7. Which dwarf in the Disney film is funnier: Sleepy, Dopey, or Doc?

8. Lucy's most favorite Disney film is *Dumbo*.

9. Her father, Tim, says that the excitingest filmmaker today is not George Lucas but Martin Scorsese.

10. Tim considered *Duck Soup* better than *A Day at the Races*, and he liked the middle film in the *Star Wars* trilogy the least.

CHAPTER 23

Effective Sentences

13. Misplaced and Dangling Modifiers   **662**
14. Incomplete Sentences   **665**
15. Mixed Constructions and Faulty Predication   **670**
16. Parallel Structure   **673**
17. Coordination and Subordination   **677**

13 MISPLACED AND DANGLING MODIFIERS

The purpose of a modifier is to give readers additional information. To do so, the modifier must be linked clearly to whatever it is meant to modify. If you wrote, "We saw a stone wall around a house on a grassy hill, beautiful and distant," your readers would be hard put to figure out whether *beautiful* and *distant* modify *wall, house,* or *hill.* When you finish writing, double-check your modifiers—especially prepositional phrases and subordinate clauses—to make sure each one is in the right place.

13a *Keep your modifiers close to what they modify.*

Misplaced modifiers—phrases and clauses that wander away from what they modify—produce results that are more likely to amuse your readers than inform them. To avoid confusion, place your modifiers as close as possible to whatever they modify.

MISPLACED   She offered handcrafted toys to all the orphans in colorful packages. [Does the phrase *in colorful packages* modify *toys* or *orphans*?]

CLEAR   She offered handcrafted toys in colorful packages to all the orphans.

MISPLACED   Today's assignment is to remove the dishes from the crates that got chipped. [Does the clause *that got chipped* modify *dishes* or *crates*?]

CLEAR   Today's assignment is to remove from the crates the dishes that got chipped.

Sometimes, when you move a misplaced modifier to a better place, an additional change or two will help you to clarify the sentence.

MISPLACED   Jim offered cream and sugar to his guests in their coffee.

CLEAR   Jim offered his guests cream and sugar in their coffee. [When *guests* is made an indirect object, *to* is cut.]

13b *Place each modifier so that it can be taken to modify only one thing.*

A **squinting modifier** is one that looks two ways, leaving the reader uncertain whether it modifies the word before it or the word after it. Don't let your modifiers squint. Make sure each modifies only one element in a sentence. A good tactic is to place your modifier close to the word or phrase it modifies and away from any others that might cause confusion.

SQUINTING   The best-seller that appealed to Mary *tremendously* bored Max.

CLEAR   The best-seller that *tremendously* appealed to Mary bored Max.

CLEAR   The best-seller that appealed to Mary bored Max *tremendously*.

Exercise 13–1

Improve the following sentences, which contain modifiers that are misplaced or squinting. Possible revisions for the lettered sentences appear in the back of the book. Example:

Miranda placed the book on the table that was overdue at the library.

Miranda placed on the table the book that was overdue at the library.

a. The team that lost miserably remained silent on the trip home.

b. Complete the writing assignment in the textbook that follows Chapter 2.

c. Those who make mistakes frequently learn valuable lessons.

d. Margaret was mortified at not having learned her lines for the duration of the rehearsal.

e. A person who snacks often gets fat.

1. Leo hid the stolen diamonds as soon as he heard the police siren under the driver's seat.
2. How can Jeannie keep that house looking so elegant at such an advanced age?
3. The city council voted to open a clinic for people with AIDS, which they can ill afford.
4. Don't ask one of the boys to carry the groceries out to the car when there are so few.
5. Horace squinted at the frog with myopic eyes.

13c *Be sure every modifier has something in the sentence to modify.*

Generally we assume that a modifying phrase that appears at the start of a sentence will modify the subject of the main clause to follow. If we encounter a modifying phrase midway through a sentence, we assume that it modifies something just before or (less often) after it.

> *Feeling sick to his stomach, Jason* went to bed.
>
> *An early bird by nature, Felix* began at eight o'clock.
>
> *Alice, while sympathetic,* was not inclined to help.

Occasionally a writer will slip up by allowing a modifying phrase to dangle. A **dangling modifier** is one that, on close inspection, is found to be shirking its job: it doesn't modify anything in its sentence.

> DANGLING *Noticing a slight pain behind his eyes*, an aspirin seemed like a good idea. [The introductory phrase cannot be said to modify *aspirin*. In fact, it doesn't modify anything.]
>
> DANGLING *To do a good job*, the right tools were needed.

To correct a dangling modifier, recast the sentence. First, figure out what noun, pronoun, or noun phrase the modifier is meant to modify and then make that word or phrase the subject of the main clause.

> CLEAR *Noticing a slight pain behind his eyes, he* decided to take an aspirin.
>
> CLEAR *To do a good job, the plumber* needed the right tools.

CORRECTING DANGLING MODIFIERS
Try either of these two strategies:

1. Figure out what noun, pronoun, or noun phrase the dangling modifier is meant to modify. Then make that word or phrase the subject of the main clause.
2. Turn the dangling modifier into a clause that includes the missing noun or pronoun.

Another way to correct a dangling modifier is to turn the dangler into a clause that includes the missing noun or pronoun.

DANGLING   Her progress, *although talented*, has been slowed by poor work habits.

CLEAR   *Although she is talented*, her progress has been slowed by poor work habits.

Sometimes a bit of rewriting will clarify what the modifier modifies and improve the sentence as well.

CLEAR   *Although talented, she* has been handicapped by poor work habits.

Exercise 13–2

Revise the following sentences, which contain dangling modifiers. Some sentences may be correct. Possible revisions for the lettered sentences appear in the back of the book. Example:

Angry at her poor showing, geology would never be Joan's favorite class.

Angry at her poor showing, Joan knew that geology would never be her favorite class.

a. After working for six hours, the job was done.

b. Unable to fall asleep, a warm bath relaxes you.

c. To join the college choir, a singer's voice has to be loud.

d. It's common, feeling lonely, to want to talk to someone.

e. Having worried all morning, relief flooded over him when his missing son returned.

1. Once gripped by the urge to sail, it never leaves you.

2. Further information can be obtained by calling the following number.

3. Passing the service station, the bank will appear on your right.

4. Having created strict ethical standards, there should be some willingness on Congress's part to live up to them.

5. Recalling Ben Franklin's advice, "hanging together" became the club members' new policy.

14 INCOMPLETE SENTENCES

A fragment fails to qualify as a sentence because it lacks a subject or a predicate or both (see 10). However, a sentence can contain these two essentials and still miss the mark. If it lacks some other key element—a crucial word or phrase—the sentence is *incomplete*. Often the problem is carelessness: the writer sets down too few words to cover a whole idea. The resulting incomplete sentence is likely to lose the reader. Like a bridge open to the public, it invites us to cross; but it has unexpected gaps that we topple through.

Incomplete sentences catch us most often in two writing situations: comparisons and the abbreviated type of parallel structure called elliptical constructions.

COMPARISONS

14a *Make your comparisons clear by stating fully what you are comparing with what.*

> INCOMPLETE   Roscoe loves spending time with a computer more than Diane.

What is the writer of this sentence trying to tell us? Does Roscoe prefer the company of a keyboard to the company of his friend? Or, of these two people, is Roscoe (and not Diane) the computer addict? We can't be sure, because the writer has not completed the comparison. Adding a word would solve the problem.

> REVISED   Roscoe loves spending time with a computer more than Diane *does*.
>
> REVISED   Roscoe loves spending time with a computer more than *with* Diane.

In editing what you write, double-check your comparisons to be sure they are complete.

> INCOMPLETE   Miami has more newcomers from Havana than New York.
>
> REVISED   Miami has more newcomers from Havana than New York *has*.
>
> REVISED   Miami has more newcomers from Havana than *from* New York.

14b *When you start to draw a comparison, finish it.*

The unfinished comparison is a favorite trick of advertisers—"Our product is better!"—because it dodges the question "Better than what?" A sharp writer (or shopper) knows that any item being compared must be compared *with* something else.

> INCOMPLETE   Scottish tweeds are warmer.
>
> REVISED   Scottish tweeds are warmer *than any other fabric you can buy*.

14c *Be sure the things you compare are of the same kind.*

The saying "You can't compare apples and oranges" makes a useful grammatical point. A sentence that draws a comparison should assure its readers that the items involved are similar enough for comparison to be appropriate. When you compare two things, be sure the terms of the comparison are clear and logical.

> INCOMPLETE   The engine of a Ford truck is heavier than a Piper Cub airplane.

What is being compared? Truck and airplane? Or engine and engine? If we consider, we can guess: since a truck engine is unlikely to outweigh an airplane, the writer must mean to compare engines. Readers, however, may not make the effort to complete a writer's incomplete thought.

> **REVISED**   The engine of a Ford truck is heavier than *that of* a Piper Cub airplane.
>
> **REVISED**   A Ford truck's engine is heavier than a *Piper Cub's*.

In this last example, parallel structure (*Ford truck's* and *Piper Cub's*) helps to make the comparison concise as well as clear. (See 16a, 16c for more on parallel structure.)

14d To compare an item with others of its kind, use any other rather than simply any.

A comparison using *any* shows how something relates to a group without belonging to the group.

> Alaska is larger than *any* country in Central America.
>
> Bluefish has as much protein as *any* meat.

A comparison using *any other* shows how one member of a group relates to other members of the same group.

> Death Valley is drier than *any other* place in the United States.
>
> Bluefish has as distinctive a flavor as *any other* fish.

Exercise 14–1

Add needed words to any of the following comparisons that strike you as incomplete. (Depending on how you interpret the sentence, there may be more than one way to complete a comparison.) Some sentences may be correct. Possible revisions for the lettered sentences appear in the back of the book. Example:

> I hate hot weather more than you.
>
> I hate hot weather more than you *do*.
>
> I hate hot weather more than *I hate* you.

a. She plays the *Moonlight Sonata* more brilliantly than any pianist her age.

b. Driving a sports car means more to Jake than his professors.

c. People who go to college aren't necessarily smarter, but they will always have an advantage at job interviews.

d. I don't have as much trouble getting along with Michelle as Karin.

e. One-eyed Bill was faster on the draw than any gunslinger in West Texas.

1. The brain of an ape is larger than a hippopotamus.

2. A more sensible system of running the schools would be to appoint a school board.

3. A hen lays fewer eggs than any turtle.

4. The town meeting form of government doesn't function as efficiently as a mayor.

5. Sex is closer to prayer than a meal of Chicken McNuggets.

ELLIPTICAL CONSTRUCTIONS

A well-known poem by Robert Frost begins:

> Some say the world will end in fire, some say in ice.

When Frost wrote that sentence, he avoided needless repetition by implying certain words rather than stating them. The result is more concise and more effective than a complete version of the same sentence would be:

> Some say the world will end in fire, some say the world will end in ice.

This common writer's tactic—leaving out (for the sake of concision) an unnecessary word—produces an **elliptical construction**. Readers can easily fill in the words that, although not written, are clearly understood. Elliptical constructions can create confusion, however, if the writer gives readers too little information to fill in those missing words accurately.

14e *When you eliminate repetition in a sentence, keep all words that are essential for clarity.*

An elliptical construction saves repeating what a reader already knows. But whenever you use this strategy, make sure to omit only words that are stated elsewhere in the sentence. Otherwise, your reader may fill the gap incorrectly.

> INCOMPLETE How can I date her, seeing that she is a senior, I a mere freshman?

This elliptical construction won't work. A reader supplying the missing verb in the last part of the sentence would get "I *is* a mere freshman." Although the writer means *am, is* is the verb already stated.

> REVISED How can I date her, seeing that she is a senior and I *am* a mere freshman?

Leaving out a necessary preposition also can produce a faulty elliptical construction.

> INCOMPLETE The train neither goes nor returns from Middletown.

Without a *to* after *goes*, readers are likely to fill in an extra *from* to complete the verb's action. Write instead:

> REVISED The train neither goes *to* nor returns from Middletown.

14f *When you eliminate repetition in a compound predicate, leave out only verb forms that have already been stated.*

Compound predicates are especially prone to incomplete elliptical constructions. Writing in haste, we accidentally omit part of a verb that is needed for the sentence to make sense. When you write a sentence with a compound predicate, check your verbs most carefully if they are in different tenses. Be sure that no necessary part is missing.

> INCOMPLETE   The committee never has and never will vote to raise taxes.
>
> REVISED   The committee never has *voted* and never will vote to raise taxes.

14g *If you mix a comparison ending in* as *with one ending in* than, *be sure to include both words.*

To contrast two things that are different, we normally use the comparative form of an adjective followed by *than: better than, more than, fewer than.* To show a similarity between two things that are alike, we normally use the simple form of an adjective sandwiched between *as* and *as: as good as, as many as, as few as.* Often we can combine two *than* comparisons or two *as* comparisons into an elliptical construction.

> The White House is smaller [than] and newer than Buckingham Palace.
>
> Some corporate executives live in homes as large [as] and as grand as the White House.

If you want to combine a *than* comparison with an *as* comparison, however, an elliptical construction won't work.

> INCOMPLETE   The White House is smaller but just as beautiful as Buckingham Palace.
>
> REVISED   The White House is smaller *than* Buckingham Palace but just *as* beautiful.
>
> INCOMPLETE   Some corporate executives live in homes as large, and no less grand, than the White House.
>
> REVISED   Some corporate executives live in homes *as* large *as,* and no less grand *than,* the White House.

Exercise 14–2

Add needed words to each of the following sentences that strikes you as incomplete. (Depending on how you interpret the sentence, there may be more than one way to fill in a gap.) Some sentences may be correct. Possible revisions for the lettered sentences appear in the back of the book. Example:

> President Kennedy should have but didn't see the perils of invading Cuba.
>
> President Kennedy should have *seen* but didn't see the perils of invading Cuba.

a. The sand pit is just as wide but deeper than the quarry.

b. Pembroke was never contacted, much less involved with, the election committee.

c. I haven't yet but soon will finish my term paper.

d. Ron likes his popcorn with butter, Linda with parmesan cheese.

e. George Washington always has been and will be regarded as the father of his country.

1. You have traveled to exotic Tahiti; Maureen, to Asbury Park, N. J.

2. The mayor refuses to negotiate or even talk to the civic association.

3. Building a new sewage treatment plant would be no more costly and just as effective as modifying the existing one.

4. We favor this proposal, Louise that one.

5. The board has not and will not accept such an unfair proposal.

15   MIXED CONSTRUCTIONS AND FAULTY PREDICATION

Sometimes a sentence contains all the necessary parts and still doesn't work. Reading it, we feel uneasy, although we may not know why. The problem is a discord between two or more parts of the sentence: the writer has combined phrases or clauses that don't fit together (a *mixed construction*) or mismatched a verb and its subject, object, or modifier (*faulty predication*). The resulting tangle looks like a sentence at first glance, but it fails to make sense.

15a Avoid mixed constructions by making sure your phrases and clauses are linked together logically.

A **mixed construction** results when a writer connects phrases or clauses (or both) that don't work together as a sentence.

> MIXED   In her efforts to solve the tax problem only caused the mayor additional difficulties.

The prepositional phrase *in her efforts to solve the tax problem* is a modifier; it cannot function as the subject of a sentence. The writer, however, has used this phrase as a noun—the subject of the verb *caused*. To untangle the mixed construction, the writer has two choices: (1) rewrite the phrase so that it works as a noun or (2) use the phrase as a modifier rather than as the sentence's subject.

> REVISED   Her efforts to solve the tax problem only caused the mayor additional difficulties. [With *in* gone, *efforts* becomes the subject of the sentence.]

> REVISED   In her efforts to solve the tax problem, the mayor created additional difficulties. [The prepositional phrase now modifies the verb *created*.]

To avoid mixed constructions, check the links that join your phrases and clauses—especially prepositions and conjunctions. A sentence, like a chain, is only as strong as its weakest link.

> **MIXED**   Jack, although he was picked up by the police, but was not charged with anything.

Using both *although* and *but* gives this sentence one link too many. We can unmix the construction in two ways.

> **REVISED**   Jack was picked up by the police but was not charged with anything.

> **REVISED**   Although he was picked up by the police, Jack was not charged with anything.

15b *Avoid faulty predication by making sure the parts of your sentences are logically related to each other.*

Faulty predication refers to a skewed relationship between a verb and some other part of a sentence.

> **FAULTY**   The temperature of water freezes at 32 degrees Fahrenheit.

At first glance, that sentence looks all right. It contains both subject and predicate. It expresses a complete thought. What is wrong with it? The writer has slipped into faulty predication by mismatching the subject and verb. The sentence tells us that *temperature freezes,* when science and common sense tell us it is *water* that freezes. To correct this error, the writer must find a subject and verb that fit each other.

> **REVISED**   Water freezes at 32 degrees Fahrenheit.

Faulty predication also can result from a mismatch between a verb and its direct object.

> **FAULTY**   Rising costs diminish college for many students.

Costs don't *diminish college.* To correct this predication error, the writer must change the sentence so that its direct object follows logically from its verb.

> **REVISED**   Rising costs diminish the number of students who can attend college.

Subtler predication errors result when a writer uses a linking verb to forge a false connection between the subject and a subject complement.

> **FAULTY**   Industrial waste has become an important modern priority.

Is it really *waste* that has become a *priority*? Or, rather, is it *working to solve the problems caused by careless disposal of industrial waste*? A writer who says all that, though, risks wordiness. Why not just replace *priority* with a closer match for waste?

> **REVISED**   Industrial waste has become a modern menace.

Predication errors tend to plague writers who are too fond of the passive voice. Mismatches between a verb and its subject, object, or another part of the sentence are easier to avoid (and to spot during editing) when the verb is active than when it is passive. To improve your sentences, cast them in the active voice whenever possible. (See 5l.)

FAULTY   The idea of giving thanks for a good harvest *was not done* first by the Pilgrims.

REVISED   The idea of giving thanks for a good harvest *did not originate* with the Pilgrims.

15c *Avoid starting a definition with* when *or* where.

Many inexperienced writers slip into predication errors when they define terms. A definition, like any other phrase or clause, needs to fit grammatically with the rest of the sentence.

FAULTY   Dyslexia is when you have a reading disorder.

REVISED   Dyslexia is a reading disorder.

FAULTY   A lay-up is where a player drives in close to the basket and then makes a usually one-handed, banked shot.

REVISED   To shoot a lay-up, a player drives in close to the basket and then makes a usually one-handed, banked shot.

15d *Avoid writing* the reason is because . . .

Anytime you start an explanation with *the reason is,* what follows *is* should be a subject complement: an adjective, a noun, or a noun clause. (See 2d.) *Because* is a conjunction; it cannot function as a noun or adjective.

FAULTY   The reason Gerard hesitates is because no one supported him two years ago.

REVISED   The reason Gerard hesitates is simple: no one supported him two years ago.

REVISED   The reason Gerard hesitates is his lack of support two years ago.

REVISED   The reason Gerard hesitates is that no one supported him two years ago.

Exercise 15–1

Correct any mixed constructions and faulty predication you find in the following sentences. Possible revisions for the lettered sentences appear in the back of the book. Example:

"Coming about" is when a sailboat makes a turn into the wind.

"Coming about" is a sailboat's turn into the wind.

A sailboat "comes about" when it makes a turn into the wind.

a. The characteristics of a balanced budget call for careful planning.

b. Among the candidates for school committee head are unimpressive this year.

c. Financial aid searches for able students and decides to pay their college costs.

d. One good reason for financial aid is because it enables capable lower-income students to attend college.

e. In one sizzling blast, the destruction of the enemy space fleet was instantly wiped out.

1. Inflation is where money keeps decreasing in value.

2. From all the debates over rising energy costs failed to accomplish any positive action.

3. The damp weather swelled Joe's arthritis.

4. Getting a job can improve a person's status symbols in the community.

5. The air force's explanation for the crash is because heavy snow forced an emergency landing.

6. Life's saddest moments are experienced by the loss of a loved one.

7. One solution to urban decay is when old neighborhoods are revitalized rather than torn down.

8. Addiction to crack cocaine has become a national crusade.

9. Market research demonstrates to a manufacturer the consumers using its products.

10. American cars try to look flashier than foreign cars.

16 PARALLEL STRUCTURE

An important tool for any writer is **parallel structure,** or parallelism. You use this tool when you create a series of words, phrases, clauses, or sentences with the same grammatical form. The pattern created by the series—its parallel structure—emphasizes the similarities or differences among the items, which may be things, qualities, actions, or ideas.

My favorite foods are roast beef, deep-dish apple pie, and linguine with clam sauce.

Louise is charming, witty, intelligent, and talented.

Jeff likes to swim, ride, and run.

Dave likes movies that scare him and books that make him laugh.

Each series is a perfect parallel construction, composed of equivalent words: nouns in the first example, adjectives in the second, verbs in the third, and adjective clauses in the fourth.

16a *In a series linked by* **and,** *or,* **or** *another coordinating conjunction, keep all elements in the same grammatical form.*

Whenever you connect items with a coordinating conjunction (*and, but, or, nor, so,* and *yet* are the most common), you cue your readers to expect a parallel structure. Whether your series consists of single words, phrases, or clauses, its parts should balance one another.

> **AWKWARD**   The puppies are *tiny, clumsily bumping* into each other, *and cute.*

Two elements in this series are parallel one-word adjectives, but the third is a verb phrase. The writer can improve this awkward sentence by making the series consistent.

> **PARALLEL**   The puppies are *tiny, clumsy, and cute.*

Don't mix verb forms in a series. Avoid, for instance, pairing a gerund and an infinitive.

> **AWKWARD**   Switzerland is a good place for a winter vacation if you like *skiing and to skate.*
>
> **PARALLEL**   Switzerland is a good place for a winter vacation if you like *skiing and skating.*
>
> **PARALLEL**   Switzerland is a good place for a winter vacation if you like *to ski and to skate.*

In a series of phrases or clauses, be sure that all elements in the series are similar in form, even if they are not similar in length.

> **AWKWARD**   The fight in the bar happens after the two lovers have their scene together but before the car chase. [The clause starting with *after* is not parallel to the phrase starting with *before.*]
>
> **PARALLEL**   The fight in the bar happens after the love scene but before the car chase.
>
> **AWKWARD**   You can take the key, or don't forget to leave it under the mat. [The declarative clause starting with *you can* is not parallel to the imperative clause starting with *don't forget.*]
>
> **PARALLEL**   You can take the key, or you can leave it under the mat.

PARALLEL STRUCTURE AT A GLANCE

- Keep all the elements in a series in the same grammatical form. (16a–16c)
- Reinforce parallelism in a series by repeating, not mixing, articles, conjunctions, or prepositions. (16d)
- In a series of clauses, repeat lead-in words to emphasize parallel structure. (16e)

16b *In a series linked by* **either . . . or, neither . . . nor, not only . . .** **but also,** *or another correlative conjunction, keep all elements in the same grammatical form.*

When you use a correlative conjunction, follow each part of it with a similarly structured word, phrase, or clause.

> AWKWARD   I'm looking forward *to either attending* Saturday's wrestling match *or to seeing* it on closed-circuit TV. [Parallel structure is violated because *to* precedes the first part of the correlative conjunction (*to either*) but follows the second part (*or to*).]
>
> PARALLEL   I'm looking forward *either to attending* Saturday's wrestling match *or to seeing* it on closed-circuit television.
>
> AWKWARD   Take my advice: try *neither to be first nor last* in the lunch line. [Parallel structure is violated because *to be* follows the first part of the correlative conjunction but not the second part.]
>
> PARALLEL   Take my advice: try to be *neither first nor last* in the lunch line.

16c *Make the elements in a comparison parallel in form.*

A comparative word such as *than* or *as* cues the reader to expect a parallel structure. This makes logical sense: to be compared, two things must resemble each other, and parallel structure emphasizes this resemblance. (See also 14g.)

> AWKWARD   Philip likes *fishing* better than *to sail.*
>
> PARALLEL   Philip likes *fishing* better than *sailing.*
>
> PARALLEL   Philip likes *to fish* better than *to sail.*
>
> AWKWARD   *Maintaining* railway lines is as important to our public transportation system as *to buy* new trains.
>
> PARALLEL   *Maintaining* railway lines is as important to our public transportation system as *buying* new trains.

16d *Reinforce parallel structure by repeating rather than mixing articles, conjunctions, or prepositions.*

When you write a series involving articles, conjunctions, or prepositions, be consistent. Try to repeat rather than to vary the word that begins each phrase or clause.

> "The time has come," the Walrus said,
> "To talk of many things:
> Of shoes—and ships—and sealing-wax—
> Of cabbages—and—kings—"

In this famous rhyme from *Through the Looking-Glass,* Lewis Carroll builds a beautiful parallel structure on three *of*'s and three *and*'s, each followed by a noun. The repetition of preposition and conjunction makes clear the equivalence of the nouns.

Sometimes the same lead-in word won't work for all elements in a series. In such cases you may be able to preserve a parallel structure by changing the order of the elements to minimize variation.

> AWKWARD The new school building is large but not very comfortable, and expensive but unattractive.
>
> PARALLEL The new school building is large and expensive, but uncomfortable and unattractive.

16e *In a series of clauses, repeat lead-in words to emphasize parallel structure.*

Parallel structures are especially useful in complex sentences expressing equivalent ideas. Whenever you write a sentence containing a series of long, potentially confusing clauses, try to precede each clause with *that, who, when, where,* or some other connective, repeating the same connective every time. To do so not only helps you to keep your thoughts in order as you write but helps readers to follow them with ease.

> No one in this country needs a government that aids big business at the expense of farmers and laborers; that ravages the environment in the name of progress; that slashes budgets of health and education; that turns its back on the unemployed, the illiterate, the mentally ill, the destitute; that constantly swaggers and rattles its sabers; that spends billions piling up missiles it would be insane to use.　　　　　—Student essay

Repeating an opening phrase can accomplish the same goal in a series of parallel sentences, as the following graceful example shows.

> The Russian dramatist is one who, walking through a cemetery, does not see the flowers on the graves. The American dramatist is one who, walking through a cemetery, does not see the graves under the flowers.　　—George Jean Nathan

Exercise 16–1

First figure out what the writer is trying to say in each of the following sentences. Then revise, substituting parallel structures for awkward ones. Possible revisions for the lettered sentences appear in the back of the book. Example:

> Not only are you wasting your time but mine.
>
> You are wasting not only your time but mine.

a. I like movies about the old West, documentaries, and I like foreign films.

b. Better than starting from scratch would be to build on what already has been done.

c. Her apartment needed fresh paint, a new rug was a necessity, and Mary Lou wished she had a neater roommate and that she had chosen quieter friends.

d. All my brothers are blond and athletes.

e. For breakfast the waiter brought scrambled eggs, which I like, and kippers, although I don't like them.

1. The United States must start either focusing more attention on education or we must accept a future as a second-rate power.

2. Not only are you a gentleman but a scholar.

3. The best teachers are kind, firm, are smart, and have a sense of humor.

4. Like Polonius in *Hamlet,* I believe neither in being a borrower nor a lender.

5. Jules contends that our science facilities are inadequate, we need a new student center, a gym, and that an arts center would add much to the quality of life on campus.

6. Melrose would rather carry his battle to the Supreme Court than he would be willing to give up without a fight.

7. My landlady is tidy, generous, easygoing, and a talker.

8. Are problem novels for the young really good for children or merely exploit them by making life appear more burdensome, chaotic, more wretched and evil than it really is?

9. When you first start out, running halfway around the track is as big a challenge as to complete several circuits.

10. Her excuses were the difficulty of the task, the instructions were awkwardly worded, and having only four hours to complete the assignment.

11. In my drama class so far we've read a Shakespearean tragedy, another by Marlowe, and one of Webster's.

12. When you are broke and unemployed and your friends have deserted you, while you have nowhere to sleep but under a bridge, then and only then should you call this number.

13. Learn both winning with grace and to lose with dignity.

14. Not only should we accept Marinda's kind offer, but thank her for making it.

15. How often Reuben has done this kind of work is less important than the quality of his output.

17 COORDINATION AND SUBORDINATION

Many inexperienced writers think that a paragraph is simply a group of sentences on the same topic. You might as well say that a symphony is simply a group of musical parts in the same key. A good piece of writing (or music) is greater than the sum of its parts. Links between sentences help the reader to see how one thought relates to another and to share the writer's overview of the topic.

When you write, you can use coordination and subordination to bring out the relationships between your ideas. Coordination clarifies the connection between thoughts of equal importance; subordination shows how one thought affects another. These two techniques will help you produce sentences, paragraphs, and essays that function as a coherent whole.

17a Use coordination to link clauses that are related in theme and equal in importance.

> The car skidded for a hundred yards. It crashed into a brick wall.

These two sentences make equally significant statements about the same subject, a car accident. Because the writer has indicated no link between the sentences, we can only guess that the crash followed from the skid; we cannot be sure.

Suppose we join the two sentences with a conjunction:

> The car skidded for a hundred yards, and it crashed into a brick wall.

Now the sequence is clear: first the car skidded, then it crashed. That's coordination.

Another way to coordinate the two sentences is to combine them into a single sentence with a compound verb. The second main clause, losing its subject, becomes a phrase.

> The car skidded for a hundred yards and crashed into a brick wall.

Now the connection is so clear we can almost hear screeching brakes and crunching metal.

Once you decide to coordinate two sentences, there are three ways you can do it: with a conjunction, with a conjunctive adverb, or with punctuation.

1. Join two sentences with a coordinating conjunction (*and, but, for, or, nor, so,* or *yet*).

COORDINATION AND SUBORDINATION AT A GLANCE

- Use coordination to link clauses that are related in theme or equal in importance. (17a1–3)
- Avoid faulty coordination by linking only sentences that are clearly and logically connected. (17b)
- Avoid excessive coordination by linking only sentences that work together to make a coherent point. (17c)
- Use subordination to link an important clause with a related but less important clause. (17d1–3)
- Avoid faulty subordination by making sure your main idea is expressed in your main clause. (17e)

UNCOORDINATED George does not want to be placed on your mailing list. He does not want a salesperson to call him.

COORDINATED George does not want to be placed on your mailing list, nor does he want a salesperson to call him.

COORDINATED George does not want to be placed on your mailing list or called by a salesperson.

2. Join two sentences with a conjunctive adverb such as *furthermore, however, moreover,* or *therefore.*

UNCOORDINATED The guerrillas did not observe the truce. They never intended to.

COORDINATED The guerrillas did not observe the truce; furthermore, they never intended to.

3. Join two sentences with a semicolon or a colon. (For details on when to use which punctuation mark, see 20, 21, 24.)

UNCOORDINATED The government favors negotiations. The guerrillas prefer to fight.

COORDINATED The government favors negotiations; the guerrillas prefer to fight.

UNCOORDINATED The guerrillas have two advantages. They know the terrain, and the people support them.

COORDINATED The guerrillas have two advantages: they know the terrain, and the people support them.

17b Avoid faulty coordination by linking only sentences that are clearly and logically connected.

Whenever you hitch together two sentences, make sure they get along. Will the relationship between them be evident to your readers? Have you chosen a coordinating conjunction, conjunctive adverb, or punctuation mark that accurately reflects this relationship?

FAULTY The sportscasters were surprised by Easy Goer's failure to win the Kentucky Derby, but it rained on Derby day.

The writer has not included enough information for the reader to see why these two clauses are connected.

COORDINATED The sportscasters were surprised by Easy Goer's failure to win the Kentucky Derby; *however, he runs poorly on a muddy track*, and it rained on Derby day.

Another route to faulty coordination is a poorly chosen link between clauses.

FAULTY   The sportscasters all expected Easy Goer to win the Kentucky Derby, and Sunday Silence beat him.

The conjunction *and* implies that both clauses reflect the same assumptions. This is not the case, so the writer should choose a conjunction that expresses difference.

COORDINATED   The sportscasters all expected Easy Goer to win the Kentucky Derby, *but* Sunday Silence beat him.

17c *Avoid excessive coordination by linking only sentences that work together to make a coherent point.*

When a writer strings together several clauses in a row, often the result is excessive coordination. Trying to pack too much information into a single sentence can make readers dizzy, unable to pick out which points really matter.

EXCESSIVE   Easy Goer was the Kentucky Derby favorite, and all the sportscasters expected him to win, but he runs poorly on a muddy track, and it rained on Derby day, so Sunday Silence beat him.

What are the main points in this passage? Each key idea deserves its own sentence so that readers will recognize it as important.

REVISED   Easy Goer was the Kentucky Derby favorite, and all the sportscasters expected him to win. However, he runs poorly on a muddy track, and it rained on Derby day; so Sunday Silence beat him.

Excessive coordination also tends to result when a writer uses the same conjunction repeatedly.

EXCESSIVE   Phil was out of the house all day, so he didn't know about the rain, so he went ahead and bet on Easy Goer, so he lost twenty bucks, so now he wants to borrow money from me.

REVISED   Phil was out of the house all day, so he didn't know about the rain. He went ahead and bet on Easy Goer, and he lost twenty bucks. Now he wants to borrow money from me.

One solution to excessive coordination is subordination: making one clause dependent on another instead of giving both clauses equal weight. (See 17d.)

Exercise 17–1

Rewrite the following sentences to add coordination where it is needed and to remove faulty or excessive coordination wherever you find it. Possible revisions for the lettered sentences appear in the back of the book. Example:

The wind was rising, and leaves tossed on the trees, and the air seemed to crackle with electricity, and we knew that a thunderstorm was on the way.

The wind was rising, leaves tossed on the trees, and the air seemed to crackle with electricity. We knew that a thunderstorm was on the way.

a. Congress is expected to pass the biotechnology bill. The president already has said he will veto it.

b. Mortgage rates have dropped. Home buying is likely to increase in the near future.

c. Find Mrs. Fellowes a seat. She looks tired.

d. I left the house in a hurry and ran to the bank so I could cash a check to buy lunch, but it was the bank's anniversary, and the staff was busy serving coffee and cake, so by the time I left, after chatting and eating for twenty minutes, I wasn't hungry anymore.

e. The U.S. Postal Service handles millions of pieces of mail every day. It is the largest postal service in the world.

1. Jackson may go through with his lawsuit. He may settle out of court.

2. If you want to take Spanish this semester, you have only one choice. You must sign up for the 8 a.m. course.

3. Peterson's Market has raised its prices. Last week tuna fish cost $.89 a can. Now it's up to $1.09.

4. Joe starts the morning with a cup of coffee, which wakes him up, and then at lunch he eats a chocolate bar, so that the sugar and caffeine will bring up his energy level.

5. I like Chinese food. I often eat it. Some Szechuan dishes are too hot for me.

17d Use subordination to link an important clause with a related but less important clause.

Subordination is one of the most useful of all writing strategies. By subordinating a less important sentence to a more important one, you show your readers that one fact or idea follows from another or affects another. You stress what counts, thereby encouraging your readers to share your viewpoint—an important goal, whatever you are writing.

When you have two sentences that contain ideas in need of connecting, you can subordinate one to the other in any of the following three ways.

1. Turn the less important sentence into a subordinate clause by introducing it with a subordinating conjunction such as *although*, *because*, *if*, or *when*. (See 1g for a list of subordinating conjunctions.)

Jason has a keen sense of humor. He has an obnoxious, braying laugh.

From that pair of sentences, a reader doesn't know what to feel about Jason. Is he likable or repellent? The writer needs to decide which trait matters more and to emphasize it.

Although Jason has a keen sense of humor, he has an obnoxious, braying laugh.

The revision makes Jason's sense of humor less important than his annoying hee-haw. The less important idea is stated as a subordinate clause opening with *although*, the more important idea as the main clause.

The writer could reverse the meaning by combining the two ideas the other way around:

Although Jason has an obnoxious, braying laugh, he has a keen sense of humor.

That version makes Jason sound fun to be with, despite his mannerism.

Which of Jason's traits to emphasize is up to the writer. What matters is that, in both combined versions of the original two separate sentences, the writer takes a clear stand by making one sentence a main clause and the other a subordinate clause.

2. Turn the less important sentence into a subordinate clause by introducing it with a relative pronoun such as *who*, *which*, or *that*. (See 1b for a list of relative pronouns.)

Jason, *who has an obnoxious, braying laugh*, has a keen sense of humor.

Jason, *whose sense of humor is keen*, has an obnoxious, braying laugh.

3. Turn the less important sentence into a phrase.

Jason, *a keen humorist*, has an obnoxious, braying laugh.

Despite his obnoxious, braying laugh, Jason has a keen sense of humor.

17e Avoid faulty subordination by making sure your main idea is expressed in your main clause.

Sometimes a writer accidentally subordinates a more important idea to a less important idea and turns the sentence's meaning upside down.

> **FAULTY SUBORDINATION** Although the Algonquin Round Table lives on in spirit, the writers who created it are nearly all dead now.

This sentence is factually accurate. Does the writer, however, really want to stress death over life? This is the effect of putting *are nearly all dead* in the main clause and *lives on* in the subordinate clause. Recognizing a case of faulty subordination, the writer can reverse the two clauses.

> **REVISED** Although the writers who created it are nearly all dead now, the Algonquin Round Table lives on in spirit.

17f Avoid excessive subordination by limiting the number of subordinate clauses you use in a sentence.

The cause of excessive subordination is usually that a writer has tried to cram too much information into one sentence. The result is a string of ideas in which readers may not be able to pick out what matters.

EXCESSIVE SUBORDINATION   Debate over the Strategic Defense Initiative (SDI), which was originally proposed as a space-based defensive shield that would protect America from enemy attack, but which critics have suggested amounts to creating a first-strike capability in space, has to some extent focused on the wrong question because it concentrates on the plan's technological flaws and thus fails to consider adequately whether SDI would in fact lower or increase the odds of nuclear war.

In revising this sentence, the writer needs to decide which are the main points and turn each one into a main clause. Lesser points can remain as subordinate clauses, arranged so that each of them gets an appropriate amount of emphasis.

REVISED   Debate over the Strategic Defense Initiative (SDI) has to some extent focused on the wrong question. The plan was originally proposed as a space-based defensive shield that would protect America from enemy attack; but critics have suggested that it amounts to creating a first-strike capability in space. However, most arguments about SDI have concentrated on its technological flaws and thus have failed to consider adequately whether SDI would in fact lower or increase the odds of nuclear war.

Exercise 17–2

Rewrite the following sentences to add subordination where it is appropriate and to remove faulty or excessive subordination wherever you find it. Possible revisions for the lettered sentences appear in the back of the book. Example:

> Some playwrights like to work with performing theater companies. It is helpful to hear a script read aloud by actors.

> Because it is helpful to hear a script read aloud by actors, some playwrights like to work with performing theater companies.

a. Although we occasionally hear horror stories about fruits and vegetables being unsafe to eat because they were sprayed with toxic chemicals or were grown in contaminated soil, the fact remains that, given their high nutritional value, these fresh foods are generally much better for us than processed foods.

b. Renata claims that cats make the best pets. They are adorable, affectionate, and easy to care for.

c. At the end of Verdi's opera *La Traviata,* Alfredo has to see his beloved Violetta again. He knows she is dying and all he can say is good-bye.

d. Violetta gives away her money. She bids adieu to her faithful servant. After that she dies in her lover's arms.

e. Some television cartoon shows have become cult classics. This has happened years after they went off the air. Examples include *Rocky and Bullwinkle* and *George of the Jungle.*

1. Cape Cod is a peninsula in Massachusetts. It juts into the Atlantic Ocean south of Boston. The Cape marks the northern turning point of the Gulf Stream.

2. Renata likes cats. However, her husband bought a German shepherd. He said it would protect their house against intruders.

3. Tim spent his last twenty dollars to buy his mother a big bouquet of flowers. He adores her.

4. Although bank customers have not yet begun to shift their money out of savings accounts, the interest rate on NOW accounts has gone up.

5. I usually have more fun at a concert with Rico than with Morey. Rico loves music. Morey merely tolerates it.

CHAPTER 24

Punctuation

18. End Punctuation   685
19. The Comma   688
20. The Semicolon   699
21. The Colon   702
22. The Apostrophe   705
23. Quotation Marks   709
24. The Dash and the Slash/Virgule   713
25. Parentheses, Brackets, and the Ellipsis Mark   716

18 END PUNCTUATION

Three marks can signal the end of a sentence: the period, the exclamation point, and the question mark.

18a *Use a period to end a declarative sentence, a directive, or an indirect question.*

In Isaac Babel's story "Guy de Maupassant," a character asserts, "No iron can pierce the heart with such force as a period put just at the right place." As a writer you will find many right places to put a period, for it is the mark we use most often to signal a full stop.

685

The great majority of English sentences are *declarative*, meaning simply that they make a statement. No matter what its topic, a declarative sentence properly ends with a period.

Most people on earth are malnourished.

The Cadillac rounded the corner on two wheels and careened into a newsstand.

A period is also used after a *directive*, a statement telling someone to do something.

Please send a check or money order with your application.

Put down your weapons and come out with your hands up.

Some readers are surprised to find a period, not a question mark, at the end of an *indirect question*. But an indirect question is really a kind of declarative sentence: it states that a question was asked or is being asked. Therefore, a period is the right way to end it.

The counselor asked Marcia why she rarely gets to class on time.

I wonder why George didn't show up.

If those sentences were written as *direct questions*, they would require a question mark.

The counselor asked, "Marcia, why do you rarely get to class on time?"

Why, I wonder, didn't George show up?

18b Use a period after most abbreviations, except at the end of a sentence.

A period within a sentence shows that what precedes it has been shortened.

Dr. Hooke's plane arrived in Washington, D.C., at 8:00 P.M.

The names of most organizations (YMCA, PTA), countries (USA, USSR), and people (JFK, FDR) are abbreviated without periods. Other abbreviations, such as those for academic degrees and designations of time, use periods. (See 26e.)

When an abbreviation that uses periods falls at the end of a sentence, follow it with just one period, not two.

Jim hopes to do graduate work at UCLA after receiving his B.A.

18c Use a question mark to end a direct question.

How many angels can dance on the point of a pin?

The question mark comes at the end of the question even if the question is part of a longer declarative sentence. (See 23h for advice about punctuating direct questions.)

"What'll I do now?" Marjorie wailed.

Only if the question is rewritten into indirect form does it end in a period.

Marjorie, wailing, wanted to know what she should do now.

You can use a question mark, also, to indicate doubt about the accuracy of a number or date.

Aristophanes, born in 450 (?) B.C., became the master comic playwright of Greece's Golden Age.

Usually, however, the same purpose can be accomplished more gracefully in words:

Aristophanes, born around 450 B.C., became the master comic playwright of Greece's Golden Age.

In formal writing, avoid using a question mark to express irony or sarcasm: *her generous (?) gift.* If your doubts are worth including, state them directly: *her meager but highly publicized gift.*

18d Use an exclamation point to end an interjection, an urgent command, or a statement that calls for emphasis.

An exclamation point signals strong, even violent, emotion. Because most essays appeal to readers' reason more than to their passions, you will rarely need to use this punctuation mark in expository writing. If you do, it may be for the kind of short, emphatic incomplete sentence known as an *interjection*. (See 1h.)

Oh, no! Fire!

Or you may use an exclamation point for an urgent directive.

Hurry up! Help me!

An exclamation point can end any sentence that requires unusually strong emphasis.

We've struck an iceberg! We're sinking! I can't believe it! This is horrible!

In newspaper parlance, exclamation points are *astonishers*. Although they can grab a reader's attention, they cannot hold it. Tossing in an exclamation point, as if it were a firecracker, is no substitute for emphatic writing that carefully selects its words.

Exercise 18–1

Where appropriate, correct the end punctuation and internal periods in the following sentences. Give reasons for any changes you make. Some sentences may be correct. Answers for the lettered sentences appear in the back of the book. Example:

Mary asked if George could manage to get to the church on time?

Mary asked if George could manage to get to the church on time.

a. Unlike Gerald Ford and L.B.J., who came to the vice-presidency from Congress, President Bush won that office after heading the C.I.A..

b. The population of California is much greater than that of Nevada!

c. Do you think I'm going to clean up this mess.

d. "When will the world end," my four-year-old nephew asked in a quavering voice?

e. Yes! The Republicans are worried about the gender gap! They fear that women in increasing numbers will vote for the Democrats! How can the Republicans fight back!

1. If you're too cold, why don't you just switch off the air conditioner.

2. "Help, help. It's a murder. Call the police," cried Jim.

3. Jim asked the officer how else the woman would have been strangled by her own scarf?

4. "Does it make sense to you?" he asked, "that she did that herself?"

5. In the history of the Cape Cod Community Players (C.C.C.P.), only one managing director has had an MA in theater.

6. Where do we go from here!

7. I didn't ask Sylvia, "Will you go to the meeting?" I told her, "You *will* go to the meeting!"

8. How do you expect me to learn the Latin names of fifty plants in an hour.

9. "Why is the sky blue" is a question that any physicist can answer.

10. Don't you think that teachers' salaries ought to be higher than they are!

19 THE COMMA

Speech without pauses would be hard to listen to. Likewise, writing without commas would make hard reading. Like a split-second pause in conversation, a **comma** helps your readers to catch the train of your thought. It keeps them, time and again, from stumbling over a solid block of words. A comma can direct readers' attention, pointing them to what you want them to notice. And a well-placed comma can prevent misreading: it keeps your audience from drawing an inaccurate conclusion about what you are trying to tell them.

Consider the following sentence:

Lyman paints fences and bowls.

From this statement, we can deduce that Lyman is a painter who works with both a large and a small brush. But add commas before and after *fences* and the portrait changes:

Lyman paints, fences, and bowls.

Now our man wields a paintbrush, a sword, and a bowling ball. What the reader learns about Lyman's activities depends on how the writer punctuates the sentence. Carefully placed commas prevent misreading and ensure that readers meet the real Lyman.

19a *Use a comma to join two main clauses with* **and, but,** *or another coordinating conjunction.*

The joint between clauses has two parts: a coordinating conjunction (*and, but, for, or, nor, so,* or *yet*) and a comma. The comma comes after the first clause, right before the conjunction.

> The chocolate pie whooshed through the air, and it landed in Lyman's face.
>
> The pie whooshed with deadly aim, but the agile Lyman ducked.

If your clauses are short and parallel in structure, you may omit the comma.

> Spring passed and summer came.
>
> They urged but I refused.

Or you may keep the comma. It can lend your words a speechlike ring, throwing a bit of emphasis on your second clause.

> Spring passed, and summer came.
>
> They urged, but I refused.

CAUTION: Don't use a comma with a coordinating conjunction that links two phrases or that links a phrase and a clause.

> FAULTY   The mustangs galloped, and cavorted across the plain.
>
> REVISED   The mustangs galloped and cavorted across the plain.

THE COMMA AT A GLANCE

USES OF COMMAS

- Between two main clauses joined with a coordinating conjunction. (19a)
- After an introductory clause, phrase, or word. (19b)
- Between items in a series. (19c)
- Between adjectives that are separate and equal modifiers of the same noun (but not between adjectives that depend on each other). (19d)
- Before and after a nonrestrictive phrase or clause. (19e)

See rules 19f–19l for further uses of the comma.
See rule 19m for inappropriate uses of the comma.

19b *Use a comma after an introductory clause, phrase, or word.*

> *Weeping,* Lydia stumbled down the stairs.
>
> *Before that,* Arthur saw her reading an old love letter.
>
> *If he knew who the writer was,* he didn't tell.

Placed after any such opening word, phrase, or subordinate clause, a comma tells your reader: "Enough preliminaries—now the main clause starts." (See 3 for a quick refresher on phrases and clauses.)

EXCEPTION: You need not use a comma after a single introductory word or a short phrase or clause if there is no danger of misreading.

> *Sooner or later* Lydia will tell us the whole story.

Exercise 19–1

Add any necessary commas to the following sentences and remove any commas that do not belong. Some sentences may be correct. Answers for the lettered sentences appear in the back of the book. Example:

> Your dog may have sharp teeth but my lawyer can bite harder.
>
> Your dog may have sharp teeth, but my lawyer can bite harder.

a. When Enrique gets to Paris I hope he'll drop me a line.

b. Beethoven's deafness kept him from hearing his own music yet he continued to compose.

c. Debbie plans to apply for a grant, and if her application is accepted, she intends to spend a year in Venezuela.

d. The cherries are overripe for picking has been delayed.

e. The robin yanked at the worm, but was unable to pull it from the ground.

1. During the summer of the great soybean failure Larry took little interest in national affairs.

2. Unaware of the world he slept, and grew within his mother's womb.

3. While across the nation farmers were begging for mortgages he swam without a care.

4. Neither the mounting agricultural crisis, nor any other current events, disturbed his tranquillity.

5. In fact you might have called him irresponsible.

19c *Use commas between items in a series.*

When you list three or more items, whether they are nouns, verbs, adjectives, adverbs, or entire phrases or clauses, separate them with commas.

> Country ham, sweet corn, tacos, bratwurst, and Indian pudding weighted Aunt Gertrude's table.

Joel prefers music that shakes, rattles, and rolls.

In one afternoon, we rode a Mississippi riverboat, climbed the Matterhorn, voyaged beneath the sea, and flew on a rocket through space.

Notice that no comma *follows* the final item in the series.

NOTE: Some writers (especially Britons and journalists) omit the comma *before* the final item in the series. This custom has no noticeable advantage. It has the disadvantages of throwing off the rhythm of a sentence and, in some cases, obscuring the writer's meaning. Using the comma in such a case is never wrong; omitting it can create confusion.

I was met at the station by my cousins, brother and sister.

Who are these people? Are they a brother-and-sister pair who are the writer's cousins or a group consisting of the writer's cousins, her brother, and her sister? One comma would clear up the confusion:

I was met at the station by my cousins, brother, and sister.

19d Use commas between adjectives that are separate and equal modifiers of the same noun, but not between adjectives that depend on each other.

Adjectives that function independently of each other, even though they modify the same noun, are called **coordinate adjectives**. Set them off with commas.

Ruth was a clear, vibrant, persuasive speaker.

Life is nasty, brutish, and short.

To check whether adjectives are coordinate, apply two tests. Can you rearrange the adjectives without distorting the meaning of the sentence? (*Ruth was a persuasive, vibrant, clear speaker.*) Can you insert *and* between them? (*Life is nasty and brutish and short.*)

If the answer to both questions is yes, the adjectives are coordinate. Removing any one of them would not greatly affect the others' impact. Use commas between them to show that they are separate and equal.

NOTE: If you choose to link coordinate adjectives with *and* or another conjunction, omit the commas.

New York City is huge and dirty and beautiful.

Cumulative adjectives work together to create a single unified picture of the noun they modify. Remove any one of them and you change the picture. No commas separate cumulative adjectives.

Ruth has two small white poodles.

Who's afraid of the big bad wolf?

If you rearrange cumulative adjectives or insert *and* between them, the effect of the sentence is distorted (*two white small poodles; the big and bad wolf*).

Exercise 19–2

Add any necessary commas to the following sentences; remove any commas that do not belong; and change any punctuation that strikes you as incorrect. Some sentences may be correct. Revisions for the lettered sentences appear in the back of the book. Example:

> Mel has been a faithful hard-working consistent pain in the neck.
>
> Mel has been a faithful, hard-working, consistent pain in the neck.

a. Mrs. Carver looks like a sweet, little, old lady, but she plays a wicked electric guitar.

b. Her bass player, her drummer and her keyboard player all live at the same rest home.

c. They practice individually in the afternoon, rehearse together at night and play at the home's Saturday night dances.

d. The Rest Home Rebels have to rehearse quietly, and cautiously, to keep from disturbing the other residents.

e. Mrs. Carver has two Fender guitars, a Stratocaster and a Telecaster, and she also has an acoustic twelve-string Gibson.

1. When she breaks a string, she doesn't want her elderly crew to have to grab the guitar change the string and hand it back to her, before the song ends.

2. The Rest Home Rebels' favorite bands are U-2, the Talking Heads and Lester Lanin and his orchestra.

3. They watch a lot of MTV because it is fast-paced colorful exciting and informative and it has more variety than soap operas.

4. Just once, Mrs. Carver wants to play in a really, huge, sold-out, arena.

5. She hopes to borrow the rest home's big, white, van to take herself her band and their equipment to a major, professional, downtown, recording studio.

19e Use commas to set off a modifying phrase or clause only when it does not restrict the meaning of what it modifies.

A **nonrestrictive modifier** adds a fact that, while perhaps interesting and valuable, isn't essential. You could leave it out of the sentence and still make good sense. When a word in your sentence is modified by a nonrestrictive phrase or clause, set off the modifier with commas before and after it.

> Potts Alley, *which runs north from Chestnut Street*, is too narrow and crowded for cars to get through.
>
> At the end of the alley, *where the street fair booksale was held last summer*, a getaway car waited.

A **restrictive modifier** is essential. Omit it and you significantly change the meaning of both the modified word and the sentence. Such a modifier is called *restrictive* because it limits what it modifies: we are talking about this specific place, person, action, or whatever, and no other. Because a restrictive modifier is part of the identity of whatever it modifies, no commas set it off from the rest of the sentence.

> They picked the alley *that runs north from Chestnut Street* because it is close to the highway.
>
> Anyone *who robs my house* will regret it.

Leave out the modifier in that last sentence—write instead *Anyone will regret it*—and you change the meaning of your subject from potential robbers to all humankind.

Here are two more examples to help you tell a nonrestrictive modifier, which you set off with commas, from a restrictive modifier, which you don't.

> White Russians, who smoke, live to be 120.
>
> White Russians who smoke live to be 120.

See what a difference a couple of commas make? The first sentence declares that all White Russians smoke, but they nevertheless live to old age. The second sentence singles out smokers from the rest of the population and declares that they reach 120.

NOTE: Use *that* to introduce (or to recognize) a restrictive phrase or clause. Use *which* to introduce (or to recognize) a nonrestrictive phrase or clause.

> The food *that I love best* is chocolate.
>
> Chocolate, *which I love*, is not on my diet.

19f Use commas to set off an appositive only if it does not restrict the noun it renames.

An **appositive** is a noun or noun phrase that renames or amplifies the noun it follows. (See 3d.) Like the modifiers discussed in 19e, an appositive can be either restrictive or nonrestrictive. If it is nonrestrictive—if the sentence still makes sense when the appositive is omitted or changed—then set it off with commas before and after.

> My third ex-husband, *Hugo,* will be glad to meet you.
>
> We are bringing dessert, *a blueberry pie,* to follow your wonderful dinner.
>
> Hugo created the recipe for his latest cookbook, *Pies! Surprise!*

If the appositive is restrictive—if you can't take it out or change it without changing your meaning—then include it without commas.

> Of all the men I've been married to, my ex-husband *Hugo* is the best cook.
>
> His cookbook *Pies! Surprise!* is selling better than his beef, wine, and fruit cookbooks.

Exercise 19–3

Add any necessary commas to the following sentences and remove any commas that do not belong. You may have to draw your own conclusions about what the writer meant to say. Some sentences may be correct. Revisions for the lettered sentences appear in the back of the book. Example:

> Jay and his wife the former Nancy Montez were high school sweethearts.
>
> Jay and his wife, the former Nancy Montez, were high school sweethearts.

a. The rain which wasn't due until tomorrow is falling right now.

b. The party, a dismal occasion ended earlier than we had expected.

c. Secretary Stern warned that the concessions, that the West was prepared to make, would be withdrawn if not matched by the East.

d. Although both of Don's children are blond, his daughter Sharon has darker hair than his son Jake.

e. Herbal tea which has no caffeine makes a better after-dinner drink than coffee.

1. The emerald, that Richard gave Elizabeth, is more valuable than the famous family diamonds, which went to his brother's wife.

2. If the base commanders had checked their gun room where powder is stored, they would have found several hundred pounds missing.

3. Brazil's tropical rain forests which help produce the air we breathe all over the world, are being cut down at an alarming rate.

4. Senator Edward Kennedy's late brothers, Joe and Jack, were older than his third brother, Bobby.

5. Mr. O'Neil told me that by next Monday, which is the day we agreed to meet, the issue already will have been decided.

19g Use commas to set off conjunctive adverbs such as furthermore, however, and nevertheless and parenthetical expressions.

A key function of the comma, as you probably have noticed, is to insert material into a sentence. To perform this service, commas work in pairs. When you drop a conjunctive adverb into the midst of a clause, set it off with commas before and after it. (See 1g for a full list of conjunctive adverbs.)

> Using lead paint in homes has been illegal, *however*, since 1973.
>
> Builders, *indeed*, gave it up some twenty years earlier.

Use a pair of commas around any parenthetical expression—that is, a transitional expression (*for example, as a result, in contrast*) or any kind of aside from you to your reader.

> Professional home inspectors, *for this reason*, are often asked to test for lead paint.
>
> The idea, *of course,* is to protect small children who might eat flaking paint.
>
> The Cosmic Construction Company never used lead paint, *or so their spokesperson says*, even when it was legal.

19h   *Use commas to set off a phrase or clause expressing contrast.*

> It was Rudolph, *not Dasher*, who had a red nose.

EXCEPTION: Short contrasting phrases beginning with *but* need not be set off by commas.

> It was not Dasher but Rudolph who had a red nose.

19i   *Use commas to set off any phrase that modifies a whole clause.*

An **absolute phrase** modifies an entire clause rather than a single word. (See 3c.) The link between an absolute phrase and the rest of the sentence is a comma, or two commas if the phrase falls in mid-sentence.

> *Our worst fears drawing us together*, we huddled over the telegram.
>
> Luke, *his knife being the sharpest*, slit the envelope.

Exercise 19–4

Add any necessary commas to the following sentences, remove any commas that do not belong, and change any inappropriate punctuation. Revisions for the lettered sentences appear in the back of the book. Example:

> The screenwriter unlike the director, believes the film should be shown unedited.
>
> The screenwriter, unlike the director, believes the film should be shown unedited.

a. Before we begin however I want to thank everyone who made this evening possible.

b. Our speaker, listed in your program as a professor, tells us that on the contrary she is a teaching assistant.

c. The discussion that followed was not so much a debate, as a free-for-all.

d. Alex insisted that predestination not free will shapes human destiny.

e. Shirley on the other hand, who looks so calm, passionately defended the role of choice.

1. Philosophy not being one of my strong points I was unable to contribute much to the argument.
2. The car rolled down the hill, a problem Bill should have anticipated when he left it in gear and crashed into a telephone pole.
3. This attic apartment its windows notwithstanding, is very hot in summer.
4. The orchard smelled fruity and felt squishy underfoot; hundreds of apples having fallen from the trees.
5. Not Jerome in the judge's opinion but Lewis was responsible for the accident.

19j Use commas to set off a quotation from your own words, and vice versa.

When you briefly quote someone, distinguish the source's words from yours with commas (and, of course, quotation marks). When you insert an explanation into a quotation (such as *he said*), set that off with commas.

> It was Shakespeare who wrote, "Some are born great, some achieve greatness, and some have greatness thrust upon them."

> "The best thing that can come with success," commented the actress Liv Ullman, "is the knowledge that it is nothing to long for."

Notice that the comma always comes *before* the quotation marks. (For more on how to use other punctuation with quotation marks, see 23h.)

> **EXCEPTION:** Do not use a comma with a very short quotation or one introduced by *that*.

> Don't tell me "yes" if you mean "maybe."

> Jules said that "Nothing ventured, nothing gained" is his motto.

Don't use a comma with any quotation that is run into your own sentence and that reads as part of your sentence. Often such quotations are introduced by linking verbs.

> Her favorite statement at age three was "I can do it myself."

> It was Shakespeare who originated the expression "my salad days, when I was green in judgment."

19k Use commas around yes and no, mild interjections, tag questions, and the name or title of someone directly addressed.

YES AND NO	*Yes*, I would like to own a Rolls-Royce, but, *no*, I didn't place an order for one.
INTERJECTIONS	*Well*, don't blame it on me.
TAG QUESTIONS	It would be fun to drive down Main Street in a Silver Cloud, *wouldn't it?*
DIRECT ADDRESS	Drive us home, *James*.

19l   *Use commas to set off dates, states, countries, and addresses.*

On June 6, 1969, Ned Shaw was born.

East Rutherford, New Jersey, seemed like Paris, France, to him.

Shortly after his tenth birthday his family moved to 11 Maple Street, Middletown, Ohio.

NOTE: Do not use a comma between a state and a zip code: *Bedford, MA 01730.*

Exercise 19–5

Add any necessary commas to the following sentences, remove any commas that do not belong, and change any inappropriate punctuation. Some sentences may be correct. Revisions for the lettered sentences appear in the back of the book. Example:

> When Alexander Graham Bell said "Mr. Watson come here, I want you" the telephone entered history.

> When Alexander Graham Bell said, "Mr. Watson, come here, I want you," the telephone entered history.

a. On October 2 1969 the future discoverer of antigravity tablets was born.

b. Corwin P. Grant entered the world while his parents were driving to a hospital in Costa Mesa California.

c. The car radio was playing that old song "Be My Baby."

d. Today ladies and gentlemen Corwin enjoys worldwide renown.

e. Schoolchildren from Augusta Maine to Azuza California can recite his famous comment "It was my natural levity that led me to overcome gravity."

1. I don't mean to prod you Belinda, but yes that was your cue.

2. Move downstage Gary, for Pete's sake or you'll run into Mrs. Clackett.

3. Vicki my precious, when you say, "great" or "terrific," look as though you mean it.

4. As your director darling I am not responsible for your props.

5. Well Dotty, it only makes sense that when you say, "Sardines!," you should go off to get the sardines.

19m   *Avoid misusing or overusing commas.*

Commas break your writing into units that your reader can absorb more easily. Used in the wrong places, however, they can puzzle or mislead your reader. When pauses would clarify your meaning, put in commas; but don't salt and pepper your prose with them.

Here is a short summary of when *not* to use commas.

1. Do not use a comma to separate a subject from its verb or a verb from its object.

FAULTY   The slim athlete driving the purple Jaguar, was the Reverend Mr. Fuld. [Subject separated from verb.]

REVISED   The slim athlete driving the purple Jaguar was the Reverend Mr. Fuld.

FAULTY   The new president should not have given his campaign manager, such a prestigious appointment. [Verb separated from direct object.]

REVISED   The new president should not have given his campaign manager such a prestigious appointment.

2. Do not use a comma between words or phrases joined by a coordinating conjunction.

Be careful not to divide a compound subject or predicate unnecessarily with a comma.

FAULTY   Neither Peter Pan, nor the fairy Tinkerbell, saw the pirates sneaking toward their hideout. [Compound subject.]

REVISED   Neither Peter Pan nor the fairy Tinkerbell saw the pirates sneaking toward their hideout.

FAULTY   The chickens clucked, and pecked, and flapped their wings. [Compound predicate.]

REVISED   The chickens clucked and pecked and flapped their wings.

3. Do not use a comma before the first or after the last item in a series.

FAULTY   We had to see, my mother's doctor, my father's lawyer, and my dog's veterinarian, in one afternoon.

REVISED   We had to see my mother's doctor, my father's lawyer, and my dog's veterinarian in one afternoon.

4. Do not use a comma to set off a restrictive word, phrase or clause.

A restrictive modifier is essential to the definition or identification of whatever it modifies; a nonrestrictive modifier is not. If you are not sure whether an element in your sentence is restrictive, review 19e.

FAULTY   The fireworks, that I saw on Sunday, were the best ones I've ever seen.

REVISED   The fireworks that I saw on Sunday were the best ones I've ever seen.

5. Do not use commas to set off indirect quotations.

When *that* introduces a quotation, the quotation is an indirect one and requires neither a comma nor quotation marks.

FAULTY   He told us that, we shouldn't have done it.

FAULTY   He told us that, "You shouldn't have done it."

REVISED   He told us that we shouldn't have done it.

This sentence also would be correct if it were recast as a direct quotation, with a comma and quotation marks.

REVISED   He told us, "You shouldn't have done that."

20   THE SEMICOLON

The semicolon has two main uses: as a weakling Clark Kent period and as a powerful Supercomma. As its appearance implies, a semicolon is a sort of compromise between a comma and a period: it creates a stop without ending a sentence.

20a   *Use a semicolon to join two main clauses that are closely related in sense but are not joined by a coordinating conjunction.*

Suppose, having written one statement, you want to add another. You could start a new sentence, but let's say that both statements are closely related in sense. You decide to keep them both in a single sentence.

> Shooting clay pigeons was my mother's favorite sport; she would smash them for hours at a time.

A semicolon is a good substitute for a period when you don't want to bring your readers to a complete stop.

> By the yard life is hard; by the inch it's a cinch.

> I never travel without my diary; one should always have something sensational to read in the train.
> —Oscar Wilde

Remember that usually, when you join two statements with a coordinating conjunction (*and, but, for, or, nor, so, yet*), no semicolon is called for—just use a comma. (For exceptions to this general rule, see 20d.)

THE SEMICOLON AT A GLANCE

USES OF THE SEMICOLON

- To join two main clauses that are closely related in sense but are not joined with a coordinating conjunction. (20a)
- To join two main clauses that are linked by a conjunctive adverb. (20b)
- To separate items in a series that contain internal punctuation or that are long and complex. (20c)
- To separate main clauses that contain internal punctuation or that are long and complex, even if they are joined by a coordinating conjunction. (20d)

Do not use a semicolon to separate a phrase or subordinate clause from the rest of the sentence; use a comma. (20e)

20b Use a semicolon to join two main clauses that are linked by a conjunctive adverb.

When the second of two statements begins with (or includes) a conjunctive adverb, you can join it to the first statement with a semicolon. Common conjunctive adverbs include *also, consequently, however, indeed, nevertheless, still, therefore,* and *thus.* (For a complete list, see 1g.)

> Bert is a stand-out player; *indeed,* he's the one hope of our team.

> We yearned to attend the concert; tickets, *however,* were hard to come by.

Note in the second sentence that the conjunctive adverb falls within the second main clause. No matter where the conjunctive adverb appears, the semicolon is placed between the two clauses.

20c Use a semicolon to separate items in a series that contain internal punctuation or that are long and complex.

In its role as Supercomma, the semicolon is especially useful for setting off one group of items from another. More powerfully than a comma, it divides a series of series.

> The auctioneer sold clocks, watches, and cameras; freezers of steaks and tons of bean sprouts; motorcycles, cars, speedboats, canoes, and cabin cruisers; and rare coins, curious stamps, and precious stones.

If the writer had used commas in place of semicolons in that sentence, the divisions would have been harder to notice.

Commas are not the only internal punctuation that warrants the extra force of semicolons between items.

> The auctioneer sold clocks and watches (with or without hands); freezers of steaks and tons of bean sprouts; trucks and motorcycles (some of which had working engines); and dozens of smaller items.

20d Use a semicolon to separate main clauses that contain internal punctuation or that are long and complex, even if they are joined by a coordinating conjunction.

Another job for Supercomma is rescuing a long sentence of two or more clauses, at least one of which contains internal punctuation.

> Though we had grown up together, laughing and playing like brother and sister, I had never regarded Spike as a possible lover; and his abrupt proposal took me by surprise.

In that sentence, an important break between clauses needs a mark stronger than a comma to give it impact. A semicolon is appropriate, even though it stands before a coordinating conjunction—where, ordinarily, a comma would suffice.

You can see the difference between a compound sentence joined with a comma and one joined with a semicolon in these examples:

> Captain Bob planned the hog-riding contest for Thursday, but it rained.
>
> Captain Bob, that old cynic, planned the hog-riding contest for Thursday despite a ban by the city council; but it rained.

You would not be wrong if you kept the original comma between clauses. The sentence is easier to read, however, with a semicolon at its main intersection.

A semicolon can do the same job for clauses that contain internal punctuation other than commas.

> Captain Bob—that cynical crowd assembler—planned the hog-riding contest for Thursday (although the city council had banned such events); but it rained.

You also can use a semicolon with a coordinating conjunction to link clauses that have no internal punctuation but that are long and complex.

> The powers behind Her Majesty's secret service occasionally deem it advisable to terminate the infiltrations of an enemy agent by ending his life; and in such cases they generally call on James Bond.

20e *Use a comma, not a semicolon, to separate a phrase or subordinate clause from the rest of a sentence.*

Remember that a semicolon has the force of a period; its job is to create a strong pause in a sentence, especially between main clauses. When your purpose is simply to add a phrase to a clause, use a comma, not a semicolon.

> FAULTY   The road is long; winding through many towns.
>
> REVISED   The road is long, winding through many towns.

Similarly, use a comma, not a semicolon, to join a subordinate clause to a main clause.

> FAULTY   Columbus sailed unknowingly toward the New World; while Ferdinand and Isabella waited for news from China.
>
> REVISED   Columbus sailed unknowingly toward the New World, while Ferdinand and Isabella waited for news from China.

Exercise 20–1

Repunctuate the following sentences as necessary, adding semicolons when they are needed and changing any that are incorrectly used. Some sentences may be correct. Revisions for the lettered sentences appear in the back of the book. Example:

> If you knew all the facts; you would see that I am right.
>
> If you knew all the facts, you would see that I am right.

a. Gasoline prices almost always rise at the start of tourist season, this year will be no exception.

b. I disagree with your point, however I appreciate your reasons for stating it.

c. The garden is a spectacular display of fountains and gargoyles, beds of lilies, zinnias, and hollyhocks, bushes shaped like animals, climbing roses, wisteria, and ivy, and lawns as wide as golf greens.

d. Luther missed the conference in Montreal; but he plans to attend the one in Memphis.

e. Dr. Elliott's intervention in the dispute was well intentioned, nevertheless it was unfortunate.

1. The banquet menu included soup; fish; roast beef; ham; a variety of vegetables; a cheese board; and salad.

2. If that shyster deceives you once, shame on him, if he deceives you twice, shame on you.

3. A Newfoundland dog is huge and furry; much like a Saint Bernard.

4. Senator Blank favors increasing state aid to small businesses, he believes however that such a bill cannot pass this year.

5. A robin's red breast is the color of rust, a grosbeak's is the rosier hue of maraschino cherries.

6. The town council voted to approve the affordable housing project, a decision that may, over time, lead to a tax increase.

7. If the residents and tourists of Athens were willing to leave their automobiles outside the city, air pollution would not threaten the caryatids on the Acropolis, but the impracticality of banning cars has forced authorities to move those stone maidens to a museum.

8. The resolution must pass by a two-thirds majority, otherwise it fails and its supporters must reintroduce it next year.

9. The Democrats on the Ways and Means Committee are hoping the bill will pass; for they are its primary supporters.

10. Don't listen to Dr. Bromberg, she doesn't understand the situation.

21 THE COLON

A colon introduces a further thought, one added to throw light on a first. In using it, a writer declares: "What follows will clarify what I've just said."

> Her Majesty's navy has three traditions: rum, sodomy, and the lash.
> —Winston Churchill

Some writers use a capital letter to start any complete sentence that follows a colon; others prefer a lowercase letter. Both habits are acceptable; but whichever you choose, be consistent. A *phrase* that follows a colon always begins with a lowercase letter.

21a *Use a colon between two main clauses if the second exemplifies, explains, or summarizes the first.*

Like a semicolon, a colon can join two sentences into one. The chief difference is this: a semicolon says merely that two main clauses are related; a colon says that the second clause gives an example or explanation of the point made in the first clause. You can think of a colon as an abbreviation for *that is* or *for example.*

> Mayor Curley was famed as a silver-tongued orator: it is said that, with a few well-chosen words, he could extract campaign contributions from a mob intent on seeing him hanged.

> She tried everything: she scoured the library, made dozens of phone calls, wrote letters, even consulted a lawyer.

21b *Use a colon after* the following *or* as follows *or to introduce a series or an appositive.*

A colon can introduce a word, a phrase, or a series as well as a second main clause. Sometimes the introduction is made stronger by *as follows* or *the following.*

> The dance steps are as follows: forward, back, turn, and glide.

> Engrave the following truth upon your memory: a colon is always constructed of two dots.

When a colon introduces a series of words or phrases, it often means *such as* or *for instance.* A list of examples after a colon need not include *and* before the last item unless all possible examples have been stated.

> On a Saturday night many different kinds of people crowd our downtown area: gamblers, drifters, bored senior citizens, college students out for a good time.

A colon also can introduce an *appositive,* a noun or noun phrase that renames another noun.

> I have discovered the key to the future: plastics.

21c *Use a colon to introduce a long or comma-heavy quotation.*

Sometimes you can't conveniently introduce a quoted passage with a comma. Perhaps the quotation is too long or heavily punctuated; perhaps your prefatory remarks demand a longer pause than a comma provides. In either case, use a colon.

> God told Adam and Eve: "Be fruitful, and multiply, and replenish the earth, and subdue it."

21d *Use a colon after the salutation in a formal letter; in citing books of the Bible; in citing the title and subtitle of a book; in citing the city and publisher of a book; and in naming times of day.*

AFTER A SALUTATION	Dear Professor James:
	Dear Sir or Madam:
BIBLICAL CITATIONS	Genesis 4:7 [The book of Genesis, chapter four, seventh verse.]
BOOK TITLES AND SUBTITLES	*In the Beginning: Creation Stories from around the World*
	Convergences: Essays on Art and Literature
SOURCE REFERENCES	Welty, Eudora. *The Eye of the Story: Selected Essays and Reviews.* New York: Random, 1978.
TIME OF DAY	2:02 P.M.

21e *Use a colon only at the end of a main clause, not after a word or phrase.*

In a sentence, a colon always follows a clause, never a phrase. Any time you are in doubt about whether to use a colon, first make sure that the preceding statement is a complete sentence. Then you will not litter your writing with unnecessary colons.

FAULTY	My mother and father are: Jill and Jim.
REVISED	My mother and father are Jill and Jim.
FAULTY	Many great inventors have changed our lives, such as: Edison, Marconi, and Hymie Glutz.
REVISED	Many great inventors have changed our lives, such as Edison, Marconi, and Hymie Glutz. *Or* Many great inventors have changed our lives: Edison, Marconi, Hymie Glutz.

Use either *such as* or a colon. You don't need both.

Exercise 21–1

Add, cut, or substitute colons wherever appropriate in the following sentences. If necessary, rewrite to support your changes in punctuation. Some sentences may be correct. Revisions for the lettered sentences appear in the back of the book. Example:

Yum-Yum Burger has franchises in the following cities; New York, Chicago, Miami, San Francisco, and Seattle.

Yum-Yum Burger has franchises in the following cities: New York, Chicago, Miami, San Francisco, and Seattle.

a. The personnel director explained that the job requirements include: typing, filing, and answering telephones.

b. The interview ended with a test of skills, taking dictation, operating the switchboard, proofreading documents, and typing a sample letter.

c. The sample letter began, "Dear Mr. Jones, Please accept our apologies for the late shipment."

d. Candace quoted Proverbs 8, 18: "Riches and honor are with me."

e. A book that profoundly impressed me was Kurt Vonnegut's *Cat's Cradle* (New York, Dell, 1963).

1. The following line is my favorite, "It is not possible to make a mistake."

2. You should have no trouble starting the car if you remember three important steps: depress the clutch, turn the key, and press briefly on the accelerator.

3. These are my dreams, to ride in a horse-drawn sleigh, to fly in a small plane, to gallop down a beach on horseback, and to cross the ocean in a sailboat.

4. The reason for the delay is: The train left Philadelphia twenty minutes late.

5. Paris at night presents an array of characters; sidewalk artists, jugglers, and break-dancers; rap musicians and one-man bands; hippies, bohemians, and amazed tourists.

6. He ended his speech with a quotation from Homer's *Iliad,* "Whoever obeys the gods, to him they particularly listen."

7. To get onto Route 6: take Bay Lane to Old Stage Road, turn right, and go straight to the end.

8. Professor Bligh's book is called *Management, A Networking Approach.*

9. George handed Cynthia a note, "Meet me after class under the big clock on Main Street."

10. She expected to arrive at 4.10, but she didn't get there until 4.20.

22 THE APOSTROPHE

Use apostrophes for three purposes: to show possession, to indicate an omission, and to add an ending to a number, letter, or abbreviation.

22a To make a singular noun possessive, add an apostrophe followed by -s.

The *plumber's* wrench left grease stains on *Harry's* shirt.

Even when your singular noun ends with the sound of *s*, form its possessive case by adding *-'s.*

Felix's roommate enjoys reading *Henry James's* novels.

Some writers find it awkward to add *-'s* to nouns that already end in an *-s,* especially those of two syllables or more. You may, if you wish, form such a possessive by adding only an apostrophe.

The Egyptian king *Cheops'* death occurred more than two thousand years before *Socrates'.*

22b *To make a plural noun ending in -s possessive, add an apostrophe.*

> A *stockbrokers'* meeting combines *foxes'* cunning with the noisy chaos of a *boys'* locker room.

22c *To make a plural noun not ending in -s possessive, add an apostrophe and -s.*

Nouns such as *men, mice, geese,* and *alumni* form the possessive case the same way as singular nouns: with *-'s.*

> What effect has the *women's* liberation movement had on *children's* literature?

22d *To show joint possession by two people or groups, add an apostrophe or -'s to the second noun of the pair.*

> I left my *mother and father's* house with our *friends and neighbors'* good wishes.

If the two members of a noun pair possess a set of things individually, add an apostrophe or *-'s* to each noun.

> *Men's* and *women's* marathon records are improving steadily.

22e *To make a compound noun possessive, add an apostrophe or -'s to the last word in the compound.*

A compound noun consists of more than one word (*commander in chief, sons-in-law*); it may be either singular or plural. (See 32a–3 for plurals of compound words.)

> The *commander in chief's* duties will end on July 1.
>
> Esther does not approve of her *sons-in-law's* professions, but she is glad to see her daughters happily married.

22f *To make an indefinite pronoun* (anyone, nobody) *possessive, add -'s.*

> What caused the accident is *anybody's* guess; but it appears to be *no one's* fault.

22g *To make a personal pronoun* (you, she, who) *possessive, use its possessive case.*

Personal pronouns are irregular; each one has its own possessive form. No possessive personal pronoun contains an apostrophe. If you are ever tempted to make a personal pronoun possessive by adding an apostrophe or *-'s,* resist the temptation.

POSSESSIVE CASE OF PERSONAL PRONOUNS

PERSONAL PRONOUN	POSSESSIVE CASE
I	my, mine
you	your, yours (*not* your's)
he	his
she	her, hers (*not* her's)
it	its (*not* it's)
we	our, ours (*not* our's)
they	their, theirs (*not* their's)
who	whose (*not* who's)

NOTE: If you learn nothing else this year, learn when to write *its* (no apostrophe) and when to write *it's* (with an apostrophe). *Its* is always a possessive pronoun.

I retreated when the Murphys' German shepherd bared *its* fangs.

It's is always a contraction.

It's [It is] not our fault.

It's [It has] been a memorable evening.

22h Use an apostrophe to show the omission of one or more letters or numbers in a contraction.

They're [They are] too sophisticated for me.

I've [I have] learned my lesson.

Pat *didn't* [did not] finish her assignment.

Bill's [Bill has] been in jail for a week.

Americans grow up admiring the Spirit of *'76* [1776].

It's nearly eight *o'clock* [of the clock].

When you are presented to the Queen, say "Your Majesty"; after that, say "*Ma'am*" [Madam].

22i Use an apostrophe to form the plural of an abbreviation and of a letter, word, or number mentioned as a word.

ABBREVIATION	Do we need I.D.'s at YMCA's outside our hometown?
LETTER	How many *n*'s are there in *Cincinnati*?
WORD	Try replacing all the *should*'s in that sentence with *could*'s.
NUMBER	Cut out two *3*'s to sew on Larry's shirt.

NOTE: A letter, word, or number named as a word is usually italicized (underlined).

EXCEPTION: To refer to the years in a decade, simply add -*s* without an apostrophe.

The 1980s differed greatly from the 1970s.

22j Use apostrophes with care and restraint when you pluralize nouns.

FAULTY　Are the Jones' coming to the barbecue?
REVISED　Are the Joneses coming to the barbecue?
FAULTY　How many kitten's did their cat have?
REVISED　How many kittens did their cat have?
FAULTY　I'm going over to the Hicks's house.
REVISED　I'm going over to the Hickses' house.

Exercise 22–1

Correct any errors in the use of the apostrophe and other related usage in the following sentences. Some sentences may be correct. Revisions for the lettered sentences appear in the back of the book. Example:

Youd better put on you're new shoes.
You'd better put on your new shoes.

a. Its not easy to be old in our society.
b. I dont understand the Jameses's objections to our plans for a block party.
c. As the saying goes, "Every dog has it's day."
d. Is this collection of 50's records your's or your roommates?
e. Alas, Brian got two Ds on his report card.

1. Joe and Chucks' fathers were both in the class of 53.
2. They're going to finish their term papers as soon as the party ends.
3. Jane deplored her mother's-in-law habit of visiting unannounced.
4. Be sure your 7s don't look like 1s.
5. Ted and Virginia's son is marrying the editor's in chief's daughter.
6. I think I know who's barn this is; that big house in the village is their's, too.
7. Its hard to join a womens' basketball team because so few of them exist.
8. I had'nt expected to hear Janice' voice again.

9. Don't give the Murphy's dog it's biscuit until it's sitting up.

10. Isnt' it the mother and fathers' job to teach kid's to mind their *p*s and *q*s?

23 QUOTATION MARKS

Quotation marks always come in pairs: one at the start and one at the finish of a quoted passage. In the United States, the double quotation mark (") is preferred over the single one (') for most uses. Use quotation marks to set off a quoted or highlighted word or words from the rest of your text.

> "Injustice anywhere is a threat to justice everywhere," wrote Martin Luther King, Jr.

23a *Use quotation marks around words you quote from another writer or speaker.*

You can enrich the content, language, and authority of your writing by occasionally quoting a source whose ideas support your own. When you do this, you owe credit to the quoted person. If you use his or her exact words, enclose them in quotation marks.

> The Arab concept of community is reflected in Egyptian leader Anwar el-Sadat's comment "A man's village is his peace of mind."
>
> Minnesota-born songwriter Bob Dylan told an interviewer, "When I was growing up in Hibbing, home was a place to run away from."

(See 27j for correct capitalization with quotation marks.)

In an indirect quotation, you report someone else's idea without using his or her exact words. Do not enclose an indirect quotation in quotation marks. Do, however, name your source; and stay as close as you can to what the source actually said.

> Anwar el-Sadat asserted that one's village is one's peace of mind.

(For punctuation of direct and indirect questions, see 18c and 18a.)

23b *Use single quotation marks to surround a quotation inside another quotation.*

Sometimes a source you are quoting quotes someone else or puts a word or words in quotation marks. When that happens, use single quotation marks around the internal quotation (even if your source used double ones), and put double quotation marks around the larger passage that you are quoting.

> "My favorite advice from Socrates, 'Know thyself and fear all women,'" said Dr. Blatz, "has been getting me into trouble lately."

23c *For a quotation of more than four lines, indent the passage*
rather than use quotation marks.

Suppose you are writing an essay about Soviet dissidents living in the United
States. You might include a paragraph like this:

> In a June 1978 commencement address at Harvard Uni-
> versity, the writer Alexander Solzhenitsyn commented:
>> I have spent all my life under a Communist re-
>> gime, and I will tell you that a society with-
>> out any objective legal scale is a terrible one
>> indeed. But a society with no other scale but
>> the legal one is not quite worthy of man
>> either.

Merely by indenting this passage, you have shown that it is a direct quotation. You need not frame it with quotation marks. Simply double-space
above and below the quoted passage, indent it ten spaces from your left
margin, and double-space the quoted lines.

Follow the same practice if your quoted material is a poem.

> Phillis Wheatley, the outstanding black poet of co-
> lonial America, expresses a sense that she is condemned
> to write in obscurity and be forgotten:
>> No costly marble shall be reared,
>>> No Mausoleum's pride--
>> Nor chiselled stone be raised to tell
>>> That I have lived and died.

Notice that not only the source's words but her punctuation, capitalization,
indentation, and line breaks are quoted exactly. (See also 27j.)

23d *For a quotation of more than one paragraph, use quotation*
marks at the start of each paragraph.

> "Let us consider," said Henry Thoreau, "the way in which we spend our lives.
> "This world is a place of business. What an infinite bustle! I am awaked almost
> every night by the panting of the locomotive. It interrupts my dreams."

23e *In dialogue, use quotation marks only around a speaker's words, and mark each change of speaker with a paragraph break.*

> Randolph gazed at Ellen and uttered a heartfelt sigh. "What extraordinary beauty."
>
> "They are lovely," she replied, staring at the roses, "aren't they?"

23f *Use quotation marks around the title of a speech, an article in a newspaper or magazine, a short story, a poem shorter than book length, a chapter in a book, a song, and an episode of a television or radio program.*

> The article "An Updike Retrospective" praises "Solitaire" as the best story in John Updike's collection *Museums and Women.*
>
> In Chapter 5, "Expatriates," Schwartz discusses Eliot's famous poem "The Waste Land."
>
> My favorite *Miami Vice* episode was "Smuggler's Blues," based on Glen Frey's song "Smuggler's Blues."

(Most other types of titles are put in italics. See 29a.)

23g *Avoid using quotation marks to indicate slang or to be witty.*

Quotation marks should not be used around slang or would-be witticisms. By "quoting" them, you make them stand out like the nose of a W. C. Fields; and your discomfort in using them becomes painfully obvious.

> INADVISABLE   Liza looked like a born "loser," but Jerry was "hard up" for companionship.
>
> REVISED   Liza looked like a born loser, but Jerry was hard up for companionship.

Stick your neck out. If you really want to use those words, just go ahead.

Some writers assume that, by placing a word in quotation marks, they wax witty and ironic:

> INADVISABLE   By the time I finished all my chores, my long-awaited "day off" was over.
>
> REVISED   By the time I finished all my chores, my long-awaited day off was over.

No quotation marks are needed after *so-called* and other words with similar meaning.

> FAULTY   Call me "a dreamer," but I believe we can win.
>
> REVISED   Call me a dreamer, but I believe we can win.

23h *Keep commas and periods inside quotation marks, and keep most punctuation that is not part of a quotation outside quotation marks.*

Many writers occasionally find their quotation marks becoming entangled with other punctuation. You will have least trouble keeping them straight if you'll remember the following guidelines.

1. A comma or a period always comes before quotation marks, even if it is not part of the quotation.

We pleaded and pleaded, "Keep off the grass," in hope of preserving the lawn.

(Also see 19j.)

2. A colon or a semicolon always follows closing quotation marks.

We said, "Keep off the grass"; they still tromped onward.

3. Parentheses that are part of the quotation go inside the quotation marks. Parentheses that are your own, not part of the quotation, go outside the quotation marks.

We said, "Keep off the grass (unless it's artificial turf)."

They tromped onward (although we had said, "Keep off the grass") all the way to the road.

4. If a question mark, exclamation point, or dash is part of the quotation, place it inside the quotation marks.

She hollered, "Fire!"

"Marjorie?" he called. "I thought you—"

If any of these marks is not part of the quoted passage, place it after the closing quotation marks.

Who hollered "Fire"?

"Marjorie"—he paused for breath—"we'd better go."

As these examples show, don't close a sentence with two end punctuation marks, one inside and one outside the quotation marks. If the quoted passage ends with a dash, exclamation point, question mark, or period, you need not add any further end punctuation. If the quoted passage falls within a question asked by you, however, it should finish with a question mark, even if that means cutting other end punctuation (*Who hollered "Fire"?*).

Exercise 23–1

Add quotation marks wherever they are needed in the following sentences, and correct any other errors. Revisions for the lettered sentences appear in the back of the book. Example:

> How do you say This is a holdup in Spanish? Etta asked the Sundance Kid.
> "How do you say 'This is a holdup' in Spanish?" Etta asked the Sundance Kid.

a. Don't think about it, advised Jason; it will only make you unhappy.

b. Should I go, Marcia asked, or should I stay here?

c. In her story The Wide Net, Eudora Welty wrote, The excursion is the same when you go looking for your sorrow as when you go looking for your joy.

d. Who's supposed to say the line Tennis, anyone? asked the director.

e. Robert Burns's poem To a Mouse opens, Wee, sleekit, cow'rin, tim'rous beastie, / O, what a panic's in thy breastie!

1. How now! a rat? exclaimed Hamlet when Polonius stirred behind the curtain.

2. That so-called "sculpture" is what I call "junk."

3. Irving Berlin wrote God Bless America, which some people think should replace The Star-Spangled Banner as our national anthem.

4. When Ann remarked that people who live in glass houses shouldn't throw stones, Bill replied, That's the pot calling the kettle black!

5. Dame Edith Sitwell wrote, Rhythm was described by Schopenhauer as melody deprived of its pitch.

24   THE DASH AND THE SLASH/VIRGULE

A **dash** is a horizontal line used to separate parts of a sentence—a more dramatic substitute for a comma, semicolon, or colon. A slash is a slanted line used mainly for separating lines of poetry.

THE DASH

To type a dash, hit your hyphen key twice. When using a pen, make your dashes good and long, so that readers can tell them from hyphens.

24a Use a dash to indicate a sudden break in thought or shift in tone.

The dash signals that a surprise is in store: a shift in viewpoint, perhaps, or an unfinished statement.

Ivan doesn't care which team wins—he bet on both.

I didn't even pay much attention to my parents' accented and ungrammatical speech—at least not at home. —Richard Rodriguez

Stunned, Jake stood there muttering, "What in the—?"

24b Use a dash to introduce an explanation, an illustration, or a series.

When you want the kind of preparatory pause that a colon provides, but without the formality of a colon, try a dash.

My advice to you is simple—stop complaining.

You can use a dash to introduce an appositive (a noun or noun phrase that renames the noun it follows) if the appositive needs drama or contains commas.

Elliott still cherishes the pastimes of the '60s—drugs, sex, and rock-'n'-roll.

Longfellow wrote about three young sisters—grave Alice, laughing Allegra, and Edith with golden hair—in "The Children's Hour."

24c Use dashes to set off an emphatic aside or parenthetical element from the rest of a sentence.

It was as hot—and I mean *hot*—as a seven-dollar pistol on Fourth of July in Death Valley.

If I went through anguish in botany and economics—for different reasons—gymnasium work was even worse. —James Thurber

Dashes set off a phrase or clause with more punch than commas or parentheses can provide. (Compare commas, 19, and parentheses, 25a–25c.)

24d Avoid overusing dashes.

Like a physical gesture of emphasis—a jab of a pointing finger—the dash becomes meaningless if used too often. Use it only when a comma, a colon, or parentheses don't seem strong enough.

EXCESSIVE   Algy's grandmother—a sweet old lady—asked him to pick up some things at the store—milk, eggs, apples, and cheese.

REVISED   Algy's grandmother, a sweet old lady, asked him to pick up some things at the store: milk, eggs, apples, and cheese.

THE SLASH/VIRGULE

The slash, or virgule (/), is a mark of separation. Although you should know its functions, you probably will need to use it only rarely.

24e *Use a slash to indicate a break between lines of poetry in a brief quotation.*

When you quote two or three lines of poetry, you generally can run them into your text, with slashes to show line breaks. Leave one space before and after each slash.

> Thomas Nashe said, "Beauty is but a flower / Which wrinkles will devour."

If you quote more than three lines of a poem, indent them and follow the author's line endings. (See 23c.)

24f *If you are tempted to use the slash for any purpose besides breaking lines of poetry, try using a conjunction or rephrasing instead.*

Some writers use (or abuse) the slash to indicate alternatives: *and/or, he/she.* What the slash usually indicates in such a case is that the writer either can't make up his or her mind or can't find a more graceful phrasing.

> AWKWARD   Everyone is entitled to his/her own opinion.
>
> REVISED   People are entitled to their own opinions.
>
> AWKWARD   The president hopes to negotiate with Japan a more favorable trade balance and/or technology exchange.
>
> REVISED   The president hopes to negotiate with Japan a more favorable trade balance, technology exchange, or both.

In a very few constructions, the slash has won fairly wide acceptance:

> I don't see this as an either/or situation.

Usually, however, you gain clarity by substituting a conjunction or rephrasing your sentence.

> I don't see this as a problem with only two possible solutions.

Exercise 24–1

Add, replace, or cut dashes and slashes wherever appropriate in the following sentences. Some sentences may be correct. Revisions for the lettered sentences appear in the back of the book. Example:

> Stanton had all the identifying marks, boating shoes, yellow slicker, khaki pants, and tennis racquet, of a preppie.
>
> Stanton had all the identifying marks—boating shoes, yellow slicker, khaki pants, and tennis racquet—of a preppie.

a. I enjoy going fishing with my friend John—whom I've known for fifteen years.

b. His new boat is spectacular: a regular seagoing Ferrari.

c. An experienced carpenter/woodworker, John refitted the boat himself.

d. We were just rounding the point when—WHAM!

e. "A rock!" I cried. "John, I'm afraid we're"

1. In spite of the jarring crash/splash, we were not in fact sinking.

2. Everything in John's tackle box, however, flies, spinners, hooks, lines, and sinkers, went flying into the water.

3. In spite of the constant up/down of an angler's fortunes, John and I plan to go fishing again next month.

4. Three-year-old Jody wrote a song, if that's the right word, consisting of two lines.

5. Here are the lyrics—"The puppies and kitties, yes, Went out in the rain."

25 PARENTHESES, BRACKETS, AND THE ELLIPSIS MARK

Like quotation marks, parentheses (singular, *parenthesis*) work in pairs. So do brackets. Both sets of marks usually surround bits of information added to make a statement perfectly clear. An ellipsis mark is a trio of periods inserted to show that some bit of information has been cut.

PARENTHESES

25a *Use parentheses to set off a word, phrase, or clause that interrupts your sentence but sharpens your thought.*

FDR (as people called Franklin D. Roosevelt) won four presidential elections.

In fact, he occupied the White House for so many years (1933 to mid-1945) that babies became teenagers without having known any other president.

The material within the parentheses may be helpful, but it isn't essential. Were the writer to omit it altogether, the sentence would still make good sense. Use parentheses when adding in mid-sentence a qualifying word or phrase, a helpful date, or a brief explanation—words that, in conversation, you might introduce in a changed tone of voice.

25b *In a sentence containing a list, use parentheses to set off numbers or letters that precede items.*

Archimedes asserted that, given (1) a lever long enough, (2) a fulcrum, and (3) a place to stand, he could move the earth.

You need not put parentheses around numbers or letters in a list that you set off from the text by indentation.

Exercise 25–1

Correct any improper use of parentheses in the following sentences. Some sentences may be correct. Revisions for the lettered sentences appear in the back of the book. Example:

> The Islamic fundamentalist Ayatollah Khomeini—1903–1989—was described as having led Iran forward into the fifteenth century.

> The Islamic fundamentalist Ayatollah Khomeini (1903–1989) was described as having led Iran forward into the fifteenth century.

a. In *The Last Crusade,* archeologist Indiana Jones, who took his name from the family dog, joins his father in a quest for the Holy Grail.

b. Our cafeteria serves the four basic food groups: white—milk, bread, and mashed potatoes—brown—mystery meat and gravy—green—overcooked vegetables and underwashed lettuce—and orange—squash, carrots, and tomato sauce.

c. The ambassador says that if, 1, the United States will provide more aid and, 2, the guerrillas will agree to a cease-fire, his government will hold free elections.

d. When Phil said he works with whales (as well as other marine mammals) for the Whale Stranding Network, Lisa thought he meant that his group lures whales onto beaches.

e. Actually, the Whale Stranding Network, WSN, rescues whales that have stranded themselves.

1. The new pear-shaped bottles will hold 200 milliliters, 6.8 fluid ounces, of lotion.

2. The letter from Agatha—not her real name—told a heart-wrenching story of abandonment and abuse.

3. Al's policeman costume was a fantastic success (even his mother was fooled).

4. Communicorp had enough applicants, 39, and enough jobs, 27, to qualify for the program, but the personnel manager failed to submit the proper paperwork.

5. Although he enjoys her company, Maxwell says he hopes to marry a better-established—meaning wealthier—woman than Lydia.

BRACKETS

Brackets, those open-ended typographical boxes, work in pairs like parentheses. They serve a special purpose: they mark changes in quoted material.

If your typewriter lacks brackets, you can draw them in by hand or you can construct passable brackets out of slashes and underlines.

```
[Franklin D.] Roosevelt
```

25c *Use brackets around any explanatory information you add or any alteration you make within a quotation.*

If you need to add or alter a word or a phrase in a quotation from another writer, place brackets around your changes. When is it appropriate to make such a change? Most often the need arises when you weave into your own prose a piece of someone else's, and you want to get rid of dangling threads.

Suppose you are writing about James McGuire's being named chairman of the board of directors of General Motors. In your source, the actual words are these: "A radio bulletin first brought the humble professor of philosophy the astounding news." But in your paper, you want readers to know the professor's identity. So you add that information, in brackets.

> "A radio bulletin first brought the humble professor of philosophy [James McGuire] the astounding news."

Be careful never to alter a quoted statement any more than you have to. Every time you consider an alteration, ask yourself: do I really need this word-for-word quotation, or should I paraphrase?

25d Follow any mistake or unlikely statement in a quotation with [sic].

When you faithfully quote a statement that contains an error and you don't want your reader to blame you for it, follow the error with a bracketed *sic* (Latin for "so" or "so the writer says").

> "President Ronald Reagan foresaw a yearly growth of 29,000,000,000 [*sic*] in the American populace."

Of course, any statement as incorrect as that one is not worth quoting. Usually you're better off paraphrasing an error-riddled passage than pointing out its weaknesses. The writer who uses *sic* is like someone who goes around with a mean dog, siccing it on fellow writers. Never unleash your dog unless your target truly deserves a bite.

THE ELLIPSIS MARK

25e Use the ellipsis mark to signal that you have cut part of a quotation.

Occasionally, in quoting a passage of prose, you will want to cite just those parts that relate to your topic. It's all right to make judicious cuts in a quotation, as long as you acknowledge them. To do this, use the *ellipsis mark*: three periods with a space before and after each one (. . .).

Let's say you are writing an essay, "Today's Children: Counselors on Marital Affairs." One of your sources is Marie Winn's book *Children without Childhood,* in which you find this passage:

> Consider the demise of sexual innocence among children. We know that the casual integration of children into adult society in the Middle Ages included few sexual prohibitions. Today's nine- and ten-year-olds watch pornographic movies on cable TV, casually discourse about oral sex and sadomasochism, and not infrequently find themselves involved in their own parents' complicated sex lives, if not as actual observers or participants, at least as advisers, friendly commentators, and intermediaries.

You want to quote Winn's last sentence, but it has too much detail for your purposes. You might shorten it by omitting two of its parts.

> Today's nine- and ten-year-olds . . . not infrequently find themselves involved in their own parents' complicated sex lives, . . . at least as advisers, friendly commentators, and intermediaries.

If you want to include parts of two or more sentences, use a period plus the ellipsis mark—four periods altogether. The period that ends the first sentence appears in its usual place, followed by the three spaced periods that signal the omission.

> Consider the demise of sexual innocence among children. . . . Today's nine- and ten-year-olds [and the rest].

25f *Use the ellipsis mark only for cuts within a quotation,
not at its start or finish; and use it judiciously.*

Even though the book *Children without Childhood* keeps on going after the quoted passage, you don't need an ellipsis mark at the end of your quotation. Nor do you ever need to begin a quotation with three dots. Save the ellipsis mark for words or sentences you omit *inside* whatever you quote.

Anytime you decide to alter a quotation, with an ellipsis or with brackets, pause to ask yourself whether the quoted material is still necessary and still effective as changed. A passage full of ellipsis marks starts to look like Swiss cheese. If you plan to cut more than one or two sections from a quotation, think about paraphrasing instead.

Exercise 25–2

The following are two hypothetical passages from original essays. Each one is followed by a set of quotations. Adapt or paraphrase each quotation, using brackets and ellipsis marks, and splice it into the essay passage.

1. ESSAY PASSAGE

Has evil lost its capacity to frighten us? Today's teenagers use words like *wicked, bad,* and *evil* not to condemn another person's behavior or style but to show that they approve of it. Perhaps the declining power of organized religion has allowed us to stop worrying about evil. Perhaps the media's coverage of war, genocide, and murder has made us feel impotent against it. Perhaps the worldwide spread of nuclear weapons has made evil too huge and uncontrollable for our imaginations to grapple with.

QUOTATIONS

a. It was as though in those last minutes he was summing up the lessons that this long course in human wickedness had taught us—the lesson of the fearsome, word-and-thought-defying *banality of evil.*
    —Philosopher Hannah Arendt, writing about the Nazi leader Adolf Eichmann

b.   I am not a pessimist; to perceive evil where it exists is, in my opinion, a form of optimism.
        —Filmmaker Roberto Rossellini

c.   The world has achieved brilliance without conscience. Ours is a world of nuclear giants and ethical infants.
        —General Omar Bradley

2. ESSAY PASSAGE

Every human life is touched by the natural world. Before the modern industrial era, most people recognized the earth as the giver and supporter of existence. Nowadays, with the power of technology, we can (if we choose) destroy many of the complex balances of nature. With such power comes responsibility. We are no longer merely nature's children, but nature's parents as well.

QUOTATIONS

a.   A land ethic for tomorrow should be as honest as Thoreau's *Walden,* and as comprehensive as the sensitive science of ecology. It should stress the oneness of our resources and the live-and-help-live logic of the great chain of life. If, in our haste to "progress," the economics of ecology are disregarded by citizens and policy makers alike, the result will be an ugly America.
        —Former Secretary of the Interior Stewart Lee Udall

b.   The overwhelming importance of the atmosphere means that there are no longer any frontiers to defend against pollution, attack, or propaganda. It means, further, that only by a deep patriotic devotion to one's country can there be a hope of the kind of protection of the whole planet, which is necessary for the survival of the people of other countries.
        —Anthropologist Margaret Mead

c.   The survival of our wildlife is a matter of grave concern to all of us in Africa. These wild creatures amid the wild places they inhabit are not only important as a source of wonder and inspiration but are an integral part of our natural resources and of our future livelihood and well-being.
        —Former President of Tanzania Julius Nyerere

d.   [Religion] is a force in itself and it calls for the integration of lands and peoples in harmonious unity. The lands wait for those who can discern their rhythms. The peculiar genius of each continent, each river valley, the rugged mountains, the placid lakes, all call for relief from the constant burden of exploitation.
        —American Indian leader Vine Deloria, Jr., a Standing Rock Sioux

Exercise 25–3: Punctuation Review

Punctuate each of the following sentences.

1.   Being a dedicated beachcomber Truman my aunts former accountant found life in Okracoke North Carolina to be just his cup of punch

2.   He would jump through waves by the hour he would shriek back at the gulls

3.   Some mornings feeling lazy hed sit in the sun and talk with shipwrecked sailors or were they dope runners whose planes had been shot down

4.   What Truman wondered was the meaning of success

5.   Lieutenant Binks officer in charge of Cape Hatteras lighthouse a Coast Guard station lent him a willing no a compassionate ear

6. One night without warning crash a colossal yacht struck the beach not far from Trumans tiny rain-drenched tent

7. Good grief he cried leaping to his feet whats happened

8. As he ran along the beach into his wondering gaze came a vision of naked loveliness

9. She seemed a moon-washed phantom her lightly stepping feet moving like a dancers through the surf

10. Such delicacy such grace Truman always a sucker for beauty instantly resolved to befriend this charming castaway

11. Shaking her sea-drenched coat she gave him a head-to-foot saltwater bath

12. Her tongue was blue which coupled with her auburn hue told Truman an expert in such matters that she must be a chow chow

13. Scoffers their eyes fixed on high-paying jobs may well laugh but Truman P Kelp CPA fugitive from society recognized love

14. With his devoted friend partner and organic bed warmer he lived to pick a trite expression happily ever after although dog food was always in scant supply

15. Heres a little saying that you really ought to know
Horses sweat and men perspire but ladies only glow
—Popular jingle, nineteenth century

CHAPTER 25

Mechanics

26. Abbreviations   722
27. Capital Letters   726
28. Numbers   730
29. Italics   733
30. The Hyphen   736
31. Spelling   740

26 ABBREVIATIONS

Abbreviations are a form of shorthand that enables a writer to include certain necessary information in capsule form. In your writing, limit abbreviations to those that are common enough for readers to recognize and understand without pausing. When a reader has to stop and ask, "What does this mean?" your writing loses impact.

If ever you're unsure about whether to abbreviate a word, remember: when in doubt, spell it out.

26a Use the abbreviated form of certain common titles when they precede proper names.

Abbreviate the following titles:

Mr. and Mrs. Hubert Collins   Dr. Martin Luther King
Rev. Martha Reading   St. Matthew

Write out other titles in full:

General Douglas MacArthur   Senator Nancy L. Kassebaum
President George Bush   Professor Shirley Fixler

Titles that are unfamiliar to readers of English, such as *M.* (for the French *Monsieur*) or *Sr.* (for the Spanish *Señor*), should be spelled out.

Spell out most titles that appear without proper names:

FAULTY   Fred is studying to be a dr.

REVISED   Fred is studying to be a doctor.

When an abbreviated title (such as an academic degree) follows a proper name, set it off from the name and from the rest of the sentence with commas.

Alice Martin, C.P.A., is the accountant for Charlotte Cordera, Ph.D., and John Hoechst, Jr., Esq.

Lucy Chen, M.D., and James Filbert, D.D.S., have moved their offices to the Millard Building.

An academic degree that appears without a proper name can be abbreviated, but it is not set off with commas.

My brother has a B.A. in economics.

Avoid repeating different forms of the same title before and after a proper name. You can properly refer to a doctor of dental surgery as either *Dr. Jane Doe* or *Jane Doe, D.D.S.*, but not as *Dr. Jane Doe, D.D.S.*

26b   Use A.M., P.M., B.C., A.D., *and $ with numbers.*

9:05 a.m.   3:45 p.m.
2000 B.C.   A.D. 1066

The words we use to pinpoint years and times are so commonly abbreviated that many English speakers have forgotten what the letters stand for. In case you are curious: *a.m.* means *ante meridiem*, Latin for "before noon"; *p.m.* means *post meridiem*, "after noon." A.D. is *anno domini*, Latin for "in the year of the Lord"—that is, since the official year of Jesus' birth. B.C. stands for "before Christ." You may also run into alternative designations such as B.P., "before present," and B.C.E., "before the common era." If you think your readers may not know what an abbreviation stands for, spell it out or add an explanation.

The ruins date from 1200 B.P. (before present).

For prices, use a dollar sign with numbers (*$17.95, $10*).

Avoid using an abbreviation together with a word or words that mean the same thing: write *$1 million* or *one million dollars*, not *$1 million dollars*. Write *9:05 a.m.* or *9:05 in the morning*, not *9:05 a.m. in the morning*.

26c *Avoid abbreviating names of months, days of the week, units of measurement, or parts of literary works.*

Many references that can be abbreviated in footnotes or citations should be spelled out when they appear in the body of an essay.

NAMES OF MONTHS AND DAYS OF THE WEEK
FAULTY   After their meeting on 9/3, they did not see each other again until Fri., Dec. 12.

REVISED   After their meeting on September 3 [*or* the third of September], they did not see each other again until Friday, December 12.

UNITS OF MEASUREMENT
FAULTY   It would take 10,000 lb. of concrete to build a causeway 25 ft × 58 in. [*or* 25′ × 58″].

REVISED   It would take 10,000 pounds of concrete to build a causeway 25 feet by 58 inches.

PARTS OF LITERARY WORKS
FAULTY   Von Bargen's reply appears in vol. II, ch. 12, p. 187.

REVISED   Von Bargen's reply appears in volume II, chapter 12, page 187.

FAULTY   Leona first speaks in Act I, sc. 2.

REVISED   Leona first speaks in Act I, scene 2 [*or* the second scene of Act I].

26d *Use the full English version of most Latin abbreviations.*

Unless you are writing for an audience of ancient Romans, translate Latin abbreviations into English and spell them out whenever possible.

COMMON LATIN ABBREVIATIONS

ABBREVIATION	LATIN	ENGLISH
et al.	*et alia*	and others, and other people, and the others (people)
etc.	*et cetera*	and so forth, and others, and the rest (things)
i.e.	*id est*	that is
e.g.	*exempli gratia*	for example, such as

Latin abbreviations are acceptable, however, for source citations and for comments in parentheses. (See also 25d.)

26e Use initials, usually without periods, for familiar organizations, corporations, and people.

Most sets of initials that are read as letters do not require periods between the letters (CIA, JFK, UCLA). You will not be wrong if you insert periods (C.I.A., J.F.K., U.C.L.A.), as long as you are consistent.

A set of initials that is pronounced as a word is called an **acronym** (NATO, UNICEF) and never has periods between letters.

To avoid misunderstanding, write out an organization's full name the first time you mention it, followed by its initials in parentheses. Then, in later references, you can rely on initials alone. (With very familiar initials, such as FBI, CBS, and YMCA, you need not give the full name.)

26f In most cases, refer to countries by their names, not their initials.

When you mention the United States or another country, give its full name, unless the name is repeated so often that it would weigh down your paragraph.

> The president will return to the United States [not *U.S.*] on Tuesday from a trip that has taken him to the Soviet Union [not *U.S.S.R.*] and the United Kingdom [not *U.K.*].

EXCEPTION: Although it is not advisable to use *U.S.* as a noun, you can use it as an adjective: *U.S. Senate, U.S. foreign policy.* For other countries, find an alternative: *Soviet aid, British ambassador.*

Exercise 26–1

Substitute abbreviations for words and vice versa wherever appropriate in the following sentences. Correct any incorrectly used abbreviations. Answers for the lettered sentences appear in the back of the book. Example:

> My history teacher, Doctor Lembas, got her doctor of philosophy degree at the University of Southwest Florida.

> My history teacher, Dr. Lembas, got her Ph.D. at the University of Southwest Florida.

a. Built for the Paris Exposition of 1889, the Eiffel Tower contains 15 million lb. of pig iron, protected by 37 T of paint.

b. Fri., 7/14, 1989, was the Eiffel Tower's 100th anniversary.

c. M. Eiffel would be pleased that Pres. Mitterrand et al. now accept his controversial "iron giraffe" as a national landmark.

d. In some Parisian tourist traps, a cup of coffee costs as much as 5 dollars.

e. France is a member of NATO, but the French historically have mistrusted some of their fellow NATO members, e.g., the U.K.

1. Amb. and Mrs. Collins stand several in. shorter than Gen. Garcia and his wife.

2. When the Senate considered whether the U.S. should aid the famine victims, Sens. Kerry, Kennedy, and Biden requested an authorization of $1.2 million dollars.

3. When John Fitzgerald Kennedy picked Lyndon Baines Johnson for VP, Democrats never guessed that three yrs. later JFK would be dead and LBJ would be in the White House.

4. At 8:20 p.m. this evening we heard that Dr. Reginald Styx M.D. had stumbled upon relics dating to 1400 B.C.

5. The children in Middletown who collected pennies for U.N.I.C.E.F. at Halloween brought in more than 70 dollars.

27 | CAPITAL LETTERS

The main thing to remember about capital letters is to use them only with good reason. If you think a word will work in lowercase letters, you're probably right.

27a *Capitalize proper names and adjectives made from proper names.*

Proper names designate individuals, places, organizations and institutions, brand names, and certain other distinctive things.

Miles Standish	University of Iowa
Belgium	a Volkswagen
United Nations	a Xerox machine

Any proper name can have an adjective as well as a noun form. The adjective form too is capitalized.

Australian beer	a Renaissance man
Shakespearean comedy	Machiavellian tactics

27b *Capitalize a title or rank before a proper name.*

Now in her second term, Senator Wilimczyk serves on two important committees.

In his lecture Professor Jones went on and on about fossil evidence.

In formal writing, titles that do not come before proper names are not capitalized.

Ten senators voted against the missile research appropriation.

Jones is the department's only full professor.

EXCEPTION: The abbreviation for the full name of an academic or professional degree is capitalized, whether or not it accompanies a proper name. The informal name of a degree is not capitalized.

Dora E. McLean, M.D., also holds a B.A. in music.

Dora holds a bachelor's degree in music.

27c *Capitalize a family relationship only when it is part of a proper name or when it substitutes for a proper name.*

Do you know the song about Mother Machree?

I've invited Mother to visit next weekend.

I'd like you to meet my aunt, Emily Smith.

CAPITALIZATION AT A GLANCE
Capitalize the following.

PROPER NAMES AND ADJECTIVES MADE FROM THEM
Marie Curie   Cranberry Island   Smithsonian Institution
a Freudian reading

RANK OR TITLE BEFORE A PROPER NAME
Ms. Olson   Professor Harvey

FAMILY RELATIONSHIP ONLY WHEN IT SUBSTITUTES FOR OR IS PART OF A PROPER NAME
Grandma Jones   Father Time

RELIGIONS, THEIR FOLLOWERS, AND DEITIES
Islam   Orthodox Jew   Buddha

PLACES, REGIONS, AND GEOGRAPHIC FEATURES
Palo Alto   the Berkshire Mountains

DAYS OF THE WEEK, MONTHS, AND HOLIDAYS
Wednesday   July   Labor Day

HISTORICAL EVENTS, PERIODS, DOCUMENTS, AND MOVEMENTS
the Boston Tea Party   the Middle Ages   the Constitution
the Abolitionist movement

SCHOOLS, COLLEGES, UNIVERSITIES, AND SPECIFIC COURSES
Temple University   Introduction to Clinical Psychology

FIRST, LAST, AND MAIN WORDS IN TITLES OF PAPERS, BOOKS, ARTICLES, AND WORKS OF ART
The Decline and Fall of the Roman Empire

THE FIRST LETTER OF A QUOTED SENTENCE
She called out, "Come in! The water's not cold."

27d *Capitalize the names of religions, their deities, and their followers.*

Christianity	Islam
Muslims	Methodists
Jehovah	Allah
Krishna	the Holy Spirit

27e *Capitalize proper names of places, regions, and geographic features.*

Los Angeles	Death Valley
the Black Hills	Big Sur
the Atlantic Ocean	the Philippines

Do not capitalize compass points unless they are parts of proper names (*West Virginia, South Orange*) or refer to formal geographic locations.

Drive south to Chicago and then east to Cleveland.

Jim, who has always lived in the South, likes to read about the mysterious East.

A common noun such as *street, avenue, boulevard, park, lake,* or *hill* is capitalized when part of a proper name.

Meinecke Avenue	Hamilton Park
Sunset Boulevard	Lake Michigan

27f *Capitalize days of the week, names of months, and holidays, but not seasons or academic terms.*

By the Monday after Passover I have to choose between the January study plan and junior year abroad.

At Easter we'll be halfway through the spring term.

27g *Capitalize historical events, periods, documents, and movements.*

Black Monday	Magna Charta
the Civil War	Declaration of Independence
the Holocaust	Atomic Energy Act
the Bronze Age	the Pre-Raphaelite Brotherhood
the Roaring Twenties	the Wobblies

27h *Capitalize names of schools, colleges, universities, formal names of departments, and course titles, but not general references to academic entities.*

West End School, Central High School [*but* elementary school, high school]
Reed College, Arizona State University [*but* the college, a university]
Department of Geography [*but* geography department, departmental meeting]
Feminist Perspectives in Nineteenth-Century Literature [*but* literature course]

27i *Capitalize the first, last, and main words in the titles of papers, books, articles, and works of art.*

When you write the title of a media product, whether it is a comic book, a television show, or a ballet, capitalize the first and last words and all main words in between. Do not capitalize articles, conjunctions, or prepositions unless they come first or last in the title or follow a colon.

ESSAY	"Once More to the Lake"
NOVEL	*Of Mice and Men*
VOLUME OF POETRY	*Poems after Martial*
POEM	"A Valediction: Of Weeping"

(For advice about using quotation marks and italics for titles, see 23f, 29a.)

27j *Capitalize the first letter of a quoted sentence or line of poetry unless the author follows another style.*

Oscar Wilde wrote, "The only way to get rid of a temptation is to yield to it."

Only the first word of a quoted sentence is capitalized, even when you break the sentence with words of your own.

"The only way to get rid of a temptation," wrote Oscar Wilde, "is to yield to it."

If you quote more than one sentence, start each one with a capital letter.

"Art should never try to be popular," said Wilde. "The public should try to make itself artistic."

(For advice about punctuating quotations, see 23h.)
If the beginning of the quoted passage blends in with your sentence, use lowercase for the first word of the quotation.

Oscar Wilde wrote that "the only way to get rid of a temptation is to yield to it."

In most poems, especially those written before the twentieth century, every line opens with a capital letter. If a poet has used a different style, follow that style. (See also 23c, 23e.)

Exercise 27–1

Correct any capitalization errors you find in the following sentences. Some sentences may be correct. Answers for the lettered sentences appear in the back of the book. Example:

> "The quality of mercy," says Portia in Shakespeare's *The Merchant Of Venice*, "Is not strained."

> "The quality of mercy," says Portia in Shakespeare's *The Merchant of Venice*, "is not strained."

a. At our Family Reunion, I met my Cousin Sam for the first time, and also my father's brother George.

b. I already knew from dad that his brother had moved to Australia years ago to explore the great barrier reef.

c. At the reunion, uncle George told me that he had always wanted to be a Marine Biologist.

d. He had spent the Summer after his Sophomore year of college in Woods Hole, Massachusetts, on cape cod.

e. At the Woods Hole oceanographic institution he studied Horseshoe Crabs.

1. "These crabs look like armored tanks," he told me. "They have populated the Northeast for millions of years."

2. "I'm writing a book," he said, "Entitled *Horseshoe Crabs are Good Luck.*"

3. I had heard that uncle George was estranged from his Mother, a Roman catholic, after he married an Atheist.

4. She told George that God created many religions so that people would not become Atheists.

5. When my Uncle announced that he was moving to a Continent thousands of miles Southwest of the United States, his Mother gave him a bible to take along.

6. My Aunt, Linda McCallum, received her Doctorate from one of the State Universities in California.

7. After graduation she worked there as Registrar and lived in the San Bernardino valley.

8. She has pursued her interest in Hispanic Studies by traveling to South America from her home in Northeastern Australia.

9. She uses her maiden name—Linda McCallum, Ph.D.—for her nonprofit business, Hands across the Sea.

10. After dinner we all toasted grandmother's Ninetieth Birthday and sang "For She's A Jolly Good Fellow."

28   NUMBERS

When do you write out a number (*twenty-seven*) and when do you use figures for it (*27*)? Unless your essay relies on statistics, you'll want in most cases to use words. Figures are most appropriate in contexts where readers are used to seeing them, such as times and dates (*11:05 P.M. on March 15*).

FIGURES AT A GLANCE

ADDRESSES	4 East 74th Street; also, One Copley Place; 5 Fifth Avenue
DATES	May 20, 1992; 450 B.C.; also, Fourth of July
DECIMALS	98.6° Fahrenheit; .57 acre
FRACTIONS	$3\frac{1}{2}$ years ago; $1\frac{3}{4}$ miles; also, half a loaf; three-fourths of voters surveyed
PARTS OF LITERARY WORKS	volume 2, chapter 5, page 37; Act 1, Scene 2 (or Act I, Scene ii)
PERCENTAGES	25 percent; 99.9 percent
PRICES	$1.99; $200,000; also, $5 million; ten cents; a dollar
SCORES	a 114–111 victory; a final score of 5 to 3
STATISTICS	men in the 25–30 age group; odds of 5 to 1 (or 5–1 odds); height 5'7"; also, three out of four doctors
TIMES	2:29 P.M.; 10:15 tomorrow morning; also, three o'clock, half past four

28a *In general, write out a number that consists of one or two words and use figures for longer numbers.*

Short names of numbers are easily read (*ten, six hundred*); longer ones take more thought (*two thousand four hundred eighty-seven*). So for numbers of more than a word or two, use figures.

> More than two hundred suckers paid twenty-five dollars apiece for that cheap plastic novelty item.
>
> A frog's tongue has 970,580 taste buds, one-sixth as many as a human being's.

EXCEPTION: For multiples of a million or more, you can use a figure plus a word.

> The earth is 93 million miles from the sun.
>
> The Pentagon has requested a $3.4 billion increase.

28b *Use figures for most addresses, dates, decimals, fractions, parts of literary works, percentages, prices, scores, statistics, and times.*

Using figures is mainly a matter of convenience. If you think words will be easier for your readers to follow, you can always write out a number.

NOTE: Any number that precedes *o'clock* should be in words, not figures. (For pointers on writing the plurals of figures [*6's, 1960s*], see 22i.)

28c *In a passage that is full of numbers, use either words or figures consistently.*

Switching back and forth between words and figures for numbers can be distracting to readers. Choose whichever form suits most of the numbers in your passage and use that form for all of them, unless to do so would create excessive awkwardness.

> Ten years ago, only a quarter of the land in town was developed; now, all but fifteen percent is occupied by buildings.

> Of the 276 representatives who voted, 97 supported a 25-percent raise, while 179 supported an amendment that would implement a 30-percent raise over 5 years.

28d *Write out a number that begins a sentence.*

Readers recognize a new sentence by its initial capital; however, you can't capitalize a figure. When a number starts a sentence, either write it out or move it deeper into the sentence. If a number starting a sentence is followed by other numbers in the same category, write them out, too, unless to do so would make the sentence excessively awkward.

> Five percent of the frogs in our aquarium ate sixty-two percent of the flies.

> Ten thousand people packed an arena built for 8,550.

Exercise 28–1

Correct any inappropriate uses of numbers in the following sentences. Some sentences may be correct. Answers for the lettered sentences appear in the back of the book. Example:

> As Smith notes on page 197, a delay of 3 minutes cost the researchers 5 years' worth of work.

> As Smith notes on page 197, a delay of three minutes cost the researchers five years' worth of work.

a. Wasn't it the 3 Musketeers whose motto was "One for all and all for one"?

b. In the 1970s, there were about ninety-two million ducks in America, but in the last 4 years their number has dropped to barely sixty-nine million.

c. Cruising around the world on a one-hundred-twenty-five-foot yacht with eight other people sounded glamorous until I saw our wooden berths, thirty-two inches wide by sixty-eight inches long.

d. Forty days and 40 nights would seem like 40 years if you were sailing on an ark with two of every kind of animal.

e. I doubt that I'll ever bowl a perfect 300, but I hope to break 250 if it takes me till I'm eighty.

1. The meeting has been rescheduled from three-thirty p.m. Tuesday to four o'clock this afternoon because ½ the members couldn't make it.

2. A program to help save the sea otter transferred more than eighty animals to a new colony over the course of 2 years; however, all but 34 otters swam back home again.

3. 1 percent or less of the estimated fifteen to twenty billion pounds of plastic discarded annually in the United States is recycled.

4. The 1983 Little League World Series saw the Roosters beat the Dusters ninety-four to four before a throng of seven thousand five hundred and fifty.

5. In Act Two, Scene Nine of Shakespeare's *The Merchant of Venice,* Portia's 2nd suitor fails to guess which of 3 caskets contains her portrait.

6. *Fourscore* means 4 times 20; a *fortnight* means 2 weeks; and a *brace* is two of anything.

7. 50 years ago, traveling from New York City to San Francisco took approximately 15 hours by plane, 50 hours by train, and almost 100 hours by car.

8. A candy bar that cost $.05 in the nineteen-fifties costs $.35 to $.50 today.

9. If the backers cannot raise a hundred and fifty thousand dollars by noon tomorrow, they lose their ten-thousand-dollar deposit.

10. Justine finished volume one of Proust's *Remembrance of Things Past,* but by the time she got to page forty of volume two, she had forgotten the beginning and had to start over.

29 ITALICS

Italic type—as in this line—slants to the right. Slightly harder to read than perpendicular type, it is usually saved for brief occasions: for emphasis or for special use of a word or phrase. In writing or typewriting, indicate italics by underlining.

29a Underline the titles of magazines, newspapers, and long literary works (books, pamphlets, plays); the titles of films; the titles of paintings and other works of art; the titles of long musical works (operas, symphonies); the titles of record albums; and the names of television and radio programs.

We read the story "Araby" in James Joyce's book *Dubliners.*

The Broadway musical *My Fair Lady* was based on Shaw's play *Pygmalion.*

Pete read reviews in the *Washington Post* and *Newsweek* magazine of the Cleveland Philharmonic's recording of Beethoven's *Pastoral* Symphony.

I saw a *Miami Vice* episode that featured cuts from two Doors albums: *The Doors* and *Strange Days.*

The names of the Bible, the books of the Bible (Genesis, Matthew), and other sacred books (the Koran, the Rig-Veda) are not italicized.

(For titles that are put in quotation marks, see 23f.)

29b Underline the names of ships, boats, trains, airplanes, and spacecraft.

The launching of the Venus probe *Magellan* was a heartening success after the *Challenger* disaster.

The *Concorde* combines the elegance of an ocean liner like the *Queen Mary* with the convenience of high-speed air travel.

29c Underline a word or phrase from a foreign language if it is not in everyday use.

Gandhi taught the principles of *satya* and *ahimsa:* truth and nonviolence.

Although there is no one-word English equivalent for the French *chez,* we can translate *chez Bob* simply as "at Bob's."

Foreign words that are familiar to most American readers need not be underlined.

After being declared passé several years ago, détente is making a reappearance in East-West politics.

I prefer provolone to mozzarella.

29d Underline a word when you define it.

The rhythmic, wavelike motion of the walls of the alimentary canal is called *peristalsis.*

ITALICS AT A GLANCE
Underline the following when typing or writing by hand.

TITLES

MAGAZINES AND NEWSPAPERS
Ms.   the *London Times*

LONG LITERARY WORKS
Heart of Darkness (a novel)   *The Less Deceived* (a collection of poems)

FILMS
Notorious   *Black Orpheus*

PAINTINGS AND OTHER WORKS OF ART
Four Dancers (a painting)   *The Thinker* (a sculpture)

LONG MUSICAL WORKS
Aïda   Handel's *Messiah*

RECORD ALBUMS
Sticky Fingers

When you give a synonym or a translation—a definition that is just one or two words long—italicize the word being defined and put the definition in quotation marks.

The word *orthodoxy* means "conformity."

Trois, drei, and *tres* are all words for "three."

29e Underline a letter, number, word, or phrase when you refer to it as a word.

George Bernard Shaw pointed out that *fish* could be spelled *ghoti*: *gh* as in *tough*, *o* as in *women*, and *ti* as in *fiction*.

Watching the big red *8* on a basketball player's jersey, I recalled the scarlet letter *A* worn by Hester Prynne.

Psychologists now prefer the term *unconscious* to *subconscious*.

29f Underline—sparingly—to place special emphasis on a word or phrase.

When you absolutely *must* stress a point, underline it; but watch out. Frequent italics can make your writing look hysterical. In most cases, the structure of your sentence, not a typographical gimmick, should give emphasis where emphasis is due.

He suggested putting the package *under* the mailbox, not *into* the mailbox.

People committed to saving whales, sea otters, and baby seals may not be aware that *forty thousand children per day* die of starvation or malnutrition.

TELEVISION AND RADIO PROGRAMS
I Love Lucy   *All Things Considered*

OTHER WORDS AND PHRASES

NAMES OF SPECIFIC VEHICLES AND SPACECRAFT
the *Orient Express*   the *Challenger*

A WORD OR PHRASE FROM A FOREIGN LANGUAGE IF IT IS NOT IN EVERYDAY USE
The Finnish sauna ritual uses a *vihta*, a brush made of fresh birch branches tied together.

A LETTER, NUMBER, WORD, OR PHRASE WHEN YOU DEFINE IT OR REFER TO IT AS A WORD
My lucky number is *12*.   What do you think *fiery* is referring to in the second line?

Note: See 23f for titles that need to be placed in quotation marks.

Exercise 29–1

Add or remove italics as needed in the following sentences. Some sentences may be correct. Revisions for the lettered sentences appear in the back of the book. Example:

> Hiram could not *believe* that his parents had seen *the Beatles'* legendary performance at Shea Stadium.
>
> Hiram could not believe that his parents had seen the Beatles' legendary performance at Shea Stadium.

a. Hiram's favorite Beatles album is "Sergeant Pepper's Lonely Hearts Club Band," but his father prefers "Magical Mystery Tour."

b. Hiram named his rowboat the "Yellow Submarine."

c. He was disappointed when I told him that the play *Long Day's Journey into Night* is *definitely not* a staged version of the movie "A Hard Day's Night."

d. I had to show him the article "Eugene O'Neill's Journey into Night" in "People" magazine to convince him.

e. Many different ethnic groups eat tomatoes and cheese in or on some form of cooked dough, whether they call this dish a *pizza*, an *enchilada*, a sandwich, or something else.

1. Is "avocado" Spanish for "lawyer"?

2. Our chorus and orchestra will perform Handel's Messiah at Christmas and Beethoven's Eroica in the spring.

3. You can pick out some of the best basketball players in the *NBA* by the 33 on their jerseys.

4. The nine musicians on the *Titanic* went down with the ship, playing "Nearer My God to Thee."

5. In one episode of "Rocky and Bullwinkle," the intrepid moose and squirrel landed on the *Isle of Lucy*.

6. "Eye" in France is "oeil," while "eyes" is "yeux."

7. "Deux yeux bleus" means "two blue eyes" in French.

8. Jan can never remember whether Cincinnati has three n's and one t or two n's and two t's.

9. My favorite comic bit in "The Pirates of Penzance" is Major General Stanley's confusion between "orphan" and "often."

10. In Tom Stoppard's play "The Real Thing," the character Henry accuses Bach of copying a *cantata* from a popular song by *Procol Harum*.

30 | THE HYPHEN

The hyphen, that Scotch-tape mark of punctuation, is used to join words and to connect parts of words. You will find it indispensable for the following purposes.

30a *Use a hyphen (or hyphens) to join words into a single compound noun or verb.*

Compound words in the English language take three forms:

1. Two or more words combined into one (*crossroads, salesperson*)
2. Two or more words that remain separate but function as one (*gas station, high school*)
3. Two or more words linked by hyphens (*sister-in-law, window-shop*)

Compound nouns and verbs fall into these categories more by custom than by rule. When you're not sure which way to write a compound, refer to your dictionary. If the compound is not listed in your dictionary, write it as two words.

30b *Use hyphens in compound adjectives that precede nouns but not in those that follow nouns.*

> Jerome, a devotee of *twentieth-century* music, has no interest in the classic symphonies of the *eighteenth century*.
>
> I'd like living in an *out-of-the-way* place better if it weren't so far *out of the way*.

In a series of hyphenated adjectives with the same second word, you can omit that word (but not the hyphen) in all but the last adjective of the series.

> Julia is a lover of eighteenth-, nineteenth-, and twentieth-century music.

The adverb *well*, when coupled with an adjective, follows the same hyphenation rules as if it were an adjective.

> It is *well known* that Tony has a *well-equipped* kitchen, although his is not as *well equipped* as the hotel's.

Do *not* use a hyphen to link an adverb ending in *-ly* with an adjective.

> FAULTY   The sun hung like a newly-minted penny in a freshly-washed sky.
>
> REVISED   The sun hung like a newly minted penny in a freshly washed sky.

30c *Use a hyphen to join most compound words of which one part begins with (or consists of) a capital letter.*

> Bill says that, as a *neo-Marxist* living in an *A-frame* house, it would be politically incorrect for him to wear a Mickey Mouse *T-shirt*.
>
> Bubba doesn't mind being labeled a *pre-Neanderthal*, but he'll break anyone's neck who calls him *anti-American*.

There are exceptions to this rule: *unchristian*, for one. If you think a compound word looks odd with a hyphen, check your dictionary.

30d *Use a hyphen after the prefixes* all-, ex-, *and* self- *and before the suffix* -elect.

> Lucille's *ex-husband* is studying *self-hypnosis*.
>
> This *all-important* debate pits Senator Browning against the *president-elect*.

Note that these prefixes and suffixes also can function as parts of words that are not hyphenated (*exit*, *selfish*). Whenever you are unsure whether to use a hyphen, check a dictionary.

30e *Use a hyphen if a compound word would otherwise create a double vowel, a triple consonant, or any potential mispronunciation.*

> The contractor told us that his *pre-estimate* did not cover any *pre-existing* flaws in the building.
>
> The recreation department favors the *re-creation* of a summer activities program.

30f *Use a hyphen in writing out fractions and in writing out compound whole numbers from* twenty-one *to* ninety-nine.

> When her sister gave Leslie's age as six and *three-quarters*, Leslie corrected her: "I'm six and *five-sixths*!"
>
> If Fred makes *ninety-nine* mistakes, he has a hundred and one excuses.

30g *Use a hyphen to indicate a series between two numbers.*

> The section covering the years 1975-1980 is found on pages 20-27.

30h *To break a word at the end of a line, divide the word between parts if it is a compound and between syllables if it is not.*

Words are divided as they are pronounced, by syllables. Break a hyphenated compound at its hyphen and a nonhyphenated compound between the words that make it up. For a noncompound word, saying it out loud usually will give you a good idea where to break it; if you still are not sure, check your dictionary.

> FAULTY   Bubba hates to be called an-
> ti-American.
>
> REVISED   Bubba hates to be called anti-
> American.
>
> FAULTY   Mr. Brown will not be in until lun-
> chtime.
>
> REVISED   Mr. Brown will not be in until lunch-
> time.

Don't split a one-syllable word, even if keeping it intact makes your line come out a bit too short or too long.

FAULTY	I'm completely drench- ed.
REVISED	I'm completely drenched.
FAULTY	Arnold is a tower of stren- gth.
REVISED	Arnold is a tower of strength.

Don't split a word after a one-letter syllable or before a one- or two-letter syllable.

FAULTY	What's that up the road a- head?
REVISED	What's that up the road ahead?
FAULTY	When did Thomas and Mari- a get married?
REVISED	When did Thomas and Ma- ria get married?

Don't split a word after a segment that looks like a whole word, even if a dictionary puts a syllable break there.

CONFUSING	The lusty sailor aimed his sex- tant at the stars.
CLEAR	The lusty sailor aimed his sextant at the stars.
CONFUSING	He is addicted to her- oin.
CLEAR	He is addicted to heroin.

Exercise 30–1

Add necessary hyphens or remove incorrectly used hyphens in the following sentences. Some sentences may be correct. Answers for the lettered sentences appear in the back of the book. Example:

Carlos presented Isabel with a beautifully-wrought silver necklace.

Carlos presented Isabel with a beautifully wrought silver necklace.

a. Do nonAmericans share our view of ourselves as a freedom loving people?

b. The dealer told George the two vases are within nine-tenths of an inch of being a perfect match.

c. Patrick Henry's words reecho down through the ages: "Give me liberty or give me death!"

d. Those well-spoken words are well-remembered today.

e. The weather forecast calls for showers followed by sunshine.

1. How are you going to fit that heavy sweater into a fully-packed suitcase?

2. Henry's exact height is six feet, four and a half inches.

3. As Joyce walked away, a voice behind her called, "You-'re under arrest!"

4. Dubowski's last film was greatly improved by reediting.

5. Critics applauded the fast moving plot and fully realized characters.

6. As part of her recovery from hand surgery, Susan has learned to crossstitch.

7. Batman fended off the Joker's surprise attack with a powerful right hook to the jaw.

8. According to Dr. Shelby, selfactualization is the highest human need.

9. The guerrillas insist that being anticapitalist doesn't mean they are proSoviet.

10. The downpour that sent everyone running for shelter ended as quickly as it had started.

31 | SPELLING

English spelling so often defies the rules that many speakers of the language wonder if, indeed, there *are* rules. You probably learned to spell—as most of us did—mainly by memorizing. By now you remember that there's a *b* in *doubt* but not in *spout,* a *k* in *knife* but not in *nine*. You know that the same sound can have several spellings, as in *here, ear, pier, sneer,* and *weird*. You are resigned to the fact that *ou* is pronounced differently in *four, round, ought,* and *double*. Still, like most people, you may have trouble with the spelling of certain words.

How many times have you heard someone say "ath-uh-lete" for *athlete,* "gov-er-ment" for *government,* or "nuc-yu-lar" for *nuclear*? Get the pronunciation right and you realize that the spelling has to be *arctic* (not *artic*), *mischievous* (not *mischievious*), *perform* (not *preform*), *surprise* (not *suprise*), *replenish* (not *replentish*), *similar* (not *similiar*).

The trouble is that careful pronunciation is only sometimes a reliable guide to English spelling. Knowing how to pronounce *psychology, whistle, light,* and *rhythm* doesn't help you spell them. How, then, are you to cope?

31a Learn and follow spelling rules.

Fortunately, there are a few rules for spelling English words that work most of the time. Learning them, and some of their exceptions, will give you a sturdy foundation on which to build.

EI OR IE?

The best way to remember which words are spelled *ei* and which ones *ie* is to recall this familiar jingle:

I before *e* except after *c*,
Or when sounded like *a*, as in *neighbor* and *weigh*.

Niece, believe, field, receive, receipt, ceiling, beige, and *freight* are just a few of the words you'll be able to spell easily once you learn that rule. Then memorize a few of the exceptions:

counterfeit	foreign	kaleidoscope	protein	seize
either	forfeit	leisure	science	weird
financier	height	neither	seismograph	

Also among the rule breakers are words in which *cien* is pronounced *shen: ancient, efficient, conscience, prescience.*

HOMONYMS

Words that sound the same, or almost the same, but are spelled differently are called **homonyms.** Here are some of the most commonly confused homonyms, briefly identified, with examples of how to use them. (Also see the Glossary of Troublemakers at the end of Part Five.)

COMMONLY CONFUSED HOMONYMS

accept (v., take); **except** (prep., other than)

Mimi could *accept* all of Lefty's gifts *except* his ring.

affect (v., influence); **effect** (n., result)

If the new rules *affect* us, what will be their *effect*?

allusion (n., reference); **illusion** (n., fantasy)

Any *allusion* to Norman's mother may revive his *illusion* that she is upstairs, alive, in her rocking chair.

capital (adj., uppercase; n., seat of government); **capitol** (n., government building)

The *Capitol* building in Washington, D.C. (our nation's *capital*), is spelled with a *capital* C.

cite (v., refer to); **sight** (n., vision or tourist attraction); **site** (n., place)

(continued)

COMMONLY CONFUSED HOMONYMS *(continued)*

Did you *cite* Mother as your authority on which *sites* feature the most interesting *sights*?

complement (v., complete; n., counterpart); **compliment** (v. or n., praise)

For Lee to say that Sheila's beauty *complements* her intelligence may or may not be a *compliment*.

desert (v., abandon); **dessert** (n., end-of-meal sweet)

Don't *desert* us by leaving before *dessert*.

elicit (v., bring out); **illicit** (adj., illegal)

By going undercover, Sonny should *elicit* some offers of *illicit* drugs.

formally (adv., officially); **formerly** (adv., in the past)

Jane and John Doe-Smith, *formerly* Jane Doe and John Smith, sent cards *formally* announcing their marriage.

led (v., past tense of *lead*); **lead** (n., metal)

Gil's heart was heavy as *lead* when he *led* the mourners to the grave.

principal (n. or adj., chief); **principle** (n., rule)

The *principal* problem is convincing the media that our school *principal* is a person of high *principles*.

stationary (adj., motionless); **stationery** (n., writing paper)

Hubert's *stationery* shop stood *stationary* for twenty years until a flood swept it down the river.

their (pron., belonging to them); **there** (adv., in that place); **they're** (contraction of *they are*)

Sue said *they're* going over *there* to visit *their* aunt.

to (prep., toward); **too** (adv., also or excessively); **two** (n. or adj., numeral: one more than one)

Let's not take *two* cars *to* town—that's *too* many unless Lucille and Harry are coming *too*.

who's (contraction of *who is*); **whose** (pron., belonging to whom)

Who's going to tell me *whose* dog this is?

your (pron., belonging to you); **you're** (contraction of *you are*)

You're not getting *your* own way this time!

PLURALS

1. To form the plural of most common nouns, add *-s*. If a noun ends in *-ch, -sh, -s,* or *-x,* form its plural by adding *-es.*

attack, attacks	umbrella, umbrellas
ridge, ridges	zone, zones
boss, bosses	trellis, trellises
sandwich, sandwiches	crash, crashes
tax, taxes	Betamax, Betamaxes

2. To form the plural of a common noun ending in *-o,* add *-s* if the *-o* follows a vowel and *-es* if it follows a consonant.

radio, radios	video, videos
hero, heroes	potato, potatoes

3. To form the plural of a common noun ending in *-y,* change the *y* to *i* and add *-es* if the *y* follows a consonant. Add only *-s* if the *y* follows a vowel.

baby, babies	sissy, sissies
fly, flies	wallaby, wallabies
toy, toys	monkey, monkeys
guy, guys	day, days

4. To form the plural of a proper noun, add *-s* or *-es* without changing the noun's ending.
Proper nouns follow the same rules as common nouns, with one exception: a proper noun never changes its spelling in the plural form.

Mary Jane, Mary Janes	Dr. Maddox, the Maddoxes
Mr. Curry, the Currys	Saturday, Saturdays
Professor Jones, the Joneses	

5. To form the plural of a compound noun, add *-s* or *-es* to the chief word, or to the last word if all the words are equal in weight.

brother-in-law, brothers-in-law	actor-manager, actor-managers
aide-de-camp, aides-de-camp	tractor-trailer, tractor-trailers

6. Memorize the plural forms of nouns that diverge from these rules. Certain nouns have special plurals. Here are a few:

alumna, alumnae	man, men
alumnus, alumni	medium, media
child, children	mouse, mice
half, halves	self, selves
goose, geese	tooth, teeth
leaf, leaves	woman, women

SUFFIXES

The *-s* added to a word to make it plural is one type of **suffix,** or tail section. Suffixes allow the same root word to do a variety of jobs, by giving it different forms for different functions. Keeping a few basic rules in mind will help you to use suffixes successfully.

1. Drop a silent *e* before a suffix that begins with a vowel.

move, mover, moved, moving
argue, arguer, argued, arguing
accrue, accruing, accrual

EXCEPTION: If the *e* has an essential function, keep it before *-ing.* In *singe,* for instance, the *e* changes the word's pronunciation from "sing" to "sinj." If you dropped the *e* in *singeing,* it would become *singing.*

singe, singed, singeing
tiptoe, tiptoed, tiptoeing

2. Keep a silent *e* before a suffix that begins with a consonant.

move, movement   hope, hopeless

EXCEPTION: In a word ending in a silent *e* preceded by a vowel, sometimes (but not always) drop the *e.*

argue, argument   true, truly

3. Change a final *y* to *i* before a suffix if the *y* follows a consonant but not if the *y* follows a vowel.

cry, crier, cried   joy, joyous, joyful
happy, happiest, happily   pray, prayed, prayer
hurry, hurried

EXCEPTION: Keep the *y* whenever the suffix is *-ing.*

hurry, hurrying   pray, praying

Drop a final *y* before the suffix *-ize.*

deputy, deputize   memory, memorize

4. Double the final consonant of a one-syllable word before a suffix if (1) the suffix starts with a vowel and (2) the final consonant follows a single vowel.

sit, sitter, sitting
flop, flopped, floppy
rob, robbed, robbery

Don't double the final consonant if it follows two vowels or another consonant.

fail, failed, failure
stack, stacking, stackable

Don't double the final consonant if the suffix starts with a consonant.

top, topless   cap, capful

5. Double the final consonant of a word with two or more syllables if (1) the suffix starts with a vowel *and* (2) the final consonant follows a single vowel *and* (3) the last syllable of the stem is accented once the suffix is added.

commit, committed, committing
rebut, rebuttal
regret, regretted, regrettable

Don't double the final consonant if it follows more than one vowel,

avail, available   repeat, repeating

or it follows another consonant,

accent, accented   depend, dependence

or the suffix starts with a consonant,

commit, commitment   jewel, jewelry

or, when the suffix is added, the final syllable of the stem is unaccented.

confer, conference (*but* conferred)
travel, traveler

PREFIXES

The main point to remember when writing a word with a *prefix* (or nose section) is that the prefix usually does not alter the spelling of the root word it precedes.

dis + appear = disappear
dis + satisfied = dissatisfied
mis + step = misstep
mis + understand = misunderstand
with + hold = withhold
un + necessary = unnecessary

For guidelines on when to use a hyphen to attach a prefix, see 30c–30e.

31b Develop your spelling skills.

Besides becoming familiar with the rules in this chapter, you can use several other tactics to teach yourself to be a better speller.

1. Use mnemonic devices.

To make unusual spellings stick in your memory, invent associations. *Weird* behaves *weirdly*. Would you rather study *ancient science* or be an *efficient financier*? Using such *mnemonic devices* (tricks to aid memory) may help you not only with *ie* and *ei* but with whatever troublesome spelling you are determined to remember. Rise ag*ain*, Brit*ain*! One *d* in *dish*, one in *radish*. Why isn't *mathe*matics like *athle*tics? You write a lett*er* on station*er*y. Any silly phrase or sentence will do, as long as it brings tricky spellings to mind.

2. Keep a record of words you misspell.

Buy yourself a little notebook in which to enter words that invariably trip you up. Each time you proofread a paper you have written and each time you receive one back from your instructor, write down any words you have misspelled. Then practice pronouncing, writing, and spelling them out loud until you·have mastered them.

3. Check any questionable spelling by referring to your dictionary.

Keep a dictionary at your elbow as you write. In matters of spelling, that good-as-gold book is your best friend. Use it to check words as you come up with them and to double-check them as you proofread and edit your work.

4. Learn commonly misspelled words.

To save you the trouble of looking up every spelling bugbear, here is a list of words frequently misspelled. This list will serve to review our whole discussion of spelling, for it contains the trickiest words we've mentioned. Check-mark those that give you trouble—but don't stop there. Spend a few minutes each day going over them. Pronounce each one carefully or have a friend read the list to you. Spell every troublesome word out loud; write it ten times. Your spelling will improve rapidly.

Everybody has at least ten or twenty bugbears. Shoot down yours.

COMMONLY MISSPELLED WORDS

absence	acknowledgment	aggravate	already
abundance	acquaintance	aggressive	although
academic	acquire	aging	altogether
acceptable	acquitted	allege	(entirely)
accessible	across	alleviate	amateur
accidentally	address	all right	analogous
accommodate	advertisement	all together (all in	analysis
accustom	advice	one group)	analyze
achievement	advise	a lot	annual

antecedent
anxiety
apology
apparatus
apparent
appetite
appearance
appreciate
appropriate
arctic
arrest
argument
ascend
assassinate
assistance
association
athlete
athletics
attach
attendance
attractive
audible
audience
average
awkward

balloon
barbarous
bearing
beginning
believe
beneficial
benefited
borne (carried)
boundary
breath (noun)
breathe (verb)
Britain
buoyant
bureaucracy
business

cafeteria
calendar
candidate
capital
capitol
   (a building)
careful
casualties

category
causal
ceiling
cemetery
certain
changeable
changing
characteristic
chief
choose
   (present tense)
chose
   (past tense)
climbed
column
coming
commitment
committed
committee
comparative
competent
competition
complement
compliment
conceive
condemn
congratulate
connoisseur
conscience
conscientious
consistent
controlled
controversy
corollary
coroner
corps (a group)
corpse (a body)
costume
criticism
criticize
cruise
curiosity
curious
deceive
decision
defendant
deficient
definite
deity

dependent
descendant
describe
description
desirable
despair
desperate
detach
develop
develops
development
device (noun)
devise (verb)
diaphragm
diary
dietitian
difference
dilemma
dining
disappear
disappoint
disastrous
discipline
discussion
disease
disparate
dissatisfied
dissipate
divide
divine
doesn't
dominant
don't
drawer
drunkenness
ecstasy
efficiency
eighth
either
eligible
embarrass
emphasize
entirety
environment
equipped
equivalent
especially
exaggerate
exceed

excel
excellence
exercise
exhaust
existence
experience
explanation
extremely

fallacious
familiar
fascinate
February
fiery
finally
financial
foreign
foremost
foresee
foreword
   (a preface)
forfeit
forward
forty
fourth
   (number four)
forth
frantically
fraternities
friend
fulfill
fulfillment

gaiety
gauge
genealogy
generally
genuine
government
grammar
grief
grievous
guarantee
guard
guidance

harass
height
heroes
hoping
   (continued)

COMMONLY MISSPELLED WORDS (continued)

humorous	losing	pastime	realize
hurriedly	lying	peaceable	rebelled
hurrying	magazine	perceive	recede
hygiene	maintenance	perform	receipt
hypocrisy	marriage	performance	receive
illiterate	mathematics	perhaps	received
illogical	medicine	permanent	receiving
imaginary	miniature	permissible	recommend
imitation	mischievous	persistence	recipe
immediately	misspell	personnel	reference
incidentally	misstep	persuade	referring
incredible	muscle	physical	regrettable
indefinite	mysterious	picnic	relevance
independence	necessary	playwright	relief
independent	neither	possession	relieve
indispensable	nickel	possibly	religious
infinite	niece	practically	remembrance
influential	ninety	precede	reminisce
inoculate	ninth	predominant	reminiscence
intelligence	noticeable	preferred	renown
intelligent	notorious	prejudice	repetition
intentionally	nuclear	preparation	replenish
interest	nucleus	prevalent	representative
interpret	numerous	primitive	resistance
interrupt	obstacle	principal (adj.,	restaurant
irrelevant	occasion	main; n., head	review
irresistible	occasionally	of a school)	rhythm
irritable	occur	principle (a rule	rhythmic
island	occurred	or standard)	ridiculous
its (possessive)	occurrence	privilege	roommate
it's (it is, it has)	occurring	probably	sacrifice
jealousy	official	procedure	sacrilegious
judgment	omission	proceed	safety
khaki	omit	professor	scarcely
knowledge	omitted	prominent	scarcity
laboratory	opinion	pronounce	schedule
led (past tense	opportunity	pronunciation	secretary
of *lead*)	originally	propeller	seize
library	outrageous	psychology	separate
license	overrun	psychological	sergeant
lightning	paid	pursue	shining
literature	pamphlet	quantity	siege
loneliness	panicky	quarantine	similar
loose (adjective)	parallel	questionnaire	sincerely
lose (verb)	particularly	quiet	sophomore
		quizzes	source

specifically
specimen
sponsor
stationary (in one
    place)
stationery (writing
    material)
strategy
strength
strenuous
stretch
studying
succeed
successful
suddenness
superintendent
supersede
suppress

surprise
suspicious
synonymous

technical
technique
temperature
tendency
therefore
thorough
thoroughbred
though
thought
throughout
tragedy
traveler
traveling
transferred

truly
twelfth
tyranny

unanimous
undoubtedly
unnecessary
unnoticed
until
useful
usually

vacancy
vacuum
valuable
vengeance
vicious
view
villain

warrant
weather
Wednesday
weird
whether
wholly
who's (who is)
whose (possessive
    of *who*)
withhold
woman
women
writing

yacht

CHAPTER 26

Word Choice

32. Appropriateness   **750**
33. Avoiding Sexism   **757**
34. Exact Words   **760**
35. Wordiness   **765**

32 APPROPRIATENESS

When you talk to people face to face, you can gauge how they are reacting to what you say. Often their responses guide your tone of voice and your choice of words: if your listener chuckles at your humor, you go on being humorous. If your listener frowns, you cut the comedy and speak more seriously.

Like a speaker's voice, a writer's voice may come across as warm and friendly or cool and aloof, furious or merely annoyed, playful or grimly serious. Its quality depends on how the writer feels toward his or her material and toward the reader. The devices the writer uses to show these feelings create the *tone* of the piece of writing.

The tone of your writing, like the tone of your speaking voice, strongly influences your audience's response to the points you are making. Judging a reader's reaction, however, is harder than judging a listener's. To know whether your presentation is successful, usually you must imagine yourself in the reader's place.

Although you may consider your readers from time to time as you gather material and as you write, you probably focus most closely on their response when you reread your writing. What attitude do you want readers to take toward your topic? What tone is likely to convey this attitude most effectively? Do your choices of sentence length, vocabulary, and other elements of style work together to create an appropriate tone?

32a Choose an approach and a level of formality that accurately reflect your attitude toward your topic.

Tone may include choice of formal or informal language, colorful or bland words, coolly objective words or words loaded with emotional connotations ("You pig!" "You angel!"). A tone that seems right (to a reader) comes when the writer has written with an accurate sense of how the reader will react. If the writer is unaware of or is wrong about the reader's responses, then the writer's tone is inappropriate. For instance, taking a humorous approach to a disease such as cancer or AIDS probably would yield an inappropriate tone. The reader, not finding the topic funny, is likely to read without sympathy.

Being aware of your audience helps you choose words that are neither too formal nor too informal. By *formal* language we mean the impersonal language of educated persons, usually written but sometimes spoken on dignified occasions. In general, formal language is marked by relatively long and complex sentences and by a large vocabulary. It doesn't use contractions (such as *doesn't*), and its attitude toward the topic is serious.

Informal (or colloquial) language more closely resembles ordinary conversation. Writers use it in letters to friends, in popular magazine articles and books, and in other types of prose meant for general readers. Its sentences tend to be relatively short and simple. Informal language may include contractions, slang, and references to everyday objects and activities (cheeseburgers, T-shirts, car repair). It may address the reader as "you."

The right language for most essays, especially those you write for class assignments, lies somewhere between formal and informal. If your topic and your tone are serious (say, for an expository paper on the United Nations), then your language is likely to lean toward formality. If your topic is not weighty and your tone is light or humorous (say, for a narrative paper about giving your dog a bath), then your language can be more informal.

32b Choose common words over jargon.

Whatever your tone and your level of formality, certain types of language are best avoided when you write an essay. **Jargon** is the name given to the specialized vocabulary used by people in a particular field (from the Middle English: *jargoun*, "meaningless chatter"). Nearly every academic, professional, and even recreational field—music, carpentry, the law, computer programming, sports—has its own jargon. In baseball, pitcher Dennis Eckersley says that when he faces a dangerous batter, he thinks: "If I throw him *the heater,* maybe he *juices it out* on me" (emphasis added). Translation: "If I throw him a fastball, he might hit a home run."[1] Among people who converse on citizens band radio, "What's your *twenty?*" means "Tell me your whereabouts," while "I'm going *double nickel*" means "I'm going the speed limit: 55 miles per hour."

To a specialist addressing other specialists, jargon is convenient and necessary. Without technical terms, after all, two surgeons could hardly discuss a patient's anatomy. To an outsider, though, such terms may be incomprehensible. If your writing is meant (as it should be) to communicate information to your readers and not to make them feel excluded or confused, you should avoid unnecessary jargon.

Commonly, we apply the name *jargon* to any private, pretentious, or needlessly specialized language. Jargon can include not only words but ways of using words. Some politicians and bureaucrats like to make nouns into verbs by tacking on suffixes like *-ize:*

> **JARGON**   Let us *prioritize* our objectives.
>
> **CLEAR**   Let us *assign priorities to* our objectives.
>
> **CLEAR**   Let us *rank* our objectives *in order of urgency.*
>
> **JARGON**   The government intends to *privatize* federal land holdings.
>
> **CLEAR**   The government intends to *sell* federal land holdings *to private buyers.*

Although *privatize* implies merely "convert to private ownership," usually its real meaning is "sell off"—as might occur, say, were a national park to be auctioned to developers. *Privatize* thus also can be called a *euphemism,* which is any pleasant term that masks an unpleasant meaning (see 32c).

Besides confusing readers, jargon is likely to mislead them. Recently, high technology has made verbs of the familiar nouns *access, boot,* and *format.* Other terms that have entered the popular vocabulary include *interface, x amount of, database,* and *parameters.* Such terms are useful to explain technical processes; but when thoughtlessly applied to nontechnical ideas, they can obscure meaning.

> **JARGON**   A democracy needs the electorate's *input.*
>
> **CLEAR**   A democracy needs the electorate *to vote and to express its views to elected officials.*

One trouble with misplaced jargon is that it is inaccurate: it transforms people into components in a system of processes. "Information is lost, not gained," declares semanticist Robert W. Hunt, "when we are told that 'feedback was obtained,' rather than 'the students complained about the policy.' "[2]

---

[1] Quoted by Mike Whiteford, *How to Talk Baseball* (New York: Dembner Books, 1983), 51.
[2] "Negative Feedback Generated by the Interface of Technical Jargon and Human Speech," *ETC.: A Review of General Semantics* 31 (June 1974): 197–99.

Why do people use technical words about nontechnical subjects? Probably they think that jargon lends their writing an air of knowledge. Rarely is this the case. Indeed, many specialists are calling for reduced jargon even in the scholarly writing of their professions. "Be brave," urge the authors of one handbook of scientific writing in their advice to medical researchers. "Say, 'It is most often found in the heart,' not 'The most frequent among its localizations is the cardiac one.' "[3] In a recent professional journal, Hanan C. Selvin and Everett K. Wilson warn their fellow sociologists against using larger words than necessary. The short word *methods*, they point out, sometimes "suffers an attack of syllabitis" and swells to *methodology*. This larger term is often too broad: it takes in not only the tactics and strategy of investigating but also the grounds for those tactics and strategies.

While a variety of methodologies have been employed to answer this question. . . .

Selvin and Wilson would suggest instead

Although various methods have been employed. . . .[4]

To improve this clause still further, the writer could substitute *used* for *employed* and choose an active rather than a passive verb.

Although researchers have used various methods. . . .

Here's how to shun needless jargon.

1. Beware of choosing any trendy new word when a perfectly good old word will do.
2. Before using a word ending in *-ize, -wise,* or *-ism,* count to ten. This will give you time either to think of a clearer alternative or to be sure that none exists.
3. Avoid the jargon of a special discipline—say, psychology or fly-fishing—unless you are writing of psychological or fly-fishing matters and you know for sure that your reader, too, is familiar with them. If you're writing for an audience of general readers about some field in which you are an expert—if, for instance, you're explaining the fundamentals of hang gliding—define any specialized terms. Even if you're addressing fellow hang-gliding experts, use plain words and you'll rarely go wrong.

Exercise 32–1

The following sentences bog down in jargon. Turn them into standard English. If you see a need to change them extensively, go ahead. If you can't tell what a sentence

[3] Maeve O'Connor and F. Peter Woodford, Foreword to *Writing Scientific Papers in English* (Amsterdam: Associated Scientific Publishers, 1975), p. 42.
[4] "Cases in Point: A Limited Glossary of Stumblebum Usage," *Sociological Quarterly* 25 (1984): 417–27.

DOONESBURY

by **Garry Trudeau**

means, decide what it might mean and rewrite it so that its meaning is clear. Possible revisions for the lettered sentences appear in the back of the book. Example:

> The proximity of Mr. Fitton's knife to Mr. Schering's arm produced a violation of the integrity of the skin.
>
> Mr. Fitton's knife cut Mr. Schering's arm.

a. Diagnosiswise, Mrs. Pitt, your husband's heart looks considerably failure-prone at this particular point in time.

b. In the heart area, Mr. Pitt is a prime candidate-elect for intervention of a multiple bypass nature.

c. Within the parameters of your insurance company's financial authorization, he can either be regimed dietwise or be bypass prognosticated.

d. We of the State Department have carefully contexted the riots in Lebanon intelligencewise, and after full and thorough database utilization, find them abnormalling rapidly.

e. Certain antinuclearistic and pacifistic/prejudicial factions have been picketing the missile conference in hopes of immobilizing these vital peacekeeping deliberations.

1. Regarding the issue as to whether foreknowledge of the operation was obtained by the secretary in this instance, it has been ascertained that no definite affirmative conclusion is warranted.

2. Engaging in a prayer situation permits an individual to maximally interface with the Lord.

3. The deer hunters number-balanced the ecological infrastructure by quietizing x amount of the deer populace.

4. "I am very grateful that we have education up where it is, high on the educational agenda of this country."

—Secretary of Education T. H. Bell, in a speech, June 1983

5. All student personnel are directed to prioritize their efforts to the *n*th degree toward minimization of excessive dormitory litter generation.

32c   *Recognize euphemisms.*

Euphemisms are plain truths dressed in attractive words, sometimes hard facts stated gently and pleasantly. To say that someone *passed away* instead of *died* is a common euphemism—useful and humane, perhaps, in breaking terrible news to an anxious family. In such shock-absorbing language, an army that retreats *makes a strategic withdrawal;* a poor old man becomes a *disadvantaged senior citizen.* But euphemisms aren't always oversized words. If you call someone *slim* whom you think *underweight* or *skinny,* you use a euphemism, though it has only one syllable.

Because they can bathe glum truths in a kindly glow, euphemisms are beloved by advertisers—like the *mortician (undertaker)* who offered *pre-need arrangements.* Euphemisms also can make ordinary things sound more impressive. Some acne medications treat not *pimples* but *blemishes.* In Madison, Wisconsin, a theater renamed its candy counter the *patron assistance center.* Over time, many euphemisms have become so familiar that we don't notice that they disguise anything. *Life insurance* might more accurately be called *death insurance,* since it prevents financial hardship only on the death of the insured. (Imagine how much harder it would be to sell "death insurance"!)

Euphemisms may serve grimmer purposes. During World War II, Jewish prisoners sent to Nazi extermination camps carried papers stamped *Rückkehr Unerwünscht* (Return Unwanted). In 1984, the Doublespeak Award of the National Council of Teachers of English went to the U.S. State Department for its announcement that it would no longer use the word *killing* in its official reports but would substitute *unlawful or arbitrary deprivation of life.* The following year, the award went to the CIA, which prepared a manual for rebels fighting the government of Nicaragua. In the manual, the rebels were told how to join a peaceful demonstration and, equipped with "knives, razors, chains, clubs, bludgeons," march along "slightly behind the innocent and gullible participants." Asked about this manual, CIA director William Casey said that its purpose was "to make every guerrilla persuasive in face-to-face communication."

Some writers, to be sure, use euphemisms ironically. As readers, we then enjoy noticing a discrepancy between a humble truth and a lofty way of putting it. The result is a comic effect—as when Mark Twain, in *Life on the Mississippi,* refers to a "fragrant town drunkard." With tongue in cheek, a sports writer calls first base "the initial hassock." Mechanically contrived, though, such euphemisms won't be funny. Most of the time, a euphemism is far less effective than direct words.

Even if you aren't prone to using euphemisms in your own writing, be aware of them when you read, especially when collecting evidence from biased sources and official spokespersons.

Exercise 32–2

Rewrite the following statements, turning euphemisms into plainer words. Possible revisions for the lettered sentences appear in the back of the book. Example:

> The president's door is always open to any employee who has first discussed his or her concern with the appropriate manager.

> The president will not talk with an employee about a problem behind his or her boss's back.

a. This entry-level position offers a challenging career opportunity with a relatively modest initial salary.

b. The ship sank because of loss of hull integrity.

c. The new K27 missile will effectively depopulate the cities of any aggressor nation.

d. In our town, sanitation engineers when making their rounds must wear professional apparel.

e. Freddie the Rocker has boarded a first-class flight for the great all-night discotheque in the sky.

1. Our security forces have judiciously thinned an excessive number of political dissidents.

2. The champion's uppercut landed, and on the challenger's lip a tea-rose bloomed.

3. To bridge the projected shortfall between collections and expenditures in next year's budget, the governor advocates some form of revenue enhancement.

4. Saturday's weather forecast calls for extended periods of shower activity.

5. Uncle Eb, a gentleman of extremely mature years, was a faithful worshiper at the Follies Bar, a shrine of progressive corporeal revelation.

32d Avoid using slang in formal writing.

Poet Carl Sandburg once said, "Slang is language that takes off its coat, spits on its hands, and gets to work." Clearly, Sandburg approved. Probably even the purists among us will concede that slang, especially when new, can be colorful ("She's not playing with a full deck"), playful ("He's wicked cute!"), and apt (*ice* for diamonds, a *stiff* for a corpse).

In fact, some coiners of slang are true poets. They notice a trait and render it vivid, occasionally in a metaphor so strong that it wins a respectable niche in the language. Most of us say that a robber *holds up* a bank or that a kind father is a *pushover,* without even knowing that such expressions long ago muscled their way into standard English through the back door, as slang. *Dropout, hacker,* and *networking* are among the more recent entries that seem bent on staying.

The trouble with most slang, however, is that it quickly comes to seem quaint, even incomprehensible. We don't hear anyone say *groovy* anymore except on reruns of *The Brady Bunch. Bad vibes* (good ones, too) and *guilt trips,* ubiquitous in the 1960s, today wear spiderwebs. Even the lately minted *bummer* and *grody to the max* already seem as old and wrinkled as the Jazz Age's favorite exclamation of glee, *twenty-three skidoo!*

In the classroom and out of it, your writing communicates your thoughts. To be understood, now and in the future, your best bet is to stick to standard English. Most slang is less than clever. The newest of it, apt though it may seem, like any fad is in danger of being quickly tossed aside in favor of something newer still. Seek words that are usual but exact, not the latest thing, and your writing will stay young longer.

Exercise 32–3

Revise the following sentences to replace slang with standard English. Possible revisions for the lettered sentences appear in the back of the book. Example:

> I can see that something is bugging you, so you may as well lay it on me.
>
> I can see that something is bothering you, so you may as well tell me about it.

a. Judy doesn't dig the way Paul's been coming on to her.

b. If large animals do not clear out of the combat zone, the army's policy is to waste them.

c. Judge Lehman's reversal of the *Smith v. Jones* verdict shows that his lights are on but nobody's home.

d. Once that eyewitness spilled his guts, Jones's goose was cooked.

e. If he can make bail, he'll probably split.

1. Otherwise he could draw five to ten in the slammer.

2. Blue-collar criminals get nailed; white-collar criminals walk.

3. The insider trading thing on Wall Street has turned out to be a major scam.

4. One honcho actually offed himself.

5. If the Iranians had the hardware, they'd probably nuke us.

33   AVOIDING SEXISM

Among the prime targets of American feminists in the 1960s and 1970s was the male bias built into the English language. Why, they asked, do we talk about *prehistoric man, manpower,* and *the brotherhood of man,* when by *man* we mean the entire human race? Why do we focus attention on the gender of an accomplished woman by calling her a *poetess* or a *lady doctor?* Why does a letter to a corporation have to begin "Gentlemen:"?

Early efforts to provide alternatives to sexist language often led to awkward, even ungrammatical solutions. To substitute "Everyone prefers their own customs" for "Everyone prefers *his* own customs" is to replace sexism with bad grammar. "Everyone prefers his or her [or his/her] own customs" is correct, but sometimes clumsy. Even clumsier is "Was it George or Jane who submitted his or her [his/her] resignation?" *Chairperson, policeperson, businessperson, spokesperson,* and *congressperson* do not flow easily from tongue or pen; and some people object to *chairwoman, policewoman,* and similar words because they call attention to gender where gender ought not to matter. *Male nurse* elicits the same objection.

Some writers try to eliminate sexual bias by alternating between the masculine and feminine genders every few sentences. Dr. Benjamin Spock, when referring to babies in later revisions of his well-known *Baby and Child Care,* uses *he* and *she* in roughly equal numbers. Some readers find this approach refreshing. Why should we, after all, think of every baby as a boy, every parent as a woman? Other readers find such gender switches confusing.

Well-meaning attempts to invent or borrow neutral third-person pronouns (*thon asks* instead of *he asks* or *she asks,* for instance) have not gained general acceptance. How then can we as sensitive writers minimize the sexist constraints that the English language places in our path? Although there are no hard-and-fast rules, no perfect solutions, we can be aware of the potholes and try to steer around them as smoothly as possible.

33a *For terms that include or imply* man, *look for alternatives that make no reference to gender.*

We all know from experience that the most obvious way to neuter *man* or a word starting with *man* is to substitute *human.* The result, however, is often clumsy.

> **SEXIST**   Mankind has always been obsessed with man's inhumanity to man.
>
> **NONSEXIST**   Humankind has always been obsessed with humans' inhumanity to other humans.

Adding *hu-* to *man* alleviates sexism but weighs down the sentence. When you run into this problem, think for a moment. Usually you can find a more graceful solution.

> **REVISED**   Human beings have always been obsessed with people's cruelty to one another.

Similarly, when you face a word that ends with *-man,* you need not simply replace that ending with *-person.* Take a different approach: think about what the word means and find a synonym that is truly neutral.

> **SEXIST**   Did you leave a note for the mailman?
>
> **REVISED**   Did you leave a note for the mail carrier?

The same tactic works for designations with a male and a female ending, such as *waiter* and *waitress.*

> **SEXIST**   Ask your waiter [or waitress] for today's specials.

| NONSEXIST | Ask your waitperson for today's specials. |
| REVISED | Ask your server for today's specials. |

33b *Avoid sexism by changing from singular to plural.*

| SEXIST | Today's student values his education. |
| REVISED | Today's students value their education. |

Sexism is not the only problem in that sentence. Anytime you let a singular noun stand for a group of people, you run the risk of creating a stereotype. Pluralizing thus can sometimes help you to avoid ethnic and racial, as well as sexual, bias.

STEREOTYPED	The Chinaman eats his rice with chopsticks.
REVISED	Chinese people eat their rice with chopsticks.
STEREOTYPED	The Native American lost his land to the white man.
REVISED	Native Americans lost their land to whites.

33c *Where possible, simply omit words that denote gender.*

SEXIST	For optimal results, there must be rapport between a stockbroker and his client, a teacher and his student, a doctor and his patient.
REVISED	For optimal results, there must be rapport between stockbroker and client, teacher and student, doctor and patient.
SEXIST	The girls in the secretarial pool bought President Schmutz a birthday cake.
REVISED	The secretarial pool [or the secretaries] bought President Schmutz a birthday cake.

33d *Avoid gender-linked words that are cute or condescending.*

A responsible writer does not call women *blondes, coeds, gals, working girls, woman drivers,* or any other names that imply that they are not to be taken seriously. Nor should an employee ever be referred to as a *girl* or *boy.*

SEXIST	I'll have my girl call your girl and make a date for lunch.
REVISED	I'll have my secretary call your secretary and make a date for lunch.
SEXIST	Mario said he'd send one of the boys to drive Linda to the airport.
REVISED	Mario said he'd send a driver to take Linda to the airport.

33e *Be on the lookout for implied sexual stereotypes.*

Sometimes gender is linked to a title or designation indirectly. Aside from a few obvious exceptions such as *mothers* and *fathers,* never assume that all the members of a group are of the same sex.

SEXIST	Astronauts have little time to spend with their wives and children.
REVISED	Astronauts have little time to spend with their families.
SEXIST	Rock musicians meet plenty of eager women, but few who are worth getting to know.
REVISED	Rock musicians meet plenty of eager members of the opposite sex, but few who are worth getting to know.

33f When writing to or about a woman who has no title that you know of, consider addressing her as **Ms.**

Ms. is a wonderfully useful form of address. Comparable to *Mr.* for a man, it is easier to use than either *Miss* or *Mrs.* for someone whose marital status you don't know. Now that many married women are keeping their original last names, either professionally or in all areas of their lives, *Ms.* is often the best choice even for someone whose marital status you do know. However, if the woman to whom you are writing holds a doctorate, a professional office, or some other position that comes with a title, use that title rather than *Ms.*

Ms. Jane Doe, Editor. Dear Ms. Doe:

Professor Jane Doe, Department of English. Dear Professor Doe:

NOTE: Accept your inability to change the English language overnight, single-handedly. As more men and women come to regard themselves as equals, the language will increasingly reflect the reality. Meanwhile, in your writing, try to be fair to both sexes without succumbing either to clumsiness or to grammatical error.

34 EXACT WORDS

What would you think if you read in a newspaper that a certain leading citizen is a *pillow of the community?* How would you react to a foreign dignitary's statement that he has no children because his wife is *inconceivable?* Good writing—that is, effective written communication—depends on more than good grammar. Just as important are knowing what words and phrases mean and using them precisely.

34a Choose words for their connotations as well as their denotations.

The **denotation** of a word is its basic meaning—its dictionary definition. *Stone,* for instance, has the same denotation as *rock. Excited, agitated,* and *exhilarated* all denote a similar state of physical and emotional arousal. When you look up a word in a dictionary or thesaurus, the synonyms you find have been selected for their shared denotation.

The **connotations** of a word are the shades of meaning that set it apart from its synonyms. We say *Phil's house is a stone's throw from mine,* not *a rock's throw.* You might be *agitated* by the prospect of exams next week, but *exhilarated* by your plans for a vacation afterward. When you choose one out of several synonyms listed in a dictionary or thesaurus, you base your choice on connotation.

Paying attention to connotation helps a writer to say exactly what he or she intends, instead of almost but not quite.

IMPRECISE   Advertisers have given light beer a macho image by showing football players *sipping* the product with *enthusiasm.*

REVISED   Advertisers have given light beer a macho image by showing football players *guzzling* the product with *gusto.*

IMPRECISE   The cat's eyes *shone* as she *pursued* the mouse.

REVISED   The cat's eyes *glittered* as she *stalked* the mouse.

34b Weed out clichés.

A **cliché** is a trite expression, worn out from too much use. It may have glinted once, like a coin fresh from the mint, but now it is dull and flat from years of passing from hand to hand. If a story begins, "It was a dark and stormy night," and introduces a *tall, dark, and handsome* man and a woman who is *a vision of loveliness,* then its author is obviously running low on change.

A cliché isn't just any old dull expression: it is one whose writer mistakenly assumes is bright. "Let's run this up the flagpole and see if anyone salutes," proposes the executive, while his or her colleagues yawn at the effort to sound clever. Stale, too, is the suggestion to put an idea *on the back burner.* Clichés abound when writers and speakers try hard to sound vigorous and colorful but don't trouble to invent anything vigorous, colorful, and new.

George Orwell once complained about prose made up of phrases "tacked together like the sections of a prefabricated henhouse." If you read newspapers, you are familiar with such ready-made constructions. A strike is usually settled after *a marathon bargaining session* that *narrowly averts a walkout,* often *at the eleventh hour.* Fires customarily *race* and *gut.* Some writers use clichés to exaggerate, giving a statement more force than they feel. The writer to whom everything is *fantastic* or *terrific* arouses a reader's suspicion that it isn't. Such word inflation once drew a protest from sports writer Ray Fitzgerald to his fellow baseball writers in the press box at Boston's Fenway Park:

> The word you hear around here is *incredible.* Everything is incredible this or incredible that. Every other play is incredible. Do you know what's incredible? If that guy turns into a swan while he's sliding into second base, that's incredible.[5]

[5]Quoted by Leigh Montville in a tribute to Fitzgerald, *Boston Globe,* August 4, 1982.

Although Fitzgerald's remark was leveled at baseball writers, college writers also can take it to heart. If in presenting evidence and illustrations you find yourself repeating words like *remarkable, unique,* or *significant,* you are probably exaggerating.

No writer can entirely avoid clichés or avoid echoing colorful expressions first used by someone else. You need not ban from your writing all proverbs ("It takes a thief to catch a thief"), well-worked quotations from Shakespeare ("Neither a borrower nor a lender be"), and other faintly dusty wares from the storehouse of our language. "Looking for a needle in a haystack" may be a time-worn phrase, yet who can put that idea any more memorably?

Nor should you fear that every familiar expression is a cliché. *Just in time, more or less, sooner or later*—these are old, dull, familiar expressions, to be sure; but they are not clichés, for they don't try to be vivid or figurative. Inevitably, we all rely on them.

When editing your writing, you will usually recognize any really annoying cliché you'll want to eradicate. If you feel a sudden guilty desire to surround an expression with quotation marks, as if to apologize for it—

In his campaign speeches for his fourteenth term, Senator Pratt shows that he cannot "cut the mustard" any longer.

—then strike it out. Think again: what do you want to say? Recast your idea more clearly, more exactly.

At age seventy-seven, Senator Pratt no longer can hold a crowd with an impassioned, hour-long speech, as he could when he first ran for Congress.

By what other means can you spot a cliché? One way is to show your papers to friends, asking them to look for anything trite. As you go on in college, your awareness of clichés will grow with reading. The more you read, the easier it is to recognize a cliché on sight, for you will have met it often before.

Meanwhile, here is a list of a few clichés still in occasional circulation. If any is a favorite of yours, try replacing it with something more vivid and original.

Achilles' heel	last but not least
acid test	Little did I dream
add insult to injury	mad as a wet hen
apple of one's eye	make a long story short
as American as apple pie	meanwhile, back at the ranch
an astronomical sum	natural inclination
at sixes and sevens	neat as a pin
beyond a shadow of a doubt	nice as pie
the Big Apple [name for	nutty as a fruitcake
New York City]	old as the hills
born with a silver spoon in one's	on the ball
mouth	on the brink of disaster

bosom companions, bosom buddies
burn the midnight oil
burn one's bridges behind
busy as a beaver (or a bee)
But that's another story.
come hell or high water
cool as a cucumber
cream of the crop
cross the Rubicon
couldn't have imagined in my wildest
    dreams
dead as a doornail
do your own thing
dressed fit to kill
dry as dust
eager beaver
easy as taking candy from a baby
easy as falling off a log
a face that would stop a clock
feeling on top of the world
few and far between
fiddle while Rome burns
fine and dandy
fly in the ointment
fresh as a daisy
from (or since) time immemorial
going like a house afire
golden years
greased lightning
hands-on learning experience
hard as a rock
high as a kite
holler bloody murder
honest as the day is long
hot and heavy
In conclusion, I would like to say . . .

over and above (or beyond) the call
    of duty
pay through the nose
piece of cake
point with pride
proud as a peacock
pull the wool over someone's eyes
pure as the driven snow
read the riot act
salad days
sell like hotcakes
a sheepish grin
since the dawn of time
skating on thin ice
a skeleton in the closet
slow as molasses
smell a rat
a sneaking suspicion
sound as a dollar
stack the deck
stagger the imagination
stick out like a sore thumb
sweet as honey
That's the way the ball bounces
    (or the cookie crumbles).
tip of the iceberg
through thick and thin
time-honored
too little and too late
tried but true
unimpeachable authority
We returned home tired but
    happy.
The worm turns.
You could have knocked me over
    with a feather.

34c When you use an idiom, be sure its form is correct.

Every language contains **idioms,** or *idiomatic expressions:* phrases that, through long use, have become standard even though their construction may defy logic or grammar. Idioms can be difficult for a native speaker of English to explain to someone just learning the language. They sound natural, however, to those who have heard them since childhood.

Many idiomatic expressions require us to choose the right preposition. We say we live *in* the city, but vacation *at* the seashore, even though we might be hard pressed to explain why we use *in* in one phrase and *at* in the other. To pause *for* a minute is not the same as to pause *in* a minute. We work *up* a sweat while working *out* in the gym. We argue *with* someone, but *about* something. We can also argue *for* or *against* it.

For some idioms we must know which article to use before a noun—or whether to use any article at all. We can be *in motion,* but we have to be *in the swim.* We're occasionally in *a tight spot* but never in *a trouble.* Certain idioms vary from country to country: in Britain, a patient has an operation *in hospital*; in America, *in the hospital.* Idioms can involve choosing the right verb with the right noun: we *seize* an opportunity, but we *catch* a plane. We *break* a law but *explode* a theory.

Sometimes even the best writers draw a blank when they confront a common idiomatic expression. Is *compared with* or *compared to* the right phrase? (The first is right in comparing two things more or less similar— "Minneapolis has spick-and-span streets, compared with New York's"—while the second is right in holding up something ordinary to a loftier ideal—"Jim isn't much of a basketball player compared to Magic Johnson.") Should you say *agree to, agree on,* or *agree with*? *Disgusted at* or *disgusted with*? *Smile about, smile at, smile on,* or *smile over*?

Depending on what you mean, sometimes one alternative is correct, sometimes another. When you're at work on a paper, the dictionary can help you to choose. Look up *agree* in *The American Heritage Dictionary,* for instance, and you will find *agree to, agree with, agree about, agree on,* and *agree that* illustrated with sentence examples that make clear just where and when each combination is appropriate. You can then pick the idiom that belongs in the sentence you are working on. In the long run, though, you learn to use idioms accurately in your writing by reading the work of careful writers, by absorbing what they do, and by doing likewise.

Exercise 34–1

Revise the following sentences to replace words that have inappropriate connotations, to eliminate clichés, and to correct any faulty idioms. Possible revisions for the lettered sentences appear in the back of the book. Example:

> The premier's tantamount objective is to defeat the guerrillas by giving them some of their own medicine.

> The premier's paramount objective is to defeat the guerrillas using their own tactics.

a. Since time immemorial, the Sahara has had a legendary reputation as one of the most overheated and arid regions on earth.

b. The intrepid explorers knew they were taking their lives in their hands as they sallied forth to cross the featureless sands.

c. After six days of travel, every member of the party was red as a beet and faint because of thirst.

d. Even the camels were on the verge to falling over in their tracks when the scouts laid their eyes on an oasis.

e. With furrowed brow, the caravan leader peered into the blinding sun.

1. As the distant speck loomed larger on the horizon, everyone could see it was no optical illusion, but a long-waited-for refuge.
2. "At last! Water!" screamed the very pleased caravan leader.
3. Cleaning his damp, dusty brow, he led the party into the welcome darkness under the palm trees.
4. Their throats felt as dry as bones, but before wetting their whistles, they watered the camels.
5. As the dead-on-their-feet explorers scurried under their mosquito netting for forty winks, their leader muttered that crossing the Sahara was a pleasure compared to searching for the North Pole.

35 WORDINESS

Writers who try to impress their audience by offering few ideas in many words rarely fool anyone but themselves. Concision takes more effort than wordiness, but it pays off in clarity. (For more on how to unpad your prose, see "Cutting and Whittling," p. 531.)

The following list contains common words and phrases that take up more room than they deserve. Each has a shorter substitute. If this list contains some of your favorite expressions, don't worry. Not even the best professional writer is perfectly terse. Still, being aware of verbal short cuts may help you avoid rambling. The checklist can be useful for self-editing, particularly if you ever face a strict word limit. When you write an article for a college newspaper where space is tight, or a laboratory report that you must squeeze into a standard worksheet, or an assignment limited to 600 words, use this list to pare your prose to the bone.

CHECKLIST OF WINDY WORDS AND PHRASES

WORDY VERSION	CONCISE VERSION
adequate enough	adequate
a period of a week	a week
approximately	about
area of, field of	[Omit.]
arrive at an agreement, conclude an agreement	agree
as a result of	because
as far as . . . is concerned	about
as to whether	whether
as you are already well aware	as you know
at an earlier point in time	before, earlier
at a later moment	after, later

CHECKLIST OF WINDY WORDS AND PHRASES *(continued)*

WORDY VERSION	CONCISE VERSION
at the present moment, at this point in time	now
basic rudiments, basic fundamentals	rudiments, fundamentals
brief in duration	brief
by means of	by
consensus of opinion	consensus *or* opinion
concerning the subject of, in connection with the subject of, with respect to the matter of	about
continuing on, continuing along	continuing
considerable amount of	much
considerable number of	many
despite the fact that, regardless of the fact that	although, though
due to the fact that, for the reason that, on account of the fact that	because
each individual person	each, each person
feel the necessity for	need
first beginnings, early beginnings	beginnings
for the most part	mostly
for the purpose of, in order to	for, to
from my own personal point of view	to me [or omit]
give consideration to	consider, think about
great amount of, large amount of	much
great number of, large number of	many
I am of the opinion that, it is my personal opinion that	I think
if it is agreeable to you	if you agree
impact on	affect
in a reckless [or any other adjective] manner (or fashion)	recklessly [or any other adverb]
in color (as in "red in color")	[Omit.]
in my personal opinion	I think
in regard to, with reference to	about
in such a way that	so that
in terms of	[Omit and rewrite.]
in the last analysis	in the end, finally
in the likely (or unlikely) event that	if
in the not-too-distant future	soon
in this modern world, in the world of today, in contemporary society	now, today
in view of the fact that	because, since
it is our considered opinion that	We believe [or omit]
I would like to request that you please	please

WORDY VERSION	CONCISE VERSION
join together	join
kind of, sort of, type of	[Omit.]
large in size, large-sized	large
a large number of	many
lend assistance to	assist, aid, help
main essentials	essentials
make contact with	call, talk with
members of the opposition	opponents
merge together	merge
numerous	many
numerous and sundry	many different
on the occasion of	on
on a once-a-month schedule	monthly
other alternatives	alternatives
past experience, past history	experience, history
persons of the female gender	women
persons of the homosexual persuasion	homosexuals, gays
persons of the Methodist faith	Methodists
pertaining to	about, on
plan ahead for the future	plan
prior to	before
put an end to, terminate	end
rarely ever, seldom ever	rarely, seldom
strongly urge	urge
sufficient amount of	enough
the reason why	the reason
refer to by the name of	call, name
refer back to	refer to
remarks of a humorous nature, remarks on the humorous side	humorous remarks
render completely inoperative	break, smash
repeat again	repeat
resemble in appearance	look like
respective, respectively	[Omit.]
returning back	returning
similar to	like
subsequent to	after
subsequently	later, then
sufficient number (or amount) of	enough
true facts	facts, truth
until such time as	until
utilize, make use of	use
very	[Omit unless you very much need it.]
wastage	waste
way in which	way
whether or not	whether

Exercise 35–1

Rewrite the following sentences to eliminate wordiness. Possible revisions for the lettered sentences appear in the back of the book. Example:

> Professor Scott assures us that as of the present moment she does not feel any necessity for an increase in bookshelf space.

> Professor Scott says she does not need more bookshelves right now.

a. It is my personal suspicion that the manner in which this inquiry is being handled has a strong likelihood of obscuring the true facts.

b. In order to begin utilization of our new computer system, all individuals are requested to make their selection of a password at their earliest possible convenience.

c. As you are already aware, there is a very low probability at this point in time of your remittance being expeditiously returned back to you.

d. If a sufficient number of people press the elevator call button within a short duration of time, the elevator will be rendered inoperative.

e. It was impossible for the secretary to ascertain whether or not Mr. Jones and Ms. Cunningham had presented to the board by telephone their respective decisions to resign.

1. Dr. Glidden wishes to urge strongly that the entertainment committee refrain from hiring any comedian who is prone to making remarks of a so-called humorous nature about persons of Italian, Irish, Polish, or other ancestry.

2. It was Ms. Howe's impression prior to accepting this job that she was assured of regular salary increases on a semiannual schedule.

3. Implementation of our organization's plan for the future will not take place on schedule due to the fact that a substantial number of the details remain to be finalized.

4. With regard to the proposal for the recycling of paper, it is management's position that restraint by all personnel in their amount of paper utilization will adequately decrease wastage.

5. Consumption of apples on a daily basis has been shown to significantly decrease the necessity for medical attention.

A Glossary
of Troublemakers

In grammatical terms **usage** refers to the ways in which literate Americans customarily employ certain words and phrases in their writing. It includes many matters of accepted practice or convention about which there isn't any law. To incorporate good usage in your writing, you can observe (as dictionary makers carefully do) the practices followed by an apparent majority of admirable writers.

This glossary lists words and phrases whose usage frequently troubles student writers. Look it over: it may clear up a few familiar problems for you. Not every possible problem is listed—only some that instructors often find in student papers. This brief list is meant not to replace your dictionary but to help you pinpoint a few sources of difficulty and wipe them out.

For advice on getting rid of long-winded expressions (*in the field of, in regards to*), see "Revising Deeply," page 523. For advice on spelling, see 31.

a, an   Use *an* only before a word beginning with a vowel sound. "*An* asp can eat *an* egg *an* hour." (Note that some words, such as *hour* and *honest*, open with a vowel sound even though spelled with an *h*.)

above   Using *above* or *below* to refer back or forward in an essay is awkward and may not be accurate. Less awkward alternatives: "the *preceding* argument," "in the *following* discussion," "on the *next* page."

accept, except   *Accept* is a verb meaning "to receive willingly"; *except* is usually a preposition meaning "not including." "This motel *accepts* all children *except* infants under two." Sometimes *except* is a verb, meaning "to exempt." "The rate of $20 per person *excepts* children under twelve."

adverse, averse   *Adverse* means "unfavorable or antagonistic" and is used to modify things, not people. *Averse* means "reluctant or strongly opposed" and is followed by *to*. "Because of the *adverse* winds, the captain is *averse* to setting sail."

advice, advise   *Advice* is a noun, *advise* a verb. When someone *advises* you, you receive *advice.*

affect, effect   Most of the time, the verb *affect* means "to act on" or "to influence." "Too much beer can *affect* your speech." *Affect* can also mean "to put on airs." "He *affected* an Oxford accent." *Effect,* a noun, means "a result": "Too much beer has a numbing *effect.*" But *effect* is also a verb, meaning "to bring about." "Beer *effected* his downfall."

aggravate   Although in speech people often use *aggravate* to mean "to annoy," in formal writing use *aggravate* to mean "to make worse." "The noise of the jackhammers *aggravated* her headache."

agree to, agree with, agree on   *Agree to* means "to consent to"; *agree with,* "to be in accord." "I *agreed to* attend the New Age lecture, but I didn't *agree with* the speaker's views." *Agree on* means "to come to or have an understanding about." "Chuck and I finally *agreed on* a compromise: the children would go to camp, but not overnight."

ain't   Don't use *ain't* in writing; it is nonstandard English for *am not, is not* (*isn't*), and *are not* (*aren't*).

allusion, illusion   An *allusion* is a reference to history, literature, music, science, or some other area of knowledge. In the statement "Two by two we hurried aboard Flight 937 as though the waters of the flood lapped at our heels," the writer makes an allusion to the biblical story of Noah's ark. An *illusion* is a misleading appearance ("an optical illusion") or a mistaken assumption. "He labors under the *illusion* that he's Romeo" (to give an example with an allusion in it).

a lot   Many people mistakenly write the colloquial expression *a lot* as one word: *alot.* Use *a lot* if you must; but in writing, *much* or *a large amount* is preferable. See also *lots, lots of, a lot of.*

already, all ready   *Already* means "by now"; *all ready* means "set to go." "At last our picnic was *all ready,* but *already* it was night."

altogether, all together   *Altogether* means "entirely." "He is *altogether* mistaken." *All together* means "in unison" or "assembled." "Now *all together*—heave!" "Inspector Trent gathered the suspects *all together* in the drawing room."

among, between   *Between* refers to two persons or things; *among,* to more than two. "Some disagreement *between* the two superpowers was inevitable. Still, there was general harmony *among* the five nations represented at the conference."

amoral, immoral   *Amoral* means "neither moral nor immoral" or "not involved with moral distinctions or judgments." "Nature is *amoral.*" "Some people think children are *amoral* and should not be held accountable for their actions." *Immoral* means "violating moral principles, morally wrong." "Stealing from the poor is *immoral.*"

amount, number   Use *amount* to refer to quantities that cannot be counted or to bulk; use *number* to refer to countable, separate items. "The *number* of people you want to serve determines the *amount* of ice cream you'll need."

an, a   See *a, an.*

and/or   Usually use either *and* or *or* alone. "Tim *and* Elaine will come to the party." "Tim *or* Elaine will come to the party." If you mean three distinct options, write, "Tim *or* Elaine, *or both*, will come to the party, depending on whether they can find a babysitter."

ante-, anti- The prefix *ante* means "preceding." An *antechamber* is a small room that leads to a larger one; *antebellum* means "before the Civil War." *Anti* most often means "opposing": *antidepressant.* It needs a hyphen in front of *i* (*anti-inflationary*) or in front of a capital letter (*anti-Marxist*).

anxious, eager Although the meanings of these two words overlap to some extent, in writing reserve *anxious* for situations involving anxiety or worry. *Eager* denotes joyous anticipation. "We are *eager* to see him, but we're *anxious* about his failing health."

anybody, any body When *anybody* is used as an indefinite pronoun, write it as one word: "*Anybody* in his or her right mind abhors murder." (*Anybody* is singular; therefore it is wrong to say "Anybody in *their* right mind." See 33 for acceptable alternatives.)

Any body, written as two words, is the adjective *any* modifying the noun *body*. "Name *any body* of water in Australia." "The coroner told his assistant to begin work on *any body* brought in from the crash site."

anyone, any one *Anyone* is an indefinite pronoun written as one word. "Does *anyone* want dessert?" The phrase *any one* consists of the pronoun *one* modified by the adjective *any* and is used to single out something in a group: "Pick *any one* of the pies—they're all good."

anyplace *Anyplace* is colloquial for *anywhere* and should not be used in formal writing.

anyways, anywheres These are nonstandard forms of *anyway* and *anywhere* and should not be used in writing.

apt Usually, *apt* means "likely." "That film is *apt* to bore you." "Jack's big feet make him *apt* to trip." *Apt* can also mean "fitting" and "quick to learn": "an apt nickname," "an apt student of French." See also *liable, likely*.

as Sometimes using the subordinating conjunction *as* can make a sentence ambiguous. "*As* we were climbing the mountain, we put on heavy sweaters." Does *as* here mean "because" or "while"? Whenever using *as* would be confusing, use a more specific term instead, such as *because* or *while*.

as, like Use *as, as if*, or *as though* rather than *like* to introduce clauses of comparison. "Dan's compositions are tuneful, *as* [not *like*] music ought to be." "Jeffrey behaves *as if* [not *like*] he were ill."

Like, because it is a preposition, can introduce a phrase but not a clause. "My brother looks *like* me." "Henrietta runs *like* a duck."

as to Usually this expression sounds stilted. Use *about* instead. "He complained *about* [not *as to*] the cockroaches."

at See *where . . . at, where . . . to*.

averse See *adverse*.

bad, badly *Bad* is an adjective; *badly* is an adverb. They are commonly misused after linking verbs (*be, appear, become, grow, seem, prove*) and verbs of the senses (*feel, look, smell, sound, taste*). Following a linking verb, use the adjective form. "I feel *bad* that we missed the plane." "The egg smells *bad*." (See 12b, 12c.) The adverb form is used to modify a verb or an adjective. "They played so *badly* they lost to the last-place team." "It was a *badly* needed victory that saved the cellar-dwellers from elimination."

being as, being that "*Being as* I was ignorant of the facts, I kept still" is a clumsy way to say "*Because* I was ignorant" or "*Not knowing* the facts."

beside, besides *Beside* is a preposition meaning "by the side of." "Sheldon enjoyed sitting *beside* the guest of honor." *Besides* is an adverb meaning "in addition." "*Besides*, he has a sense of humor." *Besides* is also a preposition meaning "other than." "Something *besides* shyness caused his embarrassment."

between, among See *among, between*.

between you and I The preposition *between* always takes the objective case. "Between *you* and *me* [not *I*], that story about the dog's eating Joe's money sounds suspicious." "Between *us* [not *we*], what's going on between Chris and *her* [not *she*] is unfathomable."

bi-, semi- These prefixes are often confused. *Bi-* means "two." *Semi-* means "half of." Thus, *semiautomatic* means "partly automatic," and *semiannual* means "happening every half year." *Biaxial* means "having two axes." Although sometimes people also use *bi-* to mean "happening twice in," avoid that use because it can be confusing (for example, it's difficult to know whether the person using *biweekly* means "twice a week" or "every two weeks").

but that, but what "I don't know *but what* [or *but that*] you're right" is a wordy, imprecise way of saying "Maybe you're right" or "I believe you're right."

can, may Use *can* to indicate ability. "Jake *can* bench press 650 pounds." *May* involves permission. "*May* I bench press today?" "You *may*, if you *can*."

capital, capitol A *capital* is a city that is the center of government for a state or country. *Capital* can also mean "wealth." A *capitol* is a building in which legislators meet. "Who knows what the *capital* of Finland is?" "The renovated *capitol* is a popular tourist attraction."

censor, censure *Censor* as a verb means "to evaluate and remove objectionable material." As a noun, it means "someone who censors." "All mail was *censored* before it left the country." *Censure* as a verb means "to find fault with, criticize." As a noun, it means "disapproval." "The governor's extreme actions were met with public *censure*."

center around Say "Class discussion *centered on* [or *revolved around*] her paper." In this sense, the verb *center* means "to have one main concern"—the way a circle has a central point. (Thus, to say a discussion centers *around* anything is a murky metaphor.)

cite, sight, site *Cite*, a verb, means "to quote from or refer to." *Sight* as a verb means "to see or glimpse"; as a noun it means "a view, a spectacle." "When the police officer *sighted* my terrier running across the playground, she *cited* the leash laws and told me I'd be fined." *Site*, a noun, means "location." "Standing at the *site* of his childhood home, he wept tears of nostalgia. He was a pitiful *sight*."

climatic, climactic *Climatic*, from *climate*, refers to meteorological conditions. Saying "climatic conditions," however, is wordy—you can usually substitute "the climate": "*Climatic* conditions are [or "The *climate* is"] changing because of the ozone hole."

Climactic, from *climax,* refers to the culmination of a progression of events. "In the *climactic* scene the hero drives his car off the pier."

compare, contrast *Compare* has two main meanings. The first, "to liken or represent as similar" is followed by *to.* "She *compared* her room *to* a jail cell." "He *compared* me *to* a summer's day." In its second meaning, *compare* means "to analyze for similarities and differences" and is generally followed by *with.* "The speaker *compared* the American educational system *with* the Japanese system."

Contrast also has two main meanings. As a transitive verb, taking an object, it means "to compare or analyze to emphasize differences" and is generally followed by *with.* "The speaker *contrasted* the social emphasis of the Japanese primary grades *with* the academic emphasis of ours." As an intransitive verb, *contrast* means "to exhibit differences when compared." "The matted tangle of Sidney's fur *contrasted* sharply *with* its usual healthy sleekness."

complement, compliment *Compliment* is a verb meaning "to praise" or a noun meaning "praise." "The professor *complimented* Sarah on her perceptiveness." *Complement* is a verb meaning "to complete or reinforce." "Jennifer's experiences as a practice teacher *complemented* what she learned in her education class."

continual, continuous *Continual* means "often repeated." "Mike was in *continual* conflict with his neighbors." *Continuous* means "uninterrupted." "Lisa's *continuous* chatter made it impossible for Debbie to concentrate on her reading."

could care less This is nonstandard English for *couldn't care less* and should not be used in writing. "The cat *couldn't* [not *could*] *care less* about which brand of cat food you buy."

could of *Could of* is colloquial for *could have* and should not be used in writing.

couple of Write "a *couple of* drinks" when you mean two. For more than two, say "a *few* [or *several*] drinks."

criteria, criterion *Criteria* is the plural of *criterion,* which means "a standard or requirement on which a judgment or decision is based." "The main *criteria* for this job are attention to detail and good typing skills."

data *Data* is a plural noun. Write "The data *are*" and "*these* data." The singular form of *data* is *datum*—rarely used because it sounds musty. Instead, use *fact, figure,* or *statistic.*

different from, different than *Different from* is usually the correct form to use. "How is good poetry *different from* prose?" Use *different than* when a whole clause follows. "Violin lessons with Mr. James were *different than* I had imagined."

disinterested, uninterested *Disinterested* means "impartial, fair, objective." "The defendant hoped for a *disinterested* judge." *Uninterested* means "indifferent." Suzanne was *uninterested* in world news.

don't, doesn't *Don't* is the contraction for *do not,* and *doesn't* is the contraction for *does not.* "They *don't* want to get dressed up for the ceremony." "*Don't* feed the grizzly bears!" "The cat *doesn't* [not *don't*] like to be combed."

due to *Due* is an adjective and must modify a noun or pronoun; it can't modify a verb. Begin a sentence with *due to* and you invite trouble: "*Due to rain,* the game was postponed." Write instead, "*Because of* rain." *Due to* works after the verb *be.* "His fall was *due to* a banana peel." There, *due* modifies the noun *fall.*

due to the fact that   A windy expression for *because*.

eager, anxious   See *anxious, eager*.

effect, affect   See *affect, effect*.

either   Use *either* when referring to one of two things. "Both internships sound great; I'd be happy with *either*." When referring to one of three or more things, use *any one* or *any*. "*Any one* of our four trained counselors will be able to help you."

elicit, illicit   *Elicit*, a verb, means "to bring or draw out." *Illicit*, an adjective, means "unlawful" or "not permissible." "Try as he might, Gus could not *elicit* details from Bob about his *illicit* nighttime activities."

emigrant, immigrant   An *emigrant* has left a country or region; an *immigrant* has moved into a country or region. The verb forms reflect the same distinction: *emigrate from*, *immigrate to*. "Even in the United States, *immigrants* often hold the lowest-paying positions." "Anders *emigrated* from Norway."

eminent, imminent   *Eminent* means "distinguished or outstanding"; *imminent* means "about to happen." "The *eminent* novelists shyly announced their *imminent* marriage."

enormity, enormousness, enormous   *Enormity* means "monstrous evil"; *enormousness* means "vastness or immensity"; and *enormous* means "vast or huge." "The *enormity* of the convicted woman's crimes baffled her acquaintances." "The *enormousness* of the lake impressed them."

enthuse   Good writers shun this verb. Instead of "The salesman *enthused* about the product," write, "The salesman *gushed* [or "*bubbled over* or *grew enthusiastic*]."

et cetera, etc.   Replace *et cetera* (or its abbreviation, *etc.*) with exact words, and you will sharpen your writing. Even translating the Latin expression into English is an improvement: *and other things*. Rather than announcing an athletic meet to feature "high-jumping, shot-putting, *etc.*," you could say, "high-jumping, shot-putting, and other field events."

everybody, every body   When used as an indefinite pronoun, *everybody* is one word. "Why is *everybody* on the boys' team waving his arms?" Keep in mind that *everybody* is singular. It is a mistake to write, "Why is *everybody* waving *their* arms?" (See 33 for acceptable alternatives.) *Every body* written as two words refers to separate, individual bodies. "After the massacre, they buried *every body* in *its* [not *their*] own grave." "From the air, Kate could see *every body* of water in the country."

everyone, every one   Used as an indefinite pronoun, *everyone* is one word. "*Everyone* has *his or her* own ideas." Remember that *everyone* is singular. Therefore it is wrong to write, "*Everyone* has *their* own ideas." (See 33 for acceptable alternatives.) *Every one* written as two words refers to individual, distinct items. "I studied *every one* of the assigned exercises."

except, accept   See *accept, except*.

expect   In writing, avoid the informal use of *expect* to mean "suppose, assume, or think." "I *suppose* [not *expect*] you've heard that half the class flunked."

fact that   This is an expression that, nearly always, you can do without. "*The fact that* he was puny went unnoticed" is wordy; write, "That [not *The fact that*] he was puny went unnoticed." "Because [not *Because of the fact that*] it snowed, the game was canceled."

famous, infamous Do something that attracts wide notice and you become cele-brated, or *famous*: "Marcia dreamed of growing up to be a *famous* inventor." But if your deeds are detestable, you may instead become notorious, or *infamous,* like Blue-beard, the *infamous* wife killer.

farther, further In your writing, use *farther* to refer to literal distance. "Chicago is *farther* from Nome than from New York." When you wish to denote additional degree, time, or quantity, use *further*: "Sally's idea requires *further* discussion."

fewer, less *Less* refers to general quantity or bulk; *fewer*, to separate, countable items. "Eat *less* pizza." "Salad has *fewer* calories."

field In a statement such as "He took courses *in the field of* economics," leave out *the field of* and save words.

firstly The recommended usage is *first* (and *second*, not *secondly*; *third* not *thirdly*; and so on).

flaunt, flout To *flaunt* is to show off. "She *flaunted* her wealth by buying much more than she needed." To *flout* is to defy. "George *flouted* the law by refusing to register for the draft."

former, latter *Former* means "first of two"; *latter*, "second of two." They are an acceptable but heavy-handed pair, best done without. Too often, they oblige your reader to backtrack. Nine times out of ten, your writing will be clearer if you simply name again the persons or things you mean. Instead of writing, "The *former* great artist is the master of the flowing line, while the *latter* is the master of color," write, "Picasso is the master of the flowing line, while Matisse is the master of color."

further, farther See *farther, further.*

get, got *Get* has many meanings, especially in slang and colloquial use. Some, such as the following, are not appropriate in formal writing:

"To start, begin": "Let's start [not *get*] painting."

"To stir the emotions": "His frequent interruptions finally started annoying [not *getting to*] me." "The puppies' pathetic whimpers really upset [not *got to*] her."

"To harm, punish, or take revenge on": "She's going to take revenge on [not *get*] him." Or better, be even more specific about what you mean. "She's going to spread rumors about him to ruin his reputation."

good, well To modify a verb, use the adverb *well,* not the adjective *good.* "Jan dives *well* [not *good*]." Linking verbs (*be, appear, become, grow, seem, prove*) and verbs of the senses (such as *feel, look, smell, sound, taste*) call for the adjective *good.* "The paint job looks *good." Well* is an adjective used only to refer to health. "She looks *well"* means that she seems to be in good health. "She looks *good"* means that her appearance is attractive. (See 12b, 12c.)

great deal of This informal expression means "much" and refers to things that come in bulk and can't be counted. "She had a *great deal of* training in psychology." Don't use it to mean "a large number." "*Many* people [or *a crowd*; not *a great deal of people*] jammed the stadium.

hanged, hung Both words are the past tense of the verb *hang. Hanged* refers to an execution. "The murderer was *hanged* at dawn." For all other situations, use *hung.* "Jane *hung* her wash on the clothesline to dry."

have got to In formal writing, avoid using the phrase *have got to* to mean "have to" or "must." "I *must* [not *have got to*] phone them right away."

he, she, he or she   Using *he* as a matter of course to refer to a person is considered sexist; so is using *she* with reference to traditionally female occupations or pastimes. However, peppering your writing with the phrase *he or she* can seem wordy and awkward. For alternatives, see 33.

herself   See *-self, -selves.*

himself   See *-self, selves.*

hopefully   *Hopefully* means "with hope." "The children turned *hopefully* toward the door, expecting Santa Claus." In writing, avoid *hopefully* when you mean "it is to be hoped" or "let us hope." "*I hope* [not *Hopefully*] the posse will arrive soon."

if, whether   Use *if* for conditional phrases. "*If* wishes were horses, beggars would ride." "*If* Dwayne calls while I'm out, please take a message." Use *whether* in indirect questions and to introduce alternatives. "Father asked me *whether* I was planning to sleep all morning." "I'm so confused I don't know *whether* it's day or night."

illicit   See *elicit, illicit.*

illusion, allusion   See *allusion, illusion.*

imminent   See *eminent, imminent.*

immoral   See *amoral, immoral.*

imply, infer   *Imply* means "to suggest"; *infer* means "to draw a conclusion." "Maria *implied* that she was too busy to see Tom. As their conversation proceeded, Tom *inferred* that Maria had lost interest in him."

in, into   *In* refers to a location or condition; *into* refers to the direction of movement or change. "The hero burst *into* the room and found the heroine *in* another man's arms." "Hiroko decided to go *into* banking."

individual   Don't use *individual* for *person.* "What kind of *person* [not *individual*] would do that?" Save the word to mean "one" as opposed to "many": "an *individual* thinker in a conforming crowd."

infer, imply   See *imply, infer.*

ingenious, ingenuous   *Ingenious* means "clever." "The *ingenious* inventor caught the mouse unharmed." *Ingenuous* has two related meanings: "naive, unsophisticated" and "frank, candid." "Little Lord Fauntleroy's *ingenuous* remarks touched even his ill-tempered grandfather."

in regards to   Write *in regard to, regarding,* or *about.*

inside of, outside of   As prepositions, *inside* and *outside* do not require *of.* "The students were more interested in what was going on *outside* [not *outside of*] the building than in what was happening *inside* [not *inside of*] the classroom." Do not use *inside of* to refer colloquially to time or *outside of* to mean "except." "I'll finish the assignment *within* [not *inside of*] two hours." "He told no one *except* [not *outside of*] a few friends."

irregardless   *Irregardless* is a double negative. Use *regardless.*

is because   See *reason is because.*

is when, is where   Using these expressions results in errors in predication. "Obesity *is when* a person is greatly overweight." "Biology *is where* students dissect frogs." *When* refers to a point in time, but *obesity* is not a point in time; *where* refers to a place, but *biology* is not a place. Write instead, "Obesity is the condition of extreme overweight." "Biology is a laboratory course in which students dissect frogs." (See faulty predication, 15.)

its, it's   *Its* is a possessive pronoun, never in need of an apostrophe. *It's* is a contraction for *it is*. "Every new experience has *its* bad moments. Still, *it's* exciting to explore the unknown."

it's me, it is I   Although *it's me* is widely used in speech, don't use it in formal writing. Write "It is *I*," which is grammatically correct. The same applies to other personal pronouns. "It was *he* [not *him*] who started the mutiny." (See pronoun case, 9.)

kind of, sort of, type of   When you use *kind, sort,* or *type*—singular words—make sure that the sentence construction is singular. "That *type* of show *offends* me." "Those *types* of shows *offend* me." In speech, *kind of* and *sort of* are used as qualifiers. "He is *sort of* fat." Avoid them in writing. "He is *rather* [or *somewhat* or *slightly*; not *sort of*] fat."

latter, former   See *former, latter*.

lay, lie   The verb *lay*, meaning "to put or place," takes an object. *Lie*, meaning "to rest or recline," does not. Their principal parts are *lay, laid, laid,* and *lie, lay, lain*. "*Lay* that pistol down." "*Lie* on the bed until your headache goes away." (See 5e.)

leave, let   *Leave* means "to go away." *Let* means "to permit." "I'll *leave* on a jet plane." "*Let* the child run—she needs the exercise."

less, fewer   See *fewer, less*.

let, leave   See *leave, let*.

liable, likely   Use *likely* to mean "plausible" or "having the potential." "Jake is *likely* [not *liable*] to win." Save *liable* for "legally obligated" or "susceptible." "A stunt man is *liable* to injury."

lie, lay   See *lay, lie*.

like, as   See *as, like*.

likely, liable   See *liable, likely*.

literally   Don't sling *literally* around for emphasis. It means "strictly according to the meaning of a word (or words)"; if you are speaking figuratively, it will wreck your credibility. "Professor Gray *literally* flew down the hall to the chairman's office" means that Gray traveled on wings. "Rick was *literally* stoned out of his mind" means that someone drove Rick insane by pelting him with mineral specimens. Save *literally* to mean that, by everything holy, you're reporting a fact. "Because chemical wastes travel on the winds, it *literally* rains poison."

loan, lend   See *lend, loan*.

loath, loathe   *Loath* is an adjective meaning "reluctant." *Loathe* is a verb meaning "to detest." "We were *loath* to say good-bye." "We *loathed* our impending separation."

loose, lose   *Loose,* an adjective, most commonly means "not fastened" or "poorly fastened." *Lose,* a verb, means "misplace" or "not win." "I have to be careful not to *lose* this button—it's so *loose*."

lots, lots of, a lot of   Use these expressions only in informal speech. In formal writing, say *many* or *much*. See also *a lot*.

mankind   This term is considered sexist by many people. Use *humanity, humankind, the human race,* or *people* instead.

may, can   See *can, may.*

media, medium   *Media* is the plural of *medium* and most commonly refers to the various forms of public communication. "Some argue that of all the *media,* television is the worst for children because it leaves so little to the imagination."

might of   *Might of* is colloquial for *might have* and should not be used in writing.

most   Do not use *most* when you mean "almost." "*Almost* [not *Most*] all of the students felt that Professor Chartrand should have received tenure."

must of   *Must of* is colloquial for *must have* and should not be used in writing.

myself   See *-self, -selves.*

not all that   *Not all that* is colloquial for *not very;* do not use it in formal writing. "The movie was *not very* [not *not all that*] exciting."

number, amount   See *amount, number.*

of   See *could of, might of, must of, should of.*

off of   *Of* is unnecessary with *off.* Use *off* alone, or use *from*: "Cartoon heroes are forever falling *off* [or *from*] cliffs."

O.K., o.k., okay   In formal writing, do not use any of these expressions. *All right* and *I agree* are possible substitutes.

one   Like a balloon, *one,* meaning "a person," tends to inflate. One *one* can lead to another. "When *one* is in college, *one* learns to make up *one's* mind for *oneself.*" Realizing that the sentence sounds pompous, the writer might be tempted to switch to the more familiar-sounding *you*: "When *one* is in college, *you* learn . . . ," but the result is inconsistency. Substituting *a person* often leads to sexist constructions (*he, himself*) or awkward alternatives (*he or she, himself or herself*). Whenever possible, substitute *people* or a more specific plural noun. "When *students* are in college, *they* learn to make up their minds for *themselves.*" Also see *you.*

ourselves   See *-self, -selves.*

outside of, inside of   See *inside of, outside of.*

per, as per   See *as per, per.*

percent, per cent, percentage   When you specify a number, write *percent* (also written *per cent*). "Eight *percent* of the listeners responded to the offer." The only time to use *percentage,* meaning "part," is with an adjective, when you mention no number: "A high *percentage* [or *a large percentage*] of listeners responded." *A large number* or *a large proportion* sounds better yet, and we urge you to strike *percentage* from your vocabulary.

per se   Translate this Latin expression into English and you'll sound less stiff. Write "Getting a good education is important *in itself* [or *by itself*; not *per se*]."

phenomenon, phenomena   *Phenomena* is plural for *phenomenon,* which means "an observable fact or occurrence." "I've read about many mysterious supernatural *phenomena.*" "Clairvoyance is the strangest *phenomenon* of all."

pore over, pour over   *Pore over* a book and you study it intently; *pour over* a book and you get it wet.

precede, proceed *Precede* means "to go before or ahead of"; *proceed* means "to go forward." "The fire drill *proceeded* smoothly; the children *preceded* the teachers into the safety of the yard."

principal, principle *Principal* means "chief," whether used as an adjective or as a noun. "Marijuana is the *principal* cash crop of Colombia." "Our high school *principal* frowns on pot." Referring to money, *principal* means "capital." "Investors in marijuana earn as much as 850 percent interest on their *principal.*" *Principle,* a noun, means *rule* or *standard.* "Let's apply the *principle* of equality in hiring." "No marijuana for her: she's a woman of strict *principles.*"

proved, proven Although both forms can be used as past participles, *proved* is recommended. Use *proven* as an adjective. "They had *proved* their skill in match after match." "Try this *proven* cough remedy: lemon, honey, whiskey, and hot water blended into a toddy."

quote, quotation *Quote* is a verb meaning "to cite, to use the words of." *Quotation* is a noun meaning "something that is quoted." "The *quotation* [not *quote*] next to her yearbook picture fits her perfectly."

raise, rise *Raise,* meaning "to cause to move upward," is a transitive verb and takes an object. *Rise,* meaning "to move up (on its own)" is intransitive and does not take an object: "I *rose* from my seat and *raised* my arm, but the instructor still didn't see me."

rarely ever *Rarely* by itself is strong enough. "George *rarely* [not *rarely ever*] eats dinner with his family."

real, really *Real* is an adjective, *really* an adverb. Do not use *real* to modify a verb or another adjective, and avoid overusing either word. "*The Ambassadors* is a *really* [not *real*] fine novel." Even better: "*The Ambassadors* is a fine novel."

reason is because, reason . . . is *Reason . . . is* requires a clause beginning with *that.* Using *because* is nonstandard. "The *reason* I can't come *is that* [not *is because*] I have the flu." But *reason . . . is* is a wordy construction that can usually be rephrased more succinctly. It is simpler and more direct to write, "I can't come because I have the flu."

respectfully, respectively *Respectfully* means "with respect, showing respect." *Respectively* means "each in turn" or "in the order given." "They stopped talking and stood *respectfully* as the prime minister walked by." "Joan, Michael, and Alfonso majored in history, sociology, and economics, *respectively.*"

rise See *raise, rise.*

seldom ever Let *seldom* stand by itself. "Martha *seldom* [not *seldom ever*] attends church."

-self, -selves Don't use a pronoun ending in *-self* or *-selves* in place of *her, him, me, them, us,* or *you.* "Nobody volunteered but Jim and *me* [not *myself*]." Use the *-self* pronouns to refer back to a noun or another pronoun and to lend emphasis. "*We* did it *ourselves.*" "Sarah *herself* is a noted musician." (See 9.)

semi- See *bi-, semi-.*

sensual, sensuous Both words have to do with stimulation of the senses, but *sensual* has more blatantly carnal overtones. "Gluttony and lust were the *sensual* millionaire's favorite sins." *Sensuous* pleasures are more aesthetic. "The *sensuous* beauty of the music stirred his soul."

set, sit *Set,* meaning "to put or place," is a transitive verb and takes an object. *Sit,* meaning "to be seated," is intransitive and does not take an object. "At the security point we were asked to *set* our jewelry and metal objects on the counter and *sit* down." (See also 5e.)

shall, will; should, would The helping verb *shall* formerly was used with first-person pronouns. It is still used to express determination ("We *shall* overcome"; "They *shall* not give in") or to ask consent ("*Shall* I let the cat out?"). Otherwise *will* is commonly used with all three persons. "I *will* enter medical school in the fall." "They *will* accept the bid if the terms are clear." *Should* is a helping verb that expresses obligation; *would,* a helping verb that expresses a hypothetical condition. "I *should* wash the dishes before I watch TV." "He *would* learn to speak English if you *would* give him a chance."

should of *Should of* is colloquial for *should have* and should not be used in writing.

sight See *cite, sight, site.*

since Sometimes using *since* can make a sentence ambiguous. "*Since* the babysitter left, the children have been watching television." Does *since* here mean "because" or "from the time that"? If using *since* might be confusing to your readers, use an unambiguous term (*because, ever since*).

sit See *set, sit.*

site See *cite, sight, site.*

sort of See *kind of.*

stationary, stationery *Stationary,* an adjective, means "fixed, unmoving." "The fireplace remained *stationary* though the wind blew down the house." *Stationery* is paper for letter writing. To spell it right, remember that *letter* also contains *-er.*

suppose to Write *supposed to.* "He was *supposed to* appear for dinner at eight o'clock."

sure *Sure* is an adjective, *surely* an adverb. Do not use *sure* to modify a verb or another adjective. If by *sure* you mean "certainly," write *certainly* or *surely* instead. "He *surely* [not *sure*] is crazy about cars."

than, then *Than* is a conjunction used in comparisons; *then* is an adverb indicating time. "Marlene is brainier *than* her sister." "First crack six eggs; *then* beat them."

that, which Which pronoun should open a clause—*that* or *which*? If the clause adds to its sentence an idea that, however interesting, could be left out, then the clause is nonrestrictive and should begin with *which* and be separated from the rest of the sentence with commas. "The vampire, *which* had been hovering nearby, leaped for Sarah's throat."

If the clause is essential to your meaning, it is restrictive and should begin with *that* and should not have commas around it. "The vampire *that* Mel brought from Transylvania leaped for Sarah's throat." The clause indicates not just any old vampire but one in particular.

Don't use *which* to refer vaguely to an entire clause. Instead of "Jack was an expert drummer in high school, *which* won him a college scholarship," write: "Jack's skill as a drummer won him. . . ." (See 19e.)

themselves See *-self, -selves.*

then, than See *than, then.*

there, their, they're *There* is an adverb indicating place. *Their* is a possessive pronoun. *They're* is a contraction of *they are.* "After playing tennis *there* for three hours, Lamont and Laura went to change *their* clothes because *they're* going out to dinner."

to, too, two *To* is a preposition. *Too* is an adverb meaning "also" or "in excess." *Two* is a number. "Janet wanted to go *too,* but she feared she was still *too* sick to travel in the car for *two* days. Instead, she went *to* bed."

toward, towards *Toward* prevails in America, *towards* in Britain. Use either; just stick to one or the other.

try and Use *try to.* "I'll *try to* [not *try and*] attend the opening performance of your play."

type of See *kind of, sort of, type of.*

uninterested, disinterested See *disinterested, uninterested.*

unique Nothing can be *more unique, less unique, really unique, very unique, or somewhat unique. Unique* means "one of a kind."

use to Write *used to.* "Jeffrey *used to* have a beard, but now he is clean-shaven."

wait for, wait on Write *wait for* when you mean "await." *Wait on* means "to serve." "While *waiting for* his friends, George decided to *wait on* one more customer."

well, good See *good, well.*

where at, where to The colloquial use of *at* or *to* after *where* is redundant. Write "*Where* were you?" not "Where were you *at?*" "I know *where* she was rushing [not *rushing to*]."

where, that Although speakers sometimes use *where* instead of *that,* you should not do so in writing. "I heard on the news *that* [not *where*] it got hot enough to fry eggs on car hoods."

whether See *if, whether.*

which, that See *that, which.*

who, which, that, whose *Who* refers to people, *which* to things and ideas. "Was it Pogo *who* said, 'We have met the enemy and he is us'?" "The blouse, *which* was lime green embroidered with silver, accented her dark skin and eyes."

  That refers to things but can also be used for a class of people. "The team *that* puts in the most overtime will get a bonus."

  Using *of which* can be cumbersome; use *whose* even to refer to things. "The mountain, *whose* snowy peaks were famous world over, was covered in a dismal fog." See also *that, which.*

who, whom *Who* is used as a subject, *whom* as an object. In "*Whom* do I see?" *Whom* is the object of *see.* In "*Who* goes there?" *Who* is the subject of "goes." (See also 9.)

who's, whose *Who's* is a contraction for *who is* or *who has.* "*Who's* going with Phil?" *Whose* is a possessive pronoun. "Bill is a conservative politician *whose* ideas are unlikely to change."

will, shall See *shall, will.*

would, should See *should, would.*

would of *Would of* is colloquial for *would have* and should not be used in writing.

you   *You,* meaning "a person," occurs often in conversation. "When you go to college you have to work hard." In writing, use *one* or a specific noun. "When *students* go to college *they* have to work hard." But see also *one.*

your, you're   *Your* is a possessive pronoun; *you're* is the contraction for *you are.* "*You're* lying! It was *your* handwriting on the envelope."

yourself, yourselves   See *-self, -selves.*

in *Academic Women on the Move* by Alice S. Rossi and Ann Calderwood. © 1973, the Russell Sage Foundation. Used with permission of the Russell Sage Foundation.

Barrie B. Greenbie. From *Spaces: Dimensions of the Human Landscape* by Barrie B. Greenbie. Copyright © 1981 by Barrie B. Greenbie. Reprinted by permission of the publisher, Yale University Press.

Charlie Haas. "Tinsel Teens," *Esquire,* June 1985. Reprinted by permission of the author.

Garrett Hardin. Reprinted with permission from *Naked Emperors: Essays of a Taboo Stalker* by Garrett Hardin. Copyright © 1982 by William Kaufmann, Inc., Los Altos, CA 94022. All rights reserved.

Mary Harris "Mother" Jones. From *The Autobiography of Mother Jones* (Charles H. Kerr Co., Chicago, 1980).

Pauline Kael. "Rocky." From "Stallone and Stahr" in *When the Lights Go Down* by Pauline Kael. Copyright © 1980 by Pauline Kael. Reprinted by permission of Henry Holt & Company, Inc.

Perri Klass. "A Textbook Pregnancy." Reprinted by permission of the Putnam Publishing Group from *A Not Entirely Benign Procedure* by Perri Klass. Copyright © 1987 by Perri Klass.

Jonathan Kozol. "Are the Homeless Crazy?" Adapted from *Rachel and Her Children* by Jonathan Kozol. Copyright © 1988 by Jonathan Kozol. Reprinted by permission of Crown Publishers, Inc.

Elisabeth Kübler-Ross. From *On Death and Dying* by Elisabeth Kübler-Ross. Copyright © 1969 by Elisabeth Kübler-Ross. Reprinted by permission of Macmillan Publishing Company.

William Least Heat Moon. "A View of Prejudice." From *Blue Highways: A Journey into America* by William Least Heat Moon. Copyright © 1982 by William Least Heat Moon. By permission of Little, Brown and Company.

Alan P. Lightman. "Time Travel and Papa Joe's Pipe." Reprinted with permission of Charles Scribner's Sons, an imprint of Macmillan Publishing Company, from *Time Travel and Papa Joe's Pipe* by Alan P. Lightman. Text copyright 1984 by Alan P. Lightman.

H. L. Mencken. From "A Libido for the Ugly" in *A Mencken Crestomathy: Edited and Annotated by the Author.* Copyright 1927, 1949 by Alfred A. Knopf, Inc. Reprinted by permission of the publisher.

Jessica Mitford. "Behind the Formaldehyde Curtain." From *The American Way of Death* by Jessica Mitford. Copyright © 1963, 1978 by Jessica Mitford. Reprinted by permission of Simon & Schuster, Inc.

Douglass C. North and Roger Leroy Miller. Excerpt from *The Economics of Public Issues,* 6th Edition, by Douglass C. North and Roger Leroy Miller. Copyright © 1983 by Harper & Row, Publishers, Inc. Reprinted by permission of the publisher.

Alexander Petrunkevitch. "The Spider and the Wasp," *Scientific American,* August 1952. Reprinted with permission. Copyright 1952 by Scientific American, Inc.

Sylvia Plath. From "Northampton" in *The Journals of Sylvia Plath,* edited by Ted Hughes and Frances McCullough. Copyright © 1982 by Ted Hughes and Frances McCullough. Reprinted by permission of Doubleday, a Division of Bantam, Doubleday, Dell Publishing Group, Inc.

David Quammen. "A Republic of Cockroaches." Reprinted by permission of David Quammen. All rights reserved. Copyright © 1983 by David Quammen.

Howell Raines. From an interview with Franklin McCain in *My Soul Is Rested.* Copyright © 1977 by Howell Raines. Reprinted by permission of the Putnam Publishing Group.

Mary Anne Raywid. From "Power to Jargon, for Jargon Is Power," *Journal of Teacher Education,* September/October 1978. Reprinted by permission.

James C. Rettie. "But a Watch in the Night" by James C. Rettie from *Forever the Land,* edited by Russell and Kate Lord. Copyright 1950 by Harper & Brothers; copyright © renewed 1978 by Russell and Kate Lord. Reprinted by permission of Harper & Row, Publishers, Inc.

Caryl Rivers. "What Should Be Done About Rock Lyrics?" Reprinted by permission of the author from *The Boston Globe,* September 15, 1985.

Phyllis Rose. "Tools of Torture." Reprinted by permission of Georges Borchardt, Inc. and the author. Copyright © 1986 by Phyllis Rose.

Bertrand Russell. "Do We Survive Death?" From *Why I Am Not a Christian* by Bertrand Russell. Copyright © 1957, 1985 by George Allen and Unwin. Reprinted by permission of Simon & Schuster, Inc. and Unwin Hyman Ltd.

Carl Sagan. "The Nuclear Winter." Copyright © 1983 by Carl Sagan. All rights reserved. First published in *Parade.* Reprinted by permission of the author. From "The Case Against SDI." Copyright © 1985 by Carl Sagan. First appeared in the September 1985 issue of *Discover.* Reprinted by permission of the author.

E. Richard Sorenson. Text excerpt and Figure 13.2 from "Cooperation and Freedom Among the Fore in New Guinea" from *Learning Non-Aggression: The Experience of Non-Literate Societies,* edited by Ashley Montagu. Copyright © 1978 by Ashley Montagu. Reprinted by permission of Oxford University Press, Inc.

Brent Staples. "Black Men and Public Space," *Harper's,* December 1987. Reprinted by permission of the author.

Ann Swidler. From *Habits of the Heart: Individualism and Commitment in American Life* by Robert N. Bellah, Richard Madsen, William M. Sullivan, Ann Swidler, and Steven M. Tipton. Copyright © 1985 by the Regents of the University of California. Reprinted by permission of the University of California Press.

Edward Teyber and Charles D. Hoffman. "Missing Fathers." Reprinted with permission from *Psychology Today* Magazine. Copyright © 1987 (P.T. Partners, L.P.).

Lewis Thomas. "The Art of Teaching Science." From *Late Night Thoughts on Listening to Mahler's Ninth Symphony.* Copyright © 1983 by Lewis Thomas. Reprinted by permission of the publisher, Viking Penguin, a division of Penguin Books USA Inc.

Wade Thompson. From "My Crusade Against Football," *The Nation,* April 11, 1959. © 1959 by The Nation Company, Inc. Reprinted by permission.

James Thurber. "If Grant Had Been Drinking at Appomattox." Copyright 1935 James Thurber. Copyright 1963 Helen Thurber and Rosemary Thurber. From *The Middle-Aged Man on the Flying Trapeze,* published by Harper & Row. Reprinted by permission.

Barbara W. Tuchman. From *A Distant Mirror: The Calamitous 14th Century* by Barbara W. Tuchman. Copyright © 1978 by Barbara W. Tuchman. Reprinted by permission of Alfred A. Knopf, Inc.

John Updike. From "Venezuela for Visitors" in *Hugging the Shore: Essays and Criticism* by John Updike. Copyright © 1983 by John Updike. Reprinted by permission of Alfred A. Knopf, Inc. Originally appeared in *The New Yorker.*

Charles Van Riper. From *A Career in Speech Pathology* by Charles Van Riper, © 1979, p. 29. Reprinted by permission of Prentice-Hall, Inc., Englewood Cliffs, N.J.

Gerald Weissmann. Excerpt from "Foucault and the Bag Lady." Reprinted by permission of Dodd, Mead & Company, Inc. from *The Woods Hole Cantata: Essays on Science and Society* by Gerald Weissmann. Copyright © 1985 by Gerald Weissmann, M.D.

Marie Winn. "The Plug-in Drug." From *The Plug-in Drug* by Marie Winn. Copyright © 1977 by Marie Winn Miller. Reprinted by permission of the publisher, Viking Penguin, a division of Penguin Books USA Inc.

Philip Zaleski. From "The Superstars of Heart Research," *Boston* Magazine, December 1982. Copyright © 1982 by Philip Zaleski. Reprinted by permission of the author.

Art and Photograph Credits

pages 46–47: Print of woodcut by The Master I.B. with the Bird (original version and forgery) from William M. Ivins, Jr., *How Prints Look,* published by Beacon Press, Boston.

page 52 (top): Peter Vandermark/Stock Boston. (*bottom*): James Holland/Stock Boston.

page 53: Eva Demjen/Stock Boston.

page 76: Excerpt from *Eating Disorders: The Facts* by Suzanne Abraham and Derek Llewellyn-Jones. © 1984. Reprinted by permission of Oxford University Press (U.K.).

page 101: Photo of Barbara Pierre. Copyright © 1982 by William Least Heat Moon. Reprinted from *Blue Highways: A Journey into America* by William Least Heat Moon by permission of the author.

pages 328–329: Drawings by Glen Baxter from *Atlas,* © 1979. Reprinted by permission of Uitgeverij De Harmonie, Amsterdam.

Figure 12.5: Entry from *The Oxford English Dictionary,* 2nd ed. © Oxford University Press 1989. Reprinted by permission.

Figure 12.6: Entries from the *Readers' Guide to Periodical Literature* 1987, Volume 47, page 2124. Copyright © 1987, 1988 by the H. W. Wilson Company. Material reproduced by permission of the publisher.

Figure 12.7: Entries from *Education Index,* June 1986–June 1987, page 1243. Copyright © 1987 by the H. W. Wilson Company. Material reproduced by permission of the publisher.

Figure 12.8: Entries from *The New York Times Index,* 1987. Copyright © 1987 by the New York Times Company. Reprinted by permission.

Answers for Lettered Exercises

EXERCISE 1–1, page 591
a. Proper noun: Lois; common nouns: paintings, husband; possessive pronoun: her; **b.** Proper noun: Lois; common nouns: price, profit; intensive pronoun: herself; **c.** Common nouns: bulk, money, supplies; relative pronoun: that; personal pronoun: she; possessive pronoun: her; **d.** Proper nouns: Lewis, Corvette; possessive pronoun: his; indefinite pronoun: someone; relative pronoun: who; personal pronoun: it; **e.** Personal pronouns: I, I, you; reflexive pronoun: myself; indefinite pronoun: no one

EXERCISE 1–2, page 593
a. Transitive: accompany; direct object: him; intransitive: goes; helping: will; **b.** Transitive: dislikes; direct object: players; linking: are; **c.** Transitive: give; direct object: roses; transitive: symbolize; direct object: infidelity; **d.** Transitive: spent; direct object: time; helping: should have; **e.** Transitive: reads; direct object: fiction; intransitive: dreams; linking: becoming

EXERCISE 1–3, page 594
a. Adjectives: mild, environmental; indefinite articles: a, a; definite article: the; adverb: greatly, modifying verb fear; **b.** Adjectives: elderly, mobile; adverb: incredibly, modifying adjective mobile; **c.** Adjectives: beautiful, wise; definite article: the; adverbs: wildly, modifying adjective beautiful; often, modifying verb made; foolishly, modifying verb act; **d.** Adjective: short; indefinite article: a; adverbs: very, modifying adjective short; fully, modifying verb lived; **e.** Adjectives: delighted, lovely; indefinite article: a; adverb: absolutely, modifying adjective delighted

EXERCISE 1–4, page 595
a. To me, adverb phrase; **b.** On the table, adjective phrase; **c.** Before the meeting, adverb phrase; **d.** According to the rules, adverb phrase; **e.** But a few troublemakers, adjective phrase

EXERCISE 1–5, page 598
a. Conjunction: when (subordinating); interjection: Oh, well; **b.** Conjunctions: and (coordinating), neither . . . nor (correlative); **c.** Conjunctions: and (coordinating), both . . . and (correlative); **d.** Interjection: Holy mackerel; **e.** Conjunctions: Although (subordinating), and (coordinating)

EXERCISE 2–1, page 600
a. Simple subject: animals; complete subject: Most wild animals; simple predicate: do make; complete predicate: do not make good pets; **b.** Simple subject: War; complete subject: War, that curse of the human race; simple predicate: has plagued; complete predicate: has plagued civilizations throughout history; **c.** Simple subject: composer; complete subject: the composer Beethoven; simple predicate: continued; complete predicate: Even after he became deaf . . . continued to write music; **d.** Simple subject: cup; com-

plete subject: One cup of coffee in the morning; simple subject: keeps; complete predicate: keeps me awake all day; **e.** Simple subject: mother; complete subject: John Updike's mother, who had been a writer herself; simple predicate: encouraged; complete predicate: always encouraged her son's literary aspirations

EXERCISE 2–2, page 603

a. Subject complement: an educated person; direct object: such a story; **b.** Direct object: his needs; indirect object: Judith; **c.** Subject complement: an evasive man; **d.** Subject complement: an interesting art; direct object: expensive equipment; **e.** Direct object: Chicago; object complement: the windy city

EXERCISE 3–1, page 608

a. Identifying parts of speech: gerund phrase, noun; **b.** In the beret: prepositional phrase, adjective; **c.** Given the situation: absolute phrase; to their mother: prepositional phrase, adverb; **d.** Through the grapevine: prepositional phrase, adverb; **e.** Gone with the wind: participial phrase, adjective

EXERCISE 3–2, page 611

a. Wherever he lived at the moment: noun clause; **b.** While we were still arguing about its value: adverb clause; **c.** That I took to the cleaner's: adjective clause; **d.** That she may fail the course: adverb clause; **e.** Whether he should invite James: noun clause

EXERCISE 4–1, page 613

a. Simple sentence. Compound subject: Not only women but also men and children; verb: benefit; **b.** Complex sentence. Prepositional phrase: Even in a life-or-death emergency; main clause: I know; subordinate clause: [that] you can count on Marlene; **c.** Compound-complex sentence. Main clauses: Biology is interesting; I prefer botany; subordinate clause: as it is taught by Professor Haines; **d.** Simple sentence. Subject: you; verb: prefer; direct object: bacon and eggs or cereal and toast; **e.** Compound-complex sentence. Main clauses: Most people believe; recent studies have shown; subordinate clauses: that poverty begets poverty; that they achieve economic independence; when children from welfare families reach adulthood

EXERCISE 5–1, page 621

   a. When Joe's mother *caught* him *lying* around the house during school hours, she *threw* him out.

   b. We woke soon after the sun *rose,* and then we *swam* to the raft.

   c. He *laid* his cards triumphantly on the table but soon found that he was not *sitting* in a lucky chair after all.

   d. Wendy knew how much Roger had *drunk,* but she *went* with him anyway.

   e. I have *lain* awake, tossing and turning, every night since exams *began.*

EXERCISE 5–2, page 625

a. Broke: simple past; was skiing: past progressive; **b.** Sleeps: simple present; is yawning: present progressive; **c.** Had seen: past perfect; run: simple present; **d.** Represents: simple present; will have performed: future perfect; split: simple past; **e.** Finish: simple present; will attend: simple future

EXERCISE 5–3, page 627

Suggested revisions:

   a. I recently read the *World Book Encyclopedia*'s article about opossums.

   b. The rat and the opossum resemble each other.

   c. The opossum hunts for food at night.

   d. Like all marsupials, opossum mothers carry their young in a stomach pouch.

   e. Passive is acceptable.

EXERCISE 5–4, page 629

   a. When Janet cooks, she insists that Tom *wash* the dishes. (Incorrect washes, indicative; correct wash, subjunctive)

   b. If Pete *wants* me to help him, he can call and ask me himself. (Incorrect want, subjunctive; correct wants, indicative)

   c. If I *were* a licensed plumber, I could install the washing machine myself. (Incorrect was, indicative; correct were, subjunctive)

   d. The IRS recommends that tax forms *be* filled out as soon as they become available. (Incorrect are, indicative; correct be, subjunctive)

   e. If that man *does* not go away, call the police. (Incorrect do, subjunctive; correct does, indicative)

EXERCISE 6–1, page 634

   a. Our foreign policy in Cuba, Nicaragua, El Salvador, and Panama *has* not been as successful as most Americans had hoped.

   b. Correct

   c. I read about a couple who *are* offering to trade their baby for a brand-new Chevrolet.

   d. A shave, a haircut, and a new suit *have* turned Bill into a different person.

e. Neither the fruit nor the vegetables *are* fresh.

EXERCISE 7–1, page 637

Suggested revisions:

a. All students are urged to complete *their* registration on time.

b. *Babies* who don't know *their* own mothers may have been born with some kind of vision deficiency.

c. Each member of the sorority has to make *her* own bed.

d. If you don't like the songs the choir sings, don't join *it.*

e. Selfish people always look out for *themselves.*

EXERCISE 8–1, page 641

Suggested revisions:

a. Every American will own a computer when it costs the same as a television set.

b. After meeting with Prime Minister Bhutto, Prime Minister Thatcher reported that she wasn't sure if Bhutto agreed with her position on freedom of speech.

c. Never having had any epileptic seizures, I cannot speak of them with firsthand knowledge.

d. Marsha didn't know Russian and had allergies, but these problems didn't stop her from summering on a Soviet kelp farm.

e. Swaying gently in his parachute, floating lazily to earth, Edgar felt pure joy. The jump had been the finest thing he'd ever tried, and he was all for this new sport.

EXERCISE 9–1, page 645

a. She can run faster than *I. (I* is the subject of the implied verb *can run.)*

b. Mrs. Van Dumont awarded the prize to Mona and *me. (Me* is an object of the preposition *to.)*

c. Jud laughed at both of us—*her* and *me.* (*Her* and *me* are appositives to the object of the preposition *us.)*

d. Were you referring to *us? (Us* is the object of the preposition *to.)*

e. Jerry, the pizza chef, and *I* regard you and *her* as the very women *whom* we wish to get acquainted with. (*I* is a subject of the verb *regard; her* is a direct object of the verb *regard; whom* is the object of the preposition *with.)*

EXERCISE 10–1, page 650

Suggested revisions:

a. Polly and Jim plan to see the new Woody Allen movie, which was reviewed in last Sunday's *New York Times.*

b. For democracy to function at all, two elements are crucial: an educated populace and a firm collective belief in people's ability to chart their own course.

c. Scholastic achievement is important to Alex, the first person in his family ever to attend college.

d. Does our society rob children of their childhood by making them aware too soon of adult ills?

e. It was one of those days: complete chaos, friends coming over in an hour, and a term paper to write.

EXERCISE 11–1, page 655

Suggested revisions:

a. Everyone had heard alarming rumors in the village about strange goings-on. We hesitated to believe them. Everyone had heard alarming rumors in the village about strange goings-on, although we hesitated to believe them.

b. Bats flew about our ears as the carriage pulled up under a stone archway. An assistant stood waiting to lead us to our host. Bats flew about our ears as the carriage pulled up under a stone archway, where an assistant stood waiting to lead us to our host.

c. We followed the scientist down a flight of wet stone steps. At last he stopped before a huge oak door. We followed the scientist down a flight of wet stone steps, until at last he stopped before a huge oak door.

d. From a jangling keyring Dr. Frankenstein selected a heavy key; he twisted it in the lock. From a jangling keyring Dr. Frankenstein selected a heavy key, which he twisted in the lock.

e. The huge door gave a groan. It swung open on a dimly lighted laboratory. The huge door gave a groan; it swung open on a dimly lighted laboratory.

EXERCISE 11–2, page 656

Suggested revisions:

a. Comma splice. As the creature lumbered toward its terrified creator, Frankenstein shrank back against a wall.

b. Fused sentence. To defend himself the scientist grabbed a wooden mallet that had been sitting on a cabinet nearby.

c. Comma splice. Frankenstein wore a smile of contemptuous superiority; however, his triumph proved brief in duration.

d. Fused sentence. With one sweep of an

arm the creature dashed aside the mallet, splintering its wooden head on the stone floor.

e. Comma splice. What followed is engraved upon my dreams; therefore, I hesitate to disclose it lest it trouble your own.

EXERCISE 12–1, page 661

a. Change *oldest* to *older;*   **b.** Change *quick* to *quickly;*   **c.** Change *correct* to *correctly* (in both places); change *trickiest* to *trickier;*   **d.** Change *sweet* to *sweetly;*   **e.** Change *the most* to *more*

EXERCISE 13–1, page 663

Suggested revisions:

a. After they lost miserably, the team remained silent on the trip home. *Or* After they lost, the team remained miserably silent on the trip home.

b. Complete the writing assignment that follows Chapter 2 in the textbook.

c. Those who frequently make mistakes learn valuable lessons. *Or* Frequently those who make mistakes learn valuable lessons.

d. For the duration of the rehearsal, Margaret was mortified at not having learned her lines.

e. A person who often snacks gets fat. *Or* Often a person who snacks gets fat.

EXERCISE 13–2, page 665

Suggested revisions:

a. After working for six hours, they finished the job. *Or* After they had worked for six hours, the job was done.

b. When you are unable to fall asleep, a warm bath relaxes you.

c. To join the college choir, a singer has to have a loud voice.

d. It's common for a person feeling lonely to want to talk to someone.

e. Having worried all morning, he felt relief flood over him when his missing son returned.

EXERCISE 14–1, page 667

Suggested revisions:

a. She plays the *Moonlight Sonata* more brilliantly than any *other* pianist her age.

b. Driving a sports car means more to Jake than *it does to* his professors. *Or* Driving a sports car means more to Jake than his professors *do.*

c. People who go to college aren't necessarily smarter *than those who don't,* but they will always have an advantage at job interviews.

d. I don't have as much trouble getting along with Michelle as *I do with* Karin. *Or* I don't have as much trouble getting along with Michelle as Karin *does.*

e. One-eyed Bill was faster on the draw than any *other* gunslinger in West Texas.

EXERCISE 14–2, page 669

a. The sand pit is just as wide *as* but deeper than the quarry.

b. Pembroke was never contacted *by,* much less involved with, the election committee.

c. I haven't yet *finished* but soon will finish my term paper.

d. Ron likes his popcorn with butter; Linda *likes hers* with parmesan cheese.

e. Correct

EXERCISE 15–1, page 672

Suggested revisions:

a. A balanced budget calls for careful planning.

b. The candidates for school committee head are unimpressive this year.

c. A college's financial aid staff searches for able students and decides to pay their costs.

d. One good reason for financial aid is that it enables capable lower-income students to attend college.

e. In one sizzling blast, the enemy space fleet was instantly wiped out.

EXERCISE 16–1, page 676

Suggested revisions:

a. I like westerns, documentaries, and foreign films.

b. Better than starting from scratch would be building on what already has been done.

c. Her apartment needed fresh paint and a new rug, and Mary Lou wished she had a neater roommate and quieter friends.

d. All my brothers are blond and athletic.

e. For breakfast the waiter brought scrambled eggs, which I like, and kippers, which I don't like.

EXERCISE 17–1, page 680

Suggested revisions:

a. Congress is expected to pass the biotechnology bill, but the president already has said he will veto it.

b. Mortgage rates have dropped, so home buying is likely to increase in the near future.

c. Find Mrs. Fellowes a seat—she looks tired.

d. I left the house in a hurry and ran to the bank so I could cash a check to buy lunch. However, it was the bank's anniversary, and the staff was busy serving coffee and cake. By the time I left, after chatting and eating for twenty minutes, I wasn't hungry anymore.

e. The U.S. Postal Service handles millions of pieces of mail every day; it is the largest postal service in the world.

EXERCISE 17–2, page 683

Suggested revisions:

a. We occasionally hear horror stories about fruits and vegetables being unsafe to eat because they were sprayed with toxic chemicals or were grown in contaminated soil. The fact remains that, given their high nutritional value, these fresh foods are generally much better for us than processed foods.

b. Renata claims that cats make the best pets because they are adorable, affectionate, and easy to care for.

c. At the end of Verdi's opera *La Traviata,* Alfredo has to see his beloved Violetta again, even though he knows she is dying and all he can say is good-bye.

d. After giving away her money and bidding adieu to her faithful servant, Violetta dies in her lover's arms.

e. Some television cartoon shows, such as *Rocky and Bullwinkle* and *George of the Jungle,* have become cult classics years after they went off the air.

EXERCISE 18–1, page 687

a. Unlike Gerald Ford and LBJ, who came to the vice-presidency from Congress, President Bush won that office after heading the CIA.

b. The population of California is much greater than that of Nevada.

c. Do you think I'm going to clean up this mess?

d. "When will the world end?" my four-year-old nephew asked in a quavering voice.

e. Yes, the Republicans are worried about the gender gap. They fear that women in increasing numbers will vote for the Democrats. How can the Republicans fight back?

EXERCISE 19–1, page 690

a. When Enrique gets to Paris, I hope he'll drop me a line.

b. Beethoven's deafness kept him from hearing his own music, yet he continued to compose.

c. Correct

d. The cherries are overripe, for picking has been delayed.

e. The robin yanked at the worm but was unable to pull it from the ground.

EXERCISE 19–2, page 692

a. Mrs. Carver looks like a sweet little old lady, but she plays a wicked electric guitar.

b. Her bass player, her drummer, and her keyboard player all live at the same rest home.

c. They practice individually in the afternoon, rehearse together at night, and play at the home's Saturday night dances.

d. The Rest Home Rebels have to rehearse quietly and cautiously to keep from disturbing the other residents.

e. Correct

EXERCISE 19–3, page 694

Suggested revisions:

a. The rain, which wasn't due until tomorrow, is falling right now.

b. The party, a dismal occasion, ended earlier than we had expected.

c. Secretary Stern warned that the concessions that the West was prepared to make would be withdrawn if not matched by the East.

d. Although both of Don's children are blond, his daughter, Sharon, has darker hair than his son, Jake.

e. Herbal tea, which has no caffeine, makes a better after-dinner drink than coffee.

EXERCISE 19–4, page 695

a. Before we begin, however, I want to thank everyone who made this evening possible.

b. Our speaker, listed in your program as a professor, tells us that, on the contrary, she is a teaching assistant.

c. The discussion that followed was not so much a debate as a free-for-all.

d. Alex insisted that predestination, not free will, shapes human destiny.

e. Shirley, on the other hand, who looks so calm, passionately defended the role of choice.

EXERCISE 19–5, page 697

a. On October 2, 1969, the future discoverer of antigravity tablets was born.

b. Corwin P. Grant entered the world while his parents were driving to a hospital in Costa Mesa, California.

c. Correct

d. Today, ladies and gentlemen, Corwin enjoys worldwide renown.
e. Schoolchildren from Augusta, Maine, to Azuza, California, can recite his famous comment "It was my natural levity that led me to overcome gravity."

EXERCISE 20–1, page 701

a. Gasoline prices almost always rise at the start of tourist season; this year will be no exception.
b. I disagree with your point; however, I appreciate your reasons for stating it.
c. The garden is a spectacular display of fountains and gargoyles; beds of lilies, zinnias, and hollyhocks; bushes shaped like animals; climbing roses, wisteria, and ivy; and lawns as wide as golf greens.
d. Luther missed the conference in Montreal, but he plans to attend the one in Memphis.
e. Dr. Elliott's intervention in the dispute was well intentioned; nevertheless, it was unfortunate.

EXERCISE 21–1, page 704

Suggested revisions:

a. The personnel director explained that the job requirements include typing, filing, and answering telephones.
b. The interview ended with a test of skills: taking dictation, operating the switchboard, proofreading documents, and typing a sample letter.
c. The sample letter began, "Dear Mr. Jones: Please accept our apologies for the late shipment."
d. Candace quoted Proverbs 8:18: "Riches and honor are with me."
e. A book that profoundly impressed me was Kurt Vonnegut's *Cat's Cradle* (New York: Dell, 1963).

EXERCISE 22–1, page 708

a. It's not easy to be old in our society.
b. I don't understand the Jameses' objections to our plans for a block party.
c. As the saying goes, "Every dog has its day."
d. Is this collection of '50s records yours or your roommate's?
e. Alas, Brian got two D's on his report card.

EXERCISE 23–1, page 713

a. "Don't think about it," advised Jason; "it will only make you unhappy."
b. "Should I go," Marcia asked, "or should I stay here?"

c. In her story "The Wide Net," Eudora Welty wrote, "The excursion is the same when you go looking for your sorrow as when you go looking for your joy."
d. "Who's supposed to say the line 'Tennis, anyone?' " asked the director.
e. Robert Burns's poem "To a Mouse" opens, "Wee, sleekit, cow'rin, tim'rous beastie, / O, what a panic's in thy breastie!"

EXERCISE 24–1, page 715

Suggested revisions:

a. I enjoy going fishing with my friend John, whom I've known for fifteen years.
b. His new boat is spectacular—a regular seagoing Ferrari.
c. An experienced carpenter and woodworker, John refitted the boat himself.
d. Correct
e. "A rock!" I cried. "John, I'm afraid we're—"

EXERCISE 25–1, page 717

Suggested revisions:

a. In *The Last Crusade,* archeologist Indiana Jones (who took his name from the family dog) joins his father in a quest for the Holy Grail.
b. Our cafeteria serves the four basic food groups: white (milk, bread, and mashed potatoes), brown (mystery meat and gravy), green (overcooked vegetables and underwashed lettuce), and orange (squash, carrots, and tomato sauce).
c. The ambassador says that if (1) the United States will provide more aid and (2) the guerrillas will agree to a cease-fire, his government will hold free elections.
d. Correct
e. Actually, the Whale Stranding Network (called WSN or "Wisson") rescues whales that have stranded themselves.

EXERCISE 26–1, page 725

a. Built for the Paris Exposition of 1889, the Eiffel Tower contains 15 million pounds of pig iron, protected by 37 tons of paint.
b. Friday, July 14, 1989, was the Eiffel Tower's hundredth anniversary.
c. Monsieur Eiffel would be pleased that President Mitterrand and others now accept his controversial "iron giraffe" as a national landmark.
d. In some Parisian tourist traps, a cup of coffee costs as much as $5.
e. France is a member of the North Atlantic Treaty Organization (NATO), but the French historically have mistrusted

some of their fellow NATO members, such as the United Kingdom.

EXERCISE 27–1, page 730
a. At our family reunion, I met my cousin Sam for the first time, and also my father's brother George.
b. I already knew from Dad that his brother had moved to Australia years ago to explore the Great Barrier Reef.
c. At the reunion, Uncle George told me that he had always wanted to be a marine biologist.
d. He had spent the summer after his sophomore year of college in Woods Hole, Massachusetts, on Cape Cod.
e. At the Woods Hole Oceanographic Institution he studied horseshoe crabs.

EXERCISE 28–1, page 732
a. Wasn't it the Three Musketeers whose motto was "One for all and all for one"?
b. In the 1970s, there were about 92 million ducks in America, but in the last four years their number has dropped to barely 69 million.
c. Cruising around the world on a 125-foot yacht with eight other people sounded glamorous until I saw our wooden berths, 32 inches wide by 68 inches long.
d. Forty days and forty nights would seem like forty years if you were sailing on an ark with two of every kind of animal.
e. Correct

EXERCISE 29–1, page 736
a. Hiram's favorite Beatles album is *Sergeant Pepper's Lonely Hearts Club Band,* but his father prefers *Magical Mystery Tour.*
b. Hiram named his rowboat the *Yellow Submarine.*
c. He was disappointed when I told him that the play *Long Day's Journey into Night* is definitely not a staged version of the movie *A Hard Day's Night.*
d. I had to show him the article "Eugene O'Neill's Journey into Night" in *People* magazine to convince him.
e. Many different ethnic groups eat tomatoes and cheese in or on some form of cooked dough, whether they call this dish a pizza, an enchilada, a sandwich, or something else.

EXERCISE 30–1, page 739
a. Do non-Americans share our view of ourselves as a freedom-loving people?
b. The dealer told George the two vases are within nine-tenths of an inch of being a perfect match.

c. Patrick Henry's words re-echo down through the ages: "Give me liberty or give me death!"
d. Those well-spoken words are well remembered today.
e. The weather forecast calls for showers followed by sunshine.

EXERCISE 32–1, page 753
Suggested revisions:
a. My diagnosis, Mrs. Pitt, is that your husband's heart may fail at any time.
b. I recommend multiple bypass heart surgery for Mr. Pitt.
c. If your insurance company will pay for it, he can be scheduled for bypass surgery; if not, he should go on a strict diet.
d. We the State Department staff have investigated the riots in Lebanon, and all our data indicate they are rapidly becoming worse.
e. Antinuclear protesters have been picketing the missile conference in hopes of stalling the negotiations.

EXERCISE 32–2, page 756
Suggested revisions:
a. This starting job involves hard work for low pay at first, but it could lead to promotion later.
b. The ship sank because of a hole in the hull.
c. The new K27 missile will kill everyone in the cities of any nation that attacks us.
d. In our town, trash collectors must wear uniforms at work.
e. Freddie the Rocker is dead.

EXERCISE 32–3, page 757
Suggested revisions:
a. Judy doesn't like Paul's sexual advances.
b. If large animals don't leave the combat zone, the army's policy is to kill them.
c. Judge Lehman's reversal of the *Smith v. Jones* verdict shows that he cannot think clearly.
d. Once that eyewitness told everything he knew, Jones's case was lost.
e. If he can get the money to pay his bail, he'll probably flee.

EXERCISE 34–1, page 764
Suggested revisions:
a. The Sahara has always been known as one of the hottest, most arid regions on earth.
b. The explorers knew they risked death as they set out to cross the desert.
c. After six days of travel, every member of

the party was sunburned and faint from thirst.

d. Even the camels were about to collapse when the scouts noticed an oasis.

e. The caravan leader squinted into the sun.

EXERCISE 35–1, page 768

Suggested revisions:

a. I suspect that this inquiry is likely to obscure the facts.

b. Please choose a password as soon as possible so that we can start using our new computer system.

c. As you know, your payment probably won't be returned to you soon.

d. If enough people press the elevator call button in a short time, the elevator will break down.

e. The secretary could not find out whether Mr. Jones and Ms. Cunningham had telephoned their resignations to the board.

Index

Abbey, Edward, 26
  "Disorder and Early Sorrow," 26–30
Abbreviation, word processing feature,
  558–559
Abbreviations, 722–726
  of academic degrees, 723
  of days and months, 724
  at end of sentence, 686
  forming plural of, 707–708
  and initials, 725
  Latin, 724
  of organizations, 686, 725
  of parts of literary works, 724
  period after, 686
  of personal titles, 722–723
  of time, 723
  of units of measurement, 724
Absolute phrases, 607, 608
  comma with, 695
Abstracts, 411
Access: The Supplementary Index to
  Periodicals, 408
Acronyms, 725
Active voice, 626–627
Addresses, commas with, 697
Adjective clauses, 610
Adjective phrases, 594–595

Adjectives, 534, 593, 657–661
  comparative, 659–661
  compound, 737
  coordinate, 691
  cumulative, 691–692
  hyphenated, 737
  made from proper names, 726
  as subject or object complement,
    658
  superlative form, 659–661
Adjectives and adverbs, deleting,
  534
Adverb clauses, 610–611
Adverb phrases, 595
Adverbs, 534, 594, 657–659, 660–661
  comparative form, 659–661
  conjunctive, 597, 612, 654, 679,
    694–695, 700
  superlative form, 659–661
Agreement
  pronoun-antecedent, 635–638
  subject-verb, 630–634
"AIDS: The Return of the Scarlet
  Letter" (Fendel), 223–227
Almanacs, 412
Alvarez, A., "Shiprock," 517
American Heritage Dictionary, 764

American Library Association Guide to Reference Books (Sheehy), 404
American Psychological Association (APA) style of documentation, 374, 436, 437, 461–467
Analogy, 143
  argument by, 527
Analysis
  literary, 212–214, 217–219
  of motives, 482
  and paragraph development, 509
  process, 181–182, 189–192, 194–195, 198, 509–510
  subject, 188–189, 190–191, 193–194
  See also Analyzing
Analyzing, 134, 181–219, 509
  anatomy application of, 197
  anthropology application of, 197–198
  applications of, 197–211
  assignment on, 187–195
  biology application of, 197, 198
  checklists for
    discovery, 188–189
    peer editing, 193, 194
    revision, 194, 195
  computer and, 193
  economics application of, 197
  education application of, 199
  geometry application of, 199
  group learning activity, 196
  and laboratory reports, 198
  and literature, 212–214, 217–219
  music application of, 207–211
  nutrition application of, 197
  political science application of, 197
  psychology application of, 199
  workplace applications of, 199–200
  See also Analysis
Anatomy, and analysis, 197
and
  antecedents joined by, 636
  subjects joined by, 631
Andrews, Deborah C., book review in *Chemical & Engineering News,* 300
Andriot, John L., *Guide to U.S. Government Publications,* 416
Annual reports, 417
Answer method, in drafting, 362

Antecedents, 635, 638
  agreement with pronoun, 635–638
  identifying, 639–640
  and subject-verb agreement, 633
Anthropology, and analysis, 197–198
APA. *See* American Psychological Association
Apostrophe, 705–708
  to form plural, 707–708
  to indicate omission, 707
  for plural of letters, words, and numbers used as words, 707–708
  in possessives, 705–707
Appositive
  colon with, 703
  comma with, 693–694
  dash with, 714
Appositive phrases, 607, 608
Appropriateness, in writing, 750–757
"Are the Homeless Crazy?" (Kozol), 315–318
Argument, 525–527
  ad hominem, 526
  by analogy, 527
  circular, 526
  data, warrant, and claim and, 527
  from dubious authority, 526
  from ignorance, 526
  and logical fallacies, 525–526
  See also Evidence; Opinion; Proposal
Art
  and evaluation, 299
  and imagination, 143
Articles (grammar), 593, 764
Art Index, 409
"Art of Eating Spaghetti, The" (Baker), 10–12
"Art of Teaching Science, The" (Thomas), 272–278
Assignments
  analyzing, 187–195
  cause and effect, 318–326
  combining resources, 149–153
  conversation, 104–113
  evaluating, 292–299
  field research, 420–435
  imagination, 131–138
  library research, 346–375
  observation, 41–49

Assignments (*cont.*)
  opinion, 227–237
  proposal, 257–266
  reading, 73–83
  recall, 16–23
Astrophysics, and imagination,
  146–148
Atlases, 412
Audience, 4–5, 35, 190, 234, 259, 319,
  751
  anticipating objections of, 261
Austin, James H., "Four Kinds of
  Chance," 517
Auxiliary (helping) verbs, 592, 615, 617

Baer, Bugs, 135
Baker, Russell, 10, 20
  "The Art of Eating Spaghetti," 10–12
  "School vs. Education," 520
Balsavias, Jennifer (peer editor),
  549–550, 553
Barber, James David, *The Presidential
  Character: Predicting Performance
  in the White House,* 504, 506
Barnet, Sylvan, *A Short Guide to
  Writing about Art,* 143
Baxter, Glen, 328–329
be, 617, 624, 649–650
Begging the question, 526
Beginnings
  and emphasis, 528–530
  and field research, 435
  and library research, 371–372
  writing, 483–490, 516–518
"Behind the Formaldehyde Curtain"
  (Mitford), 200–206
Beston, Henry, *Northern Farm,* 44–45
Betz, Jane (student writer), 214
  "A Defense of the Ending of 'The
  Story of an Hour,'" 217–219
Bible, 733
  colon used in citing, 704
*Bibliographic Index: A Cumulative
  Bibliography of Bibliographies,*
  407
Bibliography(-ies)
  annotated, 407
  in encyclopedias, 407
  printed, 354, 407

Bibliography(-ies) (*cont.*)
  working, 352–354, 357, 374
  See also Listing
Biographical sources, 411–412
Biography, interviewing and, 113
Biology
  and analyzing, 197, 198
  and library research, 395–396
  and observation, 51–54
  and recall, 25
"Black Men and Public Space"
  (Staples), 31–33
Blumberg, Albert E., *Logic,* 527
Bodanis, Paul, 185
  "What's in Your Toothpaste?"
  185–187
Book Review Digest, 411
Book reviews, 300, 411
Bouchard, Harry, and Francis Moffitt,
  Surveying, 199
Bowe, Jennifer (student writer), 127,
  135, 136–137, 492
  "If I Could Found a College,"
  127–131
Bower, T. G. R., *The Perceptual World
  of the Child,* 199
Brackets, 717–718
Brainstorming, 189, 258, 320, 471–474
  and analyzing, 189
  group, 471–472
  guidelines for, 473
  and imagination, 141
  and library research, 350
  and observation, 42
  and recall, 18
Britt, Suzanne, 221, 235, 491, 493
  "The First Person," 221–223
Brown, T. E., 299
Brumberg, Joan Jacobs, 331
  "The Origins of Anorexia Nervosa,"
  331–334
Burke, Kenneth, 233, 480–482
Business (courses), and recall, 26
Business writing
  and library research, 394
  and outlining, 501
  proposals, 266–267
  wordiness of, 532
  See also Workplace, writing in the

" 'But a Watch in the Night': A Scientific Fable" (Rettie), 122–127

Calbick, Martha (student writer), 472–474
Camera, in field research, 430
Capitalization, 726–730
  after colon, 702
  of days, months, and holidays, 728
  of educational institutions, 729
  of family relationships, 727
  of geographic names, 728
  of historical events, 728
  of names of religions, 728
  in poetry, 729
  of proper names, 726
  in quotations, 729
  of title or rank, 726
Card catalog. *See* Library catalog
Carroll, Lewis, 121
Case studies, field research and, 448–449
Catalog, library. *See* Library catalog
Cause and effect, 310–340
  applications of, 329–340
  assignment on, 318-326
  astronomy application of, 334-340
  checklists for
    discovery, 320–321
    peer editing, 325–326
    revision, 324, 325
  chemistry application of, 329
  child development application of, 329
  computer and, 322
  economics application of, 330
  and examination questions, 329, 566
  film study application of, 330–331
  group learning activity, 327
  history application of, 331–334
  immediate and remote causes, 320–321
  and paragraph development, 511–512
  social history application of, 331
  sociology application of, 329–330
  speech pathology application of, 329
CBE Style Manual, 451
CD-ROM (compact disc read-only memory), 415

Change, understanding. *See* Cause and effect
Characters, in literature, 212
Checklists. *See* Discovery checklists; Peer editing checklists; Revision checklists
Chemistry
  and cause and effect, 329
  and observation, 51–54
Chesterton, G. K., "The Two Noises," 45
Chiaramonti, Scipio, 527
Chickos, Lisa (student writer), 344–346, 350, 359–360, 363, 371
  "Educational Leadership: A Man's World," 375–391
Child development (course), and cause and effect, 329
Chomsky, Noam, 586
Chopin, Kate, 214
  "The Story of an Hour," 214–216
Chronology, establishing a, 20
Churchill, Winston, 485
Citation of sources. *See* Citing; Documentation
Citing
  APA style, 461–464
  endnotes, 454–457
  MLA style, 451–457
  of nonprint sources, 453–454, 456–457, 464
  of printed sources, 451–456, 461–464
  See also Documentation
"Citizen Reads the Constitution, A" (Doctorow), 91–94
Claim, stating a, 228. *See also* Data, warrant, and claim
Classification
  binary, 513
  paragraph development and, 512–513
Classification systems, library
  Dewey Decimal, 403–404
  Library of Congress, 403
Clauses, 609–611
  adjective, 610
  adverb, 610–611
  linked by conjunctive adverb, 700
  linking with subordination, 681–682

Clauses (*cont.*)
  main (independent), 609, 612, 682,
    689, 700–701, 704
  noun, 609–610
  pronoun as subject of, 642–643
  and sentence fragments, 653–655
  subordinate (dependent), 609, 610,
    628, 631, 649, 654, 682–683, 701
Cliché detector (word processing
    feature), 558
Clichés, avoiding, 761–763
Clustering, 496–497
Cohn, David Ian (student writer), 564,
    571, 572, 573
Coleridge, Samuel Taylor, 121
Collaborative learning, 538–553. *See
    also* Group learning activities;
    Peer editing
"Collecting the Past" (Polomsky),
    182–185
Collective noun(s)
  and singular or plural pronoun,
    637
  singular verb with, 631–632
Colon, 653, 679, 702–704, 712
  capitalization following, 702
  in citing Bible, 704
  in citing city and publisher of books,
    704
  in citing title and subtitle, 704
  at end of main clause, 704
  after introduction, 703
  between main clauses, 703
  before quotation, 703
  with quotation marks, 712
  after salutation in letter, 704
  in time of day, 704
Comma(s), 652, 654, 688–698
  to add phrase to clause, 701
  with coordinate adjectives, 691
  with coordinating conjunction, 653,
    689
  after introduction, 690
  to join main clauses, 689
  to join subordinate clause to main
    clause, 701
  misuse or overuse of, 697–698
  with quotation marks, 712
  in quotations, 696

Comma(s) (*cont.*)
  to separate phrase or subordinate
    clause, 701
  in series, 690–691
  to set off absolute phrase, 695
  to set off appositives, 693–694
  to set off conjunctive adverbs,
    694–695
  to set off contrasting elements, 695
  to set off dates, states, countries,
    and addresses, 697
  to set off nonrestrictive modifier, 692
  to set off parenthetical expressions,
    694–695
  to set off quotation, 696
Command
  exclamation point with, 687
  subject of, 600
Comma splices, 652–655
Commonly misspelled words, 746–749
Common nouns, 589
Communication disorders (course).
    See Speech pathology
Comparative form, 659–661
Comparing and contrasting
  in evaluation, 294, 296, 297
  in examination questions, 566–567
  and outlining, 296
  and paragraph development,
    510–511
  See also Evaluating
Comparisons, 666–667, 669, 675
Complements, 598, 599, 601–602
  adjectives as, 658
  object, 602, 658
  subject, 602, 658
Complete predicate, 600
Complete subject, 599
Complex sentences, 612–613, 676
Compound adjectives, 737
Compound-complex sentences, 613
Compound noun, 706, 737, 743
Compound predicate, 650, 669
Compound sentences, 612
Compound subject, 599, 612
  and agreement of verb, 631
  and pronoun-antecedent agreement,
    636
Compound verb, 612

Compound words, 737–738
Computer centers, college, 558
Computers, 554–561
  and analysis, 193
  and cause and effect, 322
  CD-ROM, 415
  and conversation, 109
  databases, 408–409, 414–415, 559
  and desktop publishing, 560
  and evaluation, 294
  and field research, 425, 432
  and grouping ideas, 497–498
  hardware and software, 557–558
  and imagination, 134
  and library research, 364, 375
  and note taking, 556
  and observation, 48
  and opinion, 234
  and peer editing, 543
  and proposal, 260
  and reading, 78
  and recalling, 19
  strategies for writing with, 554–561
  See also Word processor
Computers in libraries, 397, 398,
    408–409, 410–411, 414–415
  catalog, 398
  CD-ROM, 415
  databases, 408–409, 414–415, 559
Conclusion, 505, 518–520. *See also*
  Ending(s)
Conferences, professional, and field
  research, 430–431
"Conflicting Messages: A Look at a
  Generation Torn Two Ways"
  (Federici), 70–72
Congressional Record, 415–416
Conjunctions, 596–597, 715
  coordinating, 596, 612, 653, 674, 689,
    698, 699
  correlative, 597, 675
  subordinating, 611, 649, 681, 682
Conjunctive adverbs, 597, 612, 654, 679
  clauses linked by, 700
  commas to set off, 694–695
Connotations, 761
Construction, mixed, 670–673
Consumer Reports, 300
Contemporary Authors, 412

Contractions, apostrophe with, 707
Contrast, 669
Contrasting elements, comma with,
  695
Controversial issues. *See* Opinion
Conversation, writing from, 95–120
  applications of, 113–120
  assignment on, 104–113
  checklists for
    discovery, 104–105
    peer editing, 111
    revision, 110
  combined with other resources,
    150–153
  computer and, 109
  education application of, 118–120
  group learning activity, 112
  human development application of,
    113–114
  and interviewing, 95, 104, 105–108,
    113
  and journalism, 113, 114
  psychology application of, 114
  and recall, 20
  sociology application of, 114–115
  workplace applications of, 113
Coordinate adjectives, comma
  between, 691
Coordinating conjunctions, 596, 612,
  653, 698, 699
  clauses joined by, 689
  semicolon with, 700–701
  sentences joined by, 678–679
  series linked by, 674
Coordination, 677–680
  avoiding excessive, 680
  avoiding faulty, 679–680
Copland, Aaron, 207
  "How We Listen," 207–211
Corporations, 26, 429
  annual reports, 417
Corrections, making, 573–574, 579. *See
  also* Rewriting
Correlative conjunctions, 597
  series linked by, 675
Council of Biology Editors, *CBE Style
  Manual,* 451
Councill, Richard J., 54
Countries, avoid abbreviating, 725

Cowley, Malcolm, *The View from Eighty,* 520
Crews, Harry, "The Car," 517
Criteria, in evaluation, 279, 293–294, 295–296
Cumulative adjectives, 691–692

Dangling modifiers, 664–665
Dash, 712, 713–714
Data, warrant, and claim, 527
Databases, 408–409, 414–415, 559
   and descriptors, 414–415
   end-user searching, 414
   thesaurus and, 415
Dates, commas with, 697
Day, Robert A., *How to Write and Publish a Scientific Paper,* 422
"Defense of the Ending of 'The Story of an Hour,' A" (Betz), 217–219
Definite article, 593
Definition
   in draft, 233
   in evaluation, 295
   in examination questions, 568–569
   extended, 295
   in opening paragraph, 517
   and paragraph development, 512
   short, 295
Definitions, writing, 672
   italicizing, 734
Demonstration questions, on examinations, 567
Demonstrative pronouns, 590, 591
Denotations, 760
Dependent (subordinate) clauses, 609, 610
Dershowitz, Alan M., 304
   "Shouting 'Fire!' " 304–309
Description, 35–36. *See also* Observation
Desktop publishing, 560
Detail(s), 21, 45
Deters, Kevin (student writer), "Where Few Have Gone Before," 547–553
De Vries, Peter, 554, 555
Dewey Decimal Classification and Relative Index, 399
Dewey decimal classification system, 402–403

Dialogue, 112
   quotation marks in, 711
"Dick-and-Janing," 489–490
Dictionaries, 405–406
   biographical, 411
   and encyclopedias, 404–405
Dictionary of American Biography, 411
Dictionary of National Biography, 411
Didion, Joan, 38, 42, 46, 47
   "Marrying Absurd," 39–41
Dillard, Annie, 115
   "Encounters with Chinese Readers," 115–117
Direct address, commas with, 696
Directive, period after, 686
Direct object, 599, 601
   and transitive verb, 592, 601
Discovery checklists
   analyzing, 188–189
   cause and effect, 320, 321
   conversation, 104–105
   evaluating, 295
      evidence, 434
      exam performance, 574
   imagination, 133
   interviewing, 104–105
   library research, 349, 351, 398
   observation, 42–43
   opinion, 231, 233
   process analysis, 189
   proposal, 258, 259
   reading, 77
   recall, 17–18
Discussion questions, on examinations, 567–568
"Disorder and Early Sorrow" (Abbey), 26–30
Dissertation Abstracts, 411
Division. *See* Analysis
Division and classification, and examination questions, 568
Doctorow, E. L., 91
   "A Citizen Reads the Constitution," 91–94
Documentation, 69, 373–375, 450–467
   APA style, 374, 436, 437, 450, 461–467
   MLA style, 374, 450, 451–461

Documentation (*cont.*)
  in proposals, 261–262
"Do We Survive Death?" (Russell),
    239–243
Downey, Bill, *Right Brain . . . Write On!*,
    490
Drafting, 3, 5
  answer method, 362
  and examination questions, 571–573
  and examples, 506–508
  getting started, 483–490
  and grouping ideas, 495–498
  and narration, 521–522
  and outlining, 498–503
  and paragraphing, 503–520
  restarting, 490–491
  and stating a thesis, 491–495
  strategies for, 483–522
  and telling a story, 521–522
  thesis method, 362
  and transitions, 513–516
Drafting assignments
  and analysis, 190–192
  and cause and effect, 322–323
  and conversation, 108–110
  and evaluation, 295–296
  and field research, 431–435
  and imagination, 135–136
  and library research, 362–371
  and observation, 45–46
  and opinion, 233–235
  and proposal, 260–262
  and reading, 77–80
  and recall, 20–21
"Drinking Age, The: How We Should
    Determine It" (Ting), 254–257
Durrenberger, Robert W., *Geographical
    Research and Writing*, 141

Economics
  and analysis, 197
  and cause and effect, 330
  and imagination, 142
  and opinion, 243–249
  and recall, 25
Editing. *See* Rewriting
Education (courses)
  and analysis, 199
  and conversation, 118–120

Education (courses) (*cont.*)
  and field research, 446
  and observation, 51
  and opinion, 238–239
  and reading, 84–85
Education Index, 409
"Educational Leadership: A Man's
    World" (Chickos), 375–391
Effect, cause and. *See* Cause and effect
Ehninger, Douglas, and Wayne
    Brockriede, *Decision by Debate*,
    528
Ehrlich, Anne and Paul, *Extinction*,
    395–396
Einstein, Albert, 121
Either/or reasoning, 525–526
Eliot, T. S., 64, 296
Elkind, David, 118
  "Superkids and Super Problems,"
    118–120
Ellipsis, 79, 111, 718–719
Elliptical constructions, 668–669
Ellison, Ralph, 154
  "What America Would Be Like
    Without Blacks," 154–158
Emerson, Ralph Waldo, 478
Emphasis, 528–530
  and beginnings, 528–530
  dash to set off emphatic aside, 714
  and endings, 530
  exclamation point for, 687
  and repetition, 530
  in sentences, 529, 530
  underlining for, 735
"Encounters with Chinese Readers"
    (Dillard), 115–117
Encyclopaedia Britannica, New, 404
Encyclopedia of Associations, 416
Encyclopedia of World Art, 404
Encyclopedias, 349, 404–405, 407
  specialized, 404–405
  yearbooks, 412
Ending(s), 518–520
  and emphasis, 530
  and field research, 435
  and library research, 371–372
  quotations in, 520
  See also Conclusion
Endnotes, 454–457

Envisioning, 133–134, 138, 142–143
Erikson, Erik, 114, 506
Essay examinations, 563–574
  cause and effect questions, 329
  discovery checklist, 574
  open-book, 563
  preparing for, 563
  responding to quotations on,
    569–570
  short answer, 575
  strategies for, 571–574
  and thesis statement, 572
  time management in, 564, 571, 576
  types of questions on, 566–570. *See
    also* Question(s), examination
Essays
  in-class, 575–576
  and writing from conversation,
    115–117
  See also Essay examinations
Ethical questions, 26, 220
Euphemisms, 755–756
Evaluating, 279–309
  applications of, 299–309
  assignment on, 292-299
  checklists for
    discovery, 295, 434
    peer editing, 297
    revision, 297–298
  computer and, 294
  criteria in, 279, 293–294, 295–296
  evidence, 434
  and examination questions, 569
  fairness in, 296
  film review application of, 301–304
  group learning activity, 299
  law application of, 304–309
  and literature, 279–289, 298–299
  and note taking, 358, 362–363
  outlining and, 296
  reviews as, 300
  workplace applications of,
    299–300
Evidence, 260, 434
  citing sources of, 234–235
  in evaluations, 293, 434
  and examples, 507
  of experts, 230, 234–235
  falling in love with, 235

Evidence (*cont.*)
  interpreting, 433–434
  testing, 231–232, 354–357, 358, 362,
    433
  in writing opinion, 228–231
Exact words, choosing, 760–764
Examination questions. *See* Essay
  examinations
Examinations. *See* Essay examinations
Examples, giving, 506–508
Exclamation point, 687, 712
Expert testimony, 230, 234–235
Explanation
  brackets for, 717–718
  dash to introduce, 714
Explanation, methods of
  analyzing, 181–219
  cause and effect, 310–340

Facts, as evidence, 229–233
Facts on File, 410, 412
Fairness, in evaluation, 296
Falk, Dana (student writer), "Why
  Don't More People Donate Their
  Bodies to Science?" 545–546
Fallacies, logical, 525–528
  argument *ad hominem,* 526
  argument by analogy, 527
  argument from dubious authority,
    526
  argument from ignorance, 526
  begging the question, 526
  either/or reasoning, 525–526
  non sequitur, 232, 525
  oversimplification, 232, 264, 525
  post hoc ergo propter hoc, 527
Family science, and imagination, 142
Faulty coordination, avoiding, 679–680
Faulty predication, 670–672
Federici, Rose Anne (student writer),
  69, 75, 77–78, 79–80, 81–82
  "Conflicting Messages: A Look at a
  Generation Torn Two Ways,"
    70–72
Fendel, Susan (student writer), 228
  "AIDS: The Return of the Scarlet
  Letter," 223–227
"Fenimore Cooper's Literary Offenses"
  (Twain), 280–289

Fiction writing, 521–522
and writing from reading, 91–94
Field research, 418–449
applications of, 446–449
assignment on, 420–435
and background reading, 422
and camera or videocamera, 430
and case studies, 448–449
checklists for
discovery, 422
peer editing, 436
revision, 435
computer and, 425, 432
education application of, 446
evaluating sources for, 433–434
field trips and, 428–429
group learning activity, 445–446
and interviews, 422–424
lectures, conferences and, 430–431
and manuscript preparation,
436–437
and questionnaires, 424–428
sample paper, 437–444
sources for, 416, 421–431, 434–435
and telephone inquiry, 429
workplace applications of,
446–449
Field trips
and field research, 428–429
for observation, 43, 51
Figures, writing out, 731–732
Film Literature Index, 345
Film reviews, 300, 301
Film study, cause and effect and,
330–331
Finch, Robert, "The Tactile Land,"
151–152
"First Person, The" (Britt), 221
Fischer, Kurt W., and Arlyne Lazerson,
Human Development, 513
"Flowers for Chapel Street" (Tein),
96–99
Footnotes. *See* Endnotes
"Footprints: The Mark of Our Passing"
(Messina), 36–38
Foreign words, italics for, 734
Form, in poetry, 212
Formal language, 751, 756–757
Formal verse, 212

Formatting, 577–581
computer, 580–581
Forster, E. M., 5
Fossey, Dian, *Gorillas in the Mist,* 54
Fractions, hyphen in writing, 738
Fragments, sentence, 646–651, 665
Free verse, 212
Freewriting, 18, 259, 293, 474, 474–476,
486
guidelines for, 475
Freud, Sigmund, *Interpretation of
Dreams,* 149
Friedman, Milton, 243
"The Social Responsibility of
Business Is to Increase Its Profits,"
243–249
Frost, Robert, 298, 530
Fused sentences, 652–655

Gandhi, Mahatma, *An Autobiography,*
521
Gansberg, Martin, "38 Who Saw
Murder Didn't Call Police," 519
Gardner, Howard, *Artful Scribbles,*
300–301
Gazetteers, 412
Gender
omitting words denoting, 758–759
pronoun-antecedent agreement and,
637
Generating ideas, 2–3
and brainstorming, 471–474
and clustering, 496–497
in essay examinations, 565
and freewriting, 473, 474–476
and keeping a journal, 476–478
and reporter's questions, 478–480
and seeking motives, 480–482
strategies for, 471–482
See also Discovery checklists
Generating ideas for assignments
and analysis, 188–190
and cause and effect, 319–321
by conversation, 104–108
and evaluating, 293–295
and field research, 421–431
by imagination, 133–135
and library research, 348–361
by observation, 42–45

Generating ideas for assignments
    (*cont.*)
    and opinion, 228–233
    and proposal, 258–260
    by reading, 74–76
    by recall, 17–20
Geography, and imagination, 141
Geology, and observation, 54
Geometry, and analysis, 199
Gerund, 617, 644–645
Gerund phrases, 606
Getting started, strategies for, 483–490
Giles, Robert H., Jr., *Wildlife
    Management,* 509
good, well, 658–659, 660
Goodman, Ellen, 515
Gould, Stephen Jay, 86
    "Sex and Size," 25
    "Women's Brains," 86–91
Government documents, 415–416
Graham, Patricia Albjerg, "Status
    Transitions of Women Students,
    Faculty, and Administration,"
    358–359
Grammar, 585, 589–614
    clauses, 609–611
    defined, 585
    descriptive and prescriptive
        approaches, 585
    parts of sentences, 598–602
    parts of speech, 589–598
    phrases, 604–609
    sentence patterns, 602–604
    types of sentences, 611–614
Greenbie, Barrie B., *Spaces:
    Dimensions of the Human
    Landscape,* 152, 395–396
Gross, Feliks, "Causation of Terror,"
    331
Grouping ideas, 495–498
    by clustering, 496–497
    by linking, 495–496
    by note cards, 496
    with word processor, 497–498
Group learning activities, 538
    analysis, 196
    brainstorming as, 471–472
    cause and effect, 327
    conversation, 112

Group learning activities (*cont.*)
    evaluation, 299
    field research, 445–446
    imagination, 140–141
    library research, 392–393
    observation, 50
    opinion, 237
    proposal, 265
    reading, 84
    recall, 23

Haas, Charlie, 59
    "Tinsel Teens," 59–63
*Habits of the Heart: Individualism and
    Commitment in American Life,*
    114–115
Hairston, Maxine, 220
Hall, Donald, 485
Handbook, 583–782
Hardin, Garrett, *Naked Emperors:
    Essays of a Taboo-Stalker,*
    141–142
Hardware, computer, 557–558
Harris, Mary, *The Autobiography of
    Mother Jones,* 507–508
Hawley, Gessner G., "A Chemist's
    Definition of pH," 512
Helping (auxiliary) verbs, 592, 615,
    617
Hemingway, Ernest, 490
History
    and imagination, 141
    and observation, 51
    seeking motives and, 480
Hoffman, Charles D., and Edward
    Teyber, 268
    "Missing Fathers," 269–272
Homonyms, 741–742
"How a Bondsman Decides to Post
    Bail" (Merisotis), 438–444
"How to" (directive) writing, 199. *See
    also* Process analysis, directive
"How We Listen" (Copland),
    207–211
Human development (course)
    and conversation, 113–114
    and reading, 85
Humor, imagination and, 143–145
Hunt, Robert W., 752

Hyphen, 736–740
  to break word at end of line,
    738–739
  in compound words, 737, 738
  to indicate series between numbers,
    738
  with prefixes, and suffixes, 738

Ideas
  grouping, 495–498
  main, 492–494. *See also* Theme
  See also Generating ideas
Idioms, 763–764
"If Grant Had Been Drinking at
  Appomattox" (Thurber), 143–145
"If I Could Found a College" (Bowe),
  127–131
Illustration, dash to introduce, 714
Images, 44, 136, 212
Imagination, defined, 121–122
Imagination, writing from, 121–153
  applications of, 141–148
  assignment on, 131–138
  astrophysics applications of,
    146–148
  checklists for
    discovery, 133
    peer editing, 137
    revision, 138
  combining with other resources,
    151–153
  computer and, 134
  economics application of, 142
  and envisioning, 133–134, 138,
    142–143
  family science application of, 142
  group learning activity, 140–141
  history application of, 141
  and shifting perspective, 133,
    141–142
  and synthesizing, 134–135,
    142–143
Imperative mood, 628
In-class essay, 500, 575–576
In-class writing, 562–576
  essay examinations, 563–574
  in-class essays, 575–576
  short-answer examinations, 575
Indefinite article, 593

Indefinite pronouns, 590, 591
  and antecedent agreement, 636
  forming progressive, 706
  and verb agreement, 632
Independent (main) clauses, 609, 612,
  682, 689, 700–701, 704
Index(es)
  computerized, 408–409, 410–411
  newspaper, 403, 410–411
  periodical, 344–345, 354, 407–409
Indicative mood, 628
Indirect object, 599, 601
  to implied before, 601
Indirect question, 687
  period after, 686
Infinitive form of verb, 617, 622
Infinitive phrases, 606–607
Infinitives, 606, 617–618
Informal (colloquial) language, 751
InfoTrac, 415
Initials, 725
Intensive pronouns, 590, 591
Interjections, 597–598, 687, 696
  exclamation point with, 687
Interrogative pronouns, 590, 591
Interview(s), 95
  applications of, 113–120
  checklists for, 110, 111
  and computers, 109
  conducting, 106, 422–424
  and field research, 422–424
  follow up, 428
  preparing for, 105–106
  questions for, 105–106
  recording, 106
  telephone, 107, 429
Intransitive verbs, 592, 615
Introduction(s). *See* Beginnings
Introductory words
  comma after, 690
  dash after, 714
Invention. *See* Generating ideas
Irony, 212–213
Irregular verbs, 617, 622
  principal parts of, 618–619
Italics, 733–736
  indicate by underlining, 733
  for names of ships, trains, etc.,
    734

Italics (*cont.*)
  for titles of works, 733
  for words in foreign language, 734
it's, its, 644, 707
"I Want My MTV" (Munich), 289–292

Jackson, Jacqueline, *Turn Not Pale, Beloved Snail,* 490–491
"Japan's Closed Doors: Should the U.S. Retaliate?" (Martin), 535–537
Jargon, 751–753
Journal(s), 43, 476–478, 487–488
  keeping a, 476–478
  reading, 73, 75, 77
  specialized, 43, 478
Journals (periodicals), professional, 85, 300, 407. *See also* Periodicals
Journalism
  and field research, 446
  and interviewing, 113, 114
  and library research, 394
  and observation, 51
  See also Reporter's questions
Judging. *See* Evaluating

Kael, Pauline
  "*Rocky*" (film review), 301–304
Kafka, Franz, 143
Kennedy, Katie (student writer), 322, 323–324
  "Why We Burned a Wilderness," 311–314
Kekulé, Friedrich, 134
Kessler, Heidi (student writer), 505
King, Martin Luther, Jr., 142–143
King, Stephen, *Danse Macabre,* 330–331
Klass, Perri, 171
  "A Textbook Pregnancy," 171–178
Knox, Peter L., 85–86
Kozol, Jonathan, 315
  "Are the Homeless Crazy?" 315–318
Kübler-Ross, Elisabeth, *On Death and Dying,* 268

Laboratory reports, 54, 198
Language, formality of, 751

Language and linguistics (course), and evaluation, 299
Language development, observation and, 51
Lavenda, Robert H., and Emily Schultz, *Cultural Anthropology: A Perspective on the Human Condition,* 197–198
Law, and reading, 85–86
Lazerson, Arlyne, and Kurt W. Fischer, *Human Development,* 513
Lear, Martha Weinman, 107, 108
Least Heat Moon, William, 99, 106, 108
  "A View of Prejudice," 99–103
Lectures, and field research, 430–431
Legget, John, 488
LeGuin, Ursula, "Why Are Americans Afraid of Dragons?" 122
Lenneberg, Eric B., 526
Leonard, George B., "No School?" 518
Lesko, Matthew, *Information U.S.A.,* 416
Letter(s)
  angry, to instructor, 487
  to the editor, 238, 356–357
  in field research, 429
Letters, numbers, and words used as words
  plural of, 707–708
  underlining, 735
Lewis, Oscar, *The Children of Sanchez,* 111–112
Libraries, 397–417
  call numbers, 399
  catalog, 260, 344, 353–354, 398–402
  classification systems, 400, 402–403
  computers in, 397, 398, 408–409, 410–411, 414–415
  databases in, 408–409, 414–415
  finding a book, 399–402
  government documents in, 415–416
  microfilm and microfiche in, 398, 413
  periodicals room, 403
  reference books in, 403–412
  and reference librarian, 355, 397–398, 411
  resources of, 403–417

Library catalog, 260, 344, 353–354, 398–402
  subject headings in, 398–399, 401
Library of Congress classification system, 402
Library of Congress Subject Headings, 353–354, 399
Library research, 343–396
  applications of, 393–396
  assignment on, 346–375
  biology application of, 395–396
  checklists for
    discovery, 349, 351, 398
    peer editing, 372
    revision, 373
  computer and, 364, 375
  group learning activity, 392–393
  and manuscript preparation, 373–375
  and note taking, 357–358
  and outlining, 363–364, 375, 377–380
  and overview, 349–350
  preliminary, 352
  and reading, 343–344
  sample paper, 375–391
  schedule for, 348
  working bibliography and, 352–354
  workplace applications of, 394
Library research paper
  formatting, 578–579
  sample, 375–391
  stages in writing, 344–346
lie, lay, 619–620
Lightman, Alan P., 146
  "Time Travel and Papa Joe's Pipe," 146–148
Linking, 495–496
Linking verbs, 592, 615, 616
  to connect subject with complement, 616
  and subject agreement, 633
Listing
  APA style, 464–467
  MLA style, 457–461
  See also Citing; Documentation
List of works cited, 353, 374, 452
Lists, parentheses to set off, 716
Literary criticism, 212–214

Literature
  and analysis, 212–214, 217–219
  characters in, 212
  elements of, 212–213
  and evaluating, 279–289, 298–299
  seeking motives and, 480
Livingston, Myra Cohn, 43
Locke, John, *Second Treatise of Government,* 141

Mack, Karin, and Eric Skjei, *Overcoming Writing Blocks,* 489
Magazine Index, 408–409
Magazines. *See* Periodicals
Magazines for Libraries, 357
Mailer, Norman, 498
Main (independent) clauses, 609, 612, 682
  colon at end of, 704
  joining, 689, 700
  semicolon to separate, 700–701
Main idea, 492–494, 518. *See also* Thesis
Main verb, 592
Manchester, William, 496
Manuscript preparation, 373–375, 577–581
  and word processor, 580–581
Maps, 412
"Marrying Absurd" (Didion), 39–41
Martin, John (student writer)
  "Japan's Closed Doors: Should the U.S. Retaliate?" 534–537
Media, and field research, 430. *See also* Journalism
Medicine, and field research, 446
Memory, 9, 231, 319. *See also* Recall
Mencken, H. L., "The Libido for the Ugly," 520
Merisotis, Jamie (student writer), 419–420, 422–429
  "How a Bondsman Decides to Post Bail," 438–444
Messina, Sandy (student writer), 43, 44, 49
  "Footprints: The Mark of Our Passing," 36–38
Metaphor, 527

Michaelson, Herbert B., *How to Write and Publish Engineering Papers and Reports,* 432–433
Microfilm and microfiche, 398, 413
Miller, Roger Leroy, and Douglas C. North, *The Economics of Public Issues,* 330
Miró, Joan, 486
"Missing Fathers" (Teyber and Hoffman), 269–272
Misplaced modifiers, 662–663
Mitford, Jessica, 200
   "Behind the Formaldehyde Curtain," 200–206
Mixed construction, 670–673
MLA. *See* Modern Language Association
MLA Handbook for Writers of Research Papers, 451, 454, 558, 559
Mnemonic devices, 745–746
Modern Language Association (MLA) style of documentation, 374, 450, 451–461
Modifiers, 599, 662–665
   commas to set off, 692–693
   dangling, 664–665
   misplaced, 662–663
   nonrestrictive, 692, 693
   restrictive, 693
   squinting, 663
   See also Adjectives; Adverbs
Moffitt, Francis H., and Harry Bouchard, *Surveying,* 199
Monthly Catalog of United States Government Publications, 416
Mood, 628–630
   imperative, 628
   indicative, 628
   subjunctive, 628–629
Motives, seeking, 480–482
Ms., 760
Munich, Matthew A. (student writer) "I Want My MTV," 289–292

Names, proper
   capitalizing, 726
   in direct address, 696
Narration, 20–21, 213, 521–522
National Council of Teachers of English, Doublespeak Award, 755

National Newspaper Index, 410–411
New Century Cyclopedia of Names, 405
New Encyclopaedia Britannica, 404
News, as source of information, 258
Newspapers, 258, 403, 410
   indexes to, 403, 410–411
   style books, 450
News story, 478–479, 503
New York Times, 403, 410–411, 413
New York Times Index, 403, 410
Nonrestrictive modifiers, commas with, 692, 693
Non sequitur, 232, 525
North, Douglass C., and Roger Leroy Miller, *The Economics of Public Issues,* 330
Note cards, 231, 357–362
Note taking, 2, 231, 357–362
   computer and, 556
   and evaluating, 358, 362
   and interviews, 107–108
   for library research, 357–358
   and observation sheet, 43–44
   and reading, 74–75
Noun(s), 589
   collective, 631–632, 637
   compound, 706
   possessive, 639, 705–706
   plural, 706, 708
   proper, 589
   singular, but plural in form, 634
   subjective, objective, and possessive, 642
Noun clauses, 609–610
Noun phrases, 606, 607
"Nuclear Winter, The" (Sagan), 334–340
Number or date, question mark for doubt about, 687
Numbers, 730–732, 738
   at beginning of sentence, 732
   figures for, 731
   fractions, hyphen in, 738
Nutrition, and analysis, 197
Nutshelling, 79
   in library research, 357, 360, 365, 366, 367
   See also Summarizing

Object(s), 598, 599, 601
  direct, 599, 601
  indirect, 599, 601
  pronouns as, 643
  of transitive verb, 592, 601
Object complement, 602, 658
Objections, anticipating readers', 261
Objective pronoun, 641–642, 643–644,
  645
Observation, as evidence, 231
Observation, writing from, 35–63
  applications of, 51–63
  assignment on, 41–49
  checklists for
    discovery, 42–43
    peer editing, 48–49
    revision, 49
  combined with other resources,
    149–153
  computer and, 48
  education application of, 51
  and field trips, 43, 51
  geology application of, 54
  group learning activity, 50
  history application of, 51
  journalism application of, 51
  language development application
    of, 51
  and reading, 84
  sociology application of, 51, 59–63
  speech pathology application of,
    51
  and technical writing, 54
  workplace applications of, 51
  zoology application of, 54–59
  See also Description
"Observation sheet," 43–44, 45
Openings. *See* Beginnings
Opinion, 220–249
  applications of, 238–249
  assignment on, 227–237
  checklists for
    discovery, 231, 233
    peer editing, 235
    revision, 236
  computer and, 234
  economics application of, 243–249
  education application of, 238–239
  group learning activity, 237

Opinion (*cont.*)
  philosophy application of, 239–243
  workplace applications of, 238–239
or, nor, 631, 636
Organizations, information from, 416,
  429
"Origins of Anorexia Nervosa, The"
  (Brumberg), 331–334
Orwell, George, 531, 761
Outlining, 135, 498–503
  and analyzing, 192
  computer and, 556
  in essay examination, 571
  in evaluation, 296
  formal, 375, 501–503
  informal, 233, 499–500
  and library research, 363–364, 375
  and opinion, 233
  point by point, 296
  sample, 377–380
  scratch (or rough), 45, 498, 499
  sentence, 375, 501
  subject by subject, 296
Oversimplification, 232, 264, 525
Oxford English Dictionary (OED),
  405–406

Paleontology, and reading, 86–91
Paragraph(s), 503–520
  cause and effect, 511–512
  classifying in, 512–513
  comparing and contrasting,
    510–511
  concluding, 518–520
  defining in, 512
  development of, 509–510, 509–516
  giving examples in, 506–508
  opening, 516–518
  question and answer, 506
  and topic sentence, 504–506
  transitional, 503, 513–516
Parallel structure, 667, 673–676
Paraphrasing, 79–80
  in library research, 360–361, 365,
    368, 369
Parentheses, 712, 716–717
Parenthetical expressions, setting off,
  714
Participial phrases, 606, 607

Participles
  as main verb, 649–650
  past, 606, 607, 617–618
  present, 606, 607, 617, 619–620
Parton, Edward R. (student writer), 198
Parts of speech, 589–598
  adjectives, 593
  adverbs, 594
  conjunctions, 596–597
  interjections, 597–598
  nouns, 589
  prepositions, 594–596
  pronouns, 590–591
  verbs, 592–593
  See also Adjectives; Adverbs, etc.
Passive voice, 195, 617, 626–627, 672
Past participles, 606, 607, 617–618
Past tense of verb, 617–618, 623
Peer editing, 23, 539–540, 545–553
  computer and, 543
  guidelines for, 541–542
  reader's role in, 540–543, 545–553
  strategies for, 538–553
  writer's role in, 544–545
  See also Peer editing checklists
Peer editing checklists, 538, 549–550
  analysis, 193, 194
  cause and effect, 325–326
  conversation, 111
  evaluation, 297
  field research, 436
  imagination, 137
  library research, 372
  observation, 48–49
  opinion, 235
  proposal, 262
  reading, 82–83
  recall, 22
Peer editors, 539–540. *See also* Peer
  editing
Peer tutors, 539. *See also* Peer editing
Pentad, 481
Perfect tenses, 621, 622, 623–624
Period, 685–686
  with quotation marks, 712
Periodical indexes, 344–345, 354,
  407–409
  general, 354, 407–409
  specialized, 345, 354, 407, 409

Periodicals, 74, 403
  evaluating as sources, 355–357
  indexes to, 344–345, 354, 407–409
  news magazines, 258, 355
  specialized, 85, 409
  See also Journals
Person and number, agreement in,
  630, 635
Personal pronouns, 590, 642
  possessive case, 706–707
Perspective, shifting, 133, 141–142
Peters, Thomas J., and Robert H.
  Waterman, Jr., *In Search of
  Excellence*, 506–507
Petrunkevitch, Alexander, 54
  "The Spider and the Wasp,"
  55–59
Philosophy, and imagination, 141
Photocopying
  and library research, 357, 367
  and peer editing, 540
Phrases, 604–609, 701
  absolute, 607, 608
  as adjective, 657
  appositive, 607, 608
  following colon, 702
  gerund, 607
  infinitive, 606–607
  noun, 606, 607
  participial, 607
  prepositional, 605–606
  as sentence fragment, 648–649
  verbal, 606–607
Picasso, Pablo, 134
Plagiarism, 78, 79, 361, 369–371
Plot, in literature, 213
"Plug-In Drug, The" (Winn), 163–171
Plurals, 743
  of abbreviations, 707–708
  with apostrophe, 706, 707–708
  of letter, word, or number used as
  word, 707–708
Poetry
  capitalization in, 729
  quotation from, 710
  slash to indicate break in, 715
Point of view, 213
Political science, and field research,
  446

Polomsky, Richard (student writer)
"Collecting the Past," 182–185
Possessive nouns, 639
apostrophe with, 705–706
Possessive pronouns, 590, 641–642,
644–645
Post hoc ergo propter hoc, 527
Predicate, 598, 599, 600–601
complete, 600
compound, 650, 669
simple, 600
Predication, faulty, 670–672
Prefixes, 745
hyphen after, 738
Prepositional phrases
adjective and adverb, 594–595
and subject-verb agreement, 631
Prepositions, 594–596, 668
list of common, 595
Present participle(s), 606, 607, 617,
619–620
Problems, solutions to. *See* Proposal
Process analysis, 181–182, 189–192,
194–195, 198, 509–510
directive, 182, 190, 191, 199
and examination questions, 570
informative, 181–182, 189–190, 191,
198–199
and paragraph development,
509–510
See also Analyzing
Progressive tenses, 617, 622–623,
624–625
Pronoun-antecedent agreement,
635–638
Pronoun case, 641–646
objective, 641–642, 643–644
possessive, 641–642, 644–645
subjective, 641–643
Pronoun reference, 638–641
Pronouns, 590–591, 641–642
in apposition, 643, 644
case of, 641–646
indefinite, 590, 591, 632, 636, 706
interrogative, 590, 591
modifying a gerund, 644–645
as object, 643
objective, 641–642, 643–644, 645
personal, 590, 642, 706–707

Pronouns (*cont.*)
possessive, 590, 641–642, 644–645
reflexive, 590, 591, 642
relative, 610, 613, 633, 642, 681, 682
showing ownership, 644
as subject, 642–643
as subject complement, 643
subjective, 641–643
as transitions, 515
types of, 590–591
Pronunciation, spelling and, 740
Proofreading, 4, 235–236, 437
Proper nouns, 589
Proposal, 250–278
academic applications of, 266
applications of, 266–278
assignment on, 257–266
business applications of, 266–267
checklists for
discovery, 258, 259
peer editing, 262
revision, 264–265
computers and, 260
group learning activity, 265
psychology application of, 268–272
science application of, 272–278
thesis, 266
workplace applications of, 266
Protagonist, in literature, 213
Proust, Marcel, 485
Psychology
and analysis, 199
and conversation, 114
and field research, 446
and narration, 521–522
and proposal, 268–272
Punctuation, 685–721
apostrophe, 705–708
brackets, 717–718
colon, 653, 679, 702–704, 712
comma, 652, 654, 688–698, 701,
712
dash, 712, 713–714
ellipsis mark, 718–719
end, 685–687, 712
exclamation point, 687, 712
parentheses, 712, 716–717
period, 685–686, 712
question mark, 686–687, 712

Punctuation (*cont.*)
  quotation marks, 696, 709–713
  semicolon, 653, 655, 679, 699–702,
    712
  slash (virgule), 714–715
Purpose, in writing, 4–5, 21–22, 35, 46

Quammen, David, 65, 68–69, 78, 79,
    80, 491–492
  "A Republic of Cockroaches: When
    the Ultimate Exterminator Meets
    the Ultimate Pest," 65–68
Question(s)
  beginning paragraph with, 506, 517
  direct, 686–687
  examination, 238, 329, 566–570, 571
  indirect, 686, 687
  for interviews, 105–106
  in peer editing, 541–542
  reporter's, 18–19, 478–480, 522
  in seeking motives, 480–482
  stating, in library research, 350–351
  tag, commas with, 696
  "what if," 131–133
Question mark, 686–687
  with quotation marks, 712
Questionnaire(s), 424–428
  preparing, 424–428
  purpose of, 424–425
  response to, 427–428
  sample, 426–427
Quotation(s), 78, 83
  brackets with alterations in, 717–718
  capitalization in, 729
  colon after introduction to, 703
  commas to set off, 696
  direct, 83, 111, 365, 374
  double-checking, 111
  ellipsis in, 718–719
  in endings, 520
  in field research, 435
  indenting, 374
  indirect, 698
  in interviews, 107, 109–112
  and library research, 358–362, 365,
    374
  long, 374, 710
  from poetry, 710
  within quotations, 112, 709

Quotation(s) (*cont.*)
  responding to on examinations,
    569–570
  [*sic*] in, 718
Quotation marks, 112, 696, 709–713
  in dialogue, 711
  other punctuation with, 712
  single, 112, 709

Raines, Howell, *My Soul Is Rested,*
    114
Raven, Peter H., et al., *Biology of
    Plants,* 510
Raywid, Mary Anne, 238–239
Reader(s). *See* Audience
Readers' Guide to Periodical Literature,
    150, 260, 344, 345, 349–350, 354
  using, 352, 403, 407–408
Reading
  background, for field research, 422
  journal of, 73, 77
  and note taking, 74–75
  and observing, 84–85
  and peer editing, 540–543
  as preparation for writing, 487, 534
Reading, writing from, 64–94
  applications of, 84–94
  assignment on, 73–83
  checklists for
    discovery, 77
    peer editing, 82–83
    revision, 81
  combined with other resources,
    150–153
  computers and, 78
  and documentation, 69, 78–80
  education application of, 84–85
  group learning activity, 84
  human development application of,
    85
  law application of, 85–86
  and literature, 213
  and note taking, 74–75
  and observation, 85
  paleontology application of, 86–91
  and research, 343–344
  as starting strategy, 18, 74
Reading journal, 73, 75, 77
Reading literature, 213

Reasoning, errors in, 264. *See also* Argument; Fallacies, logical
reason is because ... , 672
Recall, writing from, 9–33
    applications of, 24–33
    assignment on, 16–23
    biology application of, 25
    and cause and effect, 319–321
    checklists for
        discovery, 17–18
        peer editing, 22
        revision, 22
    combined with other resources, 149–153
    with a computer, 19
    economics application of, 26
    group learning activity, 23
    sociology application of, 25–26
    See also Memory
Reciprocal pronouns, 590, 591
Reference books, 403–412
    abstracts, 411
    almanacs, 412
    atlases, 412
    bibliographies, 354, 407
    biographical sources, 411–412
    dictionaries, 405–406, 411
    encyclopedias, 349, 404–405
    gazetteers, 412
    indexes to periodicals, 407–409
    yearbooks, 412
Reference librarian, 355, 397–398, 411
"References," 464
Reflexive pronouns, 590, 591, 642
Relative pronoun(s), 590, 591, 642, 681
    implied, 613
    introducing adjective clause, 610
    as subject of clause, 610, 613, 633
Repetition
    eliminating, 668–669
    for emphasis, 530
    of lead-in words, 676
    to reinforce parallel structure, 676
Reporter's questions (five *W*'s and an *H*), 18–19, 478–480, 522

"Republic of Cockroaches, A: When the Ultimate Exterminator Meets the Ultimate Pest" (Quammen), 65–67
Research. *See* Field research; Library research
Restrictive modifiers, 693, 698
Rettie, James C., 122, 135
    " 'But a Watch in the Night': A Scientific Fable," 122–127
Reviews
    book, 300, 411
    movie, 300, 301
Revision. *See* Rewriting
Revision checklists
    analysis, 194, 195
    cause and effect, 324, 325
    conversation, 110–111
    evaluation, 297–298
    field research, 435
    imagination, 138
    library research, 373
    observation, 49
    opinion, 236
    proposal, 264–265
    reading, 81
    recall, 22
    rewriting, 524–525, 537
Rewriting, 3–4, 531–537
    and audience, 525
    checklists for, 524–525, 537
    and deep revision, 523–525
    and emphasis, 528–530
    on essay examinations, 573–574
    and logical fallacies, 525–528
    strategies for, 523–537
    with word processor, 556, 558–559
    See also Revision checklists
Rewriting assignments
    and analysis, 192–195
    and cause and effect, 323–326
    and computer, 555
    and conversation, 110–112
    and evaluation, 296–298
    and field research, 435–437
    and imagination, 136–138
    and library research, 372–375
    and observation, 47–48
    and opinion, 235–236

Rewriting assignments (*cont.*)
  and proposal, 262–265
  and reading, 80–83
  and recall, 21–23
Rich, Adrienne, *Of Woman Born,* 515
Rittenhouse, David, 267
Rivers, Caryl, 251
  "What Should Be Done about Rock
    Lyrics?" 251–253
"Rocky" (Kael), 301–304
Rodin, Auguste, 531
Rodriquez, Richard, *Hunger of*
  Memory, 21
Rose, Phyllis, 159
  "Tools of Torture," 159–162
Ross, Lillian, *Reporting,* 109–110
Roth, Philip, 486
Russell, Bertrand, 239
  "Do We Survive Death?" 239–243
Ruszkiewicz, John, 413

-'s, -s', 705–706
Sagan, Carl, 267–268, 334
  "The Nuclear Winter," 334–340
Sandburg, Carl, 756
Sarcasm, 212
Schedule
  research paper, 348
  for writing, 485
Schreiner, Robert G. (student writer),
  20, 21, 491
  "What Is a Hunter?" 12–16
Schultz, Emily A., and Robert Lavenda,
  Cultural Anthropology: A
  Perspective on the Human
  Condition, 197–198
Science
  and analysis, 197, 198
  and imagination, 141–142, 146–148
  and observation, 51–59
  and opinion, 239
  and proposal, 272–278
  See also individual disciplines
    (Biology, Chemistry, etc.)
Selvin, Hanan C., 753
Semicolon, 653, 655, 679, 699–702
  with conjunctive adverb, 612, 654,
    700
  with quotation marks, 712

Semicolon (*cont.*)
  to separate clauses joined by
    coordinating conjunction, 700–701
Sentence(s), 598–604, 611–614
  complements in, 599, 601–602
  complete, 646
  complex, 612–613, 676
  compound, 612
  compound-complex, 613
  declarative, 686
  emphasis in, 529, 530
  fused, 652–655
  incomplete, 665–670
  modifiers in, 599, 662–665
  object of, 598, 599, 600–601
  parts of, 598–602
  predicate of, 598, 599, 600–601
  run-on, 652–655
  sentence patterns, 602–604
  simple, 612
  subject of, 598, 599–600
  thesis, 530
  topic, 504–506
  as transitions, 514–515
  types of, 611–614
Sentence fragments, 646–651, 665
  with *being* as verb, 649–650
  as part of compound predicate, 650
  phrase as, 648–649
  revising, 648
  subordinate clause as, 649
Sentence patterns, 602–604
Series, 674–675, 698
  of clauses, 676
  colon after introduction to, 703
  commas between items in, 690–691,
    700
  dash to introduce, 714
  semicolon between items in, 700
  between two numbers, 738
Setting, in literature, 213
Sexism, avoiding, 757–760
Sexton, Anne, 5
Shakespeare, William, 122
Shaughnessy, Dan, 135–136
"Shouting 'Fire!' " (Dershowitz),
  304–309
Shriver, Rebecca (student writer), 24
[*sic*], 718

Simple predicate, 600
Simple sentences, 612
Simple subject, 599
Simple tenses, 621–623
sit, set, 619, 620–621
Skimming, 74
Slang, 711, 756–757
Slash (virgule), 714–715
Snowplowing, in drafting, 490–491
Social history, and cause and effect, 331
"Social Responsibility of Business Is to Increase Its Profits, The" (Friedman), 243–249
Social studies, and field research, 446
Sociology
  and cause and effect, 329–330
  and conversation, 114–115
  and observation, 51, 59–63
Software, computer, 558–559
Solutions
  problems and, 258–259, 260, 266
  proposing. *See* Proposal
Sorensen, E. Richard, "Cooperation and Freedom Among the Fore in New Guinea," 446–448
Source card(s), 352–354, 357–358. *See also* Note cards
Sources
  acknowledging, 69, 78–80, 234–235
  citing, 261–262, 364, 373–375, 451–457, 461–464
  citing nonprint, 453–454, 456–457
  citing printed, 451–453, 454–456, 461–464
  evaluating, 354–356, 358, 433
  honest borrowing from, 361
  for library research, 353–357, 365
  listing nonprinted, 460–461, 466–467
  listing printed, 457–461, 464–466
  nutshelling, 357, 360, 366, 367
  paraphrasing, 360–361, 368, 369
  plagiarizing, 78, 79, 361, 369–371
  primary, 355–356, 418. *See also* Field research
  quoting, 359–360, 365
  secondary, 355–356
  and working bibliography, 352–353
  writing from, 358–362

Speeches, repetition in, 530
Speech pathology
  and analysis, 199
  and cause and effect, 329
  and evaluation, 299
  and observation, 51
Spelling, 740–749
  commonly misspelled words, 746–749
  developing skills in, 745–746
  forming plurals, 743
  homonyms, 741–742
  prefixes, 745
  rules for, 741–745
  suffixes, 744–745
Spelling checkers, for word processor, 558
"Spider and the Wasp, The" (Petrunkevitch), 55–59
Sports writing, 135–136
Squinting modifier, 663
Stand, taking a. *See* Opinion
Staples, Brent, 31
  "Black Men and Public Space," 31–33
States and countries, commas with, 697
Statistics, as evidence, 230
Stereotyping, 759–760
Stevens, Wallace, 121
"Story of an Hour, The" (Chopin), 214–216
Storytelling, 521–522
Strauss, Richard, 516
Style
  APA, 374, 436, 437, 461–467
  manuscript, 577–581. *See also* Manuscript preparation
  MLA, 374, 450, 451–461
Style book, 451
Style guides, 374, 450–451
Subject complement, 602, 616
  adjective as, 658
  connecting with subject, 616
  pronoun as, 643
Subjective pronouns, 641–643
Subject of sentence, 598, 599–600, 616
  agreement with verb, 630–634
  complete, 599

Subject of sentence (*cont.*)
  compound, 599
  connecting with subject
    complement, 616
  pronoun as, 642–643
  simple, 599
  understood, 600, 612, 628
Subject analysis, 188–189, 190–191,
  193–194
Subject-verb agreement, 630–634
Subjunctive mood, 628–629
Subordinate (dependent) clauses, 609,
  610, 654, 682
  antecedent of, and agreement, 633
  comma with, 701
  as sentence fragment, 649
  subjunctive mood in, 628
Subordinating conjunctions, 596, 611,
  649, 681, 682
Subordination, 678, 681–683
  avoiding excessive, 682–683
  avoiding faulty, 682
  linking clauses with, 681–682
Suffixes, 744–745
  hyphen before, 738
Summarizing, 79, 85–86, 522. *See also*
  Nutshelling
"Superkids and Super Problems"
  (Elkind), 118–120
Superlative form, 659–661
Swidler, Ann, 115
Swift, Jonathan, "A Modest Proposal,"
  261
Syllables, and word division,
  738–739
Symbol(s)
  in literature, 213
  proofreading, 579
Syntax, 585
Synthesizing, 134–135, 143

Taking a stand. *See* Opinion
Talese, Gay, "New York," 505–506
Talking with others. *See* Conversation
Tallent, Norman, *Psychological Report
  Writing*, 434–435
Tape recorders
  in drafting, 489
  in interviews, 107, 429

Technical writing, observation and, 54
Tein, Michael R. (student writer), 106,
  108, 109
  "Flowers for Chapel Street," 96–99
Telephone interviews, 107, 429
Television. *See* Media
Television or radio programs
  italics for, 733
  quotation marks with, 711
Tenses, verb, 621–626
  past, 617, 622
  perfect, 621, 623–624
  progressive, 617, 623, 624–625
  simple, 621, 622–623
Testimony, expert, 230, 234–235
"Textbook Pregnancy, A" (Klass),
  171–178
Textbooks, 350
Teyber, Edward, and Charles D.
  Hoffman, 268
  "Missing Fathers," 269–272
than, as, in comparisons, 669, 675
that
  to introduce restrictive modifier,
    693
  quotations introduced by, 696
that clauses, 629
Theme, in literature, 213
There is, There are, 532–533
Thesaurus, database, 415
Thesis, 362, 491–495, 500
  in essay examinations, 572
  trial, 493
Thesis method, in drafting, 362
Thesis proposal, 266
Thesis sentence, 530
Thesis statement, 491–494, 500
  in essay examinations, 572
Thomas, Lewis, 272, 516
  "The Art of Teaching Science,"
    272–278
  "On Societies as Organisms,"
    504–505
  "Things Unflattened by Science,"
    197, 516
Thompson, Wade, 518
Thurber, James, 143
  "If Grant Had Been Drinking at
    Appomattox," 143–145

Time
abbreviations of, 723
colon in naming, 704
Time markers, 192, 193, 510, 514
"Time Travel and Papa Joe's Pipe"
(Lightman), 146–148
Tindall, William York, 489
Ting, Jeffrey (student writer)
"The Drinking Age: How We Should
Determine It," 254–257
"Tinsel Teens" (Haas), 59–63
Title of paper, 487
Titles of persons, 696, 760
abbreviating, 722–723
capitalizing, 726
Titles of works
capitalizing, 729
in italics, 733
quotation marks with, 711
singular verb with, 634
and subtitles, colon with, 704
to be, 533
Tobias, Sheila, *Overcoming Math
Anxiety,* 511–512
Toffler, Alvin, *The Third Wave,* 512
Tone, 750, 751
"Tools of Torture" (Rose), 159–162
Topic sentences, 504–506
Toulmin, Stephen, 527
Introduction to Reasoning, 528
The Uses of Argument, 527
Transitions, 513–516, 519, 532
and field research, 435
and library research, 365
paragraphs as, 503, 513–516
sentence as, 514
and time markers, 192, 193, 510, 514
Transitive verbs, 592, 601, 615
Traugot, Marsha, 514
Trollope, Anthony, 485, 490
Tuchman, Barbara W., *The Distant
Mirror,* 366–371
Tunney, Gene, "The Long Count," 519
Twain, Mark, 279–280, 531
"Fenimore Cooper's Literary
Offenses," 280–289

Underhill, Evelyn, *Mysticism,* 369
Underlining. *See* Italics

Updike, John, 485, 510–511
Usage, 769

van Leunen, Mary-Claire, *A Handbook
for Scholars,* 358, 365, 415
Van Riper, C., *A Career in Speech
Pathology,* 51
Verbal phrases, 606–607
Verbals, 606
Verb forms, 616–621
Verb phrase, 617
Verbs, 592–593, 615–621, 630–632
active, 533, 626
agreement with subject, 630–634
compound, 612
helping/auxiliary, 592, 615, 617
intransitive, 592, 615
irregular, 617, 618–619, 622
linking, 592, 615, 616, 633, 659,
696
main, 592
passive, 626
principal parts of, 617–621
regular, 617-618
of the senses (*feel, smell*), 616
singular or plural, 630–632
tense of, 617, 621–626
transitive, 592, 601, 615
types of, 592–593, 615
Veyne, Paul, 141
Videocamera, in field research, 430
"View of Prejudice, A" (Least Heat
Moon), 99–103
Virgule (slash), 714–715
Voice, 626–628
active, 626–627, 672
passive, 617, 626–627, 672

Wahr, Erika (student writer), 372
Waite, Donna (student writer), 528
Walker, Jill (student writer), 543
Wall Street Journal, 403, 410, 411
Warner, Edgar F., 371
Waterman, Robert H., Jr., and Thomas
J. Peters, *In Search of Excellence,*
506–507
Webster's New Biographical Dictionary,
411

Webster's Third New International (dictionary), 405

Weissmann, Gerald, "Foucault and the Bag Lady," 239

"What America Would Be Like Without Blacks" (Ellison), 154–158

"What Is a Hunter?" (Schreiner), 12–16

"What Should Be Done about Rock Lyrics?" (Rivers), 251–253

"What's in Your Toothpaste?" (Bodanis), 185–187

"Where Few Have Gone Before" (Deters), 547–553

which, to introduce nonrestrictive modifier, 693

White, E. B., "Once More to the Lake," 518–519

White, William Allen, 48

Who's Who . . . series, 411–412

Who Was Who . . . , 411

"Why We Burned a Wilderness" (Kennedy), 311–314

Wilson, Everett K., 753

Winn, Marie, 163
"The Plug-In Drug," 163–171

"Women's Brains" (Gould), 86–91

Word choice, 750–768
appropriateness of, 750–757
avoiding sexism in, 757–760
exact words, 760–765
wordiness, 765–767

Word division, 738–739

Wordiness, 531–537, 765–767

Word processor, 555–561
dedicated, 558
disadvantages of, 556–557, 560–561
grouping ideas with, 497–498
hardware and software, 557–558
tips on using, 559–560
writing with, 555–557, 558–559
See also Computers

Working bibliography, 352–354, 357, 374

Workplace, writing in the
and analyzing, 199–200
and conversation, 113
and evaluating, 299–300
and field research, 446–449
and library research, 394
and observation, 51
and opinion, 238–239
proposals, 266–267

"Works Cited," 353, 374, 452. *See also* Documentation

World Almanac and Book of Facts, 412

World Book, 404

Writer's block, 474, 489–490

Writing, 2–6
circumstances for, 484–486
as collaborative effort, 538–553
directive ("how to"), 199
about literature, 212–214
preparation for, 486–488
process of, 2–4
purpose in, 4–5, 21–22, 35, 46
while reading, 74–76, 77
schedule for, 485
strategies for beginning, 483–490
strategies for restarting, 490–491
technology of, 531. *See also* Computers

Writing community, forming a, 538–539. *See also* Peer editing

Writing process, 2–4

Yearbooks, 412

Yeats, William Butler, 138

yes, no, commas with, 696

Zaleski, Philip, "The Superstars of Heart Research," 114

Zoology, observation and, 54–59

CORRECTION SYMBOLS

Boldface numbers refer to sections of the handbook.

abbr	faulty abbreviation **26**		**om**	omitted word **14**
ad	misuse of adverb or adjective **12**		**p**	error in punctuation
agr	faulty agreement **6, 7**		⌃ ̣	comma **19**
appr	inappropriate language **32, 33**		**no ,**	no comma **19m**
awk	awkward		;	semicolon **20**
cap	capital letter **27**		:	colon **21**
case	error in case **9**		⌄	apostrophe **22**
coord	faulty coordination **17**		" "	quotation marks **23**
cs	comma splice **11**		. ? !	period, question mark, exclamation point **18**
dm	dangling modifier **13**		— ( ) [ ] . . . /	dash, parentheses, brackets, ellipsis, slash **24–26**
exact	inexact language **34**		**par, ¶**	new paragraph
frag	sentence fragment **10**		**pass**	ineffective passive **5l**
fs	fused sentence **11**		**pred**	faulty predication **15**
gl	see glossary of trouble-makers		**ref**	error in pronoun reference **8**
gr	grammar **1–4**		**rev**	revise
hyph	error in use of hyphen **30**		**sp**	misspelled word **31**
inc	incomplete construction **14**		**sub**	faulty subordination **17**
irreg	error in irregular verb **5d**		**t**	error in verb tense **5c, f–k**
ital	italics (underlining) **29**		**v**	voice **5l**
lc	use lowercase letter **27**		**vb**	error in verb form **5**
mixed	mixed construction **15**		**w**	wordy **35**
mm	misplaced modifier **13a–b**		**//**	faulty parallelism **16**
mood	error in mood **5m–o**		∧	insert
ms	manuscript form pp. 577–581		**x**	obvious error
nonst	nonstandard usage **32, 34**		**#**	insert space
num	error in use of numbers **28**		◡	close up space

A Guide to the Handbook

21. BASIC GRAMMAR   589

1. Parts of Speech gr   589
a. Nouns
b. Pronouns
c. Verbs
d. Adjectives / articles
e. Adverbs
f. Prepositions
g. Conjunctions
h. Interjections

2. Parts of Sentences and Sentence Patterns gr   598

PARTS OF SENTENCES   598
a. Subject
b. Predicate
c. Objects
d. Complements

SENTENCE PATTERNS   602

3. Phrases and Clauses gr   604

TYPES OF PHRASES   604
a. Prepositional
b. Verbal
c. Absolute
d. Appositive

TYPES OF CLAUSES   609
e. Noun
f. Adjective
g. Adverb

4. Types of Sentences gr   611
a. Simple
b. Compound
c. Complex
d. Compound-complex

22. GRAMMATICAL SENTENCES   615

5. Verbs vb   615

VERB FORMS   615
a. Linking verbs
b. Helping verbs
c. Principal parts
d. Irregular verbs
e. *Lie* and *lay* / *sit* and *set*

TENSES   621
f. Simple present
g. Simple past
h. Simple future
i. Present, past, and future perfect
j. Present, past, and future progressive
k. Present, past, and future perfect progressive

VOICE   626
l. Active / passive

MOOD   628
m. Indicative
n. Imperative
o. Subjunctive

6. Subject-Verb Agreement agr   630
a. Person and number
b. Intervening words
c. Subjects with *and*
d. Subjects with *or* or *nor*
e. Collective nouns
f. Indefinite pronouns
g. *all*, *any*, and *some*
h. *who*, *which*, *that*
i. Subject following verb
j. Linking verbs
k. Titles
l. Singular nouns plural in form

7. Pronoun-Antecedent Agreement agr   635
a. Person and number
b. Antecedents joined by *and*
c. Antecedent joined by *or* or *nor*
d. Indefinite pronouns
e. Collective nouns
f. Gender

8. Pronoun Reference ref   638
a. Implied antecedents
b. Antecedents of *it*, *this*, *that*, or *which*
c. Ambiguous reference
d. Keeping pronouns and antecedents together

9. Pronoun Case case   641
a. Subjects
b. Subject complements
c. Appositives to subjects
d. Objects
e. Appositives to objects
f. Possessive case
g. With gerunds

10. Sentence Fragments frag   646
a. Phrases
b. Subordinate clauses
c. With *being* or another participle
d. Compound predicates

11. Comma Splices and Fused Sentences cs/fs   652
a. Repair by separating sentences
b. With a comma and a coordinating conjunction
c. With a semicolon or colon
d. By subordinating
e. With a conjunctive adverb

12. Adjectives and Adverbs ad   657
a. Adverbs to modify verb, adjective, or adverb
b. Adjectives as subject or object complements
c. *Good* and *well*
d. Form of comparatives and superlatives
e. Redundant comparatives and superlatives
f. Use of comparatives and superlatives

23. EFFECTIVE SENTENCES   662

13. Misplaced and Dangling Modifiers mm/dm   662
a. Misplaced modifiers
b. Squinting modifiers
c. Dangling modifiers

14. Incomplete Sentences inc   665

COMPARISONS   666
a. Making full comparisons
b. Finishing comparisons
c. Comparing things of the same kind
d. Using *any other*

ELLIPTICAL CONSTRUCTIONS   668
e. Words essential for clarity
f. In a compound predicate
g. With *as* and *than*

15. Mixed Constructions and Faulty Predication mixed   670
a. Mixed constructions
b. Faulty predication
c. Definitions with *when* or *where*
d. *The reason is because* . . .

16. Parallel Structure //   673
a. Coordinating conjunctions
b. Correlative conjunctions
c. In comparisons
d. Repeating words
e. Repeating lead-in words

17. Coordination and Subordination coord/sub   677
a. Uses of coordination
b. Faulty coordination
c. Excessive coordination
d. Uses of subordination
e. Faulty subordination
f. Excessive subordination